The **Rough Guide** to

Moscow

written and researched by

Dan Richardson

with additional contributions by

Jonathon Reynolds

NEW YORK • LONDON • DELHI

www.roughguides.com

Contents

Moscow: the new New York colour section following p.176

The Moscow metro colour section following p.336

Colour maps following p.480

◄◄ St Basil's Cathedral ◄ Moscow at night

Introduction to Moscow

In Siberia, they call Moscow "the West", with a note of scorn for its bureaucrats and politicians. To Westerners, the city looks European, but its unruly spirit seems closer to Central Asia. For Muscovites, Moscow is both a "Mother City" and a "big village", a tumultuous community with an underlying collective instinct that shows itself in times of trouble. Nowhere else reflects the contradictions and ambiguities of the Russian people as Moscow does – nor the stresses of a country undergoing meltdown and renewal.

The city is huge, surreal and exciting. After a few weeks here, the bizarre becomes normal and you realize that life is – as Russians say – *bespredel* (without limits). Traditionally a place for strangers to throw themselves into debauchery, leaving poorer and wiser, Moscow's puritan stance in Soviet times was seldom heartfelt, and with the fall of Communism it has reverted to the lusty, violent ways that foreigners have noted with amazement over the centuries, and Gilyarovsky chronicled in his book, *Moscow and the Muscovites*. No excess is too much for Moscow's new rich, or *novye bogaty* – the butt of countless "New Russian" jokes.

As the nation's largest city, with some twelve million inhabitants (one in fifteen Russians lives there), Moscow exemplifies the best and worst of Russia. Its beauty and ugliness are inseparable, its sentimentality the obverse of a brutality rooted in centuries of despotism and fear of anarchy. Private

▲ Cathedral of Christ the Saviour

and cultural life is as passionate as business and politics are cynical. The irony and resilience honed by decades of propaganda and shortages now help Muscovites to cope with "wild" capitalism. Yet, for all its assertiveness, Moscow's essence is moody and elusive, and uncovering it is like opening an endless series of *Matryoshka* dolls, or peeling an onion down to its core.

Both images are apposite, for Moscow's concentric geography mirrors its historical development. At its heart is the Kremlin, whose foundation by Prince Dolgoruky in 1147 marked the birth of the city. Surrounding this are rings corresponding to the feudal settlements of medieval times, rebuilt along European lines after the great fire of 1812, and ruthlessly modernized in accordance with Stalin's vision of Moscow as the Mecca of Communism. Further out lie the fortified monasteries that once guarded the outskirts, and the former country estates of tsars and nobles, now well within the 880-square-kilometre urban sprawl encircled by the Moscow Ring Road.

Moscow's identity has been imbued with a sense of its own destiny since the fourteenth century, when the principality of Muscovy took the lead in the struggle against the Mongols and Tatars who had reduced the Kievan state to ruins. Under Ivan the Great and Ivan the Terrible – the "Gatherers of the Russian Lands" – its realm came to encompass everything from the White Sea to the Caspian, while after the fall of Constantinople to the Turks, Moscow assumed Byzantium's suzerainty over the Orthodox world. Despite the changes wrought by Peter the Great – not least the transfer of the capital to St Petersburg, which Slavophiles have always abhorred – Moscow kept its mystique and bided its time until the Bolsheviks made it the fountainhead of a new creed. Long accustomed to being at the centre of an empire, and being misled that their society was the envy of the world,

Muscovites felt the disillusionments of the 1990s more keenly than most Russians – although some have prospered beyond their wildest dreams.

All this is writ large in Moscow's architecture and street life. The Kremlin's cathedrals are Byzantine, like its politics. Ministries and hotels the size of city blocks reach their apotheosis in the "Seven Sisters" – Stalin-Gothic skyscrapers that brood over the city like vampires. Limousines cruise past *babushki* whose monthly pensions wouldn't cover the cost of admission to a nightclub (the city has more casinos than any capital in the world). Fascists and Communists march together, bankers live in fear of contract killers and life is up for grabs. From all this, Muscovites seek solace in backstreet churches and shady courtyards; in the steamy conviviality of the bathhouse; and over tea or vodka. Discovering the private, hidden side of Moscow is as rewarding as visiting the usual tourist sights.

◀ Souvenir stalls around Red Square

What to see

Despite its size, Moscow's concentric layout is easier to grasp than you'd imagine, and the city's famous **metro** ensures that almost everywhere of interest is within fifteen minutes' walk of a station. **Red Square and the Kremlin** (Chapter 1) are the historic nucleus of the city, a magnificent stage for political drama, signifying a great sweep of history that includes Ivan the Terrible, Peter the Great, Stalin and Gorbachev. Here you'll find Lenin's Mausoleum and St Basil's Cathedral, the famous GUM department store, and the Kremlin itself, whose splendid cathedrals and Armoury Museum head the list of attractions. Immediately east of Red Square lies the **Kitay-gorod** (Chapter 2), traditionally the commercial district, and originally fortified like the Kremlin. Stretches of the ramparts remain behind the *Metropol* and *Rossiya* hotels, and the medieval churches of Zaryade and the shops along Nikolskaya ulitsa may tempt you further into the quarter, where you'll find the former headquarters of the Communist Party.

The Kremlin and Kitay-gorod are surrounded by two quarters defined by ring boulevards built over the original ramparts of medieval times, when Moscow's residential areas were divided into the "White Town" or **Beliy Gorod** (Chapter 3), and the humbler "Earth Town" or **Zemlyanoy Gorod** (Chapter 4). Situated within the leafy **Boulevard Ring** that encloses the Beliy Gorod are such landmarks as the Bolshoy Theatre and the Lubyanka headquarters of the secret police – with its "KGB Museum" – while the Zemlyanoy Gorod that extends to the eight-lane **Garden Ring** is enlivened by the trendy old and new Arbat streets, with three Stalin skyscrapers dominating the Ring itself.

Beyond this historic core Moscow is too sprawling to explore on foot, which is why our division of the city is based mostly on transport connections and ease of access. **Krasnaya Presnya, Fili and the south-west** (Chapter 5) describes a swathe which includes the former Russian Parliament building (known as the White House); Tolstoy's house and the Novodevichie Convent and Cemetery; Victory Park, with its war memorials and Jewish museum; and Moscow State University in the Sparrow Hills – the largest of the Stalin skyscrapers.

Across the river from the Kremlin, **Zamoskvareche and the south** (Chapter 6) are the site of the old and new Tretyakov Gallery's superlative collection of Russian art. Here too you'll find Gorky Park, the Donskoy and Danilov monasteries that once stood guard against the Tatars, and the romantic ex-royal estates of Tsaritsyno and Kolomenskoe – the latter known for staging folklore festivals and historical pageants. **Taganka and Zayauze** (Chapter 7), east of the centre, likewise harbour fortified monasteries – the Andronikov, Novospasskiy and Simonov – and the erstwhile noble estates of Kuskovo and Kuzminki, but the main lure for tourists is the Izmaylovo art market. Moscow's **Northern Suburbs** (Chapter 8) cover a vast area with a sprinkling of sights. Foremost is the VVTs, a huge Stalinist exhibition park

Moscow's skyscrapers

Among Moscow's most distinctive landmarks are the "Seven Sisters" – Stalin skyscrapers bristling with statuary, spires and illuminated red stars, which form an arc around the city centre. These totemic symbols of Soviet power were intended to surround the never-built Palace of Soviets that was envisaged as the tallest building in the USSR, topped by a statue of Lenin that would raise its height to surpass the Statue of Liberty and the Empire State Building put together. Although this colossal edifice never materialized – and the Cathedral of Christ the Saviour that was demolished to clear the site has now been rebuilt to affirm the victory of Christianity over Communism – the Stalin skyscrapers still dominate Moscow's Garden Ring. Today, they have inspired a new generation of skyscrapers, from the neo-Stalinist Triumph Palace in the northern suburbs to the futuristic twin towers of Gorod Stolitsa in the Krasnaya Presnya district, and the Gazprom Building in the southern suburbs.

with amazing statues and pavilions, in the vicinity of the Ostankino Palace, Moscow's Botanical Gardens and TV Tower.

Outside Moscow there's scope for **day-excursions** to the **Trinity Monastery** of St Sergei, the **Abramtsevo** artists' colony, Tchaikovsky's house in **Klin**, Lenin's estate at **Gorki Leninskie**, and the battlefield of **Borodino** (Chapter 9), where the battle is re-enacted every September. Further afield, the historic towns of **Vladimir** and **Suzdal** (Chapter 10) are graced by splendid cathedrals and monasteries attesting that they were the seat of a principality when Moscow was merely an encampment. Suzdal is one of the loveliest towns in Russia, and definitely merits an overnight stay. It's also possible to visit the Aviation Museum at Monino air base, en route to Vladimir, if you take the trouble to get permission ahead of time.

▶ Glass portrait of Lenin

When to go

Moscow lies on about the same latitude as Edinburgh in Scotland, but its **climate** is closer to that of Edmonton in Canada (a bit further south), due to its location far from the sea, on a great continental land mass. Summers are hot and winters cold by Western European standards – although the dry, often sunny weather makes the latter tolerable, if not pleasurable.

▲ The Space Obelisk at the VVTs

As most foreigners have an exaggerated fear of the cold in Russia, the most popular time to go is **summer**, lasting from the beginning of June to mid-September. Days and nights are warm and sultry, with heat waves likely during August, when Muscovites leave in droves for their *dachas* in the countryside. Culturally, things are rather slack during this period, with the Bolshoy Ballet away from June until early September and many other theatres closed for the duration.

Spring is chiefly rewarding for the rituals and candle-lit processions marking Orthodox **Easter**, when cathedrals are so packed that people wait for hours to get in. (Christmas services are as splendid yet not nearly so crowded.) Several major **music festivals** start around this time, or in May, accompanied by such national holidays as Victory Day and May Day. **Autumn** is likewise excellent for festivals, despite cloudy skies and falling temperatures, and you can still look forward to a week or two of *Babe leto* ("Granny's Summer"), when Moscow is an Impressionist's vision of autumnal hues, in the final glow of warmth.

Subzero temperatures and snow can set in up to two months before **winter** officially begins in December. Blanketed in fresh snow, Moscow is magically hushed and cleansed, and Muscovites revel in the crispness of the air. Days are often gloriously sunny, and the temperature only a few degrees below zero, so skiing and sledging are popular pursuits. The secular **New Year** and **Orthodox Christmas** in early January are occasions for shopping and merrymaking, but at some point a cold snap will send the temperature down to -20°C or lower, while traffic and thaws turn the snow into mounds and lakes of black ice or brown slush, which linger on until late March.

Finally, make sure you bring the right gear. Lots of layers, a hat and waterproof footwear with nonslip soles are essential for winter. A compact rainproof jacket will protect you from showers in the spring or autumn. Shorts and t-shirts are fine for summer, but pack long trousers or a skirt for visiting monasteries, the ballet or dining out – and a mosquito net to drape over your bed if you're unsure that your lodgings have screens on the windows.

Average daily temperatures and rainfall in Moscow

	Jan	Feb	Mar	Apr	May	June	July	Aug	Sept	Oct	Nov	Dec
Max. temp. (°C)	-7	-5	0	8	15	20	21	20	15	9	2	-3
Min. temp. (°C)	-13	-12	-8	0	6	11	13	13	9	4	-2	-8
Rainfall (mm)	35	30	31	36	45	50	72	78	64	76	46	4

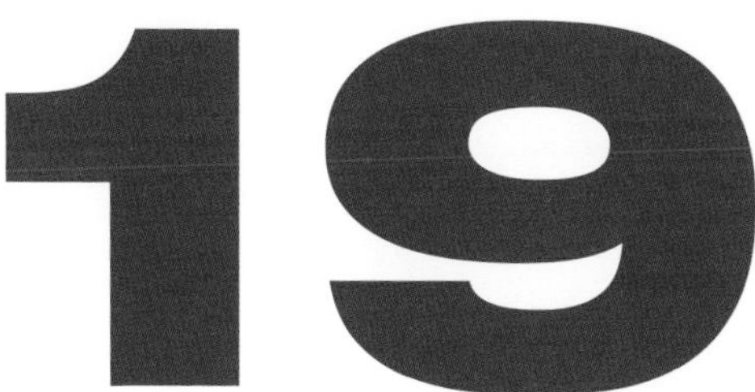

things not to miss

It's not possible to see everything that Moscow has to offer on a short trip – and we don't suggest you try. What follows is a subjective selection of the city's highlights, shown in no particular order, ranging from the medieval splendour of the Kremlin to the hedonistic heights of Moscow's clubland, all arranged in colour-coded categories to help you find the very best things to see, do and experience. All entries have a page reference to take you straight into the guide, where you can find out more.

01 Moskva River cruise Page **46** • In summertime, river cruises afford superb views of the Kremlin, the Cathedral of Christ the Saviour, the monument to Peter the Great, some of the Stalin skyscrapers, and fortified monasteries.

02 GUM Page **73** • GUM's elegant Victorian-era arcades are now full of designer-label stores rather than the shoddy products and queues for which it was known in Soviet times. A fine place for window-shopping in its colonnades, or sipping coffee by its fountains.

03 Kolomenskoe Page **234** • The eerie Church of the Ascension (featured in Eisenstein's film *Ivan the Terrible*) and hulking wooden watchtowers and cabins make this former royal estate beside the Moskva River a fabulous spot, which looks quite unearthly in the winter. Folkloric and historical pageants are staged here throughout the year.

04 The Metro Page **42** • Take a ride on Moscow's showcase metro, whose stations are the most decorous in the world. Styles range from High Stalinist to ballroom glitz.

05 Ballet, opera and classical music Page **366** • While the Bolshoy is Moscow's most famous venue, there is a wealth of companies, theatres and orchestras providing world-class entertainment.

06 The Arbat Page **163** • Once the heart of bohemian Moscow, this cobbled street buzzes with souvenir sellers, buskers and photographers (who'll snap you beside a life-size Putin, Schwarzenegger or Mickey Mouse).

07 Izmaylovo Market Page **265** • A cornucopia of Soviet memorabilia, icons, paintings, wood carvings, vintage cameras and samovars, the outdoor Vernissazh (as locals call it) is Moscow's best source of souvenirs. Performing bears appear at weekends.

08 The Kremlin palaces and Armoury Page **95** • The seat of Russian power features seventeenth-century and Neoclassical interiors, and treasures ranging from Fabergé eggs to the sable-trimmed Crown of Monomakh.

09 Georgian cuisine Page **340** • The healthiest and tastiest of Russia's diverse culinary traditions, due to its emphasis on fresh herbs, vegetables, pulses, nuts and garnishes such as pomegranate seeds – but with plenty to satisfy carnivores too. Best washed down with a robust red wine or a bottle of Borzhomi mineral water.

10 The VVTs Page **280** • The Stalinist theme park that once extolled the achievements of the Soviet economy, with mosaic-encrusted fountains and pavilions, and two iconic monuments.

11 Tretyakov Gallery Page **211** • Its two buildings showcase nearly a thousand years of Russian art, from icons to Futurism and Socialist Realist art.

12 Red Square Page **67** • The heart of Mother Russia, where St Basil's Cathedral, Lenin's Mausoleum, the Kremlin walls and GUM department store stand magnificently juxtaposed.

13 Clubbing Page **359** • Whether it's jazz-fusion, trance, grunge, S&M or gender bending, there are clubs for any taste in Moscow – the more way-out or extravagant, the better.

14 Banya Page **390** • An essential Russian experience, the *banya* (bathhouse) is a sauna with a masochistic twist that leaves you gasping for more and feeling wonderfully relaxed afterwards.

15 Suzdal Page **315** • A beautiful small town of fortified monasteries and wooden houses, used as a location for filming historical epics such as *Andrei Rublev*, and currently a popular place to spend Christmas and New Year.

16 Pushkin Museum of Fine Arts Page **125** • This wonderful museum boasts Schliemann's discoveries from "Troy", several Rembrandts, some of Gauguin's best-loved Tahitian paintings, and works by Monet, Van Gogh, Picasso and Cézanne.

17 Peter the Great monument Page **206** • A 95-metre-high, monstrously kitsch waterfront homage to the founder of the Russian navy, by Mayor Luzhkov's favourite artist, Tsereteli.

18 Novodevichie Convent and Cemetery Page **194** • A high-walled, golden-domed convent that unwanted wives or sisters of the tsars were once obliged to enter as nuns. In the adjacent cemetery, Gogol, Shostakovich, Eisenstein, Khrushchev and a host of other luminaries are buried beneath elaborate funerary sculptures.

19 Orthodox choral music Page **367** • This music is otherworldly and perfectly in keeping with the rituals of the faith. Visitors can attend evening service at any church; saint's day festivals, Christmas or Easter at Moscow's cathedrals and monasteries are far grander events.

Basics

Basics

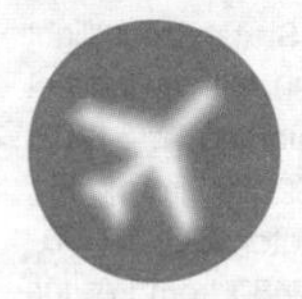

Getting there

Moscow's distance from Western Europe – never mind North America or Australasia – makes flying the obvious way of getting there. Travelling overland to Moscow is unlikely to work out cheaper than flying unless you're coming from Poland or the Baltic States, but the lure of riding the Trans-Siberian Railway across the vastness of Russia, or adventures along the way from Eastern Europe, are reason enough to consider other approaches than flying. The need to obtain a visa makes it hard to take advantage of last-minute offers, but you should be able to save money on both tickets and Russian visas by booking months in advance. For short visits to Moscow, a package tour may well be cheaper than doing things independently, once you've taken the cost of accommodation and visas into account.

Booking flights online

Many airlines and discount travel websites offer you the opportunity to book your tickets online, cutting out the cost of agents and middlemen, and giving you a discount at the same time. Good deals can often be found through discount or auction sites, as well as through the airlines' own websites – the airport codes to input are DME for Domodedovo, SVO for Sheremetevo-2, or MOW for all Moscow airports. It's worth bearing in mind, however, that many online deals permit little or no flexibility, so you need to make sure that your flight dates match exactly with the dates of your Russian visa, which may take several weeks to obtain (see p.30).

Online booking agents and general travel sites

Ⓦ www.cheapflights.com (US), Ⓦ www.cheapflights.co.uk (UK and Ireland) Flight deals, travel agents, plus links to other travel sites.
Ⓦ www.cheaptickets.com Discount flight specialists.
Ⓦ www.expedia.com (US), Ⓦ www.expedia.co.uk (UK), Ⓦ www.expedia.ca (Canada) Discount airfares, all-airline search engine and daily deals.
Ⓦ www.in-russia.com Discount flight and hotel bookings in Russia, from the US only.
Ⓦ www.lastminute.com (UK), Ⓦ www.lastminute.com.au (Australia) Offers good last-minute holiday package and flight-only deals.
Ⓦ www.priceline.com (US), Ⓦ www.priceline.co.uk (UK) Name-your-own-price website that has deals at around forty percent off standard fares.
Ⓦ www.travelocity.com Destination guides, cheap fares and best deals for car hire, accommodation and lodging.
Ⓦ www.travelonline.co.nz The best site for New Zealanders to find worldwide flights from their country.

Flights from Britain and Ireland

Between them, **British Airways** (BA), **BMI** and the Russian airlines **Aeroflot** and **Transaero** operate about thirty **direct flights** a week **from London** to Moscow. BA, BMI and Aeroflot each have 2–3 flights daily from Heathrow; Transaero, a daily flight from Gatwick in summer, 3–4 weekly at other times. An important difference between them is that BA, BMI and Transaero fly into **Domodedovo airport**, linked by a cheap shuttle train to the centre of Moscow, whereas Aeroflot uses **Sheremetevo-2**, from which the journey into town is slow, if not costly – something to keep in mind when comparing **fares**.

Discount and specialist travel agents sell direct flights below the headline rate, and offer **indirect flights** with other European carriers, changing planes at a hub city before flying on to Moscow. Possibilities include Luftansa via Frankfurt or Munich, KLM via Amsterdam, Air France via Paris, Brussels Airlines via Brussels, Austrian Airlines via Vienna, Air Berlin via Berlin, and Aerosvit via

Kiev. **Fares** are rarely lower than Transaero's but may undercut Aeroflot, BA or BMI, and allow departures from Birmingham, Glasgow or Manchester. It's also worth keeping an eye out for special offers and cheap flights on **budget airlines** to new members of the European Union that border Russia, such as Estonia or Latvia – both easyJet and Ryanair, for example, fly from Stansted and Glasgow to Riga and Tallinn from £20 one-way, if you book well in advance, while Air Baltic flies from Gatwick to both cities for a similar price. From these cities, you can travel overland fairly easily to Moscow (see "By Train" and "By coach", pp.26–28).

There are currently no direct scheduled flights **from Ireland** to Moscow, and the cheapest way to get there from either Belfast or Dublin Is via England – ideally Manchester or London. The best options **from Dublin** are to Manchester on Ryanair, and from there to Moscow on Transaero, which will cost from around €200, or Dublin to Heathrow on BA or BMI, then Aeroflot to Moscow, from around €250. **From Belfast** the cheapest option Is with Ryanair to Manchester then Transaero to Moscow which costs about £220.

Flights from the US and Canada

Four airlines offer **direct flights** to Moscow from the US and Canada. Delta and American Airlines fly **from New York**'s JFK to Moscow's Sheremetevo-2 airport (9hr 30min), as does Russia's national carrier, Aeroflot, which also has nonstop flights **from Seattle** (11hr 20min), **Washington DC** (12hr 20min) and **Los Angeles** (12hr 20min). Additionally, Aeroflot has flights from San Francisco (10–15hr) and Montreal (12–15hr), connecting with their LA or east-coast departures, or using another airline to cross the Atlantic. **From Canada**, Aeroflot flies direct from **Toronto** (9hr 30min), while Air Canada flies from Toronto and **Montreal**. Transaero also flies direct from Toronto and Montreal to Moscow's Domodedovo airport three times a week in summer, less frequently in winter.

Return **fares** vary from low (mid-Jan, Feb, Oct & Nov) to high (June–Sept, Christmas & New Year) season, with Delta generally being the cheapest **from the US**: its direct flight from JFK costs $1155–1600, with an indirect flight from Los Angeles starting at $1402. Aeroflot fares start at $2058 from JFK, $1740–2850 from Washington DC, $2300–2600 from Seattle, and $2480 from LA (the last costing more in low season, strangely). **From Canada**, Aeroflot fares from Toronto range from C$1030–1200, while Transaero flights from Toronto or Montreal start at C$1070. Air Canada flights are more expensive at C$1760–2250.

Alternatively, you may wish to fly to a European capital and **continue overland** from there. Good candidates include Riga, Tallinn, Helsinki, Warsaw or Berlin (in that order of distance from Moscow). If Moscow is part of a longer European trip, you'll also want to check out details of the Eurail pass (see p.27).

Flights from Australia and New Zealand

Flight time **from Australia and New Zealand** to Moscow is over twenty hours, and some routings take nearer thirty; with no direct flights, you're likely to touch down somewhere in Asia or the Middle East. Given the length of the journey, you might be better off including a night's stopover in your itinerary – some airlines include one in the price of the flight. Finnair, Cathay Pacific, Emirates, Aeroflot, Korean Air, Scandinavian Airlines and Austrian Airlines seem to offer the best deals, in tandem with Qantas, BA or KLM. There's a plethora of airline combinations online, so shop around and be flexible.

Fares vary from low (mid-Jan, Feb, Oct & Nov) to high (June–Sept, Christmas & New Year) season. Average return fares to Moscow **from eastern gateways** are A$1900–2350 in low season, A$2265–3000 in high season. Fares **from Perth or Darwin** cost A$120–180 more. Flights **from Auckland** are in the region of NZ$2643 in low season, NZ$3373 in high season.

Airlines

Aeroflot UK ⓣ 0207/355 2233, US ⓣ 1-888/340-6400, Canada ⓣ 416/642-1653, Australia ⓣ 02/9262 2233; ⓦ www.aeroflot.com, ⓦ www.aeroflot.co.uk, or book online ⓦ www.england.aeroflot.aero/eng, ⓦ www.aeroflot.com.au. No NZ office.

Aerosvit US ⓣ1/212 661 1620, Canada ⓣ1/416 961 5948, Australia & NZ ⓣ02/9505 9698; ⓦwww.aerosvit.ua/eng.html.
Air Baltic UK ⓣ0911/598 0599, ⓦwww.airbaltic.com.
Air Berlin UK ⓣ0871/500 0737, US ⓣ1-866/266-5588, Canada ⓣ866 705 9127; ⓦwww.airberlin.com.
Air Canada Canada ⓣ1-888/247-2262, ⓦwww.aircanada.ca.
Air France UK ⓣ0870/142 4343, Ireland ⓣ01/814 4060, US ⓣ1-800/237274, Canada ⓣ1-800/667 2747; ⓦwww.airfrance.com.
American Airlines US ⓣ1-800-433-7300, ⓦwww.aa.com.
Austrian Airlines UK ⓣ0870/124 26 25, Ireland ⓣ1-800 509 142, US ⓣ1-800/843-0002, Australia ⓣ1800/642 438 or 02/92004800; ⓦwww.aua.com.
British Airways UK ⓣ0844/493 0787, Ireland ⓣ01/890 626 747, US & Canada ⓣ1-800/247-9297, Australia ⓣ1300/767 177, New Zealand ⓣ09/966 9777; ⓦwww.british-airways.com.
bmi UK ⓣ0870/607 0555 or 0870/607 0222, Republic of Ireland ⓣ01/283 0700, US ⓣ1-800/788-0555; ⓦwww.flybmi.com.
Brussels Airlines UK ⓣ0905/60 95 609, Ireland 01/844 6006, ⓦwww.brussels-airlines.com.
Cathay Pacific Australia ⓣ13 17 47, New Zealand ⓣ0800/800 454; ⓦwww.cathaypacific.com.
Delta Airlines US & Canada ⓣ1-800/221-1212, ⓦwww.delta.com.
easyJet UK ⓣ0905/821 0905, ⓦwww.easyjet.com.
Emirates Australia ⓣ02/9290 9700 or 1300/303 7777, New Zealand ⓣ05/0836 4728; ⓦwww.emirates.com.
Finnair UK ⓣ0870/241 4411, Republic of Ireland ⓣ01/844 6565, US & Canada ⓣ1-800/950-5000, Australia ⓣ1300/798 188; ⓦwww.finnair.com.
KLM UK ⓣ0871 222 7474, Ireland ⓣ01/850 747 400, US & Canada ⓣ1-800/225 2525 (Northwest), Australia ⓣ1300/392 192, New Zealand ⓣ09/921 6040; ⓦwww.klm.com.
Korean Air Australia ⓣ02/9262 6000, New Zealand ⓣ09/914 2000; ⓦwww.koreanair.com.au.
Lufthansa UK ⓣ0871/945 9747, Ireland ⓣ01/ 844 5544, US ⓣ1-800/3995-838, Canada ⓣ1-800/563-5954; ⓦwww.lufthansa.com.
Qantas Australia ⓣ13 13 13, ⓦwww.qantas.com.au, New Zealand ⓣ0800/808 767; ⓦwww.qantas.co.nz.
Ryanair UK ⓣ0871/246 0000, Ireland ⓣ01818/303 030; ⓦwww.ryanair.com.
Scandinavian Airways (SAS) UK ⓣ0871/521 2772, Ireland ⓣ01/844 5440, US & Canada ⓣ1-800/221-2350, Australia ⓣ1300/727 707, New Zealand agent: Air New Zealand ⓣ09/357 3000; ⓦwww.flysas.com.
Transaero UK ⓣ0208/887 0394, Canada ⓣ1/905 405 1999; ⓦwww.transaero.ru/en.

Agents and operators

ebookers UK ⓣ0871/223 5000, Republic of Ireland ⓣ01/431 1311; ⓦwww.ebookers.com, ⓦwww.ebookers.ie. Low fares on an extensive selection of scheduled flights and package deals.
Flight Centres Australia ⓣ13 31 33, ⓦwww.flightcentre.com.au. Promises to beat any other discount fare quoted online.
Joe Walsh Tours Ireland ⓣ01/ 241 0800, ⓦwww.joewalshtours.ie. General budget fares agent.
North South Travel UK ⓣ01245/608 291, ⓦwww.northsouthtravel.co.uk. Friendly, competitive travel agency, offering discounted fares worldwide. Profits are used to support projects in the developing world, especially the promotion of sustainable tourism.
On the Go Tours UK ⓣ020/7371 1113, ⓦwww.onthegotours.com. Runs group and tailor-made tours, including Moscow city breaks, and a variety of tours including Moscow as part of a wider Russian itinerary.

STA Travel US ⓣ1-800/781-4040, UK ⓣ0871/2300 040, Australia ⓣ134 782, New Zealand ⓣ0800/474 400, South Africa ⓣ0861/781 781; ⓦwww.statravel.com. Worldwide specialists in independent travel; also student IDs, travel insurance, car rental, rail passes and more. Good discounts for students and under-26s.

Trailfinders UK ⓣ0845/058 5858, Republic of Ireland ⓣ01/677 7888, Australia ⓣ1300/ 780 212; ⓦwww.trailfinders.com, ⓦwww.trailfinders.com.au. One of the best-informed and most efficient agents for independent travellers, offering discounted flights, car rental, tailor-made tours and rail passes.

Travel Avenue US & Canada ⓣ1-800/333-3335, ⓦwww.t100g.com. Full-service travel agent that offers trips to Moscow as part of a variety of wider Russian tours.

Travel Cuts Canada ⓣ1866/246 9762, US ⓣ1-800/592 2887; ⓦwww.travelcuts.com. Canadian student-travel organization.

Package tours

Given the price of flights to and hotels in Moscow, there's a strong incentive to look for a **package tour** – an easy way of cutting the cost and trouble of organizing a trip. There are all kinds of possibilities, from city breaks to Trans-Siberian tours and luxury cruises. Unless otherwise stated, all prices below are land-only rates for one person in a twin share; where two prices are given, these refer to low- and high-season rates.

From the UK, a **city break** makes sense if you just have a few days, although the visa costs will make the trip much pricier than to other Eastern European cities (the prices quoted below include visa support, but not the cost of the visa itself). Go Russia runs an escorted four-day tour for £680 (year round), and unescorted three-day tours from £370–560, depending on the hotel, while Intourist has a three-night tour for £530–630, or £750–990 in a superior hotel.

Several operators offer **two-city tours of Moscow and St Petersburg**: the cheapest eight-day package comes from Intourist (£990–1240). Both Intourist and Go Russia run tours combining the two cities with historic towns on the **Golden Ring**, such as Kostroma, Uglich, Suzdal and Novgorod, which start at around £630. From the US or Canada, you can do an eight-day Moscow and St Petersburg tour, with an overnight train journey between them – ranging from the low-budget land-only Adventure Center ($1490) to deluxe tours ($9000–12,700 for ten days, flights included) from Exeter International. From Australia, a similar two-city tour with overnight train costs from A$1146 with Passport Travel, up to A$2112 with Eastern European Travel Bureau.

A more leisurely approach is a **Volga cruise** between Moscow and St Petersburg. Cosmos, for example, offers a twelve-day tour (£1230–1310) spending three days in each city with stopovers at Kostroma, Uglich and Yaroslavl, plus the wooden churches of Kizhi on Lake Onega. From the US, the Russian National Group offers a similar tour from $2465 ($3900 including flights), while from Australia, Abercrombie and Kent runs an equivalent deluxe tour from A$8975. Alternatively, Intourist does an eight-day tour (£1429) focusing on Moscow, St Petersburg and Kizhi (which is reached by hydrofoil from Petrozavodsk, rather than by cruise boat).

The other main area of tourism is **Trans-Siberian Railway packages** and "soft adventure" spin-offs in Siberia or Mongolia. The Trans-Siberian Railway links Beijing, Ulan Bator (in Mongolia) and Vladivostok (on Russia's Pacific coast) with Moscow, and many companies offer diverse experiences such as staying in a Mongolian nomad's tent, as part of the package or optional extras. The Russia Experience offers numerous trips starting in Moscow or St Petersburg and ending up in China, Mongolia or Vladivostok, from a thirteen-day trip to Beijing that includes staying in a felt tent on the Mongolian steppes (£1050) to forays into Buryatia or Tuva to witness Buddhist and shamanistic traditions, or the Altay Mountains to go whitewater rafting. GW Travel runs private "nostalgia" trains from Moscow to Mongolia for the Naadam festival (£3995), and along the Silk Road from Beijing to Moscow (£4815). From the US, Mir Corporation offers Beijing to Moscow by the Silk Road in a luxurious private train for $10,995. From Australia, China-based Monkey Business Shrine Tours arranges no-stopover trips from Beijing to Moscow, via Manchuria (from A$1563) or Mongolia (from A$1479), while Passport Travel offers the same routes with stopovers for A$1487 and A$1761 respectively.

Specialist tour operators

Abercrombie and Kent UK ⓣ0845/618 2200, Australia ⓣ613 9536 1800, New Zealand ⓣ618/0044 1638; ⓦwww.abercrombiekent.co.uk,

Fly less – stay longer! Travel and climate change

Climate change is perhaps the single biggest issue facing our planet. It is caused by a build-up in the atmosphere of carbon dioxide and other greenhouse gases, which are emitted by many sources – including planes. Already, **flights** account for three to four percent of human-induced global warming: that figure may sound small, but it is rising year on year and threatens to counteract the progress made by reducing greenhouse emissions in other areas.

Rough Guides regard travel as a **global benefit**, and feel strongly that the advantages to developing economies are important, as are the opportunities for greater contact and awareness among peoples. But we also believe in travelling responsibly, which includes giving thought to how often we fly and what we can do to redress any harm that our trips may create.

We can travel less or simply reduce the amount we travel by air (taking fewer trips and staying longer, or taking the train if there is one); we can avoid night flights (which are more damaging); and we can make the trips we do take "climate neutral" via a carbon offset scheme. **Offset schemes** run by climatecare.org, carbonneutral .com and others allow you to "neutralize" the greenhouse gases that you are responsible for releasing. Their websites have simple calculators that let you work out the impact of any flight – as does our own. Once that's done, you can pay to fund projects that will reduce future emissions by an equivalent amount. Please take the time to visit our website and make your trip climate neutral, or get a copy of the *Rough Guide to Climate Change* for more detail on the subject.

www.roughguides.com/climatechange

Ⓦwww.abercrombiekent.com.au. Tailor-made deluxe city breaks in Moscow and St Petersburg, plus upmarket tours featuring Moscow, Uglich, Kostroma, St Petersburg and the Imperial Palaces.

Adventure Center US & Canada Ⓣ1-800/228 8747, Ⓦwww.adventurecenter.com. Moscow to St Petersburg cruises, the Silk Route plus tours of Tallinn, Moscow, Suzdal, Kostroma, St Petersburg and Helsinki.

Affordable Tours US & Canada Ⓣ1-866/265 2651, Ⓦwww.affordabletours.com. Agent for many companies, including Abercrombie and Kent, offering luxury tours to Russia and Moscow.

Cosmos Tourama UK Ⓣ0871/423 8472, Ⓦwww.cosmostourama.co.uk. Mainstream tour operator offering Moscow and St Petersburg tours, as well as Russian River Cruises between the two cities stopping off at Kizhi and Yaroslavl.

Eastern European Travel Bureau Australia Ⓣ02/9262 1144, New Zealand Ⓣ03/ 3653 910; Ⓦwww.eetbtravel.com. Trans-Siberian and twin-centre packages, homestays in St Petersburg and Moscow, and river cruises.

Exeter International US Ⓣ800/633 1008 or 813/251 5355, Ⓦwww.exeterinternational.com. Deluxe St Petersburg-Kizhi-Moscow cruises, and tours of the Imperial Palaces.

General Tours US & Canada Ⓣ1-800/221-2216, Ⓦwww.generaltours.com. Cruises from St Petersburg to Moscow via Kizhi, and from Kiev to Odessa, Sevastopol and the River Dnieper, plus a Jewish heritage tour of Moscow and St Petersburg.

Geographic Expeditions US & Canada Ⓣ1-800/777-8183 or 415/922-0448, Ⓦwww.geoex.com. Adventure tours of Far Eastern Siberia (including reindeer trekking), and a Moscow-Golden Ring–St Petersburg package.

Go Russia UK Ⓣ0208/434 3496, Ⓦwww.justgorussia.co.uk. Specialist operator running trips to Moscow and St Petersburg as well as longer wilderness trips, the Trans-Siberian and Golden Ring tours. It also offers day-trips outside Moscow and a wide range of services including visa support.

GW Travel UK Ⓣ0161/928 9410, Ⓦwww.gwtravel.co.uk. Tours in private trains from Moscow to St Petersburg and Vladivostok; to Mongolia; and from Beijing to Moscow via the Silk Road.

Interchange UK Ⓣ020/8681 3612, Ⓦwww.interchange.uk.com. Tailored short breaks, flights, hotel and homestay bookings in Moscow and St Petersburg.

Intourist UK Ⓣ0870/1121232, Ⓦwww.intouristuk.com. Moscow and St Petersburg city breaks, twin centre and Golden Ring tours; tailor-made Trans- Siberian and adventure holidays.

Intours Corporation Canada Ⓣ1 416/766-4720, Ⓦwww.intours.ca. Canadian company offering tours of Moscow, St Petersburg, the Golden Ring, Siberia and the Russian Far East.

Mir Corporation US Ⓣ800/424-7289, Ⓦwww.mircorp.com. Small-group tours on themes such as Siberian shamanism or the Gulag Archipelago; the Silk Road by private train; Moscow, St Petersburg and the Golden Ring.

Monkey Business Shrine Beijing Ⓣ8610/6415 1954, Hong Kong Ⓣ852/2723 1376; Ⓦwww.monkeyshrine.com. Reliable, low-cost Trans-Siberian operator, based in China. Only accepts payment in euros, US dollars or Chinese yuan.

Page & Moy Holidays UK Ⓣ0870/833 4012, Ⓦwww.page-moy.com. Specializes in Moscow and St Petersburg city breaks.

Passport Travel Australia Ⓣ613/9500 0444, Ⓦwww.travelcentre.com.au. Trans-Siberian itineraries and Moscow-St Petersburg packages, based on homestay accommodation (hotel upgrades are available).

Pioneer Tours and Travel US & Canada Ⓣ1-800/369-1322, Ⓦwww.pioneerrussia.com. Customized individual tours, special-interest and educational tours to Russia and the CIS. Phone for information as their website is useless.

Russian Gateway (UK) Ltd UK Ⓣ01926/426460, Australia Ⓣ0800/700 333; Ⓦwww.russiangateway.co.uk, Ⓦwww.russian-gateway.com.au. Luxury city breaks and tours of St Petersburg and Moscow, river cruises, Trans-Siberian packages and school tours.

The Russia Experience UK Ⓣ020/8566 8846, Ⓦwww.trans-siberian.co.uk. Trans-Siberian specialists in individual and small-group travel in Russia, Mongolia, China and Tibet. Operates the Beetroot Backpackers Bus between Moscow and St Petersburg over summer (see p.29).

Russia House US & Canada Ⓣ202/364 0200, Ⓦwww.russiahouse.org. Arranges visas, tickets and accommodation in Russia, mainly for business travellers.

The Russia House Ltd UK Ⓣ020/7403 9922, Ⓦwww.therussiahouse.co.uk. Visa support, hotel bookings and other services, mainly for business travellers.

Russian National Group Inc US & Canada Ⓣ877/221 7120 or 646 473 2233, Ⓦwww.russia-travel.com. Affiliated to the Russian National Tourist Office in New York. All kinds of tours, including cruises to Solovki. Visa support, accommodation and flight bookings in Russia.

Scantours Inc US & Canada Ⓣ1-800/223-7226, Ⓦwww.scantours.net. Scandinavian ferry agent selling cruises and land-only Russian city breaks.

Scott's Tours UK Ⓣ020/7383 5353, Ⓦwww.scottstours.co.uk. Specialists in discount flights to Russia, visa support, accommodation and other services.

Space tourism

Russia is the only country in the world that currently offers rich tourists the out-of-this-world experience of **space travel**, and several tourists a year now head off into space. Alternatively, you can buy tickets ($102,000) for rides on a **sub-orbital shuttle** at the Zhukovsky air-force base outside Moscow. The C-21 shuttle ascends 100km from the earth's surface – beyond the atmosphere – enabling passengers to experience weightlessness and see the world from outer space. Other programmes currently available include a free-fall simulation of **zero gravity** in an IL-76 cargo plane ($7,000); flying to the **edge of the atmosphere** (where the earth's curvature is visible) in a MiG-25 fighter, plus a simulated rocket launch in the world's largest centrifuge at Star City ($19,000); or **supersonic** and **high-G flights** in a MiG-29 fighter and an L-39 jet trainer ($19,000). All these packages include deluxe hotels and tours in Moscow, pre-flight training at Zhukovsky and/or Star City, and various fancy souvenirs – but not flights to Russia. All the details are on ⓦwww.spaceadventures.com.

Space Adventures US & Canada ⓣ888-85-SPACE, ⓦwww.spaceadventures.com. US partners of Russia's Space Agency, whose deluxe packages feature sub-orbital, zero-gravity, supersonic and high-G flights.
Steppes Travel UK ⓣ01285/880 980, ⓦwww.steppestravel.co.uk. Offers Moscow and St Petersburg city breaks, as well as the Golden Ring, the Trans-Siberian and trips further east.
Sundowners Australia ⓣ613/9672 5300, ⓦwww.sundownersoverland.com. Offers various Trans-Siberian and Silk Road itineraries.
Travel for the Arts UK ⓣ020/8/799 8350, ⓦwww.travelforthearts.co.uk. Deluxe tours for music lovers, including the Russian Easter festival in Moscow and other opera and dance tours.
VisitRussia.com US & Canada ⓣ1-800/755-3080, ⓦwww.visitrussia.com. Online Russian travel agency with a sales office in New York.
Voyages Jules Verne UK ⓣ020/7616 1000, ⓦwww.vjv.co.uk. Moscow and St Petersburg city breaks and tours between the capitals including Waterways of the Tsars.

By train

Travelling **by train** from London takes two days and two nights, and costs easily as much as flying, so going by rail only really makes sense if you're planning to visit Moscow as part of an extensive European trip. The city's main international rail gateways are Berlin, Warsaw, Prague, Riga, Tallinn and Helsinki – but there are trains from as far away as Bulgaria, Romania and Ukraine if you happen to be coming from that direction.

Routes

There are no direct train services **from London** to Moscow, but there is a direct service from Paris three times a week, which takes 52 hours. Alternatively, there are through-trains from Brussels four or five days a week that enable you to connect with a Moscow train at **Cologne**. Taking Eurostar through the tunnel, you need to arrive in Brussels in time to catch the 5.25pm high-speed Thalys train to Cologne, where you change to the 10.28pm train to Moscow, which arrives two nights later. It's a good idea to bring food and drink for the journey, since there's nothing available in Russian sleeper wagons except hot water from the *samovar*, and the odd can of beer, and many of the stops at stations are in the small hours when buffets are closed, or passengers sleeping. Both the Paris and Brussels trains pass through Belarus, so you'll need to have got your **visas** for Belarus (see box, p.28) and Russia (p.30) before leaving: no visas are issued at the border crossings.

Starting **from Warsaw or Prague** is another possibility. There's a nightly train from Warsaw's Central Station to Moscow, connecting with a train from Prague (Fri & Sat) – though this has a bad reputation for robberies. Travel **from Estonia** is quicker (17hrs) and comfier, and doesn't require a Belarus visa. The daily *EVR* express from Tallinn leaves shortly before 5pm and arrives at 9.30am next day; see ⓦwww.gorail.ee for details. A second-class sleeper costs €82 one-way; tickets are sold by EVR Ekspress Reisid, Toompuiestee 37 (Ⓣ315/615 6722). More distantly, there's the daily *Tolstoy* express **from Helsinki**, at 5.45pm, which travels via Vyborg and St Petersburg, arriving in Moscow at 8.30am next day. The one-way fare is €56 with a supplement of €13 in high season. For details, see the Finnish Railways website, Ⓦwww.vr.fi.

Tickets and passes

You cannot buy **tickets** to Russia online, only by phone from certain UK rail agents, up to sixty days ahead. The best ones to call are German Railways' UK office, or Real Russia, which don't charge for quotes (unlike European Rail). It is possible to book the entire outward journey to Russia by using the computer reservation system for trains starting in Germany, but booking a return journey may be impossible in Britain. In that case, ask them to book you the outward journey with a return ticket on Eurostar and the Brussels–Cologne train and buy a ticket from Moscow back to Germany using a local agent, such as Svezhy Veter (see listings below).

Eurostar tickets from London to Brussels or Paris start at around £60 return and the Brussels to Cologne or Berlin ticket starts at around £38 each way. The prices from Cologne or Berlin to Moscow vary by the season but at time of writing cost around £174 to £257. The Paris to Moscow train costs about £230 one-way. On top of these fares, don't forget to factor in the cost of a Belarus transit visa (see p.28).

There are various European rail passes, but none covers Russia, Belarus or the Baltic States. With **InterRail**, for example, their Global Pass can take you as far as Warsaw or Helsinki; the onward fare to Moscow is about the same from either city (about £75/£51 in first/second class), but the journey from Helsinki is much faster and doesn't require a Belarus transit visa. A ten-day Global Pass costs £359/£265/£179 travelling first/second class/student rate; for a one-month pass, the rates are £599/£445 and £295. InterRail isn't valid in the UK, though you're entitled to discounts in Britain and on Eurostar and cross-Channel ferries. To qualify for the pass you must have been resident in Europe for six months.

North Americans, Australians and **New Zealanders** who don't qualify for InterRail can obtain a **Eurail pass**, which comes in various forms, and must be bought before leaving home. For more information, and to reserve tickets, contact Rail Europe or STA Travel (see p.23) in North America, CIT World Travel or Trailfinders (see p.23) in Australia and New Zealand.

Rail contacts

CIT World Travel Australia & New Zealand Ⓣ1300/361 500 or 03/9650 5510, Ⓦwww.cittravel.com.au. Sells Eurail and other European rail passes.

European Rail UK Ⓣ020 /7619 1083, Ⓦwww.europeanrail.com. Rail specialists that offer competitive international railway tickets from anywhere in the UK to most European cities, including Moscow.

Eurostar UK Ⓣ08705/186 186, Ⓦwww.eurostar.com. Latest fares and youth discounts (plus online booking) on the London–Paris and London–Brussels Eurostar service, and competitive add-on fares from the rest of the UK.

German Railways (Deutsche Bahn) UK Ⓣ0871/880 8066, Ⓦwww.bahn.de. Competitive fares for any journey from London across Europe, with very reasonable prices for those journeys that pass through Germany. Their website can't give prices for tickets to Moscow, but does allow journey-planning.

International Rail UK Ⓣ08700/84 14 10, Ⓦwww.international-rail.com. Agent for all European railways and rail passes.

Rail Europe UK Ⓣ0844/8484 064, US Ⓣ1-877/456 7245, Canada Ⓣ1-800/361 7245, Australia Ⓣ03/9642 8644; Ⓦwww.raileurope.co.uk, Ⓦwww.raileurope.com. SNCF-owned information and ticket agent for all European passes, and journeys from London as far as Warsaw. Sells Eurail passes to North Americans.

Real Russia Ⓣ0207/100 7370 or 100 4985, Ⓦwww.realrussia.co.uk. UK-based company with offices in Moscow who offer visa support, full tours and access to train tickets both within Russia and in the UK.

Svezhy Veter Ⓣ3412/45 00 37, Ⓦwww.sv-agency.udm.ru. Russian-based company selling tickets on domestic and international trains, as well as many other forms of transport and visa support.

The Man in Seat 61 ⓦwww.seat61.com. The best and most up-to-date online information about train travel, this wonderful site features virtually all the information you need to plan a journey by train from London to Moscow.

By coach

Travelling **by coach** instead of flying is unlikely to save you any money starting from Britain, but fares from Germany, Estonia and Latvia are significantly lower, and with cheap flights to Berlin, Riga and Tallinn, any of these could be a springboard for overland travel to Moscow. The network of bus services may also be useful for anyone roving round north-eastern Europe, if they don't qualify for InterRail or Eurail.

Coaches **from Germany** are run by Eurolines Russia and travel via Poland and Belarus. The coaches leave from various cities on Tuesday, Friday, Saturday and Sunday, arriving in Moscow at 10am two days later. The bus from Berlin leaves at 10.30pm, and costs €242 return; tickets can be booked through BEX (ⓣ030/3022 5294) in Berlin's central bus station, or online at ⓦwww.eurobusexpress.de.

The best way to get to Moscow **from the Baltic States** is via Latvia. Eurolines Latvia coaches runs regular direct services from Riga, which leave the central bus station on Monday (3.30pm) and Thursday (9.30pm), arriving in Moscow next morning. The fares are €37 one-way and €65 return. You can buy tickets from Baltijas Autobusu Linijas in the bus station (ⓣ371/721 4080) and check schedules on ⓦwww.eurolines.lv. There are currently no direct coaches from either Lithuania or Estonia to Moscow, but there are services from both Vilnius and Tallinn to St Petersburg, from where you can get a train or a further bus onto Moscow (see p.29 for details). From Tallinn, services to St Petersburg run several times a day (€18 one-way) and there are plans to reintroduce a direct service to Moscow in 2009: check Eurolines website for the latest schedules (ⓦwww.eurolines.ee).

If you're calculating savings, bear in mind the hidden costs of travelling by coach, such as transit **visas** for Belarus (see box below), and food and drink for the journey. You'll also need to obtain visas for both Russia and Belarus, if relevent, in advance (see p.30).

Coach operators

Eurobus Germany ⓦwww.eurobusexpress.de. Covers Germany and Eastern Europe.
Eurolines Estonia ⓦwww.eurolines.ee. Covers Germany, Latvia and Estonia, with services from Tallinn to St Petersburg.
Eurolines Latvia ⓦwww.eurolines.lv. Covers Germany and the Baltic States, and from Riga to Moscow.
Eurolines Lithuania ⓦwww.eurolines.lt. Connects Vilnius to most capitals in Europe, except Moscow.
Eurolines Russia ⓦwww.eurolines.ru. Coach operators to the Baltic States and Germany.

Belarus transit visas

All foreigners crossing Belarus by road or rail require a **transit visa**, which must be obtained in advance from a Belarus consulate abroad; ask for a double-entry visa if you're returning by the same route. You have to submit your passport with a Russian visa already in place to apply for a Belarus transit visa.

Belarus consulates

Australia/New Zealand No embassies or consulates; Belarus visas may be applied for online at ⓦwww.visatorussia.com.

Canada 130 Albert St, Suite 600, Ottawa, ON K1P 5G4 ⓣ613/233-9994, ⓔbelamb@igs.net. Single/double-entry transit visa C$100/C$177 (allow 5 working days).

UK 6 Kensington Court, London W8 5DL ⓣ0207/937 32 88, ⓦwww.uk.belembassy.org. Single/double-entry transit visa £44/£79 (5–10 working days).

US 1619 New Hampshire Ave NW, Washington, DC 20009 ⓣ202/986-1604, ⓦwww.belarusembassy.org. Downloadable form. Single/double-entry transit visa $100/$177 (5 working days).

By car

It doesn't make much sense to **drive** from Britain to Moscow, especially since foreign vehicles are so vulnerable to unwelcome attention in Poland, Belarus and Russia, but if you're intent on doing so, it's just about possible to make the journey in under three days. However, since this allows little time for stopping and sleeping, it is sensible to spread the journey out over a longer period and take in a few places en route.

The quickest and often the cheapest way to **cross the Channel** is via Eurotunnel (ⓣ0870/535 3535, ⓦwww.eurotunnel.com), which runs to Calais 24 hours a day, every fifteen minutes at peak times, and takes around 35 minutes. Off-peak fares start at around £50 each way for a car and one passenger.

Once across the Channel, the most **direct route** is through Germany, Poland and Belarus, broadly sticking to the following itinerary: Calais–Berlin–Warsaw–Brest–Minsk–Smolensk–Moscow. Note that you will need to obtain a Russian **visa** and a transit visa for Belarus in advance: see box on p.28 for details. Driving licence and insurance requirements in Russia are covered on p.45.

Coming from St Petersburg

Visitors entering Russia from Finland or the Baltic States may well reach Moscow **via St Petersburg**. Of the fourteen **trains** from St Petersburg's Moscow Station, the fastest are the evening *Nevskiy Express* (daily) and train #163 200 (Mon, Tues, Thurs, Fri), which take just under five hours, arriving shortly after 11pm. However, most people prefer an **overnight train** (8–9hr), arriving between six and nine o'clock next morning, namely the *Smena*, *Nikolaevskiy Express*, *Krasnaya Strela*, *Express* or *Afanasiy Nikitin*, which depart around midnight with the city hymn playing on the platform and smartly uniformed guards waving batons. Their unisex two- or four-berth coupés are overheated but otherwise quite comfortable; secure the door handle with the plastic device provided, or insert a wedge into the flip-lock in the upper left corner of the door. Shortly after leaving Moscow, an attendant will come around dispensing sheets and offering tea to passengers in first class. Mineral water, sweets and paper towels are provided gratis in all coupés.

While the journey is easy enough, buying **tickets** in St Petersburg is another matter, as speculators sometimes scoop the lot and bookings offices can be bewildering. Buy them through a local travel agency to avoid the hassle – it's well worth paying a small surcharge. Bring your passport, since tickets are sold to named individuals only, and conductors make identity checks before allowing passengers on board. Foreigners no longer pay more than Russians (for whom fares have doubled) nor need pay in hard currency.

Alternatively, you could consider a more leisurely journey to Moscow, with stopovers en route, aboard the **Beetroot Bus**, an enjoyable compromise between packaged and independent travel. Since you can join the bus in either city, it's ideal for people arriving in Moscow on the Trans-Siberian, or in St Petersburg from the Baltic States, who plan to visit the other city later. From July to September, the **classic tour** (£400) features three days' sightseeing in each city, a day relaxing at Lake Mets with a barbecue and a sauna, and a day and a night in Novgorod, with its medieval Kremlin. All their tours include airport or station transfers and superior budget accommodation: see ⓦwww.beetroot.org for details, or contact The Russia Experience in London (ⓣ0208/566 8846, ⓔinfo@beetroot.org) or Moscow (ⓣ095 453 43 68, ⓔinfo@trans-siberian.co.uk).

Red tape and visas

Bureaucracy has always been the bane of Russia, and visas are the greatest deterrent to would-be visitors; the system seems designed to make you spend money to get round the obstacles it creates. Visas must be obtained in advance from a Russian embassy or consulate in the country where you hold citizenship or have right of residence. If you're not travelling on a package tour, this requires some kind of visa support, which is available from B&B agencies, hostels and hotels in Moscow for their guests, or from specialist travel agents or visa brokers abroad. Then there's the fee for the visa itself – which varies from country to country according to type of visa and the speed at which it's issued – plus an extra sum if you pay an agency to deliver and collect your documents at the consulate rather than applying by post and allowing more time for the process, or queuing in person. At the minimum, you're looking at £45/€70/$100/C$75/A$85 for a visa, and could spend a lot more if you're in a hurry. Note that children travelling on their own passports also require a separate visa.

Visas

There are various kinds of **visa** (all in the form of a one-page sticker in your passport), and it's important to know which will suit you best. It's perfectly acceptable to use a tourist visa for a business trip, or a business visa for a vacation, if it's more convenient or works out cheaper that way. Russian officials don't care which kind you travel under providing the stated purpose of the trip matches the type of visa, all the paperwork is in order, and you don't overstay. Broadly speaking, a tourist visa is the cheapest, simplest option for a single visit of up to one month, while business visas are for those wishing to stay longer or travel back and forth without getting a new visa each time. However, regulations can (and do) change, upsetting the calculus; check consulate websites and the visa forum on Way to Russia (ⓦwww.waytorussia.net) for the latest facts.

Tourist, business, student or private visas each require some kind of supporting documentation from Russia, generically known as **visa support** – the exact form varies according to the type of visa. Most consulates accept faxed or emailed visa support for tourist and single- or double-entry business visas. Visitors on package holidays get this from their tour operator; many hotels in Russia can provide it if you make a booking with them for the duration of your stay; or local agencies can supply it for €20–30, if you're planning to stay in a flat or with friends.

A single-entry **tourist visa** is valid for an exact number of days up to a maximum of thirty, covered by a tourist voucher and confirmation of pre-booked accommodation in Russia for the entire period. If you're on a package tour, the formalities can be sorted out for you by the tour operator, though they may charge extra for this. If you're travelling independently, visa support can be provided by specialist travel agents in your own country (see "Getting There", pp.24–26), or by some agencies, hostels and hotels in Moscow for their clients (see Chapter 11, "Accommodation"). You have to email or fax them the following information: nationality, date of birth, passport number and date of expiry, length of stay at the hotel or hostel, date of arrival and departure from Russia, and credit card details. The visa support documentation should be faxed or emailed to you the following day, though some consulates demand the original visa support documentation, in which case you will have to allow enough time for it to be sent by post. The procedure is essentially the same whether you get your visa support from a travel agency in Russia or online.

A single- or double-entry **business visa** (specify which you want at the outset) is valid for up to 90 days. There is no obligation to pre-book accommodation, so you can rent a flat or stay with friends if you wish, though you must still register: some visa support services, such as Ⓦ www.visahouse.com, can register you for a business visa as well as providing visa support papers. You don't have to be doing business in order to get one; you simply need to provide the consulate with a stamped letter of invitation (or fax or email in some cases) from an organization in Russia that's accredited to the MID (Ministry of Foreign Affairs) and MVD (Ministry of the Interior). There are lots of foreign and Russian travel agencies and visa brokers that can provide this for a fee. **Multi-entry** business visas valid for a year are now only issued to people who have travelled to Russia before on a single- or double-entry business visa (enclose a copy of this with your application), and only allow you to stay up to 90 days within a 180-day period.

Foreigners wishing **to live in Russia** without spending an equivalent time abroad must now leave every 90 days to obtain a new business visa in another country. Otherwise, the only solution is to obtain a Russian residence permit, or a work permit from a local employer – which isn't an option for most people – or to come here on a student or private visa. A **student visa** is issued to people who come to study at a Russian school or institution, whose "foreign department" will post or fax an invitation directly to the consulate. A **private visa** is the hardest kind to obtain, requiring a personal invitation (*izveschenie*) from your Russian host – authorized by the PVU (see p.33) – guaranteeing to look after you for the duration of your stay. A faxed copy is not acceptable, so the original has to be posted to your home country, and the whole process can take three or four months to complete. By law, foreigners wishing to stay in Russia for longer than three months must obtain a **doctor's letter** certifying that they are not HIV-positive, and submit the original with their application – make a copy to take to Russia, as the letter will not be returned by the consulate.

If you are planning only to pass through Russia en route to another country, you can apply for a **transit visa**, valid for a 72-hour stopover in one city. You'll need to show a ticket for your onward journey from Russia, and a visa for the destination country (if required).

Russian embassies and consulates abroad

Australia 78 Canberra Ave, Griffith, Canberra, ACT 2603 Ⓣ 02/6295 9474; 7–9 Fullerton St, Woollahra, Sydney, NSW 2025 Ⓣ 02/9326 1866; Ⓦ www.sydneyrussianconsulate.com.
Canada 52 Range Rd, Ottawa, Ontario K1N 8J5 Ⓣ 613/236 7220, Ⓕ 613/238-6158, Ⓔ ruscons@rogers.com; 175 Bloor St East, South Tower Suite 801, Toronto, Ontario M4W 3R8 Ⓣ 416/962-9911, Ⓦ www.toronto.mid.ru; 3655 Avenue du Musee, Montreal, Quebec H3G 2EL Ⓣ 514/843-5901, Ⓦ www.montreal.mid.ru
Ireland 186 Orwell Rd, Rathgar, Dublin 14 Ⓣ 01/492 2048, Ⓦ www.ireland.mid.ru.
New Zealand 57 Messines Rd, Karori, Wellington Ⓣ 04/476 6113, Ⓦ www.russianembassy.co.nz.
UK 5 Kensington Palace Gdns, London W8 4QS Ⓣ 0207/499 1029, Ⓕ 0207/229 3215, Ⓦ www.rusemblon.org; 8 Melville St, Edinburgh EH3 7HF Ⓣ 0131/225 7098, Ⓦ http://edinburgh.rusembassy.org.
US 2650 Wisconsin Ave NW, Washington, DC 20007 Ⓣ 202/939 8907; 9 East 91st St, New York, NY 10128 Ⓣ 212/348 0926; 2790 Green St, San Francisco, CA 94123 Ⓣ 415/928 6878; 2323 Westin Bldg, 2001 6th Ave, Seattle, WA 98121 Ⓣ 206/728-1910; Ⓦ www.russianembassy.org.

Applying for a visa

The current official position is that you can only apply for a visa **in the country where you hold citizenship** or a country where you can prove **right of residence** for 90 days. EU citizens can thus apply for a visa in any EU state, but will need to prove right of residence to apply in the US or Australia, as will North Americans, Australians or New Zealanders anywhere abroad. This ruling is a huge blow to Trans-Siberian tourism, and Russia chat forums are buzzing as operators try to figure out a response: see Ⓦ www.waytorussia.net for advice if you are facing this difficulty

Aside from that, your **passport** must be valid for at least six months after your intended date of departure from Russia, and contain at least one blank page for the visa to be stuck into place. Some consulates have a website with a downloadable **application form** and detailed instructions on what documents to send. Others steer you towards visa brokers, with the consulate taking a cut of the profits. Apply as far ahead as possible, because the cost of processing your application rises the faster it's done.

With all applications, you need to submit two photos (signed on the back) and your passport. Applying to the consulate rather than through a travel agent or visa broker, you'll also need to include the fee (money order only by post, or cash in person, no cheques), plus a prepaid SAE envelope (preferably registered) for postal applications. Postal applications are preferable to delivering or collecting in person, when you may have to queue for ages outside the consulate, but will add three or more days to the **visa-processing times** given below. These refer to working days (excluding weekends and Russian holidays) *after* the day on which your application is received – though at some consulates you can get a visa in 48 hours or even on the same day if you're willing to pay enough. Just be sure to submit the right documents to support your application, which can differ in small but crucial details from country to country.

In Britain, applications from England, Wales and Northern Ireland are handled by the London consulate: the one in Edinburgh deals with Scotland. Forms can be downloaded from ⓦwww.rusemblon.org. Applications for a tourist visa require a tourist voucher, and a fax or copy of the confirmation from an accredited Russian or foreign travel agency. Applying for a business visa, a fax or photocopy of your invitation is required, plus a letter of introduction from your employer (or yourself, if self-employed, in which case you must also submit copies of bank statements for the last three months). For a transit visa, you need to include both the original and a copy of your ticket for onward travel from Russia. The fee for a single-entry (tourist or business), double-entry or multi-entry visa is directly related to the speed of processing: £45/55/110 for seven working days; £95/105/160 for same-day processing.

With the exception of Britain, Ireland and Denmark, **other EU countries** have signed an agreement with Russia on a unified tariff, with all types of visa costing €35 for seven-day processing, €70 for three days. Though some consulates nudge applicants towards a visa broker by refusing to accept postal applications, in theory these tariffs apply to EU citizens in any country, even outside the EU. Citizens of the **Schengen states** (Austria, Belgium, France, Germany, Holland, Italy, Portugal and Spain) must also fill in and submit an **insurance card** (downloadable from ⓦwww.russianvisas.org) with their application.

In the US, you must apply to the Russian consulate that has "jurisdiction" over your home state. Separate application forms for US citizens and other nationals are downloadable from ⓦwww.ruscon.com. If not delivered in person, all documents must be posted (and returned) using a certified courier. It's left to the consulate's discretion whether applicants can send a fax or photocopy of their invitation, or must submit the original – it's wiser to follow the latter course if the consulate hasn't specified. There's a flat fee of $100 for any kind of visa in six working days. Otherwise, the cost of a single-/double-/multi-entry tourist or business visa is $150/200/300 in three working days; $200/250/350 next day; and $300/350/450 for same-day issue.

In Canada, three consulates hold jurisdiction over different provinces, two with websites from which you can download the application form. Canadians must have two blank pages in their passport and include a photocopy of the page with their personal details. An original or downloaded and printed email voucher and confirmation is required for a tourist visa, and the original invitation for a double- or multi-entry business visa. Applying by post or in person, the fee must be paid with a money order (no cash or cheques). A single-entry tourist or business visa costs C$75 in fourteen working days, C$150 in seven days, C$180 in three days, C$210 next day, and C$300 the same day. For a double-entry visa the rates are: C$100, C$175, C$205, C$235 and C$325; for a multi-entry, C$205, C$290, C$305, C$335 and C$425. It is worth noting that it is sometimes possible for Canadians to get a visa at the Russian Embassy in London, but make sure you check before you leave Canada as it is not always the case.

In **Australia**, copies of the tourist voucher or business invitation are okay for a single- or double-entry visa, but multi-entry visas require the original document. A single-/double-/multi-entry visa costs A$85/140/350 in fifteen working days; A$110/170/370 in ten days; A$140/200/400 in five days; A$170/255/430 in two days; A$200/285/460 in one day; and A$400/485/600 for same-day issue.

Migration cards and registration

On arrival in Russia, foreigners must fill out a **Migration card** (Migratsionnaya karta) similar to the "landing card" given to non-EU citizens arriving in Europe, which will be stamped by an immigration official. Your stated reason for travel should correspond with the type of visa you are travelling under (tourism, business, etc). You also need to specify the organization that issued your invitation and your address in Russia: if you don't know your address, you can put the name of any hotel in Moscow, though it's a good idea to have a reservation as they sometimes ask for confirmation. Guard the card as carefully as your passport, as you'll need to produce it when leaving Russia; make a photocopy to show if you're stopped by the police (see pp.54–55), or lose the original.

By law, all foreigners must **register** their visa within 72 hours of arrival (excluding weekends and public holidays, but including the day when you arrive, even if this is after office hours). It used to be a stamp on your visa or Migration card, but is now a slip of paper (which should be photocopied as a precaution). Hotels are legally obliged to register guests (and may charge a small fee) however they obtained their visa support, but visitors who opt for homestay or flat rental can only be legally registered by the company that issued their invitation (and it has a responsibility to do so), so it's vital that it has an office (or accredited partner) in Moscow. Similarly, hostels may only register guests who got their visa support from the hostel (or its partner). As a result of the registration process becoming so complex, many hostels and some of the cheaper hotels are now reluctant to accept foreign guests unless they are staying for a week or more.

If renting from a private landlord, they must provide you with a letter to submit to your local Passport and Visa Service or **PVU** (*Passport i Viza Upravlenie* – still universally known by its old acronym, **OVIR**), which charges R1000–1500 to register you: check the address of your local office on ⓦwww.fmsmoscow.ru, or to find out more information on the process, see ⓦwww.waytorussia.net.

While not registering within the 72-hour limit is an infringement for which the police can detain you up to three hours and/or fine you R1000 (under Federal Law #195-FZ, Article 18.3), officers have been known to try to extort more during ID checks (see p.55). The easiest way to get belatedly registered is to check into a hotel for one night. This might not cover your whole time in Russia, but at least you'll have some evidence of registration. Some tourist agencies may be willing to register you for up to 30 days at a fictitious address for around R600. When it comes to leaving Russia, immigration officials may not even bother asking for your registration slip – but there are enough tales of people being stopped, fined or missing their plane to make it wise to get properly registered.

Currency declaration and customs

Another form available at the airport and border crossings is the **currency declaration**, for listing valuables brought into and out of Russia. You don't need one and can simply walk through the Green customs channel unless you're carrying over $10,000 in cash, in which case you must declare it on a form and get it stamped going through the Red channel. This also goes if you're travelling with hypodermic needles; bring a prescription for them and declare them under "Narcotics and appliances for use thereof". GPS devices may not be brought into Russia. It is not necessary to register cameras, laptops and other items if you are planning on staying within Moscow.

Export controls change so frequently that even customs officials aren't sure how things stand. The official line is that you can currently export 250 grams of black caviar and any amount of red, and there are no limits on alcohol or cigarettes – though the last two are subject to allowances set by other countries. You can currently take up to R250,000 out of the country in any currency, though for traveller's cheques there is no limit and no need to make a declaration.

The main restriction is on exporting **antiques and contemporary art**, though it's unclear where they draw the line between artwork and souvenirs (which aren't liable to controls). However, you can be fairly sure of encountering problems if you try to take out antique icons, samovars, porcelain or jewellery. Permission to export contemporary art and antiques (anything pre-1960, in effect) must be applied for to the Ministry for Culture at Neglinnaya ul. 8/10, room #298 (Ⓣ921 32 58), but you would be advised to ask the seller to do the paperwork for you, if possible. If the export is approved, you can be liable for tax of up to one hundred percent of the object's value. The export of pre-1960 books must be approved by the Russian National Library, 3/5 ul. Vozdvizhenka, Beliy Gorod (Mon–Fri 9am–7pm Sat 9am–6pm closed last Mon of each month).

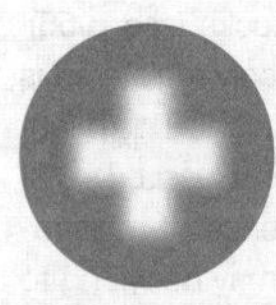

Health

Visitors to Moscow are advised to get booster shots for diphtheria, polio and tetanus, but there's no need to be inoculated against typhoid and hepatitis A unless you're also planning to visit remote rural areas. Though there's no danger of malaria, mosquitoes can be fierce during the summer months, so a mosquito net or a locally available repellent is advisable. The most likely hazard for a visitor, however, is an upset stomach.

Pollution, SADS and stress

Moscow's **water** supply is obtained from four reservoirs outside the city rather than the polluted Moskva River, but even so, few Muscovites will drink tap water unless it has been boiled first. It is regarded with particular suspicion in the spring, when the melting snow cover is believed to cause manure and other pollutants to enter the reservoirs. To play safe, use only bottled water for drinking and cleaning your teeth, or tap water that has been boiled for fifteen minutes and then allowed to stand overnight. Bottled water is widely available in kiosks and supermarkets.

While the authorities maintain that the concentrations of heavy metals, nitrates, phenol, ammonia and other chemicals in the water supply are well below the limits set by the World Health Organization, **air pollution** is acknowledged as a serious problem. In many areas of Moscow, the level is thirty to fifty times above WHO limits – or even higher. Though brief exposure shouldn't do you any harm, visitors may feel inexplicably tired after a day or two, while long-term residents can suffer from apathy and skin complaints as a result.

The commonest visitor's ailment is **diarrhoea**, caused by spoilt food or poor hygiene. While restaurants and cafés are generally safe, street food should be regarded with more caution. Always wash your hands before eating or preparing food, and avoid using the reusable towels in restaurants or public toilets.

You don't have to believe in **SADS** (Seasonally Affected Disorder Syndrome) to feel its effect during the long Russian winter. Anyone staying more than a month can easily get run-down owing to a lack of vitamins, and depressed by the darkness and ice. According to a survey of Moscow's expat community, the chief problems are alcoholism, nervous breakdowns and sexually transmitted diseases. A lot of this stems from the **stress** of living in an exhilarating, brutal and bewildering city, where foreigners can take little for granted. If you're going to be here awhile, pace yourself and adapt to the rhythms of Russian life. Because Moscow is, as Russians say, "without limits", you must determine your own in order to stay sane here.

Mosquitoes, roaches and ticks

When there isn't snow on the ground, many parts of the city near rivers or marshes are plagued by **mosquitoes**. The best solution for a good night's sleep is to bring a mosquito net, but, failing that, you should invest in a mosquito-zapping device known as an Ezalo, taking tablets under the generic name of Raptor, both of which are sold at pharmacies, supermarkets and household goods shops. As in New York, there are few apartment blocks without **cockroaches** lurking in the heating and ventilation shafts and behind kitchen fittings. Don't leave food uncovered overnight, and try to put the critters out of your mind.

More seriously, forested areas outside the city are potentially infested with encephalitis-bearing **ticks** (*kleshy*) during May and June. Russians take care to cover their heads, shoulders and arms at this time of year when walking in forests, so you should do the same or, failing that, check all over your body (particularly your neck and shoulders) for signs of burrowing ticks. If you find them, press around the tick's head with tweezers, grab it and gently pull outwards; avoid pulling the rear of the body or smearing chemicals on the tick, which increases the risk of infection and disease.

Bootleg liquor and sexually transmitted diseases

If you drink alcohol, it's hard to avoid the national drink, vodka – and frankly, you can't hope to relate to Russia without at least one vodka-fuelled evening with Russians. Getting drunk and speaking *dushe po-dushe* (soul-to-soul) goes with the territory. Unfortunately, so does **bootleg liquor** – a hazard that can be avoided by following the advice on p.342.

Vodka and a rampant sex industry make Moscow one of the most hedonistic cities on Earth. Just keep in mind that the large number of intravenous drug users and prostitutes has made it a nexus of **AIDS/HIV**, so you would be very rash to have any sexual encounter without using a condom. In the event of being found to be HIV-positive or carrying an infectious disease such as syphilis or hepatitis, you risk being incarcerated in a locked isolation ward and treated like a subhuman. If you suspect you're infected, seek treatment outside Russia.

Pharmacies, doctors and hospitals

For minor complaints, it's easiest to go to a high-street **pharmacy** (*aptéka*), which stocks a wide range of Western and Russian products; most are open daily from 8am to 9pm and identifiable by the green cross sign. It goes without saying, however, that if you are on any prescribed medication, you should bring enough supplies for your stay. This is particularly true for diabetics, who should ensure that they have enough needles. Both Russian and western brands of **condoms** (*prezervativiy*) can be found in all pharmacies as well as many 24-hour shops and kiosks. **Tampons** can also be bought from pharmacies: local chemists sell Ukrainian-made Tampax, while imported ones can be found in large supermarkets.

The standard of **doctors** varies enormously, so seek recommendations from friends or acquaintances before consulting one. Some Russian specialists are highly skilled diagnosticians who charge far less for a private consultation than you'd pay in the West.

If your condition is serious, public **hospitals** will provide free emergency treatment to foreigners on production of a passport (but may charge for medication). However, standards of hygiene and care are low by Western standards and horror stories abound. Aside from routine shortages of anaesthetics and drugs, nurses are usually indifferent to their patients unless bribed to care for them properly. Long-term expats advise, "Get an interpreter first, then a doctor". On the whole, however, foreigners rely on special clinics with imported drugs and equipment, and American-standard charges – a powerful reason to take out insurance. Many foreign clinics have their own ambulances, and can arrange medical evacuations. For a regular public **ambulance** phone ⓣ01 and demand "*Skoraya pomosh*" – the more urgent you sound, the better the chance of a speedy response. All of the clinics listed below have English-speaking doctors and accept major credit cards.

Clinics in Moscow

American Medical Center Prospekt Mira 26, build. 6 (entrance from Grokholsky Pereulok) ⓣ933 77 00, ⓦwww.amcenter.ru/en; Prospekt Mira metro. All medical and dental care at very high prices; OK if you're insured. Consultants work 8am–8pm. Daily 24hr.

European Dental Centre 1-y Nikoloschepovskiy per. 6, str. 1 ⓣ933 00 02, or 933 66 55 (for emergencies); Smolenskaya metro. Mon–Fri 9am–8pm, Sat 9am–4pm.

European Medical Centre Spiridonievsky per. 5 ⓣ933 66 55, ⓦwww.emcmos.ru/en; Pushkinskaya, Tverskaya or Mayakovskaya metro. Consultants work Mon–Sat 8am–9pm. Daily 24hr.

International SOS Clinic Grokholskiy per. 31, 10th floor ⓣ937 57 60, ⓦwww.sosclinic.ru; Prospekt Mira or Komsomolskaya metro. Family practice; trauma unit with ultrasound and CAT scan. Daily 24hr.

Mediclub Moscow Michurinskiy pr. 56 ⓣ931 50 18, or 932 23 16 (for emergencies); bus #661 or #715 from Prospekt Vernadskovo metro. Canadian joint-venture with family doctor, testing facilities, pharmacy and ambulance. Mon–Thurs 9am–8pm, Fri 9am–6pm, Sat 10am–2pm.

24-hour pharmacies

36.6 Tverskaya ul. 25/9, str. 2 ⓣ299 24 59; Mayakovskaya, Belorusskaya or Mendeleevskaya metro.

Stariy Lekar ul. Arbat 54/2 ⓣ244 00 21; Smolenskaya metro.

Information and websites

Russian tourist offices abroad are few in number and poorly stocked with maps and brochures. If you want to do some research or whet your appetite for Moscow before you go, there are various websites worth checking out. In Moscow, the local foreign-language press and listings magazines are the best sources of information, unless you can read Russian.

Information

Moscow is one of the few capitals in Europe with **no tourist information centre** where you can walk in and get a map or an answer to a question. Intourist, the former state agency, no longer even has a downtown office, and the plethora of private tour companies across the city are into selling holidays abroad, rather than catering to foreign visitors. It is worth asking the **hotel service bureaux** at the luxury hotels for advice, and you can sometimes pick up a free listings magazine and map of the city there; hotel guests get a more helpful response than walk-in enquirers, though, and the scruffily dressed may not get past the doormen. Backpackers' **hostels** (see p.335) also provide a raft of information for their guests, as well as low-priced excursions and services for a modest commission.

For reviews of restaurants, clubs, concerts and exhibitions, check out the free **English-language papers** the *Moscow Times* or the *eXile*, which can be found in hotels, restaurants, bars and shops frequented by foreigners. The *Moscow Times* features arts and club listings on Fridays, while the *eXile* reviews clubs and restaurants in each issue. You may also run across the monthly colour magazines *Where Moscow* and *Pulse*, whose reviews can also be useful. For those with some knowledge of the language, there are several weekly **listings magazines in Russian**, including the trend-setting *Afisha* and the more family-oriented *Vash Dosug*, sold at newspaper kiosks all over the place.

If you're planning to stay several months it's worth investing in the pocket-sized *Moscow Traveller's Yellow Pages*, listing all kinds of businesses and services, with lots of maps and advice on diverse aspects of life. It is regularly updated and sold for R1500–2000 at major hotels and Sheremetevo-2 airport; a Russian version, *Luchsee v Moskve* ("Best in Moscow"), is more widely available, or there's an online version in English, at ⓦwww.infoservices.com/moscow/.

Websites

There are myriad **websites** about Russia; the trick is finding ones that are up to date, relevant and accurate. Official tourist sites are notably lacking in all these respects: the Russian National Tourist Office site ⓦwww.interknowledge.com/russia hasn't been updated since 2006, though its US branch's site, ⓦwww.russiatravel.com, is up to date on visa regulations and the package tours it offers, but with little specific information on Moscow. This leaves the field clear for sites belonging to tourist agencies, hotels and hostels, which have more of an interest in providing up-to-date info, though this can't be taken for granted. Details of what's currently on in the city can be obtained from the *Moscow Times* website. See below for some of the most useful sites; a list of Russian media websites appears, while other sites are given in the text as appropriate.

Useful websites

Accommodation ⓦ**www.all-hotels.ru**, ⓦ**www.allrussiahotels.com**, ⓦ**www.hotelsrussia.com** and ⓦ**www.waytorussia.net**. Good sites for booking hotel rooms at discount rates. Other accommodation sites are listed under "Tourism" below, or "Accommodation agencies" in Chapter 11 (see p.326).

Ballet ⓦ**www.bolshoi.ru**. Official site of the Bolshoy Ballet, with news, features, schedules of performances (more up to date on the Russian-language version than the English one), and online booking. ⓦ**www.aha.ru/%7Evladmo/** is strong on ballet history and biographies, but lacks current news and listings.

Classical music ⓦ**www.classicalmusic.ru** is an audio archive of Russian composers and musicians. ⓦ**www.classicalmusic.spb.ru** is the last word on musical life in St Petersburg; a parallel site devoted to Moscow is under construction. For Russian choral music, check out ⓦ**www.musicarussica.com**.

eXile ⓦ**www.exile.ru**. The lurid lowdown on Moscow nightlife and politics, with a who's who of oligarchs and social stereotypes, but less current listings than in the *eXile* newspaper.

Gay & Lesbian ⓦ**www.gay.ru**. Advice, listings and contacts, including gay-friendly guides and homestay accommodation through their partner travel agency.

Moscow Times ⓦ**www.themoscowtimes.com**. Russia's leading English-language newspaper (see p.48).

MosNews.com ⓦ**www.mosnews.com**. An English-language spin-off from the Russian newspaper *Gazeta* (see p.48), featuring local and national news.

Restaurants, bars and clubs ⓦ**www.eng.menu.ru**. A useful site for restaurant, bar and club listings with excellent reviews.

Theatre ⓦ**www.theatre.ru**. Covers Moscow's stage world; mainly in Russian, but with some links to theatres in English.

Tourism ⓦ**www.waytorussia.com** and ⓦ**www.moscowcity.com** are best for practical advice, though German-speakers may find the webzine ⓦ**www.moskau.ru** equally useful. Low-budget travellers should check out ⓦ**www.hostels.ru** or ⓦ**www.cheap-moscow.com**.

Yellow Pages ⓦ**www.infoservices.com**. Traveller's Yellow Pages for Moscow, St Petersburg, Novgorod and Vyborg. Comprehensive listings for each city, plus theatre seat-plans.

Arrival

Arriving by air, there's a big difference between getting into town from Moscow's two main airports. While a shuttle train whisks you into the centre from Domodedovo, getting in from Sheremetevo means at least an hour on the traffic-choked Leningrad highway, passing a monument in the form of giant anti-tank obstacles that marks the nearest that the Nazis got in 1941. Arriving by train at one of the city's main-line stations, you'll be pitched straight into street life at its rawest, and the Moscow metro. Relatively few tourists arrive by bus or boat.

Airports

The gateway of choice, **Domodedovo** has been recently refurbished and Is linked to Pavelets Station in central Moscow by a **shuttle train**, which covers the 35km in 45 minutes. To board the train, turn left in the Arrivals terminal (which has currency exchange, car rental and ATMs) and keep going through the Departures terminal until you see the ticket office for the train, shortly before its platforms. You'll need to change money before buying a ticket as they only take rubles. Trains run hourly from 6am to 11pm; the fare is around R300. Several airlines have agreements with the train company by which passengers get a free ticket if they show their boarding pass: check with your airline to see if your ticket is covered. Alternatively, **bus** #405 and **minibuses** leave from the car park outside Departures to Domodedovskaya metro, in southeast Moscow (30–40min; R200) from 6am to 10pm. In the event that you'll arrive after either the train or buses and the metro have ceased working, a **taxi** into the city centre costs R1400 upwards and takes from one to one and a half hours, depending on traffic.

Sheremetevo-2, 28km northwest of the centre, hasn't been upgraded since it was built for the 1980 Olympics and is notoriously bottlenecked and depressing – though with all the usual facilities on its concourse. Getting into town **by public transport** involves travelling to Rechnoy Vokzal (bus #851 or minibus #48) or Planernaya (bus #817 or minibus #49) metro station in the northwest suburbs and thence into the centre by metro. The buses and minibuses run every 10–15 minutes from 6am to midnight; the journey to Planernaya takes 30 minutes (almost half the time it takes to reach Rechnoy Vokzal), but the metro ride into the centre takes 15–20 minutes from either station. If that sounds too gruelling or you know that you'll be arriving late or with a lot of baggage, **arrange to be met**. Most hotels offer this service for R1500–2500; hostels charge in the region of R1500, and firms such as Logus 88 (☎911 97 47) or Taxi Bistro (☎324 99 74) even less. If you don't pre-book a car, you'll be at the mercy of a cartel of **taxis** charging R2000–2800 for a ride into the centre – and probably fated to fume in a traffic jam on Leningradskiy prospekt, too.

Flights from St Petersburg, the Baltic States or Central Asia arrive at **Sheremetevo-1** airport, which is linked by the same buses and minibuses to Rechnoy Vokzal and Planernaya as its sister airport across the runway (see above).

Two other airports handle flights from elsewhere in the Russian Federation. **Bykovo**, west of the city, is linked by suburban train (5am–10pm; every 20min; 1hr) to Vykhino metro in the southeast suburbs and Kazan Station in the centre. From **Vnukovo**, south of Moscow, express trains run to Klevskaya Station (7am–10.30pm; every 10min; 20min), while regular buses #611 (6am–1am; every 10min; 35min) and minibuses #45 (7am–11pm; every 10–15min) run to Yugo-Zapadnaya metro, thirty minutes' ride from the centre. Taxis from Bykovo or Vnukovo cost R1200–2000.

Leaving Moscow

Allow plenty of time to reach the airport, if only because formalities are time-consuming.

Airport enquiries

Domodedovo ⓣ495 933 66 66, ⓦwww.domodedovo.ru/en.

Sheremetevo-1 & 2 ⓣ495 578 91 01, ⓦwww.sheremetevo-airport.ru.

Bykovo ⓣ495 558 47 38.

Vnukovo ⓣ495 436 28 13, ⓦwww.vnukovo.ru/eng.

Getting to Domodedovo is easy: Paveletsk Station has a special lounge for shuttle travellers, and passengers on some airlines get free train tickets by showing their boarding pass. Providing you get there in time for the hourly departure, it should be hassle-free. With all the other airports, details of public transport are given above; a pre-booked taxi or hotel transfer to Sheremetevo usually costs less than being met at the airport.

Unless you're told otherwise, **check-in** opens two and a half hours before the scheduled time of departure, and closes forty minutes before boarding. Err on the side of caution; there may be long queues to pass luggage through scanners before you can enter the hall where the check-in desks are. Once checked in, a customs officer will expect to see your original **currency declaration** (see p.33) and a duplicate form detailing what you're taking out of the country (forms are available in the hall) before you pass through Immigration control into the departure lounge, with its overpriced bar and "duty-free" shops.

Train stations

Most of Moscow's eight main-line **train stations** are on the Circle line of the metro, and relatively central. Don't hang around, as they're full of beggars, thieves and drunks, and have nothing useful aside from left-luggage facilities and exchange bureaux.

Arriving by train **from London, Berlin or Warsaw**, you'll end up at **Belarus Station** (Belorusskiy vokzal), about 1km northwest of the Garden Ring, which is served by Belorusskaya metro. Most trains **from the Baltic States** arrive at **Riga Station** (Rizhskiy vokzal), 2km north of the Garden Ring (Rizhskaya metro), while services **from Prague, Budapest or Kiev** terminate at **Kiev Station** (Kievskiy vokzal), south of the Moskva River (Kievskaya metro).

Trans-Siberian trains from China or Mongolia pull into **Yaroslav Station** (Yaroslavskiy vokzal) on Komsomolskaya ploshchad. Services **from St Petersburg** and some trains **from Finland and Estonia** arrive at the neighbouring **Leningrad Station** (Leningradskiy vokzal), while trains **from Central Asia and western Siberia** terminate at **Kazan Station** (Kazanskiy vokzal), across the square. All three stations are linked to Komsomolskaya metro.

Trains **from Crimea and the Caucasus** arrive at **Kursk Station** (Kurskiy vokzal), on the southeastern arc of the Garden Ring (Kurskaya metro), while services **from central southern Russia** wind up at **Pavelets Station** (Paveletskiy vokzal), further round the Ring to the south of the river (Paveletskaya metro).

Bus terminals

Passengers arriving in Moscow disembark at the Intercars Russia office on Ukrainskiy bulvar, near Kievskaya metro, while **Eurolines** coaches terminate outside Leningrad Station near Komsomolskaya metro. Either is more central than the so-called **Central Bus Station** (Tsentralniy Avtovokzal) used by Russian intercity buses, which is actually in the far northeastern suburbs near Shchelkovskaya metro (15 min ride from Kurskaya metro, on the Circle line). It's not that bad a place to arrive, however.

River terminals

Passengers arriving by boat **from St Petersburg or Nizhniy Novgorod** dock at one of Moscow's river terminals, far from the centre. The **Northern River Terminal** (Severniy rechnoy vokzal) is ten minutes' walk from Rechnoy Vokzal metro on the Zamoskvoretskaya line, while the **Southern River Terminal** (Yuzhniy rechnoy vokzal) lies a similar distance from Kolomenskaya metro, at the other end of the same line. In both cases, the route to the metro station is signposted at the terminal.

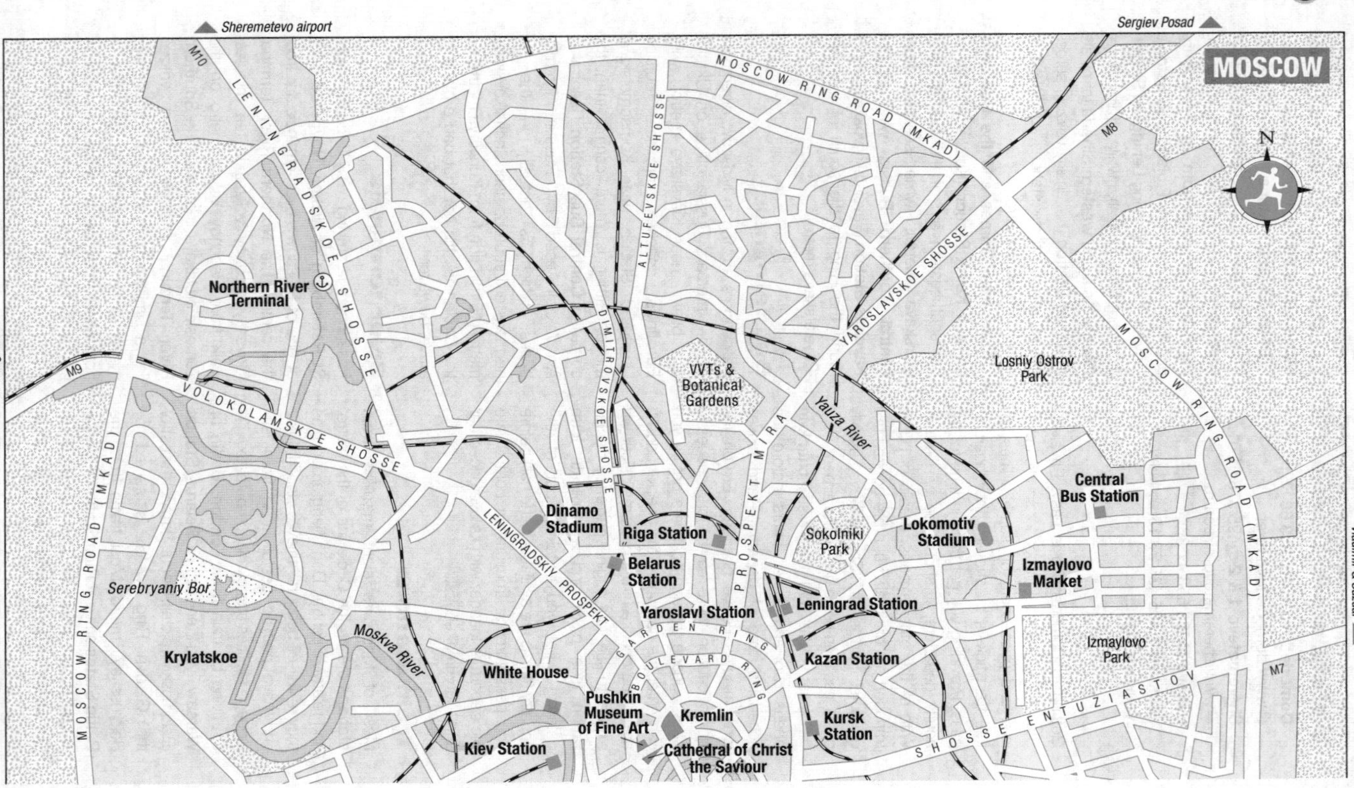
MOSCOW
N
Sergiev Posad
Sheremetevo airport
Arkhangelskoe
Vladimir & Suzdal
MOSCOW RING ROAD (MKAD)
M8
M10
M9
M7
LENINGRADSKOE SHOSSE
VOLOKOLAMSKOE SHOSSE
ALTUFEVSKOE SHOSSE
DIMITROVSKOE SHOSSE
YAROSLAVSKOE SHOSSE
PROSPEKT MIRA
LENINGRADSKIY PROSPEKT
SHOSSE ENTUZIASTOV
GARDEN RING
BOULEVARD RING
Northern River Terminal
Losniy Ostrov Park
VVTs & Botanical Gardens
Yauza River
Central Bus Station
Lokomotiv Stadium
Sokolniki Park
Izmaylovo Market
Izmaylovo Park
Dinamo Stadium
Riga Station
Belarus Station
Yaroslavl Station
Leningrad Station
Kazan Station
Kursk Station
Serebryaniy Bor
Krylatskoe
Moskva River
White House
Pushkin Museum of Fine Art
Kremlin
Kiev Station
Cathedral of Christ the Saviour

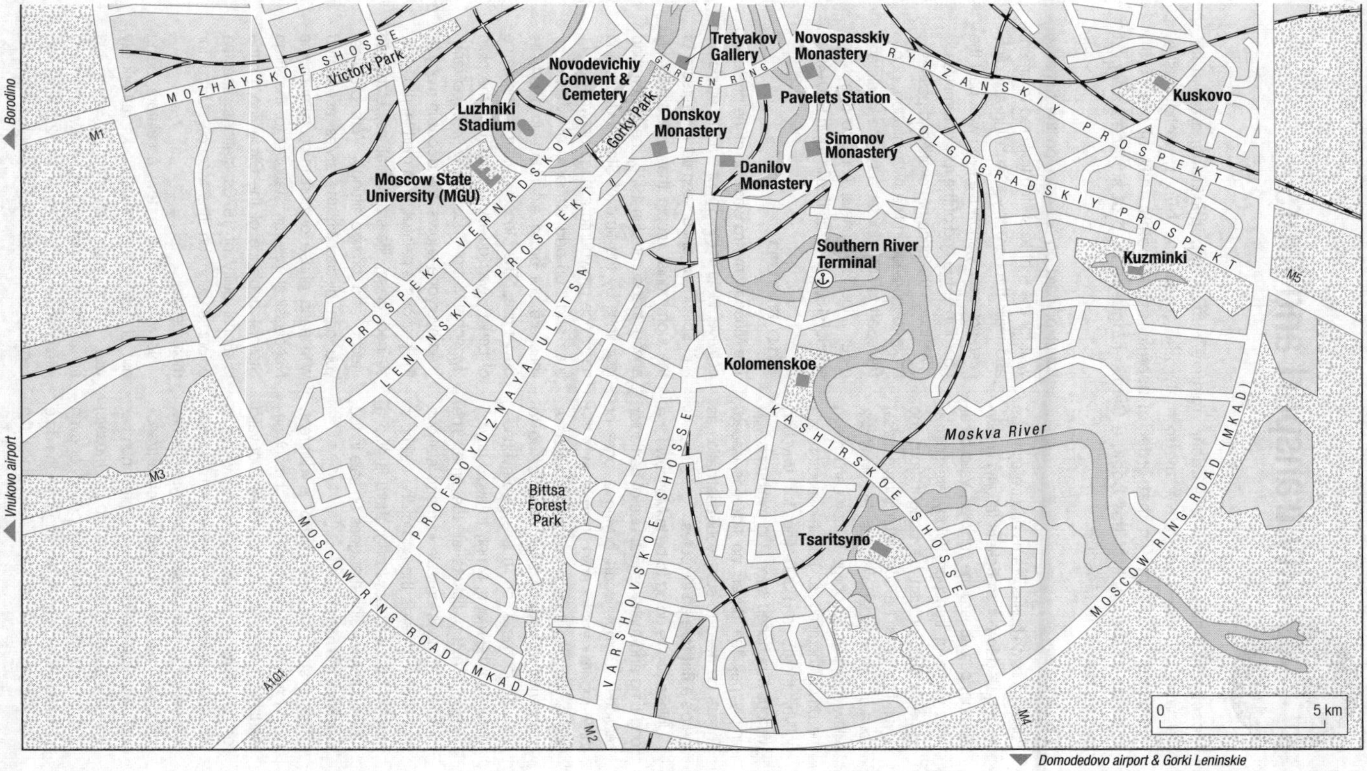

Domodedovo airport & Gorki Leninskie

Vnukovo airport

Borodino

0 5 km

MOSCOW RING ROAD (MKAD)

M1

M2

M3

M4

M5

A101

MOZHAYSKOE SHOSSE

Victory Park

Moscow State University (MGU)

Luzhniki Stadium

Novodevichiy Convent & Cemetery

Gorky Park

GARDEN RING

Donskoy Monastery

Tretyakov Gallery

Danilov Monastery

Pavelets Station

Novospasskiy Monastery

Simonov Monastery

Southern River Terminal

Kolomenskoe

RYAZANSKIY PROSPEKT

VOLGOGRADSKIY PROSPEKT

Kuskovo

Kuzminki

Moskva River

KASHIRSKOE SHOSSE

Tsaritsyno

VARSHOVSKOE SHOSSE

Bittsa Forest Park

PROFSOYUZNAYA ULITSA

LENINSKIY PROSPEKT

PROSPEKT VERNADSKOVO

City transport and tours

Moscow is a huge city, with a cheap, relatively efficient public transport system. As well as the superlative metro network, there are buses, trolleybuses, minibuses and trams (in that order of usefulness). A colour map of the metro appears at the back of this book; a Cyrillic-language map of surface transport routes is sold in Moscow.

Tickets

Passengers on buses, trams and trolleybuses are required to punch **tickets** (*talony*) in low-tech devices aboard the vehicles. Valid on all three forms of transport, *talony* are sold at some kiosks, or can be bought from the driver if there isn't a conductor (*provodnitsa*) aboard. On crowded vehicles, Russians ask fellow travellers to oblige if they can't reach the driver themselves. Ticket inspectors are active; there's a R300 fine for travelling without a punched *talon*. On minibuses you simply pay the driver; no ticket is issued. There's no need to state your destination as there's a **flat fare** on all routes.

Unless you're going to be in Moscow for a long time and make regular use of particular services, it's not worth buying a one- or three-month pass for any combination of the above vehicles, though you might purchase a one-month **yediniy bilet**, valid for up to seventy journeys on buses, trolleybuses, trams and the metro, simply to avoid buying *talony* or metro tickets all the time. The *yediniy bilet* goes on sale in metro stations and kiosks towards the end of the calendar month, for a few days only; there is also a half-monthly version that goes on sale in the middle of the month.

The system on the **metro** is different, insofar as you buy various kinds of machine-readable tickets. There is a *prisnoy bilet* valid for ten, twenty or sixty journeys within a thirty-day period, or a one-month *prisnoy bilet* valid for up to seventy journeys. Alternatively, you can buy a **transport card** (*transportnaya karta*) valid for an unlimited number of journeys within a one-month (*na mesats*) or three-month (*tri mesyatsa*) period, or even an entire year (*na god*), starting from the date of issue. With all of these, you place the ticket or card on a reader on the turnstile, wait for the light to switch from red to green, and walk through. If you're using a *yediniy bilet*, you simply show it as you walk past the guardian at the end of the row of turnstiles.

Although the price of tickets and passes is liable to increase in line with inflation, public transport is still affordable for the locals and great value for tourists. A metro ride costs about R15, a minibus ride in town R20–40.

The metro

The Moscow **metro** was one of the proudest achievements of the Soviet era – its efficiency and splendour once seemed a foretaste of the Communist utopia that supposedly lay ahead. Inaugurated in 1935, the system had four lines by the time of Stalin's death and has since grown into a huge network of 11 lines and 165-odd stations, of which four lines are still being extended. In 1994, its Soviet title, "The Moscow Metro in the name of Lenin", was quietly replaced by the plain "Moscow Metro" (*Moskovskiy Metropolitan*).

As everyone knows, the **decor** in many of the stations is palatial, with marble, mosaics, stained glass, life-sized statues, elaborate stucco and bronze fittings. With practice, you can distinguish the styles associated with each phase of construction, from the Neoclassical prewar stations to the High Stalinist opulence of the Circle line, or the lavatorial utility of 1970s stations: see the colour section on the Moscow Metro for more details.

Notwithstanding a few escalators being out of action, the metro works remarkably well. Trains run daily from 5.30am; the entrances and underground walkways linking interchange stations close at 12.30am, and services stop about half an hour afterwards, though on festivals and holidays they may run until later. There are trains every 1–2 minutes during the day and every 7 minutes at night.

Stations are marked with a large "M" and have separate doors for incoming and outgoing passengers. Many have two or three **exits**, located 500–700m apart at street level, which can be disorienting if you pick the wrong one. Though each exit is signposted with the appropriate street names (and even bus routes) at platform level, this is of no help if you can't read Cyrillic. Where **directions in the text** advise that you use the exit near the front (or rear) of the train, it's assumed that you're travelling out from the centre.

It's a peculiarity of Russian metros that where two or three lines meet, the **interchange stations** often have different names. In a quirk of its own, the Moscow metro also has two sets of stations called "Arbatskaya" and "Smolenskaya", on different lines (the Filyovskaya and Arbatsko-Povarskaya).

Though carriages now feature bilingual maps of individual lines, other **signs** and **maps** are in Russian only, so you'll have to learn to recognize the Cyrillic form of the words for "entrance" (*vkhod*), "exit" (*vykhod*) and "passage to another line" (*perekhod*). If the station names seem incomprehensible, concentrate on recognizing the first three letters only (our colour metro map at the back of this book shows both the English and Cyrillic versions).

Since the platforms carry few signs indicating which station you're in, it's advisable to pay attention to Tannoy **announcements** in the carriages (in Russian only). As the train pulls into each station, you'll hear its name, immediately followed by the words *Sléduyushchaya stantsiya* – and then the name of the next station. Most importantly, be sure to heed the words *Ostorozhno, dvéry zakryvayutsa* – "Caution, doors closing" – they slam shut with great force. Should anyone ask if you are getting off at the next stop – *Vy vykhodite?* – it means that they are, and need to squeeze past.

Due to Moscow's swampy subsoil – and the prospect of war – many of the lines were built extremely deep underground, with vertiginous **escalators** that almost nobody walks up, although the left-hand side is designated for that purpose. Interchange stations are often on several levels, with intermediary passages and transit halls where vendors have staked out their patch. Muggings are rare, but obvious foreigners may be targeted by pickpockets, so try to be inconspicuous and avoid speaking unless necessary.

Generally, however, the main problem is being jostled by **crowds** – during rush hour, you can well believe that nine million people travel on the metro each day (more than the number of passengers on the London and Paris systems put together). Beware of trolleys that can bruise your ankles. The problem is worst on the **Circle line**, which connects seven main-line stations; their respective metros are choked by passengers in transit with vast amounts of luggage.

Buses, trams, trolleybuses and minibuses

In theory, Moscow has a fully integrated network of buses, trolleybuses and trams, covering almost every part of the city. The reality is an overstretched and dilapidated system that battles on somehow, but is hardly user-friendly. Aside from the clapped-out vehicles, the **overcrowding** on some routes is such that you may find it physically impossible to get on board. Many visitors are also discouraged by the pushing and shoving, but Russians rarely take this personally, and once inside the vehicle will cheerfully help each other to punch tickets or buy them from the driver.

As a rule, buses and trolleybuses operate from 6am to 1am, and trams from 5.30am to 1.30am. Some routes are good for **sightseeing** on a Saturday or Sunday morning when there aren't many passengers. These are: bus б (circling the Garden Ring) and trolleybuses #1 (Belarus Station–Tverskaya ulitsa–Manezhnaya ploshchad–Zamoskvareche), #2 (circling the Kitay-gorod and the Kremlin before heading along Noviy Arbat and Kutuzovskiy prospekt to Victory Park), #5 (1905 Goda metro–Barrikadnaya–Nikitskiy bulvar–ulitsa Prechistenka and on to the Novodevichiy Convent), #8 (past the churches in Zamoskvareche) and #15 (around the Boulevard Ring and along Prechistenka to Novodevichiy). Trams mostly take roundabout routes, and don't run in the centre at all.

Stops (*ostankovki*) are relatively few and far between, so getting off at the wrong one can mean a lengthy walk. Bus stops are marked with an "A" (for *avtobus*); trolleybus stops with what resembles a squared-off "m", but is in fact a handwritten Cyrillic "t" (for *trolleybus*). Both are usually attached to walls, and therefore somewhat inconspicuous, whereas the signs for tram stops (bearing a "T" for *tramvay*) are suspended from the overhead cables above the road.

In addition to the services outlined above, Moscow is also covered by a network of **minibuses**, which Russians call *marshrutnoe taksi* (*marshrutki* for short). Operated by various firms, they mostly leave from metro or main-line stations and serve outlying residential areas, making them of little use to tourists. They can be flagged down at any point along their route but don't take standing passengers. You pay the driver the flat fare posted on the window, which is slightly above the regular bus fare.

Taxis

Registered taxis are usually Volgas or Fords with a chequered logo on the doors. If the domed light on the roof is on, the taxi is unoccupied. Those working through taxi companies (see box below) can be ordered by phone an hour or two ahead; dispatchers often speak a little English, but it helps to know Russian. They'll want to ring you back shortly before the pick-up is due to confirm that you still want a taxi and give you the vehicle's licence number. Like taxis that simply cruise for clients, they no longer use meters, so if you don't agree on a price first you're liable to pay whatever the driver demands at the end of the journey. Some drivers are happy to make opening bids of R1500 or more, before coming down a bit; others refuse to bargain at all. Though obviously open to abuse, this laissez-faire system is kept within bounds by strong competition from ordinary vehicles acting as taxis (see below), except at airports and hotels, where the "taxi mafia" has a stranglehold. At the airport it can be difficult to avoid their clutches, but at hotels you can always walk a block or so away and then look for an ordinary car.

Most Russians prefer **hitching rides in private vehicles**, which enables ordinary drivers to earn extra money as *chastniki* (moonlighters). You simply stand on the kerb and flag down any likely looking vehicle heading in the right direction. When one stops, state your destination and what you're willing to pay ("*Mozhno* [say the destination] *za* [specify the sum in rubles] *rubley?*"); the driver may haggle a bit, but there's so much competition that it's a buyer's market. Between R80–150 should suffice for any destination on or within the Garden Ring. Foreigners may be asked for more, but can usually get the same price by remaining firm.

As the above system is unregulated, it's as well to observe some **precautions**. Don't get into a vehicle which has more than one person in it, and never accept lifts from anyone who approaches you – particularly outside restaurants and nightclubs. Instances of drunken foreigners being robbed in the back of private cars are not uncommon, and women travelling alone would be best advised to give the whole business a miss.

Driving

You don't really need a **car** in Moscow, since public transport is cheap and efficient. Traffic

Taxi companies (24hr)

Allo Taxi ⓣ745 50 49, ⓦwww.allotaxi.ru.

Avtovozov Taxi ⓣ725 00 66, ⓦwww.avtovozov.su.

Stolichniy Izvozchik ⓣ971 53 00, ⓦwww.citytaxi.ru.

Taxi Audi ⓣ991 56 34 ⓦwww.taxi-audi.ru/en.

Taxi Blues ⓣ105 51 15, ⓦwww.taxi-blues.ru.

Taxi-Milady ⓣ785 81 81, ⓦwww.taxi-milady.ru.

Taxi 749 ⓣ991 61 73 ⓦwww.taxi749.ru/en.

is heavy, one-way systems abound, and local motorists act like rally drivers, swerving at high speed to avoid potholes or tramlines, and overtaking in any lane. Some drivers are likely to have purchased their licence, rather than passed a test. Driving yourself, therefore, requires a fair degree of skill and nerve.

To drive a car in Moscow you should carry with you all of the following **documents**: your home driving licence and an international driving permit with a Russian-language insert (available from the AA and other motoring organizations); an insurance certificate from your home insurer, or from your travel company; your passport and visa; the vehicle registration certificate; and a customs document asserting that you'll take the car back home when you leave (unless, of course, you rented it in Moscow).

Petrol (*benzin*) is easy to come by, and cheaper than in Western Europe. Foreign cars require 95 octane (4-star) or 98 octane (premium) but most Russian models use 92 octane (3-star) fuel. **Lead-free petrol** and high-octane fuel suitable for cars fitted with catalytic converters are sold at LUKoil and BP service stations, which take major credit cards as well as rubles. At all gas stations, you pay before filling up; if a pump attendant does the job, give him 10 rubles. Should you break down, 24-hour emergency repairs or tow-away is provided by Angel-NSA (☎747 00 22), Buksirov (☎936 25 55) and AvtoSOS (☎228 04 10).

Rules of the road – and the GIBDD

Rules and regulations tend to be ignored on the rare occasions when there are no traffic cops around. Traffic coming from the right, or onto roundabouts, has **right of way**, while **left turns** are only allowed in areas indicated by a broken centre line in the road, and an overhead sign. If you are turning into a side street, pedestrians crossing the road have right of way. **Trams** have right of way at all times, and you are not allowed to overtake them when passengers are getting on and off, unless there is a safety island.

Unless otherwise specified, **speed limits** are 60km (37 miles) per hour in the city and 80km (50 miles) per hour on highways. It is illegal to drive after having consumed *any* **alcohol** – the rule is stringently enforced, with heavy fines for offenders. **Safety-belt use** is mandatory (though most Russians only drape the belt across their lap, and drivers may be insulted if you belt up), and **crash helmets** are obligatory for motorcyclists. Take extra care when driving in **winter** (between Oct and March), when snow and ice make for hazardous road conditions.

Rules are enforced by the **GIBDD**, a branch of the Militia (see p.55) recognizable by their white plastic wands tipped with a light, which they flourish to signal drivers to pull over. They are no longer allowed to levy on-the-spot fines, but may give you a ticket which you will have to pay at a police station.

Vehicle crime is on the increase and Western cars are a favourite target – never leave anything visible or valuable in your car. Guarded parking (*avtostoyanka*) is available at all top hotels (free for guests) and in many locations around the city centre.

Car rental

If you have Russian friends or acquaintances, asking around may well get you a car with a driver for a lot less than you'd pay for self-drive hire at a car rental agency. Otherwise, it's worth checking out major rental firms in your own country, which may have special offers or reductions for advance booking, and comparing rates with those of Moscow agencies (see below). A foreign car is preferable to a Russian one if you're driving yourself. Many rental agencies insist on payment by credit card and require the full range of documentation (see opposite) for self-drive rental.

Rental agencies in Moscow

Avis Meshchanskaya ul. 7/21 (☎284 19 37) and Sheremetevo-2 (☎578 71 79), Ⓔrentacar@avis-moscow.ru. Self-drive and chauffeur rental.

Budget Tverskaya ul. 26, *Marriott Grand Hotel* (☎495 937 08 80); 1-ya Tverskaya-Yamskaya ul. 23, *Sheraton Palace Hotel* (☎931 97 00); Olympiyskiy pr. 18/1, *Renaissance Hotel* (☎931 90 00); Sheremetevo-2 airport (☎578 73 44). Ⓦwww.budgetrentacar.com. Self-drive Ford, Mercedes and minivan rental.

Hertz Domodedovo (☎797 46 72) and Sheremetevo-2 (☎578 56 46) airports, Ⓦwww.hertz.ru. Car reservations with or without driver.

Olga-Limousine Teatralniy pr. 1/4, *Metropol Hotel* (Ⓣ927 69 72); ul. Balchug, *Baltschug Kempinski* (Ⓣ230 65 00); Sheremetevo-2 (Ⓣ578 09 64). Mercedes, Hundai, Skoda and minibus rental, with or without driver.

Cycling

In Russia, **cycling** is seen as more of a leisure activity than a means of transport. Moscow has a handful of intrepid cyclists, but the combination of potholed roads, manic motorists, tramlines and air pollution is enough to put most people off. If you're leaving your bike somewhere, be sure to secure it with a Kryptonite or other U-shaped lock, rather than just a chain and padlock. To be inspired for longer journeys, read Dan Buettner's *Sovitrek: A Journey by Bicycle Across Russia* (published in 1994) or contact the Bicycle Club of Russia (Ⓦwww.bigfoot.com/~rctc), which organizes cycling expeditions. There are many dealers in foreign bikes in Moscow, most of which are based in the suburbs and offer **repair services.**

River cruises

From late April to early October (weather permitting), **river boat cruises** offer a superb view of such landmarks as the Kremlin, the monument to Peter the Great, the Cathedral of Christ the Saviour, Moscow University, the Novodevichiy Convent and Novospasskiy Monastery – plus swathes of Moscow's new business districts, with snazzy postmodern architecture. The boats (called *kater*, or cutters) have an enclosed lower deck with a snack bar and an open-air top deck, so you can enjoy the trip in any weather – the only distraction being nonstop commentary in Russian. **Tickets** are sold at the river **termini** beside ploshchad Yevropy (see p.184) and the bridge near the Novospasskiy Monastery (p.253). You can get off (or board, if you have a ticket) at any of the **landing stages** in between: at the foot of the Sparrow Hills; Frunzenskaya naberezhnaya; Gorky Park near Krymskiy val; Bolshoy Kamenniy most across the river from the Kremlin; or Ustinskiy most near the *Rossiya Hotel* and Red Square.

On weekends and holidays, boats sail every half hour from 10am–8pm; weekday **schedules** are a lot less frequent. If you can't find a timetable posted, you could try asking the Capital Shipping Company (Ⓣ277 39 02) that operates the service.

Walking

The historic centre within the Boulevard and Garden Rings is best explored on foot, starting from a convenient metro station. Off the Stalinist squares and avenues that were imposed in the 1930s and 1950s, you'll find a mellower Moscow of courtyards and lanes in every hue of brick and stucco, with gaunt trees that burst into greenery as the slush of winter recedes. Moscow is a city of hidden charms, and whenever you least expect it localities are enlivened by a fairytale church, or some glimpse into a private world.

Less metaphysically, there are several minor **hazards** to bear in mind. Traffic is unpredictable and only respects zebra crossings at traffic lights, while the surface underfoot can't be taken for granted, either. Watch out for potholes, crevices, open storm drains and protuberant bits of metal. In winter everything is covered with snow or ice, causing hundreds of Muscovites to slip and break their legs each week. With the spring thaw, beware of roofs shedding their layers of snow or needle-like icicles; where roof-cleaning is in progress, the pavement below is marked as a danger zone (*opasnaya zona*) by red-and-white tape or a plank laid across two benches.

Tours

If you don't speak Russian and you find Moscow a bit daunting, guided tours can make things a lot easier. The obvious first choice is **Capital Tours** (Ⓣ232 24 42, Ⓔcapitaltours@col.ru, Ⓦwww.capitaltours.ru) in the Gostiniy dvor on ul. Ilinka, just off Red Square (see map, pp.68–69). Their three-hour **city tour** (daily 11am & 2.30pm) will familiarize you with such landmarks as the Bolshoy Theatre, the Cathedral of Christ the Saviour and the Sparrow Hills, while their walking tour of the **Kremlin and the Armoury Museum** (daily except Thurs 10.30am & 3pm; R2100) is an ideal introduction to Moscow's historic seat of power. It's advisable to book by phone or online (payment by Amex, MC, Visa or rubles only).

A wider range of excursions is offered by their sister company, **Patriarshy Dom**

Tours (Ⓣ&Ⓕ795 09 27, Ⓔalanskaya@co.ru, Ⓦwww.russiatravel-pdtours.netfirms.com), whose office (Mon–Fri 9am–5pm) is in School #1239, Vspolniy per. 6, just off the Garden Ring near Barrikadnaya metro. As well as tours of the old **Tretyakov Gallery** (R560) and the **Pushkin Museum of Fine Arts** (R510), the company offers exclusive access to the otherwise off-limits **Great Kremlin Palace** (R2100). They also run **themed tours**, such as Jewish Moscow (R840), Stalin's Moscow (R620) and the *War and Peace* trail (R2000).

Patriarshy Dom also runs **out-of-town excursions** (R1540–2100) to the Trinity Monastery of St Sergei, Lenin's estate at Gorkie Leninskie, Tchaikovsky's home at Klin and the battlefield of Borodino (on the anniversary of the battle), plus a twelve-hour excursion to Vladimir and Suzdal (R2655) – places covered in Chapters 9 and 10 of this book. The Trinity Monastery is scheduled every fortnight, the others only once a month.

For those that understand the lingo, **Russian-language tours** are another option. Transaero Tours (Mon–Fri 9am–7.30pm, Sat & Sun 10am–4pm) at Nikolskaya ul. 9, near Capital Tours, offer a similar Moscow tour (daily 11am and 2pm; R2000) and walking tour of the Kremlin and Armoury (daily except Thurs 10.30am and 3pm; R2140), while the Moscow City Bureau for Excursions, at ul. Rozhdestvenka 5, behind Detskiy Mir (daily 9.30am–6pm; Ⓣ924 94 96), has an even longer list of themed tours than Patriarshy Dom.

The media

The city's major hotels sell a limited range of foreign newspapers, generally a day or more old. Local English-language papers are useful for finding out what's on, and the *Moscow Times* features some national and international news, but to keep up with world events it's better to go online at an Internet café, or tune into foreign radio or satellite TV.

Russian TV is partially accessible to those with a limited grasp of the language: game show formats are familiar and news programmes gorily explicit. The press requires a real knowledge of the language. Besides sensationalism, its main flaw is peddling propaganda for business and political ends. While glasnost and the collapse of Soviet power led to almost total media freedom, it wasn't long before Russia's new financial oligarchs were bundling TV stations and newspapers into media empires. Most journalists shared the oligarchs' aim of getting Yeltsin re-elected, for fear of what a Communist victory would mean for their own careers; having colluded in one campaign to mould opinion, it was natural to go along with the wave that swept Putin into power, and then acquiesce when he stripped three oligarchs of their media empires, and control passed into the hands of others, closer to the Kremlin.

The press

If you can understand the language, the **Russian press** holds some surprises for those who remember it from olden days. *Pravda*, the Communist Party daily, fell into the hands of "Greek swindlers who claimed to be Communists" in the mid-1990s, and now only a rebel version exists in cyberspace. *Izvestiya*, once the organ of the Soviet government, and the erstwhile Young Communists' daily, *Komsomolskaya Pravda*, are now a pro-business sheet and a popular tabloid respectively, both owned by the oligarch Potanin. The elite peruse *Kommersant*, a liberal paper that's the last remnant of Berezovsky's media empire, or *Nezavisimaya Gazeta*, independent by name and allegiance. *Gazeta* is likewise critical of the Kremlin but its sensationalism detracts from the credibility of intrepid investigative reporters such as Anna Politovskaya, who is widely believed to have been murdered for her work. Russia's angry dispossessed buy *Sovetskaya Rossiya* or *Zavtra*, both unashamedly far right, xenophobic hate-sheets. *Limonka*, published by the National Bolshevik Party, is a more amusing vehicle for the ego of its leader, Limonov. However, Moscow's best-selling daily is a local paper, *Moskovskiy Komsomolets*, which specializes in crime, sex and showbiz scandals. Since one of its journalists was murdered after exposing corruption in the Army high command, the paper has shied away from serious investigative journalism.

While **foreign newspapers** aren't widely available in Moscow, you can be sure of finding them in major hotels at heavily marked-up prices, and often up to a week old. If you're staying a while and desperate to have foreign papers delivered, contact the subscription service IPS (Malaya Dmitrovka st., 29/1 ⓣ733 90 73, ⓦwww.ips.ru).

Many tourists prefer the **local English-language press**, which is better distributed, free, and will tell you **what's on**. The *Moscow Times* is a hardy perennial published from Monday to Friday, with listings and reviews supplement, *Metropolis*, in its Friday edition. Written for the expat business community, it combines local news with press agency reports and prim editorials. Similar but duller are the weekly English/German *Moscow Kurier* whose *LifeStyle* supplement is a cross between the reviews in the *Moscow Times* and the racy listings in the *eXile* – an "alternative" paper published every other Wednesday, which flaunts its commitment to partying, whoring and drugs. Though sure to offend some, its view of Russia is a welcome affront to the bland consensus peddled by the others. Additionally, there's a weekly entertainments sheet, *Element*, and the tourist-oriented monthly magazine *Where Moscow*. All these are available free of charge at Western watering holes and eateries like the *American Bar & Grill* and *Starlite Diner* (see Chapter 12 for addresses) – and you can also find the *Moscow Times* and *eXile* online.

Russian media online

Afisha ⓦwww.afisha.ru. Influential monthly style and listings magazine with reviews and listings, in Russian only.

eXile ⓦwww.exile.ru. Off the scale in terms of political incorrectness, but its club and restaurant reviews and political analyses are often nearer the mark than rival papers.

Gateway2Russia ⓦwww.gateway2russia.com. News and information portal, run in partnership with the UK *Financial Times*.

Moscow Times ⓦwww.themoscowtimes.com. The best source of local and national news.

Moskau.Ru ⓦwww.moskau.ru. A lively German-language webzine combining local and national news, features and facts for tourists.

NTV ⓦwww.ntv.ru. News, features and schedules for the NTV channel. Some of the website is in English.

Pravda.ru ⓦhttp://english.pravda.ru. English-language edition of the erstwhile Communist Party paper, in cyberspace.

RIA Novosti ⓦwww.rian.ru. Multilingual, state-owned Russian International News Agency. Putin-speak rules.

St Petersburg Times ⓦwww.sptimes.ru. The paper isn't distributed in Moscow, but is worth reading if you're also visiting St Petersburg.

TV and radio

Television in the Yeltsin era was outrageously biased, yet rivalry between media moguls made for some plurality and criticism. Putin ended that by using the financial giants Gazprom and LUKoil to prise the networks from their owners, ensuring that the Kremlin no longer needs favours to get its message across nor has much to fear from critical coverage. **ORT** (Channel 1) is the nation's favourite for its soaps, game shows and classic Soviet films. Its former owner Berezovsky was the *eminence grise* of Russian politics until he fled abroad to avoid being jailed on suspicion of fraud like his rival Gusinsky, whose **NTV** (Channel 3) angered the Kremlin with its reportage of the war in Chechnya, till Gazprom took over. While NTV news has since lost its edge, the station's slick thrillers, drama and documentaries make better viewing than

Channel 4's equivalents and are streets ahead of the wholly state-owned **RTR** (Channel 2), whose mix of soaps, tedious state events and servile news gives it the lowest rating of the lot.

Viewers in Moscow can also receive **Kultura** (Channel 5), the St Petersburg arts and culture channel, and **STS** (Channel 6), a light entertainment channel founded with the help of Ted Turner; several secondary channels, available only with the aid of a subsidiary aerial, which are heavy on game shows and US, Brazilian and Mexican films and soaps; and local cable TV stations delivering **OTV** (European news and documentaries), MTV-Russia and Sky.

As far as **radio** goes, most cafés and bars tune into one of the many FM music stations. The most popular are Europa Plus, which dishes out "the best of the West" on 106.2 FM, Radio Maximum (103.7), Hit FM (107.4) and Serebryaniy Dozhd (100.1) – all playing mainstream Russian and foreign pop – and the techno-oriented Stanitsiya 2000 (106). Russkoe Radio (107.8) and Radio Retro (72.92) are devoted to Russian music of the 1960s, 1970s and 1980s, while Nashe Radio specializes in jazz and blues (101.7). For classical music, tune in to Klassika (102.1) or Orpheus (72.14). Should you have a short-wave radio, it's also possible to pick up the BBC World Service (see Ⓦ www.bbc.co.uk/worldservice for frequencies), or you can listen to almost any radio station worldwide on the Internet if you have a fast connection.

National holidays and festivals

National holidays (*prazdnik*) have been a contentious issue since the end of Communism. All the major Soviet ones are still observed, and in Moscow (if nowhere else) there are once again parades of gymnasts, school kids and soldiers across Red Square on **May Day**, while the wishfully renamed anniversary of the Bolshevik Revolution on **November 7** sees Communists, nationalists and anarchists march into the centre, as rival, state-sponsored events take place on Red Square. While **New Year** remains a family and friends affair, and International Women's Day on **March 8** a chance for Russian men to give flowers to their spouses and female acquaintances and make a big fuss of doing the housework for one day of the year, the Putin era has seen increasingly lavish parades, fireworks and fly-pasts on **May 9** (Victory Day, marking the defeat of Nazi Germany) and **February 23** (Defenders of the Motherland Day), while Russian Independence Day on **June 12** – the anniversary of Russia's secession from the Soviet Union – has become a feel-good event that tries to please everyone, called Russian Flag Day. in 2006 an extended **New Year** holiday (**Jan 1–5**) was declared almost right up to the Russian Orthodox Christmas (**Jan 7**), in recognition of the fact that many Russians skipped work anyway: in practice, of course, many people take January 6 off too. Good Friday is still a working day, much to the Church's annoyance. As **Easter** is a moveable feast according to the Orthodox calendar, it may coincide with public holidays in May, giving rise to an extended holiday period of three to four days. If public holidays fall at the weekend, a weekday will often be given off in lieu.

Festivals

No publication or website gives the full rundown of the city's festivals throughout the year. Some events are sure to occur at a certain time, but others drift across the calendar, or vanish in some years. A few have websites or contact numbers, but with others the best you can hope for is a month's notice in *Where Moscow*, *Pulse*, *Afisha* or

Calendar of holidays, festivals and events

January

New Year's Day (Jan 1)*.
Orthodox Christmas (Jan 6–7)*.
Old New Year (night of Jan 13/14), according to the Julian calendar, is celebrated by traditionalists.
Christmas at the Kremlin concerts by the Chamber Orchestra Kremlin (second half of Jan).
Svyatki Masquerades, bell-ringing and the blessing of the water at Kolomenskoe (Sun nearest to Jan 19).
CIS Cup indoor finals, if any Moscow team is in the running (sometime in Jan).

February & March

Defenders of the Motherland Day (Feb 23)*. Wreath-laying at war memorials all over Moscow.
Maslenitsa Festivities, handicrafts and pancakes at Kolomenskoe (Sat a week before the onset of Lent, usually in late Feb).
Buddhist New Year (late Feb/early March).
Golden Mask awards for drama, opera, dance and puppetry (late Feb/early March).
International Women's Day (March 8)*.
St Patrick's Day party at the Tochka club (mid-March).

April & May

Russian Championship and Russian Cup qualifying matches at local stadiums (early April onwards).
Orthodox Easter (date varies).
Easter Festival of classical music, Orthodox choirs and bell-ringing (date varies).
Moscow Forum international festival of contemporary music at the Conservatory (April).
SKIF festival of indie and avant-garde music, DJs and performance artists from Russia and abroad (April).
Vertical Festival of mountaineering and extreme sports films (mid-April).
International Labour Day/Spring Festival (May 1 and 2)*. Local festivities, especially at Kolomenskoe.
Moscow Stars Festival of classical music (throughout May).
Victory Day (May 9)*. Military parades on Red Square and/or Park Pobedy.
Long Arms festival of modern classical, fusion and experimental music (May).
Boheme Jazz festival at the Moscow International House of Music (late May).
Day of Slav Culture (May 24). Religious procession from the Kremlin to Slavyanskaya ploshchad.
Peter the Great's birthday pageant at Kolomenskoe (May 30).

June–August

Chekhov International Theatre Festival, anytime from May to August (every three years; next in 2009).
Troitsa Folk rituals at Kolomenskoe, marking the day of the dead (first Sun in June).
Beer festival at Luzhniki (first weekend in June).
Kupava festival held in Suzdal (early June) with bonfires and swimming.
Tchaikovsky piano competition at the Conservatory (every four years; next in 2011).
Russian Independence Day or Russian Flag Day, with concerts and fireworks (June 12)*.
Orthodox spiritual music festival at Kolomenskoe (June).
US Independence Day party at Kuskovo (July 4).
Ethnic Music Festival in the Hermitage Garden (early July) – Moscow's WOMAD.
Bastille Day outdoor pop concert (July 14).

Cucumber festival of food and drink in Suzdal (mid-July).
Navy Day (last Sun in July).
Airborne Forces Day (first Sat in Aug).Veterans drink and brawl in Gorky Park.
Spartak Cup ice-hockey matches (during Aug).
MAKS airshow at the Zhukovsky Airbase (mid-Aug every odd-numbered year).
Pusto open-air festival of video art, near the Tretyakov Gallery (late Aug).
Jazz at the Hermitage Garden – ethno-jazz and rock fusion (late Aug).
Spas Yablochni Medovy harvest festival at Kolomenskoe (Aug 30 till Sept 2).
Goldfish international children's animation festival (late Aug/early Sept).

September

Ice hockey season begins.
City Day (Sept 6). Carnival on Tverskaya ulitsa and a historical pageant at Kolomenskoe.
Battle of Borodino memorial ceremonies and a re-enactment of the battle at Borodino (first Sun).
Art Klyzama open-air festival of contemporary art and cinema, beside the Klyazminskoe Reservoir outside Moscow (early/mid-Sept).
Autumn Divertimenti at Arkhangelsoe – classical and early music (mid-Sept).
Solomon Mikoels International Festival of music, film, drama and literature (late Sept/early Oct).

October & November

French Music Festival at the Kremlin and major concert halls (throughout Oct).
Ibero-American Festival of dance, music and art from Latin America, Spain and Portugal (throughout Oct).
Dance Inversion international festival of modern dance (throughout Oct).
Kremlin Cup international tennis tournament at the Olympiyskiy Sports Complex (early Oct).
Talents of Russia festival of young classical musicians at the Rossiya concert hall (first half of Oct).
International Puppet festival at the Obraztsov Theatre and other venues (mid-Oct).
Mixed Fight world championships at Luzhniki Sports Complex (mid-Oct).
Rokfest international rock festival at the Luzhniki (mid-Oct).
International Folk Music Festival at the Central House of Artists (second half of Oct).
Festival of Japanese Music at various venues (late Oct).
Halloween Night celebrations at clubs (Oct 31).
Feast day of Our Lady of Kazan at her church at Kolomenskoe (Nov 4).
Day of Reconciliation and Accord (Nov 7)*. March by Communists from Oktyabrskaya ploshchad into the centre of town.
Baltic House international drama festival (late Nov/early Dec).

December

December Evenings of classical concerts at the Pushkin Museum of Fine Arts (all month).
Jazz Voices international festival of jazz vocalists (all month).
Christmas at the Kremlin Chamber concerts in the Armoury Hall and Patriarch's Palace (mid-Dec, continuing in the second half of Jan).
Russian Winter Festival at Izmaylovo Park, with *troyka* rides and folk dancing, and a festival of ice sculptures at the VVTs (late Dec, continuing early Jan).
New Year's Eve (Dec 31). A family feast, then party time.

Note: National holidays are marked with an asterisk.

the *Moscow Times*. Nearer the time, events are advertised by posters and banners on the streets.

Moscow City Government funds a number of **carnivals** and festivities. **City Day** (Sept 6 or the nearest Sat) sees a parade of floats down Tverskaya ulitsa and Militia men embracing samba dancers rather like at London's Notting Hill Carnival, and a historical pageant at Kolomenskoe (see p.235). This royal estate also hosts traditional folk festivals: **Svyatki** masquerades and bell-ringing in January, and **Spas Yablochni Medovy**, a harvest celebration with dancing and games. **Russian winter** festivals are also fun, with sleigh-rides, dancing and drinking in Izmaylovo Park (ⓣ499 166 50 24, ⓦwww.kremlin-izmailovo.com for information) and ice sculptures at the VVTs (ⓣ495 544 34 00, ⓦwww.vvcentre.ru/eng) in the run-up to New Year and in early January. September sees the start of the lavishly funded **Solomon Mikoels International Festival** (ⓦhttp://festival.gluz.ru) of drama, music, cinema and literature, followed by an **Ibero-American Culture** festival of dance, music and painting in October.

There are **music festivals** throughout the year: **jazz** in late May, late August and December; **ethnic** music in July; **rock** and **folk** in October; and **indie and avant-garde** in April and May. Lovers of **classical** music are spoilt for choice. Moscow's **Easter Festival** (ⓦwww.easterfestival.ru) features Orthodox choirs and bell-ringing, and the orchestra of St Petersburg's Mariinskiy Theatre, conducted by maestro Gergiev. Top conductors, soloists and ensembles from Russia and abroad perform at the Conservatory, the Tchaikovsky Concert Hall and International House of Music during **Moscow Stars** in May; at the Pushkin Museum of Fine Arts (ⓦwww.museum.ru/gmii) during **December Evenings**, and at the French and Japanese music festivals in October; while every four years the Conservatory hosts the world-class Tchaikovsky piano competition (ⓦwww.tchaikovsky.org.ru) – next scheduled for 2011.

Moscow's international **film** festival (ⓦwww.moscowfilmfestival.ru) is now an annual event (late June or Aug) that attracts foreign stars and directors as well as Russian ones. The main venue is the Pushkin cinema on Pushkinskaya ploshchad, but the closing ceremony is held at Gorky Park. Besides smaller festivals of children's animation (late Aug/early Sept) or extreme sports films (mid-April), there are two outdoor events, devoted to video-art (late Aug) and contemporary art and independent films (early/mid-Sept), the first near the old Tretyakov Gallery, the second by a reservoir to the north of Moscow.

Otherwise, the stellar event on the **performing arts** calendar is the Golden Mask festival, awarding prizes for the previous year's best drama, opera, dance and puppetry in Russia (late Feb/early March). **Drama** lovers should also pencil into their diaries the Baltic House international festival, which comes to Moscow from St Petersburg in late November or early December; or the Chekhov festival, staged every three years (next scheduled for May to Aug 2009). Foreign ballet and modern **dance** companies visit Moscow throughout the year, but especially during the Dance Inversion festival in October, which coincides with a long-established international **puppetry** festival at the Obraztsov Theatre.

The **sports** calendar revolves around soccer, ice hockey and tennis. Depending on how well local **football** teams Spartak, Dinamo, TsKA and Lokomotiv do in the qualifying rounds of the Russian Championship (starting in March and ending in Nov) and the Russian Cup (starting and finishing in May), or the indoor CIS Cup finals (Jan), there may be more or less action at their respective stadiums. **Ice hockey** comes a close second in popularity: TsKA and Krilya Sovetov are often favourites in the run-up to the Spartak Cup in August. **Tennis** doesn't have a long-established fan base, but the success of Russian players abroad has captivated the younger generation, ensuring an audience for the international Kremlin Cup (Oct). While the notion of bringing Formula-1 racing to Moscow seems to have fallen by the wayside, the Russian capital is a natural host for **martial arts** events like the no-holds-barred Mixed Fight championships (mid-Oct).

If you're hankering for Soviet-style **parades**, **Victory Day** (May 9) sees regiments and tanks mass at Victory Park, while **May Day** has gymnasts and folk dancers doing their stuff on Red Square. On a smaller scale, **Navy Day** (last Sun in July) is heralded by patrol boats on the Moskva River and fireworks near the monument to Peter the Great. **Airborne Forces Day** (first Sat in Aug) sees parachute displays, benefit concerts and veterans wearing stripy uniform vests zooming around in armoured cars or brawling in Gorky Park (not a time to wander the streets). And at **Borodino**, west of Moscow, military re-enactment clubs replay the epic battle between Napoleon and Kutuzov on the first Sunday of September.

During spring, the run-up to the Orthodox Easter overshadows the **Day of Slav Culture** (May 24), marked by a procession of monks and nuns from the Kremlin to the statue of Cyril and Methodius on the edge of the Kitay-gorod. **Easter** (*Paskha*) is the high point of the Orthodox calendar: Moscow's churches and cathedrals are packed with worshippers, who exchange triple kisses and the salutation "Christ is Risen!" – "Verily He is Risen!". At midnight they circle the church holding candles – an unforgettable sight. Whereas Easter is a moveable feast whose date changes each year, the **Russian Orthodox Christmas** (*Rozhdestvo*) starts at midnight on January 6 and goes on until dawn the following day. The choir, the liturgy, the candles and the incense combine to produce a hypnotic sense of togetherness, which Russians call *sobornost*. Despite their emotional charge and Byzantine splendour, Orthodox services are come-and-go as you please, allowing non-believers to attend without embarrassment, but women should cover their heads and wear a skirt.

Less obviously, the **festivals of other faiths** are celebrated in their places of worship: Rosh HaShana, Yom Kippur and Hannuka at the Choral and Lubavitch synagogues; Ramadan at the Central Mosque; and Catholic festivals at the Church of the Immaculate Conception (see p.63 for addresses).

Muscovites have taken to some expatriate celebrations. **St Patrick's Day** is celebrated by clubbers in mid-March, while thousands of people attend the **US Independence Day** party at Kuskovo (see p.260) and the outdoor pop concert with fireworks on **Bastille Day** (the location varies) – held on the nearest Saturday or Sunday to July 4 and July 14, if not on the exact day. And **Halloween** (Oct 31) has been adopted by students as a chance to dress up and party, ignoring gripes about its "satanic influence" by the Orthodox Church.

Despite all the Christmas trees and bunting (and partying among the expat community), Russians largely ignore the Western Christmas in the rush to prepare for **New Year** (*Noviy God*). This remains a family occasion until midnight, when a frenzied round of house-calling commences, getting steadily more drunken and continuing until dawn. In residential areas, you may see people dressed as *Dyed Moroz* (Grandfather Frost, the Russian equivalent of Father Christmas) and his female sidekick, Snegurochka (Snow Maiden), who do the rounds wishing neighbours a Happy New Year (*s Novim Godom!*). To enjoy it all over again, many Russians also celebrate the Orthodox New Year or **Old New Year** on the night of January 13/14 – though this isn't an official holiday.

Trouble and the police

Moscow's lurid reputation for mafia killings, police corruption and terrorism is based on fact, but exaggerates its effect on everyday life for most people. Personal security is generally in inverse proportion to personal wealth; those with most to fear are local politicians or rich businessmen. The average citizen – or visitor – is no more likely to be a victim of crime than in any other large European city. Pickpockets are the main hazard, on the metro and around the major tourist sites.

Avoiding trouble is mostly commonsense. Keep your money in a money-belt under your clothing, and don't carry cameras or other valuables in a bag on your back. Most street robberies involve gangs of child-pickpockets rather than stick-ups or muggings. Sensible precautions include making photocopies of your passport and visa, and noting down traveller's cheque and credit card numbers. If you have a car, don't leave anything in view when you park it, and take the cassette/radio with you. Luggage and valuables left in cars make a tempting target and foreign or rental cars are easy to spot. Vehicles get stolen, too; use guarded parking lots, or park in the inner courtyard of buildings.

Changing money with street hustlers is a sure way to get ripped off, and the Militia couldn't care less about it. Getting blind drunk or going back to strange flats with prostitutes is also asking for trouble, and neither the Militia nor foreign consulates have much sympathy in such cases. If you're unlucky enough to be robbed you'll need to **go to the police**, if only because your insurance company will require a police report. Few Militia speak any language but Russian; try the phrase *Menya obokrali* – "I've been robbed". There are Militia posts in every metro station.

Generally, **the law** in Russia is Janus-faced. Bribery is widespread, and few Russians expect cops or judges to be honest, while many regard the police as a predatory force with links to organized crime. There's no doubt that police corruption at a lower level is manifest in petty shakedowns. In a neat Catch-22, people aren't obliged to carry **identification** by law, but the police can demand ID and, if not satisfied, take them to a Militia station. Some use this as a licence to hassle people, especially those with darker skins (on grounds of "security") or tourists who might pay a "fine" when something is found to be "wrong" with their documents. It's best to carry your passport and Immigration Card at all times and be ready to point out that your visa, registration stamp and currency declaration are all in order – which makes it hard for them to find a pretext. If you have a mobile phone, pull it out and tell the officer you'd like to call your embassy (see p.58) to have somebody meet you at the police station. Do not surrender your passport.

Terrorism

Terrorism isn't an abstract threat in Moscow. The mysterious 1999 apartment block bombings that were the *casus belli* for Russia's reoccupation of Chechnya have since been echoed by other terrorist acts in the capital. In 2002, Chechen terrorists took over 800 people hostage at a musical; 130 are thought to have died from the effects of the gas that was pumped in to subdue the Chechens as Special Forces stormed the building (see p.256). The following year, female suicide bombers (dubbed "Black Widows" by the media) killed thirteen people at a rock festival and six passers-by outside the *National Hotel*. In 2004 a bomb on the metro in February left 39 dead and 122 injured, while in August, two suicide-bombers bribed their way through security at Domodedovo Airport and brought down two passenger planes, killing everyone on board. In 2006, a further two planes heading from Moscow to the Black Sea came down in mysterious circumstances, killing 147 people, though the last four years has seen little terrorist activity in Moscow itself. Despite this, Muscovites are well accustomed to metal detectors in the foyers of concert halls, museums and hotels, and spot ID-checks at metro stations (where photography has been prohibited for security reasons).

Sexual harassment and racism

Sexual harassment is no worse than in Western Europe, but the tendency of Russian men to veer between extreme gallantry and crude chauvinism – and of Russian women to exploit their femininity – makes for misunderstandings when foreigners are involved. Russian women feel secure enough to flag down cars as taxis (see p.44), but foreign women shouldn't risk it. At some clubs and hotels, unaccompanied women are liable to be viewed as prostitutes, hassled by security guards or even by pimps, mistaking them for freelance operators. **Prostitution** is not illegal under Russian law, and most upmarket hotels, bars and nightclubs have prostitutes who'll proposition foreign males and even married couples.

Russians of both sexes regard striptease acts as normal entertainment. Political correctness has barely a toehold in Russian society. **Racism** is a casual and common phenomenon, sometimes expressed violently, mostly against Roma, Chechens, Azerbaijanis and Central Asians, but also Africans and Arabs. Anyone dark-skinned can expect to be stopped by the Militia on a regular basis. Some years, gangs of neo-Nazis have rampaged through the streets on Hitler's birthday (April 20) – many embassies advise their nationals to keep off the streets at this time.

The police

The Ministry of the Interior (MVD) maintains several law-and-order forces, all of them armed and with a high profile on the streets. Foremost are the regular police, or **Militia** (*Militsiya*), in blue-grey uniforms with red bands on their caps, or jumpsuits and parkas in shades of grey. Militiamen are much in evidence around metro stations, where they often conduct spot ID-checks.

The other main branch of the Militia is the **GIBDD**, or traffic police – still universally known by its former title, the GAI – who you're only likely to run into if you're driving or happen to be involved in an accident. They wear Militia uniforms emblazoned with a badge, armband or large white letters reading ДПС (standing for *Dorozhno Patrulnaya Sluzhba*, or Highway Patrol Service).

Some checkpoints are also manned by the **OMON**, a paramilitary force charged with everything from riot control to counter-insurgency. In Moscow, they guard important state buildings, patrol crowds and lend muscle to Militia crackdowns on mafia gangs. Dressed in green or grey camouflage and toting Kalashnikovs or pump-action shotguns, they look fearsome but are unlikely to bother tourists unless they get caught up in a raid of some kind. Should you be so unlucky, don't resist in any way – even verbally. The same goes for operations involving **RUOP**, the smaller Regional Force Against Organized Crime, whose teams wear civilian clothes or paramilitary uniforms like the OMON's, only the patch on the back reads РУОП instead of ОМОН.

Aside from maybe having your passport scrutinized by a plainclothes agent at the airport, you shouldn't have any contact with the once-feared KGB in its post-Soviet incarnation as the **Federal Security Service (FSB)** unless you get involved in environmental activism or high-tech acquisitions. The FSB has regained the powers of the KGB in the 1970s, thanks to its former boss, Putin, but it no longer intervenes in the lives of ordinary Russians, who are happy to ignore it. Visitors are free to do likewise, or saunter past the Lubyanka (see p.139) out of curiosity (taking photos is not advised).

You're far more likely to encounter **private security guards** in banks, stores, clubs or restaurants. They are allowed to carry guns, but have no powers of arrest and you're not legally obliged to show them ID. However, since many wear paramilitary garb, you may find it hard to distinguish them from the OMON (who have full police powers); private guards usually wear an ОХРАНА badge.

Emergencies

The emergency number for the police, ambulance and fire services is ⓣ01.

Travel essentials

Addresses

In Russian usage, the street name is written before the number in **addresses**. When addressing letters, Russians start with the country, followed by a six-digit postal code, then the street, house and apartment number, and finally the addressee's name; the sender's details are usually written on the bottom of the envelope. The number of the house, building or complex may be preceded by *dom*, abbreviated to *d*. Two numbers separated by an oblique dash (for example, 16/21) usually indicate that the building is on a corner; the second figure is the street number on the smaller side street. However, if a building occupies more than one number (for example, 4/6), it is also written like this; you can usually tell when this is the case as the numbers will be close to each other and will both be even or odd. *Korpus* or *k.* indicates a building within a complex, *stroinie* or *str.* a detached part of a complex, *podezd* (*pod.*) an entrance number, *etazh* (*et.*) the floor and *kvartira* (*kv.*) the apartment. **Floors** are numbered in American or Continental fashion, starting with the ground floor, which Russians would call *etazh 1*. To avoid confusion we have followed the Russian usage throughout this book.

Apartment blocks in the centre of Moscow are typically arranged around an inner courtyard or *dvor*, off which numbered *podezdy*, or communal entrance stairways, give access to flats in different wings of the complex. Out in the suburbs, high-rise blocks are the norm and it's customary for several to share the same street number, with each block being given a subsidiary number or Cyrillic letter to distinguish it from the others.

The main **abbreviations** used in Moscow (and in this book) are: ul. (for *ulitsa*, street); nab. (for *naberezhnaya*, embankment); pr. (for *prospekt*, avenue); per. (for *pereulok*, lane or side street) and pl. (for *ploshchad*, square). Other common terms include *most* (bridge), *bulvar* (boulevard), *shosse* (highway), *alleya* (alley) and *sad* (garden). In the city centre most of the streets now have **bilingual signs** (Cyrillic and Latin script), which make it easier to find your way around.

Cyrillic addresses

alleya	аллея
bulvar	бульвар
dom	дом
dvor	двор
etazh	таж
kvartira	квартира
korpus	корпус
most	мост
naberezhnaya	набережная
pereulok	переулок
ploshchad	площадь
podezd	подьезд
prospekt	проспект
sad	сад
shosse	шоссе
ulitsa	улица
Email	лектронная почта
Internet	Интернет

Airlines

Aeroflot Leningradskiy pr. 37, korp. 9 ☎735 55 55; Sheremetevo-1 ☎578 73 76.
Air China ul. Kuznetskiy most 1/8, str. 5 ☎292 54 40.
Air France ul. Koroviy val 7 ☎937 52 81; Sheremetevo-2 ☎578 32 567.
Air India ul. Koroviy val 7 ☎237 74 94.
American Airlines Sadovaya-Kudrinskaya ul. 20 ☎234 40 74.
British Airways 1ya Tverskaya Yamskaya ul. 23 ☎263 25 25.
Delta Gogolevskiy bul. 11 ☎937 90 90.
KLM ul. Usacheva 33/2 str. 6 ☎258 36 00; Sheremetevo-2, office #616 ☎578 35 53.
Korean Air Bolshoy Gnezdikovskiy per. 1, str. 2 ☎725 27 27.
LOT Tverskoy bul. 26/5 ☎229 57 71; Sheremetevo-2, office #632 ☎956 46 58.
Lufthansa, *Baltschug-Kempinski Hotel*, ul. Baltschug 1 ☎737 64 04; *Renaissance Hotel*, Olimpiyskiy pr. 18/1 ☎737 64 00; *Sheraton Palace Hotel*,

1-ya Tverskaya Yamskaya ul. 19 ⓣ737 64 05; Sheremetevo-2 ⓣ737 64 15.
Malév Povarskaya ul. 21 ⓣ202 84 16; Sheremetevo-2 ⓣ578 27 10.
SAS 1-ya Tverskaya Yamskaya ul. 5 ⓣ775 47 47.
South African Airlines Sadovaya-Chernogryaznaya ul. 13, str. 3 ⓣ937 59 53.
Thai Airways Sadovaya-Chernogryaznaya ul. 13, str. 3 ⓣ937 59 20.
Transaero Paveletskaya pl. 2, str. 3 ⓣ800 200 23 76 (freephone); Nikolskaya ul. 11/13 str. 2 ⓣ298 02 52.

Churches

Churches and other places of worship are open for services, if not all day. It often depends on how valuable their icons are and whether there are enough parishioners, since few churches can afford to hire guards. In Soviet times, many were converted into museums, swimming pools, cinemas or workshops. Most have now reverted to their former purpose but many are still being repaired or redecorated, which may limit access. **Orthodox churches** celebrate the Divine Liturgy (*Bozhestvennaya Liturgia*) at 8am, 9am or 10am Monday to Saturday, and at 7am or 10am on Sunday and saints' days; most also hold **services** at 5pm or 6pm daily, some with an *akafist* or series of chants to the Virgin or saints. Both services last about two hours. Additional services occur on saints' days (*Prestolniy prazdnik*). Orthodox believers cross themselves with three fingers (first the head, then the stomach, followed by the right shoulder and then the left). See p.63 for details of religious services at non-Orthodox churches.

Costs

With over eighty percent of the nation's wealth flowing into Moscow, it's hardly surprising that it ranks as one of Europe's most expensive cities: huge new malls in every residential district attest to a Muscovite middle class outnumbering that of all the other cities in Russia put together. For visitors, **costs** in general terms are comparable to Paris or London, though transport is significantly cheaper. By far the biggest expense is **accommodation**, for except for a few hostels and cheap hotels, you're looking at £90/$180 a night minimum, or upwards of £270/$600 at classy establishments. For those staying longer than a few weeks, renting a flat works out much cheaper, if not less than you'd pay for a bed in a hostel. Another factor is discriminatory ticket pricing at museums and other major attractions, whereby foreigners pay up to ten times what Russians do. An ISIC **student card** gives a fifty percent discount at most museums, while student cards issued in Russia entitle the holder to even lower rates, or even free entry.

Package tourists with prepaid accommodation including full- or half-board really only need money for tickets to museums and palaces, buying gifts and the odd snack or drink. Unless you go overboard in expensive places, £45/$90 a day should suffice. Independent travellers will of course have to add accommodation costs and food on top of this figure. Staying in a cheap hotel and sticking to inexpensive bars and restaurants, you could get away with a total daily budget of £150/$300, but patronizing fancier places will easily triple or quadruple this figure. Alternatively, if you rent a flat and live as Russians do, you could spend £30/$55 a day or less on the whole works, including lodging, food and drink.

Cultural Institutes

American Center Nikoloyamskaya ul. 1 ⓣ777 65 30, ⓦwww.amc.ru; 10min from Taganskaya metro or trolleybus #45 from Kitay-Gorod metro. Anyone can use their library; lending rights and Internet access (1hr per day) are limited to members (passport with 3-month Moscow registration stamp and one photo required). Regular lectures (Mon 6pm), movies (Tues 5pm) and occasional poetry readings or concerts, open to the public. Mon–Fri 10am–7.45pm, Sat & Sun 10am–5.45pm (closed Sun over summer).
British Council ⓣ782 02 34, ⓦwww.britishcouncil.org.russia. Currently closed, but check website for the latest situation.
Cervantes Institute Novinskiy bul. 20a ⓣ937 19 54, ⓦwww.cervantes.es; Barrikadnaya or Smolenskaya metro. Spanish magazines and books, films and other cultural events. Mon–Fri 11am–2pm & 3–7pm, plus Sat 11am–6pm on alternate weekends.
Foreign Literature Library Nikoloyamskaya ul. 1 ⓣ915 35 28, ⓦwww.libfl.ru; Taganskaya metro or trolleybus #45 from Kitay-Gorod metro. Besides housing the American, British and French cultural centres, this library has Moscow's largest collection of

literature in foreign languages. Passport with a Moscow registration stamp required. Mon–Fri 9am–8pm, Sat & Sun 10am–6pm.

Institut Français Nikoloyamskaya ul. 1 ⓣ915 79 74, ⓦwww.ccfmoscou.net. Has a lending library (free membership; passport and two photos required), and organizes all kinds of cultural events, from French films and music to Bastille Day celebrations. Mon & Wed 2–6.30pm, Tues & Thurs 2–8pm, Fri noon–5pm.

Goethe Institut Leninskiy pr. 95a ⓣ936 24 57, ⓦwww.goethe.de/moskau; Prospekt Vernadskovo or Novye Cheremushkiy metro. Organizes film showings and lectures, and diverse extramural events. Mon–Thurs 9am–5pm, Fri 9am–4pm.

Drugs

Grass (*travka*) and **cannabis resin** (*plastylin*) from the Altay Mountains are commonplace on the club scene, as are acid, ecstasy and heroin (which, at only R50 a wrap, is responsible for the soaring addiction rate). At some clubs, the merest whiff will draw the bouncers; at others, dope-smokers are stolidly ignored. While simple possession of dope may incur only a caution, hard drugs – and smuggling – are still punishable by a long term of hard labour. The safest policy is to avoid all drugs entirely.

Electricity

A standard Continental 220 volts AC; most European appliances should work as long as you have an adaptor for Continental-style, two-pin round plugs. North Americans will need this plus a transformer.

Embassies

Australia Podkolokolny Pereulok 10A/2 ⓣ956 6070, ⓦwww.russia.embassy.gov.au; Kitay-Gorod metro. Mon–Fri 9am–5pm.

Belarus ul. Maroseyka 17/6 ⓣ6287813, ⓦwww.embassybel.ru; Kitay-Gorod metro. Mon, Tues & Thurs 9.30am–noon & 3–5pm, Fri 9.30 am–noon & 3–4pm.

Britain Smolenskaya nab. 10 ⓣ956 72 00, ⓦwww.britemb.msk.ru; Smolenskaya metro. Mon–Fri 9am–5pm.

Canada Starokonyushenniy per. 23 ⓣ105 60 00, ⓦwww.russia.gc.ca; Kropotkinskaya or Arbatskaya metro. Mon–Fri 8.30am–1pm & 2–5pm.

China ul. Druzhby 6 ⓣ938 20 06, ⓦwww.chinaembassy.ru; Universitet metro. Mon–Fri 8.30am–noon & 3–6pm.

Czech Republic ul. Yuliusa Fuchika 12/14 ⓣ251 05 44, ⓦwww.mzv.cz/moscow; Mayakovskaya metro. Mon–Fri 9am–11am & 1.30–3.30pm.

Estonia 5 Maly Kislovsky Pereulok ⓣ737 36 40, ⓦwww.estemb.ru/eng/embassy; Arbatskaya metro. Mon–Fri 9am–5pm.

Finland Kropotkinskiy per. 15–17 ⓣ787 41 74, ⓦwww.finland.org.ru; Park Kultury metro. Mon–Fri 9am–11am & 1.30–3.30pm.

Germany Mosfilmovskaya ul. 56 ⓣ937 95 00, ⓦwww.moskau.diplo.de; trolleybus #17 or 34 from Kievskaya metro. Mon–Thurs 8am–1pm & 1.45–5pm, Fri 8am–1pm & 1.45–3pm.

Ireland Grokholskiy per. 5 ⓣ937 59 11; Prospekt Mira metro. Mon–Fri 9.30am–1pm & 2.30–5.30pm.

Latvia ul. Chapygina 3 ⓣ232 97 60, ⓦwww.am.gov.lv/en/Moscow; Turgenevskaya/Chistye Prudy metro. Mon–Fri 9am–6pm.

Lithuania Borisoglebskiy per. 10 ⓣ785 86 25; Arbatskaya metro. Mon–Fri 9am–noon & 2–4pm.

Netherlands Kalashniy per. 6 ⓣ797 29 00, ⓦwww.netherlands-embassy.ru; Arbatskaya metro. Mon–Fri 9am–1pm & 2–5pm.

New Zealand Povarskaya ul. 44 ⓣ956 35 79, ⓦwww.nzembassy.com; Barrikadnaya metro. Mon–Fri 9am–12.30pm & 1.30–5.30pm.

Poland ul. Klimashinka 4 ⓣ231 15 00, ⓦwww.moskwa.polemb.net; Belorusskaya metro. Mon–Fri 9am–5pm.

Ukraine Leontevskiy per. 18 ⓣ629 47 04, ⓦwww.mfa.gov.ua/russia/ru; Pushkinskaya metro. Mon–Thurs 9am–1pm & 2–6pm, Fri 9am–1pm & 2–4.45pm.

US Novinskiy Bulvar 21 ⓣ728 55 77, ⓦmoscow.usembassy.gov; Barrikadnaya metro. Mon–Fri 9am–noon & 2–6pm.

Feminist contacts

The best places to start looking are the Russian Feminist Resources website ⓦwww.geocities.com/Athens/2533/russfem.html, which has a lot of links and material in English; the Women Information Network has a regularly updated news site in Russian (ⓦwww.womnet.ru) and a database of women's organizations throughout Russia in English (ⓦwww.womnet.ru/db/English/English.html).

Film and photos

Outlets for imported **film** and one-hour **processing** services are getting harder to find as almost everyone has switched to digital. Only the professional shops carry film now: FotoLab, ul. Rozhdestvenka 11

Ⓣ234 48 86 (Kuznetsky most metro; Mon–Sat 10am–10pm, Sun 10am–9pm), is a good central option. Do not take photos of foreign embassies or metro stations – you might have your film or camera confiscated.

Hairdressers

If you need a haircut and don't speak Russian, you can avoid potentially embarrassing results by going to the unisex Expat Salon, Skaterniy per. 3 Ⓣ495 291 64 67, off Tverskaya ulitsa (daily 10am–9pm), where all the staff speak English.

Insurance

Medical insurance is obligatory for citizens of Australia and the Schengen states and is strongly advisable for other nationalities, even if covered by reciprocal state healthcare agreements.

Travel insurance is also highly recommended in the event of unforeseen curtailment or cancellation of your trip, or for lost or stolen baggage or valuables. When considering baggage cover, make sure that the per-article limit – typically under £500 – will cover your most valuable possession. Rough Guides has teamed up with Columbus Direct to offer you travel insurance that can be tailored to suit your needs. Products include a low-cost **backpacker** option for long stays; a **short break** option for city getaways; a typical **holiday package** option; and others. There are also annual **multi-trip** policies for those who travel regularly. Different sports and activities (trekking, skiing, etc) can usually be covered if required. See our website (Ⓦwww.roughguides.com/website/shop) for eligibility and purchasing options. Alternatively, UK residents should call Ⓣ0870/033 9988; Australians should call Ⓣ1300/669 999 and New Zealanders should call Ⓣ0800/55 9911. All other nationalities should call Ⓣ+44 870/890 2843.

If you need to make a claim, you should **keep receipts** for medicines and medical treatment, and in the event you have anything stolen, you must obtain an official **theft report** (*spravka*) from the police (see p.54).

Internet

One of the best ways to keep in touch while travelling is to sign up for a **free internet email address** that can be accessed from anywhere, for example Google mail (Ⓦwww.googlemail.com), YahooMail (Ⓦwww.yahoo.com) or Hotmail (Ⓦwww.hotmail.com). Once you've set up an account, you can use these sites to pick up and send mail from any Internet café, or hotel with Internet access.

You can go **online** at numerous cafés in Moscow (see below), many of which are open 24 hours. Hourly **rates** vary, but are rarely more than R50 at peak times and as little as R20 after midnight. At most places the staff speak some English and can reset the on-screen language format so that you don't have to grapple with instructions in Cyrillic. The Russian word for @ is *sobachka* (literally "dog"); a dot is a *tochka*.

Wi-fi is also common in Moscow at many cafés, hotels and hostels: a good number are free, while some use a voucher purchase system. If you need help, there are computer dealers all over Moscow – though warranty agreements on hardware or software bought abroad don't apply within Russia. Pirated software is widely available in shops and markets.

Internet cafés in Moscow

Mediateka Abelmanovskaya ul. 11; Proletarskaya/Krestyanskaya Zastava metro. Daily 11am–7pm.
MMMT ul. Arbat 46; Smolenskaya metro. Mon–Fri 9am–5.45pm.
NetCity Kamegerskiy per. 6, Teatralnaya metro; Paveletskaya pl. 2, str. 1, Paveletskaya metro. 24hr.
Ostrov Formoza Bolshoy Trekhsvyatitelskiy per. 2 Ⓦwww.island-formoza.ru; Kitay-Gorod metro. Mon–Fri 10am–8pm, Sat 10am–7pm.
TimeOnLine Okhotniy ryad mall, lower level Ⓦwww.timeonline.ru; Okhotniy Ryad metro. With over 200 fast terminals (R35/hr), it claims to be the biggest Internet facility in Eastern Europe. No drinks served. Enter from the Okhotniy Ryad metro underpass facing the Alexander Garden after the mall is closed. Daily 24hr.

Language courses

Russian language courses in Moscow can be arranged through the Center of Russian Language Study, Minaevskiy per. 2 Ⓣ495 978 91 01; Language Link, Novoslobodskaya ul. 5, str. 2 Ⓣ495 232 02 25, Ⓦwww.languagelink.ru; Moscow Linguistic Centre, ul. Presnenskiy val 17, office #515

(☎737 01 83) and ul. Seleznevskaya 11A, bld2 (☎495 221 21 72), Ⓦwww.language-learning.ru; Patriarshy Dom Tours (see p.46); or the St Petersburg-based tourist agency HOFA (see p.320). All these centres can provide visa support for their students.

Laundry

Zolushka (☎495 424 38 22; Mon–Sat 9am–8pm) is a dry-cleaning and laundry service that collects and delivers washing, but requires one day to take the order and three days to process it. The service costs about R200 per kilo of laundry. Many hotels have a laundry service, but you'd be unwise to entrust them with anything valuable.

Left luggage and lost property

Most bus and train stations have lockers and/or a 24-hour **left-luggage office**. Anything you lose on public transport is unlikely to end up at the **lost-property depots** (*stol nakhodok*) handling documents (3-y Kolobovskiy per. 8 ☎495 200 99 57; Mon–Thurs 9am–2pm, Fri 9am–2pm & 3–5pm) or other items lost on the metro (at Sportivnaya metro ☎222 20 85; Mon–Thurs 9am–noon & 1–6pm, Fri 9am–4pm). Only Russian is spoken and both numbers are usually engaged.

Mail

The Russian **postal system** is notoriously inefficient, and there's little sign of modernization yet. Incoming international mail takes up to three weeks to arrive, while the outbound service is even less reliable. As a result, most Russians entrust letters to someone travelling abroad, for safer postage there, while foreigners either emulate them or employ an **express mail** or **courier firm** (see below): Fedex and DHL promise to deliver mail to Europe in three to five days and cost around R200 per letter.

Parcels must be taken unwrapped to the Main or International post office (see below); there they'll be inspected and wrapped for you, whereupon you can send them from any **post office** (Почта), or by courier (see below). If you only want **stamps**, it's easier to go to the postal counters in major hotels rather than queue in a post office, though there's a mark-up on the price.

American Express card or traveller's cheques holders can use their client mail service, which is more reliable than the **poste restante** (До Востребования) in public post offices. If you do use poste restante, the most centrally located facilities are in the Central Telegraph Office (*tsentralniy telegraf*) at Tverskaya ul. 7 (daily 8am–10pm; ☎495 504 4444), and the Main Post Office (*glavniy pochtamt*) at Myasnitskaya ul. 26 (Mon–Fri 8am–8pm, Sat 8am–7pm, ☎924 02 50), near Chistye Prudy metro. The International Post Office at Varshavskoe shosse 37 (daily 8.30am–8pm; ☎114 45 84, Ⓦwww.interpost.ru) is further out, so seldom used by visitors.

International express mail and courier services

DHL *Radisson Slavyanskaya Hotel*, 2nd floor ☎941 84 17, Ⓦwww.dhl.ru; Kievskaya metro. Mon–Fri 9am–2pm & 3–6pm.

Federal Express Aviatsionniy per. 8/17 ☎937 77 77, Ⓦwww.fedex.com; Aeroport metro. Mon–Fri 8am–8pm, Sat 9am–6pm.

Pony Express MGU, "Visokiy energii" Bldg. room #407 ☎745 50 55, Ⓦwww.ponyexpress.ru; Universitet metro. Mon–Fri 9am–6pm.

TNT ul. Svobody 31 ☎797 27 77, Ⓦwww.tnt.ru; Sokol metro. Mon–Fri 8am–8pm, Sat 9.30am–1.30pm.

UPS Bolshoy Tishinskiy per. 8, str. 2 ☎961 22 11, Ⓦwww.ups.com; Ulitsa 1905 metro. Mon–Fri 9am–7pm.

Maps

The **maps** in this book should be okay for most purposes, but if you need more detail, or are staying outside the centre, it's worth buying a detailed street plan. Don't bother with maps produced abroad, which cost more than you'd pay in Moscow for an up-to-date Russian map. The best locally produced one in English is the 1:25,000 scale *Moscow City Map* published by Traveller's Yellow Pages (see above). If you can read the Cyrillic alphabet, the 1:15,000 *Moscow-Center* map published by TsEVKF imeni Dunayev details everything from restaurants to bus and trolleybus routes. Another publisher, Rubber Map, produces *Moskva Tramvay, Trolleybus, Bus*, detailing their routes across the city, while the pocket-sized *Atlas Moskva s kazhdym domom* identifies the street number of every building, and would be great for locating clubs or residential blocks if the print wasn't so tiny that you need a magnifying glass. All of these are sold at newspaper kiosks and bookshops in Moscow for R400–500 apiece: Biblio-Globus, Myasnitskaya ul. 9 (ⓣ495 781 1900, ⓦwww.biblio-globus.ru) has a particularly good selection. Conversely, visitors could get by using the **free** *Cultural Map* available from Capital Tours (see p.47) or major hotels, which covers the centre of Moscow on a generous scale.

Money

Russia's currency, the **ruble**, has been relatively stable since the 1998 crash and has recently been getting stronger, leading to increased inflation. The **denominations** in circulation are coins of 5, 10 and 50 kopeks and 1, 2 and 5 rubles; and notes of 5, 10, 50, 100, 500 and 1000 rubles.

At the time of writing the **exchange rate** was £1=R46, €1=R37, $1=R23. To find out the current Central Bank rate, check in the financial section of the *Moscow Times*, or on the currency converter websites ⓦwww.xe.com and ⓦwww.oanda.com. The designation-code for Russian rubles is "RUR". Inside Russia, ruble prices are written with a Cyrillic ру or р, followed by a decimal point and a к for kopeks – so that 12 р. 50 к means twelve rubles and fifty kopeks.

Though almost everywhere specifies prices in rubles and you will always be expected to pay in rubles, some restaurants, bars, clubs and hotels quote in so-called "**standard units**" or "conditional units" (*uslovnye yedenitsy*, abbreviated to УЕ in Cyrillic), which can mean dollars, euros or some midway point between the two – usually whichever is most advantageous for them. So far as restaurants go – and sometimes hotels and bars as well – this is often an indication that the establishment is overpriced, and best avoided.

Rubles can't be obtained abroad: you must change money or draw on your plastic in Russia. Changing money with street hustlers is a sure way to be cheated, and there's no reason to exchange money anywhere other than in a proper **bank** or a **currency exchange bureau** (*obmen valuty*). These can be found all over Moscow, including inside shops and restaurants (usually open the same hours as the host establishment). Most banks set fairly similar rates, and commission should be negligible. Many banks and exchange bureaux will only change US dollars or euros, so bringing any other currency will limit your options as to where you can change money. Moreover, due to **counterfeiting** many places insist on new-style US dollars in good condition – notes in other currencies may also be refused if they're in a dodgy state. Likewise, guard against receiving any torn ruble notes in return. Counterfeiting tends to be limited to 100 ruble notes (fakes are recognizable by their thick paper, dull serial numbers and unclear watermarks), due to the security features on higher denomination notes – so you needn't worry much about it.

By far the easiest way to get money, however, is from bank **ATMs** (*bankomat*), which are widely available and accept most foreign cards. **Credit and debit cards** can be used in ATMs, as well as in most hotels and restaurants and quite a few shops. Almost all banks and many exchange bureaux will give cash in rubles on Visa, MasterCard or Maestro; Guta-Bank and Gazprombank accept Union Card, and Baltiyskiy Bank, Diners Club. Cash withdrawn on a credit card is treated as a loan, with interest accruing daily from the date of the withdrawal, plus a 1–4 percent commission charge. Therefore, a debit card is best for withdrawals, as the flat transaction fee is usually quite small, and there are no interest payments. Always keep the **receipts** from ATM withdrawals or card transactions, and be sure to note down the overseas emergency number for reporting

Changing money

bank	Банк
currency exchange	обмен валюты
convertible currency	СКВ
standard units	УЕ
ruble	рубль
buying rate	покупка
selling rate	продажа
exchange rate	курс

lost or stolen cards. Surplus rubles can be converted back into hard currencies at most banks

Traveller's cheques (TCs) no longer have any real benefit, with commission charges ranging from 1–4 percent. The only brand that's readily replaceable if lost or stolen in Moscow is **American Express** (GUM, Vetoshny per. 17 ⓣ495 543 94 00, ⓦwww.americanexpress.com/russia/en; Ploshchad Revolyutsii metro; daily 10am–9.30pm), which can be cashed at branches of Bank Moskvy, Baltiyskiy Bank, Guta-Bank and Vneshtorgbank, as can Thomas Cook and Visa cheques.

Wiring money to Russia is expensive but easily done via Western Union, available at American Express (see above), most banks and some exchange bureaux (see ⓦwww.westernunion.ru for a full list).

Museums

Ticket prices to museums are higher for foreigners than for Russians; minor museums charge R75–125, and major attractions such as the Kremlin and the Tretyakov Gallery R125–300. An ISIC **student card** entitles you to a fifty percent discount at all museums, while a card issued by a Russian educational establishment entitles you to even lower rates or free admission. Many museums require you to buy a **photography permit** (cameras R25–75; videos up to R250; no discounts) or leave your camera in the cloakroom (*garderob*), and some make visitors put on felt or plastic overshoes (*tapochki*) to protect their parquet floors.

At some museums you can rent an audioguide (*player*) at the ticket desk (*kassa*), or arrange a **guided tour** (*beseda*) in English or other foreign languages through the museum's excursions bureau. There are no set rules about how far in advance you should book a tour, and a lot may depend on whether a member of staff who speaks English will be on duty that day (which is less likely in the summer holidays). Some museums have set rates for tours; others prefer to negotiate rates on an ad hoc basis.

Opening hours

Twenty-four-hour food and liquor stores exist in residential areas of the city (many take an hour's break in the morning), alongside bakeries, butchers and fish **shops**, which open Monday to Saturday from 9am to 6pm or 7pm (with an hour or two's break between 1pm and 4pm). Retailers in the downtown area keep similar hours, while **malls and department stores** may stay open until 9pm or later, even on Sundays. Kiosks near metro stations stay open all night or close by mid-evening, depending on what they're selling. Opening hours for **museums and galleries** tend to be from 10am or 11am to 5pm or 6pm. They are closed at least one day a week, but there are no hard-and-fast rules as to which. In addition, one day in the month will be set aside as a *sanitarniy den* or "cleaning day", and it's not unusual to find museums unexpectedly closed "for repairs" (*na remont*) or "technical reasons" (*po tekhnicheskim prichinam*), usually due to staff shortages. Full opening hours are detailed in the text.

Phones

Mobile phones are wildly popular in Moscow. Europeans using the GSM system can use their own phones in the city, but Americans must rent a special phone from their dealer before leaving; in either case calls will be expensive. Anyone intending to use a mobile extensively, or over several months, will save money by buying or renting a *mobilnik* from a local dealer and using a Russian network. Shopping around is essential, but it's better to pay more for a reliable service with MTS (ⓦwww.mts.ru) or MegaFon (ⓦwww.megafon.ru) than suffer

Signs

Communications centre	Переговорный пункт
Intercity telephone	Междугородный телефон
International telephone	Международный телефон
Local telephone	Таксофон щк телефон

Moscow phone number changes

Moscow is currently changing its **seven-digit phone numbers** to **ten-digit numbers**, a process which is due to be completed by the end of 2008. At the time of writing, some companies had already been issued with their new numbers, and others not. Where possible we have included the new ten-digit numbers, but bear in mind that all the seven-digit numbers listed in the guide are liable to change: if in doubt, check the website for the hotel or restaurant you are calling.

the spotty coverage of cut-price operators. MTS has the slightly better coverage and can provide **WAP** services, while Megafon is slightly cheaper.

Public phonecard phones have largely superseded the old-style payphones that used *zhetony* (tokens). The most common are the blue MTTS phones, found in metro stations and other public places, which can be used for local, intercity and international calls; press the black-flagged button for instructions in English. MTTS **phonecards** (*telefonaya karta*) are sold in metro stations, post offices and banks in various denominations of units, costing from R200 upwards. The cheapest ones may not allow you to call abroad.

The big hotels and flashier restaurants also have **BCL card phones**, which use satellite links for international connections. These sometimes have an echo and are expensive, although still cheaper than calling from your **hotel room or business centre**, where the cost of an international call can be anything from R200 to R500 a minute. Another way to make an international call is to go to a **communications centre** (*peregovorny punkt*) – there's one in every district. If you're lucky enough to have access to a **private phone**, you'll find that local calls are cheap, while rates for intercity and international calls are about as low as you'll find in Russia, without buying an international discount phonecard or signing up for IP telephony (see below).

If you have access to a touch-tone phone you can choose between a plethora of **discount phonecards** (from phone dealers and kiosks; the Pushinskaya metro underpass has the widest selection) that let you call selected countries at reduced rates – though you'll need some knowledge of the language or help from Russian friends to check out what's on offer.

To **make a direct international call** dial 8, wait for the tone to change and then dial 10, followed by the country code, city code (omitting the initial zero if present) and subscriber number. To call anywhere in Russia, or most of the former Soviet republics (except the Baltic States), dial 8, pause, and then the city code (with any zeros). Calls placed through the international operator (Ⓣ079/Ⓣ073 for outside/inside the CIS) cost twice as much and may take time to come through.

Visitors with their own computer would be wise to sign up for web-based, or **IP, telephony**: Skype (Ⓦwww.skype.com), for example, charges around 1–2p a minute for calls to North America, the UK and Australia, and if the person you are calling has Skype too it is free. All you need is a high-speed internet connection which is easier to get than phone service in much of Moscow.

Direct dialling codes

To Moscow
From Britain Ⓣ00 7 095
From Ireland Ⓣ00 7 095
From the US and Canada Ⓣ011 7 095
From Australia and New Zealand Ⓣ0011 7 095
From Moscow
Australia Ⓣ8 (pause) 10 61
Ireland Ⓣ8 (pause) 10 353
New Zealand Ⓣ8 (pause) 10 64
UK Ⓣ8 (pause) 10 44
US and Canada Ⓣ8 (pause) 10 1

Religious worship

Adventist Maliy Tryokhsvyatitelskiy per. 3 Ⓣ917 05 68; Wed & Sat 6.30am & 10pm.
Anglican Church of St Andrew, Voznesenskiy per. 8/5 Ⓣ229 09 90; Thurs 6.30pm, Fri 6.30pm, 7pm & 8pm, Sat 6.30pm & 9.30pm, Sun 8.30am, 10am & 6.30pm.
Baptist Maliy Tryokhsvyatitelskiy per. 3 Ⓣ917 33 63; Tues, Thurs, Sat & Sun 10am–6pm.

Catholic Church of the Immaculate Conception, Malaya Gruzinskaya ul. 27 ⓣ252 39 11; daily 9am–6pm.
Jewish Choral Synagogue, Bolshoy Spasoglinishchevskiy per. 10 ⓣ923 96 97; Mon–Fri 8.30am, Sat & holy days 9am, evening services after sunset.
Lutheran Sts Peter and Paul Church, Starosadskiy per. 7/10 ⓣ928 32 62; daily 10.30am & 12.30pm.
Muslim Central Mosque, Vypolzov per. 7 ⓣ281 38 66; daily noon–5pm.

Smoking

Nearly all Western brands of **cigarettes** are available, though many of the packets sold at kiosks are made under licence (or counterfeited) in Russia or Turkey. It is normal to be approached by strangers asking for a light (*Mozhno pokurit?*) or a cigarette. While museums and public transport are **no-smoking** (*ne kurit*) zones, Russians puff away everywhere else, and see nothing wrong with it. However, many fast-food chains have a no-smoking policy.

Superstitions

Russians consider it bad luck to kiss or shake hands across a threshold, or return home to pick up something that's been forgotten. Before departing on a long journey, they gather their luggage by the door and sit on it for a minute or two, to bring themselves luck for the journey. When buying flowers for your hostess, make certain that there's an odd number of blooms; even-numbered bouquets are for funerals. It's considered unlucky to whistle indoors, or put a handbag on the floor.

Time

Moscow Time is generally three hours ahead of Britain and eight hours ahead of US Eastern Standard Time, with the clocks going forward on the last Saturday of March and back again on the last Saturday of October.

Tipping

In **taxis**, the fare will usually be agreed in advance so there's no need to tip; in **restaurants**, no one will object if you leave an extra ten percent or so, but in most places it's not compulsory. Check, too, that it hasn't already been included. In those places where a **service charge** is compulsory, it ranges from ten to fifteen percent; the exact figure will be stated on the menu.

Toilets

It's generally acceptable for non-customers to use the toilets in restaurants and hotels, since **public toilets** (*tualet* or *WC*) are few and far between – despite efforts to boost numbers by locating Portaloo-type cabins in parks and squares. There is a small charge, which includes a wad of toilet paper given out by the attendant. Otherwise, make for the nearest *McDonald's*. Men's facilities are marked M; ladies Ж. You can buy **toilet paper** (*tulatenaya bumaga*) in any supermarket or pharmacy.

Travellers with disabilities

The needs of disabled citizens in Russia were largely ignored in the past, and the chronic shortage of funds has hindered progress even now in places where attitudes have changed. **Wheelchair access** to most of the top international hotels in Moscow is possible with some assistance, but only the *Metropol*, *Marriott Grand* and *Radisson Slavyanskaya* are fully wheelchair-accessible. **Public transport** is a big problem, since buses, trams and trolleybuses are virtually impossible to get onto with a wheelchair, and the metro and suburban train systems are only slightly better. Though major sights like Red Square, the Kremlin, the Tretyakov Gallery and the Novodevichiy Convent are wheelchair-accessible, churches and museums often require you to negotiate steps. Museum staff are keen to assist but unsure how (or embarrassed to suggest using a freight elevator), so it's best to have an interpreter to smooth things over. The **webzine** *Disability World* (ⓦwww.disabilityworld.org) is worth checking out as it sometimes features articles about the situation for disabled people in Russia.

The City

The City

Red Square and the Kremlin

Every visitor to Moscow is irresistibly drawn to **Red Square and the Kremlin**, the historic and spiritual heart of the city, so loaded with associations and drama that they seem to embody all of Russia's triumphs and tragedies. Exalted by the poet Mayakovsky as the centre of the world, the vast square has a slight curvature that seems to follow that of the earth's surface. On one side, the Lenin Mausoleum squats beneath the ramparts and towers of the Kremlin, confronted by the long facade of GUM, while St Basil's Cathedral erupts in a profusion of onion domes and spires at the far end. For sheer theatricality, Red Square is only surpassed by the Kremlin itself, whose fortifications, palaces and cathedrals are an amalgam of European and Asiatic splendour, redolent of the Italian Renaissance and the court of Genghis Khan alike. While the treasures of its Armoury Palace and other museums are a must for visitors, it's the frisson of proximity to power and the sense that history is being made here that sets the Kremlin apart from other palatial citadels the world over.

This chapter begins with Red Square, as you can and should visit it at any time of the day or night, without worrying about opening times and admission tickets. The Kremlin is different, insofar as it's only open at set times, and requires tickets. Moreover, the visitors' entrance is around the far side, in the Alexander Gardens, rather than on Red Square as you might expect. Otherwise, access is simple, with three metro stations (Ploshchad Revolyutsii, Okhotniy Ryad and Teatralnaya) within a few-minutes' walk of Red Square, and two others (Aleksandrovskiy Sad and Biblioteka Imeni Lenina) equally near the entrance to the Kremlin.

Starting from Okhotniy Ryad or Teatralnaya metro, you'll probably approach Red Square via a long pedestrian underpass running beneath Manezhnaya ploshchad, which brings you out within sight of the square's Resurrection Gate.

Red Square (Krasnaya ploshchad)

The name **Krasnaya ploshchad – Red Square** – has nothing to do with Communism, but derives from *krasniy*, the old Russian word for "beautiful", which probably came to mean "red" due to people's thirst for bright colours

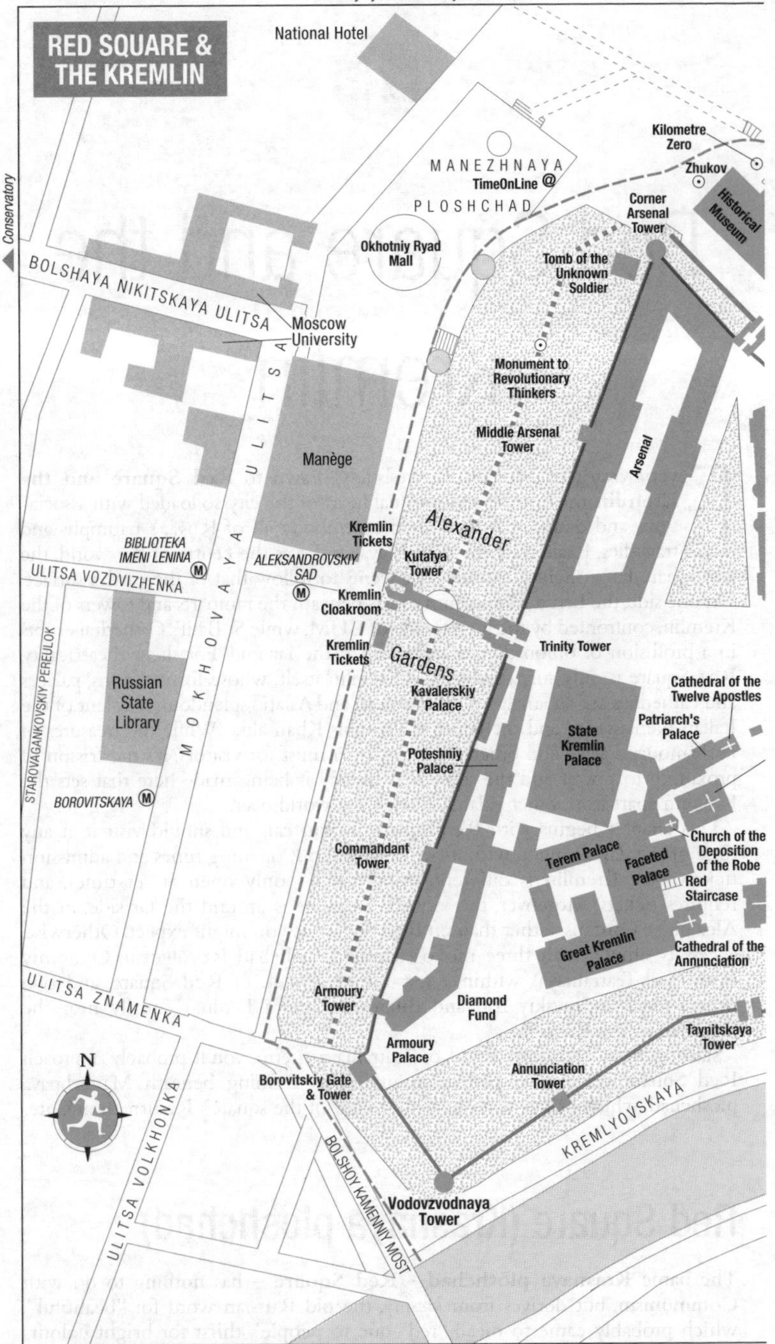
Okhotniy Ryad & Teatralnaya metros
RED SQUARE & THE KREMLIN
National Hotel
Kilometre Zero
Zhukov
Historical Museum
MANEZHNAYA
TimeOnLine @
PLOSHCHAD
Corner Arsenal Tower
Conservatory
Okhotniy Ryad Mall
Tomb of the Unknown Soldier
BOLSHAYA NIKITSKAYA ULITSA
Moscow University
Monument to Revolutionary Thinkers
Middle Arsenal Tower
Manège
Arsenal
MOKHOVAYA ULITSA
Alexander
Kremlin Tickets
BIBLIOTEKA IMENI LENINA
Kutafya Tower
ALEKSANDROVSKIY SAD
ULITSA VOZDVIZHENKA
Kremlin Cloakroom
Kremlin Tickets
Trinity Tower
STAROVAGANKOVSKIY PEREULOK
Gardens
Russian State Library
Kavalerskiy Palace
State Kremlin Palace
Cathedral of the Twelve Apostles
Patriarch's Palace
Poteshniy Palace
BOROVITSKAYA
Church of the Deposition of the Robe
Commandant Tower
Terem Palace
Faceted Palace
Red Staircase
Great Kremlin Palace
Cathedral of the Annunciation
ULITSA ZNAMENKA
Armoury Tower
Diamond Fund
Taynitskaya Tower
Armoury Palace
N
Borovitskiy Gate & Tower
Annunciation Tower
KREMLYOVSKAYA
ULITSA VOLKHONKA
BOLSHOY KAMENNIY MOST
Vodovzvodnaya Tower
Pushkin Museum of Fine Arts & Cathedral of Christ the Saviour

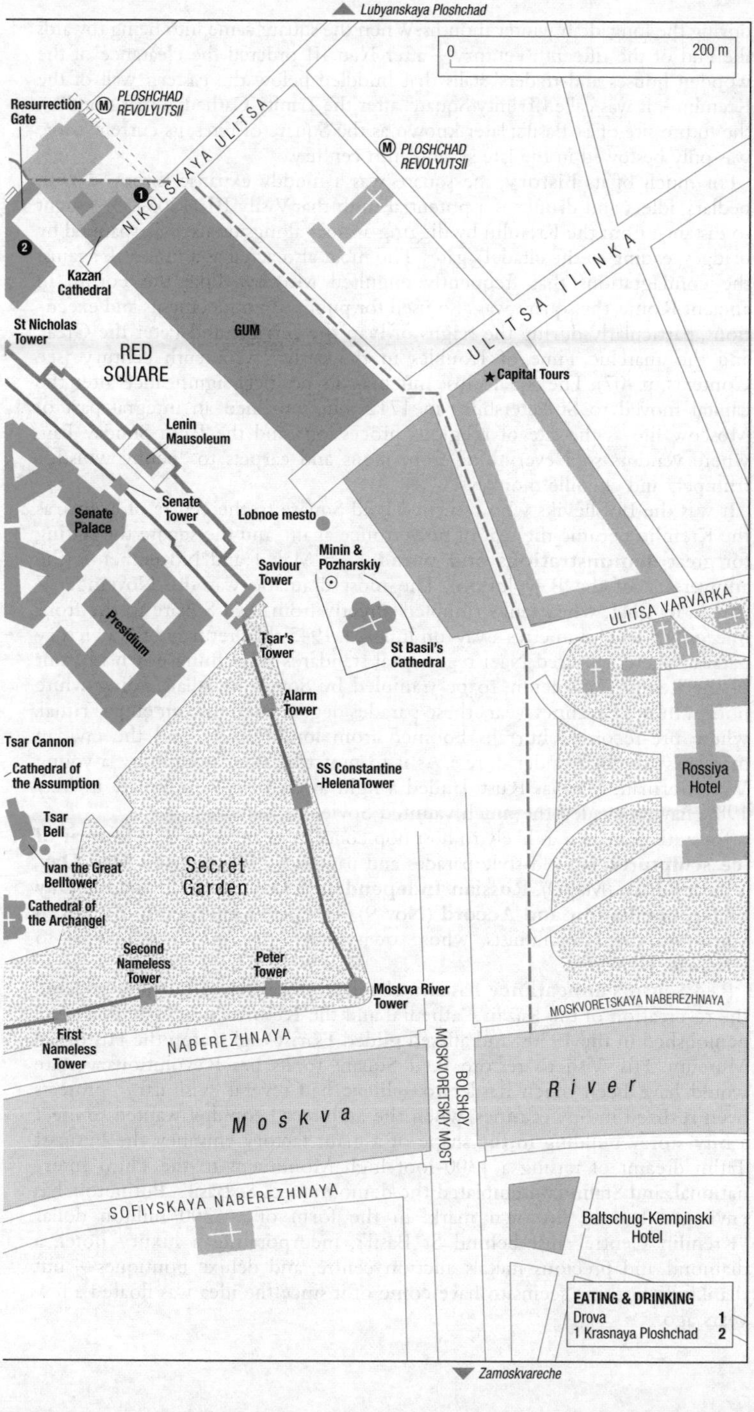

Lubyanskaya Ploshchad

0 200 m

Resurrection Gate

PLOSHCHAD REVOLYUTSII

NIKOLSKAYA ULITSA

PLOSHCHAD REVOLYUTSII

Kazan Cathedral

ULITSA ILINKA

St Nicholas Tower

GUM

RED SQUARE

Capital Tours

Lenin Mausoleum

Senate Tower

Senate Palace

Lobnoe mesto

Minin & Pozharskiy

Saviour Tower

Presidium

Tsar's Tower

St Basil's Cathedral

ULITSA VARVARKA

Alarm Tower

Tsar Cannon

Cathedral of the Assumption

SS Constantine -HelenaTower

Rossiya Hotel

Tsar Bell

Ivan the Great Belltower

Secret Garden

Cathedral of the Archangel

Second Nameless Tower

Peter Tower

Moskva River Tower

MOSKVORETSKAYA NABEREZHNAYA

First Nameless Tower

NABEREZHNAYA

BOLSHOY MOSKVORETSKIY MOST

River

Moskva

SOFIYSKAYA NABEREZHNAYA

Baltschug-Kempinski Hotel

EATING & DRINKING	
Drova	1
1 Krasnaya Ploshchad	2

Zamoskvareche

during the long, drab winter months. When the square came into being towards the end of the fifteenth century – after Ivan III ordered the clearance of the wooden houses and traders' stalls that huddled below the eastern wall of the Kremlin – it was called Trinity Square, after the Trinity Cathedral that stood on the future site of St Basil's; later known as the Square of Fires, its current name was only bestowed in the late seventeenth century.

For much of its **history**, the square was a muddy expanse thronged with pedlars, idlers and drunks – a potential mob that Vasily III (1505–33) sought to distance from the Kremlin by digging a moat alongside its wall, spanned by bridges leading to the citadel's gates. The moat also acted as a firebreak against the conflagrations that frequently engulfed Moscow. Like the Forum in ancient Rome, the square was also used for public announcements and executions, particularly during the reigns of Ivan the Terrible and Peter the Great, and the anarchic Time of Troubles in the early seventeenth century (see Contexts, p.407). The square lost much of its political significance after the capital moved to St Petersburg in 1712, but remained an integral part of Moscow life as the site of religious processions and the Palm Sunday Fair, where vendors sold everything from icons and carpets to "penny whistles, trumpets and chenille monkeys".

It was the Bolsheviks who returned Red Square to the centre of events, as the Kremlin became the seat of power once again, and the square the setting for great **demonstrations and parades** on May 1 and November 7 (the anniversary of the Revolution). The most dramatic was the November 7 parade in 1941, when tanks rumbled directly from Red Square to the front line, only a few kilometres away; on June 24, 1945 they returned for a victory parade where captured Nazi regimental standards were flung down in front of the Lenin Mausoleum, to be trampled by Soviet Marshals riding white horses. In the Brezhnev years these parades degenerated into an empty ritual, where pre-recorded hurrahs boomed from loudspeakers, and the civilian marchers attended under duress. As if to puncture their pomposity, a young West German, Mathias Rust, landed a light aircraft on Red Square in May 1987, having evaded the much vaunted Soviet air defences.

Today, the square is as likely to host pop concerts or the New Year **festival of ice sculptures**, but old-style parades and pageantry still occur on **May Day**, **Victory Day** (May 9), **Russian Independence Day** (June 12) and the **Day of Reconciliation and Accord** (Nov 9) – the latter intended to deny Red Square to the Communists, whose own march (see p.226) is obliged to terminate elsewhere.

Red Square's **appearance** has also changed, since Mayor Luzhkov ordered the re-creation of the Kazan Cathedral and the Resurrection Gate that were demolished in the 1930s, and affixed gilded Tsarist eagles atop the Historical Museum. His wish to restore Red Square to its pre-Revolutionary state would have been much harder to achieve had several "visionary" projects been realized in Soviet times, when the architect Leonidov wanted to erect a fifty-storey building in the shape of a giant factory chimney, the Futurist Tatlin dreamt of raising a 1300-foot-high Monument to the Third International, and Stalin contemplated the demolition of St Basil's. Putin, too, has envisaged leaving his own mark, in the form of a $300 million dollar "Kremlin Centre" just behind St Basil's, incorporating a luxury hotel, a diamond and precious metals auction centre, and deluxe boutiques – but thankfully nothing seems to have come of it since the idea was floated a few years ago.

The Resurrection Gate and the Kazan Cathedral

Most people approach Red Square from the north, via one of the cobbled streets that slope uphill beside the Historical Museum, for a thrilling first glimpse of Lenin's Mausoleum alongside the Kremlin wall, and St Basil's Cathedral looming at the far end of the square. The view of St Basil's is framed

▲ The Resurrection Gate

by the **Resurrection Gate** (Voskresenskie vorota), a 1990s replica of a sixteenth-century gateway that was pulled down in 1931 as part of Stalin's campaign to rid Moscow of its holy relics and churches, and make Red Square more accessible for tanks and marchers. While its twin towers with their green spires topped by Tsarist eagles could be described as something from a fairytale, the external chapel, with its portal flanked by gilded reliefs of SS Peter and Paul, is simply kitsch. The chapel of the original gateway held a revered icon, the Iberian Virgin, to which every visitor to Moscow paid their respects before entering Red Square. Today, Russian tourists have their photo taken standing on a brass relief set into the ground in front of the gate, marking **Kilometre Zero**, whence all distances from Moscow are measured.

Passing through the gate, the entrance to the Historical Museum (see below) is on your right, while the sky-blue building on your left once contained a prison known as "the Pit", where the eighteenth-century writer Alexander Radishchev awaited exile for his critique of Catherine the Great's autocracy. Though a decrepit red-brick Mint founded by Peter the Great can still be seen by venturing into its courtyard, your eyes will inevitably be drawn instead to the diminutive Kazan Cathedral, on the corner of Nikolskaya ulitsa.

The original **Kazan Cathedral** (Kazanskiy sobor) was built in 1636 to commemorate Tsar Mikhail Romanov's victory over the Poles, and dedicated to the Virgin of Kazan, whose icon was carried into battle by Prince Pozharsky during the Time of Troubles. Demolished on Stalin's orders and replaced by a public toilet, its belated reconstruction owed much to the architect Pyotr Baranovsky, who secretly made plans of the building even as it was being pulled down, and later risked his life to save St Basil's from a similar fate (see p.78). The modern-day Kazan Cathedral sports a strawberry-and-cream coloured exterior replete with the ornate window frames (*nalichniki*) and ogee-shaped gables (*kokoshniki*) characteristic of early Muscovite church architecture, crowned by a cluster of green and gold domes. Inaugurated in 1993 on the feast day of the Icon of Kazan (Nov 4), the cathedral is open daily from 8am–7pm. As at all Orthodox places of worship, you are not allowed in wearing shorts.

The Historical Museum

Though you'll probably want to wander around Red Square first, the **Historical Museum** (Istoricheskiy muzey; 10am–5pm; closed Tues & the first Mon of each month; R230, camera or video permits R100) is definitely worth a visit at some point. Established by order of Alexander III, and opened in 1894, the museum occupies a liver-red building cluttered with pinnacles, chevrons and saw-toothed cornices, whose interior is lavishly decorated with murals and carvings harking back to medieval Russia.

The ticket office, on the right inside the entrance, stocks a free brochure in English and rents audioguides (R110) that cover the highlights of the permanent exhibition, which is captioned in five languages. It's possible to book a guided tour in English (group rate R1000 with a translator, or R700 if you have your own translator, plus tickets: call ⓣ692 37 31 a week to ten days in advance). Concerts of historical music are held at the museum as advertised.

To reach the exhibition rooms on the second floor, you ascend the stairs of a grand hall that used to be the ceremonial entrance from Red Square. Its ceiling features a pictorial family tree of Russian monarchs from Vladimir and Olga of Kiev (shown watering the roots of the tree) to Alexander III, which was white-washed over in the 1930s.

The first two rooms are notable for a pair of mammoth tusks, a replica of a grave containing the remains of a boy and girl, and scenes of Paleolithic life by Viktor Vasnetsov. Room 3 boasts a 5000-year-old oak **longboat** that was unearthed beside the River Volga, while Room 4 opens with a haunting wooden idol from the Gorbunkovsky peat bogs, and concludes with nephrite axe heads and gold-inlaid silver spearheads, used for ritual purposes. Also notice the Bronze Age **stele** with a sun face, from the Altay Mountains of southern Siberia.

Room 5, covering the Iron Age, has many wonderful exhibits, such as the **Kazbeksky Hoard** of deer and bird figurines. The first millennium BC was the heyday of the Scythians, warlike nomads whose veneration for horses was expressed in **gold bridle ornaments** shaped like horses' heads or dragons – a style that influenced other nomadic cultures. From the Altay come **funerary masks** of diverse ethnic groups, a leather coat decorated with painted fur and wooden studs, and two stelae carved with deer, such as are erected on the Mongolian steppes to this day.

The hybrid nature of steppe culture is further emphasized by the **Turmansky Sarcophagus**, shaped like a Greek temple with Chinese-style decorations on its "roof"; and glassware that once circulated between the Scythians and Sarmatians and the Hellenized and Roman trading cities on the Black Sea coast (Room 6). Whereas the Finno-Ugrians, Mordovians and Khazars left tumuli containing bronze and amber **jewellery** during the Age of Migrations, the earliest Slavs left nothing more sophisticated than hand-moulded pots, attesting to their isolation from other cultural influences (Room 7).

In the ninth century AD these disparate peoples gave rise to the **Kievan Rus**, or Old Russian state, ruled by Scandinavian warriors known as the Varangians, who used the Volga and Dniepr as trade routes from northern Europe to Byzantium. Room 8 displays artefacts from this period and the conversion of the Kievan Rus to Christianity by Prince Vladimir in 988. On the walls hang two huge canvases depicting *The Night of Sacrifice* of infants to the pagan gods, and the *Funeral of the Great Rus*, a Varangian ruler surrounded by human and animal sacrifices.

Behind the museum, facing Manezhnaya ploshchad, a stiffly poised equestrian **statue of Marshal Zhukov** tramples a Nazi battle-standard under his horse's hooves, as occurred at the Victory Parade on Red Square in 1945. Zhukov was the most successful Soviet commander of World War II, who fell from grace under Khrushchev, but never lost his place in the pantheon of Soviet heroes. Erected in 1996, the monument is by Vyacheslav Klykov, the creator of a controversial statue of Nicholas II that he hoped would stand outside the Kremlin, but which ended up in a village outside Moscow, where it was blown up by neo-Bolsheviks the same year.

GUM

GUM (daily 10am–10pm) is to Moscow what Harrods is to London, a flagship emporium that every tourist wants to visit, patronized by rich locals when they're not shopping somewhere more exclusive. But that isn't its stereotypical image: for anyone who recalls Soviet times, GUM (pronounced "Goom": the initials stand for "State Department Store") evokes memories of shelves of unsold *brak* (junk) and queues for "deficit" items like tampons (imported from Hungary, since the USSR never got around to manufacturing them). The difference between then and now is a measure of how much Russia has changed.

Architecturally, GUM makes a perfect foil for the Kremlin. Its ornate neo-Russian facade – drawing on motifs from the medieval churches of Borisoglebsk and Rostov Veliky in the Volga region of Russia – conceals an elegantly utilitarian interior, employing the same steel-frame and glass construction techniques as the great train stations of London and Paris. Executed by Alexander Pomerantsev in 1890–93, this three-storey, modern arcade replaced the old hall of the Upper Trading Rows that burned down in 1825, whose 1200 shops shared a common roof "so awkwardly constructed, that in the strongest sunshine people stumble in darkness, and after the slightest shower wade through mud".

Nationalized and renamed GUM after the 1917 Revolution, it continued to function as a shop until bureaucrats overseeing the First Five-Year Plan took over the building. In 1932 it was used for the lying-in-state of Stalin's wife, Nadezhda, after her suicide; Stalin stayed there for days, silently noting who came to pay their respects. Here, too, the giant photographic portraits of Communist leaders that emblazoned Red Square were assembled, having been developed in swimming pools. Not until 1952 was GUM reopened as an emporium famed throughout the world. Less well known was "Section 100", a special clothing store for the Party elite, tucked away on the top floor. With the advent of perestroika, GUM received an infusion of investments from Western firms keen to get a prestigious foothold on the Russian market, and is now privately owned and more akin to a luxury mall.

GUM is laid out in three parallel arcades or "lines" (designated 1-ya liniya, 2-ya liniya, 3-ya liniya), which meet at a central fountain, overlooked by galleries. Glass canopy roofs flood the whole complex with light, or give a startling view of the stars on winter nights. The first and second floors have been entirely colonized by the likes of Estée Lauder and Body Shop, but a few old, Soviet-style shops survive on the third floor. You can enter GUM at either end of lines 1 and 3, from the street behind the store, or from Red Square itself.

Lenin's Mausoleum

For nearly seventy years, the Soviet state venerated its founder by acts of homage at the **Lenin Mausoleum** (Mavzoley V.I. Lenina) – an image associated with Soviet Communism the world over. Yet when Lenin died on January 21, 1924, his widow Krupskaya pleaded: "Do not let your sorrow for Ilyich find expression in outward veneration of his personality. Do not raise monuments to him, or palaces to his name, do not organize pompous ceremonies in his memory." Nonetheless, a crude wooden mausoleum was hastily erected on Red Square for mourners to pay their respects, and the Party leadership decided to preserve his body for posterity. In the Orthodox tradition, an un-decayed corpse is proof of sainthood; and Stalin – a former seminarian – made Lenin's cult a secular religion. (Another practice was having a "Lenin corner" with a votive lamp, where icons would have hung in olden days.)

The **embalming** was carried out by biochemist Boris Zbarsky and anatomist Vladimir Vorybov, who overcame the problem that Lenin's veins (the usual conduit for embalming fluid) had been removed at the autopsy, by bathing the corpse in a vat of preservatives and making cuts in the body to help the chemicals penetrate (details kept a secret until Zbarsky's son revealed them in a book in 1998). By August 1924 the body was fit to be viewed in a newly built wooden mausoleum, which was replaced by a permanent stone one in 1930, once it became clear that the embalming process had been successful.

Designed by Alexei Shchusev, the **mausoleum** is a step-pyramid of cubes, a form revered by Russian avant-gardists that was also fashionable for its association with ancient Egyptian architecture, following the discovery of Tutankhamun's tomb. Faced with red granite and black labradorite, it bears the simple inscription *Lenin* above its bronze doors, which were traditionally flanked by a guard of honour (changed every hour, as the Saviour Tower clock chimed). After Stalin's death in 1953 he too was displayed in what became the Lenin-Stalin Mausoleum, but in 1961 it reverted to its old title after Stalin's body was spirited away one night and reburied by the Kremlin wall. For decades, the Politburo reviewed anniversary parades from its podium (with a supply of machine guns stashed behind them in case of trouble), and diplomats noted who stood nearest the General Secretary as an indication of their influence. The septuagenarian Chernenko contracted fatal pneumonia from standing there on a chilly day, and the swan song of such events occurred when Gorbachev was booed during the October Revolution parade in 1989, and on May Day the following year.

Radical democrats called for Lenin's body to be removed from Red Square and reburied with his mother and sisters in St Petersburg – as he (or Krupskaya) is said to have wished, though no proof has been found. The fall of Communism raised expectations and a Russian impresario proposed sending Lenin on a "farewell world tour". But it wasn't until Yeltsin had crushed parliament in 1993 that he felt bold enough to strip the mausoleum of its guard of honour and pledge the removal of Lenin's body "within months" – an idea that was quietly dropped after the elections returned a majority of Communist and ultra-nationalist Deputies. When Yeltsin raised it again four years later the Communist leader Zyuganov threatened to bring tens of thousands of loyalists to stand vigil, and a neo-Bolshevik group vowed to blow up the monument to Peter the Great (see p.206) in retaliation.

Today, Lenin's position seems as assured as it was in Soviet times. A nationwide survey in 2000 rated him the "Russian man of the century" on the basis of fourteen percent of votes cast (Stalin came second), and millions still venerate him. "To take Lenin out and bury him would say to them that they have worshipped false values, that their lives were lived in vain," said Putin (whose own grandfather had been a cook for Lenin and Stalin); "I cherish stability and consensus in society, and I will try not to do anything to upset civil calm" – sentiments echoed by the Orthodox Patriarch and even some who once campaigned for Lenin's reburial.

Maintaining Lenin costs taxpayers $1 million a year. The body is dabbed with embalming fluid twice a week and receives a lengthy soaking every eighteen months at a special laboratory in the bowels of the Kremlin. Besides Lenin, the Kremlin Centre for Biological Structures has embalmed such foreign Communists as Enver Hoxha, Ho Chi Minh and Kim Il Sung, and it's alleged that dozens of mafiosi have been restored "by the Lenin method" after being shot or blown up. Fees reputedly start at $300,000 – sarcophagus not included.

Visiting the Mausoleum

Official **opening hours** (10am–1pm; closed Mon & Fri; free) may be suspended at short notice, and the mausoleum shuts for six weeks every eighteen months while Lenin gets the full treatment (to find out when, call Ⓣ623 55 27). Would-be visitors must stash their bags and cameras in the cloakroom beneath the Kutayfa Tower in the Alexander Gardens, before joining the queue at the northwest corner of Red Square. Visitors are expected to line up in pairs, remove their hats, take their hands out of their pockets, and refrain from talking except in whispers – a regime enforced by humourless guards. Descending into the bowels of the mausoleum, past motionless sentries and doors that emit the crackle of walkie-talkies, one enters the funerary chamber, faced in grey and black labradorite inset with carmine zigzags. Softly spotlit in a crystal casket, wearing a polka-dot tie and a dark suit-cum-shroud, Lenin looks shrunken and waxy, his beard wispy and his fingers discoloured. (Sceptics think that Lenin is partly, or entirely, a waxwork.) The chamber's layout ensures that it's impossible to linger, so that visitors emerge blinking into the daylight less than a minute later.

The Kremlin wall and its towers

The Kremlin wall behind the mausoleum constitutes a kind of Soviet pantheon, containing the remains of up to 400 bodies. Visitors exiting the mausoleum pass a mass grave of Bolsheviks who perished during the battle for Moscow in 1917, to reach an array of luminaries whose ashes are interred in the Kremlin wall. These include the American journalist **John Reed**; Lenin's wife **Krupskaya**, and his lover **Inessa Armand**; the writer **Maxim Gorky**; the founder of the secret police, **Felix Dzerzhinsky**; various foreign Communist leaders; and the world's first cosmonaut, **Yuri Gagarin**. Beyond lies a select group of Soviet leaders, distinguished by idealized busts on plinths. The first to be encountered is **Chernenko**'s (looking smarter than he ever did in real life), followed by an avuncular **Andropov**, a pompous **Brezhnev** and a benign-looking **Stalin** (whose tomb is marked by lilies, as well as red roses). Conspicuously absent from this roll call of leaders is Khrushchev, who died out of office in relative obscurity and was buried in the Novodevichie Cemetery (see p.194).

The **Kremlin wall** averages 19m high and 6.5m wide, topped with swallow-tailed crenellations and defended by eight towers mostly built by Italian architects in the 1490s. The distinctive jade-green spires were added in the seventeenth century, and the ruby-red stars (which revolve in the wind) in 1937. At the northern end is the round **Corner Arsenal Tower**, which takes its name from the adjacent Kremlin Arsenal. Further along is the triple-tiered St Nicholas Tower, built by Pietro Antonio Solari. The tower's massive red star (3.75m wide and 1.5 tonnes in weight) gives it a total height of 70.4m.

Beyond the **Senate Tower**, named after the green-domed building visible behind Lenin's Mausoleum, looms the Gothic-spired **Saviour Tower**. In Tsarist times, an icon of the Saviour was installed above its gate and everyone who entered doffed their hats; when Napoleon rode in without doing so his horse shied and his hat fell off, confirming the Russians' belief in its miraculous powers. On Lenin's orders, the chimes of the tower's clock were adjusted to play the Internationale; in 1944, they were changed to play the stirring Soviet anthem, which Yeltsin replaced by a melody by Glinka, before Putin restored the former anthem. It was from the Saviour Gate that soldiers formerly goose-stepped to the mausoleum to change the guard at what was known as Sentry Post No.1, while in the post-Communist era, a **procession** of clerics and nuns bearing icons and banners emerges on the Day of Slavic Culture (May 24), bound for the statue of SS Cyril and Methodius on Slavyanskaya ploshchad (see p.109).

The small **Tsar's Tower**, erected in 1680, gets its name from an earlier wooden tower whence the young Ivan the Terrible used to hurl dogs to their deaths and watch executions on Red Square. Also opposite St Basil's is the **Alarm Tower**, whose bell warned of fires; Catherine the Great had the bell's tongue removed as a "punishment" after it was rung to summon a dangerous mob during the Plague Riot of 1771. In medieval times, the chunky **SS Constantine-Helena Tower** served as the Kremlin's torture chamber; the screams of victims were audible on Red Square. The circular **Moskva River Tower**, built by Marco Ruffo in 1487, protects the southeastern corner of the Kremlin wall, which was usually the first part of the fortress to be attacked by the Tatars.

To withstand sieges, artesian wells were dug beneath the **Vodovzvodnaya** (Water-Drawing) and Corner Arsenal towers, and a concealed passage from the **Tanitskaya** (Secret) Tower to the riverside, for covert egress or sudden sallies. The defenders could move from one tower to another by passages within the walls. In Soviet times, a secret **Kremlin metro line** was created as an escape route for the Politburo, linked to the regular metro system at Biblioteka Imeni Lenina, Borovitskaya and other stations, by unobtrusive "maintenance" doors.

The Lobnoe mesto

Crossing Red Square towards St Basil's, you'll see a circular stone platform known as the **Lobnoe mesto**, whose name (derived from *lob*, meaning "forehead") is usually translated as the "place of executions" or the "place of proclamations", since it served for both. Early in his reign, it was here that Ivan the Terrible begged for the people's forgiveness after Moscow was razed by a fire that the Patriarch pronounced to be God's punishment for his misdeeds. In 1570, however, Ivan staged a festival of torture on the square, where two hundred victims perished in a man-sized frying pan or on ropes stretched taut enough to saw bodies in half; on another occasion, he amused himself by letting loose wild bears into the crowd. In 1605, the False Dmitri proclaimed his accession here; after his downfall, his mutilated corpse was burned to ashes and fired from a cannon in the direction of Poland, from the same spot. Most famously, in 1698 Peter the Great carried out the mass execution of the mutinous Streltsy regiments on scaffolds erected nearby – personally wielding the axe on a score of necks (see box below).

St Basil's Cathedral

No description can do justice to the inimitable **St Basil's Cathedral** (sobor Vasiliya Blazhennovo; May–Oct daily 11am–6pm; Nov–April Mon, Wed–Sun 11am–5pm; R100, camera or video permits R130). Foreigners have always seen it as a cryptic clue to the mysterious Russian soul. The French diplomat, the Marquis de Custine, thought its colours combined "the scales of a golden fish, the enamelled skin of a serpent, the changeful hues of the lizard, the glossy rose

The Streltsy

In medieval times, Red Square and the suburbs across the river teemed with thousands of **Streltsy**, the shaggy pikemen and musketeers who guarded the Kremlin and were Russia's first professional soldiers. Garbed in caftans, fur-trimmed hats and yellow boots, their banners emblazoned with images of God smiting their foes, they made a fearsome host whenever they assembled at the tsar's bidding – or in revolt. In 1682, when Peter was ten years old, they butchered several of his relatives on the Red Staircase in the Kremlin – an experience that crystallized his hatred for Old Muscovy and its raggle-taggle army. It was to beat them that Peter later formed his own "toy" regiments drilled in European tactics by foreign officers, which routed the Streltsy when they revolted again in 1698. A famous painting by Surikov (in the Tretyakov Gallery) depicts the tsar gazing pitilessly over the wives and children of the condemned, in the shadow of St Basil's.

and azure of the pigeon's neck", and questioned whether "the men who go to worship God in this box of confectionery work" could be Christians.

St Basil's was commissioned by Ivan the Terrible to celebrate his capture of the Tatar stronghold of Kazan in 1552, on the feast day of the Intercession of the Virgin. Officially named the Cathedral of the Intercession of the Virgin by the Moat (after the moat that then ran beside the Kremlin), its popular title commemorates a "holy fool", St Basil the Blessed (1468–1552), who came to Ivan's notice in 1547 when he foretold the fire that swept Moscow that year, and was later buried in the Trinity Cathedral which then stood on this site. St Basil's was built in 1555–60, most likely by Postnik Yakovlev (nicknamed "Barma" – the Mumbler) who, legend has it, was afterwards blinded on the tsar's orders so that he could never create anything to rival the cathedral (in fact he went on to build another cathedral in Vladimir).

In modern times this unique masterpiece was almost destroyed by Stalin, who resented that it prevented his soldiers from leaving Red Square en masse. Its survival is due to the architect Baranovsky, whose threat to cut his own throat on the cathedral's steps in protest changed Stalin's mind, though he was punished by five years in prison. More recently St Basil's was threatened by subsidence, and it wasn't until the millennium that funds were allocated to underpin the cathedral's foundations and restore its flaking domes and interior.

Despite its apparent disorder, there is an underlying **symmetry** to the cathedral, which has eight domed chapels (four large and octagonal, the others smaller and squarish) symbolizing the eight assaults on Kazan, clustered around a central, lofty tent-roofed spire, whose cupola was compared by the poet Lermontov to "the cut-glass stopper of an antique carafe". In 1588 Tsar Fyodor added a ninth chapel on the northeastern side, to accommodate the remains of St Basil; its small yellow-and-green cupola is studded with orange pyramids. Rather than using the main arcaded staircase, visitors enter through an inconspicuous door near the ticket kiosk (which closes for thirty minutes at lunchtime, and an hour before the cathedral does).

The **interior** is a psychedelic maze of galleries painted with floral or geometric patterns, that wends from one chapel to another and from level to level via narrow stairways whose low arches were designed to make even the most exalted worshipper stoop in humility. St Basil occupies a silver casket in a chapel on the lower floor, whose gaudy magnificence is echoed by the red, blue and gold iconostasis in the Chapel of the Intercession, upstairs. Other chapels such as the one dedicated to the Velikoretskiy icon of St Nicholas are more restrained, or even quite austere in their decor.

In the garden out in front stands an impressive bronze **statue of Minin and Pozharsky**, who rallied Russia during the Time of Troubles. They made a curious team: Dmitri Pozharsky was a prince, while Kuzma Minin was a butcher from Nizhniy Novgorod, whose citizens funded the volunteer army that drove out the invading Poles in 1612, after he took their womenfolk hostage. Erected in 1818 by public subscription, the statue was Moscow's first monumental sculpture, and originally stood in front of what is now GUM.

The Alexander Gardens

To visit the Kremlin, leave Red Square to the northwest and turn left around the corner into the **Alexander Gardens** (Aleksandrovskiy sad; daily 24hr) that were laid out in 1819–22, after the Neglina River that ran beside the Kremlin's western wall was channelled into an underground pipe. Just inside the gates is the **Tomb of the Unknown Soldier**, whose eternal flame was kindled from the Field of Mars in Leningrad when the memorial was unveiled in 1967. Beneath a granite plinth topped by a giant helmet and furled banner lie the remains of a nameless soldier disinterred from the mass grave of those who died halting the Nazi advance at Kilometre 41 on the Leningrad highway; the inscription reads: "Your name is unknown, your feat immortal". Nearby is a line of porphyry blocks containing earth from the "Hero Cities" of Leningrad, Kiev, Stalingrad, Sevastapol, Minsk, Smolensk, Odessa, Novorossisk, Tula, Murmansk, Kerch and the Brest Fortress. Newlyweds and VIPs come here to lay flowers at the monument, which is carpeted with bouquets on Victory Day (May 9). The **changing of the guard** is a popular spectacle, introduced since the ritual at Lenin's Mausoleum was scrapped (every hour on the hour; half hourly during winter).

On the far side of the gardens, **statues** based on Russian fairytales such as the Prince and the Frog and the Fox and the Stork, spotlit amid mosaic-encrusted basins and balustraded walkways linked to a mall beneath Manezhnaya ploshchad (see p.114), evince Mayor Luzhkov's desire to transform Moscow's image from that of a drab metropolis into a prosperous fun city.

Previously, the only note of levity was a whimsical arched **Grotto** near the **Middle Arsenal Tower**; it was more typical of the Soviet Union that an obelisk erected to mark the 300th anniversary of the Romanov dynasty should be converted on Lenin's orders into a **Monument to Revolutionary Thinkers**, inscribed with the names of Bakunin, Marx, Engels, Hume and other personages. In Bulgakov's famous novel, *The Master and Margarita*, it was on one of the nearby benches that the grieving heroine Margarita met the Devil's sidekick, Azazello, and accepted an invitation to Satan's Ball, which led to the release of her beloved from a mental asylum.

Midway along the ramparts, a brick ramp with swallow-tailed crenellations descends to the white **Kutafya Tower**, the last survivor of several outlying bastions that once protected the bridges leading to the Kremlin, whose decorative parapet was added in the seventeenth century. The bridge leads up to the

▲ Changing of the Guard at the Tomb of the Unknown Soldier

eighty-metre-high Trinity Tower, the tallest of the Kremlin towers, whose gateway admits visitors to the citadel (see p.82). Further south, the Commandant's Tower and the Armoury Tower abut the Kremlin's Armoury Palace, while another rampway leads up to the multi-tiered Borovitskiy Tower, whose name derives from the pine-grove (*bor*) covered hillock on which the citadel was founded. In winter, when the steep hillside is covered with snow, kids zoom down on sledges and shoot across the path of unsuspecting tour groups heading for the Borovitskiy Gate.

The Kremlin

This curious conglomeration of palaces, towers, churches, monasteries, chapels, barracks, arsenals and bastions ... this complex functions as fortress, sanctuary, seraglio, harem, necropolis and prison, this violent contrast of the crudest materialism and the most lofty spirituality – are they not the whole history of Russia, the whole epic of the Russian nation, the whole inward drama of the Russian soul?

Maurice Paléologue, *An Ambassador's Memoirs*

Brooding and glittering in the heart of Moscow, the Kremlin thrills and tantalizes whenever you see its towers stabbing the skyline, or its cathedrals and palaces arrayed above the Moskva River. Its name* is synonymous with Russia's government, and in modern times assumed connotations of a Mecca for believers, and the seat of the Antichrist for foes of Communism. Hostile foreign perceptions long predate the Soviet era, for as far back as 1839 the Marquis de Custine fulminated: "To inhabit a place like the Kremlin is not to reside, it is to protect oneself. Oppression creates revolt, revolt obliges precautions, precautions increase dangers, and this long series of actions and reactions engenders a monster." Unsurprisingly, Russians generally feel more respectful than paranoid, being inclined to agree with Lermontov, who rhapsodized: "What can compare to the Kremlin which, having ringed itself with crenellated walls and adorned itself with the golden domes of cathedrals, sits on a high hill like the crown of sovereignty on the brow of an awesome ruler."

A brief history

According to **legend**, a band of boyars (nobles) hunting in the forest saw a giant two-headed bird swoop down on a boar and deposit its corpse on a hilltop overlooking two rivers. That night, they dreamt of a city of tent-roofed spires and golden domes, where people shuffled in chains towards huge gallows – and waking next morning, they resolved to build upon the site. More prosaically, the **founding of the Kremlin** is attributed to Prince **Yuri Dolgoruky**, who erected a wooden fort above the confluence of the Moskva and Neglina rivers in about 1147 – although the site may have been inhabited as long ago as 500 BC. Crammed with wooden houses, churches and stables, Dolgoruky's Kremlin was razed to the ground by the Mongols in 1238 but, like the city that had grown up around it, soon arose from the ashes, bigger and stronger than before.

*In Russia, kreml means fortress, and every medieval town had one. The origin of the word is obscure: some think it derives from the Greek kremn or krimnos, meaning a steep hill above a ravine; others from a Slav term for thick coniferous woods in a swampy place.

Between 1326 and 1339 the Kremlin was surrounded by oaken walls and the first stone cathedral appeared in its midst; some forty years later the original fortifications were replaced by stone walls, whose colour earned Moscow the sobriquet "the White City". Despite being sacked by the Tatars in 1382, its development proved unstoppable. During the reign of Grand Duke **Ivan III** (1462–1505) – dubbed "the Great" – the realm of Muscovy quadrupled in size and threw off the Tatar yoke, becoming pre-eminent among the Russian states. To confirm Moscow's stature Ivan embarked on an ambitious building programme, using craftsmen from Pskov, Tver and Novgorod, supervised by Italian architects, who arrived in 1472.

It was the Italians who built most of the cathedrals and fortifications that exist today, which were subsequently embellished by Ivan III's grandson Ivan IV (1553–84) – better known as **Ivan the Terrible** (Ivan Grozny) – who first assumed the title of "Tsar", and made the Kremlin notorious for murders and orgies. The demise of his son Fyodor I brought the Rurik dynasty to an end, and the wily **Boris Godunov** to power in 1598. His unpopularity with the nobility encouraged a pretender, claiming to be the youngest son of Ivan the Terrible, to invade Russia from Poland and proclaim himself tsar following Godunov's death in 1605. This so-called **False Dmitri** soon alienated his supporters and was murdered by a mob; the ensuing **Time of Troubles** saw Russia ravaged by famine, civil wars and invasions. After the Kremlin was recaptured from the Poles by Minin and Pozharskiy in 1612, the nobility elected **Mikhail Romanov** as tsar, inaugurating the dynasty that would rule Russia until 1917.

Under Mikhail and his successors, Alexei and Fyodor II, the Kremlin was rebuilt and order restored; the Terem and Patriarch's Palaces date from this era. The next tsar, **Peter the Great** (1682–1725), changed everything by spurning Moscow and the Kremlin for the new city that he founded by the Gulf of Finland, and by enforcing reforms that struck at everything held dear by traditionalists. Henceforth, the tsars and the government dwelt in St Petersburg, only visiting the Kremlin for coronations, weddings and major religious celebrations. Although **Catherine the Great** added the Senate building and commissioned a vast new palace that was never built, the Kremlin was otherwise neglected until the French invasion of 1812, when the great fire that destroyed Moscow and forced **Napoleon** to withdraw, necessitated major repairs to the parts of the Kremlin that he had spitefully blown up.

During the reign of the arch-conservative **Nicholas I** (1825–55), the Russo-Byzantine-style Armoury and Great Kremlin Palaces were constructed, and the Terem Palace was refurbished in a re-creation of early Romanov times. However, St Petersburg remained the capital and the focus of events until after the fall of the Romanov dynasty and the overthrow of the Provisional Government by the **Bolsheviks**, whose Moscow contingent took the Kremlin by storm on November 3, 1917.

In March 1918, **Lenin** moved the seat of government back to Moscow and into the Kremlin, as if anticipating how a party founded in the spirit of internationalism would later, under the rule of **Stalin** (1929–53), identify itself with Ivan the Terrible and other "great Russian patriots". Like "Genghis Khan with a telephone", Stalin habitually worked at night, obliging his ministers and their staffs to do likewise, giving rise to the pasty "Kremlin complexion". As purges decimated the Party, fear and secrecy pervaded the Kremlin, which remained closed to outsiders until 1955. Yet, despite the murderous decisions taken here, it saw little actual blood spilt, the most dramatic moment being the arrest of Lavrenty Beria, the dreaded chief of the secret police, following Stalin's demise.

Under later Soviet leaders, the Kremlin retained an aura of power and mystery, but gradually lost its terrible associations. In the aftermath of the break-up of the Soviet Union it seemed that the occupants of the Kremlin wielded less power than at any time in its colourful history, but autocratic mastery and subterfuge have definitely made a comeback since then.

Visiting the Kremlin

In general, **visiting the Kremlin** is quite easy. Unless closed without notice for state occasions or security alerts, the complex is open to the public from 10am to 5pm every day except Thursday. While its cathedrals are accessible from opening to closing time, the Armoury Palace and Diamond Fund can only be entered at set times, and the Faceted, Terem and Great Kremlin palaces only on special tours (detailed on p.91). Tour groups usually enter through the Borovitskiy Gate at the far end of the western wall, rather than via the Kutafya and Trinity gates, as other visitors do.

Assuming you're not with a group, the procedure is to buy tickets outside the Kutafya gate before figuring out what size restrictions currently apply to bags being brought into the Kremlin and only stashing yours at the luggage office below the gate-tower's southern side (open 9am–6.30pm; R60 per bag) if you must. A single **ticket** covers admission to the Kremlin precincts and cathedrals (R300), but you need another one for the Armoury Palace (R350); **photo permits** are required to take pictures in the cathedrals and the Armoury (R110 each). Visitors wearing shorts will be refused entry to the Kremlin.

The larger ticket kiosks sell illustrated **guidebooks** (R250) and rent **audioguides** (R200, plus ID as security), so there's no need to sign up for a tour unless you want to. Capital Tours runs English-language **tours** of the Kremlin cathedrals and Armoury starting at its office off Red Square (see map on, p.68–69) at 11am and 2pm every day except Thursday (R1400 per person plus admission charges). Alternatively, you can engage a **personal guide** from the hopefuls that wait near the Kutafya Tower. Rates are negotiable (R500–700 an hour) and the quality variable; accredited guides should wear a badge issued by the City Government. If you're seriously interested in icons or history, the English-speaking consultants on duty inside the Assumption and Annunciation cathedrals can answer most questions for free, and the Kremlin museum's **website**, Ⓦwww.kremlin.museum.ru, features plenty of historical information.

Visitors' **movements** within the Kremlin are strictly controlled, with white lines and whistle-tooting cops marking the limits beyond which you can't stroll – the descriptions in this book are structured to take account of these restrictions. Those with the energy should also try viewing the Kremlin from **different vantage points**. The view from across the Moskva River is the finest in Moscow, with a glorious panorama of palaces and cathedrals. From high up on Bolshoy Kamenniy bridge, you can glimpse the secretive Terem Palace. You might even brave the traffic to walk right around the outside of the Kremlin walls, which total 2235m in length.

Restricted zones and the State Kremlin Palace

Roughly two-thirds of the Kremlin is off limits to tourists, namely the trio of buildings in the northern half of the citadel, and the wooded Secret Garden sloping down towards the river. Entering via the Trinity Gate, the "government zone" lies to your left, where cannons captured during the Napoleonic Wars are ranged alongside the **Arsenal**. Commissioned by Peter the Great, but virtually redundant by the time it was completed in 1736, this occupies the site of the medieval boyars' quarter, where the higher nobility resided until the fifteenth century.

Opposite the Arsenal stands the imposing **Senate Palace**, erected in 1776–87 by Matvei Kazakov, whose Neoclassical design was cleverly adapted to the awkward triangular site. The edifice was commissioned by Catherine the Great for meetings of the Moscow branch of the Senate, an advisory body established in 1711; since 1991 it has been the official residence of Russia's president. From Red Square you can see the green cupola of its grand hall, formerly used for meetings of the USSR Council of Ministers and the awarding of Lenin Prizes. During the late 1990s, the modernization of its interior gave Yeltsin an excuse to get rid of Lenin's quarters, which had been preserved as a hallowed shrine, and revealed a secret passage beneath Stalin's study, that may have enabled the secret police chief, Beria, to eavesdrop on his boss. The staggering cost of the modernization – at least $457 million, or $13,125 a square metre – was equalled by its tackiness; the inner courtyard being turned into a winter garden of artificial trees made from green and yellow glass.

To the southeast is another Neoclassical structure, built in 1934 as a school for "Red Commanders", which subsequently housed the Presidium of the Supreme Soviet and is still referred to as the **Presidium**. In June 1953, it was here that Beria was arrested at gunpoint by Marshal Konev during a meeting. Some say that he was shot on the premises, and the body smuggled out in a carpet for fear that his bodyguards would take revenge on the other ministers. Previously, in Tsarist times, the site was occupied by the Monastery of Miracles and the Convent of the Ascension, which many royal daughters were forced to enter as nuns, owing to a lack of suitably Orthodox foreign rulers whom they could marry. By the nineteenth century, the convent had become so disreputable that one visitor described it as a "complete bagnio", where "the favours of any particular nun may be had for the asking".

To the right of the Trinity Gate a narrow lane runs parallel to the Kremlin wall; also out of bounds, this contains the former **Kavalerskiy Building** where Lenin and Krupskaya lived after they first moved into the Kremlin, before moving into a modest suite of rooms in the Senate. Across the way is the seventeenth-century **Poteshniy Palace**, where Stalin had his private apartments, and his wife Nadezhda shot herself in 1932. The yellow palace is recognizable by its protruding bay window; its name derives from the word for "amusements" (*potekhi*), as Tsar Alexei had a theatre here.

Further east stands the **State Kremlin Palace** (previously the Palace of Congresses), a 120-metre-long glass and concrete box sunk 15m into the ground so as not to dwarf the other buildings in the Kremlin. Built in 1959–61 to host Party congresses, the stage of its 6000-seat auditorium was formerly adorned by a giant bas-relief of Lenin's head, and the foyer still flaunts the crests of the Soviet Republics. Performances by the Kremlin Ballet Company are held here; for details, see p.369.

The Patriarch's Palace and Cathedral of the Twelve Apostles

As far as tourists are concerned, the accessible part of the Kremlin begins around the corner from the State Kremlin Palace, where the **Patriarch's Palace** (Patriarshie palaty) and the **Cathedral of the Twelve Apostles** (sobor Dvenadtsati Apostolov) come into view. The two form one structure, with an arched, covered balcony inset with polychrome tiles, and gilt frills on the three rounded gables and the balcony roof, surmounted by five small domes. Though the palace was begun in 1640, it is chiefly associated with **Patriarch Nikon**, who split the Russian Orthodox Church by his reforms during the years that he held the post (1652–58). While Nikon desired to restore the Church to the purity of its Byzantine origins, many Russians saw him as a heretic bent on imposing foreign ways. He also tried to assert the primacy of the Church over the state, thus angering Tsar Alexei, who refused to reinstate Nikon as Patriarch after he resigned in a fit of pique.

Today, the palace is a **Museum of Seventeenth-century Life and Applied Art**, displaying ecclesiastical regalia, period furniture and domestic utensils – an English-language guide tape can be rented inside. The palace's highlight is the vaulted **Cross Chamber** (Krestovnaya palata), measuring 19m by 13m, which was the first hall of such size to be built in Russia without a central supporting column. Its inauguration occasioned a day-long feast where guests placed their empty goblets on their heads between toasts, while monks chanted the *Life of the Saints*. Among the goblets in case 3 is one without a base which can't stand up, and which was given to guests who arrived late, to drain in one go. Decades later, the chamber was used for the preparation of *miro*, or holy oil, which explains the huge stove.

Other **exhibits** worth noting include a box for wine bottles made in the shape of an Evangelistary, and a wine ladle with a capacity of 100 litres, belonging to Peter the Great's "Drunken Synod", whose riotous parties mocked Church rituals. The exhibition concludes in the former Cathedral of the Twelve Apostles, which was built above the archway leading to Sobornaya ploshchad, as it was deemed sacrilegious to site an altar above rooms used for everyday life. The cathedral's Baroque iconostasis was moved here from the now-demolished Convent of the Ascension; on the wall to the left hangs the *Passion of the Apostles*, depicting a dozen martyrdoms in detail. Also notice the small window high up on the west wall, through which Nikon could observe services from his private chapel on the floor above. Like all the windows in the palace, this is glazed with mica instead of glass, imparting a frosty hue to views of the outside world.

The Tsar Bell and Cannon

Before passing through the archway into Sobornaya ploshchad, you can make a brief detour to find two of the Kremlin's most famous sights. The **Tsar Cannon** (Tsar-pushka) is one of the largest cannons ever made; its bronze barrel (bearing a relief of Ivan the Terrible's son, Fyodor) is 5.34m long, weighs 40 tonnes and has a calibre of 890mm. Cast by Andrei Chokhov in 1586, it was intended to defend the Saviour Gate, but has never been fired in battle (though it was used to fire the ashes of the False Dmitri back towards Poland). Its enormous chassis, decorated with a lion and a snake fighting on either side, and a snarling lion's head beneath the barrel, was cast in 1835, like the cannonballs piled in front (which are purely ornamental, as the cannon was originally meant to fire stone case shot).

Further along, behind the Ivan the Great Belltower, looms the earthbound **Tsar Bell** (Tsar-kolokol), the largest in the world, weighing 200 tonnes (almost fifteen times as much as London's Big Ben) and measuring 6.14m in height and 6.6m in diameter. Its bronze surface is emblazoned with portraits of Tsar Alexei and Empress Anna, who decreed the creation of the original and existing versions of the bell. The first, 130-tonne, version was cast in 1655, during

▲ The Tsar Cannon

Alexei's reign, but nineteen years elapsed before anyone could work out how to hoist it into the belfry, whence it fell to the ground and shattered in the fire of 1701. Thirty years later, Anna ordered the fragments to be used for a much larger bell, which lay in its casting pit for over a century, having cracked in 1737, when fire once again swept the Kremlin and water was poured on the red-hot bell. Finally, in 1836, the Tsar Bell was excavated and installed in its present location, accompanied by a chunk that broke off, itself weighing 11 tonnes.

The nineteenth-century dissident Pyotr Chaadaev mused that "in Moscow every foreigner is taken to look at the great cannon and the great bell – the cannon which cannot be fired and the bell which fell down before it was rung. It is an amazing town in which the objects of interest are distinguished by their absurdity, or perhaps that great bell without a tongue is a hieroglyph symbolic of this huge, dumb land."

Sobornaya ploshchad and the Ivan the Great Belltower

Beyond the Patriarch's Palace lies the historic heart of the Kremlin, surrounded by a superb array of buildings that gives the square its name. **Sobornaya ploshchad** (Cathedral Square) was first laid out in the early fourteenth century, making it the oldest square in Moscow, although the buildings that you see today were erected later. Throughout Tsarist times the square was used for Imperial coronations and weddings, and before the capital was transferred to St Petersburg it was also the setting for court life and political dramas. Every morning the boyars and gentry converged here in carriages or sledges to assemble in order of rank; the *ploshchadniki* or "people of the square" being inferior to the *komnatniki* or "people of the apartments", who enjoyed access to the tsar's palace. At other times commoners were free to gather on the square – providing they prostrated themselves whenever the monarch appeared.

Soaring above the square, the magnificent white **Ivan the Great Belltower** (Kolokolnya Ivana Velikovo) provides a focal point for the entire Kremlin, being the tallest structure within its walls. The main belltower was erected in

1505–08 by the Italian architect **Marco Bono** (known in Russia as Bon Fryazin), whose octagonal tower was increased to its present height of 81m during the reign of Boris Godunov, as proclaimed by the inscription in gold letters beneath its gilded onion dome. It remained the tallest structure in Russia until 1707, and dominated Moscow's skyline for long after that. Adjacent is the four-storey belfry (Zvonitsa), added in 1532–43 by the architect Petrok Maliy, which also has a gilded dome. The 64-tonne Resurrection Bell, dating from the nineteenth century, is the largest of its 21 bells. On the ground floor of this section is a hall used for **temporary exhibitions**; tickets (R100) are sold on the spot. The final, tent-roofed part of the building – known as the Filaret Annexe, after the Patriarch who commissioned it in 1624 – was badly damaged in 1812, when the French attempted (but failed) to blow up the entire belltower.

The Cathedral of the Assumption

Across the square from the Ivan the Great Belltower stands the oldest and most important of the Kremlin churches, whose massive walls and gilded helmet-shaped domes have the stern serenity of a warrior monk. The **Cathedral of the Assumption** (Uspenskiy sobor) has symbolized Moscow's claim to be the protector of Russian Orthodoxy ever since the seat of the Church was transferred here from Vladimir in 1326, together with a revered icon that was installed in a small cathedral erected by Ivan I.

By the 1470s this cathedral had become so decrepit that Ivan III ordered a replacement worthy of Moscow's stature; unfortunately the first effort by native builders collapsed before completion, so Ivan hired the Bolognese architect **Alberti Fioravanti** – dubbed "Aristotle" – who arrived in 1475, bringing engineering techniques a century ahead of any in Russia. Having visited the ancient cities of Vladimir, Suzdal and Novgorod to study Russian architectural traditions, he took only four years to finish the cathedral, which so harmonized with native forms that Patriarch Nikon would later recommend it as a model for Russian architects. Fioravanti's reward was to be thrown in prison after he begged permission to return to Italy; he died, still there, in 1486.

The cathedral's subsequent **history** reflects its role as Russia's premier church, used throughout Tsarist times for coronations and solemn acts of state. Here, Ivan III tore up the charter that bound Russia's princes to pay tribute to the Tatar Khans; divine intercession was invoked during calamities; Te Deums were sung to celebrate victories; and the Patriarchs of the Orthodox Church were inaugurated and buried. In times of woe, the cathedral also suffered: Napoleon's cavalry stabled their horses here in 1812, while in 1917 it was shelled during fighting between the Bolsheviks and White troops. Following the Revolution, no services took place for more than seven decades (unless you believe the story that Stalin ordered a secret one to invoke divine protection when the Nazis were at the gates of Moscow), until a special Mass was permitted in honour of the tercentenary of the Russian Patriarchate in 1989.

Given the cathedral's exalted status, its **exterior** is remarkably plain, like that of the Cathedral of the Assumption in Vladimir, which Fioravanti was ordered to emulate. Built of limestone with brick drums and vaulting, its rectangular form incorporates portals on three sides and barely protuberant apses on the eastern facade. The only decorative features are a horizontal belt of blind arcading punctuated by slit windows, a series of frescoes added in the 1660s beneath the gables on the east and west sides, and the ogee-shaped porches on the north and south facades. The current entrance is through the doorway sited

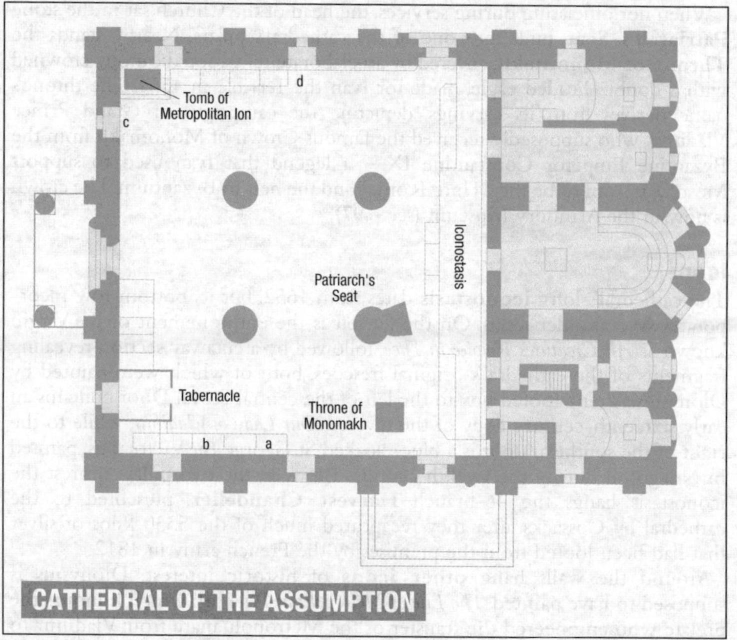

opposite the Church of the Deposition of the Robe (see opposite), which has now been enclosed to form a vestibule.

Frescoes, tombs and thrones

The **interior** is spacious, light and echoing, its walls, roof and pillars entirely covered by frescoes applied onto a gilt undercoating that gives them the richness of an illuminated manuscript – the predominant colours are amber, russet, indigo, green and scarlet. Originally the cathedral was decorated by a team of artists led by the famous icon painter Dionysius; most of the **frescoes** extant today, however, date from the cathedral's first restoration in the 1640s, and were restored in Soviet times. As is usual in Orthodox churches, the west wall bears a huge Apocalypse, with Christ flanked by the saintly host floating above a pair of scales. Notice the infernal serpent writhing in coils of iron, prodded by angels (below), and sinners being scourged and fed into the maw of Satan (bottom right). The upper three tiers on the north and south walls depict the life of the Virgin, while the pillars are adorned with five rows of paintings portraying saints and martyrs (which decrease in height towards the roof, so as to accentuate the loftiness of the cathedral).

Around the walls are the **tombs of the Metropolitans and Patriarchs**, encased in metal caskets resembling caterers' hotboxes, with the conspicuous exceptions of a bronze Tabernacle containing the remains of Patriarch Hermogenes, who perished in prison for opposing the Polish occupation in 1612 and was later canonized; and the tomb of Metropolitan Ion in the northwest corner, surmounted by a gold and silver arch. Aside from Patriarch Nikon, who lies in the New Jerusalem Monastery, the only absentees are Tikhon and Alexei I, two Patriarchs of Soviet times.

When not officiating during services, the head of the Church sat in the stone **Patriarch's Seat**, built into one of the cathedral's pillars. Nearby stands the **Throne of Monomakh**, covered by an elaborate tent-roofed canopy crowned with a double-headed eagle, made for Ivan the Terrible in 1551. The throne's name derives from its carvings, depicting the campaigns of Grand Prince Vladimir, who supposedly received the famous Crown of Monomakh from the Byzantine Emperor Constantine IX – a legend that Ivan used to support Moscow's claim to be the "Third Rome" and the heir to Byzantium. The crown is now in the Armoury Museum (see p.97).

Icons

The cathedral's lofty **iconostasis** dates from 1652, but its bottom row incorporates several older icons. On the far left is the enthronement of the Virgin known as *All Creatures Rejoice in Thee*, followed by a cutaway section revealing fragments of the cathedral's original frescoes, both of which were painted by Dionysius. A tent-roofed box to the left of the central Royal Door contains an early sixteenth-century copy of the revered *Our Lady of Vladimir*, while to the right of the southern door is a blue-cloaked St George the Victorious, painted in Novgorod during the twelfth century. Between the two pillars nearest the iconostasis hangs the 46-branch **Harvest Chandelier**, presented to the cathedral by Cossacks after they recaptured much of the 5330 kilos of silver that had been looted from the premises by the French army in 1812.

Around the walls hang **other icons** of historic interest. Dionysius is supposed to have painted *The Life of Metropolitan Peter* [**a**], which honours the prelate who engineered the transfer of the Metropolitanate from Vladimir to Moscow; the foundation of the original Cathedral of the Assumption is depicted near its bottom left corner. Nearby hangs *The Apostles Peter and Paul*, painted by an unknown Greek master of the fourteenth or fifteenth century [**b**]. By the west wall, an early fifteenth-century Crucifixion is followed by another copy of *Our Lady of Vladimir* [**c**] which, like the copy in the iconostasis, was venerated almost as much as the original (now held by the Tretyakov Gallery), believed to have been painted by St Luke and to have saved Moscow from the army of Timerlane. The aptly named *Saviour with the Severe Eye*, painted in the 1340s, hangs nearby, while along the north wall are *St Nikolai and his Life*, by the school of Novgorod, and several icons from the Solovetskiy Monastery in the White Sea [**d**].

The Church of the Deposition of the Robe

Almost hidden behind the Cathedral of the Assumption, the lowly white **Church of the Deposition of the Robe** (tserkov Rizpolozheniya) was built by craftsmen from Pskov in 1484–86, on the foundations of an older church erected to celebrate the prevention of a Tatar attack on Moscow some thirty years earlier. Its name refers to the festival of the deposition of the robe or veil of the Virgin Mary in Constantinople, which was believed to have saved the city from capture on several occasions; the miraculous relic was paraded around the city walls in times of danger, as was an icon of the same name in Moscow during medieval times.

Externally, the church is notable for the slender pilasters and intricate friezes that decorate its apses, and the ogee-shaped portal on its south side, reached by an open stairway. Nowadays visitors enter by a covered stairway facing the Cathedral of the Assumption, which leads up to an **exhibition of wooden figures**, which believers once imbued with almost as much holiness as icons.

The effigies of Nikita Muchenik (wearing armour and hefting a flail) and Patriarch **Nikola** (carrying a model of a cathedral) are particularly striking.

Inside the chapel there's hardly room to swing a censer, but it's worth lingering over the **frescoes**, which were painted in 1644 by Sidor Osipov and Ivan Borisov, and restored in the 1950s. Above the door as you come in are Mary and Joseph in the wilderness and the Adoration of the Magi; on the other walls, the uppermost tiers depict scenes from the apocryphal life of the Virgin, while the bottom two rows illustrate the 25 stanzas of the *Hymn to the Virgin*. Christ, the Virgin and the prophets cover the ceiling, while the pillars bear portraits of Prince Vladimir, Alexander Nevsky and other heroes of Russian Christianity.

The Cathedral of the Archangel

The last of the great churches to be erected on Sobornaya ploshchad, the **Cathedral of the Archangel** (Arkhangelskiy sobor) was built in 1505–08 as the burial place for the rulers of Muscovy, who claimed the Archangel Michael as their celestial guardian. Unlike the vernacular Cathedral of the Assumption,

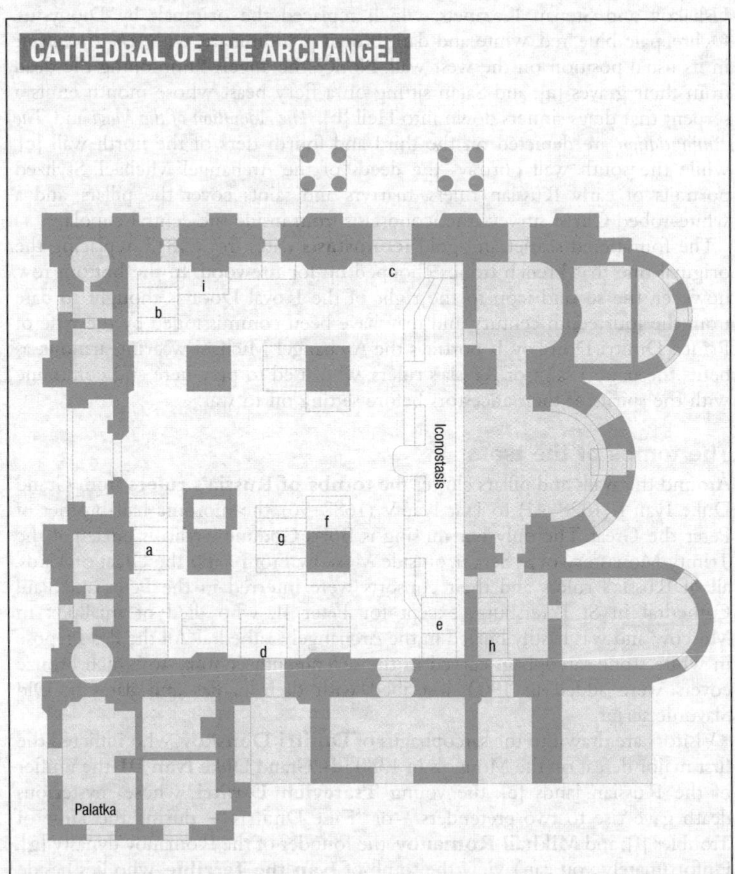

its debt to the Italian Renaissance is obvious, for the architect **Alevisio Novi** incorporated such features as Corinthian capitals and the Venetian-style shell scallops that form the gables. Another characteristic is its asymmetrical layout, with the east and west walls being divided into three sections, and the north and south walls into five. To compensate for this, the western pair of domes is larger than the eastern pair; both sets are clad in silvery iron, in contrast to the gilded central dome. The cathedral's plan was further complicated by the addition of chapels to the apses during the sixteenth century; buttresses along the south wall were added after it cracked in 1773; and an annexe or *palatka* was attached to the southwest corner in 1826.

You enter the cathedral through its west **portal**, whose archway is framed by carvings of plants and a faded fresco depicting Christ and the saints (above), and the mass baptism of the Russians during the reign of Prince Vladimir (at the bottom, on either side).

The frescoes and iconostasis

Four heavy square pillars take up much of the dimly lit interior, which is covered in frescoes executed (1652–66) by a team of artists under Simon Ushakov and Stepan Rezanets, which replaced the originals by Dionysius. Ochre, pale blue, red, white and dark brown predominate, with *The Apocalypse* in its usual position on the west wall. Notice the angels summoning the dead from their graves [**a**], and Satan sitting on a fiery beast whose mouth emits a serpent that drags sinners down into Hell [**b**]. *The Adoration of the Magi* and *The Annunciation* are depicted on the third and fourth tiers of the north wall [**c**], while the south wall portrays the deeds of the Archangel Michael. Stylized portraits of early Russian rulers, martyrs and saints cover the pillars, and a white-robed Christ surveys the iconostasis from inside the central cupola.

The four-tiered scarlet and gold **iconostasis** dates from 1813, replacing the original one that French troops chopped up for firewood. In the bottom row, however, the second icon to the right of the Royal Door is thought to date from the fourteenth century and may have been commissioned by the wife of Prince Dmitri Donskoy. It portrays the Archangel Michael wearing armour, as befits the patron saint of Russia's rulers, who used to pray here and commune with the spirits of their ancestors before setting off to war.

The tombs of the tsars

Around the walls and pillars cluster the **tombs of Russia's rulers** from Grand Duke Ivan I (1328–41) to Tsar Ivan V (1682–96), the moronic half-brother of Peter the Great. The only tsar missing is Boris Godunov, who is buried at the Trinity Monastery of St Sergei, outside Moscow. From Peter the Great onwards, all of Russia's rulers and their consorts were interred in the Peter and Paul Cathedral in St Petersburg, except for Peter II, who died of smallpox in Moscow and was hastily buried in the Archangel Cathedral. All the dead repose in white stone sarcophagi carved in the seventeenth century, to which bronze covers were added in 1903, inscribed with their names and dates in Old Slavonic script.

Visitors are drawn to the sarcophagus of **Dmitri Donskoy**, who inflicted the first major defeat on the Mongols in 1380 [**d**]; Grand Duke **Ivan III**, the unifier of the Russian lands [**e**]; the young **Tsarevich Dmitri**, whose mysterious death gave rise to two pretenders – or "False Dmitris" – during the Time of Troubles [**f**]; and **Mikhail Romanov**, the founder of the Romanov dynasty [**g**]. Unfortunately, you can't view the tomb of **Ivan the Terrible**, who lies beside his sons Ivan (whom he killed in a fit of rage) and Fyodor, in a chapel behind the iconostasis [**h**]. In 1963 Ivan the Terrible's tomb was exhumed and a model of his head was created by the anthropologist Gerasimov, an expert at reconstructing the features of unidentified corpses from their skulls, who makes a pseudonymous appearance in Martin Cruz Smith's novel *Gorky Park*.

The Faceted, Terem and Great Kremlin palaces

These fabulous palaces are only accessible on a **special guided tour**, run by Patriarshy Dom Tours (☎795 09 27; see p.46), two or three times a month. The excursion is limited to 25 people and tickets sell out fast despite the cost (R2100), so book as far ahead as possible. Visitors must submit their passport and visa details and bring both documents to be verified by security; cameras are locked away in the foyer. The itinerary switches back and forth between the three palaces rather than focusing on each in turn (as our account does), since the Great Kremlin Palace's St Vladimir Hall provides access to the upper levels of the other two palaces.

The Faceted Palace and the Red Staircase

The white **Faceted Palace** (Granovitaya palata) jutting out between the cathedrals of the Assumption and the Annunciation is so-called for its diamond-patterned facade. Built for Ivan III in 1487–91 by Marco Ruffo and Pietro Antonio Solario, its outstanding feature is the 500-square-metre **chamber** that forms its upper storey, whose vaults are supported by a single massive pillar. Every centimetre is gilded and frescoed with biblical and "historical" scenes by Palekh artists. Look out for Prince Vladimir telling his twelve sons to rule Russia in peace (they soon fell out), and Tsar Fyodor with his advisor Boris Godunov (who commissioned the murals, and was believed to have murdered Fyodor's heir to seize the throne for himself). The boyars occupied benches around the walls while the tsar sat enthroned in the corner where the sun stayed longest. It was both an audience chamber and a banqueting hall; Ivan the Terrible treated foreign ambassadors to roast swan and elks' brains, with dwarves and jesters for entertainment.

When the tsar ventured forth in olden days, he passed through a Porch Hall with four gilded doors surmounted by lions and dragons, and descended to Sobornaya ploshchad by the **Red Staircase** (Krasnaya lesnitsa). During the Streltsy revolt of 1682, the ten-year-old Peter the Great saw several of his relatives thrown from the stairs onto the pikes of the mutineers – but its name has nothing to do with bloodshed; as with Red Square, it originally meant "beautiful". The medieval staircase was demolished in the 1930s; what you see today is a 1990s re-creation, complete with Tsarist eagles above its arches and lions on the balustrade.

The Terem Palace

The most intriguing edifice is the archaic **Terem Palace** (Teremnoy dvorets), which was the Imperial residence until Peter the Great moved the capital to St Petersburg in 1712. It incorporates two medieval churches built one on top of the other and two levels of service quarters, above which is the royal suite created for Mikhail Romanov in 1635–36 – *terem* means "tower-chamber". All the rooms were connected by a corridor used for the *smotriny*, the selection of the tsar's bride from a parade of eligible virgins, ostensibly asleep on eiderdowns.

The palace fell into disuse in the eighteenth century and might have crumbled away had not Nicholas I commissioned Fyodor Solntsev to restore it in a re-creation of the seventeenth-century style, in 1837.

Nicholas's initial appears on the shields held by lions flanking the stairs from the so-called **Golden Porch** to the royal suite, while access from the floor below is via a grill-work door crawling with dragons and demons (a medieval feature, perhaps meant to ward off evil). Low-vaulted **anterooms** with ornate tiled stoves and murals lead to a **Cross Chamber** where the inner circle of boyars watched buffoons or listened to monks chanting while they forged a consensus, before filing into the red and gold **Throne Chamber**, to present it to their sovereign. Whereas tsars Fyodor, Mikhail Romanov and Alexei Mikhailovich were willing to let the boyars make policy, Ivan the Terrible only let them decide the menu for banquets, and other trivial matters.

The tsar and tsarevna slept in separate quarters, giving the tsar the choice of visiting his wife or a mistress downstairs. The four-poster **bed** in this room was an early sign of westernization (Russians traditionally slept on benches, wrapped in furs), imported from Germany via Arkhangelsk – a staggering distance to transport such a mundane item.

The Great Kremlin Palace

The aptly named **Great Kremlin Palace** (Bolshoy Kremlevskiy dvorets) stretches for 125m along the crest of the Kremlin hill. Commissioned by Nicholas I, who revered ancient Russia and preferred Moscow to St Petersburg, its yellow-and-white facade employing Russo-Byzantine motifs according to the rules of classical harmony hides five magnificent halls dedicated to the chivalric orders of the empire. Architect Konstantin Ton exploited the newly invented technique of *faux mabre*, whereby powdered marble was applied to stucco and polished to simulate solid stone on a scale where the real thing would need massive foundations to bear the weight. The result is overpoweringly splendid: when George W. Bush was shown around by Putin, his jaw dropped at the sight – and for once you can't blame him.

The white **St George Hall** is 61m long and 18m tall; its vaults are adorned with the cross and star of St George; its benches upholstered in the orange and black of the order's ribbon; the walls inscribed with 200,000 names of individuals and regiments awarded the honour (which was reinstated in the mid-1950s); and the columns topped by female figures representing territories conquered by the Russian empire.

Adjacent are two still larger halls that were knocked through in the 1930s to create a meeting place for the Supreme Soviet, which Yeltsin restored at vast expense, adding foyers and galleries that never existed before. The rose-pink **Alexander Nevsky Hall** is awash with gilding, its dome studded with the star and cross of the order (awarded for military genius) and its walls festooned with Tsarist eagles and the crests of old Russian principalities – an exalted backdrop for conclaves of the Federation Council (the upper chamber of the Duma). Grander still is the green and gold **St Andrew Hall**, named after the highest award in the Tsarist empire, bestowed at the monarch's discretion – which Putin has conferred on such figures as Mikhail Kalashnikov (inventor of the Kalashnikov rifle) and the Nobel laureate Solzhenitsyn. The hall is also used for swearing-in Russia's president, who has yet to utilize the thrones once occupied by the tsar, tsarevna and tsarevich, beneath an ermine and cloth-of-gold canopy.

The octagonal **St Vladimir Hall**, faced in white and pale mauve marble, originally served for awarding a special order to Tsarist bureaucrats, and for signing treaties in Soviet times. Today, diplomatic summits are held in the

Malachite Vestibule, whose lustrous green columns are offset by oxblood walls, hung with laughably bad portraits of Russian rulers by Ilya Glazunov (see p.131) – the ones of Peter and Catherine the Great are only differentiated by a moustache. Visitors seldom see the white, gold and malachite **St Catherine Hall**, which is regularly used for diplomatic and ministerial functions.

Downstairs, you're led through an enfilade of rooms in various styles. Highlights include the **Rococo Room**, with its silver silk wallpaper, "pineapple" chandeliers and azure porcelain lamp stands; the crimson and gold Baroque **Music Room**, with its mother-of-pearl-inlaid doors; a boudoir with a malachite fireplace (purely for show), and a Blue Study with a divan used by Alexander III, whose kidney problems obliged him to lie down a lot. Sadly, you can't see the **Imperial Bedrooms**, which are always offered to visiting heads of state – the only ones to have accepted are Britain's Queen Elizabeth II and the North Korean dictator Kim Il Sung.

The Cathedral of the Annunciation

To the south of the Faceted Palace glints the golden-domed **Cathedral of the Annunciation** (Blagoveshchenskiy sobor), which served as the private church of the Grand Dukes and Tsars. It stands on the site of a church built by Dmitri Donskoy's son, Vasily I, the foundations and undercroft of which

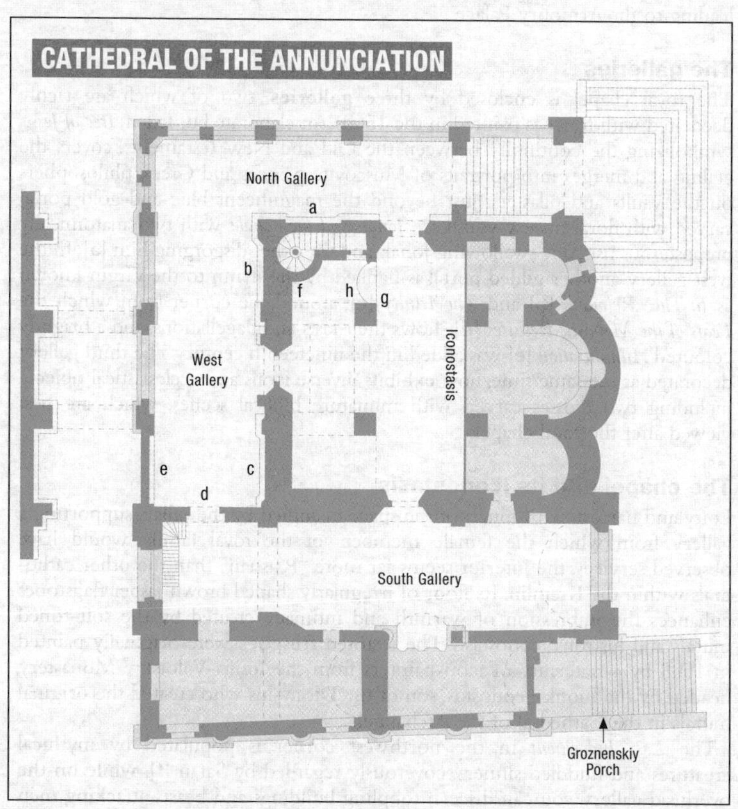

were incorporated into the existing structure, erected in 1448–49 by master stonemasons from Pskov at the behest of Ivan III. The cathedral was badly damaged in the conflagration that swept Moscow in 1547, shortly after the coronation of Ivan the Terrible, and it was restored in 1562–64. The tsar had the cathedral's gallery enclosed, a domed chapel added to each corner, and two false domes erected, bringing the total to nine. The domes, roof and tops of the apses were then sheathed in gold (supposedly looted from Novgorod, after Ivan sacked the city), giving rise to the cathedral's nickname, "gold-topped". Notice the inverted crescents at the base of the crosses above the domes, symbolizing the triumph of Orthodoxy over Islam. Its tiers of gables and *kokoshniki* reflect the influence of early Moscow architecture, while the intricately carved frieze below the domes is a typical feature of Pskov churches.

Visitors enter via the steps at the northeast corner; the other, covered, porch was added in 1572, after Ivan the Terrible married for the fourth time, contrary to the rules of the Orthodox faith, which allow only three marriages. The Church Council dared not refuse him a special dispensation, but salved its conscience by stipulating that the tsar henceforth attend services via a separate entrance, and observe them from behind a grille. You can follow in his footsteps by climbing the steps of the **Groznenskiy Porch** (whose name derives from the sobriquet *Grozny*, meaning "Awesome" or "Terrible") alongside the road leading to the Armoury Palace.

The galleries

The royal chapel is enclosed by three **galleries**, two of which are richly decorated with frescoes painted in the 1560s. An elaborate but faded *Tree of Jesse*, symbolizing the continuity between the Old and New Testaments, covers the ceiling and merges into portraits of Muscovite princes and Greek philosophers on the vaults and pilasters. Just beyond the magnificent blue-and-gold portal carved with floral tracery, you'll see *Jonah and the Whale*, with two anatomically preposterous fish, one swallowing Jonah and the other disgorging him [**a**]. In the west gallery, another gilded portal is flanked by the hymn to the Virgin known as *In Thee Rejoiceth* [**b**] and *The Trinity* [**c**], around the corner from which the *Feats of the Monastic Recluses* [**d**] shows their fasts and flagellations, and a brightly coloured *Annunciation* [**e**] was added in the nineteenth century. The third gallery, decorated at the same time, now exhibits diverse icons and ecclesiastical objects, including two crosses carved with miniature biblical scenes, which are best viewed after the royal chapel.

The chapel and its iconostasis

Lofty and narrow, with much of the space occupied by the pillars supporting a gallery from which the female members of the royal family would have observed services, the interior seems far more "Russian" than the other cathedrals within the Kremlin. Its floor of irregularly shaped brown jasper flagstones enhances the impression of warmth and intimacy created by the soft-toned murals and lustrous iconostasis. The restored **frescoes** were originally painted in 1508 by a fraternity of icon-painters from the Iosifo-Volotskiy Monastery, headed by the monk Feodosius, son of the Dionysius who created the original murals in the Cathedral of the Archangel.

The *Last Judgement* in the northwest corner is populated by mythical creatures and huddled sinners, covetously regarded by Satan [**f**], while on the overhead gallery you can discern toppling buildings and beasts attacking men in *The Apocalypse* [**g**]. Portraits of Russian princes, including Dmitri Donskoy and Vasily I, adorn the nearby pillar [**h**]; the other one features the Byzantine Emperors and their families. Scenes from the lives of Christ and the Virgin cover the north and south walls, while angels, patriarchs and prophets cluster around Christ Pantokrator in the central dome.

The **iconostasis** – which dates from 1405 and survived the fire of 1547 – is regarded as the finest in Russia, containing as it does the work of three masters: Theophanes the Greek, Andrei Rublev and Prokhor of Gorodets. In the bottom row to the right of the Royal Door are *Christ Enthroned* and the *Ustyug Annunciation* (whose central panel is a copy of the twelfth-century original now in the Tretyakov Gallery). To the left of the Royal Door are icons of the *Hodegetria Virgin* and *Our Lady of Tikhvin* (far left), both dating from the sixteenth century. Theophanes created most of the icons in the third, Deesis, Row, where Christ is flanked by John the Baptist and the Virgin, next to whom is an Archangel Michael attributed to Rublev, who collaborated with Prokhor on the Festival Row, above. This is surmounted by a row devoted to the prophets, topped by ogee-shaped finials containing small images of the patriarchs.

The Armoury Palace

Situated between the Great Kremlin Palace and the Borovitskiy Gate, the **Armoury Palace** (Oruzheynaya palata) conceals a staggering array of treasures behind its Russo-Byzantine facade. Here are displayed the tsars' coronation robes, carriages, jewellery, dinner services and armour – made by the finest craftsmen with an utter disregard for cost or restraint – whose splendour and curiosity value outweigh the trouble and expense involved in seeing them. As an institution, the Kremlin Armoury probably dates back to the fourteenth century, if not earlier, though the first recorded mention was in 1508. Initially, its purpose was utilitarian – one foreigner described it as being "so big and so richly stocked that twenty thousand cavalry men could be armed with its weapons" – but it soon became a storehouse for state treasures and, in 1806, a semi-public museum. The existing building was completed in 1851 in the same style as the Great Kremlin Palace, by Nicholas I's favourite architect, Ton.

Visiting the Armoury requires a little planning. Admission is limited to four times a day (10am, noon, 2.30pm & 4.30pm), and you can only remain inside for a single session of an hour and a half's duration. It's best to buy a ticket before you enter the Kremlin and start queuing outside the Armoury entrance at least 15 minutes before the time specified on your ticket, otherwise you'll waste time waiting to buy one in the foyer (which has an ATM) or trying to get through the crowd of visitors.

Beyond the cloakroom is an **information** desk, followed by stalls selling books and souvenirs, where you can rent an **audioguide** (R200), buy an illustrated **guidebook** to the Armoury (R250) or a CD-ROM tour of the Kremlin. Stairs at the far end lead to a small foyer from which you ascend to a larger one with two staircases, the left-hand one leading to the lower floor of the Armoury, the other to the upper floor.

The lower floor

Although guided tours often start on the floor above, it's the **lower floor** that holds the most appeal, as it displays the fabulous costumes, thrones, crowns and carriages of Russia's rulers, from medieval times onwards. Besides their sheer sumptuousness, one is struck by the abrupt stylistic change from Russo-Byzantine forms to the fashion of Western European courts, introduced by

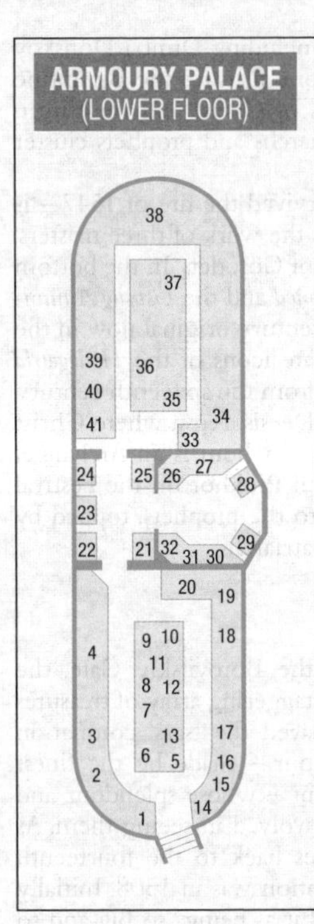

Peter the Great in the early eighteenth century. Though each section has an explanatory note in English, the actual exhibits are labelled in Russian only, but the keyed plan on this page should help you to figure out what's what.

Court dress and vestments

The first room is largely devoted to **court dress**. In the left-hand case are a black velvet caftan worn by Peter the Great whilst working in the shipyards of Amsterdam, and his thigh-boots and cane [**1**]; a falconry outfit with a Tsarist eagle on its breast [**2**]; typical long-sleeved, old-style caftans [**3**]; the gold brocade robes and jewellery worn by Peter at his coronation, and the house-caftans that he relaxed in [**4**]. The central display is fronted by an archaic gold caftan and sable hat worn by Nicholas II at a costume ball in 1903 [**5**], with Peter the Great's Dutch-style frock coat nearby. Beyond the cerise coronation dress of Catherine I [**6**] are the frock coat and stockings of Peter II; the gold-embroidered coronation dresses of empresses Anna [**7**] and Elizabeth [**8**]; and the wasp-waisted wedding dress of the future Catherine the Great [**9**]. Finest of all are Catherine's coronation dress [**10**] and the ermine-trimmed cape [**11**] of Nicholas II's wife Alexandra. The coronation dresses of Alexandra Fyodorovna [**12**] and Maria Alexandrova [**13**] are in the French Empire style of the 1820–50s.

Along the right wall are **ecclesiastical vestments and fabrics**, the oldest of which is the pale blue and silver satin *sakkos* (ceremonial robe) of Metropolitan Peter, made in 1322 [**14**]. Metropolitan Photius had two sakkos [**15**]: the Maliy, decorated with Crucifixions, saints and royal portraits; and the Bolshoy, with similar designs outlined in pearls (a symbol of good luck in old Russia). Past a *sakkos* given by Ivan the Terrible to Metropolitan Dionysius [**16**] are the pearl-embroidered Venetian velvet robes, mantle, cuffs and crowns of Patriarch Nikon [**17**] – the mantle alone weighs 24 kilos. Imported European fabrics began to be used from the seventeenth century onwards, as evinced by the cloth-of-gold pearl-hemmed cape given by Mikhail Romanov to the Novospasskiy Monastery [**18**]; Patriarch Adrian's Italian robe, embroidered with Tsarist eagles [**19**]; and an Italian velvet cape crisscrossed with pearl tracery and emblazoned with a diamond and emerald cross, given by Catherine the Great to Metropolitan Platon [**20**].

Crowns and thrones

The corridor beyond showcases **crowns and thrones**. Ivan the Terrible's ivory throne, carved with battle and hunting scenes, stands beside a low golden throne studded with turquoises, given to Boris Godunov by Shah Abbas I of Persia [**21**]. Opposite are the throne of Mikhail Romanov, made in the Kremlin Armoury, and the Diamond Throne of his son Alexei, adorned with silver

The Crown of Monomakh

The Cap or **Crown of Monomakh** (Shapka Monomakha) symbolized the tsars' claim to heritage of Byzantium and Moscow's boast of being the "Third Rome". Legend has it that the crown was presented to Prince Vladimir of Kiev (1053–1125) by his grandfather, the Byzantine Emperor Constantine IX Monomachus, though experts believe that the existing crown actually dates from the late thirteenth or early fourteenth century. In any event, it visibly differs from other European crowns, consisting of eight gold-filigree triangles joined to form a cone, studded with rough-cut gems and trimmed with sable. It served for the coronation of every tsar from the end of the fifteenth century to 1682; some years later Peter the Great introduced Western-style crowns, which were used thereafter. However, his successors retained Mikhail Romanov's original orb and sceptre, symbolizing the tsar's dominion over the earth.

elephants and over eight hundred diamonds, a gift from Armenian merchants [**22**]. The huge silver double throne [**23**] was made for the dual coronation in 1682 of the young Peter the Great and his feeble-minded half-brother Ivan V, who were prompted by their elder sister Sofia from a secret nook behind the throne (now exposed). The hefty Empress Elizabeth sat on a wide Empire-style "armchair" throne, while the runty Tsar Paul had a smaller one with a foot-tuffet [**24**].

Best of all are the **crowns and imperial regalia** in the last case [**25**]. On the top shelf are the famous Crown of Monomakh (see box above); the eighteenth-century European-style Silver Crown that belonged to Empress Anna, encrusted with 2500 diamonds; and a cruder "second" Crown of Monomakh that was made for the joint coronation of Peter and Ivan V. On the lower shelf can be seen the latter's Siberian Crown, trimmed in silver sable; the gold-leafed Kazan Crown of Ivan the Terrible, made to celebrate the capture of that city from the Tatars in 1552; and Mikhail Romanov's emerald-topped Dress Crown and enamelled orb and sceptre.

Saddlery and coaches

The adjacent octagonal room displays **equestrian regalia**, including Ivan the Terrible's saddle, covered in dark red velvet, turquoises and gold embroidery [**26**]. Beyond the saddles of Prince Pozharsky and Boris Godunov (the latter embossed with lions' heads) is a saddle decorated with gems, given by the Persian Shah to Mikhail Romanov in 1635 [**27**]. The stuffed horse in ceremonial attire was one of a hundred such horses that used to precede the Imperial coach during processions. Catherine the Great received jewelled harnesses and saddles from sultans Abdul Hamid [**28**] and Selim III [**29**], as did Alexei and Mikhail Romanov from earlier Turkish rulers [**30**], and tsars Fyodor and Boris Godunov from the monarchs of Persia [**31**] and Poland [**32**]. Also notice the splendid saddle from Gdansk, embroidered with hunting scenes in silver wire.

The oldest of the **carriages and coaches** in the end room is an English carriage presented to Boris Godunov by James I, decorated with hunting scenes on the sides [**33**]. Nearby stand an early seventeenth-century Russian coach with mica windows [**34**] and tiny summer and winter coaches made for the son and niece of Peter the Great, which had dwarves for coachmen and were drawn by ponies [**35**]. The French coach with paintings of cherubs by Boucher [**36**] was given to Empress Elizabeth by the Hetman of the Ukraine; she also owned a winter coach whose sleds were carved with dolphins [**37**], a

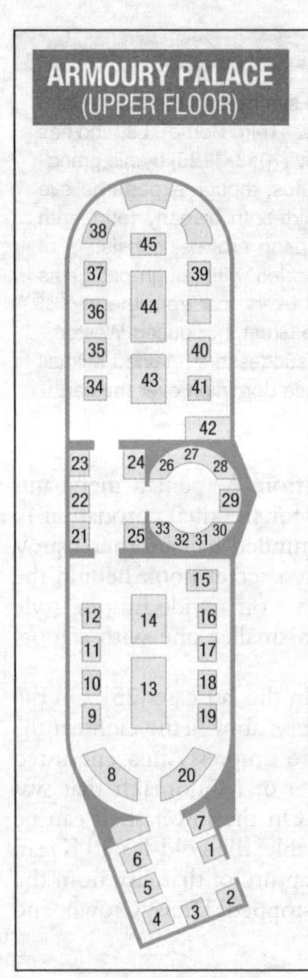

fleet of travel coaches [38] and a coronation coach that was a present from Frederick II of Prussia [39]. By comparison, Catherine the Great's collection seems modest, consisting of two carriages for travel and state occasions [40], and a summer coach that was a gift from her favourite, Orlov [41].

The upper floor

From the same lobby, a grand staircase with brass balustrades ascends to the **upper floor**, whose landing is decorated with paintings of parades and processions outside the Kremlin, with the Soviet crest incongruously inset above a massive doorway. The rooms that follow are crammed with treasures and armour, which soon overwhelm visitors, and eventually pall. As on the lower floor, each case has an explanatory note in English, although individual pieces are only labelled in Russian.

Russian gold and silver

The first room contains the **Russian gold and silver** collection ranging from the twelfth to the sixteenth centuries, plus a few rare items from the Age of Migrations, such as a silver-gilt jug decorated with figures of the nine Muses [1]. Though many medieval treasures disappeared during the Mongol invasion, two buried troves of jewelled pectorals and necklaces were found at Ryazan and Tula in the nineteenth century [2]. Bibles and icons often used to be encased in gold covers like the foliage-engraved *okhlad* for Our Lady ofVladimir [3], while holy relics were kept in cathedral-shaped receptacles such as the Great Sion [4].The sixteenth century was the golden age of Russian jewellery [5]. Notice the Evangelistary studded with gems as big as grapes, which Ivan the Terrible gave to the Cathedral of the Annunciation, and the pearl-rimmed crucifix that he bestowed upon the Solovetskiy Monastery [6]. The life-size gold tomb covers [7] from the shrines of Tsarevich Dmitri and St Cyril, the founder of the Belozersk Monastery, are unique specimens of this form of art.

The dark green hall beyond exhibits more of the same, from the seventeenth century onwards. Near a squinting *Our Lady of the Don* with a pearl choker is a gold cover for an icon of The Trinity, featuring three face-shaped ovals suspended in mid-frame [8]. At court, mead was drunk from a scoop-shaped *kovsh*, while guests toasted each other with a shared friendship cup, or *bratina* [9]. Moscow craftsmen specialized in the technique of niello, whereby etched grooves were filled with a powder that turned a soft black after firing, highlighting the designs that appeared on the surface [10]. At Solvychedosk, they excelled at enamelling, with tiny birds a favourite motif [11], whereas the Volga towns went in for minutely detailed silverwork [12]. The Kremlin workshops produced the enamelled chalice given by Boyarina Morozova to the

Monastery of Miracles, and the gold goblet presented by Tsar Alexei to the Monastery of the Ascension [**13**].

The early eighteenth-century inlay and enamel work on display [**14**] is less striking, as is the collection of French Empire-style stuff [**15**, **16** & **18**], snuff-boxes and Evangelistaries [**17**].

However, don't miss the **Fabergé eggs** that were exchanged as Easter gifts by the tsar and tsaritsa every year from 1884 until the fall of the Romanov dynasty [**19**]. Among the fourteen examples owned by the Armoury are the *Clock Egg*, with its bouquet of diamond lilies; the *Shtandart* and *Azov* eggs, containing models of the Imperial yacht and the cruiser *Azov*; and the *Kremlin Egg*, which played the anthem God Save the Tsar. Even more ingenious was the *Grand Siberian Railway Egg*, produced to mark the completion of the line to Vladivostok, which held a tiny replica of the Trans-Siberian Express, which ran for 20m when its clockwork locomotive was wound up (until broken by the Imperial kids). The *Dandelion* and *Pansies* are so artfully carved from crystal that they resemble jars full of water; the latter bears portraits of the tsar's children on its stamens, revealed by squeezing the stem.

A sauce boat surmounted by a beetle and a Style Moderne cup, jug and sugar bowl are the highlights of the twentieth-century display case [**20**].

Weapons and armour

Among the **foreign weapons and armour** in the next room are arquebuses and plate armour from Germany [**21**]; a complete set for a horse and rider, presented to Tsar Fyodor by King Stephen Bathory of Poland [**22**]; and a miniature suit of armour made for Tsarevich Alexei in 1634 [**23**]. Across the way are jewelled maces and Egyptian sabres, rifles inlaid with ivory and mother-of-pearl, gilded helmets and arm-guards studded with turquoises and carnelians – all hailing from various parts of the Ottoman Empire [**24**]. Also notice the spiked helmets with sinister face-masks, and the gem-encrusted dagger presented by the Shah of Persia to Mikhail Romanov, in the showcase of Persian arms and armour [**25**].

The adjacent circular chamber – decorated by a frieze of royal portraits – displays **Russian weapons and armour**. To the left are the spiked helmets and chain mail armour of Boris Godunov and Prince Shuyskiy, and a teardrop-shaped helmet made for Ivan Ivanovich, the three-year-old son of Ivan the Terrible [**26**]. The *saadak* (weapons case) and quiver of Mikhail Romanov are made of gold and encrusted with jewels [**27**], while his gold-chased helmet appears beyond the mail-and-plate armour of his son, Alexei [**28**]. Russian cavalrymen customarily wore a mixture of Russian-made and Turkish or Persian armour, as on the life-sized model [**29**]. Beyond various products of the Kremlin Armoury [**30**] is a host of drums, trumpets and officers' throat guards, captured from the Swedes during the Northern War [**31**]. Brilliants glitter on the hilt and scabbard of Alexander I's sword, made in Tula [**32**], and a display of the chivalric orders of the Tsarist empire concludes the exhibition [**33**].

European gold and silver

The final hall is stuffed with **European gold and silver**, much of it presented as ambassadorial gifts. The Dutch gave Count Stroganov ewers, tankards and a leaf-shaped wall candelabra [**34**], while Tsar Alexei received a silver banqueting set from the Poles, which included a bird-figure that poured water on guests' hands [**35**]. In 1644, the Danes lavished similar gifts in the hope of marrying their Crown Prince to Tsarevna Irina, and the Hanseatic League sent huge goblets with gryphons on the lids [**36**]. Nuremberg goldsmiths devised receptacles moulded to fit pineapples [**37**] and a drinking vessel in the form of a cockerel [**38**], while Hamburg specialized in "smoking hills" that wafted aromatic fumes across the table [**39**]. From France came gold *toilette* sets for the Stroganovs and Trubetskoys [**40**], the *Tête-à-Tête* tea service [**41**], and the *Olympic* dessert service that Napoleon gave to Alexander I to commemorate the Treaty of Tilsit [**42**]. Among the Armoury's peerless collection of English Tudor silver are two leopard-shaped flagons and a pair of jugs with dragon spouts [**43**]. Finally, don't miss the triple-layer Swedish table fountain [**44**], nor the caseful of *objets* fashioned from shells, bone and other unusual materials [**45**].

The Diamond Fund

The Armoury Palace also houses the **Diamond Fund** (Almazniy Fond; daily except Thurs 10am–12.30pm & 2–4.30pm; R500), which contains the most valuable gems in Russia. Every two hours, guided tours are run for groups (R1400 for up to 6 people; call ⓣ629 20 36 to book in advance, or buy tickets shortly before the tour starts). Photography is not allowed; cameras and mobile phones must be left at the ticket booth.

The exhibition features such treasures as the diamond-encrusted **Coronation Crown** of Catherine the Great, and the 190-carat **Orlov Diamond** that she was given by Count Grigory Orlov, in an attempt to revive their relationship; she never wore it, but had it set into the **Imperial Sceptre**. Another notable gem is the 89-carat **Shah Diamond**, presented to Nicholas I by the Shah of Persia as compensation for the murder of the Russian diplomat and playwright Griboedov by a mob in Teheran. Besides this, there are dozens of jewelled necklaces and earrings, the world's largest sapphire (258.8 carats), and a gold nugget weighing 36kg. You can also see the Tsarist orders that were bestowed in the Great Kremlin Palace and diamond-encrusted victory orders awarded to Stalin's marshals.

Streets and Squares	
Krasnaya ploshchad	Красная площадь
Sobornaya ploshchad	Соборная площадь
Metro stations	
Aleksandrovskiy Sad	Александровский сад
Biblioteka Imeni Lenina	библиотека имени Ленина
Borovitskaya	Боровицкая
Okhotniy Ryad	Охотный ряд
Ploshchad Revolyutsii	Площадь Революции
Teatralnaya	Театральная
Museums	
Armoury Palace	Оружейная палата
Historical Museum	Исторический музей
Kremlin	Кремль
Lenin Mausoleum	мавзолей В.И. Ленина

The Kitay-gorod

To the east of Red Square lies the **Kitay-gorod** quarter, whose mix of churches and palaces, banks, workshops and offices reflects its 800-year-old history. Although Kitay-gorod means "China Town" in modern Russian, there's no evidence that Chinese merchants ever resided here, and most scholars believe that the name derives from *kita*, an old word meaning "wattle", after the palisades that reinforced the earthen wall erected around this early Kremlin suburb. In the fifteenth century nobles began to settle here in preference to the Kremlin, displacing the original population of artisans and traders, but the nobility later moved further out to escape the risk of fires and plagues, leaving the quarter to rich merchants. Finally, the merchants too relocated to more salubrious areas, and the Kitay-gorod became what it still is today, predominantly commercial, with new banks and emporiums replacing the older shops and dwellings.

Aside from the busy **street life** on thoroughfares like Nikolskaya ulitsa, the main attractions are the quarter's churches, particularly the **Church of the Trinity**; the interior of the **Palace of the Romanov Boyars** and the **Old English Court** in the Zaryade area shouldn't be missed either. The **Archeological Museum** and two sections of the **fortified walls** that once ran for 2.6km around the Kitay-gorod attest to its ancient history, while the former Lenin Museum and Communist Party headquarters are reminders of the not-so-distant Soviet era.

Being just off Red Square, **ploshchad Revolyutsii** is a good place to start, with access from Ploshchad Revolyutsii or Okhotniy Ryad metro stations; or you can approach the quarter from its periphery instead, starting from the Kitay-gorod or Lubyanka stations. As the Kitay-gorod is small and contained, you can walk around the whole quarter in an hour or so.

Around ploshchad Revolyutsii

Proximity to Red Square makes **ploshchad Revolyutsii** (Revolution Square) a meeting place for Communist and far-right agitators – particularly on Sundays, when "Red Grannies" and black-shirts hawk Soviet memorabilia and anti-Semitic tracts outside the **former Lenin Museum**. This red-brick, neo-Russian edifice, built for the Tsarist City Duma, once boasted the world's largest collection of Leninalia, including his Rolls-Royce Silver Ghost – expropriated from a millionaire – and a replica of his study in the Kremlin. After the 1991 putsch, it lost its state funding and was forced to shed 150 staff, but struggled on until 1993, when Luzhkov decreed its eviction. The building hasn't been open since then. The flight of **steps** alongside leads through a passage to Nikolskaya ulitsa (see p.103).

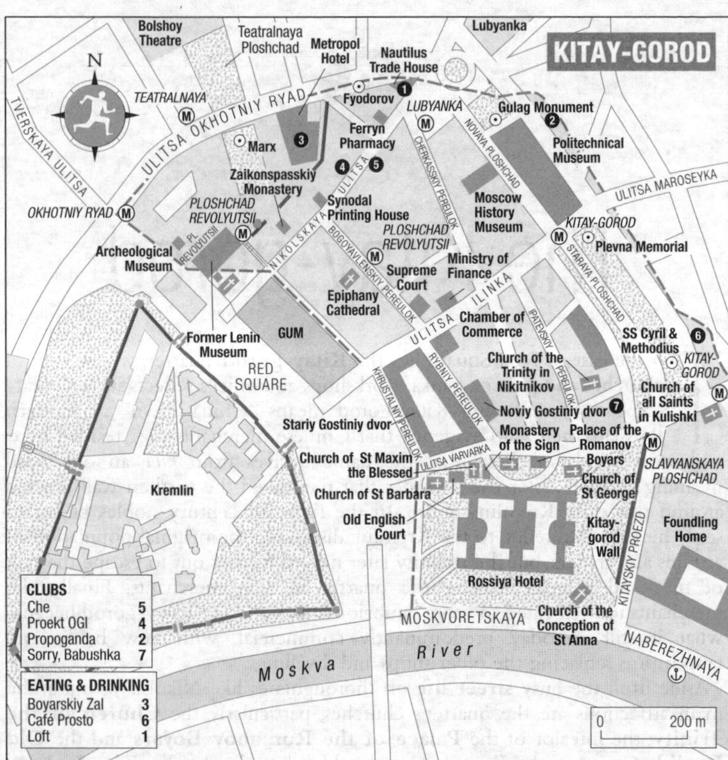

At present, the ploshchad is a dreary expanse bordering a building site where a plush new hotel is being built on the site where the **Moskva Hotel** stood until 2004. This dour monolith was built in the 1930s to accommodate delegates to Party congresses; the British defector Guy Burgess lived there until his death in 1963. Famously, its asymmetrical facade facing Manezhnaya ploshchad arose because its architect submitted two variations to Stalin, who approved both, not realizing that he was supposed to choose between them – no one dared correct his mistake. Had the 1935 city reconstruction plan been fully realized, it would have faced the Palace of Soviets (see p.132) down a wide avenue, intended as the focal point of the city. When the US architect Frank Lloyd Wright was asked for his opinion of the hotel, he replied "It's the ugliest thing I have ever seen" – which his interpreter tactfully translated as "I'm very impressed".

The Archeological Museum of Moscow

Near the former *Moskva Hotel* site, a wrought-iron and marble pavilion covers the entrance to the subterranean, wheelchair-accessible **Archeological Museum of Moscow** (muzey arkheologii Moskvy; Tues, Thurs, Sat & Sun 10am–6pm, Wed & Fri 11am–7pm; closed Mon & the last Fri of each month; R60, students R25). Opened in 1997, the museum's highlight is a substantial section of the limestone arches of the **Voskresenskiy bridge** over the Neglina River, which led from the Beliy gorod quarter to the Resurrection Gate of

Red Square. The bridge was uncovered during the construction of the mall beneath Manezhnaya ploshchad, which also exposed the foundations of houses on the far bank of the Neglina. The oldest artefacts are earrings and necklaces from the twelfth century, when Moscow was founded – though most date from the fifteenth century onwards and include a hoard of Spanish doubloons found in the Kitay-gorod. Birch-bark shoes and vessels, leather purses and a spiked helmet are among the humbler objects displayed alongside scale models of the Kremlin and Kitay-gorod, the Voskresenskiy bridge and Okhotniy ryad in olden days.

Teatralnaya ploshchad, the medieval walls and the Metropol

Teatralnaya ploshchad (Theatre Square) is the next part of downtown Moscow set to be transformed now that Manezhnaya ploshchad has been finished, so you'll have to see what the outcome is. There's certainly room for improvement, as the square was cut in half by ulitsa Okhotniy ryad in the 1930s, leaving the Bolshoy and other theatres isolated from the greenery that did them justice. In the park on the Kitay-gorod side of the avenue, a **statue of Karl Marx** looms out of a granite menhir, flanked by testimonials reading: "His name will endure through the ages, and so will his work" (Engels); "Marxist doctrine is omnipotent because it is true" (Lenin).

As a foretaste of what's to come, the end of the square is now dramatized by a replica of the **medieval walls** of Kitay-gorod, complete with swallow-tailed crenellations and a tent-roofed tower, added to a genuine portion that runs off behind the **Metropol Hotel** due to a bend in the now-buried Neglina River. While the Proofreading House in the Synodal Printing House and belltower of the Zaikonspasskiy Monastery above the ramparts are accessible by a stairway, you're more likely to be drawn to the hotel. A Style Moderne masterpiece built (1899–1903) by the Odessa-born British architect William Walcott, its north wall features a huge ceramic panel, *The Princess of Dreams*, designed by the Symbolist artist Mikhail Vrubel in his characteristic palette of indigo, violet and bottle green. Notice the wrought-iron gateway, and the two plaques beside the main entrance, attesting to the hotel's role as the "Second House of Soviets", where the Central Executive of the Soviets of Workers' and Peasants' Deputies met in 1918–19. Famous guests have included Tolstoy, Chaliapin, George Bernard Shaw, JFK and Michael Jackson.

As an alternative route back into the Kitay-gorod you can continue uphill past the *Metropol* and cut in through **Tretyakovskiy proezd**, where an ornamental gateway leads to Nikolskaya ulitsa. This passage is named after the merchant Sergei Tretyakov, who knocked it through in 1871, for quicker access to the banks along Kuznetskiy most. Just uphill from the gateway is an appealing **statue of Ivan Fyodorov**, Russia's first printer (see opposite). At the top of the hill, the curvaceous, polychrome-tiled **Nautilus Trade House** embodies the tastes of today's New Russians, with boutiques, offices, a fitness club and restaurant under one roof. When its foundations were dug in 1999, medieval coins, jewellery and tombstones were found at the site, which archeologists called **Starie Pola** (Old Fields) as it once lay just outside the Kitay-gorod walls.

Nikolskaya ulitsa

Running off from Red Square either side of GUM are the two main thoroughfares of the Kitay-gorod, Nikolskaya ulitsa and ulitsa Ilinka. Named after the St Nicholas Gate of the Kremlin, facing the end of the street, **Nikolskaya ulitsa** bustles with shoppers emerging from GUM, yet despite its prime location and fetching pre-Revolutionary buildings, its tone is set by cheap eateries such as *Drova* (see p.348) and far-from-glamorous shops, with a handful of historic monuments and a clandestine subculture of its own.

On the left-hand side, the iron gateway of no. 9 leads into a shadowy courtyard harbouring the remains of the **Zaikonspasskiy Monastery**. Founded in 1600, the monastery supported itself by selling icons on the street outside – hence its name, "Behind the Icon of the Saviour". In 1687, its seminary was converted into Russia's first institution of higher education, the Slavo-Greco-Latin Academy, where the "Russian Leonardo", Mikhail Lomonosov, later studied. Now slowly being restored, the monastery's cathedral has a red-and-white octagonal belltower crowned by a gilded finial, linked to the adjacent monks' quarters by an overhead arcade.

It's indicative of how many monasteries there were in Moscow that just up the road and around the corner is the Monastery of the Epiphany. Its hulking **Epiphany Cathedral** (Bogoyavlenskiy sobor) is decorated with crested *nalichniki* and an intricate cornice, while the crimson-and-white belltower is inset with mosaic portraits of saints, and topped by a gilded dome. Although the cathedral was constructed in the 1690s, the monastery itself was founded by Prince Daniil in the thirteenth century, making it the second oldest in Moscow. Now fully restored, the cathedral not only holds services, but also occasional **bell-ringing** concerts.

Returning to Nikolskaya ulitsa, you'll catch sight of the **Synodal Printing House**, a sky-blue edifice with Gothic pinnacles and lacy stuccowork, erected on the site of the sixteenth-century Royal Print Yard, where Ivan Fyodorov produced Russia's first printed book, *The Apostle*. Ivan the Terrible took a keen interest, visiting nearly every day until the book was completed in 1564, whereupon superstitious Muscovites, incensed by this "Satan's work", stormed the press, forcing Fyodorov to flee to Poland. In 1703, Russia's first newspaper, *Vedomosti*, was produced here without any mishap. The heraldic lion and unicorn of the old print yard appear over the existing building's central arch. Until the early nineteenth century, the Kitay-gorod was home to 26 of Moscow's 31 bookshops.

Of equal significance to Moscow's cultural life was the **Slavyanskiy Bazaar** restaurant, which stood at no. 17, and was famous for hosting an eighteen-hour discussion between Konstantin Stanislavsky and Vladimir Nemirovich-Danchenko, that led to the foundation of the Moscow Art Theatre (see p.116) – the restaurant obligingly stayed open till they had finished, at two o'clock in the morning. It also had rooms for guests; in Chekhov's story, *The Lady with a Lapdog*, Gurov's lover stayed here when she came to Moscow. Unfortunately it burned down in 1994, and you'll find nothing but a shoe shop where it once stood.

Further along at no. 21, the nineteenth-century **Ferryn Pharmacy** is worth a look for its Empire-style facade and the gilded, pillared room upstairs. Now housing a luxurious restaurant and crystal boutique, it was designated Pharmacy #1 in Soviet times, and has long been associated with drug trafficking; still today prescription opiates diverted onto the black market are sold in the vicinity by innocent-looking pensioners, whose customers identify themselves by scratching their forearms. Surprisingly, this happens only 250m from the Lubyanka headquarters of the secret police (see p.139), where the *Chekisti* fortified themselves for executions in the 1920s with cocaine and vodka. Assuming you don't cross the square for a closer look at the Lubyanka, a right turn will bring you to the Moscow History and Politechnical museums (see pp.109–110).

Ulitsa Ilinka

Parallel to Nikolskaya ulitsa, **ulitsa Ilinka** used to be the financial centre of the Kitay-gorod. Its name derives from the tiny sixteenth-century **Church of St Elijah** (tserkov Ili) – which worshippers are slowly restoring – across the road from the oval-shaped **Stariy Gostiniy dvor** that occupies the entire block between Khrustalniy (Crystal) and Rybniy (Fish) pereulok. The Russian equivalent of an oriental caravanserai for visiting merchants and their wares, the Gostiniy dvor was designed in the 1790s by Catherine the Great's court architect, Quarenghi, who embellished its facade with colonnades of Corinthian pilasters. After decades of neglect its interior has been refurbished as a deluxe car showroom, which sold its entire stock of Ferraris and Maseratis (averaging $300,000 apiece) on its opening day in 2004 – a sign of how much wealth exists in Moscow, which now has more resident billionaires than New York, according to Russian *Forbes* magazine, whose editor was murdered shortly after he identified them.

On the other corner of Rybniy pereulok stands the former Stock Exchange that now serves as Moscow's **Chamber of Commerce**. Painted tangerine and white, its Ionic pillars and bas-relief gryphons confront a small square flanked by buildings of equal probity. Across the way stand the **Supreme Court** – housed in another neo-Russian pile – and the former **Ryabushinsky Bank**, a pale green edifice with glazed brick facings, designed by the Style Moderne architect Fyodor Shekhtel. Pavel Ryabushinsky, the Chairman of the pre-Revolution Stock Exchange, also commissioned Shekhtel to build him a house that is one of the glories of Moscow (see p.159). Take a brief look down Rybniy pereulok, where the **Noviy Gostiniy dvor** bears a kitsch bas-relief of a merchant's ship sailing into the sunset.

Continuing along Ilinka, you'll pass a striking pair of buildings: to the right, a pistachio facade upheld by writhing atlantes and caryatids, facing the austere grey tiers of the **Ministry of Finance**, across the road. Further on, gates bar access to the side streets leading to the complex previously occupied by the Communist Party's Central Committee – beyond which Ilinka emerges on to Novaya and Staraya squares (see p.109).

Zaryade

The most interesting part of the Kitay-gorod is the area known as **Zaryade**, situated due east of St Basil's. From the twelfth century onwards, the swampy slope above the Moskva River was settled by craftsmen and artisans, whose homes lay behind the rows (*za ryade*) of stalls that covered what is now Red Square. Though nobles and foreign merchants displaced them during the fifteenth and sixteenth centuries, the quarter gradually reverted to being the heart of popular Moscow, crammed with booths and huts, and smelling of "perfumed Russian leather, spiritous liquors, sour beer, cabbages, and grease of Cossacks' boots", and undrained cesspits that rendered it prone to epidemics. In *War and Peace*, Tolstoy wrote of peasants lying unconscious in the mud, and drunken soldiers staggering after prostitutes.

Today, Zaryade's main sights lie along or just off **ulitsa Varvarka** (St Barbara St), which is the oldest street in Moscow, dating back to the fourteenth century. During Soviet times it was called ulitsa Razina, after the leader of the 1670 peasant revolt, Stenka Razin, who was led along it to his execution on Red Square. Seen from Red Square, Varvarka's vista of onion domes and gilded crosses is marred only by the **Rossiya Hotel**, a 1960s eyesore covering nearly ten acres, whose architects originally intended to demolish the churches and medieval residences lining the street's south side. The hotel itself recently faced demolition, but seems to have been spared for now, while the appeal of the churches owes less to their interiors than to the totality of their variegated facades, which appear taller on the hotel-facing side, being built against a steep bank.

The first that you reach is the compact salmon-pink-and-white **Church of St Barbara** (tserkov Varvary; Mon–Sun 11am–6pm, except during services; free), built in 1796–1804, on the site of an earlier church by Alevisio Novi, the architect of the Archangel Cathedral in the Kremlin. Having suffered decades of neglect under the stewardship of the All-Russia Society for the Protection of Monuments of History and Culture, it is now back in the hands of the Orthodox Church, which has renovated and reopened it.

The Old English Court

At the bottom of the slope beyond the Church of St Barbara stands a chunky white building with a steep wooden roof and narrow windows of varying sizes, identified by a plaque on the wall facing the *Rossiya* hotel as the **Old English Court** (Palaty starovo angliyskovo dvora; 10am–6pm, Wed & Fri 11am–7pm; closed Mon & the last Fri of each month; R50). As the exhibition inside relates, trade between England and Russia began in 1553 with the arrival of Richard Chancellor's merchant ship in the White Sea and the foundation of the Muscovy Company, which was granted duty-free privileges by Ivan the Terrible and given the house as a kind of embassy. While the first two envoys were warmly received, the third incurred Ivan's wrath by prevaricating over his demand to marry Queen Elizabeth I, and was confined under house arrest until Ivan's anger had abated. In return for English muskets, gunpowder and broadcloth, the Company exported furs, honey, caviar and mica, until it was expelled from Russia in 1649 by Tsar Alexei, who was outraged by the English Parliament's execution of Charles I.

The collection of old prints and coins is less interesting than the house itself, whose narrow staircases and extremely low doorways are typical of early Muscovite architecture. Its vaulted Official Hall has a huge fireplace-cum-stove made of bricks incised with zoomorphic designs, and was once used for banquets; it now hosts monthly **concerts** of medieval music (Ⓣ298 39 52). The final section of the exhibition tells how the house was saved from demolition in the 1960s by the architect Baranovsky, who recognized its medieval origins beneath what was by then an apartment block. It was restored to coincide with the state visit of Queen Elizabeth II in 1994.

St Maxim the Blessed and the Monastery of the Sign

The nearby **Church of St Maxim the Blessed** (tserkov Maksima Blazhennovo) is a simple Novgorod-style church with a yellow belltower, erected by merchants from Novgorod in 1690–99 as a repository for the mortal remains of the fifteenth-century "holy fool", St Maxim, venerated for his mortification and self-denial. Behind the church rises another, pointed, belltower, belonging to the **Monastery of the Sign** (Znamenskiy monastyr), established on the Romanov family estate in 1634, following the death of the tsar's mother. The monastery's red-brick Cathedral, beyond the overpass leading to the *Rossiya* hotel, is decorated with intricate *nalichniki* and *kokoshniki*, surmounted by four onion domes covered in green and red shingles, and a central, gilded dome. Like most of the churches on Zaryade, it was founded on oak piles that became harder than stone when wet. During Soviet times it was converted into a concert hall, but religious services are now once again held in the lower level of the church.

The Palace of the Romanov Boyars

Ulitsa Varvarka's most interesting building is the rambling **Palace of the Romanov Boyars** (muzey Palaty v Zaryade; Mon & Thurs–Sun 10am–7pm, Wed 11am–7pm; closed Tues & the first Mon of each month; R100, students R50). Built in the sixteenth century by Nikita Romanov (Ivan the Terrible's brother-in-law), it once formed the nucleus of a vast complex of seven thousand households stretching down to the river, made almost entirely of wood, with the exception of the palace.

Romanov menfolk used the first floor, built of stone, whose rooms are low and vaulted, with mica windows, tiled stoves and gilded, embossed leather "wallpaper", in contrast to the spacious, airy women's quarters upstairs, panelled in blonde wood. Here, married couples slept on benches against the walls, while unmarried daughters spent the daytime weaving in the adjacent *svetlitsa* or "light room", with its latticed windows overlooking the street. The residence was abandoned after Mikhail Romanov was elected tsar in 1613, and the whole family and their retainers moved into the Kremlin. In 1859, it was restored on the orders of Nicholas I as a tribute to his ancestors, and opened as a public museum.

Beyond the palace rises the sky-blue belltower of the **Church of St George** (tserkov Georgiya na Pskovskoy Gorke), whose sea-green onion domes spangled with gold stars and sprouting intricate crosses add a final touch of colour to the street. Although dedicated to the patron saint of Moscow, it was erected by merchants from Pskov in 1657, the belfry being a nineteenth-century addition.

From here you can cross the road and walk up Ipatevskiy pereulok to find the wonderful Church of the Trinity, or head downhill towards Slavyanskaya ploshchad (see p.109).

▲ Palace of the Romanov Boyars

The Church of the Trinity on Nikitnikov

By following Ipatevskiy pereulok uphill and turning right, you'll come upon the **Church of the Trinity on Nikitnikov** pereulok (tserkov Troitsy v Nikitnikakh), whose exuberant colours and asymmetrical form are all the more striking for being hemmed in by the anonymous premises of the Moscow Regional Council and the former Central Committee of the Communist Party. The church defies its confinement with an explosion of decorative features: white ogee-shaped *nalichniki* and *kokoshniki*, columns and cornices contrasting with crimson walls, green roofs and domes. Its height and dynamism are accentuated by a tent-roofed stairway climbing above a deep arcaded undercroft, and an open pyramid-spired belfry that would have soared above the wooden houses of the medieval Kitay-gorod.

Erected in 1635–53 by the wealthy merchant Grigory Nikitnikov, who stashed his valuables in its basement, the church was squatted by numerous families after the Revolution, before being turned into a museum in 1967 (it is still classified as a museum rather than a church). Due to slow, long-overdue repairs, the only part of the church open to the public is the lower side-altar (11am–3pm), where you can see beautiful **frescoes** by Simon Ushakov and other icon painters from the Kremlin Armoury.

Due to the proximity of many government institutions, Nikitnikov pereulok is patrolled by **plainclothes security agents**, who may demand that you produce some ID, and object to anyone taking photographs.

Down towards the river

Downhill from the Church of St George and around the corner to the right, another remnant of the **Kitay-gorod wall** runs alongside Kitayskiy proezd. Though its swallow-tailed crenellations resemble those of the Kremlin, the Kitay-gorod walls were constructed a century later, when Russian fortifications became lower and thicker owing to the advent of cannons in siege warfare, and they were originally wide enough for a carriage to drive along the top. The pedestrian subway exposes some fragments of the **Varvarka Gate** that once straddled this exit under the protection of a supposedly miraculous icon of the Virgin. During the plague of 1771, this was taken down and repeatedly kissed in frenzied services that spread contagion; when Archbishop Amvrosy realized this and tried to replace the icon above the gate, he was pursued by a mob to the Donskoy Monastery and torn to bits.

Visible through the trees across the road from the ramparts is the vast classical edifice of the **Foundling Home**, established by Catherine the Great to discourage infanticide and teach orphans trades useful to the state. At one time, over 13,000 children resided here; in 1812 as the French army approached, the older ones were evacuated but the toddlers and babies were left behind in the care of a general and, amazingly, survived. It now houses the Dzerzhinsky Artillery Academy and the grounds are off limits.

Beside the embankment below the *Rossiya Hotel* stands the small white **Church of the Conception of St Anna** (tserkov Zachatiya Anny), where Salomonia Saburova, Grand Duke Vasily III's barren wife, often prayed for a child. In 1526 she was confined to a convent so that he could marry Yelena Glinskaya, who gave birth to the future Ivan the Terrible four years later.

From Slavyanskaya ploshchad to the Lubyanka

Slavyanskaya ploshchad (Slav Square), at the foot of ulitsa Varvarka, takes its name from an imposing **statue of Cyril and Methodius** (Kiril i Metodi), the "Apostles of the Slavs" who invented the Cyrillic alphabet in order to bring them Christianity and let them write in their own language – honoured on the Day of Slavic Culture (May 24) by a **procession** of clerics and nuns bearing icons from the Kremlin's Saviour Gate to the monument. In Tsarist times this was the site of an outdoor "winter market", heaped with deep-frozen Crimean oxen, Caspian sheep, Siberian deer and fish from the White Sea, which purchasers stored in their ice cellars and thawed as needed. The Royal Salt Yard (Solyaniy dvor) that once stood here has left its name to ulitsa Solyanka, nearby.

With the Kitay-gorod's transformation into a modern financial centre early last century, the market was superseded by the **Delovy dvor** (Business House), on the corner of Kitayskiy proezd. During the "heroic phase" of Socialist construction during the 1930s, it housed the Commissariat for Heavy Industry, whose boss, Sergei Ordzhonikidze, also had a hand in building the first line of the metro system. Almost next door is the small but striking blood-red, gold-domed **Church of All Saints in Kulishki** (tserkov Vsekh Svyatykh na Kulishkakh), erected by Ivan III to replace a wooden church built in a forest clearing (*kulishki*) by Prince Dmitri Donskoy, whose army passed by en route to the battle of Kulikovo on the River Don (1380), where the Russians defeated the Mongols for the first time.

Behind Cyril and Methodius, **Staraya ploshchad** (Old Square) slopes up an embankment crowned by a row of office blocks dating from the 1900s. On the corner stands the former Moscow Insurance Company building, an early design by Shekhtel, distinguished by its sea-green tiles and sinuous balconies. In Soviet times, this became the headquarters of the Moscow Regional Party organization, while the adjacent edifice (no. 4) housed the **Central Committee of the Communist Party**, the nexus of power in the Soviet Union. The day after the failure of the 1991 putsch, its nervous *apparatchiki* frantically shredded compromising documents, afraid to burn them lest the smoke cause the angry crowd outside to storm the building. Now flying the Russian tricolour, the buildings harbour the Prime Minister's office and Moscow regional government.

At the top end of the wooded Ilinskiy Gardens that run down the middle of the hill stands the bell-shaped **Plevna Memorial**, honouring the Russian Grenadiers who died in the 1878 siege of Plevna, which liberated Bulgaria from the Turkish yoke. Financed by battle veterans, it was designed by Vladimir Sherwood, the architect of the Historical Museum on Red Square. The gardens are named after the former Ilinskiy Gate, which was demolished in the 1930s, like the other gates in the Kitay-gorod wall.

The Politechnical Museum

The hill levels out at **Novaya ploshchad** (New Square), flanked by a mustard-coloured neo-Russian pile housing the **Politechnical Museum** (Politekhnicheskiy muzey; Tues–Sun 10am–6pm; closed Mon & last Fri of each month; R200, students R80). Founded in the 1870s to promote science and technology, the museum hosted experiments in telepathy in the 1960s that were subsequently conducted in secret under the auspices of the KGB. It has an endearingly old-fashioned character, with archaic instruments and models rather than VDUs. The first floor covers everything from the development of lamps and typewriters to mining and the petroleum industry, while the floor above deals with space travel, antique music boxes, clocks and computers. Among the "classics" of Soviet design are a TV set the size of a fridge with a screen so small it required a magnifying glass; and a hilarious ghetto blaster from the 1980s. There are also models and plans of futuristic buildings conceived in the 1920s and 1930s, which never got beyond the drawing board.

Don't overlook the **monument to the victims of the Gulag** in a garden on the Lubyanka side of the museum: a boulder taken from the Solovetskiy Isles, whose ancient monastery became one of the earliest Soviet concentration camps.

The Moscow History Museum

Across Novaya ploshchad is a building with a green cupola that was once the Church of St John the Divine Under the Elm and is now the **Moscow History Museum** (muzey Istorii Goroda Moskvy; Tues, Thurs, Sat & Sun 10am–6pm, Wed & Fri 11am–7pm; closed last Fri of each month; R50). Its permanent exhibition charts the city's growth since the seventeenth century, with scale models of the Kremlin and boyars' compounds in Zaryade, and meticulously researched scenes of medieval life by the historical painter Apollinarius Vasnetsov (see p.173). The corner of a log house with wooden water pipes from the same era can be seen on the first floor.

Streets and squares	
Ipatevskiy pereulok	Ипатьевский переулок
Kitayskiy proezd	Китайский проезд
Nikitnikov pereulok	Никитинов переулок
Nikolskaya ulitsa	Никольская улица
Novaya ploshchad	Новая площадь
ploshchad Revolyutsii	площадь Революции
Slavyanskaya ploshchad	Славянская площадь
Staraya ploshchad	Старая площадь
Teatralnaya ploshchad	Театральная площадь
Tretyakovskiy proezd	Третьяковский проезд
ulitsa Ilinka	улица Ильинка
ulitsa Varvarka	улица Варварка
Metro stations	
Kitay-Gorod	Китай-Город
Lubyanka	Лубянка
Okhotniy Ryad	Охотный ряд
Ploshchad Revolyutsii	Площадь Революции
Museums	
Archeological Museum of Moscow	музей Археологии Москвы
Old English Court	Палаты старого английского дора
Palace of the Romanov Boyars	музей Палаты в Зарядье
Moscow History Museum	музей Истории Города Москвы
Politechnical Museum	Политехнический музей

The Beliy Gorod

The **Beliy Gorod**, or "White Town", is the historic name of the residential district that encircled the Kremlin and the Kitay-gorod – derived from the white stone ramparts erected around it at the end of the sixteenth century. It remains a useful designation for the area within the horseshoe-shaped **Boulevard Ring** (Bulvarnoe koltso), laid out on the rampart sites after the great fire of 1812. Despite widening and modernization, many of the boulevards are still divided by elongated parks with wrought-iron lampposts and fences, statues and urns redolent of nineteenth-century Moscow, and many squares bear the names of the original gate-towers. The Futurist El Lissitzky dreamt of buildings suspended above the Ring on giant legs (trumpeted as "architecture for world revolution", to "raise human consciousness"), but his ideas survive only as drawings in the Tretyakov Gallery on Krimskiy val (see p.222).

Much of the cultural life and other pleasures of Moscow are found in the Beliy Gorod, from the **Bolshoy Theatre**, the **Pushkin Museum of Fine Arts** and the **Conservatory**, to restaurants, nightlife, and piquant juxtapositions of old and new Russia – which often turn out to be much the same. The rebuilding of the **Cathedral of Christ the Saviour**, decades after Stalin destroyed the original, is only the tip of the iceberg when it comes to reinventing the past, as brash new banks pose as pre-Revolutionary financial houses, and casinos and nightclubs call themselves *Chekhov* and *Stanislavsky*. The discordances are echoed by the architecture: Stalinist behemoths with Italianate loggias stitched across a patchwork of Neoclassical and Style Moderne backstreets, studded with **medieval monasteries**. A visit to the **Sandunovskiy Baths** or the "KGB Museum" attached to the infamous **Lubyanka** is not to be missed, nor a wander around the one-time **Ukrainian quarter**.

The Beliy Gorod's web-like layout and hilly topography make orientation quite difficult. This account starts with Manezhnaya ploshchad and the **central axis** of Tverskaya ulitsa, before covering the remainder of the Beliy Gorod in **wedge-shaped sections** – first the western and then the eastern sectors. Each sector is described starting from the point nearest the Kremlin or the Kitay-gorod and working outwards to the Boulevard Ring – a distance of between one and two kilometres. In practice, you'll probably zigzag across several "wedges" rather than follow a single one to the end.

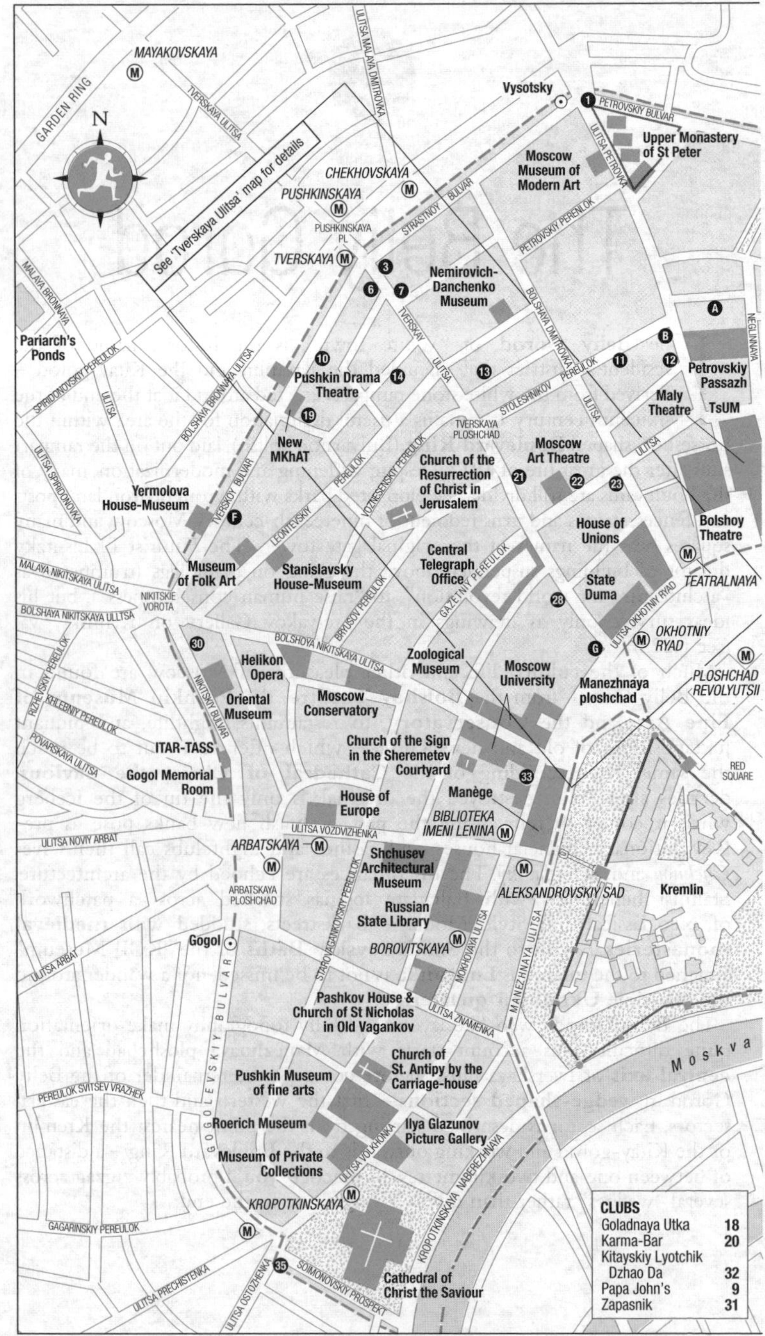

MAYAKOVSKAYA
GARDEN RING
TVERSKAYA ULITSA
ULITSA MALAYA DMITROVKA
Vysotsky
PETROVSKIY BULVAR
Upper Monastery of St Peter
ULITSA PETROVKA
Moscow Museum of Modern Art
See 'Tverskaya Ulitsa' map for details
CHEKHOVSKAYA
PUSHKINSKAYA
PUSHKINSKAYA PL
STRASTNOY BULVAR
PETROVSKIY PERELOK
TVERSKAYA
Nemirovich-Danchenko Museum
MALAYA BRONNAYA
BOLSHAYA DMITROVKA
NEGLINNAYA
Pariarch's Ponds
SPIRIDONOVSKIY PERELOK
BOLSHAYA BRONNAYA ULITSA
Pushkin Drama Theatre
TVERSKAY ULITSA
STOLESHNIKOV PERELOK
Petrovskiy Passazh
Maly Theatre
TsUM
ULITSA SPIRIDONOVKA
New MKhAT
TVERSKAYA PLOSHCHAD
Moscow Art Theatre
Church of the Resurrection of Christ in Jerusalem
VOZNESENSKIY PERELOK
LEONTEVSKIY PERELOK
Yermolova House-Museum
TVERSKOY BULVAR
House of Unions
Bolshoy Theatre
MALAYA NIKITSKAYA ULITSA
Museum of Folk Art
Stanislavsky House-Museum
Central Telegraph Office
GAZETNIY PERELOK
State Duma
TEATRALNAYA
NIKITSKIE VOROTA
BOLSHAYA NIKITSKAYA ULITSA
BRYUSOV PERELOK
ULITSA OKHOTNIY RYAD
OKHOTNIY RYAD
BOLSHOYA NIKITSKAYA ULITSA
Helikon Opera
Zoological Museum
Moscow University
Manezhnaya ploshchad
PLOSHCHAD REVOLYUTSII
RZHEVSKIY PERELOK
KHLEBNIY PERELOK
NIKITSKIY BULVAR
Oriental Museum
Moscow Conservatory
POVARSKAYA ULITSA
ITAR-TASS
Church of the Sign in the Sheremetev Courtyard
RED SQUARE
Gogol Memorial Room
Manège
House of Europe
BIBLIOTEKA IMENI LENINA
ULITSA NOVIY ARBAT
ULITSA VOZDVIZHENKA
ARBATSKAYA
Shchusev Architectural Museum
ARBATSKAYA PLOSHCHAD
ALEKSANDROVSKIY SAD
Kremlin
STAROVAGANKOVSKIY PERELOK
Russian State Library
MOKHOVAYA ULITSA
Gogol
BOROVITSKAYA
ULITSA ARBAT
MANEZHNAYA ULITSA
Pashkov House & Church of St Nicholas in Old Vagankov
ULITSA ZNAMENKA
GOGOLEVSKIY BULVAR
Moskva
Church of St. Antipy by the Carriage-house
Pushkin Museum of fine arts
PEREULOK SVITSEV VRAZHEK
Roerich Museum
Ilya Glazunov Picture Gallery
Museum of Private Collections
ULITSA VOLKHONKA
KROPOTKINSKAYA NABEREZHNAYA
KROPOTKINSKAYA
GAGARINSKIY PEREULOK
ULITSA PRECHISTENKA
ULITSA OSTOZHENKA
SOIMONOVSKIY PROSPEKT
Cathedral of Christ the Saviour
Peter the Great Monument
CLUBS
Goladnaya Utka 18
Karma-Bar 20
Kitayskiy Lyotchik Dzhao Da 32
Papa John's 9
Zapasnik 31

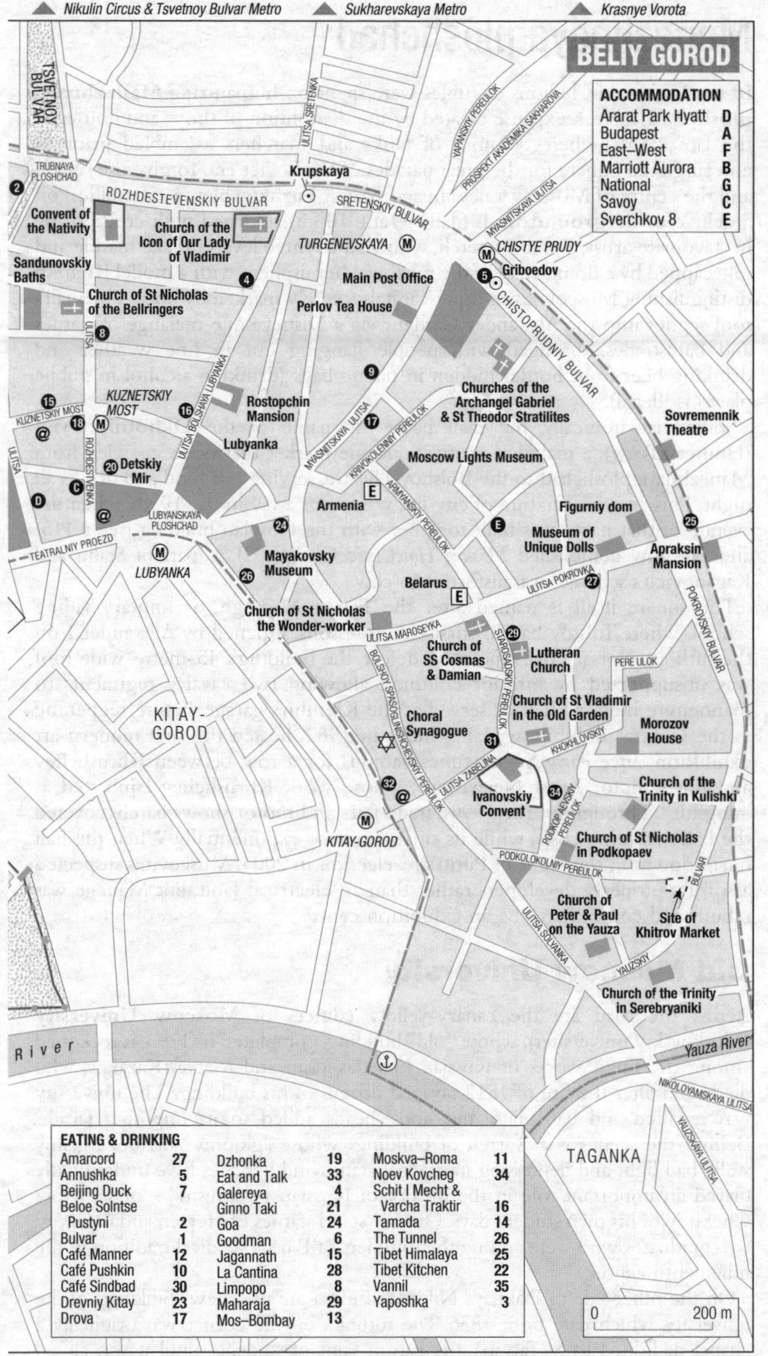
Nikulin Circus & Tsvetnoy Bulvar Metro
Sukharevskaya Metro
Krasnye Vorota
BELIY GOROD
ACCOMMODATION
Ararat Park Hyatt D
Budapest A
East–West F
Marriott Aurora B
National G
Savoy C
Sverchkov 8 E
TSVETNOY BULVAR
TRUBNAYA PLOSHCHAD
ROZHDESTEVENSKIY BULVAR
ULITSA SRETENKA
YAPANSKIY PEREULOK
PROSPEKT AKADEMIKA SAKHAROVA
MYASNITSKAYA ULITSA
Krupskaya
SRETENSKIY BULVAR
Convent of the Nativity
Church of the Icon of Our Lady of Vladimir
TURGENEVSKAYA
CHISTYE PRUDY
Sandunovskiy Baths
Griboedov
Main Post Office
Church of St Nicholas of the Bellringers
Perlov Tea House
CHISTOPRUDNIY BULVAR
KUZNETSKIY MOST
ULITSA BOLSHAYA LUBYANKA
Rostopchin Mansion
Churches of the Archangel Gabriel & St Theodor Stratilites
Sovremennik Theatre
Lubyanka
MYASNITSKAYA ULITSA
KRIVOKOLENNIY PEREULOK
Moscow Lights Museum
ULITSA
ROZHDESTVENKA
Detskiy Mir
ARMYANSKIY PEREULOK
Armenia
Figurniy dom
LUBYANSKAYA PLOSHCHAD
Museum of Unique Dolls
Apraksin Mansion
TEATRALNIY PROEZD
Mayakovsky Museum
LUBYANKA
Belarus
ULITSA POKROVKA
POKROVSKIY BULVAR
Church of St Nicholas the Wonder-worker
ULITSA MAROSEYKA
Church of SS Cosmas & Damian
STAROSADSKIY PEREULOK
Lutheran Church
PERE ULOK
BOLSHOY SPASOGLINISHCHEVSKIY PEREULOK
KITAY-GOROD
Choral Synagogue
Church of St Vladimir in the Old Garden
KHOKHLOVSKIY
Morozov House
ULITSA ZABELINA
Church of the Trinity in Kulishki
Ivanovskiy Convent
PODKOP AEVSKIY PEREULOK
KITAY-GOROD
Church of St Nicholas in Podkopaev
PODKOLOKOLNIY PEREULOK
BULVAR
Church of Peter & Paul on the Yauza
Site of Khitrov Market
ULITSA SOLYANKA
YAUZSKIY
Church of the Trinity in Serebryaniki
River
Yauza River
NIKOLOYAMSKAYA ULITSA
YAUZSKAYA ULITSA
TAGANKA
EATING & DRINKING
Amarcord 27
Annushka 5
Beijing Duck 7
Beloe Solntse Pustyni 2
Bulvar 1
Café Manner 12
Café Pushkin 10
Café Sindbad 30
Drevniy Kitay 23
Drova 17
Dzhonka 19
Eat and Talk 33
Galereya 4
Ginno Taki 21
Goa 24
Goodman 6
Jagannath 15
La Cantina 28
Limpopo 8
Maharaja 29
Mos–Bombay 13
Moskva–Roma 11
Noev Kovcheg 34
Schit I Mecht & Varcha Traktir 16
Tamada 14
The Tunnel 26
Tibet Himalaya 25
Tibet Kitchen 22
Vannil 35
Yaposhka 3
0 200 m

Manezhnaya ploshchad

In the last decade, billions of rubles were spent on humanizing **Manezhnaya ploshchad**, a bleak expanse created by the demolition of shops and houses in the late 1920s, where columns of tanks and marchers assembled prior to entering Red Square for the great parades of the Soviet era. To give the square and the centre of Moscow a new image, Mayor Luzhkov blew $350 million on a deluxe **underground mall** (daily 11am–10pm), adorned with creations by his favourite artist, Zurab Tsereteli, who clad its three levels in fake marble and gilt, capped by a dome-map of the northern hemisphere with a model Kremlin distinguishing Moscow from other capitals (merely marked by dots). The mall's roof segues into the Alexander Gardens via a Disneyesque melange of statues and balustrades, thronged with people hanging out in fine weather and drinking beer from bottles hidden in plastic bags (drinking alcohol in public places is illegal).

Somewhat ironically, the mall bears the name of the **Okhotniy ryad** (Hunters' Row), a malodorous meat and pie market that once sprawled from Manezhnaya ploshchad to the Bolshoy Theatre, serving hot food and drinks all night. This convivial fixture of city life was swept away in the 1930s, when the avenue of that name was built together with the Gosplan building (see p.115) and the now demolished *Moskva Hotel* (see Chapter 2), as part of Stalin and Kaganovich's scheme to transform Moscow.

The square itself is named after the Tsarist **Manège**, or military riding school, where Tolstoy had his first riding lessons. Opened by Alexander I on the fifth anniversary of Napoleon's defeat, the building's 45-metre-wide roof was unsupported by interior columns, allowing two cavalry regiments to manoeuvre indoors. It later served as the Kremlin's garage, before reopening as the Central Exhibition Hall which, in 1962, hosted the first modern art exhibition since early Soviet times, famous for a row between Khrushchev and the sculptor Ernst Neizvestniy, whose work Khrushchev lambasted as "dogshit". Throughout the 1990s, trade fairs and motor shows barely covered the hall's running costs, while its site value rose exponentially. When the hall burnt down on the night of Putin's re-election in 2004, Muscovites suspected arson by property developers rather than an electrical fault, but Manège was rebuilt and continues to be an exhibition centre.

Old Moscow University

Across the road are the canary-yellow edifices of **Moscow University** (Moskovskiy universitet), whose "old" building, completed in 1793, is reckoned among the finest works of Russian Neoclassicism and Matvei Kazakov, who died soon after the fire of 1812 ravaged dozens of his buildings. The university was repaired and bas-reliefs and lions' heads added to its imposing facade. Behind the scenes is a warren of buildings whose "gloomy corridors, grimy walls, bad light and depressing stairs, coat stands and benches have undoubtedly played an important role in the history of Russian pessimism" – or so wrote Chekhov of his own student days. Outside stand statues of Herzen and Ogaryov, two graduates who were among the founders of Russia's radical tradition in the nineteenth century.

On the other side of Bolshaya Nikitskaya ulitsa are the "new" buildings of the university, which date from 1836. The rotunda on the corner was originally a chapel dedicated to St Tatyana, the patron saint of students, until it was closed down after the Revolution; it was returned to the Church in 1994. In front of the main college building is a **statue of Mikhail Lomonosov**, the "Russian Leonardo" who founded Moscow University in 1775. Amid the lesser buildings around the back rises the belltower of the **Church of the Sign in the Sheremetev Courtyard** (tserkov Znameniya na Sheremtevom dvore), a lovely example of seventeenth-century Moscow Baroque with a filigreed spire. Earlier still, this was the site of Ivan the Terrible's **Oprichniy dvor**, a great fortified palace whence his infamous *Oprichniki* (see p.406) sallied forth to murder, rape and rob.

National Hotel, State Duma and the House of Unions

Before heading up Tverskaya ulitsa, look at the buildings that flank its juncture with Manezhnaya ploshchad and Okhotniy ryad. On the left-hand corner stands the **National Hotel**, an eclectic-style edifice with a tiled frieze that was Moscow's finest hotel before the Revolution. In 1918, Lenin lived in room 107 before moving into the Kremlin; as the "First House of Soviets", it accommodated Party officials and fellow travellers, such as John Reed and Anatole France. Since being refurbished in the 1990s, the *National* has vied with the *Metropol* for the title of Moscow's premier hotel, boasting views of the Kremlin its rival can't match. This proximity has its downside: in 2003, a Chechen suicide-bomber killed six passers-by when she was stopped by police outside the hotel, bound for Red Square.

On the far side of Tverskaya looms a grey 1930s building erected for Gosplan, the agency that oversaw the Soviet economy, which is now used by the **State Duma**, or lower house of the Russian parliament – known for its brawls during the Yeltsin era. It totally dwarfs the adjacent **House of Unions**, a green-and-white Neoclassical edifice of the 1780s, which served as the Club of the Nobility until the Revolution. In Soviet times its glittering Hall of Columns was used for the show trials of veteran Bolsheviks (see p.424) and "Trotskyite wreckers", and the lying in state of Lenin and Stalin, which occasioned mass demonstrations of genuine grief. The queue to bid farewell to Lenin lasted for three days and nights, despite arctic weather conditions; while nobody knows how many people were crushed to death in the crowd at Stalin's funeral – estimates range as high as 1500.

Tverskaya ulitsa

As its name suggests, **Tverskaya ulitsa** originated as the road leading to the old town of Tver, continuing to Novgorod and (after 1713) on to St Petersburg. Inns and smithies soon grew up alongside, until they were displaced during the sixteenth century by the stone palaces of the boyars and merchants. The road was surfaced with logs and varied in width from 8m to 15m along its zigzag course. As Moscow's main thoroughfare from the seventeenth century onwards, it boasted two monasteries and four churches, past which the tsars proceeded on arrival from St Petersburg; for victory parades, Tverskaya was bedecked with carpets, flowers and icons. During the nineteenth century it became more commercial, as the point of departure for stagecoaches to St Petersburg, and notable for being the first street in Moscow to be lit by lampposts and feature billboards.

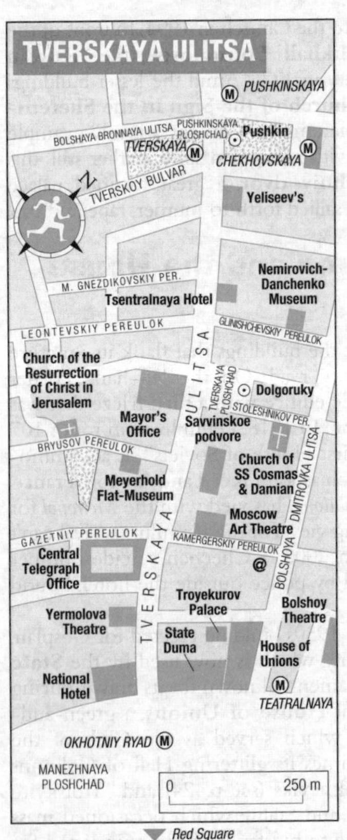

Its present form is due to a massive reconstruction programme in the mid-1930s, when Tverskaya was also renamed in honour of the writer Maxim Gorky (it reverted to its old name in 1990). To straighten and widen the street, rows of houses were demolished, while other buildings were moved back to create a new avenue 40 to 60m wide, lined with gargantuan buildings. Despite their scale, the variety of ornamentation and the older, often charming side streets that are visible through their huge archways give the avenue a distinctive character. At night, Tverskaya is thronged with window-shoppers and theatre-goers; sushi bars and cyber cafés are packed; and festive **illuminations** enhance the buzz of Moscow's Fifth Avenue.

The initial, uphill, stretch is best covered on the eastern side of the avenue, where a huge archway leads to Georgievskiy pereulok, where the fence behind the State Duma building allows a glimpse of the modestly sized **Troyekurov Palace**, a rare surviving example of a seventeenth-century boyar's townhouse. On the other side of Tverskaya are the diminutive pre-Revolutionary **Yermelova Theatre**, and the brooding **Central Telegraph Office**, with its illuminated globe. During Brezhnev's time, the Telegraph Office's ill-paid female staff were renowned for moonlighting as prostitutes, imbuing the globe with the significance of a red light in a seedy neighbourhood; in the Yeltsin years, streetwalking flourished under the nose of the Mayor's office on Tverskaya, until Luzhkov finally cleaned up the avenue's image.

MKhAT and the Meyerhold Museum

Kamergerskiy pereulok is one of the most inviting turnings off Tverskaya, blending culture and café society. A **statue of Chekhov** presages the famous **Moscow Art Theatre** – known here by its Russian initials as **MKhAT** (pronounced "Em-*Khat*") – that was founded in 1898 by Konstantin Stanislavsky and Vladimir Nemirovich-Danchenko. MKhAT pioneered the methodical training of actors and directors, and the doctrine that acting should express inner feelings, rather than merely consist of gestures and vocal tricks. Its foundation coincided with the advent of Chekhov's plays, the first modern drama, which required a new style of acting. Having flopped in St Petersburg when first performed by hammy old thespians, *The Seagull* became an overnight sensation thanks to MKhAT's production; Chekhov's congratulatory telegram to Stanislavsky read: "You have brought my seagull back to life".

In Soviet times, MKhAT specialized in the plays of Gorky and became increasingly conservative, but nevertheless produced outstanding directors like Meyerhold (see below) and brilliant actors such as Inokennty Smoktunovsky, famous for his portrayal of Hamlet in particular. Its playhouse was converted by Fyodor Shekhtel according to Stanislavsky's belief that nothing should distract audiences from the stage. Its foyer and auditorium are extremely simple, and the exterior decorations are limited to a stylized seagull on the pediment and a bas-relief wave above the doorway. Playbills, photos and designs for sets by Roerich, Benois, Serov and Kustodiev are displayed in a **museum** (Nov–March Wed–Sun noon–6pm; R70). For details of performances see Chapter 14, "The Arts".

Returning to Tverskaya, check out the courtyard of no. 6, which harbours a spectacular neo-Russian residential complex whose silver tent-roofed towers and pale-green-and-lilac-tiled frontage contrast with the Stalinist gloom that now surrounds it. Built in 1905–07 as a speculative venture by the Orthodox Church, the **Savvinskoe podvore**'s huge apartments, turned into communal flats after the Revolution, have now been converted back into luxury residences and offices.

Opposite are two mammoth brownstone buildings (nos. 9–11) erected just after the war, united by a great **arch** made from granite intended for a Nazi victory memorial, captured in 1941. Behind this, on Bryusov pereulok, a 1920s Constructivist building (no. 11) that was the first Soviet apartment block for "cultural workers" now contains the **Meyerhold Flat-Museum** (muzey-kvartira V.E. Meyerkholda; Wed–Sun noon–7pm; closed the last Fri of each month; R100). Input #011 at the door to gain access to flat #11, where the avant-garde director Vsevolod Meyerhold lived with Zinaida Reich and two children from her previous marriage to the poet Yesenin until 1939, when Meyerhold was arrested by the NKVD (to be shot the following year) and Reich was killed during a "burglary" the very next day. Their flat was divided into lodgings for NKVD officers, which Moscow's Theatre Museum later purchased to create this exhibition. Only the bookcase and four wineglasses in

▲ Tverskaya's upmarket shops

the study belonged to Meyerhold – the rest is a reconstruction based on reminiscences and other sources. Set designs by Golovin and Popova show how revolutionary his productions were. Today, his work is once again celebrated in Moscow – imparting a cultural gloss to the Meyerhold Centre in the Northern Suburbs (see Chapter 8) – and the museum organizes **films** and seminars (☎629 53 22 for details).

Further down the lane, the pretty orange-and-white **Church of the Resurrection of Christ in Jerusalem**, dating from 1629, was one of the few Moscow churches that functioned throughout Soviet times.

Tverskaya ploshchad to the Boulevard Ring

Soon afterwards the avenue levels out at **Tverskaya ploshchad**, as if in awe of the **Mayor's Office** (Merya), a crimson edifice with a golden crest that bears little relation to Kazakov's original design of 1782, for when the avenue was widened in Stalin's time the building was moved back 14m, its wings were removed, and two storeys and a new entrance added. Originally the residence of Moscow's Tsarist governor generals, it was "sold" sometime in the nineteenth century to an English lord by a gang of con men, with the help of the notoriously gullible Governor Dolgorukov. After the October Revolution it housed the Moscow Soviet of Workers' and Soldiers' Deputies and the Military-Revolutionary Committee, which Lenin addressed on occasions now commemorated by sculpted plaques. Before perestroika, it was traditional to register him as deputy no. 1 whenever a newly elected City Council convened. Since its powers were vested in a Mayor, the office has become synonymous with **Yuri Luzhkov**, who has been elected four times running and likens himself to Mayor Daley of Chicago. A glassy, pyramid-roofed tower behind the old City Hall marks the first stage of a massive new extension to the Mayoralty's office space.

Across the road prances an equestrian **statue of Yuri Dolgoruky**, the founder of Moscow, belatedly unveiled seven years after the city's 800th anniversary in 1947. The large building on the right, with a fruity cornice, was once the *Dresden Hotel*, where Schumann, Chekhov and Turgenev stayed. Since Soviet times it has housed the **Aragvi Restaurant**, giving rise to a Georgian joke that Dolgoruky had the sense to found his city near a good place to eat. Next door to the *Aragvi* is the small seventeenth-century **Church of SS Cosmas and Damian** (tserkov Kosmy i Damiana) whose congregation includes many dissidents from the Brezhnev era, vindicated by the demise of the Institute of Marxism-Leninism at the end of the square.

Off to the east

Running downhill from the SS Cosmas and Damian, the cobbled **Stoleshnikov pereulok** takes its name from the tablecloth weavers (*stoleshniki*) who resided here in the sixteenth century. A sculpted plaque on the wall of no. 9 commemorates the journalist Vladimir Gilyarovsky, whose book *Moscow and the Muscovites* captured the city's life before the Revolution and during the NEP era. A *bon viveur* and a dandy, Gilyarovsky would surely welcome the return of chic shops to Stolesnikov pereulok, which is now one of the most elegant streets in Moscow, with a tiny **chapel** at the bottom near the *Marriott Aurora Hotel* on Bolshaya Dmitrovka ulitsa.

Returning to Tverskaya ulitsa and continuing northwards, you'll pass the dingy **Tsentralnaya Hotel**, which served as a residential hostel for many members of the Communist International during the 1930s, when their ranks were decimated by Stalin's purges. Victims were arrested at night and hustled out through the kitchens into a waiting prison van, disguised as a bread delivery van, whereupon their families were moved into worse rooms and shunned by everyone else in the hostel.

In those days the street around the corner was home to many esteemed People's Artists, including the co-founder of the Moscow Art Theatre, whose flat is preserved as the **Nemirovich-Danchenko Museum** (muzey-kvartira V.I. Nemirovicha-Danchenko; Tues–Sat noon–6pm; R50). Vladimir Nemirovich-Danchenko was an actor, war correspondent, novelist, playwright and drama critic, whose meeting with Stanislavsky in 1897 led him to abandon his literary career after the publication of his first novel and devote all his energies to directing and promoting the Moscow Art Theatre. To find the flat (#52), walk through the arch of the Stalinist block at Glinishchevskiy pereulok 5/7, head upstairs to the left, through the door beneath the pipes to a second lift shaft and take the elevator to the third floor. If you need to get past an intercom, press 052.

Chekhov's widow, the actress **Olga Knipper-Chekhova**, lived in a similar apartment one block downhill from 1938 until her death in 1959. As yet, there is no plaque to mark the flat where **Solzhenitsyn** lived before his expulsion from the Soviet Union: apartment #169, in the block behind Tverskaya 12.

Yeliseev's and the Nikolai Ostrovsky Museum

Nearer Pushkinskaya ploshchad, Tverskaya 14 houses a couple of institutions. **Yeliseev's** (open 24/7) used to be Moscow's foremost delicatessen, and certainly boasts the finest interior of any shop in the city, replete with stained-glass skylights, floral chandeliers and mahogany counters, its ceiling upheld by voluptuous buttresses – all lovingly restored for the store's 150th anniversary. The entrance hall displays a bust of Pyotr Yeliseev, a serf-gardener who won his freedom by growing a perfect strawberry, and traded so successfully in St Petersburg that in 1843 his sons were able to found the *Brothers Yeliseev*, opening branches in Moscow and Kiev. After the Revolution, they reputedly tried to save their gold by making it into rods and connections for the lamps in the chandeliers that illuminated their stores.

The entrance just up the road leads to the **Nikolai Ostrovsky Museum and Humanitarian Centre** (muzey-kvartira i gumanitarniy tsentr Nikolya Ostrovskovo; Wed–Sun 11am–7.30pm, closed last Fri of the month; R200). Ostrovsky (1904–36) was a true believer who sacrificed everything for Communism, becoming a Party activist at the age of thirteen, and contracting a wasting disease while laying a railway line after the Civil War. By the age of 25 he was blind and paralyzed; having contemplated suicide, he dictated his semi-autobiographical novel, *How the Steel was Tempered*, a classic of Stalinist literature. The museum preserves his Spartan study and bedroom, while the centre showcases the achievements of disabled people like Ludmilla Rogova, who overcame multiple sclerosis by devising exercises that she later taught to children with cerebral palsy, and Nikolai Fenomenov, who helped build more than ten metro stations despite being severely injured in the war.

To Pushkinskaya ploshchad

Further uphill, Tverskaya crosses the heavily trafficked Tverskoy and Strastnoy sections of the Boulevard Ring at Pushkinskaya ploshchad. This is a good place to take the city's pulse and savour its contrasts. Affluent Muscovites frequent the marbled **Galereya Aktyor** mall (daily 11am–9pm) on the corner of Strasnoy bulvar, while ordinary commuters and traders throng the maze of **underpasses** beneath the square, leading to Pushkinskaya, Tverskaya and Chekhovskaya metro stations and a dozen locations above ground. At one of the underpass junctions on the eastern side, a white marble **plaque** commemorates twelve Muscovites killed and scores injured by a bomb in August 2000.

For a description of Pushkinskaya ploshchad and beyond, see p.149.

Bolshaya Nikitskaya, Nikitskie vorota and Tverskoy bulvar

Another promising route from Manezhnaya ploshchad to the Boulevard Ring is **Bolshaya Nikitskaya ulitsa**, a narrow street lined with university buildings in various shades of yellow, which looks fetchingly nineteenth-century when blanketed with snow. In Soviet times the street was named after the radical journalist Alexander Herzen, who set Ogaryov's salon at no. 23 buzzing in the early 1820s. Today, the initial stretch is notable for the **Zoological Museum** (Zoologicheskiy muzey; Tues–Sun 10am–5pm; closed Mon & the last Sun of each month; R70), recognizable by its mural and stucco frieze of animals cavorting in flora. The collection includes a mammoth's skeleton from Yakuta, stuffed bison and bears, and a mongoose fighting two cobras at once.

The Moscow Conservatory

Across the road further on is Russia's foremost music school, the **Moscow Conservatory** (Moskovskaya konservatoriya). Founded in 1866 by Nikolai Rubenstein, the Conservatory occupies an eighteenth-century mansion fronted by a statue of Tchaikovsky waving his hands as if to conduct an orchestra – its railing is in the form of notes from six of his works, including *Swan Lake*. Tchaikovsky taught for twelve years at the Conservatory, which now bears his name. Although some Western biographers have argued that he committed suicide to avoid a scandal over an affair with his nephew, it is now reckoned that he actually died from cholera, which was the cause of death recorded at the time – but there are enough unexplained questions to keep the debate running.

Try to attend a concert in the **Grand Hall** (Bolshoy zal), decorated with giant medallions of composers. It was here that one of Shostakovich's most virulent critics suffered a fatal heart attack during the premiere of a symphony that expressed the composer's torment at the years when his works were branded "formalist perversions". Every four years it hosts the Tchaikovsky Competition, one of the most prestigious contests in the world of classical musicianship; the winner's professional success is assured.

Nikitskie vorota and the Stanislavsky Museum

Beyond the Conservatory, Bolshaya Nikitskaya ulitsa meets the Boulevard Ring, as a dozen roads converge on the site of the medieval St Nicholas Gate – still called **Nikitskie vorota**, although the gate was demolished in Stalin's time. The concrete-honeycombed offices of the **ITAR-TASS** news agency on the corner of Tverskoy bulvar will help you get orientated before pushing on to the amazing Gorky house (see p.159) beyond Nikitskie vorota, or turning up the side street beside ITAR-TASS, to find a veritable shrine to Method Acting.

The **Stanislavsky House-Museum** (dom-muzey K.S. Stanislavskovo; Wed & Fri 2–8pm, Thurs, Sat & Sun 11am–6pm; closed Mon, Tues & the last Thurs of each month; R50) at Leontovskiy pereulok 6 occupies a Neoclassical mansion that was assigned to "cultural workers" in 1921. After his own home on Karetniy ryad was requisitioned as a chauffeurs' club, Stanislavsky was allocated five rooms here to live and tutor actors from the Moscow Art Theatre and Bolshoy opera studio. They signed in at the top of the stairs before applying their make-up in the Red Room and setting to work in his study, bisected by bookcases that served as "wings". Performances were staged in the Onegin Hall, named after the premiere of Tchaikovsky's opera *Yevgeny Onegin*, which took place in 1922. You can still see the armchair from which he oversaw rehearsals, and the bedroom where the ailing director wrote *An Actor Prepares* – the bible of the Method school of acting – before his death in 1938.

Diagonally across the road, a small **Museum of Folk Art** (muzey narodnovo iskusstva; Mon–Thurs & Sat 10am–6pm; closed last Thurs of the month; R50) mounts temporary exhibitions of ethnic crafts from across the former Soviet Union. It's housed in a neo-Russian edifice with a steepled porch, financed in the 1890s by Savva Morozov (see p.158), who also bankrolled the Moscow Art Theatre.

Along Tverskoy bulvar

The streets radiating from Nikitskie vorota have long been associated with Moscow's stage world. At Tverskoy bulvar 11, the **Yermolova House-Museum** (dom-muzey M.N. Yermolovoy; Mon & Wed–Sun 11am–7pm; closed last Mon of each month, in summer closed every Mon; R120) commemorates a legendary actress from the Maly Theatre, resident there from 1880 until 1928. Its terracotta and yellow Empire frontage hides a charming period interior that conveys how affluent Russians lived before the Revolution. While her lawyer husband fled into exile, Maria Yermelova ended her illustrious career as a People's Artist of the USSR. Her personality pervades the house upstairs, especially the study, filled with statues and biographies of Joan of Arc, her favourite role. There are two grand pianos, a palmy conservatory, and a covered balcony from which she greeted admirers. Head straight upstairs, leaving the exhibition on the ground floor till last, but don't miss seeing the clockwork puppet-stage, nor the diorama of Teatralnaya ploshchad in the early nineteenth century.

In the 1920s, Tairov and Meyerhold pioneered Expressionist drama and Constructivist stage designs and introduced the plays of Brecht, Shaw and O'Neill to Russia, at what is now the **Pushkin Drama Theatre**, midway along the boulevard. On the other side of Tverskoy looms the Brutalist-style **New MKhAT** playhouse, built in the 1970s to stage dramas by Maxim Gorky. Retracing your steps to the corner of Tverskoy bulvar and Nikitskie vorota, you'll be just around the corner from the Theatre on Malaya Bronnaya, where the State Yiddish Theatre once existed (see p.157).

Towards the Arbat

Another route to the Boulevard Ring – and the Arbat beyond it – is to head along **ulitsa Vozdvizhenka**, which starts beside the gigantic Russian State Library (see p.123). Like nearby ulitsa Znamenka, this is prime real estate – right on the Kremlin's doorstep – and Moscow property developers have used every means going to grab it, from demolishing listed buildings like the Tsarist Military Department Store to threatening tenants in residential buildings with "gas leaks". One building that's survived so far is the eighteenth-century Talyzin mansion that still nominally houses the **Shchusev Architectural Museum** (muzey arkhitektury imeni A.V. Shchuseva; Tues–Sun 10am–7pm; R100), boasting a host of models and photos of buildings from medieval times to the Soviet era, when its namesake, Alexei Shchusev (1873–1949), designed such varied structures as the Lenin Mausoleum and the *Moskva Hotel*. For over a decade, however, the museum has been "under refurbishment" (while being leased out as offices) and reduced to mounting temporary exhibitions in the Apothecary's Palace in the yard behind the mansion, where statues and wrought-ironwork gather dust. The whitewashed palace once served the German apothecaries who laid out the tsar's medicinal herb garden on Vagankov Hill, further along Starovagankovskiy pereulok (see p.124), a picturesque backstreet that leads towards the Cathedral of Christ the Saviour in the distance. The Palace of Soviets that Stalin intended to stand there (see p.132) was only one of the colossal edifices dreamt up by Soviet architects in the 1920s and 1930s, documented by a fascinating online Museum of Paper Architecture (Ⓦwww.utopia.ru).

The "Pentagon" and the House of Europe

Slightly further along Vozdvizhenka on the corner of Bolshoy Znamenskiy pereulok stands a two-storey **house** with a floral cornice (no. 9) that once belonged to **Tolstoy's grandfather**. Though he died before Tolstoy's birth, in 1821, Prince Nicholas Volkonsky was imaginatively resurrected in *War and Peace* as the irascible Prince Bolkonsky, with his "gloomy house on the Vozdvizhenka". He should not be confused with Tolstoy's second cousin, the other real-life Prince Volkonsky, who was exiled to Siberia for his part in the Decembrist revolt.

Immediately beyond are the marble-clad modular offices of the Armed Forces **General Staff** (Generalniy Shtab), familiarly known to Muscovites as the "Pentagon". Its concrete bowels contain the decorative 1930s **Arbatskaya metro** station on the Arbatsko-Pokrovskaya line, whose exit brings you out opposite the **House of Europe** (dom Yevropy). This bizarre mansion was built in 1898 for a dissipated heir, Arseny Morozov; its lace-trimmed towers and sculpted seashells were inspired by the Casa de las Conchas in Salamanca. When his mother saw it, she declared, "Until now, only I knew you were mad; now everyone will". Arseny died of septicemia at the age of 24, after shooting himself in the foot to see whether he could bear the pain. After the Revolution the mansion was taken over by Anarchists before becoming the headquarters of Proletcult, an organization involving Mayakovsky and Meyerhold that aimed to turn workers and peasants into agitprop artists – one of whom made himself a home in Morozov's bathroom. Since the 1950s the building has housed the Union of Friendship Societies – now renamed the Centre for Scientific and Cultural Cooperation – which during Soviet times was responsible for staging meetings between foreign visitors and approved artists. Occasional **exhibitions** are your only chance of getting inside. Check on the notice board outside (in Russian only) for details.

Arbatskaya ploshchad and Nikitskiy bulvar

Further up the road, **Arbatskaya ploshchad** (Arbat Square) bears the scars of several bouts of redevelopment. It has a 1950s underpass serving traffic on the Boulevard Ring, and another, multi-branched pedestrian **subway** where thrash rockers busk till late at night. On the surface, you'll also notice the pavilion of **Arbatskaya metro** station on the Filyovskaya line, built in the shape of a five-pointed star (a favourite architectural conceit of the 1930s), and the **Praga Restaurant**. Founded before the Revolution, it was long regarded as Moscow's top restaurant and hosted diplomatic banquets in Soviet times till it fell out of fashion in the 1980s. Having hit rock bottom in the early 1990s, the *Praga* was refurbished by Ismailov Telman, a magnate whose astrological sign is emblazoned on all the plates and rugs.

While visitors are usually drawn into the Arbat district beyond the *Praga* (covered on p.162), a few sights beg a detour **along the Boulevard Ring** itself. At the head of Gogolevskiy bulvar, beside the square, stands what locals call the "Happy" **Gogol statue**, since it replaced a statue that the Soviet authorities deemed too gloomy for the late 1940s. The original, by the sculptor Andreev, was banished to the open courtyard of no. 7, Nikitskiy bulvar, where the "Sad" **Gogol statue** huddles in a cape, eyes downcast, while the plinth bears a jolly frieze of characters from *The Government Inspector* and *Taras Bulba*. In the public library on the right, devoted scholars have created the **Gogol Memorial Room** (closed until 2009; call Ⓣ291 15 50 or check Ⓦwww.domgogolya.ru for new opening hours) in what was Gogol's study during his last years. Here he burned the second part of *Dead Souls* in the fireplace and lapsed into religious melancholia, eating only pickled cabbage. A sufferer from cataleptic fits, he was mistakenly buried alive in the Novodevichie Cemetery (see p.197).

Across the road and 150m further north at no. 12a Nikitskiy bulvar, a pale yellow, Corinthian-pilastered mansion contains the **Oriental Museum** (muzey Vostoka; Tues–Sun 11am–8pm; R100). Its superb collection includes Caucasian rugs, Indonesian shadow-puppets, Vietnamese silver Buddhas, Samurai swords, lacquer-ware, porcelain, Chinese screens and robes. Reproduction pictures by Roerich, a mystic Russian Orientalist (see p.131), are sold in the foyer. As the museum is located south of Nikitskie vorota, it's also easy to reach from there. There are several good ethnic cafés (see Chapter 12) along this stretch of Nikitskiy bulvar, which used to be a gay cruising area in the 1920s and 1930s.

From the Russian Library to the Pushkin Museum

The corner of Vozdvizhenka and Mokhovaya streets is dominated by the immense **Russian State Library** (Mon–Fri 9am–8pm, Sat 9am–7pm; closed last Mon of each month; free) – better known by its former title, the Lenin Library or – "Leninka" – where some forty million books and periodicals repose on 200km of shelving. Looming above a hillock behind a lanky arcade of black pillars, the library's main building was actually a reworking of a design for a hydroelectric power station, which became progressively more encrusted with reliefs and statues as its construction (1928–50) was influenced by the Palace of Soviets that was supposed to arise in the vicinity. The black marble **statue of Dostoyevsky** at the top of the steps was added in 1997.

Although you can't go beyond the cloakrooms without a reader's pass, have a look at the grand staircase (entrance #1) that ascends to the library's four main halls, decorated in the apogee of Soviet Classicism. (To obtain a pass, or *chitatelskiy bilet*, bring your passport and one photo along.) Bibliophiles can also visit the **Museum of Books** (muzey knigi; Mon–Sat 10am–6pm; closed last

Mon of each month; free) on the fourth floor of wing U (entrance #3). Its collection ranges from ancient Egyptian papyri and clay tablets bearing the Olympic Oath to some of the earliest books in the Cyrillic alphabet, including Fyodorov's *The Apostle* (1562) and the first all-Russian Bible (1581).

Downhill lies **Borovitskaya metro station**, whose inauguration in 1985 caused subsidence beneath the library's huge depository and the loss of some forty thousand books. Ensuring its structural integrity had to come before anything else at a time of shrinking budgets; for a while the library couldn't even afford to heat its premises. Borovitskaya is reputedly linked to the secret Kremlin metro line by a nondescript door at the end of one of its platforms.

The Pashkov House and Mokhovaya ulitsa

Subsidence also badly affected the impressive **Pashkov House** (dom Pashkova) that overlooks the Kremlin's Borovitskiy Gate from a hilltop, and once had a garden running down to the Kremlin moat, where peacocks strutted. When built by Bazhenov in the 1780s it was the finest private house in Moscow and constituted a bridge between Baroque and Neoclassical architecture. Mortgaged away by the gambling-mad Count Pashkov, it was purchased by a book-loving Marshal and turned into the Rumyantsev Library, whose collection of one million volumes later formed the core of the Lenin Library, located on the premises until 1950. It was from the rooftop of this building that the Devil and his entourage surveyed the chaos they had sown across Moscow in Bulgakov's *The Master and Margarita*.

Despite its grand facade facing the Kremlin, the main entrance actually lies round the back on **Starovagankovskiy pereulok**, where the adjacent walled **Church of St Nicholas in Old Vagankov** (tserkov Nikolaya v Starom Vagankove) sports a plaque boasting that Gogol was a regular worshipper in the 1840s. While the church's title recalls the village of Vagankov that existed here in the Middle Ages, the main road below the library, **Mokhovaya ulitsa**, is named after the moss (*mokh*) once sold here for caulking the chinks in wooden houses, and later for inserting between the panes of double-glazed windows to prevent fogging from condensation. If you're heading for the Pushkin Museum of Fine Arts, crossing the busy intersection of Mokhovaya ulitsa and Borovitskaya ploshchad will require an irksome detour up ulitsa Znamenka, since there are no underpasses in the vicinity.

The "Arts Zone"

Ulitsa Volkhonka is the core of the "Arts Zone" that culture-lovers would like to establish in the vicinity of the Kremlin – in the face of property developers with different ideas. Its bedrock is the **Pushkin Museum of Fine Arts**, which is such a revered national institution that no speculator could hope to shift it. The Yeltsin era saw the arrival of two privately endowed museums – the **Nikolai Roerich Museum** and the **Museum of Private Collections** – at the same time as the rebuilding of the Cathedral of Christ the Saviour, making this the most talked-about location in Moscow. The inauguration of the **Glazunov Picture Gallery** in 2004 and the **Gallery of nineteenth- and twentieth-century European and American Art**, three years later, set the seal on the area's status as a cultural must-see.

While the museums here are readily accessible from Kropotkinskaya **metro** station (see p.168), anyone approaching the Pushkin Museum from the backstreets via Starovagankovskiy pereulok (see p.124) will pass by a minor curiosity. The asymmetrical corner **Church of St Antipy by the Carriage-house** (tserkov Antipa na kolymazhnom dvore) was reputedly commissioned by Malyuta-Skuratov – the psychopath who ran Ivan the Terrible's *Oprichniki* – after the tsar's own habit of absolving his heinous sins by ostentatious acts of piety.

The Pushkin Museum of Fine Arts

As the Imperial capital, St Petersburg had a head start on Moscow when it came to the acquisition of foreign art. The Hermitage became a semi-public museum in 1852, whereas it took years of campaigning by the father of the poetess Marina Tsvetaeva to establish a similar museum in Moscow in 1912, named after Alexander III. Following the Revolution, its collection of casts of antique, medieval and Renaissance sculptures was augmented by works from private collections and the Hermitage, prior to it being renamed in 1937 and bearing the indignity of being turned over to an exhibition of gifts received by Stalin, prompting the resignation of its director.

Today, the **Pushkin Museum of Fine Arts** (muzey Izobrazitelnykh Iskusstv imeni A.S. Pushkina; Tues–Sun 10am–7pm, Thurs open til 9pm; R300) prefers to recall hosting exhibitions of Tutankhamun's treasures and works from the Louvre and the Prado, and trumpets its own holdings of art and antiques. While not covering such a broad sweep as the Hermitage or having many thousands of exhibits in hundreds of rooms, it still boasts everything from Greek antiquities to Picasso and has far more in its storerooms than can ever be displayed, despite the rotation of pictures in the rooms devoted to nineteenth- and twentieth-century paintings, and **temporary exhibitions** on the upper level of the Zholtovsky Staircase of anything from engravings by Kathe Kollwitz to contemporary European art. Besides the constraints imposed by lack of space, politics have also played a part, as in the decades when abstract works were ideologically taboo. Not until the mid-1990s did the museum reveal much of the "trophy art" that was seized from the Nazis in 1945 and hidden for decades afterwards, such as the Treasure of Troy (see p.126).

Although the majority of paintings are labelled in English (or French) as well as Russian, there aren't many explanatory captions, so anyone wishing to learn something about the artworks should sign up for the weekly two-hour **guided tour** in English (R600 per person plus admission charge) run by Patriarshy Dom Tours (see p.46), or rent an **audioguide** (R250 plus ID as a deposit) in the museum basement, where the cloakrooms, **toilets** and a **café** (reserved for staff from 1–2pm) are located. **Photography** is allowed except in rooms 7 and 1. Since the rooms are numbered in a way that bears little relation to their **layout** in terms of access, the following account is loosely structured on a thematic basis, starting on the ground floor, which is approached from the basement. It's also worth bearing in mind that the museum is currently undergoing a major expansion which will see its exhibition space more than triple, so some of the artworks mentioned in this account may have moved from the rooms described below.

The museum hosts annual concerts of classical music, known as the **December Evenings**. For a preview of its collection and news of forthcoming temporary exhibitions, visit its **website** at Ⓦwww.museum.ru.gmii.

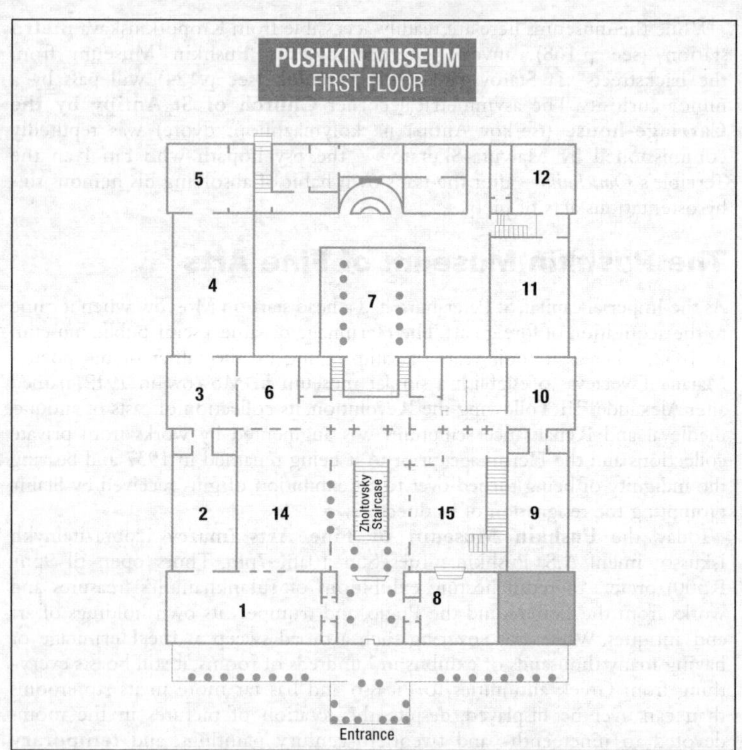

Antiquities and Byzantine art

Most visitors head straight for **Room 3** and the famous **Treasure of Troy** (Sokrovishcha Troy) found by Schliemann, which vanished from a Berlin bunker to surface at the Pushkin Museum fifty years later. As Russian legislators are at one with public opinion in opposing the return of any "trophy art" to Germany until Russian claims for treasures despoiled by the Nazis are settled, it's set to remain here. The gold diadems, torques and nephrite axeheads come from Hissarlik in Turkey, where Schliemann believed that he had found the Troy of Homer's *Iliad* but actually uncovered the Mycenean-era city. By coincidence, he made the fortune that financed his excavations while trading as an indigo merchant in Russia during the Crimean War.

Next door, **Room 2** opens with a fine display of **Coptic textiles** and funerary masks, and sixteen amazingly vivid **Fayoum portraits**, which were painted while their subjects were alive and then pasted onto their mummies – all from Egypt, between the first and sixth centuries AD. On the far wall are several glorious **Byzantine icons**, most notably a serene *Christ Pantokrator* from the mid-fifteenth century. Apart from an eclectic mix of pre-Columbian and Hindu sculptures, the rest of the room is largely devoted to magnificent limestone **Babylonian bas-reliefs** from the Palace of Ashurnaziral (885–860 BC), whose portal flanked by winged bulls forms the entrance to the hall. At the far end lies Room 1, decorated like an Egyptian temple and filled with **Pharaonic artefacts** from the Old, Middle and New Kingdoms, collected by the orientalist Golenischev. They include funerary figures, Canopic chests, a mummified woman's head and the mummy of Hor-Ha.

The other eye-grabber – though hardly valuable or controversial – is the life-sized plaster casts of **ancient monuments** in **Room 14**, including a corner of the Parthenon and a gigantic bull-headed capital from the palace of Artaxerxes II in Susa.

Gothic and Renaissance art

Italian art of the sixteenth century kicks off in **Room 6**, where a diminutive *Minerva* by **Paolo Veronese** is accompanied by larger works of his school. Here too you'll find a sinuous *St John the Baptist* by **El Greco**, which was thought to have vanished during World War II, and a *Portrait of a Man* in an ermine-trimmed robe by **Tintoretto**.

Rooms 11 and 12 feature **Italian**, **German and Dutch art** of the fifteenth and sixteenth centuries. Here, you can admire Vittore Crivelli's sumptuously decorative *Virgin and Child with Saints*, a sadistic *Flagellation of Christ* by Johann Koerbecke, and St Michael trampling a hairy demon, attributed to the Catalonian master Pedro Espalargues. Beyond here, Giulio Romano's *Woman at her Toilet* faces a tiny, sublime *Annunciation* by **Sandro Botticelli** and a lovely *St Sebastian* by da Vinci's pupil and assistant, Giovanni Boltraffio; while on the wall across the way is a magnificently pain-wracked *Golgotha* by the mysteriously named Master of the Prodigal Son.

The following section features four small works by **Lucas Cranach the Elder**, the most striking being *The Fall of Man* and *The Results of Jealousy*. On the right-hand wall of the final section hangs a *Winter Landscape with Bird Trap* by **Pieter Brueghel the Younger** – actually a copy of a like-named painting by his father, Brueghel the Elder, in Brussels – while beside the doorway is an over-the-top *Solomon and the Queen of Sheba* by Hans Vredeman de Vries, where figures in Renaissance dress are posed against an oddly metallic-looking palazzo.

Rubens, Rembrandt and Baroque art

Room 11 also contains seventeenth-century **Flemish and Spanish art**, including a trio of paintings by the Spaniard **Bartolomé Murillo**, whose *Archangel Raphael and Bishop Domonte* was commissioned to adorn the bishop's own cathedral. You can also see here a *Still life with Swans* by **Frans Snyders** hanging beside a portrait of the corpulent merchant Adriaen Stevens, by **Anthony van Dyck**. Both Snyders and Van Dyck worked as assistants at the studio of **Peter Paul Rubens**, whose three works owned by the Pushkin Museum include *Bacchanalia*, featuring an intoxicated Bacchus supported by his slaves while a cloven-hoofed woman suckles a brood of baby satyrs. On the facing wall are *Ulysses in the Cave of Poliphemus* and *The Flight into Egypt*, by Jacob Jordaens.

Room 12 also contains **Italian art** of the seventeenth and eighteenth centuries. On the right as you enter are Salvatori Rossa's cruel *Old Coquette*, followed by Domenico Gargiulo's action-packed *The Ark brought by King David to Jerusalem*, which leads one towards *Buccentoro's Return to the Pier at the Doge's Palace* – a sumptuous vista of gilded barges and Venetian palazzi by **Canaletto**.

Room 10 is devoted to **seventeenth-century Dutch art**, where everyone makes a beeline for works by **Rembrandt**. His mastery of dark tones and free brushwork is evinced by *Ahasuerus, Haman and Esther*, where the males are almost lost in the shadows, while Esther's embroidered bodice is rendered by merely scratching the paint's surface. On the other side of the partition, two religious works – *Christ Cleansing the Temple* and *The Incredulity of Thomas* – face a trio of portraits depicting Rembrandt's mother (*An Old Woman*), brother (*An Old Man*) and sister-in-law (*An Elderly Woman*), all painted in 1654, when the artist was struggling to come to terms with bereavement and poverty.

Copies of masterpieces

Room 15 contains bronze and plaster **copies of Medieval and Renaissance masterpieces** such as the Bishop's Seat of Ulm Cathedral, Michelangelo's *David*, and the famous *condottieri* statues from Padua and Venice.

Its stairway leads **upstairs** into a gallery displaying ancient Cretan statues, from where a door leads into **Room 16**, filled with plaster casts of ancient Greek sculptures and friezes from the Temple of Zeus at Olympia and other sites. This marks the start of a series of rooms devoted to copies of statues by Michelangelo (**Room 29**); other Renaissance masterpieces, such as Ghiberti's "Doors of Paradise" from the Florentine Baptistry (**Room 28**); medieval cathedral art from France and Germany (**Room 26**); and Greek and Roman statuary (**Rooms 24 & 25**) – whose period decor complements the exhibits.

Barbizon, Orientalist and Academic painters

Room 23 exhibits a fraction of the museum's huge collection of **Barbizon painters**, which rivals the Louvre's. Though nowadays unfashionable, they paved the way for the Impressionists by abandoning the studio in favour of

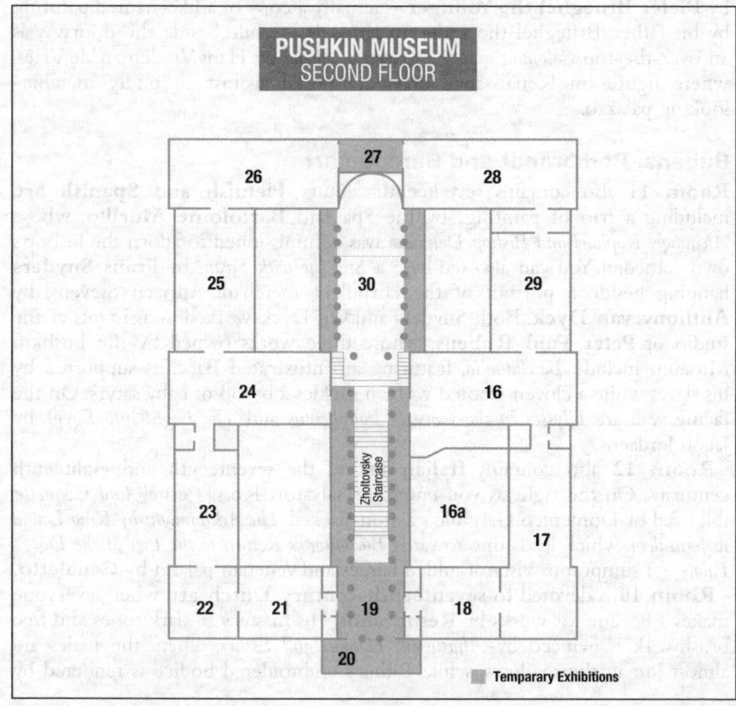

plein air painting. The emphasis on spontaneity and naturalism is particularly evident in landscapes by Jean-Baptiste-Camille **Corot**, such as *Stormy Weather* and *A Gust of Wind*, and in Jules Bastien Lepage's romantic *Rural Love*.

In the same room are picturesque **Orientalist paintings** like Jean Fromentin's *Awaiting the Boat to Cross the Nile* and Honore Daumier's *The Revolt*; a small *View of the Mountains* by one of the greatest German Romantic painters, **Caspar David Friedrich**; and a copy of one of Rodin's Burghers of Calais.

At the far end of the room is a host of works in the **Academic style** that Russian artists were obliged to ape during the eighteenth and nineteenth centuries, including a serene *Virgin with the Host* by **Ingres**, commissioned by Tsar Alexander II; an equestrian *Portrait of Prince Yusupov* by Antoine-Jean **Gros**; and *After the Shipwreck* by Eugène **Delacroix**.

Thirteenth- to fifteenth-century Italian Art

Back through the main hallway, which hosts temporary exhibitions, **Rooms 17 and 18** exhibit **Italian art** from the thirteenth to the fifteenth centuries, as it evolved from Byzantine to Gothic forms. Look out for the splendid *Madonna and Child Enthroned* with a gem-studded halo, framed with scenes from Christ's life, by an anonymous Florentine artist (c.1280), and the brilliantly coloured *Madonna Enthroned with Angels* by Giovanni di Bartolomeo Cristiani. There are also two small yet exquisite altar triptychs from the second half of the fourteenth century, as well as a skeletal *Crucifixion* by Jacobello del Fiore. Notice the jealous expressions in Pietro di Giovanni Lianori's rose- and yellow-hued triptych of the *Virgin and Child with Saints*.

The Gallery of nineteenth- and twentieth-century European and American Art

In the early 1900s, the Moscow millionaires Sergei Shchukin and Ivan Morozov bought scores of paintings by Picasso, Matisse and the **French Impressionists**, which now form the core of the modern European art collections of the Hermitage and the Pushkin Museum. The latter's collection of French Impressionists is concentrated in a new **Gallery of nineteenth- and twentieth-century European and American Art**, at Volhkana 14, across the road from the main Pushkin building (Tues–Sun 10am–7pm, Thurs open til 9pm; R250).

Fine works by **Monet** include *Luncheon on the Grass*, *The Rocks of Belle-Ille*, foggy views of the River Thames and *Rouen Cathedral at Sunset* (one of a series that captured the changing light on the cathedral's facade throughout the day). You can also see landscapes and Parisian street scenes by **Pissarro**; vivid pastels by **Degas**, such as *Ballet Rehearsal* and *Dancers in Blue*; and a *Portrait of Yvette Guilbert* by **Toulouse-Lautrec**, who often sketched this chanteuse at the Moulin Rouge. The museum's large collection of works by **Renoir** includes various portraits of actresses and a gorgeous plump nude known as "The Pearl", while small versions of *The Burghers of Calais* and *The Kiss* are numbered among its sculptures by **Rodin**.

Post-Impressionism and Modernism

The gallery is also home to the finest display of **Post-Impressionist art** outside of the Hermitage – mostly from the collections of Morozov and Shchukin, both of whom bought more than fifty works apiece by Picasso and Matisse. Those by **Picasso** range from a Cézanne-like *Cottage with Trees* and the *Cubist Violin* and *Queen Isabeau*, to paintings from his Blue, Rose and Spanish periods, such as *Young Acrobat on a Ball*, *Portrait of Sabartès*, *Old Jew and a Boy* and *Spanish Woman from Mallorca*. The paintings by **Matisse** include a *Moroccan Triptych* in saturated blues, several still lifes with vases, and *The Goldfish*; the museum also owns his bronze sculpture *Jaguar and Hare*. The museum's collection of works by **Cézanne** is equally rich, ranging from landscapes and self-portraits to still lifes and pictures from his Pierrot and Harlequin series, such as *Mardi Gras*.

Equally impressive is the breadth of work by **Van Gogh**, from the doleful *Prisoners at Exercise* to the coruscating *Red Vineyard at Arles*. The latter was the only painting he sold in his lifetime, about which he wrote: "Oh, the beautiful sun of midsummer! It beats upon my head, and I do not doubt that it makes one a little queer" – shortly before cutting off his ear and leaving it in a brothel. Likewise, the amazing selection of Tahitian works by **Gauguin** – including *Relax*, *Gathering Fruit*, *The Great Buddha*, *Still Life with Parrots*, *Landscape with Peacocks* and *The Queen* – and the two enormous canvases by **Bonnard** – *Autumn* and *Early Spring in the Country*.

In addition, you can see a host of diverse works by later artists, ranging from the pioneer of abstract art, **Vasily Kandinsky**, to the Surrealists **de Chirico** and **Miró**. The gallery also features three colourful compositions by the card-carrying Communist **Léger**, and the dream-like *Nocturne* and *The Artist and his Bride*, by the Russian-Jewish artist **Chagall**.

The Museum of Private Collections

Next door to the Pushkin Museum stands a subsidiary **Museum of Private Collections** (muzey Lichnykh Kollektsiy; Wed–Sun noon–7pm; closed last Fri of each month; R50). The brainchild of Ilya Zilbershtein, a collector himself, it displays private collections of antique and modern art that were amassed during Soviet times. The individual tastes and limited resources of a score of collectors make for a well-rounded, quirky exhibition, flattered by a stylish interior. Although some rooms host temporary exhibitions, the rest shouldn't change much. All the artworks are clearly labelled in English. **Photography** is not allowed inside.

The exhibition

The permanent exhibition begins on the **second floor** with **Salvador Dalí**'s pen-and-wash drawings from the series *Mythology* and *The Hippies*, and anthropophagic illustrations to *Faustus* and *The Songs of Maldoror*. Next door features drawings of vases and women by **Matisse**, and the artist's own palette. Look out for the portraits of Lydia Delektorskaya, Matisse's model and secretary from 1928 until his death, who donated many of his works to Russian museums.

The **third floor** is more Russian in spirit, with nineteenth-century works by the Wanderers, such as **Ilya Repin**, whose lurid pink and gold *Duel* is counterposed by **Vasily Polonev**'s gentle *Christ* musing over the Sea of Galilee. You will also find set designs by **Boris Kustodiev** and **Alexander Benois** from the golden age of Russian ballet; views of Moscow and St Petersburg in the eighteenth century; and a score of sixteenth- and seventeenth-century icons. Of historical interest are the tiny **portraits of the Decembrists** exiled to Siberia in 1825, drawn by fellow prisoner Nikolai Bestuzhev, and a painting of Countess Maria Volkonskaya, who followed Tolstoy's second cousin into exile.

The **fourth floor** offers a feast of twentieth-century art, to which the concert pianist Svatoslav Richter contributed his own pastels and grand piano, and still lifes by **Robert Falk**. Look out for Kustodiev's *After the Storm with a Rainbow* and Grabar's *Women Merchants*, in the room that brings together *fin-de-siècle* artists fascinated by Parisian nightlife, and rural Russia. Beyond a hoard of whimsical canvases and woodcarvings by **Alexander Tyshler** are two rooms devoted to **Alexander Rodchenko** and his wife **Varvara Stepanova** – arguably the museum's prime attraction. Rodchenko pioneered photo-collage and unorthodox perspectives, and his photos, posters and Constructivist book jackets are now classics of the genre, while Stepanova's textile designs have equal retro appeal. You can also see a snazzy red-and-black chess table, designed by Rodchenko for a workers' club.

The Glazunov Gallery

Across the road stands the **Ilya Glazunov Picture Gallery** (Kartinnaya galereya Ilyi Glazunova; Tues–Sun 11am–7pm; R160), showcasing the work of Russia's most popular living artist. A child of the Soviet system (orphaned during the siege of Leningrad), Glazunov was taught by Boris Ioaganson, the head of the Artists Union, and looked set for success until his fascination for Orthodox and Tsarist culture led to him being "exiled" to Kazan in the 1970s. His status as a dissident was enhanced by tales of a gigantic canvas, *The Mystery of the Twentieth Century* – featuring Hitler, Stalin, Nicholas II, Pushkin, Dostoyevsky and a host of other historical and cultural figures – and of how senior *apparatchiki* secretly collected his works. By 1980 retro-patriotism was celebrated: Glazunov was awarded the title of Peoples' Artist; UNESCO chose his painting *The Contribution of the Soviet Peoples to World Culture and Civilization* for its permanent art collection, and later gave him their Picasso Gold Medal. His view of the Yeltsin era is embodied by another huge painting, *The Market of Our Democracy*, which shows Yeltsin waving a conductor's baton as two lesbians kiss and the oligarch Berezovsky flaunts a sign reading "I will buy Russia", while charlatans rob a crowd of refugees and starving children. Subtle it's not – but his 2002 exhibition at the Manège drew over two million visitors in a month, so his art clearly resonates with many even if Moscow's intelligentsia shudder with distaste and liken him to Tsereteli (see p.208). A better comparison might be Dalí, with whom Glazunov shares an Old Master's draughtsmanship (his early illustrations for Dostoyevsky's novels are superb) and far-right sympathies.

The Roerich Museum

Nearby, but not owned by the Pushkin, is the **Nikolai Roerich Museum** (muzey N. Rorikha Ⓦ www.roerich-museum.ru; Tues–Sun 11am–7pm; R180) – which has to be the only museum in Moscow that's scented by joss sticks. Opened in 1997, it is dedicated to the ideals of Nikolai Roerich (1874–1947), an artist and scholar whose passion for Eastern philosophy led him to Central Asia, Tibet and India in the 1920s, and Manchuria and Mongolia in the 1930s. Another aspect of his idealism was the Roerich Pact for the preservation of cultural values during wartime, which became the basis of the Hague Convention of 1954. The museum displays his paintings of mystics, steppes and the Himalayas, intermingled with photos of Ladakh and Tibet and items of gear from his expeditions, on which Roerich was accompanied by his wife Helene and their son Georgi (the only one of the family to return to Soviet Russia, and be buried in the Novodevichiy Cemetery). A shop in the grounds sells Asian handicrafts and philosophical tracts.

The Cathedral of Christ the Saviour

One of the most prominent features of Moscow's skyline is the gigantic **Cathedral of Christ the Saviour** (khram Khrista Spasitela; daily 6.30am–10pm; closed last Mon of each month; free), near the Pushkin Museum, whose gilt onion domes are visible from Manezhnaya ploshchad. Clad in marble and granite, with colossal bronze doors covered in repoussé saints, the cathedral is an awesome statement of the refound power and prestige of the Orthodox Church – and Mayor Luzhkov's intention to leave his mark on Moscow as surely as Stalin did. It was Stalin who was responsible for destroying the original Cathedral of Christ the Saviour that Luzhkov rebuilt, in tandem with the erection of an equally vast monument to Peter the Great (visible across the river, and detailed on p.206).

The re-creation of Christ the Saviour struck a chord in the national psyche as an act of atonement for the sins of Communism and the reaffirmation of spiritual values: "Russia is freeing itself from evil. Good is triumphing!" was a typical comment in the visitors' book on the construction site. Only a small minority were opposed for aesthetic reasons, arguing that the original cathedral was derided as "a samovar" when it was built (1839–83) to commemorate Russia's victory over Napoleon, and that it entailed the destruction of the medieval Alexeevsky convent (whose abbess reputedly cursed the site) – so that the Orthodox Church and Alexander II were guilty of the same vandalism as the Communists.

Stalin's destruction of the cathedral in 1933 was intended to make way for the centrepiece of his new Moscow – a gargantuan **Palace of Soviets**, envisaged as the most important building in the USSR. As conceived by its architects, it was to be 315m high and crowned by a one-hundred-metre-tall aluminium statue of Lenin that would make it higher than the Empire State Building and the Statue of Liberty combined. Legend has it that the statue was added at Stalin's bidding, and its eyes were intended to emit a bright red beam. Work progressed as far as sinking the foundations, but the girders were ripped out to make anti-tank "hedgehogs" in 1941, and when construction resumed after the

▲ Cathedral of Christ the Saviour

war it was with less conviction. Ultimately the palace was never realized because the high water table made the ground unstable, so in 1959 the plan was dropped and an open-air **swimming pool** was built instead. Pious Russians whispered that it was God's revenge that smote Stalin's Tower of Babel, while the pool itself was later believed to be cursed after several swimmers drowned or were stabbed to death in the fog that shrouded its surface (which also threatened art works in the Pushkin Museum).

Today's cathedral was built between 1995 and 1997; the **interior** took another three years to decorate, bringing the total cost to $360 million. Its murals are gilded with 103kg of gold leaf, and – according to Tsereteli, who directed the project – identical to the originals, "only better". God, the Christ child and the Apostles stare down from the main cupola on a gilded, crown-shaped tabernacle, while biblical scenes and episodes from Russian history cover the walls and pillars, offset by red, black and beige marble in the nave, and alabaster in the enfilades where the names of thousands of soldiers decorated for their part in the Patriotic War are inscribed, along with the cathedral's sponsors, a roll call of oligarchs and multinational corporations.

Beneath the cathedral is a **museum** (daily 10am–6pm; free), which is accessible from Soimonovskiy proezd, if not directly by a stairway from the enfilades. This exhibits relics and plans of the original cathedral and a gouache of the Palace of Soviets, plus many pictures on religious themes, which look like they were painted in the nineteenth century but actually date from the 1990s – affirming the regressive spirit underlying the whole project.

Theatreland to the Lubyanka

East of Tverskaya is a wedge of the Beliy Gorod that encompasses some of Moscow's oldest monasteries and most treasured cultural landmarks. The Bolshoy Theatre and the fashionable shops of ulitsa Kuznetskiy most and ulitsa Petrovka were the hub of Moscow's social life before the Revolution; and the whole area seethes with activity today. Although its hot-dog vendors and renovation work might seem a far cry from how you'd imagine it in Anna Karenina's day, rubbish and mud were a bigger problem then, as the Neglina River – channelled into an underground pipe – often flooded the whole area with putrid sludge. The wealth flaunted by the banks, bars and boutiques that mushroomed here in the 1990s is something that Tolstoy's heroine would have recognized as a familiar aspect of Moscow.

The Bolshoy Theatre

Bolshoy means "big" or "great", and the **Bolshoy Theatre** (Bolshoy teatr), dominating Teatralnaya ploshchad, is both – with a massive eight-columned portico, surmounted by Apollo's chariot. Alas, its problems are also on a grand scale, from subsidence due to the theatre's position above the underground Neglina River, to the inferiority of dancers' wages and the quality of performances compared to St Petersburg's Mariinskiy Theatre. Since Putin appointed Anatoly Iksanov to rescue the theatre from its decline in 2002, there are signs that the Bolshoy has turned a corner – including three awards at the Golden Mask festival – but the overhaul of its choreography and sets has just begun and the reconstruction of the old theatre will not be finished until 2009.

The Bolshoy's **New Stage** (Novaya Stena), on a terrace facing the side of the old theatre, has been criticized for being too small to stage certain ballets or operas with a full cast of dancers or singers – dismaying those who cherish the Bolshoy's tradition of "big" productions – but at least the company has somewhere to perform until the renovation of the historic theatre is completed at the end of 2009. Subsidence first appeared in 1906 (when part of the auditorium sagged during a matinee) but remained untreated until 1921; when it returned in the late 1980s, action was likewise delayed for lack of money. Besides this, the stage machinery, lighting and fire-prevention systems are antiquated and unfit for modern productions. Yet conservationists fear the loss of features such as the "rotunda" of pillars that forms the structural core, or a kitsch makeover by Tsereteli.

Its **auditorium** seats 2000, with five tiers of balconies rising towards a chandelier weighing 1.5 tonnes (a gift from Napoleon III) and a circular mural of Apollo and nine Muses that was going to be replaced with the hammer and sickle, had not the Nazi invasion occurred. Cherry-red upholstery and hangings highlight the gilded mouldings on the boxes and balconies; the Imperial Box is dead centre, while heads of state and the artistic director occupy the ones to the left and right of the stage. Balletomanes should ask about the **backstage tour** offered by Patriarshy Dom Tours (p.46), which may be suspended depending on building work. This includes a visit to the Bolshoy's rehearsal studio, directly above the auditorium, and various nooks and crannies of the building.

For details of how and where to buy **tickets**, see the entry on the Bolshoy in "The Arts" (p.367) or visit the theatre's **website** (Ⓦwww.bolshoi.ru), which allows online booking. The English-language part isn't always up to date with regard to **performances** (unlike the Russian version), but you can see what's scheduled from posters outside the old and new stage's respective ticket offices, or listings in the *Moscow Times* and *Pulse*.

Some history

The Bolshoy's origins go back to 1776, when the English showman Michael Maddox founded a company that became established on the corner of ulitsa Petrovka as the first permanent theatre in Moscow. Its licence stipulated that all the dancers had to be Russian and all plays had to be performed in that language. The company's ballet tradition was firmly established after it came under state control in 1806, while some of the first Russian operas were performed here in the 1890s. However, the Bolshoy played second fiddle to St Petersburg's Mariinskiy Theatre until the early 1900s and only became supreme following the return of the capital to Moscow in 1918. Its international reputation was gained in the period from the 1950s to the 1970s by new works such as Khachaturian's *Spartacus* and star dancers like **Maya Plisetskaya** and **Vladimir Vasilev**. It was also famous for defections in protest at the autocratic management and conservative choreography associated with **Yuri Grigorovich**, the artistic director for thirty years until his abrupt dismissal in 1995. His successor, the revered dancer Vasilev, failed to arrest the Bolshoy's decline, and five years later he too was fired – only hearing the news from the radio – while the esteemed conductor **Gennady Rozhdestvensky** lasted only a year in the job, worn out by intrigues within the theatre and Moscow's cultural bureaucracy. News agencies gleefully reported the case of a ballerina who sued the Bolshoy for $920,000 in damages after she was fired for being too heavy for her dancing partners to lift – she lost the court action, however.

Besides opera and ballet, the Bolshoy has been a stage for **political dramas**, the stormiest of which was the Fifth Party Congress of July 1918, which witnessed the final split between the Bolsheviks and the Left Socialist Revolutionaries, whose leader Maria Spiridonova denounced Lenin for treating the peasantry like "dung" and called for war. The Left SR delegation were held prisoner in the Bolshoy while the Bolsheviks put down an uprising by their followers; in the words of Bruce Lockhardt, "the revolution, which was conceived in a theatre, ended in the same place".

Other theatres and the TsUM

The **Russian Academic Youth Theatre** (RAMT) beside the New Stage traces its history back to 1921, which makes it a stripling compared to the **Maly Theatre** (Maliy teatr) across the square. This long, low-slung edifice was originally built as a warehouse for Moscow's only honest army provisioner – who was jailed on false charges – whereupon it was sold off and converted into a theatre in 1838. Its drama company traces its origin back to the university theatre founded in 1757, but really came of age in tandem with the playwright Alexander Ostrovsky (1823–86), who is honoured by a seated statue outside. The actress Maria Yermolova (1853–1928) spent five decades at the Maly, providing a continuity from the age of Ostrovsky into the Soviet era, when she was the first person to be awarded the title of People's Artist.

Opera buffs should also note the **Moscow Operetta Theatre** (Moskovskiy teatr Operetty), on the corner of Bolshaya Dmitrovka ulitsa and the alleyway that exits the square behind the New Stage. In the 1890s, the composer Rachmaninov and the singer Chaliapin began their careers at what was then the avant-garde Private Opera of Savva Mamontov, which hired leading artists to design the costumes and sets (some of which can be seen at the Museum of Private Collections and the Moscow Museum of Modern Art).

There's also something theatrical about the **TsUM** (pronounced "tsoom") department store (Mon–Sat 10am–10pm, Sun 11am–10pm), sandwiched between the Maly Theatre and ulitsa Petrovka. Built as Moscow's first modern store in 1908 by the Scottish trading firm Muir & Mirrielees, its spiky neo-Gothic exterior conceals the pioneering use of reinforced concrete and curtain walls; it was also the first building in Russia to be fitted with lifts. Chekhov bought his writing paper here and named his dogs Muir and Mirrielees. During Soviet times it became a downmarket version of GUM, frequented by black-market traders in women's wear, who had their own "changing rooms" in a ladies' toilet behind the store, on the corner of ulitsa Kuznetskiy most.

Ulitsa Kuznetskiy most

As a connoisseur of bookshops, cafés and scandal, Mayakovsky wrote: "I love Kuznetskiy most … and then Petrovka" – two streets whose buzz is definitely back. **Ulitsa Kuznetskiy most** is where the aristocracy used to take their afternoon promenade and browse in shops selling everything from Fabergé bracelets to English woollens. Tolstoy listened to an early phonograph in what used to be the music shop at no. 12, and wrote of Anna Karenina shopping in Gautier's at no. 20.

Today, the street still meanders picturesquely over hills and across thoroughfares, past arresting buildings like the crested Style Moderne structure on the corner of Neglinnaya ulitsa. The banks are back in force and the **bookshops** (see p.379) are as busy as ever, while cybercafés and ethnic **eateries** (p.348) are mushrooming. Seedier commerce in CDs, liquor and peepshows flourishes in the arcades between Kuznetskiy Most metro and ulitsa Rozhdestvenka, where the infamous club formerly known as the *Hungry Duck* is located (see p.360).

Ulitsa Petrovka

Long before the Bolshoy was built, **ulitsa Petrovka** was one of the most aristocratic streets in Moscow, as the boyars emulated Grand Duke Vasily III, who built a palace with grounds extending between today's Boulevard and Garden Rings. It was also a major thoroughfare leading to the St Peter's Gate in the city's walls, which was protected by a fortified monastery.

Gradually, the aristocracy moved out and merchants took over – a process culminating with the opening in 1903 of the **Petrovskiy Passazh** (Mon–Sat 10am–8pm, Sun 11am–6pm), an elegant twin-arcaded mall along the lines of GUM. Restored by Turkish contractors in the early 1990s, it set a benchmark for retailing in Moscow that later rivals have tried to surpass. The figure of the heroic proletarian outside the Petrovka entrance is a rare surviving example of the "Monumental Propaganda" decreed by Lenin in 1920. In Ilf and Petrov's satire *The Twelve Chairs*, it was in the Passazh that most of the said objects were auctioned off to buyers unaware of the diamonds secreted within them.

The Upper Monastery of St Peter

From the Passazh, you can walk 600m uphill to the **Upper Monastery of St Peter** (Vysoko-Petrovskiy monastyr; daily 9am–8pm; free). Enclosed by a high red-brick wall whose blank lower half contrasts with the ornately framed windows above, the fortified complex is a superb example of late Moscow Baroque architecture – a style promoted by the Naryshkin relatives of Peter the Great who financed its reconstruction in the 1680s.

Passing through the gateway of its Baroque **bell tower**, you'll see the multi-domed **Church of the Icon of the Virgin of Bogolyubovo** (tserkov Bogolyubskoy Bogomateri), commemorating three of Peter's uncles killed in the 1682 Streltsy revolt, who are buried in its vaults. Other Naryshkins lie beneath the low stone building alongside, beyond which stands the single-domed **Church of Metropolitan Peter** (tserkov Petra-Mitropolita), which Peter's mother Natalya founded to celebrate their defeat of the Regent Sofia in 1689. The ensemble is completed by a large red-and-white **Refectory Church** with five green cupolas on tall drums, linked by a shadowy arcade to the **Naryshkin Palace** inside the outer walls. In Soviet times the palace was turned into a workers' hostel and a factory, and many rooms are still occupied by workshops. Since being returned to the Church, the complex now houses the Moscow Patriarchate's Seminary administration, and is being restored by volunteers.

The Museum of Modern Art

Across the road from the monastery in a converted eighteenth-century merchant's house, the **Moscow Museum of Modern Art** (Moskovskiy muzey Sovremenovo iskusstva; daily noon–8pm; closed last Mon of month; R200, photo permit R150, video permit R300) is the only venture by Luzhkov and Tsereteli that's been welcomed by all. Although the sculptures in the yard veer towards kitsch, what's on show indoors is a stimulating mix of avant-garde art up to 1917, and the end of Soviet power, when "underground" art flourished ever more openly.

Among those at art school in the 1980s were the Marilyn Monroe-impersonator Vlad Mamyshev-Monroe, and Alexander Kosalapov, whose take on Warhol's soup cans, *Blue Caviar*, is an ironic salute to the pop culture that conquered the USSR without a shot being fired. Tsereteli was, by this time, a successful Soviet artist, whose faux naïve graphics and tapestries (in the corridor and on the stairs) show far more talent than his later sculptures do. Other names on the "underground" scene are represented on the third floor, where 1970s Mytki Primitivists are juxtaposed with contemporary artists like Olga Tobreluts and Andrei Zhelanov, next door to a series of rooms used for temporary exhibitions, often devoted to individual retrospectives.

But the real draw is the second floor, with its Primitivist and Futurist works by Goncharova (*Cyclist* and *Bathing Boys*), Filonev (*Composition with 11 Heads*), Tatlin (*Portrait of a Worker*), Popova and Lentulov; sumptuous set designs and an Odalisque's costume from the Ballet Russes and other masterpieces from the World of Art movement; and lithographs by Chagall. Foreign Surrealists are also featured, with prints by Léger, de Chirico and Ernst, and bronzes by Dalí.

If you feel like a stroll afterwards, it's not far to the Boulevard Ring junction named **ploshchad Petrovskiy vorota**, after the St Peter's Gate that stood here in medieval times, by a market called the Skorodom ("quick house"), specializing in everything needed to assemble a house within two or three days. Business thrived, thanks to the fires that regularly gutted whole districts of Moscow; citizens preferred their traditional wooden houses to European-style stone dwellings, which were colder and damper in winter. Today, there's nothing much to see but an ugly **statue of Vysotsky**, which does no justice to the memory of the beloved bard (see p.248).

Neglinka and Rozhdestvenka ulitsa

Neglinka is the popular diminutive for the Neglina River that once flowed into the heart of Moscow, encircling the Kremlin and the Kitay-gorod; *neglina* means "without clay". In Catherine the Great's time the river was channelled into a pipe running underneath what is now Neglinnaya ulitsa, but continued to flood due to infrequent cleaning and the locals' habit of dumping rubbish – and victims of robberies – into the storm drains. Today, this hilly area is only hazardous for its icy slopes in winter, and otherwise invites a wander ending at the Convent of the Nativity near the Boulevard Ring. As you ascend the hill, banks and sushi bars gradually give way to small shops, such as characterized the area during Soviet times.

The Sandunovskiy Baths

One establishment spanning the pre- and post-Communist eras with ease is the **Sandunovskiy Baths** (Sandunovskie bani), two blocks north of Kuznetskiy. Traditionally favoured by merchants, and writers like Tolstoy and Chekhov, the baths grew shabby during Soviet times but were fully refurbished for the centenary of their inauguration (in 1896). You first notice a grandiose Beaux Arts facade, whose great arch fronts a courtyard modelled on the Moorish Alhambra Palace in Andalucía, which originally formed the main entrance but is now off limits. The baths occupy a pale-lime, colonnaded building in a lane behind it, and are entered by an alley with separate doors for either sex, leading to foyers rich in majolica. While most punters opt for the "first-class" *banya* on the floor above, wealthy Muscovites patronize the "luxe" ones on the top floor, with their vaulted pool and private rooms, stained-glass windows and mahogany benches. See Chapter 17, "Sports", for bathing details.

Up ulitsa Rozhdestvenka to the Convent of the Nativity

Running parallel to Neglinnaya ulitsa along what was once a high riverbank, a steeper road, **ulitsa Rozhdestvenka**, ascends to the Convent of the Nativity from which it takes its name. At the lower end of the street is the **Savoy Hotel**, whose Style Moderne and Baroque interior rivals the *Metropol*'s for splendour, where the French socialist Henri Barbusse stayed while writing his sycophantic biography of Stalin.

Further uphill, students gather outside the blue-and-yellow Beaux Arts facade of the **Architectural Institute** at no. 9, followed by the seventeenth-century **Church of St Nicholas of the Bellringers** (tserkov Svyatitelya Nikolaya v Zvonaryakh), whose name refers to the street's old settlement of bellringers from the Ivan the Great Belltower in the Kremlin. In medieval Russia, holy days were celebrated by ringing all the bells of Moscow's "forty times forty" churches in unison, until "the earth shook with their vibrations like thunder".

At the end of Rozhdestvenka a gilt-spired Baroque belltower proclaims the **Convent of the Nativity** (Rozhdestvenskiy monastyr; daily 8am–8pm; free), which otherwise retires behind a wall. Duck in through the arch to find a complex of nuns' cells surrounding the sixteenth-century **Cathedral of the Nativity** and the eighteenth-century **Church of St John Chrysostom**. In medieval times, the convent had a dual role as a perimeter fortress, as a corner turret and brick ramparts along Rozhdestvenskiy bulvar attest.

Lubyanka and around

The name Lubyanka resounds like a gunshot at the far end of a darkened corridor – the traditional method of killing prisoners in the **headquarters of the secret police** on Lubyanka Square. For Russians, the building represents a historically malevolent force that's best ignored whenever possible, whereas foreigners can afford to be curious and genuinely blasé – in the old days it was

▲ The Lubyanka

almost a sport to bait Intourist guides with awkward questions whenever KGB HQ came into sight at the top of the long rise from Okhotniy ryad. The secret police are still ensconced here – though nowadays called the FSB.

While it's common knowledge that the building is named after its location on **Lubyanskaya ploshchad**, few Muscovites know that Catherine the Great's secret police had its headquarters on the same spot – its memory having been effaced in the nineteenth century, when the square was surrounded by stables and dens for the refreshment of coachmen, until the 1890s, when insurance companies transformed the neighbourhood with residential and office buildings. Expropriated after the Revolution, these formed the nucleus of a 1930s redevelopment plan that included the demolition of the Kitay-gorod's Vladimir Gate.

Today, you're struck by the grotesque decision to construct in 1957 Moscow's largest toy shop just across the square from the Lubyanka – supposedly as a tribute to the founder of the Soviet secret police, who also chaired a commission on children's welfare. Located on the site of the medieval cannon foundry where the giant Tsar Cannon in the Kremlin was cast, the **Detskiy Mir** (Children's World; Mon–Sat 9am–9pm, Sun 10am–9pm; Dec open daily til 11pm) now sells everything from Barbie and Lego to lingerie, and has an internet café on the fourth floor.

The Lubyanka

The Lubyanka rises in sandstone tiers from a granite-faced lower storey emblazoned with Soviet crests. Built as the head office of the Rossiya Insurance Company in 1897, it was taken over by the Bolshevik Cheka in March 1918, only months before the repression of the Anarchists and Left SRs. In Stalin's time, generations entered its maw via the infamous Lubyanka "kennel", a whitewashed cellar used for body searches. Such was the volume of arrests that the versatile Shchusev was commissioned to design an extension that doubled its size by 1947. Even so, its bureaucracy engulfed neighbouring buildings as the security service burgeoned through successive name changes, into the KGB of Cold War notoriety. Under Yeltsin, the KGB was divided into two agencies: the **Federal Security Service** (FSB) that monitors the home front, and the **External Intelligence Service** (SVR), which is now based in a modern block at Yasenevo, beyond the Moscow Ring Road.

Both the FSB and SVR have greatly improved their image in recent years, thanks to Russians' fear of terrorism and organized crime, and their suspicion of Western meddling. While catching CIA and MI6 agents makes for good publicity, the FSB's strongest card has been the threat of **Chechen terrorism**. Even before becoming president, Putin vowed to strengthen the FSB, whose boss he had been from 1998 to 1999, having spent sixteen years in its Soviet predecessor. Since then, it has regained control of the Border Guards and the bugging agency, FAPSI (which Yeltsin made separate entities), and ex-KGB officials have been installed at the highest levels of government throughout the Russian Federation, to form the backbone of Putin's "vertical" (see p.437).

For several decades, a six-metre-tall statue of "Iron Felix" **Dzerzhinsky**, the Cheka's founder, loomed from its massive pedestal on the grassy knoll in the middle of Lubyanskaya ploshchad. The night after the collapse of the 1991 putsch, crowds cheered as the statue was toppled by a crane, its head in a wire noose, a symbol of the end of Soviet Communism. It's a sign of how far Russia has travelled since then that the Duma recently debated (but rejected) a motion to replace Dzerzhinsky's statue there. (It remains in the sculpture park behind the New Tretyakov Gallery.) However, the organization that he created is still going strong, as you can see from the hordes of people that leave its headquarters at 5pm. The FSB is actually based in the sinister-looking dark grey 1980s block to the west of the "old" Lubyanka (which now houses the Border Police); their computer centre is above the Mayakovsky Museum (see below), and their social club and private museum are beside a supermarket on Bolshaya Lubyanka ulitsa.

Behind the Lubyanka

The **Tsentralniy** supermarket, behind the Lubyanka, was created as a food store for the secret police and opened to ordinary citizens after the war. Like several former flagship stores, its counters where citizens queued to buy fish or butter have now been replaced by self-service aisles crammed with imported goods, and the original High Stalinist decor of marble, friezes and chandeliers largely sacrificed to the imperatives of commerce.

Just uphill past the entrance to Lubyanka 12, a fence topped by urns preserves the privacy of the crumbling **Rostopchin mansion**, a longtime haunt of the secret police whose exterior matches the colour of the epaulettes worn by the KGB. It once belonged to Count Rostopchin, the governor who ordered Moscow to be burned in 1812, and escaped from a mob besieging his home by throwing them an alleged traitor. During the first night of the French occupation, Rostopchin's agents set fire to wine stalls in the Kitay-gorod and the carriage-workshops on Karetniy ryad. By the next morning, a powerful wind had fanned the flames and the fire had spread to engulf half of Moscow – ironically, Lubyanka was one of the few quarters to survive, owing to vigorous firefighting by its residents.

From the Rostopchin mansion, Bolshaya Lubyanka runs 500m uphill to the Boulevard Ring, where the small white **Church of the Icon of Our Lady of Vladimir** nestles in a leafy walled compound. This was once the fortified Sretenskiy Monastery, erected on the spot where Muscovites had welcomed the arrival of a miraculous icon of the Virgin in 1395 (see p.214). Suppressed in Soviet times, the monastery has now been revived; its brethren live in the pistachio-and-white buildings at the rear of the compound.

The only inducement to walk along **Sretenskiy bulvar** is the **statue of Nadezhda Krupskaya** (1869–1939), Lenin's wife. The lithe, gamine figure bears little resemblance to the real dumpy, fish-eyed Krupskaya – just like the hagiographies that failed to mention Lenin's infidelity before the Revolution. When Krupskaya protested against the death sentence on Kamenev in 1934, Stalin warned her, "The Party can always find another widow for Comrade Lenin" – and even had a substitute lined up. During the 1930s, the boulevard was a gay cruising ground.

The Mayakovsky Museum

Across the road to the east of the Lubyanka, a granite head gazing from a portal at Myasnitskaya ulitsa 3–6 betrays the **Mayakovsky Museum** (muzey V.V. Mayakovskovo; Ⓦ www.museum.ru/Majakovskiy; Mon, Tues & Fri–Sun 10am–7pm, Thurs 1–8pm; closed last Fri of each month; R90). Vladimir Mayakovsky (1893–1930) was an enthusiastic supporter of the Bolsheviks from an early age, who got into Futurism at the Moscow School for Painting and Sculpture after meeting the Burlyuk brothers. Together they published a manifesto called *A Slap in the Face for Public Taste* and embarked on a publicity tour, Mayakovsky wearing earrings and a waistcoat with radishes in the buttonholes. In 1917 he threw himself into the October Revolution, founding the Left Front of Art with Alexander Rodchenko and Osip Brik, and producing more than six hundred giant cartoon advertisements with pithy verse captions for the Russia Telegraph Agency. Mayakovsky's suicide at the age of 37 has been variously ascribed to despair over his love for Osip's wife, Lili, to disillusionment with Soviet life and its censors, or to hostile reviews of his last exhibition. Thousands filed past his open coffin at the Writers' Union, and Stalin would later decree that "Mayakovsky was and remains the most talented poet of our Soviet epoch. Indifference to his memory and to his work is a crime."

Opened in 1990, and run by the poet's granddaughter, the Mayakovsky Museum is quite unlike other memorial museums in the ex-residences of writers or artists, with their period decor and display cases. Rather, it feels like walking around inside Mayakovsky's head during a brainstorm. Melting chairs and Constructivist vortices breathe life into editions of his poetry and agitprop posters, mixed in with personal effects and symbolic *objets* – viewed as you ascend a spiral ramp towards the upper floor. Although nothing remains of the original flat, it was here that Mayakovsky lived from 1919 onwards, and ultimately committed suicide with a stage prop revolver, leaving an unfinished poem beside him.

Towards Chistye prudy

The section of the Boulevard Ring known as **Chistye prudy** is notable for several architectural curiosities, mostly within five-minutes' walk of Chistye Prudy or Turgenevskaya metro stations. Another approach is to walk up **Myasnitskaya ulitsa** (Butchers' St), where at no. 19, on the left, the **Perlov Tea House** (Mon–Fri 8am–1.30pm & 2–8pm, Sat 9am–6pm) has a facade crawling with bronze dragons and pagoda-like flourishes, matched inside by lacquered columns and Chinese vases. Legend has it that the shop was decorated in this fashion by the wealthy tea merchant Perlov, who desired to impress the young emperor of China during his visit to Russia in 1893. Sadly for Perlov, the emperor chose to visit a rival tea merchant instead. There's a wonderful aroma of tea and coffee inside.

The pale-peach-and-white building next door played an important role in Russian art after the Moscow School of Painting and Sculpture was established here in 1844. By 1872, when it hosted the first major exhibition of the Wanderers movement, the Moscow School had begun to outshine the Academy of Arts in St Petersburg; four decades later, it was at the forefront of the avant-garde. The teaching staff included Leonid Pasternak, whose son Boris – the future author of *Doctor Zhivago* – spent his childhood in a nearby annexe. In 1920, it was transformed into the Higher Technical-Artistic Workshop or VKhuTeMas, the short-lived Soviet equivalent of the Bauhaus, whose radical Futurism dismayed Lenin.

Apart from the Tea House, the best sights are located along or just off Chistoprudniy bulvar, round the corner from the **Main Post Office** (Glavpochtamt). The boulevard and the locality are named after the pond at the far end, which was used for the disposal of butchers' waste until 1703, when it was mucked out on the orders of Prince Menshikov and henceforth known as Chistye prudy (Clean Ponds). Given Menshikov's notorious corruption, it seems fitting that the far side of the boulevard is now dominated by the beige and smoked-glass **headquarters of LUKoil**, the scandal-prone oil company created during the privatization binge of the 1990s. At the entrance to the park that runs along the boulevard stands a **statue of Alexander Griboedov**, an army officer turned playwright and diplomat who was murdered by a mob in Teheran in 1829. The pedestal is decorated with reliefs of characters from his celebrated drama, *Woe from Wit*.

Menshikov's Tower

In the early eighteenth century, this part of Moscow belonged to **Prince Menshikov** (1673–1729), who rose from being a humble pie-seller to fortune and power, owing to Peter the Great's appreciation of his ruthless ability and artful blend of "servility, familiarity and impertinence". Menshikov understood Peter's impatience with Muscovite conservatism and the Orthodox Church, and surpassed the tsar in ostentatious gestures. Accordingly, he commissioned Ivan Zarudny to build (1705–07) an outstanding edifice that incorporated secular Western forms into Orthodox architecture – the salmon-pink **Church of the Archangel Gabriel** (tserkov Arkhangela Gavriila).

Popularly known as **Menshikov's Tower** (Menshikova bashnya), this boasted a wooden-spired belfry holding fifty bells and crowned by a gilded statue of the Archangel, 3m higher than the Ivan the Great Belltower in the Kremlin – hitherto the tallest building in all Russia. His hubris was punished in 1723, when lightning set the spire ablaze. Since Menshikov was then living at Oranienbaum, and shortly had to fight for survival following Peter's death, no rebuilding took place until 1766–80, when the Freemason Izmaylov devised a belfry with only two of the three original octagonal tiers and a gilded coronet instead of a spire. However, many features of Zarudny's design remain, such as the Bible-clutching seraphim that flit across the salmon-pink facade, and the massive buttresses scrolling upwards beside the door on the left-hand side. The **interior** looks more Catholic than Orthodox, its frescoes offset by swags and cherubs – but Izmaylov's Masonic symbols were removed after the Freemasons were banished from the church in 1863. The tower is set back from the street directly behind the lower Neoclassical **Church of St Theodor Stratilites** (tserkov Fyodora Stratilata).

By turning right after both churches, you'll find yourself in **Krivokolenniy pereulok** (Double Knee-Bend Lane), so-called because it has two sharp bends instead of one. Its cute name aside, this is a nice, quiet way into the Ukrainian quarter, coming out on Armyanskiy pereulok (see p.144). There are several attractive Style Moderne buildings along the way.

Along the Ring to the Apraksin Mansion

Alternatively, you can return to the Boulevard Ring and carry on to the limpid pond that gives Chistye prudy its name. On the far side stands the **Sovremennik Theatre**, occupying a former cinema with an elegant, rounded portico flanked by bas-reliefs of Greek deities. Further along at no. 23 is a florid sky-blue apartment building where the film director Sergei Eisenstein lived from 1920 to 1934. On the near side of the boulevard, don't miss the **Figurniy dom** (Figured House) at no. 14, built by Sergei Vashkov at the beginning of the last century, whose frontage crawls with a bestiary of supernatural creatures.

While in the area, it's worth a short detour beyond the Ring to see the former **Apraksin Mansion** near the corner of ulitsa Pokrovka. Erected in the 1760s, overlooking the Pokrovka Gate and the road leading to the royal palaces in the old foreigners' quarter, the mansion was Moscow's ultimate in decorative Baroque: a rambling mass of bay windows and scalloped niches, clusters of angels and Corinthian pilasters, modelled on the Winter Palace in St Petersburg. The archway into its courtyard is lined with plaques listing technical journals based at the premises – a legacy of the Industrial Academy for "Red managers" that existed here after the Revolution. Its students included Stalin's wife Nadezhda Allilueva, and Nikita Khrushchev, who was the school's Party secretary.

The Ukrainian quarter

The erstwhile **Ukrainian quarter** to the east of the Kitay-gorod no longer has a distinct ethnic flavour, but its hilly, winding lanes are a reminder of the time when Moscow's residential quarters consisted of "quiet lanes where wooden gates open into courtyards planted with lilacs, acacias and senna". In late medieval times this area was prosperous and cosmopolitan, for scores of Westerners chose to settle here after Tsar Mikhail Romanov allowed non-Orthodox believers to live where they pleased. But as income for local Orthodox churches declined, protests impelled the tsar to order the demolition of their chapels and a ban on further settlers; his successor, Alexei, later banished them to a colony beyond the city walls. Ukrainians began moving in after the Russo-Polish war of 1654–67 left Ukraine under Russian control, followed by other races as the empire grew. Today, embassies and diverse places of worship maintain something of this tradition, but the area's real charm lies in its meandering backstreets and odd juxtapositions of medieval, nineteenth-century and Soviet architecture. The nearest metro stations are Kitay-gorod and Chistye Prudy.

Along Maroseyka and Pokrovka

Running from the edge of the Kitay-gorod through the heart of the quarter, **ulitsa Maroseyka** takes its name from *Malorosseyka* or "Little Russia", the old Tsarist title for Ukraine, which came under the jurisdiction of the Little Russian Office. During Soviet times, the street was named after Bogdan Khmelnitskiy, the Cossack Hetman who transferred control of Ukraine from Poland to Russia in 1653. Nowadays far too narrow for its heavy traffic, Maroseyka is shabby and congested, but redeems itself with some fine old buildings and picturesque lanes before becoming ulitsa Pokrovka, nearer the Boulevard Ring.

Starting from the vicinity of Staraya ploshchad, the first sight is the small salmon-pink **Church of St Nicholas the Wonder-worker** (tserkov Nikolay Chudotvortsa), characterized by chunky *nalichniki*, green roofs and a cobalt onion dome. The church dates from 1687, its belltower from 1748. Further on at no. 17 stands a sky-blue mansion dripping with caryatids. Originally the Little Russian Office, it now contains the **Belarus Embassy**, which maintains a hotel for visiting dignitaries around the corner. Across the main road is the sage-green **Church of SS Cosmas and Damian** (tserkov Kosmy i Damiana), built by Kazakov in 1791–1803, which is unique among Moscow churches for its central cylinder, topped by a gilt-knobbed cupola and abutted by several rounded chapels.

Beyond the church, the road becomes Ulitsa Pokrovka, home to the **Museum of Unique Dolls** (muzey redkikh kukol; Tues–Sun 10am–2pm & 2.30–6pm; free), at 13-2. Opened in 1996, it displays some 250 dolls from the private collection of Yulia Vishnevskaya, manufactured in Russia, France, England and Germany between the 1830s and the 1950s. The rarest is one made by the pre-Revolutionary Russian firm Zhuravlov & Kocheshkov, whose dolls were banned by the Commissariat of Enlightenment for being "excessively bourgeois". Bonnets, frills and big hair are certainly ubiquitous, but there are also such exceptions as a "granny doll" doing her knitting, as well as model locomotives and clockwork cars. Some captions are in English, and it's possible to arrange a **guided tour** in English (☎625 75 12; free).

Armenians' Lane

Back at the junction of ulitsas Maroseyka and Pokrovka, around the corner from the Belarus embassy, lies the original heart of the foreign quarter, **Armyanskiy pereulok** (Armenians' Lane), whose security was half-assured by the fact that Artamon Matveev, Tsar Alexei's foreign minister, lived here with his Scottish wife, Mary Hamilton, surrounded by mirrors, clocks and paintings that attested to his fascination with European ways. Although this didn't stop Alexei from evicting all the foreigners in 1652, it was here that he later met his second wife, Natalya Naryshkina – the upshot being a child who upset the dynastic ambitions of the **Miloslavsky boyars**, whose intrigues against Matveev and Natalya led to the Streltsy revolt of 1682. The rival families lived directly opposite each other: Matveev where the Belarus Embassy stands today; the Miloslavskys in a pale-grey house that still exists (albeit much remodelled) around the corner. During the late nineteenth century this was inhabited by the Slavophile poet **Fyodor Tyutchev**, who famously wrote that you cannot understand Russia, only believe in her.

At the far end of the lane, the **Armenian Embassy** occupies a pale yellow mansion (no. 2) that retires behind an elegant portico and wrought-iron gates, which was formerly the Lazarev Institute for Oriental Languages, established by a wealthy Armenian family. Armenians have lived here since the time of the Miloslavskys, who also owned a house across the road at no. 3. Unlike their other place, this looks more of its time, having low brick vaulted rooms at several levels, and is now given over to a **Moscow Lights Museum** (Moskovskiy muzey sveta; Mon–Fri 9am–5pm; free), covering the history of illuminating the city. If antique gas lamps don't get you going, there are switchboards from the metro and an album of photos showing Moscow ablaze with neon and fireworks at the victory celebrations in 1945. The museum is now sponsored by the energy monopoly, UES, whose chief executive, Chubais, masterminded the privatization of state assets in the 1990s.

To the Ivanovskiy Convent and the Choral Synagogue

By turning off ulitsa Maroseyka beside SS Cosmas and Damian, you can follow **Starosadskiy pereulok** (Old Garden Lane) downhill past a neo-Gothic **Lutheran Church** (used as a recording studio in Soviet times) to the **Church of St Vladimir in the Old Garden** (tserkov Vladimira v Starykh sadakh). The only surviving example of the dozen or so stone parish churches built for Grand Duke Vasily III by the Italian Alevisio Novi (creator of the Archangel Cathedral in the Kremlin), it was truncated in the 1680s and thereafter nicknamed "domeless" (*bez glavy*) – though it actually has six small domes, resting on drums carved with anthropomorphic figures.

Across the slope looms the high-walled **Ivanovskiy Convent** (Ivanovskiy monastyr), whose fanged belltowers and scabrous cupolas reflect its sinister history. Founded in the sixteenth century, it was used as a dumping ground for unwanted wives and daughters and as a prison for noblewomen guilty of heinous crimes or vaguely defined political offences. Among those detained in the reign of Catherine the Great were the notorious Countess Dariya Saltykova – confined for thirty years in an underground cell for murdering 139 of her serfs – and the tragic Princess Tarakanova, who fell foul of the empress (see box, p.254). In Soviet times the convent was disbanded and the complex turned into a police training school, onto which a modern block was grafted. Now back in Orthodox hands, it has been restored as a working convent, which isn't open to outsiders.

The Choral Synagogue

From the convent, ulitsa Zabelina slopes down to the Kitay-gorod, off which a steep, narrow lane called Spasoglinishchevskiy pereulok harbours Moscow's **Choral Synagogue** (Khoralnaya sinagoga; Mon–Fri 10am–6pm; free). Its location – just behind, but not visible from, a major thoroughfare – reflects the ambivalent status of Moscow's Jewish community when the synagogue was built in 1886 (financed by a railway tycoon, Polyakov). Only five years earlier, 20,000 Jews had been expelled to the Pale in the wave of reaction that followed the assassination of their emancipator, Alexander II. Yet the regime needed their skills and officials desired bribes, so Jews soon re-established themselves in the capital. By bribing Moscow's Governor, the community was later able to erect a Star of David above its synagogue, which could be seen over the rooftops – as Nicholas II was startled to notice as he drove by during his coronation in 1896.

The building's exterior is quite austere and gone to pot, but its interior is a lovely example of the Moorish style of synagogues across Eastern Europe, swirling with arabesque mouldings and murals, recently restored with funds from the city. Its rabbi is reportedly disgusted that none of the oligarchs who've attended the synagogue has ever donated anything, and Moscow's Orthodox Rabbinate resents the wealthier Lubavitch sect for trying to lure away its congregation (see pp.188–189). Ironically, the "Choral" designation of the Orthodox synagogue refers to the fact that it incorporates several shrines, for the use of Armenian, Georgian or Bukharan Jews visiting Moscow, allowing "many voices to sing in unison".

Tourists are welcome during visiting hours providing they're properly attired, but anyone attending **services** (Mon–Fri 8.30am, Sat & holidays at 9am; evening services after sunset) is expected to know the ropes and behave accordingly.

Down towards the Yauza River

If you're still keen on exploring, try the lane running uphill to the east of St Vladimir's Church, whose name, **Khokhlovskiy pereulok**, comes from *khokhli*, an old Russian nickname for Ukrainians, derived from their traditional hairdos (*khokhol* means "tuft" or "crest").

At the triple fork beyond the first bend you'll see a terraced garden, overlooked by a turquoise mansion whose ornamental neo-Russian archway invites a closer look. The **Morozov House** once belonged to Maria Morozova, a fervent Old Believer who inherited her husband's textile empire and ran it regardless of her sons, leaving them to patronize the arts. While Savva bankrolled the Moscow Art Theatre and resided elsewhere, Sergei lived here with his mother and her ban on baths and electricity. However, he did sponsor a museum, took up art himself and built a studio in the garden, which he later gave as a sanctuary to the painter Isaak Levitan, who would otherwise have been included in the mass expulsion of Jews from Moscow in 1881. After the Revolution the Morozovs fled and the house was seized by Left SRs, who transformed it into a fortress. During their abortive "Bolshoy coup" of July 6, 1918, they held Dzerzhinsky a prisoner here until he was freed by Latvian sharpshooters. It now serves as a playschool.

On a parallel side street stands the **Church of the Trinity in Kulishki** (tserkov Trekh Svyatiteley na Kulishkakh), whose deep undercroft supports a nest of chapels and shingled domes, their ogee-gables picked out in red. Finished in 1674, this multi-level structure once contained an upper "summer" church, and a smaller, warmer one for winter worship, below – a functional division common in those times. Turned into an NKVD prison in the 1930s and more recently used as offices, it is now again a place of worship.

From here there's a choice of routes down to **Podkolokolniy pereulok** (Under the Bells Lane), which slopes gently uphill from ulitsa Solyanka to the Boulevard Ring. Khitrovskiy pereulok, running off behind the Church of the Trinity, gets its name from the infamous Khitrov Market that once existed in the vicinity, while Podkpaevskiy pereulok lends its name to the **Church of St Nicholas in Podkopaev** (tserkov Nikoly v Podkopae), which blithely defies the rules of Classical harmony by juxtaposing a tiny church with a bulbous dome and a chunky freestanding belfry.

Across the main road from St Nicholas, the first turning to the east (Petropavlovskiy pereulok) will lead you to the **Church of Peter and Paul on the Yauza** (tserkov Petra i Pavla chto na Yauze). Erected on a hill near one of the city gates in 1700, this once enjoyed a lovely view across the river to the churches of Zayauze, extending upstream as far as the Andronikov Monastery. Though its view has been curtailed by high-rise apartments, the church remains peacefully aloof from the city, its visual appeal enhanced by a deep red paint job, against which its crested *nalichniki* and golden domes stand proud.

One final church worth seeing rises just beyond the Boulevard Ring near ploshchad Yauzkie vorota, where the gate once stood. The **Church of the Trinity in Serebryaniki** (tserkov Troitsy v Serebryanikakh) takes its name from the quarter of silversmiths (*serebryanki*) that existed here when Karl Blank built the church in 1781. Its lofty freestanding belfry of three tiers buttressed by Corinthian pilasters and jutting pediments is a local landmark, painted a bright cerulean blue; the refectory and chapel are secluded behind it. At this point, you might be drawn across the Yauza by the looming mass of the Stalin-Gothic Kotelnicheskaya Apartments, described on p.250.

Streets and squares

Arbatskaya ploshchad	Арбатская площадь
Armyanskiy pereulok	Армянский переулок
Bolshaya Nikitskaya ulitsa	Большая Никитская улица
Bolshoy Spasoglinishchevskiy	Больой Спасоглищевский переулок
pereulok Chistoprudiy bulvar	Чистопрудный бульвар
Georgievskiy pereulok	Георгиевский переулок
Gogolevskiy bulvar	Гоголевский бульвар
Kamergerskiy pereulok	Камергерский переулок
Khokhlovskiy pereulok	Хохловский переулок
Krivokolenniy pereulok	Кривоколенный переулок
Lubyanskaya ploshchad	Лубянская площадь
Manezhnaya ploshchad	Манежная площадь
Mokhovaya ulitsa	Моховая улица
Myasnitskaya ulitsa	Мясницкая улица
Neglinnaya ulitsa	Неглинная улица
Nikitskiy bulvar	Никитский бульвар
Nikitskie vorota ploshchad	Никитские ворота площадь
Petrovskiy vorota ploshchad	Петровские ворота площадь
Podkolokolniy pereulok	Подколокольный переулок

Streets and squares	
Pokrovskiy bulvar	Покровский бульвар
Pushkinskaya ploshchad	Пушкинская площадь
Rozhdestvenskiy bulvar	Рождественский бульвар
Serebryanicheskiy pereulok	Серебрянический переулок
Starosadskiy pereulok	Старосадский переулок
Stoleshnikov pereulok	Столешников переулок
Tverskaya ploshchad	Тверская площадь
Tverskaya ulitsa	Тверская улица
Tverskoy bulvar	Тверской бульвар
Teatralnaya ploshchad	Театральная площадь
ulitsa Bolshaya Lubyanka	улица Большая Лубянка
ulitsa Malaya Lubyanka	улица Малая Лубянка
ulitsa Kuznetskiy most	улица Кузнецкий мост
ulitsa Maroseyka	улица Маросейка
ulitsa Petrovka	улица Петровка
ulitsa Pokrovka	улица Покровка
ulitsa Rozhdestvenka	улица Рождественка
ulitsa Vozdvizhenka	улица Воздвиженка
ulitsa Zabelina	улица Забелина
ulitsa Znamenka	улица Знаменка
Metro stations	
Arbatskaya	Арбатская
Biblioteka imeni Lenina	Библиотека имени Ленина
Borovitskaya	Боровицкая
Chekhovskaya	Чеховская
Chistye Prudy	Чистые пруды
Kropotkinskaya	Кропоткинская
Lubyanka	Лубянка
Okhotniy Ryad	Охотный ряд
Ploshchad Revolyutsii	Площадь Революции
Pushkinskaya	Пушкинская
Teatralnaya	Театральная
Turgenvskaya	Тургеневская
Tverskaya	Тверская
Museums	
Gogol Memorial Room	музей-квартира Н.В. Гоголя
Ilya Glazunov Picture Gallery	Картинния галерея Ильи Глазунова
Mayakovsky Museum	музей В.В. Маяковского
Meyerhold Flat-Museum	музей-квартира В.И. Мейерхольда
Moscow Lights Museum	Московский музей свтеа
Museum of Books	музей Книги
Museum of Folk Art	музей Народново искусства
Museum of Private Collections	музей Личных Коллекций
Museum of Unique Dolls	музей редких кукол
Nemirovich-Danchenko Museum	музей-квартира Немировичф-Данченка
Nikolai Ostrovskiy Museum	музей-квартира Николя Островского
Oriental Museum	музей Востока
Pushkin Museum of Fine Art	музей изобразительных искусств им. А.С. Пушкина
Shchusev Architectural Museum	музей архитектуры им. А.В. Щусева
Stanislavsky House-Museum	дом-музей К.С. Станиславского
Yermolova House-Museum	дом-музей М.Н. Ермоловой
Zoological Museum	Зоологический музей

The Zemlyanoy Gorod

In medieval times, the white-walled Beliy Gorod was encircled by a humbler **Zemlyanoy Gorod**, or "Earth Town", ringed by an earthen rampart 15km in diameter. Its wooden houses and muddy lanes proved impervious to change until its total destruction in the fire of 1812. Reconstruction presented an ideal opportunity for gentrification, as former artisans' quarters were colonized by the nobility and the old ramparts were levelled to form a ring of boulevards, where anyone building a house was obliged to plant trees – the origin of the **Garden Ring** (Sadovoe koltso) that marked the division between the bourgeois centre and the proletarian suburbs.

Although Moscow's growth eroded this distinction and the Revolution turned it inside out, the area's cachet endured. Its roll call of famous residents includes Pushkin, Lermontov, Chekhov, Gorky and Bulgakov, all of whom are associated with certain neighbourhoods – in particular, Bulgakov and the **Patriarch's Ponds**. Besides its **literary associations**, this is one of the best-looking parts of Moscow, with Empire and Art Nouveau **mansions** on every corner of the backstreets off the **Arbat**. This quarter has inspired poet-musicians like Bulat Okudzhava, giving rise to a vibrant **street life** that was unique in Moscow during the 1980s and is still more tourist-friendly than anything else currently on offer.

The modern Garden Ring is a Stalinist creation whose name has been a misnomer since all the trees were felled when it was widened to an eight-lane motorway in the 1930s (said to have been envisaged as an aircraft runway in wartime). Vast avenues, flanked by leviathan blocks and the **Stalin-Gothic skyscrapers** whose pinnacles and spires dominate Moscow's skyline, exude power and indifference. In 1944, hordes of German POWs were herded along the Ring en route to Siberia; some Muscovites jeered, others threw them bread. The Ring witnessed barricades and bloodshed during the crises of 1991 and 1993 – but under normal circumstances, traffic is the only real hazard.

Approaches

The size of the Zemlyanoy Gorod and its uneven distribution of sights call for two approaches. Whereas the western half – particularly the Arbat district – repays exploration **on foot**, the rest is best tackled on a hit-and-run basis, making forays from the nearest **metro** station. Some Circle line stations coincide with the Garden Ring, but most are sited further out. Travelling overground is an experience in itself. Despite the Ring's heavy traffic and brutal functionalism, its sheer width and roller-coaster succession of underpasses and flyovers make for a dramatic ride by car, or a slow parade of skyscrapers aboard **trolleybus** Б which takes about an hour to circle the Ring, stopping at all the main intersections.

Each section of the Ring is individually named (eg Bolshaya Sadovaya ulitsa, Sadovaya-Triumfalnaya ulitsa) and numbered in a clockwise direction with the odd numbers on the outer rim. Our account follows the pattern of the previous chapter by starting with Tverskaya ulitsa and dividing the rest into wedge-shaped sectors. Many of these tie in with points on the Boulevard Ring, mentioned in the previous chapter, although in other cases the starting point is the Garden Ring or a metro station.

Pushkinskaya ploshchad and beyond

The long, flat stretch of Tverskaya ulitsa beyond the Boulevard Ring starts with an elongated slab of greenery underlaid by pedestrian subways and three metro stations (Pushkinskaya, Tverskaya and Chekhovskaya), one of which takes its name from the statue of the poet that gazes over **Pushkinskaya ploshchad** (Pushkin Square).

Alexander Opekushin's bronze **statue of Pushkin** is Moscow's best-loved monument. Paid for by public donations and unveiled in 1880 to eulogies by Ivan Turgenev and other writers, the statue was moved from its original location on the other side of Tverskaya ulitsa to its present site in 1950. Floral tributes always lie at the foot of its plinth, while on Pushkin's birthday (June 6), thousands of admirers gather to recite his poetry.

Behind Pushkin's statue looms the bronzed pediment and glass facade of a **cinema** that was one of the first daringly modern buildings in postwar Moscow when it was erected in 1961, on the site of the demolished Strastnoy Convent. Previously called the Rossiya (Russia) Cinema, it was long alleged by nationalists to be a devious ploy whereby Pushkin was made to turn his back on Russia, till it was renamed the **Pushkin Hall** (Pushkinskiy zal) in 1997. The Moscow international film festival and Russia's equivalent of the Oscars are held here. Beneath the cinema, a casino offers the chance of winning the cars mounted on plinths outside and there's a 24-hour pawnbrokers for hardened gamblers; behind it are the offices of **Noviy Mir**, the monthly literary journal that printed Solzhenitsyn's *One Day in the Life of Ivan Denisovich* during Khrushchev's "thaw", and Orwell's *Nineteen Eighty-four* under glasnost.

The northern side of the square is flanked by the offices of **Izvestiya** ("News"), founded as the organ of the Soviet government, whose original Constructivist premises with asymmetrical balconies and circular upper windows abut a 1970s extension, standing beside the yellow-tiled Style Moderne **Sytin dom**, where the Communist Party newspaper *Pravda* ("Truth") was printed in the 1920s. Their proximity inspired the quip that "There is no news in *Pravda* and no truth in *Izvestiya*". Around the corner of the Sytin dom, the concrete premises of a third newspaper, *Trud* ("Labour"), face the flamboyant **Ssudnaya kazna**, a neo-Russian pile with a faceted facade that was once the Tsarist Central Bank. The Museum of Modern History is visible from the corner of the main road (see p.152).

Up Malaya Dmitrovka ulitsa

Before checking out the Museum of Modern History, it's a good idea to take a look around the corner of the old wing of the *Izvestiya* building, where a delightful church stands at the beginning of **Malaya Dmitrovka ulitsa**.

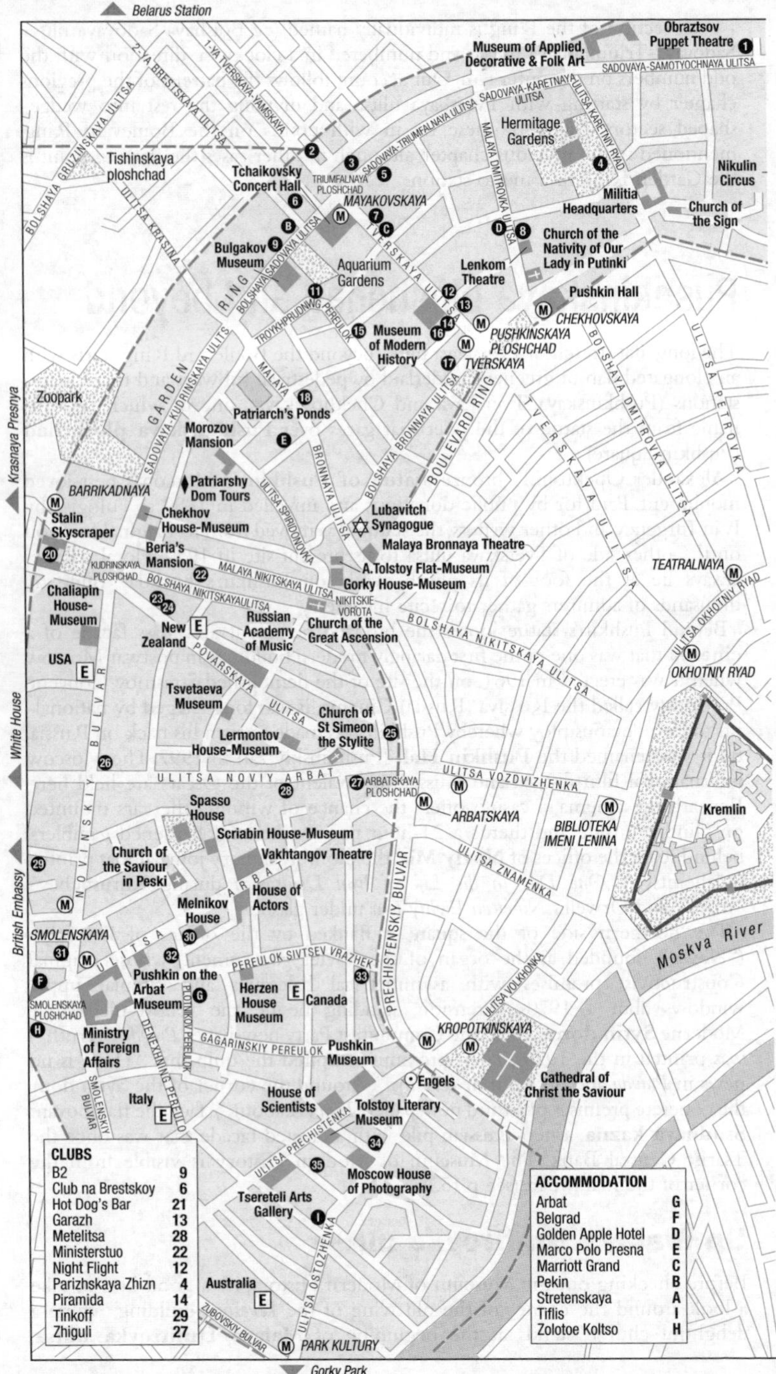
Belarus Station
Obraztsov Puppet Theatre
Museum of Applied, Decorative & Folk Art
SADOVAYA-SAMOTYOCHNAYA ULITSA
SADOVAYA-KARETNAYA ULITSA
ULITSA KARETNIY RYAD
1-YA TVERSKAYA-YAMSKAYA
2-YA BRESTSKAYA ULITSA
BOLSHAYA GRUZINSKAYA ULITSA
SADOVAYA-TRIUMFALNAYA ULITSA
MALAYA DMITROVKA ULITSA
Hermitage Gardens
Nikulin Circus
Tishinskaya ploshchad
Tchaikovsky Concert Hall
TRIUMFALNAYA PLOSHCHAD
MAYAKOVSKAYA
Militia Headquarters
Church of the Sign
ULITSA KRASINA
Church of the Nativity of Our Lady in Putinki
Bulgakov Museum
BOLSHAYA SADOVAYA ULITSA
TVERSKAYA ULITSA
Aquarium Gardens
Lenkom Theatre
Pushkin Hall
CHEKHOVSKAYA
TROYKHPRUDNIY PERELOK
Museum of Modern History
PUSHKINSKAYA PLOSHCHAD
TVERSKAYA
GARDEN RING
SADOVAYA-KUDRINSKAYA ULITSA
MALAYA
Zoopark
Patriarch's Ponds
BOLSHAYA BRONNAYA ULITSA
BOULEVARD RING
ULITSA PETROVKA
BOLSHAYA DMITROVKA ULITSA
Morozov Mansion
BRONNAYA ULITSA
Krasnaya Presnya
Patriarshy Dom Tours
BARRIKADNAYA
ULITSA SPIRIDONOVKA
Lubavitch Synagogue
Stalin Skyscraper
Chekhov House-Museum
Malaya Bronnaya Theatre
Beria's Mansion
KUDRINSKAYA PLOSHCHAD
MALAYA NIKITSKAYA ULITSA
A.Tolstoy Flat-Museum
Gorky House-Museum
TEATRALNAYA
BOLSHAYA NIKITSKAYA ULITSA
Chaliapin House-Museum
NIKITSKIE VOROTA
ULITSA OKHOTNIY RYAD
New Zealand
Russian Academy of Music
Church of the Great Ascension
OKHOTNIY RYAD
USA
POVARSKAYA ULITSA
Tsvetaeva Museum
White House
Church of St Simeon the Stylite
Lermontov House-Museum
NOVINSKIY BULVAR
ULITSA NOVIY ARBAT
ARBATSKAYA PLOSHCHAD
ULITSA VOZDVIZHENKA
Kremlin
Spasso House
ARBATSKAYA
BIBLIOTEKA IMENI LENINA
Scriabin House-Museum
British Embassy
Church of the Saviour in Peski
Vakhtangov Theatre
ULITSA ZNAMENKA
ARBAT
House of Actors
Melnikov House
SMOLENSKAYA
ULITSA
PERELOK SIVTSEV VRAZHEK
Moskva River
Pushkin on the Arbat Museum
PRECHISTENSKIY BULVAR
SMOLENSKAYA PLOSHCHAD
PLOTNIKOV PERELOK
Herzen House Museum
Canada
ULITSA VOLKHONKA
KROPOTKINSKAYA
Ministry of Foreign Affairs
DENEZHNIY PERELOK
GAGARINSKIY PERELOK
Pushkin Museum
Engels
SMOLENSKIY BULVAR
Cathedral of Christ the Saviour
Italy
House of Scientists
Tolstoy Literary Museum
ULITSA PRECHISTENKA
Moscow House of Photography
Tsereteli Arts Gallery
Australia
ULITSA OSTOZHENKA
ZUBOVSKIY BULVAR
PARK KULTURY
Gorky Park
CLUBS
B2 9
Club na Brestskoy 6
Hot Dog's Bar 21
Garazh 13
Metelitsa 28
Ministerstuo 22
Night Flight 12
Parizhskaya Zhizn 4
Piramida 14
Tinkoff 29
Zhiguli 27
ACCOMMODATION
Arbat G
Belgrad F
Golden Apple Hotel D
Marco Polo Presna E
Marriott Grand C
Pekin B
Stretenskaya A
Tiflis I
Zolotoe Koltso H

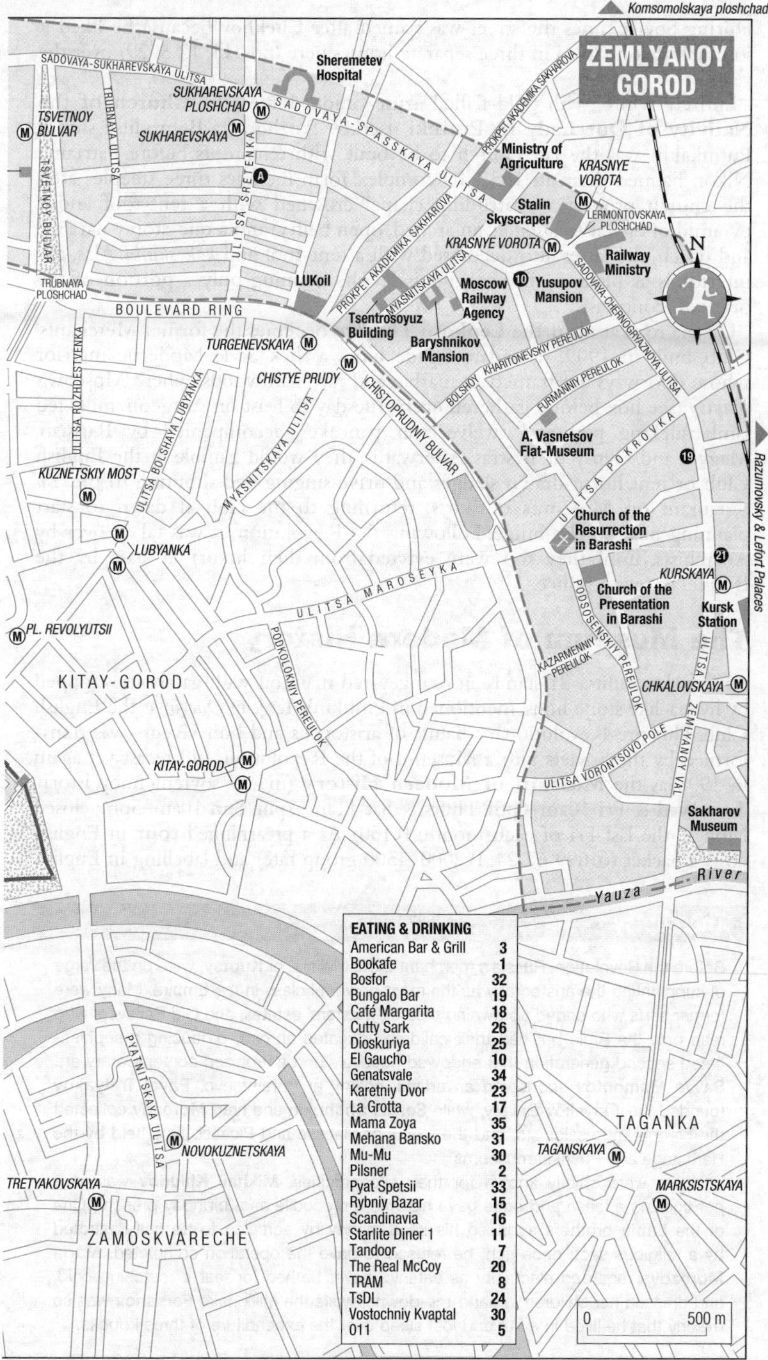
Komsomolskaya ploshchad
ZEMLYANOY GOROD
SADOVAYA-SUKHAREVSKAYA ULITSA
Sheremetev Hospital
SUKHAREVSKAYA PLOSHCHAD
SADOVAYA-SPASSKAYA ULITSA
TSVETNOY BULVAR
SUKHAREVSKAYA
TRUBNAYA ULITSA
ULITSA SRETENKA
PROKPET AKADEMIKA SAKHAROVA
Ministry of Agriculture
KRASNYE VOROTA
LERMONTOVSKAYA PLOSHCHAD
Stalin Skyscraper
KRASNYE VOROTA
Railway Ministry
TRUBNAYA PLOSHCHAD
BOULEVARD RING
LUKoil
MYASNITSKAYA ULITSA
Moscow Railway Agency
Yusupov Mansion
SADOVAYA-CHERNOGRYAZNOVA ULITSA
Tsentrosoyuz Building
Baryshnikov Mansion
TURGENEVSKAYA
CHISTYE PRUDY
BOLSHOY KHARITONEVSKIY PEREULOK
FURMANNIY PEREULOK
ULITSA ROZHDESTVENKA
ULITSA BOLSHAYA LUBYANKA
CHISTOPRUDNIY BULVAR
A. Vasnetsov Flat-Museum
ULITSA POKROVKA
Razumovsky & Lefort Palaces
KUZNETSKIY MOST
LUBYANKA
Church of the Resurrection in Barashi
KURSKAYA
Church of the Presentation in Barashi
Kursk Station
ULITSA MAROSEYKA
PL. REVOLYUTSII
KAZARMENNIY PEREULOK
PODSOSENSKIY PEREULOK
KITAY-GOROD
PODKOLOKOLNIY PEREULOK
CHKALOVSKAYA
ULITSA
ZEMLYANOY VAL
ULITSA VORONTSOVO POLE
KITAY-GOROD
Sakharov Museum
Yauza River
EATING & DRINKING
American Bar & Grill 3
Bookafe 1
Bosfor 32
Bungalo Bar 19
Café Margarita 18
Cutty Sark 26
Dioskuriya 25
El Gaucho 10
Genatsvale 34
Karetniy Dvor 23
La Grotta 17
Mama Zoya 35
Mehana Bansko 31
Mu-Mu 30
Pilsner 2
Pyat Spetsii 33
Rybniy Bazar 15
Scandinavia 16
Starlite Diner 1 11
Tandoor 7
The Real McCoy 20
TRAM 8
TsDL 24
Vostochniy Kvaptal 30
011 5
PYATNITSKAYA ULITSA
TAGANKA
NOVOKUZNETSKAYA
TAGANSKAYA
TRETYAKOVSKAYA
MARKSISTSKAYA
ZAMOSKVARECHE
0 500 m

During Soviet times the street was named after Chekhov because he liked it so much that he lived in three separate houses here (nos. 11, 12 & 29) over the years.

Entirely white, with gold-frilled azure onion domes, the **Church of the Nativity of Our Lady in Putinki** (tserkov Rozhdestva Bogroditsy shto v Putinkakh) was the last church to be built with tent-roofs before Patriarch Nikon banned them in 1652. Its complex form includes three steeples atop the church proper; a protruding chapel crowned with a tent-roof and a pyramid of ogival *kokoshniki*; an arched, open belfry; and a one-storey narthex and porch, the latter also decorated with a tent-roof and *kokoshniki*. Alas, the interior is as plain as the exterior is lavish, retaining only a portion of the original iconostasis.

Up the road at no. 6, the **Lenkom Theatre** occupies the former Merchants' Club, built in 1909. Its sedate facade hides a slick Style Moderne interior whose doorways are framed in marble and rare hardwoods, where Moscow's *Kuptsy* (see box below) gathered every Tuesday to feast on sturgeon, milk-fed lamb, sucking pigs and twelve-layer pancakes, accompanied by Russian, Magyar and Gypsy orchestras. Afterwards, they would gamble at the English Club or rent horse-drawn sledges and drive singing and shouting to the *Yar* restaurant on Moscow's outskirts, returning to the club at dawn to start planning next week's binge. Following the Revolution, it was taken over by Anarchists, until they too were evicted from their luxurious base by the Bolshevik secret police.

The Museum of Modern History

At Tverskaya ulitsa 21 stands an orangey-red mansion with gatehouses topped by hyena-like stone lions, mentioned in Pushkin's *Yevgeny Onegin* as the English Club. This pre-Revolutionary haunt of aristocrats and bon viveurs was transformed by the Soviets into a Museum of the Revolution, and recast yet again in 1998 as the **Museum of Modern History** (muzey sovremennoy istorii; Tues, Wed & Fri 10am–6pm, Thurs & Sat 11am–7pm, Sun 10am–5pm; closed Mon & the last Fri of each month; R150). As a prearranged **tour** in English costs a packet (Ⓣ699 67 24; R2000–4500 group rate) and labelling in English

The Kuptsy

Before the Revolution, Russia's merchant-industrialists, or **Kuptsy**, were on the verge of supplanting the aristocracy as the most powerful class in the Empire. Many were former serfs who ended up owning their ex-masters' estates, and Old Believers who read only the Bible but had their children educated abroad, producing a sophisticated second generation that endowed hospitals and patronized contemporary art. **Savva Mamontov** sponsored an artists' colony at Abramtsevo, **Pavel Tretyakov** founded the Tretyakov Gallery, while **Sergei Shchukin** and **Ivan Morozov** collected the French Impressionists, and the works of Matisse and Picasso now held by the Hermitage and Pushkin museums.

Others were chiefly known for their eccentricities. **Mikhail Khludov** walked a pet tiger on a leash and once gave his wife a crocodile as a birthday present. One of the **Lapin** brothers acquired his seed-money by agreeing to be half-castrated by a religious sect; once rich, he refused to have the operation completed. **Maria Morozova** regarded electricity as satanic, never bathed for fear of catching cold, and dressed her children in hand-me-downs, while the millionaire **Fersanov** was so miserly that he lived in a hut and lost sleep over the expenditure of three kopeks.

is limited, the significance of some exhibits may be lost on visitors, but many are eye-catching enough for it not to matter.

This is especially true of the Soviet propaganda posters agitating against capitalists, counter-revolutionaries and kulaks, or extolling collectivization and Stalin, and the roomful of gifts and tributes to the "Wise Father of all the Peoples", including a huge wireless with his portrait on it. Look out for artists' impressions of the never-built Palace of Soviets that was meant to be the focal point of Moscow (see p.132). Cobblestones thrown at the police in 1905, an armoured car from the street battles of 1917 and numbered grave posts from the Karaganda labour camp are among the many artefacts on permanent display – augmented by temporary exhibitions on diverse themes.

The museum concludes with a re-creation of the **library** of the **English Club**, which was founded in 1831 and "so called because hardly any Englishman belongs to it". Virtually the only place where political discussions were tolerated during the reign of Nicholas I, the club soon became a "cathedral of idleness" where Tolstoy lost 1000 rubles and Mikhail Morozov blew more than a million in one night, in the card room called "Hell". In 1913 it hosted a costume ball in honour of the tricentenary of the Romanov dynasty that was the last truly grand social event before the Revolution.

A **shop** off the foyer stocks Soviet posters, stamps and badges, at collectors' prices.

On to Triumfalnaya ploshchad

The final stretch of Tverskaya ulitsa is fairly unremarkable, featuring the **Moscow Dramatic Theatre** (next to the Museum of Modern History), the swanky **Marriott Grand Hotel**, and pretentious shops directed at new Russians.

Shortly afterwards, Tverskaya ulitsa meets the Garden Ring at **Triumfalnaya ploshchad**, named after the festive arches that were erected here to greet monarchs in the eighteenth century. As these were surmounted by a statue of a charioteer, Muscovites joked that there were only two coachmen in Moscow who weren't drunk: the one on the arch and the one on top of the Bolshoy Theatre. The square is, in fact, better known by its former Soviet name – ploshchad Mayakovskovo – and for its craggy **statue of Mayakovsky**, unveiled in 1958. Its truculent pose and baggy trousers call to mind Mayakovsky's eulogy on the first Soviet passport, issued in the 1920s: "I take from the pocket of my wide trousers my red-skinned passport, the priceless object I carry. Read it and envy me! I am a citizen of the Soviet Union."

Behind it rises the **Pekin Hotel** (see p.330), a yellow-and-white wedding cake adorned with motifs from the era of Sino-Soviet Friendship. This was actually built as a postwar headquarters for the secret police, but never used as such – the only sign of its intended function being red and green lights above the doors on corridors, meant for signalling when interrogations were in progress inside what are now the guest bedrooms.

Above the main entrance to Mayakovskaya metro looms the massive square-pillared portico and diamond-patterned facade of the **Tchaikovsky Concert Hall**. Originally built as a theatre for the avant-garde director Meyerhold, who wished to design it "for the wonderful future a hundred years ahead", it was to have two circular stages – able to revolve, descend or rise as the director wished – and a "creative tower" on the corner of Tverskaya ulitsa, for artistic experiments. Then Meyerhold was arrested and shot, and in 1938 the theatre was converted into a concert hall, now used by the State Symphony Orchestra.

That same year saw the completion of **Mayakovskaya metro station**, internationally acclaimed for its light and silvery ribbed hall. As one of the deepest stations on the metro, this hosted a dramatic meeting on the eve of the anniversary of the Revolution in November 1941, when the Nazis were on the outskirts of Moscow, at which Stalin gave a sombre briefing to the assembled generals and Party activists. It also served as a public air-raid shelter.

By heading on past the **Satirical Theatre** and the **Aquarium Gardens** – the site of the **Mossovet Theatre** and the 24-hour *Starlite Diner* – you'll be on the right track for the next itinerary.

Around Patriarch's Ponds, Kudrinskaya and Nikitskie vorota

The quarter to the southwest of Tverskaya is notable for its pretty, leafy backstreets and **literary associations**, which make the Patriarch's Ponds one of the priciest neighbourhoods in Moscow. Admirers of Bulgakov, Chekhov, Gorky, Pushkin or Alexei Tolstoy will find their former homes preserved as museums, and fans of *The Master and Margarita* can retrace locations from the novel. A monument to the Yiddish writer Sholem Aleichem and the Lubavitch Synagogue attest to Moscow's **Jewish heritage**. There's also some fabulous **architecture**, namely the Style Moderne Ryabushinskiy mansion near Nikitskie vorota and the Stalin-Gothic skyscraper on Kudrinskaya ploshchad, visible from Triumfalnaya ploshchad around the curve of the Ring.

Patriarch's Ponds and Malaya Bronnaya

Past a row of kiosks beyond the Aquarium Gardens, a plaque beside the archway of no. 10 Bolshaya Sadovaya ulitsa attests that **Mikhail Bulgakov** (see box below) lived here from 1921 to 1924. His satirical fantasy *The Master and*

Bulgakov and *The Master and Margarita*

Born in Kiev in 1891, **Mikhail Bulgakov** practised medicine and experienced the Civil War in Ukraine and the Caucasus before he settled in Moscow in 1921 and became a full-time writer. His early success as a satirist and playwright aroused a backlash from RAPP (Russian Association of Proletarian Artists), which attacked his sympathetic portrayal of White characters in *The Days of the Turbins*, and his anti-Bolshevik allegory, *The Heart of a Dog*. Luckily for Bulgakov, *The Days of the Turbins* was Stalin's favourite play, so despite being blacklisted his life was spared. Eventually, he asked Stalin's permission to emigrate; Stalin refused, but authorized the staging of his play *Molière*.

Bulgakov began **The Master and Margarita** in 1928, knowing from the outset that it wouldn't be published. Its progress reflected his personal life: the Master's affair with Margarita echoed Bulgakov's own with Yelena Shilkovskaya, who left her husband after they met at a party in 1932, while the fiendish cat Behemoth was based on their own pet, Flyushka. The book was completed just days before his death in 1940, and Yelena was obliged to hide the manuscript, which wasn't published in Russia until 1966. Its huge popularity in the 1980s owed much to the Taganka Theatre's amazing production of the novel – but its enduring fame rests on its piquant absurdities, as the Devil and his gang sow chaos across Moscow. Tellingly, it contains many instances of behaviour and dialogue that ring as true in the New Russia as they did when Bulgakov satirized *Homo Sovieticus* in the 1920s and 1930s.

Margarita is indelibly associated with Moscow – and this area in particular – as Bulgakov transposed his own flat to "302a Sadovaya Street" and made it the setting for Satan's Ball and other events in the novel. During the 1980s it became a place of pilgrimage, to the annoyance of residents, who grew sick of fans gathering on the stairway and covering the walls with **graffiti** and images of the impish cat Behemoth. In his former flat (no. 50), **Bulgakov's House** (Dom Bulgakova; daily 1–11pm, open all night on Fri & Sat in summer; free), you can see photos of the author and illustrations of his works donated by admirers. It also organizes literary events, meetings and excursions, such as a night trip around the centre of the city called "Following the characters of *The Master and Margarita*" (book in advance ⓣ775 94 61, ⓦwww.dombulgakova.ru).

To pursue *The Master and Margarita* trail a step further, walk on past the Aquarium Gardens – where the bewitched audience of Woland's magic show suddenly realized their nakedness – and turn left down a path between some kiosks. Turn right at the far end along Yermolaevskiy ulitsa, and hang left at the first corner and you'll find yourself at **Patriarch's Ponds** (Patriarshiy prudy). Readers of the novel will know this from its opening chapter as the place where two literary hacks meet Woland on a park bench. His prediction that one of them will die soon is borne out when the editor Berlioz slips on spilt sunflower oil just outside the park on the corner of Malaya Bronnaya and Yermolaevskiy streets, and falls under a tram.

A commemorative plaque here would be fine, but Mayor Luzhkov has outraged residents by having the whole area re-landscaped, to include **outsized sculptures** illustrating the novel – with Jesus walking on columns across the water towards a figure of Bulgakov on a park bench, and a giant primus stove inscribed with scenes from the lives of the novel's evil spirits at the other end of the pond. As the whole area is currently still a building site, it remains to be seen what the outcome is – but few expect it to be an improvement on what previously existed. Generations of Muscovites cherished it as an oasis of calm off the frenetic Garden Ring – children especially loved its **monument to Ivan Krylov** (1769–1844), a pensive bronze figure surrounded by creatures from his Aesopian fables. Before the Revolution, the stately apartment blocks surrounding the pond were popular with students and intellectuals, earning it the soubriquet of Moscow's "Latin Quarter". Its name comes from three ponds that were dug to drain a reputedly haunted swamp, by Patriarch Iov in the sixteenth century – hence its association with evil spirits and Christian sanctity in the novel.

On the corner of the Garden Ring and Malya Bronnaya ulitsa (which leads to the Ponds) stands another addition to the neighbourhood that's raised eyebrows. An eclectic **pastiche of Soviet architecture** combining offices and luxury apartments under one roof, its tiers of colonnades evoke the Stalin skyscraper further round the Ring, while its summit is crowned by a scaled-down version of Tatlin's un-built *Monument to the Third International.*

Malaya Bronnaya and the Lubavitch Synagogue

To see more of the area, follow **Malaya Bronnaya ulitsa** past Patriarch's Ponds. Like nearby Bolshaya Bronnaya, its name comes from the quarter of armourers (*bronoviki*) that existed here in medieval times. A haunt of Moscow's literary and artistic intelligentsia since the mid-nineteenth century, today it's the local equivalent of Hampstead or Greenwich Village. Beyond a slew of antique shops and trendy restaurants stands a **memorial to Sholem Aleichem**, the popular Yiddish writer (1859–1916) whose tales were the basis for *Fiddler on the Roof* (characters from which decorate the statue's plinth). Though he never lived in

▲ Sculpture illustrating a scene from Bulgakov's novel

Moscow, adaptations of his work are still performed there, and it seems fitting to honour him here, near the former State Yiddish Theatre.

Another reminder of Russia's Jewish heritage stands near the junction of Bolshaya and Malaya Bronnaya: a pale-green-and-white Neoclassical edifice, dwarfed by a concrete monstrosity. The Agndas Chassidei Chabad, or **Lubavitch Synagogue**, was built as an Orthodox synagogue in 1863 (after the emancipation of the Jews by Alexander II), financed by a railway tycoon, Polyakov. In the early 1920s it was given to the Hassidim, whom the Communists initially favoured over the "bourgeois" Orthodox Jews – but this uneasy coexistence came to an end after World War II, with purges of "cosmopolitans" and the closure of the synagogue. When Yeltsin restored it to the Hassidim in 1991, he shrewdly allowed relics of Rabbi Schonberg – the founder of the Lubavitch sect – that had been seized by the KGB in the 1960s, to go on display there, thereby ensuring the devotion of wealthy émigré Lubavitchers. The interior of the synagogue is austere and only remarkable for a concealed hideaway beneath the altar, but no expense has been spared on a huge **cultural centre** next door, which was nearing completion as this book went to press.

Further down the road, the **Malaya Bronnaya Theatre** occupies the building that once housed the State Yiddish Theatre, whose brilliant actor-director Solomon Mikhoels was secretly murdered by the NKVD, before the theatre was dissolved (see box, pp.188–189). The existing theatre's repertoire includes Ilf and Petrov's sympathetic (but excruciatingly named) 1920s satire about Jewish life and anti-Semitism in Russia, *A Yid in the City of Peter*.

Around Kudrinskaya ploshchad

Kudrinskaya ploshchad is a jumping-off point for several sights in the vicinity and one of the most distinctive junctions on the Garden Ring – but you'll probably think twice about getting there from Triumfalnaya ploshchad. It's a bit far to walk (1.2km) and you can wait ages for a trolleybus around the Ring, while the metro journey involves changing at Belorusskaya station. As you can see from afar, Kudrinskaya is dominated by a 22-storey **Stalin skyscraper** laden with pinnacles but relatively free of reliefs and statuary. Built in 1950–54, it was the last of Moscow's skyscrapers. According to Khrushchev, Stalin justified their erection on the grounds that "We've won the war and are recognized the world over as the glorious victors. We must be ready for an influx of foreign visitors. What will happen if they walk around Moscow and find no skyscrapers? They will make unfavourable comparisons with capitalist cities." The Kudrinskaya block was originally reserved for Party bigwigs, but its large, stylish flats are now favoured by rich New Russians.

Shortly before you reach the square, look out for a pink two-storey building sandwiched between two taller ones, at Sadovaya-Kudrinskaya ulitsa no. 6. The recently restored **Chekhov House-Museum** (dom-muzey A.P. Chekhova; Tues, Thurs, Sat 11am–6pm; Wed, Fri 2–8pm; R40; ⓣ291 61 54) is where Anton Chekhov, his parents and his brother lived from 1866 to 1890, during which time he wrote *Ivanov*, three one-act farces and over 100 short stories, while practising as a doctor. He also found time for an active sex life, as evinced by letters that discuss the pros and cons of making love on the floor, in bed, or over a trunk – and what to do if the servants walked in. The museum has been carefully restored to how it would have been when Chekhov lived there, with much of the furniture re-created from descriptions in his writings. Aside from a few collections of pens and some original novels, there is little for lovers of the writing itself, but the ambience of the rooms gives visitors a good sense of life in Chekhov's time.

Not far beyond this, on the corner of **Malaya Nikitskaya ulitsa**, the **Tunisian Embassy** was abashed to make news in 1993 when workmen found a dozen skeletons buried outside, reminding Muscovites that this was once **Beria's mansion**. The most odious and feared of Stalin's cohorts, Lavrenty Beria headed the secret police from 1938 onwards, and oversaw high-priority projects such as the construction of Moscow's skyscrapers and the development of the Soviet atomic bomb. His favourite recreation was raping pre-pubescent girls in his mansion. After Stalin's death, Beria's Politburo colleagues feared for their lives and had him arrested at a meeting in the Kremlin. It's unclear whether he was shot at once, or first tried *in camera* as a "foreign agent", but the outcome was the same. A few years ago, Russia's Supreme Court debated whether to posthumously pardon him as the victim of false charges, but decided that his genuine crimes made any such absolution risible. The mansion features in Robert Harris's thriller *Archangel*.

Chaliapin's house and the US Embassy

Further round the Ring – past the skyscraper – you can visit the **Chaliapin House-Museum** (dom-muzey F.I. Shalyapina; Tues 10am–6pm, Wed & Thurs 11.30am–7pm, Sat 10am–6pm, Sun 10am–4pm; R50) at Novinskiy bulvar 25. The Pavarotti of his day, Fyodor Chaliapin worked as a riverboat stevedore before his talents were recognized, and cared little for conventions. In Moscow, he married a ballerina who gave up dancing to be a housewife, while in St Petersburg he had another family by a woman whom he bigamously wed in 1927. His first wife had to move upstairs after their house was turned into a *komunalka*, and their children emigrated to the West. It was they who financed the house's restoration and supplied the mementos, leading to the opening of the museum in 1988; it also hosts **concerts** in September (Ⓣ205 62 36 for details).

The house is richly decorated in a mixture of French Empire and Style Moderne. His **wife's room** is papered with silk, and enshrines the candles from their wedding. After his operatic performances, Chaliapin loved to throw parties in the gilded white **ballroom**, but hated to be beaten in the **billiard room**. When he was feeling low, his wife would invite friends over who would deliberately lose. You can see his costumes from *Prince Igor*, *Faust* and *Judith*; his blue **study** hung with self-portraits of him as Don Quixote; and a replica of his **green room**, awash with wigs, cosmetics and trunks. Upstairs is an exhibition of dull portraits by his son Boris, who worked as an illustrator for *Time* magazine in the 1950s.

Immediately beyond, the **US Embassy** occupies a massive block whose Soviet-crested pediment and custard- and bile-coloured paint job might have been designed to make its occupants feel nauseous. In fact, they had worse reasons for feeling so, as from the 1970s the embassy was subjected to a constant bombardment of microwaves from KGB listening posts in the vicinity. The Americans' discovery of this coincided with the fiasco over their new embassy annexe, which was riddled with bugs from the outset (see p.180).

To Nikitskie vorota

There are several possible routes from the Patriarch's Ponds or the Garden Ring to **Nikitskie vorota**, not to mention approaching it from the Boulevard Ring (see p.120). Perhaps the most obvious – and nicest – is **ulitsa Spiridonovka**, a long, quiet, residential street. Walking down from the Patriarch's Ponds, you'll pass the former **Savva Morozov mansion** at no. 17. The first of over a dozen mansions designed by the prolific architect Shekhtel, this yellow neo-Gothic edifice with mock crenellations was built (1893–98) for a liberal scion of the Morozov textiles dynasty, who sponsored the Moscow Art Theatre and funded Lenin's newspaper *Iskra*. In 1905, with revolution raging in Russia and his own contradictions pulling him apart, Morozov committed suicide while on a visit to France. The mansion now belongs to the Ministry of Foreign Affairs, which holds press conferences in its neo-Gothic grand hall.

Further along the street are several mid-rise blocks that look nothing special from outside, but are finished to a high standard within. When **Gorbachev** joined the Politburo as a candidate member in 1979, he and Raisa were allotted an apartment in one of these enclaves; after he became Soviet leader, they moved to the Lenin Hills. Soon afterwards, you'll reach a small park containing a **statue of Alexander Blok** (1880–1921) looking every inch the Symbolist poet that he was, in a flowing overcoat and cravat. Just beyond stands the house where Blok lived before World War I, while a little further on you'll come to two literary museums.

Alexei Tolstoy's flat

The **Alexei Tolstoy Flat-Museum** (muzey-kvartira A.N. Tolstovo; Thurs, Sat & Sun 11am–6pm, Wed & Fri 1–6pm; closed the last Fri of each month; R40) is tucked away around the back of the Gorky Museum (see below), mirroring the way its owner lived in the shadow of his illustrious distant relative, Lev Tolstoy. Count Alexei Tolstoy (1882–1945) was a White émigré who returned in 1923 to establish himself as a popular author and later as a Deputy of the Supreme Soviet, occupying this flat from 1941 until his death.

It is decorated in the haut-bourgeois style of the nineteenth century, making the copy of *Pravda* in the drawing room seem an anachronism. In his columned salon, Tolstoy entertained friends at the grand piano or Lombard table like an aristocrat, while his study was a cosy world of history books, Chinese tea urns and pipes, with a copy of Peter the Great's death mask for inspiration. Here he wrote *Peter I*, *Darkness Dawns* and half an epic about the time of Ivan the Terrible. In the hallway hang a tapestry picture of Peter crowning Catherine I, and a portrait of the tsar made of seeds.

Gorky's house

Next door, the **Gorky House-Museum** (dom-muzey A.M. Gorkovo; Wed & Sun 11am–5.30pm; free) is worth seeing purely for its amazing decor, both inside and out. Still widely known as the **Ryabushinsky mansion**, the house was built in 1900 for the art-collecting chairman of the Stock Exchange, Stepan Ryabushinsky, who fled after the Revolution. If not unquestionably the finest Style Moderne creation of the architect Fyodor Shekhtel, it is certainly his most accessible, as the others are now embassies.

Its glazed brick exterior has sinuous windows and a shocking-pink floral mosaic frieze, while inside there's hardly a right angle to be seen, nor a square foot unadorned by mouldings or traceries. It seems ironic that this exotic residence should have been given to such an avowedly "proletarian" writer as Maxim Gorky (see box, p.160), who lived here from 1931 to 1936. The first room you encounter belonged to his secretary, who screened his visitors and reported to the NKVD. In Gorky's own study, notice the thick coloured pencils that he used for making notes and revisions. His library is installed in Ryabushinsky's salon, whose ceiling is decorated with stucco snails and flowers. Repeated wave-like motifs are a feature in both the parquet flooring and the ceiling of the **dining room**, while the crowning glory is a limestone **staircase** that drips and sags like molten wax, as if melted by the stalactite-lamp atop its newel post. The ugly wooden cabinets on the stairs were installed at Gorky's request; as he confessed to his daughter, Style Moderne was not to his taste. Notice the pillar on the landing, whose capital is decorated with giant lizards. The upstairs rooms are plainer and devoted to Gorky memorabilia, including his Chinese gown and skullcap.

Maxim Gorky

Orphaned and sent out to work as a young boy, Alexei Peshkov achieved literary success in his thirties under the *nom de plume* of **Maxim Gorky**, and took a leading role in the 1905 Revolution. After protests from Western writers, his subsequent prison sentence was commuted to exile abroad, where he raised funds for the Bolsheviks from his villa on Capri. Returning home in 1913, Gorky's joy at the overthrow of Tsarism soon turned to apprehension and disgust at the savagery unleashed by the Revolution, and the violence and cynicism of the Bolsheviks, whom he fiercely criticized in articles.

Having left Russia in 1921 – ostensibly on the grounds of ill health – Gorky was wooed back home by Stalin in 1928 to become chairman of the new Union of Soviet Writers. His own novel *Mother* was advanced as a model for **Socialist Realism**, the literary genre promulgated by the Union in 1932, and he also collaborated on a paean to the White Sea Canal, built by slave labour. As a murky finale, his death in 1936 was used as a pretext for the arrest of Yagoda, the head of the NKVD, who was charged with killing Gorky by seating him in a draught until he caught pneumonia. (Another version has it that Gorky was slowly poisoned by the toxic paint used in his bedroom.) Despite allegations of foul play, it is now thought that Gorky really did die of natural causes.

Lastly, you can visit a tiny Old Believers' **chapel** secreted in the attic (reached by a stairway just inside the mansion's entrance), which contains an exhibition on Stepan Ryabushinsky and his eight brothers. Their father was an industrialist who had eight daughters by his first wife, before divorcing her to marry another woman, in order to have male heirs.

The Church of the Great Ascension and the embassy quarter

Across the road from Gorky's house stands the bronze-domed **Church of the Great Ascension** (tserkov Bolshovo Vozneseniya), where Pushkin, aged 32, married 17-year-old Natalya Goncharova on February 18, 1831. During the ceremony one of the wedding rings was dropped and the candle that he was holding blew out, causing the superstitious writer to mutter in French, "All the omens are bad" – as indeed they were, for he was killed in a duel over his wife's honour six years later (see p.166). During Soviet times, the church was turned into a sports club used for table-tennis tournaments. A **Rotunda fountain** with a gilded cupola surmounting bronze statues of the newlyweds (who don't look happy) was erected outside the church on the bicentenary of Pushkin's birth. From here, you can orientate yourself vis-à-vis Nikitskie vorota and cross over to the south side, where any lane will take you into an **embassy quarter** full of Style Moderne and neo-Gothic mansions, whence you should emerge somewhere along Povarskaya ulitsa.

Povarskaya and Noviy Arbat

The area to the south of Kudrinskaya and Nikitskie vorota bears the stamp of two distinct epochs: the twilight of the Romanov era and the apogee of the Soviet period.

Povarskaya ulitsa and its side streets reflect a time when the old aristocracy was being supplanted by a new class of merchants and financiers, whose preference for Style Moderne and neo-Gothic was a rejection of the classical aesthetic revered by the nobility. Picturesque and on a human scale, it is one of the nicest areas in Moscow to wander around.

By contrast, Noviy Arbat (New Arbat), south of Povarskaya, is a brutal 1960s slash of traffic lanes, mega-blocks and stores, meant to prove that the Soviet capital was as racy, modern and consumerist as anywhere in the West, but only realized those Brezhnevite aspirations in the post-Soviet era. Today, its main attraction is the spectacular neon light displays.

Povarskaya ulitsa

Povarskaya ulitsa (Cooks' St) once served the royal household, together with nearby settlements on Khlebniy (Bread), Stoloviy (Table) and Skaterniy (Tablecloth) lanes. During the eighteenth century it became as fashionably aristocratic as the Old Equerries' quarter beyond the Arbat – and enjoyed the same complacent decline until revitalized by an influx of Kuptsy in the late nineteenth century. In 1918, a dozen local mansions were seized by Anarchists, who held wild orgies there until flushed out by the Bolshevik Cheka, leaving the interiors riddled with bullet holes and smeared with excrement. Under Soviet rule the mansions were refurbished and put to institutional uses; today, most have long since been privatized, as their real-estate value is astronomical.

From the House of Writers to Noviy Arbat

Near the Kudrinskaya ploshchad end of the street, the graceful Neoclassical mansion with a horseshoe-shaped courtyard (no. 52) is thought to have been the model for the Rostov family house in Tolstoy's *War and Peace*. In 1932 it became the **House of Writers**, the headquarters of the Writers' Union that dispensed *dachas* and other perks to authors who toed the Party line. Yet, contrary to what Bulgakov fans might imagine, this is not the setting for the fictional "Massolit" in *The Master and Margarita* – he actually modelled it on the other House of Writers building on Tverskoy bulvar.

Across the road stands an asymmetrical Constructivist building created (1931–34) by the Vsenin brothers for the Society of Former Political Prisoners. After the Society was dissolved a few years later it became the **Studio Theatre of Cinema Actors** (Kinoakter). Further along at no. 25, the pink-and-white Empire-style Gagarin mansion is notable for its stucco eagles and a statue of Gorky in peasant dress outside. It houses the **Gorky Institute of World Literature**, which he founded to publish cheap translations of foreign classics, and provide a livelihood for starving intellectuals after the Revolution.

The corner of Povarskaya and Noviy Arbat juxtaposes a huge, striking 24-storey block and the small white **Church of St Simeon the Stylite** (tserkov Simeon Stolpnika). Built in the mid-seventeenth century on the model of the Church of the Trinity on Nikitnikov (see p.108), the nave is capped by tiers of *kokoshniki* and green domes. It was here that Count Sheremetev secretly married the serf actress Parasha Kovalyeva-Zhemchugova (their romance is related on p.282), and Gogol was a regular worshipper when he lived in the vicinity (see p.123).

Before emerging onto Noviy Arbat, consider a brief detour off to the right to visit the **Lermontov Museum** (muzey M.Yu. Lermontova; Wed & Fri 2–6pm, Thurs, Sat & Sun 11am–5pm; closed last day of each month; R40, students R30), at Malaya Molchanovka ulitsa 2. This two-storey clapboard house was where the poet Mikhail Lermontov lived from 1829 to 1832, while he was a student at Moscow University; he spent so much time writing poems and dramas that he never sat his exams. Among these was an early version of *The Demon*, a theme that haunted Lermontov for years, and would later obsess the artist Vrubel.

The Tsvetaeva Museum

Lovers of Russian literature may embrace a longer detour to the **Tsvetaeva Museum** (muzey M. Tsvetayevoy; Mon & Fri–Sun noon–5pm, closed the last Fri of each month; free) on Borisoglebskiy pereulok, an earlier turning off Noviy Arbat. The yellow-and-white, two-storey house at no. 6 doubles as a literary centre and shrine to Marina Tsvetaeva (1892–1941), one of the finest poets of the Silver Age, whose tragic life enhanced her iconic status as the symbol of a generation who supported the Whites. Flat no. 3 partially reconstructs the six-room apartment that Tsvetaeva's family enjoyed before the Revolution – with a grand piano in the salon and a stuffed eagle in her husband Sergei's study – rather than the bare, unheated *kommunalka* that it became during the Civil War, when Sergei fought in the White Army while she struggled to feed their two daughters, whom she finally placed in an orphanage, where one died. After Marina, Sergei and their remaining daughter emigrated to Paris in 1922, Sergei became a Soviet spy and she left him after discovering his treachery, returning to Russia where she lived in desperate poverty and killed herself during the war. Tsvetaeva's work was banned but circulated in underground literature until glasnost restored her to her rightful place in the literary pantheon; the museum was opened on the centenary of her birth. By calling a day or two ahead you can arrange a guided **tour** in English (Ⓣ202 35 43).

Noviy Arbat (New Arbat)

Among its many changes to the capital, the 1935 General Plan for Moscow envisaged an arterial avenue linking the Boulevard and Garden Rings to create a cross-town route between the Kremlin, Kiev Station and points west. By Khrushchev's time this had become imperative since the narrow Arbat could no longer cope with the volume of traffic. Between 1962 and 1967, a one-kilometre-long swathe was bulldozed through a neighbourhood of old wooden houses, and a wide avenue flanked by high-rise complexes was laid out. Though officially named prospekt Kalinina (after the titular Bolshevik head of state, Kalinin) until 1991, Muscovites called it the **Noviy Arbat** – or **New Arbat** – from the outset.

Its inhuman scale and assertive functionalism won the architects a prize in 1966. Along the northern side are ranged five 24-storey apartment blocks awarded to People's Artists and other favoured citizens, which featured in 1970s Soviet films as symbols of *la dolce vita*; the gap-toothed appearance that they gave to the street led to it being nicknamed "The Dentures". Moscow's largest bookshop, **Dom knigi** (House of Books), is located between the first and second blocks, while the **Oktyabr Cinema** fills the gap between the penultimate and final blocks, its entire facade covered with a Revolutionary mosaic. The other side of the avenue is flanked by four 26-storey administrative blocks shaped like open books, overlaid by a synchronized **neon light display** which you can view from aboard **trolleybus** #2, running the length of the avenue. In the 1970s, residents of the tower blocks along Noviy Arbat were obliged to turn their lighting on or off, so that their windows spelled out "Glory to the Communist Party". The 850-metre-long glass-fronted gallery that runs beneath them briefly embodied Moscow's mall culture, before other, fancier emporiums stole its limelight. Further along, the Arbat entertainments complex is recognizable by a large rooftop **globe** that once showed Aeroflot's routes.

At the far end of the avenue, beyond the Garden Ring, the Mayoralty building presages the White House beside the river (see p.180).

On and off the Arbat

Oh Arbat, my Arbat, you are my destiny,

You are my happiness and my sorrow.

Bulat Okudzhava

Celebrated in song and verse, the **Arbat** once stood for bohemian Moscow in the way that Carnaby Street represented swinging London. Narrow and cobbled, with a tramline down the middle, it was the heart of a quarter where writers, actors and scientists frequented the same shops and cafés. This cosy world of the Soviet intelligentsia drew strength from the neighbourhood's identity a century earlier, when the **Staraya Konyushennaya** or **Old Equerries' quarter** between the Arbat and Prechistenka was the home of the *ancien* nobility, who still measured their wealth by the number of "souls" (male serfs) that they owned (women didn't count), training them to cook French pastries or play chamber music so as to be able to boast that their estate provided every refinement of life.

Divided into communal flats after the Revolution, each household felt Stalin's Terror, as recalled in Anatoly Rybakov's novel *Children of the Arbat*, which wasn't published until glasnost. By then, the Arbat was established as the hippest place in Moscow, having been pedestrianized in the early 1980s (for the worse, many thought). Perestroika made it a magnet for young Muscovites and tourists in search of something happening, while the Yeltsin years saw its real-estate value soar as businesses moved in and residents left. At street level, however, it's anything but staid, with lots of cafés and beer tents, souvenir stalls catering to both Russians and foreigners, and people of all ages strolling or hanging out, watching the street performers and singsongs over a few bottles of beer until midnight or later.

Getting to the Arbat

Most visitors approach the Arbat via the pedestrian underpass on **Arbatskaya ploshchad** (p.122). If you're coming by metro, bear in mind that there are two pairs of identically named stations on separate lines. On the Arbatsko–Pokrovskaya line, Arbatskaya station exits opposite the House of Europe on ulitsa Vozdvizhenka, while Smolenskaya brings you out behind *McDonald's* at the far end of the Arbat. Arbatskaya station on the Filyovskaya line is also conveniently situated, but the other Smolenskaya is way off on the Garden Ring and best avoided.

Beyond the Peace Wall

Aside from a huge new office/residential complex and an array of fast-food outlets and antique shops, there's nothing especially remarkable until you reach the **Peace Wall** (Stena Mira). A cute example of propaganda against Reagan's

▲ Street life in the bohemian Arbat quarter

Star Wars, the wall consists of scores of tiles painted by Soviet schoolchildren, expressing their hopes for peace and fears of war. The names of the side streets beyond recall the era when the neighbourhood served the tsar's court: Serebryaniy (Silver) and Starokonyushenniy (Old Stables) lanes. As you pass by the latter, notice the green **wooden house** with carved eaves, dating from 1872, a model of which won a prize at the Paris Exhibition as the epitome of the "Russian Style".

Thereafter, the Arbat gets busier with portrait artists, buskers, and photographers offering a range of props, while the buildings bloom with bright colours and quirky details. Stuccoed ivy flourishes above the lilac Style Moderne edifice at no. 27, while the next block consists of a neo-Gothic apartment complex guarded by statuesque knights and containing the **House of Actors**. Opposite stands the **Vakhtangov Theatre**, named after its founder, Yevgeny Vakhtangov (1883–1922), who split from MKhAT to pursue a fusion of Realism and the Meyerhold style. The postwar building is notable for its heavy Stalinist facade, and a slender gilt **Turandot fountain**, added alongside in the 1990s.

Around the backstreets

While Vakhtangov himself lived on the Arbat, the neighbouring Bolshoy Nikolopeskovskiy pereulok is more tangibly associated with the composer Alexander Scriabin (1872–1915), who spent his last years at no. 11 before dying of a septic boil on his lip. The **Scriabin House-Museum** (dom-muzey A.N. Skryabina; Wed & Fri noon–7pm, Thurs, Sat & Sun 10am–5pm; closed last Fri of each month; R150) preserves his sound and light laboratory, an apparatus with which he tried to match notes with colours, in accordance with his musical and philosophical theories, which the curators are happy to explain if you're interested (and speak Russian). They also hold **concerts** in the house, which sometimes feature the apparatus in action (call ⓣ241 19 01 for information).

The next lane on the right – Spasopeskovskiy pereulok – retains a seventeenth-century church with a tent-roofed belfry and an ornamental gate. The **Church of the Saviour in Peski** (tserkov Spasa na Peskakh) gets its name from the site (*peski* means "sand") of an earlier wooden church that caught fire from a votive candle in 1493; igniting the neighbourhood, it grew into a city-wide conflagration. The locality still looked rural as late as the nineteenth century, as depicted by Vasily Polonev in his popular painting *A Moscow Courtyard* (now in the Tretyakov Gallery). Off to the right at the far end is a guarded green dignified by the Neoclassical **Spaso House**, the residence of US ambassadors since 1933. Bulgakov once attended a reception here and was so struck by its opulence and frivolity – at a time of terror in the Soviet Union – that it inspired Satan's Ball in *The Master and Margarita*. Recently, Russians were outraged to learn that the Americans pay an annual rent of only $2.50 (due to the devaluation of the ruble since the lease was last signed) – a paltry sum that the Russian government rejects on principle.

Back on the Arbat, look out for **Krivoarbatskiy pereulok** (Crooked Arbat Lane), around the far side of the House of Actors. The walls of the building are luridly covered in **graffiti about Viktor Tsoy**, the lead singer of the group Kino (Film), whose fatal car crash in 1990 ensured his immortality as a cult hero. Though fans gather here to sing his songs and contemplate (or add to) the graffiti, nobody seems to know why this spot became a shrine in the first place.

The Melnikov House

Around the corner past the Tsoy graffiti, the lane's Art Nouveau buildings are interrupted by the defiantly Constructivist **Melnikov House** (no. 10). Konstantin Melnikov (1890–1974) was one of the most original architects of the 1920s, who was granted a plot of land to build a house after winning the

Gold Medal at the Paris World Fair in 1925. Though his career nose-dived once the Party spurned Modernism, he was allowed to keep his home – the only privately built house in Moscow after the Revolution – but died in obscurity. Belatedly honoured owing to the efforts of his children, his unique house was declared a historic monument in 1987, though it isn't open to visitors.

Consisting of three interlocking cylinders pierced by scores of hexagonal windows, it predated (1927–29) the breakthroughs of Melnikov's contemporaries, Le Corbusier and Mies van der Rohe, with self-reinforcing floors that eliminated the need for internal load-bearing walls. The rooms are divided up by slim partitions and feature built-in furniture (as in peasant cottages), while the intersection of the cylinders creates a space for the staircase that spirals up through the core of the house. Despite its revolutionary design, the materials are simple and traditional: timber, brick and stucco. Sadly, the house looks rather dilapidated and its cylindrical rear facade can only be seen from around the back of the *Vostochniy Kvartal* restaurant on Plotnikov pereulok, at the far end of the street.

The Okudzhava memorial

Turning right onto Plotnikov pereulok – back towards the Arbat – you'll encounter a larger-than-life **statue of Bulat Okudzhava**, mooching through a bronze archway, the back of which is inscribed with lyrics from his song, *My Arbat*, which launched the Bard movement of the 1960s. The Georgian poet became a songwriter after accompanying one of his satirical verses on the guitar – unbothered by the fact that he only knew three chords. As Okudzhava recalled, "The composers hated me. The singers detested me. The guitarists were terrified by me. And that is how it went on, until a very well-known poet of ours announced: 'Calm down, these are not songs. This is just another way of presenting poetry.'" His songs and those of his fellow Bards expressed the reformist hopes of the post-Stalinist generation. When Okudzhava died in Paris, in 1997, hundreds of thousands of Muscovites sang *My Arbat* as they queued to pay their last respects outside his house at ulitsa Arbat 43.

Pushkin and Bely on the Arbat

On the next block of the Arbat, beyond the childhood home of the novelist Anatoly Rybakov (no. 51) – marked by a bronze plaque – a sky-blue Empire-style house enshrines the fleeting domicile of Russia's most beloved writer as the **Pushkin on the Arbat Museum** (muzey-kvartira A.S. Pushkina; Wed–Sun 10am–6pm; closed last Fri of each month; R80). In the spring of 1831, it was here that Pushkin held his stag night and spent the first months of married life with Natalya Goncharova. They then moved to St Petersburg, where Pushkin was later killed in a duel with a French officer whose advances to Natalya were the talk of the town. After Pushkin's death their apartment was preserved as an evocative museum, which is worth seeing should you visit St Petersburg. The Arbat museum, however, is strictly for manuscript buffs, offering few insights into their lifestyle other than a taste for gilded chairs – and they would probably have been embarrassed by the bronze **statue of Natalya and Pushkin** that now stands on the other side of the street, resembling Barbie and Ken dressed for a costume ball.

Given that Moscow fondly devotes two museums to him, it's ironic that Pushkin scorned the city as a "Tatar nonentity" where "nobody receives periodicals from France", and lamented being "condemned to live among these orang-utans at the most interesting moment of our century". Worse for newlyweds, he wrote, s Б, so unless you're aiming for somewhere specific you're npted by the leafy streets adjacent to the Boulevard Ring svetnoy bulvar itself.

arden Ring

th noting till the junction with Karetniy ryad, where the **Museum of Applied, Decorative and Folk Art** -prikladnovo i narodnovo iskusstva; Mon–Thurs, Sat & ed the last Thurs of each month; R300) on the corner a. Its diverse collection occupies the main wing of the Dsterman mansion, and an annexe off to the right of the r you begin, keep your ticket for the other bit. The star nexe, upstairs) is Soviet porcelain of the 1920s and 1930s, rist designs or metro-building motifs; among the figurines, nily rejoicing over the Stalin Constitution. Downstairs are es, painted with fairytale scenes, along with nineteenth- s and contemporary tapestries.

g is named Sadovaya-Samotyochnaya ulitsa and known he **headquarters of the GIBDD**, or traffic police. The 3) contains the famous **Obraztsov Puppet Theatre**, braztsov, whose concrete facade is enlivened by a decora- of twelve little houses. Every hour one of them opens to pet; at noon all the figures dance to a Russian folk song. dents and Western reporters often arranged to meet here l over news stories or underground literature. The spot he journalists since many lived nearby on the other side twar block (no. 12) nicknamed "Sad Sam", which formed tto for the foreign press corps. A 677-metre-long flyover ss the old valley of the Neglina River at Samotyochnaya noy bulvar on the right (see opposite), and the wonderful se (see p.269) in the other direction.

d

ryad (Coach Row) gets its name from the carriage- and hops that lined the road during the nineteenth century, d their vehicles rather than let them be stolen by the ned into state garages after the Revolution, they are still the arched houses along the eastern side. No. 4 was the he director Stanislavsky until it was requisitioned as a 918.

ky first achieved professional success in the **Hermitage** where his Moscow Art Theatre premiered *The Seagull* in e pleasure-garden was founded by Yakov Shchukin, an nsured that it remained respectable by spreading rumours into the pond; he later invited the Lumière brothers to n Moscow there. Today, Muscovites come to loll in the mmer teahouse, attend performances at the **New Opera**, **theatres** (see Chapter 14), or hang out at *Parizhskaya* 3).

of the avenue is designated as a continuation of ulitsa dominated by the vast beige **headquarters of the**

"here you live, not as you wish but as aunties wish. My mother-in-law is just such an auntie. It's a quite different thing in Petersburg! I'll start living in clover, as a petty bourgeois, independently, and taking no thought of what Maria Alexeevna will say."

The *kassa* for the Pushkin Museum also sells tickets for the sparsely furnished **Bely Memorial Room** (muzey-kvartira Andreya Belovo; same hours; R80) in the house next door, where the Symbolist writer Andrei Bely was born and grew up. Originally named Boris Bugaev, he adopted the pseudonym Bely (White) to disassociate himself from his father – a well-known professor – and express his identification with spiritual values. Most of his novels were autobiographical and concerned with consciousness; visitors can see four graph-like charts, representing his material and spiritual lives, his friends and his influences (classified as good or evil), drawn by Bely. Surprisingly, his novels continued to be published after the Revolution, and he wasn't persecuted by the authorities – not least because he died in 1934, before the Great Terror began.

Smolenskaya ploshchad and further south

Smolenskaya ploshchad, at the far end of the Arbat, was once Moscow's haymarket, ankle-deep in straw and dung and thronged with ostlers and farriers. Today, it bears the stamp of Stalinist planning, dominated by 1940s monoliths and the Stalin-Gothic skyscraper of the **Ministry of Foreign Affairs**. Known by its initials as the **MID**, the central block is 172m high, with three portals surmounted by bas-reliefs of furled flags, fronted by granite propylaea and lamps. The original design was without a spire; when Stalin remarked on this, one was immediately added. Having been led by Molotov (known to Western diplomats as "Old Stony-face") and Gromyko ("Mr Nyet") during the Cold War, and at the forefront of perestroika with Sheverdnadze ("The Silver Fox"), the ministry enjoyed its last spell in the limelight under the veteran spymaster Primakov, since when its bosses have been relative nonentities.

In October 1993, Smolenskaya ploshchad witnessed two days of clashes between riot police and supporters of the White House, which ended with the police surrendering en masse, the breaking of the blockade of Parliament, and a victory rally where Khasbulatov urged the seizure of the TV Centre and the Kremlin. Though the "desertion" of the police seemed a sign of Yeltsin's weakness at the time, it was actually a ruse to make the rebels overconfident, and tempt them into a rash move that would ensure their downfall (see p.180).

South towards Prechistenka

You can follow almost any street running off the Arbat and emerge on ulitsa Prechistenka.

Although a bit of a detour, **pereulok Sivtsev Vrazhek** (Grey Mare's Lane) boasts an array of stuccoed wooden houses with literary connections. The poet Maria Tsvetaeva and her fiancé Sergei Efron stayed in a "huge, uncomfortable flat" at no. 19; Tolstoy made his first attempts at writing fiction at no. 34; Mikhail Sholokhov – author of the Soviet classic *Quiet Flows the Don* – lived for many years at no. 33; and no. 30 is the former house of the Slavophile writer Sergei Aksakov (see p.298). The ponderous Stalin-style edifice next door is the former **Kremlin Polyclinic**, where senior *apparatchiki* enjoyed the best medical treatment that the Soviet Union could offer. Further along and across the street at no. 27, the **Herzen House-Museum** (dom-muzey Gertsena; currently closed for restoration; call ☎241 58 59 for further information) records Alexander Herzen's odyssey around Europe, during which he was expelled from France after the 1848 Revolution, moved to London and founded the radical newspaper *Kolokol* (The Bell) which, although published in London, had a great impact in Russia despite being banned – even the tsar read it.

One direct route to ulitsa Prechistenka is **Denezhniy pereulok**, which turns off the Arbat just before the MID and brings you to a typical wooden house of the early nineteenth century (no. 9), painted turquoise and white. Halfway down the next block, the **Italian Embassy** (no. 5) occupies the former Berg mansion, a sandstone pile whose interior manifests every style from Baroque to neo-Gothic. Confiscated from its owner after the Revolution, the mansion was given to Imperial Germany as an embassy just after the Bolsheviks signed the humiliating Peace of Brest-Litovsk. By following the road to the very end, across Lyovshinsky pereulok, you'll emerge on ulitsa Prechistenka.

Along Prechistenka

Ulitsa Prechistenka (Communion St), the medieval road leading from the Kremlin to the Novodevichiy Convent, has been one of Moscow's most prestigious avenues since the sixteenth century, delineating the southern edge of the Old Equerries' quarter. Its array of mansions in the Russian Empire style – newly built after the fire of 1812 – can really only be appreciated by walking along Prechistenka. If you're not coming from the direction of the Arbat, the best starting point is **Kropotkinskaya metro**, whose stylish platform is itself an attraction. In Soviet times, the avenue was also named "Kropotkinskaya", after the Anarchist Prince Kropotkin (see opposite), who was born nearby.

Prechistenka starts at the bottom of the hill with a **statue of Friedrich Engels**, erected in 1976. The idea was that this would be "united" with the statue of Marx on Teatralnaya ploshchad by prospekt Marksa, to form a kind of Communist ley line. Behind the statue rises the **Golovin palace**, a simple brick structure with crested *nalichniki* and a steeply pitched roof, built at the end of the seventeenth century by a family associated with Peter the Great. The house across the road at no. 10 was the headquarters of the wartime Jewish Anti-Fascist Committee that was liquidated by Stalin in 1948 (see box, p.188–189).

The Pushkin and Tolstoy museums and the House of Photography

Further uphill and across the road at no. 12, the former Khrushchev mansion contains the **Pushkin Museum** (muzey A.S. Pushkina; Tues–Sun 10am–6pm; closed last Fri of each month; R80), with ten rooms devoted to the life and works of the poet. Besides his sketches and first editions, the mansion's interior is notable for its elegant fireplaces and ceiling frescoes. Built of wood covered in stucco, its exterior is colonnaded on two sides; the entrance is on Khruschevskiy pereulok, around the corner. Here you'll find a large, modern glass-roofed extension that hosts temporary exhibitions on diverse aspects of Russian culture – from Symbolist poetry to Soviet pop music (for details, see Ⓦwww.pushkinmuseum.ru).

On the next block is another impressive pile whose gates and walls are topped by lions and urns, which now serves as the **House of Scientists** and is an occasional venue for classical concerts. Directly opposite at no. 11, the former Lopukhin mansion has been turned into a **Tolstoy Literary Museum**

Militia and the Criminal Investigations Department. "**Petrovka 38**" is as famous in Russia as Scotland Yard is in Britain, having been acclaimed in Soviet pulp fiction and TV dramas since the 1970s, and more recently featured in the best-selling novels of Alexandra Marinina (a former police criminologist) and Nikolai Leonov.

Around the corner on 2-y Kolobovskiy pereulok stands a battered relic of law enforcement from the years before Peter the Great. The multi-domed **Church of the Sign** was erected by a company of Streltsy in the late seventeenth century, when several companies were settled in this quarter to defend the ramparts and keep order in the Earth Town.

Tsvetnoy bulvar

Tsvetnoy bulvar is the prettiest radial avenue along this stretch of the Ring, having a wooded park with wrought-iron railings running up the middle from Trubnaya ploshchad. From 1851, when flowers (*tsvety*) began to be sold on Trubnaya ploshchad, the boulevard became Moscow's flower market, and its red-light district. The side streets to the east harboured dozens of brothels coyly referred to in the 1875 *Murray's Handbook* as "several *guinguettes* where the male traveller may study 'life'". There, Chekhov wrote from personal experience: "No one hurried, no one hid his face in his coat, no one shook his head reproachfully. This unconcern, that medley of pianos and fiddles, the bright windows, wide open doors – it all struck a garish, impudent, dashing, devil-may-care note."

Today, the boulevard offers more wholesome entertainment in the form of the **Yuri Nikulin Circus** (better known abroad as the Moscow State Circus). The circus is named after its late director, a lanky, craggy-faced giant beloved as a clown and a comic actor (in such classic films as *Diamond Arm*), but also adept at serious roles, like the officer in *They Fought for the Motherland* (for which he drew on his own wartime experiences). A life-size **statue of Nikulin** beside a battered roadster portrays him as his best-known clown persona, on the pavement outside the circus, where his body lay in state beneath its big top before being buried with full honours in the Novodevichiy Cemetery in 1997. For details of performances at this and other circuses, see Chapter 14, "The Arts".

To Krasnye vorota, Kursk Station and beyond

The **eastern half of the Garden Ring** – from Tsvetnoy bulvar to Krasnye vorota, and on to Kursk Station – is the least appealing part of the Zemlyanoy Gorod, and anyone in a hurry could take the **metro** straight to Krasnye vorota to see its Stalin skyscraper, before checking out a few attractions in the back-streets towards the Boulevard Ring (also accessible from Chistye Prudy metro), or heading on to the Sakharov Museum beyond Kursk Station.

Sukharevskaya ploshchad and Sadovaya-Spasskaya ulitsa

If you opt for a trolleybus ride around the Ring, the first notable junction is **Sukharevskaya ploshchad** which – like the local metro station – is named after the bygone **Sukharev Tower** (Sukhareva bashnya). Erected in honour of Colonel Sukharev – whose soldiers had escorted the young Peter the Great and his mother to safety during the Streltsy mutiny of 1682 – this was designed in the form of a ship, with the tower representing a mast and its surrounding galleries a quarterdeck. Reputedly, Peter's private Masonic lodge held rituals in the tower, which was thereafter regarded as unlucky. It was converted in 1829 into an aqueduct-cum-fountain for supplying Moscow with water piped in from 16km away, and subsequently demolished during the widening of the Garden Ring in the 1930s. A small **replica** of the tower rises above one of the buildings on the northern side of Sukharevskaya ploshchad. Before and after the Revolution the square was known for its huge flea market for stolen goods, causing Lenin to lament that in the soul of every Russian there was "a little Sukharevka". Today, there's a vast **computer mall** where you can buy almost any software, DVD or CD-ROM (mostly pirated) – a Sukharevka for the cyber age.

Further on appears the former **Sheremetev Hospital**, a huge curved edifice painted sea-green and turquoise. Founded by Count Nikolai Sheremetev, the hospital was built (1794–1807) by the serf architect Elizvoi Nazarov, and had a poorhouse in its left wing. After the death of his beloved serf actress wife, the Count commissioned Catherine the Great's court architect Quarenghi to change the hospital's church into a memorial chapel, which he enhanced by adding a semicircular portico. Since Soviet times the building has housed the Sklifosovskiy Institute, named after a pioneering surgeon of the late nineteenth century.

Finance and bureaucracy are the keynotes on **Sadovaya-Spasskaya ulitsa**, with the triple bronzed-glass towers of the **International Banking Centre** visible off to the right, just before you sight the rust-red **Ministry of Agriculture**. One of the last Constructivist edifices built (1928–33) in Moscow, the ministry was designed by Shchusev, the architect of Lenin's Mausoleum. The prospekt between them is named after Dr Andrei Sakharov (1921–90), the nuclear physicist and human rights campaigner who lived at no. 47 after he and his dissident wife, Yelena Bonner, were allowed to return from exile by Gorbachev. The 1980s Banking Centre opposite their flat is a logical outgrowth of the older economic administration blocks that flank the section of the prospekt nearer the Boulevard Ring, where fans of Brutalist architecture will go for the **Tsentrosoyuz** building designed by Le Corbusier. Built in 1929–36 for the Union of Consumer Societies, this hideous clinker-block structure is now occupied by the State Statistical Commission, which produced 30,000 million forms a year during Soviet times. Its obverse facade overlooks Myasnitskaya ulitsa, where the former **Baryshnikov Mansion** at no. 42 houses the editorial staff of the magazine *Argumenty i Fakti* ("Arguments and Facts"), a torchbearer of glasnost in the mid-1980s.

Krasnye vorota and the backstreets

The junction known as **Krasnye vorota** (Beautiful Gate) takes its name from a Baroque triumphal arch erected in honour of Empress Elizabeth in 1742. For the coronation of Tsar Paul in 1796 the streets were lined with tables spread with food and drink for the populace all the way from here to the Kremlin. Although the arch was demolished in 1928, the locality is still popularly called Krasnye vorota – which means "Red Gate" in modern Russian and seems an apt name for a square dominated by a **Stalin skyscraper** with a huge red-granite portal. Erected in 1947–53, its 24-storey central block is shared by the Transport Construction Ministry and the Directorate for the Exploitation of Tall Buildings, while the wings contain communal flats. Typically, the portal is flanked by propylaea and urns, and the towers festooned with heroic statuary. A plaque on the wall around the southeast corner attests that the Romantic poet Mikhail Lermontov was born on this spot in 1814, which accounts for the triangular-shaped square being named **Lermontovskaya ploshchad**, with its **monument to Lermontov**, a frock-coated statue.

The **backstreets** within the Garden Ring represent an older Moscow that turns its back on Stalinist gigantism, preserving an intimate, residential character. Once-elegant mansions turned into institutes or communal flats are juxtaposed with postwar low-rises, schools and clinics. Though specific sights are limited, it's a nice area to wander around, like the Ukrainian Quarter within the Boulevard Ring.

▲ Stalinist skyscraper, Krasnye Vorota

The Yusupov Mansion

By heading 500m south from Krasnye Vorota metro and turning off onto Bolshoy Kharitonevskiy pereulok, you'll find the **Yusupov Mansion** behind a swirly iron fence and a grove of trees. Painted a deep red, with its pilasters and *nalichniki* picked out in white, the mansion's melange of undercrofts, wings and annexes typifies the multi-cellular architecture of the late seventeenth century, unified by a checkerboard roof. One of its earliest occupants was Peter Tolstoy, the head of Peter the Great's Secret Chancellery. It is entered via an enclosed porch around the back, added in the 1890s, like the ceremonial gateway that bears the Yusupov crest. An immensely rich family descended from the Nogai Tatar Khans – now chiefly remembered for the last of the dynasty, Prince Felix, who murdered Rasputin – the Yusupovs acquired the mansion in 1727, but preferred to live in St Petersburg and rent it out; Pushkin lived here as a child. After the Revolution it became the Academy of Agriculture, where the eminent geneticist Vavilov worked from 1929 to 1935. Though it's not open to the public, you could try begging a peep at its romantic interior, a warren of pseudo-medieval chambers furnished with tiled stoves.

The Vasnetsov Flat-Museum

A few-minutes' walk from the Yusupov Mansion, a nondescript brownstone at Furmanniy pereulok 6 harbours the **Apollinarius Vasnetsov Flat-Museum** (muzey-kvartira A.M. Vasnetsova; Tues–Sat 11am–5pm; R160). The historical artist Apollinarius Vasnetsov (1856–1933) lived here from 1903 until his death, an "internal exile" from Soviet life and Socialist art, like his brother, Viktor (whose own fairytale house is also a museum: see p.269). Flat no. 22 displays Apollinarius's carefully researched drawings of Old Muscovy and the Simonov Monastery, plus a portrait of him by Viktor. His living quarters are preserved across the landing, where the drawing room is festooned with pictures given as gifts by Savrasov, Polonev and other artist friends, while the study contains an ingenious chair that "changes sides" (demonstrated by the curator). The tour ends in Vasnetsov's studio, hung with cloud and light studies; notice his travelling painting kit, and the preparatory drawing for his last work, on the easel.

The Barashi quarter

If you're still in the mood for walking, head south into the quarter where the tsar's tent-makers (*Barashi*) lived in the fifteenth century, which gives its name to the former **Church of the Resurrection in Barashi**, where Empress Elizabeth is said to have secretly married her lover Alexei Razumovsky in 1742. Much altered since then and now a fire station, the shocking-pink edifice will set you in the direction of the **Church of the Presentation in Barashi** (tserkov Vvedeniya v Barashakh), down a lane to the right. Built in 1701, its strawberry facade is decorated with cable-mouldings, and crested, scalloped *nalichniki*, while ventilation flues and builders' rubble attest to the church's use as a factory in Soviet times, and efforts to restore it. By walking around to the rear side of the church and along Yakovaposttolskiy pereulok, you'll emerge on the Garden Ring to the north of Kursk Station, on the stretch of the Ring called ulitsa Zemlyanoy val (Earth Town Rampart St).

Kursk Station and the Sakharov Museum

The difference between Moscow in Brezhnev's time and nowadays is writ large around **Kursk Station** (Kurskiy vokzal). Last modernized in 1972, the vast steel-and-glass shed might have been even larger, under a 1930s plan to combine all of Moscow's mainline stations into a single mega-terminal serving every point in the USSR. Fortunately this never happened; the existing station (for Vladimir, Crimea, the Caucasus and eastern Ukraine) is bad enough, with a dank labyrinth of underpasses where travellers slump amid their baggage. In spirit, little has changed since it featured in Yerofeev's 1970s novel *Moscow Stations* as the starting point of his hero's alcoholic odyssey (see "Books", p.445). Beneath the station lies **Kurskaya metro**, whose splendid vestibule upheld by massive ornamental pillars justifies a visit using the Circle line.

The other side of the coin is represented by the 24-hour **Atrium Mall**, just up the road, whose fashion and fast-food outlets, bowling lanes and glittering atrium are a Mecca for Moscow's middle classes. Around midnight, the underpasses between Kurskaya metro's exits are full of prostitutes and punters, picking their way to the *Boarhouse* past homeless alcoholics.

The Sakharov Museum

Beyond the station, Zemlyanoy val plunges downhill towards the River Yauza, its fringes getting greener as it goes. Bilingual signposts ensure that you'll be able to find your way to the **Andrei Sakharov Museum and Public Center** (muzey i obshchestvenniy tsentr imeni Andreya Sakharova, Ⓦ www.sakharov-center.ru; Tues–Sun 11am–7pm; free) beside the embankment, fronted by a chunk from the Berlin Wall. Opened in 1996 by Sakharov's widow and fellow human rights crusader, Yelena Bonner, it documents the evils of the Soviet era and upholds their ideals in present-day Russia. In 2001, an exhibition entitled "Caution: Religion" was trashed by Orthodox activists.

On the lower floor are a multilingual **library** of Gulag-related material and a centre for research and civic outreach. Upstairs is a well-laid-out **exhibition**, juxtaposing the myths and realities of Communism with artefacts from camps, dossiers of victims and other documentation that brings home the scale and brutality of the Gulag (with archive footage on the monitors, if they're working). The 1950s cultural "thaw" and the 1960s Bards movement are represented by photos, *samizdat* editions of forbidden books and bootlegged Beatles LPs; the Jewish *refuseniki* and the Moscow Helsinki Group complete its "Resistance to the Regime" section. Sakharov's own life – a physicist decorated for creating the Soviet H-Bomb, who became the USSR's leading dissident – is detailed in the final part, along with photos of memorials to the victims of Soviet repression and horrific images from present-day Chechnya, where human rights abuses are still routine. As Sakharov said at his Nobel Prize lecture in 1975, "Peace, progress and human rights – these three goals are inextricably linked. It is impossible to achieve any one of these goals while ignoring the others".

Streets and squares

Bolshaya Nikitskaya ulitsa	Большая Никитская улица
Bolshoy Nikolopeskovskiy pereulok	Большой Николопесковский переулок
Bolshaya Sadovaya ulitsa	Большая Садовая улица
Bolshoy Kharitonevskiy pereulok	Большой Харитоньевский переулок
Delegatskya ulitsa	Делегатская улица
Denezhniy pereulok	Денежный переулок
Furmanniy pereulok	Фурманный переулок
Karetniy ryad	Каретный ряд
Krivoarbatskiy pereulok	Кривоарбатский переулок
Kropotkinskiy pereulok	Кропоткинский переулок
Kudrinskaya ploshchad	Кудринская площадь
Lermontovskaya ploshchad	Лермонтовская площадь
Malaya Bronnaya ulitsa	Малая Бронная улица
Malaya Dmitrovka ulitsa	Малая Дмитровка улица
Malaya Nikitskaya ulitsa	Малая Никитская улица
Novinskiy bulvar	Новинский бульвар
pereulok Sivtsev Vrazhek	переулок Сивцев Вражек
Povarskaya ulitsa	Поварская улица
Pushkinskaya ploshchad	Пушкинская площадь
Sadovaya-Karetnaya ulitsa	Садовая-Каретная улица
Sadovaya-Kudrinskaya ulitsa	Садовая-Кудринская улица
Sadovaya-Triumfalnaya ulitsa	Садовая-Триумфальная улица
Sadovaya-Samotyochnaya ulitsa	Садовая-Самотёчная улица
Sadovaya-Spasskaya ulitsa	Садовя-Спасская улица
Spasopeskovskiy pereulok	Спасопесковский переулок
Smolenskaya ploshchad	Смоленская площадь
Sukharevskaya ploshchad	Сухаревская площадь
Triumfalnaya ploshchad	Триумфальная площадь
Tsvetnoy bulvar	Цветной бульвар
Trubnaya ploshchad	Трубная площадь
Tverskaya ulitsa	Тверская улица

Streets and squares	
ulitsa Arbat	улица Арбат
ulitsa Malaya Molchanovka	улица Малая Молчановка
ulitsa Noviy Arbat	улица Новый Арбат
ulitsa Petrovka	улица Петровка
ulitsa Prechistenka	улица Пречистенка
ulitsa Spriridonovka	улица Спиридоновка
Vspolniy pereulok	Вспольный переулок
Metro stations	
Arbatskaya	Арбатская
Chkalovskaya	Чкаловская
Krasnye Vorota	Красные ворота
Kurskaya	Курская
Mayakovskaya	Маяковская
Pushkinskaya	Пушкинская
Smolenskaya	Смоленская
Tsvetnoy Bulvar	Цветной бульвар
Tverskaya	Тверская
Museums	
Andrey Sakharov Museum and Public Center	музей и общественный центр имени Андрея Сахарова
Apollinarius Vasnetsov Flat-Museum	музей-квартира А.М. Васнецова
Alexei Tolstoy Flat-Museum	музей-квартира А.Н. Толстого
Bulgakov Museum	музей Булгакова
Chaliapin House-Museum	дом-музей Ф.И. Шаляпина
Chekhov House-Museum	дом-музей А.П. Чехова
Gorky House-Museum	дом-музей А.М. Горького
Herzen House-Museum	дом-музей А.И. Герцена
Lermontov Museum	музей М.Ю. Лермонтова
Moscow House of Photography	Московский дом фотографии
Museum of Applied, Decorative and Folk Arts	музей декоративно -прикладного и народного искусства
Museum of Modern History	музей современной истории
Museum of Unique Dolls	музей редких кукол
Pushkin Museum	музей А.С. Пушкина
Pushkin on the Arbat Museum	музей-квартира А.С. Пушкина
Scriabin House-Museum	дом-музей Скрябина
Tolstoy Literary Museum	музей Л.Н. Толстого
Tsvetaeva Museum	музей М. Цветаевой

Moscow: the new New York

Thirty years ago, as capital of the USSR, Moscow would never have been associated with glamour and glitz. Today, however, there are few places in the world which can claim to have more style – indeed, Moscow is often referred to as the "new New York". Watching the comings and goings on a Moscow metro platform is like sitting in the front row of a designer fashion show – groups of incredibly beautiful women dressed in eye-catching outfits stop, twirl and then disappear onto the trains as if performing for an audience.

Arbat Street ▲

GUM shopping centre on Red Square ▼

Music and art

In this city which never sleeps it is possible to find any musical style you like in almost any venue – a far cry from the days of Soviet censorship of music. In Soviet times, **Arbat Street** was one of the few places where a little more freedom was tolerated, and today it is still a popular centre for musicians to meet and jam on the street late into the night, while artists sell their paintings and photographs. In the winter the street becomes a playground with dozens of snowmen forming a crowd of constantly changing faces – passers-by mould the snowmen into brides, grooms, children and old people and whole groups playing guitars. This is a classically Muscovite approach to street art – unexpected, humorous and inclusive.

Designers

Boutiques from every major fashion house in the world now grace the boulevards where once only small soviet stores stood. GUM, the huge shopping centre on Red Square, has all the top designer stores from Paris, London and New York. But it is not the imported fashions that make Moscow so stylish – it is the resident designers and the millions of Muscovites themselves. Some **home-grown designers** such as Denis Semachev or Alyona Akhmadulina have developed international reputations, others, like Julia Dalakian and Masha Tsigal, are known only locally. But despite a low profile outside Russia, in Moscow they enjoy celebrity status and have a great deal of influence, owning clothing stores, restaurants, clubs and couture houses, and appearing regularly on TV and in magazines. Their designs embrace the quirkier side of Russian taste – the love of skin-tight leopard skin prints, for example – playfully poking fun at Muscovites at the same time as making them look good.

Many new designers start out in places such as **Winzavod** (see p.377). Once home to Moscow's largest wine warehouse and liquor distribution company, this complex of refurbished industrial buildings (close to the Kurskaya and Chkalovskaya metros) is now a vibrant community of galleries, design studios, designer clothing shops, interior design businesses and architects' offices. In the evenings it often hosts concerts of both local Russian bands and international indie groups.

▲ Top international designer stores abound

▼ Muscovites wrap up warm in style

Architecture

Winzavod's industrial buildings are a world away from the beautiful Style Moderne (Russian Art Nouveau) architecture of early 1900s Moscow. Displaced first by the palatial but austere **Stalinist style**, seen in the seven towers scattered around the city centre – the biggest, the forbidding Moscow University building, looms over the river – and then by the ugly utilitarian Khrushchev era apartment blocks, many **Style Moderne** buildings have now been demolished to make way for new developments, though there are still some fine examples left (see box on next page). New towers are shooting up from the rubble all over Moscow and especially in the World Trade Centre area near Kievskaya Train station: fantasies of steel and glass, their sheer exuberance is a metaphor for the way in which modern oligarchs have sprung from the ruins of the Soviet state.

▼ New high-rise apartment blocks

Ceramic frieze by Vrubel at the *Metropol* ▲

The great staircase at the Ryabushinsky Mansion ▼

Moscow's top Style Moderne buildings

Isakov Mansion Designed by leading Style Moderne architect, Kekushev, the Isakov Mansion was his last major work. Look out for the two ladies sculpted into the wall below the curving eaves, and the plastic flowing forms on the exterior walls.

Metropol Hotel See p.103. The *Metropol* is one of Moscow's most accessible Style Moderne buildings – wander though its lobby and restaurants to admire the many statues incorporated into its structure, and also check out the exterior with its ceramic friezes by Vrubel and Golovin.

MKhAT theatre Kamergersky lane 4. The entrance of the theatre's features huge wooden doors whose frames soar above a large flowing sculpture by Ann Golubkina, contrasting with the geometric designs on the walls.

Ryabushinsky Mansion. See p.159. The architect Shekhtel's masterpiece, the Ryabushinsky Mansion is Moscow's best example of the Style Moderne movement. Don't miss the curves of the stained-glass windows that call to mind cloaked figures, or the railing of the great staircase which flows like melted wax.

Smirnov Mansion Tverskoy boulevard 18. Also by Shekhtel, the Smirnov Mansion was once home to the Smirnov vodka family and is notable for its exquisite wrought-iron balconies. It is often used for receptions and events, when you can view its stained-glass windows and panelled wainscoting, as well as the Egyptian-inspired hieroglyphs on the square pillars in the main reception area.

Yaroslavsky railway station Another Shekhtel building, Yaroslavsky station looks more like a chateau or mini-Kremlin. Its entrance – flanked by two towers and a curving roof – leads into an interior replete with plaster sculptures of dolphins, birds and animals, with elaborate moldings capping pillars and walls.

5

Krasnaya Presnya, Fili and the southwest

Beyond the Garden Ring, Moscow seems an undifferentiated sprawl of blocks and avenues, attesting to its phenomenal growth in Soviet times. Yet on closer inspection, each arc of the city contains a scattering of monuments and institutions that deserve attention. This is particularly true of **Krasnaya Presnya, Fili and the southwest** – a swathe of the city defined by the loops of the Moskva River and the approaches to the Sparrow Hills.

Krasnaya Presnya is chiefly notable for the ex-Parliament building known as the **White House** – whose role in the crises of the 1990s invested it with symbolic potency – but also harbours the lovely **Vagankov Cemetery**. Over the river, a showpiece avenue that epitomizes Stalinist planning forges out past the **Borodino Panorama Museum** and **Victory Park** which commemorates the USSR's triumphs and sacrifices during World War II. The lovely **Church of the Intercession at Fili** is a sole reminder of the estates and villages that once flanked Moscow's western approaches, where Napoleon marched into the city in 1812, and the Red Army advanced to confront the Nazis in 1941. An earlier vestige of military history is the reconstructed medieval fortress of **Setunskiy Stan**.

Closer to the centre, a peninsula defined by the oxbow Moskva River boasts **Tolstoy's House** and the fairytale **Church of St Nicholas of the Weavers** in the Khamovniki district, while further out lies the **Novodevichie Convent and Cemetery**, the grandest of Moscow's monastic complexes. Further south, across the river, a magnificent view of the city is afforded by the **Sparrow Hills**, dominated by the titanic Stalin skyscraper of **Moscow State University** (MGU). And if science museums are your thing, don't miss the **Darwin and Paleontology museums** out beyond the university.

This chapter is largely structured with **transport** in mind, each major section corresponding to a metro line used to reach the sights. All of them connect with the Circle line, enabling you to switch from one itinerary to another with relative ease.

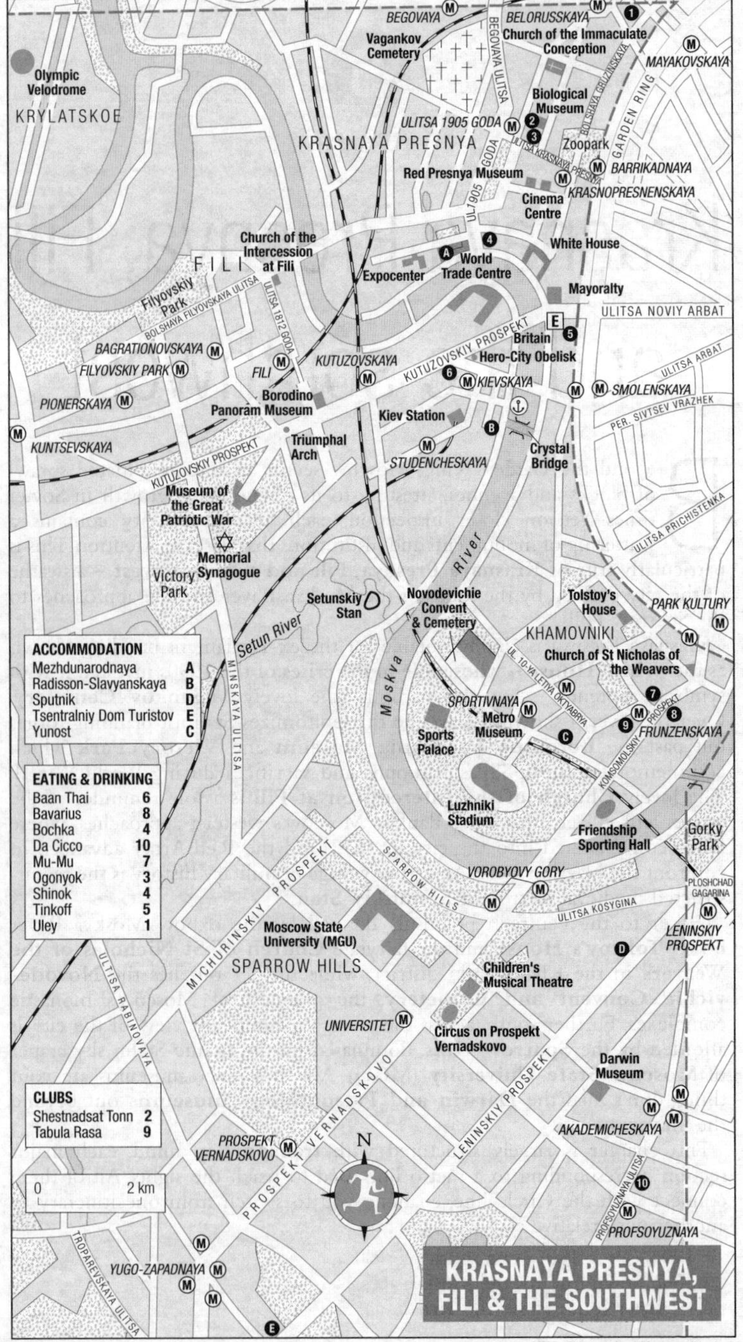
KRASNAYA PRESNYA, FILI & THE SOUTHWEST
ACCOMMODATION
Mezhdunarodnaya A
Radisson-Slavyanskaya B
Sputnik D
Tsentralniy Dom Turistov E
Yunost C
EATING & DRINKING
Baan Thai 6
Bavarius 8
Bochka 4
Da Cicco 10
Mu-Mu 7
Ogonyok 3
Shinok 4
Tinkoff 5
Uley 1
CLUBS
Shestnadsat Tonn 2
Tabula Rasa 9
0 2 km
N
Olympic Velodrome
KRYLATSKOE
BEGOVAYA
Vagankov Cemetery
BEGOVAYA ULITSA
BELORUSSKAYA
Church of the Immaculate Conception
MAYAKOVSKAYA
Biological Museum
BOLSHAYA GRUZINSKAYA
GARDEN RING
ULITSA 1905 GODA
KRASNAYA PRESNYA
Zoopark
ULITSA KRASNAYA PRESNYA
BARRIKADNAYA
Red Presnya Museum
KRASNOPRESNENSKAYA
UL 1905 GODA
Cinema Centre
Church of the Intercession at Fili
FILI
White House
World Trade Centre
Expocenter
Mayoralty
ULITSA NOVIY ARBAT
Filyovskiy Park
BOLSHAYA FILYOVSKAYA ULITSA
ULITSA 1812 GODA
Britain
KUTUZOVSKIY PROSPEKT
BAGRATIONOVSKAYA
Hero-City Obelisk
ULITSA ARBAT
FILYOVSKIY PARK
FILI
KUTUZOVSKAYA
KIEVSKAYA
SMOLENSKAYA
Borodino Panoram Museum
PIONERSKAYA
Kiev Station
PER. SIVTSEV VRAZHEK
KUNTSEVSKAYA
Triumphal Arch
Crystal Bridge
STUDENCHESKAYA
KUTUZOVSKIY PROSPEKT
Museum of the Great Patriotic War
ULITSA PRICHISTENKA
Memorial Synagogue
River
Victory Park
Setunskiy Stan
Novodevichie Convent & Cemetery
Tolstoy's House
PARK KULTURY
Setun River
KHAMOVNIKI
Church of St Nicholas of the Weavers
UL. 10-YA LETIYA OKTYABRYA
Moskva
SPORTIVNAYA
Metro Museum
KOMSOMOLSKIY PROSPEKT
FRUNZENSKAYA
Sports Palace
MINSKAYA ULITSA
Luzhniki Stadium
Friendship Sporting Hall
Gorky Park
SPARROW HILLS
VOROBYOVY GORY
MICHURINSKIY PROSPEKT
PLOSHCHAD GAGARINA
ULITSA KOSYGINA
Moscow State University (MGU)
LENINSKIY PROSPEKT
SPARROW HILLS
Children's Musical Theatre
ULITSA RABINOVAYA
UNIVERSITET
Circus on Prospekt Vernadskovo
Darwin Museum
LENINSKIY PROSPEKT
PROSPEKT VERNADSKOVO
AKADEMICHESKAYA
PROSPEKT VERNADSKOVO
PROFSOYUZNAYA ULITSA
PROFSOYUZNAYA
TROPAREVSKAYA ULITSA
YUGO-ZAPADNAYA
Palaeontology Museum (5km)

Krasnaya Presnya

The **Krasnaya Presnya** district beyond Kudrinskaya ploshchad (see p.157) is a former working-class quarter that was once Moscow's most radical and has now become one of its better neighbourhoods. Besides amenities, the district has political and financial clout, harbouring the Russian White House, Moscow's World Trade Center and other corporate megaliths. These all seem a far cry from the proletarian militancy evoked by huge sculptures, faded murals and names bestowed on streets and metro stations in honour of the 1905 uprising, until one remembers how Russia's fate has twice been decided here in the 1990s.

The district's early history reads like a Marxist tract, as the local textiles industry boomed and slum landlords made fortunes by exploiting rural migrants, creating an urban proletariat receptive to revolutionary agitation. Originally called simply Presnya after a tributary of the Moskva River running through the district, it earned the name "Red" (*Krasnaya*) during the December uprising of 1905, when local workers heeded the Moscow Soviet's rash call to overthrow the Tsarist government, which had just suppressed the Soviet in St Petersburg. The poorly armed insurgents failed to break through into central Moscow and withdrew behind barricades in Presnya, only surrendering after nine days of bombardment and close-quarter fighting, whereupon hundreds more fell to army firing squads. During the Brezhnev era, Presnya's profile was transformed by new housing, as bureaucrats awoke to the potential of a waterfront site only fifteen-minutes' drive from the Kremlin.

Barrikadnaya and the Zoopark

As its name suggests, **Barrikadnaya** was the site of a major barricade during the 1905 Revolution, where the workers retrenched after failing to break through into the bourgeois districts within the Garden Ring. The barricade stood beside the Presnya River, which was channelled underground in 1908; the only part that's still visible forms a large pond just inside the entrance to Moscow's Zoopark.

Fronted by a fairytale tower and a rusticated arch, the **Zoopark** (Tues–Sun: summer 10am–7pm, winter 10am–5pm; R150) consists of two sections linked by a pedestrian bridge spanning Bolshaya Gruzinskaya ulitsa. Though money has been spent on improving some of the enclosures and building an **Exzotarium** to display exotic wildlife, the environment for many of the animals remains poor. Still, youngsters are likely to enjoy it, especially the touchy-feely encounters in the children's zoo on the eastern side of Bolshaya Gruzinskaya. On a more macabre note, the area's violent past was dramatically highlighted during the zoo's refurbishment in the 1990s, when the skeletons of several hundred Muscovites secretly killed in Stalin's time were discovered.

Down towards the river

Emerging from the Krasnopresnenskaya metro pavilion across the road from the zoo, turn left around the corner to find the **Cinema Centre** (Kino tsentr), a traditional venue for art-house movies (see p.375), then either head down Druzhinnikovskaya ulitsa, directly behind it – past the shrine to the "martyrs" of 1993 (see p.180) – or south along Konyushovskaya ulitsa, the main road running down towards the Moskva River.

The latter route passes the **Krasnaya Presnya Stadium** and the red-brick blocks of the **new US Embassy**, across the road. In the mid-1980s, this caused grave embarrassment when it was found to be riddled with KGB bugs, implanted during construction. The US reckoned that it would be cheaper to tear the whole place down and start afresh rather than de-bug it, until Gorbachev handed the Ambassador a stack of plans 15cm thick. Naturally, the Americans never believed that all the bugs had been exposed, so the building remains largely empty, and most embassy business is still conducted at the old embassy on the Garden Ring (p.158).

The White House

The **White House** or **Beliy dom**, a marble-clad hulk crowned by a gilded clock and the Russian tricolour, is known around the world for its starring role in two confrontations broadcast by CNN. When the building was completed in 1981 to provide spacious offices for the Council of Ministers of the Russian Federation, nobody dreamed that its windowless Hall of Nationalities would serve as a bunker ten years later, despite the paranoid foresight that specified the construction of a network of escape tunnels from the building. All this changed after the Russian Parliament took up residence and Yeltsin was elected president with a mandate to take on the *apparat*. When the old guard staged a putsch against Gorbachev on August 19, 1991, the democratic opposition made the White House their rallying point, and a hundred thousand Russians from all walks of life formed human barricades fifty layers deep around the building, where Yeltsin, Rutskoy and Khasbulatov were holed up on the third floor, phoning around the garrisons and broadcasting defiance.

Two years later, the White House became the crucible of conflict between parliament and president, culminating in what Russians call the **October events**. The dubious legality of Yeltsin's dissolution of parliament and his sanctions against the deputies who occupied the White House enabled Khasbulatov and Rutskoy to claim that they were only defending the constitution when they urged a mob of supporters to seize the Ostankino TV centre on October 3. Next day, the army bowed to Yeltsin's orders and shelled the White House into submission.

Since then the building has been renamed the **House of Government** (dom Praiteltsva) and its occupants have taken precautions against future trouble by erecting a tall ornamental fence around the perimeter through which you can peer. The White House is best seen from the embankment side, where an outpost flying the Iraqi flag added a bizarre touch to the defences in 1993. From here you also have a striking view of the Stalin-Gothic *Ukraina Hotel* (see p.185) across the river, and the World Trade Center, 700m west along the embankment (see p.183).

The Gorbaty most and shrine to the October events

Beside the main road behind the White House lies the **Gorbaty most** (Hunchback Bridge), a small cobbled structure that workers barricaded in December 1905, to bar Tsarist troops from Presnya, until artillery blew them away. Later, the bridge was covered over and forgotten till it was unearthed and restored in 1979, when a **monument** showing three generations of workers fighting side by side was erected nearby. This proved apposite when the barricades went up again in the 1990s, as people gathered to defend the White House.

"Patriots were killed here" reads the inscription on a cross behind the White House, a belief manifest in an **outdoor shrine** on Druzhinnikovskaya ulitsa, where the flags of the Soviet Union and the Tsarist army and navy fly above the portraits of 100 "martyrs", accompanied by photos of bullet-riddled corpses and a miniature barricade. An annual **remembrance service** (Oct 2–4), charged with grief and hatred, symbolizes the pain of Russia's change from communism to "democracy". The atmosphere during the service is fairly anti-foreign and tourists may not feel very welcome: if possible, avoid visiting on these dates. At other times the shrine is deserted, so you can look around without being approached by old ladies who declare themselves to be "patriots, not Communists", before ranting about how Russia was plundered by the oligarchs and the US with the connivance of Yeltsin, Luzhkov and Patriarch Alexei – all of whom are "really Jews".

The Mayoralty

To the east of the White House looms a glassy 31-storey block housing Moscow's **Mayoralty**, which also played a part in the bloody events of 1993. On the afternoon of October 3, Rutskoy and Khasbulatov's supporters were holding a triumphal rally outside the White House to celebrate the breaking of the police blockade when they were fired on by snipers from the Mayoralty and the adjacent *Mir Hotel*. At that point, the rebels were on the verge of a political victory, as the Federation Council had just agreed on a compromise solution to the crisis that would have cast Yeltsin in the role of provocateur and his opponents as moderates. Instead, the sniping goaded them into storming the Mayoralty – whose lower floors were set ablaze – and this easy victory convinced them that power was ripe for the taking, causing Rutskoy and Khasbulatov to issue the fateful order to seize the TV centre (see p.283).

The Red Presnya Museum

Cutting a swathe through the hinterland of Barrikadnaya, **ulitsa Krasnaya Presnya** was dubbed the "Murder Strip" in the mid-1990s due to the regularity with which owners of its nightclubs got shot, but is nowadays only dangerous for its traffic and devoid of interest. However, there are several attractions in the backstreets, about a fifteen-minute walk from Krasnopresnenskaya metro.

South of the avenue, an ugly concrete block at Bolshoy Peredtechenskiy pereulok 4 contains the intriguing **Red Presnya Museum** (muzey Krasnaya Presnya; Tues–Fri & Sun 10am–6pm, Sat 10am–5pm; closed last Fri in each month; R70). An offshoot of the Museum of Modern History (see p.152), its first (ground) floor displays photos of the 1905 Revolution and the 1991 putsch. Exhibits upstairs represent the triumphs and tragedies of the Soviet era, from the flying suit worn by Chkalov on his pioneering flight across the North Pole in 1937, to a prisoner's mug and spoon from the Sakhalin labour camp and the rehabilitation certificates posthumously issued to victims of the purges. From World War II there are prisoners' clothes from Auschwitz and the personal telephone of German Field Marshal von Paulus, captured at Stalingrad. You can also see Gagarin's overcoat and the spacesuit used to send a dog – Laika – into orbit prior to his epic voyage. Last but not least, there's a huge **diorama** of the barricade at the Hunchback Bridge in 1905, with commentary in various languages, complete with the sound of shell fire and the strains of the *Internationale* – clearly unchanged since the museum opened in the 1970s.

Malaya Gruzinskaya ulitsa

Across the avenue, **Malaya Gruzinskaya ulitsa** offers another perspective on Presnya. Its Soviet name, Little Georgian Street, belied its pre-Revolutionary character as an enclave of Polish engineers and railway workers, who ran Belarus

Station. Many left in the 1920s or fell victim to the purges; a heritage mutely acknowledged by the opening of a Polish embassy and cultural centre in the era of "fraternal relations". A grander Polish symbol is the neo-Gothic **Church of the Immaculate Conception**, whose steeple and spires are boldly spotlit at night, while its stained-glass rose window catches the eye by day. Built in 1906 with donations from the 30,000-strong Polish community, it was plundered in 1930 and only returned to Catholic hands in 1991. Services are held in Polish, Russian, Spanish, Korean and English (Sunday Mass at 3pm).

En route to the church you pass a striking townhouse (no. 15) built in the seventeenth-century Moscow Baroque style for the industrialist Pavel Shchukin in the 1890s. Expropriated after the Revolution and turned into a **Biological Museum** (Biologicheskiy muzey imeni K.A. Timiryazeva; Tues & Thurs–Sat 10am–6pm, Wed 10am–8pm, Sun 11am–6pm; closed last Tues of each month; R70) named after the botanist Timiryazev, it boasts a unique collection of life-size model **prehistoric hominoids** made by the anthropologist Mikhail Gerasimov, who invented the technique of reconstructing faces from skulls now widely used by forensic scientists (demonstrated here by computer graphics). Visitors can also watch wildlife videos (Sat & Sun at 2pm) or sign up for tours of the museum's greenhouse (R100 group rate; ⓣ252 07 49 for information).

Around ulitsa 1905 goda

The other jumping-off point for exploring Krasnaya Presnya is **Ulitsa 1905 goda** (1905 St) metro station, which has multiple exits around a major intersection. The main one brings you out on Krasnopresnenskiy Zastavy ploshchad, where shoppers ignore a huge Brezhnev-era **Monument to the 1905 Revolution**, featuring workers unhorsing a gendarme and waving rifles. Another surfaces near Bolshaya Dekabrskaya ulitsa, which is the one to take if you're aiming for the Vagankov Cemetery, the area's main attraction.

Vagankov Cemetery

Sited at the far end of Bolshaya Dekabryskaya ulitsa, the Vagankov Cemetery (Vagankovskoe kladbishche; daily: summer 9am–7pm, winter 9am–6pm; free) is an oasis of mournful beauty. In Moscow's hierarchy of prestigious burial grounds, it runs a close second to the Novodevichie cemetery, which takes people who never quite made it into the Kremlin Wall. Though it doesn't have such a profusion of sculptural monuments, there are enough architectural surprises to make wandering round a pleasure. The cemetery itself dates from 1771, when an outbreak of plague impelled the authorities to dig up all the graveyards in central Moscow and establish new ones beyond the city limits. It takes its name from the parish cemetery that belonged to the Church of St Nicholas in Old Vagankov, near the Borovitskiy Gate of the Kremlin.

Off to the right just inside the entrance is the flower-strewn grave of **Vladimir Vysotsky**, the maverick actor-balladeer of the Brezhnev era (see p.248). Though hundreds of fans braved police cordons to attend his hushed-up funeral in 1980, no monument was permitted until the advent of perestroika. It portrays Vysotsky garbed in a martyr-like shroud, his guitar forming a halo behind his head. Nearby lies the grave of the mafia boss **Otari Kvantrishvili**, shot by a contract sniper as he left a local bathhouse in 1994, whose funeral was shown on TV accompanied by the theme tune from *The Godfather*. His brother (killed the year before) is buried alongside, with a sculpted angel watching over their graves.

Further in, you can head down a path to the left of the **Church of the Resurrection** to find Plot 17, where a tender sculpture marks the grave of the heart-throb poet **Sergei Yesenin**, who in 1925 apparently cut his wrists and hanged himself, leaving a final poem written in his own blood (some suspect the Cheka of killing him and faking a suicide). An admirer, **Galina Benislavskaya**, shot herself on his grave a year later and is buried behind him. In the same area are the graves of the historical painter **Vasily Surikov** – marked by a palette and brushes – the botanist **Klement Timiryazev** (Plot 14), and the lexicographer **Vladimir Dal**, whose work is known to every student of the Russian language (signposted off Timiryazevskaya alleya).

It's also worth seeking out the graves of various **Soviet sporting heroes** – marked with footballs, ice hockey sticks and suchlike – on the alley leading to the modern Columbarium at the centre of the cemetery.

The riverside business district

A kilometre from the cemetery, the **riverside business district** is of little interest to the average tourist but a focal point for Moscow's financial community. Its genesis was the **World Trade Center** (Tsentr Mezhdunarodnoy Torgovli, or TsMT), initiated by Armand Hammer, the founder of Occidental Petroleum, who began doing business with the USSR in the 1920s and personally knew every Soviet leader from Lenin to Gorbachev. Inaugurated in 1980, the glass and concrete complex was an early beachhead of Western business culture, in tandem with the adjacent *Mezhdunarodnaya* (International) **hotel**, whose expatriate clientele dubbed it "the Mezh". Notwithstanding the murder of the director of the company that bought both enterprises in the mid-1990s, in 2004 a 21-storey **World Trade Center II** was erected between the original complex and an **Expocenter** linked by a shopping arcade-cum-**footbridge** to the vicinity of Kutuzovskiy prospekt, across the river. And if all goes according to plan, the district will soon boast Moscow's first real skyscraper, the futuristic **Gorod Stolits**, with two asymmetrical towers of 72 and 61 floors (with luxury apartments from the nineteenth floor upwards). Projected to cost $250 million, it was started in 2003 and, at the time of writing, is still unfinished.

To Victory Park and beyond

Across the river from the business district, the hand of postwar Stalinist planning is writ large in gigantic avenues and residential blocks whose pomposity is underscored by the vibrant Church of the Intercession in Fili and a string of Napoleonic and World War II memorials culminating in the grandiose Victory Park. Though relatively low on Moscow's list of tourist attractions, they say much about Soviet aesthetics and Russian patriotism and almost every sight is within walking range of a metro station on the Filyovskaya line.

Around Ploshchad Yevropy

Emerging from **Kievskaya metro** – an interchange on the metro line that serves everywhere else covered below – you'll find yourself at the **Kiev Station** (Kievskiy vokzal) that handles trains from Ukraine and Moldova. In Soviet

▲ The Crystal Bridge

times, the square outside seemed an apt site for a monument commemorating the unification of Ukraine and Russia in the seventeenth century. Today, its vandalized plinth lurks on the edge of **ploshchad Yevropy** (Square of Europe), a silvery sculptural ensemble ringed by fountains and the flags of the nations of the European Union and the Commonwealth of Independent States, symbolizing Russia's wish to be respected by both. Its exhibition pavilion has been closed due to leaks since being unveiled in 2002, underscoring the vainglory of the whole ensemble.

More eye-catching is the **Crystal Bridge**, a humpbacked, glass-roofed structure that straddles the river, giving direct access to the centre. The escalators on either side operate from 8am to 10pm, but you can climb the steps to cross over at any time. If the view of the steep embankment on the far side of the river – crowned by snazzy office blocks – sets you wondering about the waterfront further downriver, **river cruises** depart from the embankment not far away, offering fabulous views of the monument to Peter the Great, the Cathedral of Christ the Saviour, the Kremlin, and several monasteries (see p.46 for details).

In the other direction lies the **Radisson Slavyanskaya Hotel**, notorious among Moscow's expat business community for the feud between the US entrepreneur Paul Tatum and his Russian partners, which led to Tatum's murder outside Kievskaya metro in 1996. Although some harboured suspicions, nothing was said until a spate of TV "exposés" on Mayor Luzhkov's links with organized crime suggested that Luzhkov sanctioned the contract killing – claims that tarnished his image in the run-up to the 2000 presidential election which saw Putin coast to victory.

Kutuzovskiy prospekt

Kutuzovskiy prospekt was laid out in the mid-1950s as a prestigious residential area for diplomats, top scientists and even the Soviet leadership, whose town apartments were conveniently located midway between the Kremlin and their suburban *dachas* to the west of Moscow. The avenue is named after

Field Marshal Kutuzov, whose troops marched this way to confront Napoleon's *Grande Armée* at Borodino and retreated back along the road after Kutuzov's fateful decision to abandon Moscow. In 1941, Stalin evoked the shades of 1812 as Soviet regiments streamed towards the advancing *Wehrmacht*; the sacrifices and victories of both wars are commemorated by a series of monuments along several kilometres of the avenue.

Kutuzovskiy's initial stretch is notable for the **Ukraina Hotel**, a tawny-coloured Stalin-Gothic leviathan that boasts one thousand rooms. Designed by Arkady Mordvinov and completed in 1957, its 39-storey central tower is flanked by turreted wings and culminates in a 73-metre-high spire crowned with a Soviet star, giving it a total height of 206m. Among those who've stayed there are Robert de Niro and Marcelo Mastroiani, singers Patricia Kass and Boris Grebeshnikov, and the composer Michel Legrand. During the crises of 1991 and 1993, the hotel's guests had a ringside view of events at the White House, across the river – one was even killed by a stray bullet.

If you want to see more of the prospekt, trolleybus #39 or any bus going west will take you past the **Moscow-Hero-City Obelisk** erected at the junction of Bolshaya Dorogomilovskaya ulitsa in 1977. The Stalinist blocks on either side of the prospekt contain high-ceilinged apartments of up to a dozen rooms that are each the size of an entire flat for the average Muscovite family. The right-hand ones were built over the Dorogmilskaya Cemetery, Moscow's Jewish burial ground. Number 26 used to be known as the **Politburo block**: Brezhnev had an opulent two-floor apartment and his Interior Minister, Shchelokov, an entire floor – in contrast to the ascetic KGB chief, Andropov, with his three-bedroom flat. The properties now sell for around R45,000,000, though, like all the prestigious Stalinist buildings, they are badly infested with cockroaches.

The Borodino Panorama

The first of the Patriotic Wars that shaped Russia's destiny is commemorated midway along Kutuzovskiy prospect, beyond Kutuzovskaya metro station; take the exit near the front of the train, turn right outside and head towards the Triumphal Arch 500m away. Shortly before this is the circular blue pavilion of the **Borodino Panorama Museum** (muzey Panorama Borodinskaya Bitva), inaugurated in 1962 on the 150th anniversary of the Battle of Borodino against Napoleon. Its 115-metre-long circular painting by Franz Roubaud depicts a critical moment in the battle, which occurred 129km west of Moscow on August 26, 1812. Casualties were unprecedented, with forty thousand Russians and thirty thousand French killed in fifteen hours – but neither side emerged the winner. The painting depicts the battle from the standpoint of Russian troops holding the village of Semyonovskaya; Napoleon can be identified in the distance by his white horse. Real cannons, carts and stuffed horses have been placed at strategic points, and there are sound effects. Individual **visitors** (R160) are only admitted on Saturdays and Sundays, either in groups formed on the spot (noon–2pm), or as individuals (2.30–6pm); pre-booked **groups** have the run of the museum from Monday to Thursday (10am–6pm; closed last Thurs of each month; group rate R2100; ⓣ 148 19 27 for bookings, English and German spoken; photo permit R50, video permit R100).

Outside the pavilion, an equestrian **statue of Kutuzov** bestrides a pedestal flanked by bronzes of Russian soldiers and peasant guerillas. Mikhail Kutuzov (1745–1813) was a one-eyed giant who used to close his good eye and pretend to be asleep so that his aides could express their opinions freely. Five days after Borodino, with the French still advancing, a council of war was held in the *izba* (hut) of a peasant named Frolov, at which Kutuzov resolved to withdraw from Moscow to avoid being outflanked, and preserve his army. His decision aroused anger but was soon vindicated by events: the burning of Moscow left Napoleon's *Grande Armée* bereft of shelter as winter approached, and obliged to retreat under the constant threat of Russian attacks. Behind the pavilion stands the **Kutuzov Hut**, a replica of the historic *izba*, created as a museum in 1887, but currently closed for repairs.

The Triumphal Arch

Russia's victory over Napoleon is commemorated on a grander scale by a **Triumphal Arch** designed by Osip Bove, originally erected (1829–34) where the St Petersburg road entered Moscow, near what is now Belarus Station. Imperial processions passed beneath it and along Tverskaya ulitsa, towards the Kremlin until, like the Triumphal Arch in Leningrad, it was deemed an impediment to traffic and demolished in the 1930s. Vitali's sculptures were preserved at the Donskoy Monastery until it was decided to reconstruct the arch in the patriotic upsurge that followed World War II. Completed in 1968, the stone arch is bracketed by Corinthian columns flanking Vitali's Classical warriors, decorated with the coats of arms of 48 Russian provinces and surmounted by the winged figure of Glory urging his chariot westwards.

To inspect it at closer quarters, follow the underpass that surfaces near the arch in the middle of the avenue, or walk there from **Park Pobedy metro**. One of Moscow's deepest metro stations (the escalator ride takes over two minutes), it resembles an ancient Egyptian temple crossed with the Starship *Enterprise*, and is linked by a pedestrian subway to Victory Park on the far side of the highway.

Victory Park

Moscow's **Victory Park** (Park Pobedy) was conceived in the Era of Stagnation, when the Party erected ever-larger war memorials in an effort to overcome ideological apathy among the masses. In 1983 the Politburo approved a design by Nikolai Tomsky that involved levelling the **Poklonnaya gora** (Hill of Greetings), where generations of travellers had exclaimed with joy as they reached its summit to suddenly behold Moscow ahead of them, and where Napoleon had waited in vain to be presented with the keys to the city. The intention was to erect a 75-metre-high monument to Mother Russia, supported by a host of allegorical figures, like the hilltop memorial at Volgograd (Stalingrad). With the advent of glasnost, the project was decried as a waste of money and cancelled – only to be revived by Yeltsin's government in an effort to restore Russia's battered national pride. Billions of rubles and battalions of conscripts were committed to "storm" the final stage, so that the park could be ready for the 49th anniversary of Victory Day, in 1994, while the 50th anniversary saw yet more additions to the complex, and the grandest military parade since Stalin's days.

Indeed, if you can, it's best to come here on **Victory Day** (May 9) – the only anniversary in Soviet times that was genuinely heartfelt – when crowds stream towards the park carrying bouquets. Bemedalled old women and bow-legged ex-cavalrymen in archaic uniforms reminisce, weep, sing and dance to accordion music. The mood is deeply sentimental, dwelling less on the triumphs of Stalingrad and Berlin than on the terrible autumn of 1941, when the Red Army was repeatedly savaged and forced back towards Moscow – as in a poem by Konstantin Simonov, whose opening lines are known to every Russian:

Do you remember Alyosha

The Smolensk roads

Where the dank rains fell unending.

At other times, the park is a popular **meeting place** for young Muscovites, with rollerbladers taking advantage of its ramps and paved expanses, and groups drinking and hanging out till the small hours if the weather allows. Even in winter, newlyweds come to be photographed by a 142-metre-high **memorial obelisk** topped by an angel and cherubs blowing trumpets, with St George beheading a Nazi dragon at its base – a typically kitsch design by Tsereteli. Supposedly, every ten centimetres of the obelisk represents a day in the war.

The Museum of the Great Patriotic War

Behind the obelisk looms a vast concave structure raised on stilts and surmounted by a spiked bronze dome, containing the ultimate exposition of World War II from the Soviet perspective: the **Museum of the Great Patriotic War** (muzey Velikoy Otechestvennoy voyny; Tues–Sun 10am–7pm; closed last Thurs of each month; R120). What Russians call the Great Patriotic War is only deemed to have begun in 1941 with Hitler's invasion of the USSR, and ended with the liberation of Prague two days after the formal German surrender that's taken in the West as VE Day. This ethnocentric bias is more excusable than most, since Soviet losses – of approximately 27 million – were greater than any other country's, and even Churchill acknowledged that it was the Red Army that "tore the guts from the Nazi war machine". Don't miss the **dioramas** behind the Hall of Memory in the basement, depicting the critical battles of Moscow, Stalingrad, Kursk and the Dnieper, the siege of Leningrad and the fall of Berlin. Upstairs, the main exhibition is arranged in chronological order round the outside of a Hall of Glory whose dome is 50m in diameter.

Downhill from the museum, dugouts of the kind that once defended Moscow and artillery and vehicles from both sides of the conflict are deployed in an outdoor **Weaponry and Fortifications Exhibition** (same hours; R80). On Victory Day elders nod sagely as loudspeakers play wartime radio broadcasts, such as the famous call to arms by Stalin that opened with the Orthodox salutation "Brothers and Sisters", and went on to invoke the warrior-saints of Holy Russia. A memorial **church**, built in the medieval Pskov style, stands nearby.

The memorial synagogue and Jewish Museum

Postwar Soviet historians obscured the racial nature of the Nazi genocide against the Jews and subsumed the dead of the Holocaust into the greater total of victims of Fascism – an ideological stance which finds an echo in Tsereteli's monument, **Peoples' Tragedy**, with its lines of dehumanized figures lurching from a stylized maw. The consecration of an Orthodox church on Poklonnaya gora made the omission of a Jewish shrine all the more glaring, yet Moscow's Metropolitan tried to block Yeltsin's belated addition of a synagogue at the rear of Victory Park (together with a **mosque**, in honour of the Muslim peoples that fought for the USSR).

Funded by the Russian Jewish Congress, the **memorial synagogue** is seldom used and its guards are loath to unlock the door except for pre-arranged school parties or tour groups (such as the "Jewish Moscow" excursion run by Patriarshy Dom Tours; see p.46). The synagogue's **Jewish Museum** (no set hours; free) deserves to be visited more often and to be captioned in other languages besides Russian. On the top floor, items of antique Judaica, including

Jewish history in Russia

The rulers of **Old Muscovy** regarded Jews as enemies of Christianity and forbade them from entering the kingdom. Although Peter the Great made a baptized Jew, Peter Shafirov, his foreign minister, Jews only became statistically visible in the late eighteenth century, when Russia annexed the eastern part of the kingdom of Poland that had welcomed Jews expelled from Germany and the Czech lands centuries earlier. This swathe of small towns and *shtetls* (villages) – known as the Jewish Pale or **Pale of Settlement** (Cherta Osledosti) – was the origin of the Jewish population of the Russian Empire. Jewish traditions were seen as an affront to Orthodoxy and Jewish craftsmen and traders as unwelcome competitors. Tsarist policy swung between enforced isolation and assimilation. In 1861, the Tsar Liberator, Alexander II, allowed Jews with useful skills to settle in towns outside the Pale, and others to enter new professions such as banking and industry, or join the army. While Jewish commerce, education and philanthropy took off, it wasn't until 1917 that a Jew became an officer in the Tsarist army – only after winning the highest honour for valour four times (he later emigrated to Palestine and fought against the Arabs).

Alexander II's assassination in 1881 led to a wave of reaction. His successor, Alexander III, and his ultra-reactionary minister, Pobedonostsev, blamed Jews for causing dissent, and the police stood by as mobs of "**Black Hundreds**" looted, raped and murdered in Jewish communities. The **pogroms** were followed by a roundup of Jews in Moscow; 20,000 were expelled to the Pale. Nicholas II was equally anti-Semitic and willing to scapegoat Jews. His secret police fabricated the infamous *Protocols of the Elders of Zion* – cited by anti-Semites ever since – and the Orthodox Church supported the notorious **Beiliss trial** of 1912–1913 in which a Jewish factory clerk in Kiev stood accused of the "ritual murder" of a 13-year-old boy. Witnesses were forced to lie by the local district attorney, a fanatical anti-Semite, and even after two policemen discovered the real culprit, the trial went ahead, to demonstrations at home and abroad – it was Russia's equivalent of the Dreyfus Affair in France. It's to the credit of Russia's civic opposition that Beiliss was eventually acquitted.

Unsurprisingly, Jews were at the forefront of the **revolutionary movement** from the 1880s onwards. Lenin's old comrades Sverdlov and Zinoviev – and his Menshevik rival Martov – were Jewish, as was **Leon Trotsky**. Trotsky's role was pivotal, for the experience that he gained from organizing the **Jewish Bund** (militia) against pogroms in the 1900s enabled him to forge the Red Army and lead it to victory in the Civil War. Many Jews also served in the Cheka (alongside Latvians, Estonians and Russians). Yet, although the Old Bolshevik elite took pride in their internationalism, Lenin said of the Party at large, "Scratch a Bolshevik and you'll find a Russian chauvinist". Whereas the Tsarist empire had classified citizens by religion and rank, the Soviet state made class and **ethnicity** the criteria. To declare oneself Jewish was (initially) a matter of choice – 31 percent of Party members did in 1918. Adopting Russian or Ukrainian nationality was easy, however. Many saw the writing on the wall and quietly changed their names and ethnicity; by 1937, only 11 percent of Party members identified themselves as Jewish (only 0.3 percent did so in 1956). **Lazar Kaganovich** sat on the Politburo throughout the 1930s and 1940s, and is chiefly remembered for building the Moscow metro and dynamiting the Cathedral of Christ the Saviour (which he pleaded not to do, rightly fearing that the destruction would arouse anti-Semitism, and he would be personally blamed later).

During World War II, the Nazis **massacred** around 1.5 million Jews in the occupied territories of the Soviet Union, assisted by local puppet regimes in Ukraine, Belarus

a sixteenth-century Torah and synagogue silverware, are juxtaposed with maps and photos relating the history of Jews in Russia, from the Pale and the pogroms of the Tsarist regime to involvement in the revolutionary underground and the and the Baltic States. Jews resisted as **partisans** (leading 90 of the 1400 groups active in Belarus) and served at every level in the **Red Army** (which had 19 Jewish generals). A **Jewish Anti-Fascist Committee** – whose members included the world-famous actor Solomon Mikoels, and the wife of Stalin's foreign minister, Polina Molotova – toured the United States and raised $200 million for the postwar reconstruction of Soviet Jewry. The apotheosis of Soviet-Jewish amity came at the United Nations, in 1947, when the USSR endorsed the creation of the state of **Israel**. Stalin's hope that "a Socialist-Zionist state" would "be a nail in the arse of the British Empire" and side with the Soviet camp, only came to light with the opening of diplomatic archives in the 1990s.

The postwar years saw anti-Semitism become official policy. In 1947, Jews were quietly purged from the *apparat*, the diplomatic service and judiciary, and quotas set on their entry to universities. Early in 1948, Stalin secretly ordered the **murder of Mikoels**, in a staged car accident on the road to Minsk, where he had gone to see the results of the first tranche of reconstruction funds – which had been misappropriated. While Mikoels was publicly mourned as Kirov had been, Stalin dropped any pretence after the rapturous welcome given by Russian Jews to the new Israeli ambassador, Kiev-born **Golda Meir**, who spoke at rallies alongside Molotova. The media assailed "rootless cosmopolitans" and identified all those who had Russified their names, printing the original Jewish names in brackets. The Anti-Fascist Committee was arrested (Molotov continued to serve Stalin while his wife was in the Gulag) and thirteen Jewish generals were shot. Further purges heightened the hysteria, casting Jewish physicians as "assassins in white coats". Only Stalin's death stopped the "**Doctors Plot**" (see p.189) from becoming an orchestrated, nationwide pogrom, which would be used as a pretext for deporting the Jews *en masse* to Siberia for "their own protection".

While Khrushchev was less repressive, anti-Semitism was an inherent part of the system throughout the 1950s and 60s, prompting a minority of Jews to risk all by demanding the **right to emigrate** (afforded by the Soviet Constitution, but regarded as akin to treason). The *refuseniki* (those refused exit visas) were at the forefront of the dissident movement of the 1970s and a major irritant in US-Soviet relations until Gorbachev signalled a change in policy by allowing the veteran *refusenik* **Anatoly Scharansky** to emigrate in 1986. Between 1987 and 1991, 500,000 Soviet Jews emigrated to Israel and 150,000 to the United States. In Moscow, this resulted in the Jewish community shrinking from 3.6 to 2 percent of the city's population, and Ukrainians becoming the second-largest ethnic group in the city (according to official statistics).

Today there's a modest flow the other way. Computer savvy, Russian-born Israelis now find that Moscow offers more opportunities than Israel. More significantly, since 1991, 50,000 **Hassidim** have settled in Russia, reviving the Hassidic culture that was wiped out in its spiritual heartland, only surviving among the diaspora that fled the Tsarist pogroms. The **Lubavitch** sect has poured money into welfare programmes, infuriating Moscow's Jewish Orthodox leadership, which accuses them of luring worshippers from the Choral Synagogue (see p.145) by offering free meals at the Lubavitch Synagogue in Marina Roshcha (p.156). While secular Jews regard the feud with amusement – noting how many pensioners attend both synagogues – they're less blasé about Putin's crackdown on the **oligarchs** of the Yeltsin years, whose chief targets to date have all been Jewish (Berezovsky, Guisinsky and Khodorkovsky).

Soviet state (vouchsafed by the Party cards of Sverdlov and Kaganovich). A subterranean hall commemorates the Holocaust with horrific images from the ghettos in Nazi-occupied territory (where the bread ration was only an eighth of the amount for citizens of Leningrad during the Blockade) and the killing ground of Babi Yar in Ukraine. Jewish partisans in Belarus and armed resistance in the concentration camps are recalled with pride, and credit is given to Righteous Gentiles who saved Jewish lives.

Setunskiy Stan

Amid the high-rise zone between Victory Park and the Moskva River, a hillock within an oxbow loop of a tributary called the Setun has been identified as the site of **Setunskiy Stan** (Sat & Sun noon–2pm; groups only; for reservations phone ⓣ240 35 33 or 109 77 85; R200 per person), a twelfth-century **Slav fortress** reconstructed with one eye on historical authenticity and the other on attracting visitors. It features a forge where you can see weapons being made, mock duels and displays of jousting and cavalry tactics from the era of the Mongol invasion. Dressing up in period costumes and eating medieval-style banquets can be arranged for a fee. The fort can be reached by taking bus #91 from Kievskaya metro to the "Krepost Setun" stop, shortly before the flyover and railway bridge cross the river to Luzhniki.

Fili

While the estates and villages that once flourished to the west of Moscow vanished long ago, an outstanding church of the pre-Petrine era survives in the 1950s suburb of **Fili**. It can be reached on foot from the Borodino Panorama via ulitsa 1812 goda (1.5km; no access to cars), but it's easier to catch the metro to Fili station instead. Leave by the exit nearest the front of the train, turn left outside, and head for the golden dome just 350m away.

The **Church of the Intercession at Fili** (tserkov Pokrova v Filyakh; 11am–5pm; closed Tues & the last Fri of each month; R30) is the first real masterpiece of Naryshkin Baroque. Delightfully exuberant yet firmly controlled, it seems a world apart from the gloomy, rambling Upper Monastery of St Peter that the Naryshkins endowed a few years earlier. Nobody knows the identity of the

Stalin's final years

For the last twenty years of his life, Stalin inhabited a secluded *dacha* near the village of Kuntsevo, outside Moscow. His intimates called it *Blizhnoe* – the **"Near Dacha"** – as it was closer to the Kremlin than his former villa at Zubalovo, abandoned after his wife's death. Besides hundreds of guards, Stalin had several sleeping quarters which he used at random; servants and staff knew better than to creep up on him or fail to make eye contact. Hating solitude, Stalin made his cronies watch films until the small hours or drink endless alcoholic toasts while he consumed mineral water and jovially accused them of being British agents, or snarled: "Why are your eyes so shifty?" Yet only belatedly did he realize that he was surrounded by staff chosen by Beria, whom some suspect of hastening **Stalin's death** from a brain hemorrhage in 1953. As they feared to disturb him, hours passed before Stalin was found unconscious in his bedroom on March 1, and a further ten elapsed before any treatment (with leeches) was authorized, which kept him barely alive until March 5. At 4am next day, Moscow Radio announced that "the heart of the comrade-in-arms and continuer of the genius of Lenin's cause, of the wise leader and teacher of the Communist Party and the Soviet Union, has ceased to beat". Within a few years, the Party elite had abandoned Kuntsevo for a new *dacha* colony beyond the Ring Road – leaving Kuntsevo to be swallowed up by the city. The dacha still exists somewhere in the suburbs, protected by the FSB, who keep its whereabouts a closely guarded secret.

▲ Church of the Intercession at Fili

architect who was commissioned by Prince Lev Naryshkin, but his design was inspired. Constructed from 1690–93 in the form of a Greek cross with short rounded arms, the church rises in wedding-cake tiers of red brick ornamented with engaged columns and "cockscomb" cornices, offset by gilded rhomboids above the second level and a larger dome crowning the belltower. The locked summer church, above, is reached by three stairways incorporating sharp turns that were intended to heighten the drama of processions. In 1812, the French turned it into a tailors' workshop and stabled their horses in the lower winter church, which now contains some fragmentary murals and **temporary exhibitions** of religious art. You may feel it's not worth buying a ticket from the hut nearby, as the exterior can be admired for free. Occasional **concerts** in the summer are advertised on the spot.

Khamovniki and Luzhniki

The **Khamovniki** and **Luzhniki** districts are somewhat removed from the rest of the city, covering a peninsula bounded by the Moskva River and the Garden Ring, and best approached by metro. From Park Kultury station, it's a short walk to the lovely Church of St Nicholas of the Weavers and from there to Tolstoy's House. But the star attraction has to be the Novodevichie Convent and Cemetery, a magnificent fortified complex with a history of intrigues, next to a necropolis that numbers Gogol and Shostakovich among its dead. This lies within walking distance of Sportivnaya metro, which also serves for reaching the Luzhniki sports complex at the far end of the peninsula. An exploration of the sights in this area can easily be combined with a visit to nearby Gorky Park and the New Tretyakov Gallery (see Chapter 7), just across the river from Park Kultury metro station.

St Nicholas of the Weavers

Emerging from Park Kultury station, the swathe of flyover along Komsomolskiy prospekt makes the **Church of St Nicholas of the Weavers** (tserkov Nikolay v Khamovnikakh) appear even more striking by contrast. A fine example of the colourful parish churches of the mid-seventeenth century, its long refectory and elaborate tent-roofed belltower are painted a snowy white, while all the *nalichniki*, gables, drums, pendentives and columns are outlined in dark green or maroon, like a chromatic negative of a Russian church in winter. The exterior is rounded off with wrought-iron porches and strategically placed images of St Nicholas. A protector of those in peril (and the saint from whom Father Christmas originated), St Nicholas is regarded in Russia as the patron of weavers, farmers and sailors. His name day (Dec 19) and the day on which his relics were removed to Bari in Italy (May 22) are both celebrated here in the church.

The church was founded by a weavers' (*khamovniki*) settlement that was established in the 1620s. One of many settlements (*slobody*) in Moscow based on crafts guilds, it forbade non-weavers from living there and marriages outside the community. Their prized looms occupied the **Palace of Weavers**, 50m up a side road from the church (closed to the public). This whitewashed brick edifice with a wooden roof counted as a palatial workplace by the standards of seventeenth-century Moscow.

Tolstoy's House

Further north, on the left-hand side of ulitsa Lva Tolstovo, a tall brown fretwork fence with a plaque announces the **Tolstoy House-Museum** (muzey-usadba L.I. Tolstovo; 10am–6pm; closed Mon & the last Fri of each month; R200). Count Lev Tolstoy purchased the wooden house in October 1882 to placate his wife, Sofia Andreevna, who was tired of provincial life at Yasnaya Polyana and feared that their children's education was suffering. By this time, Tolstoy had already written *War and Peace* and *Anna Karenina*, and seemed bent on renouncing his wealth and adopting the life of a peasant – to the fury of Sofia. The children generally sided with her but felt torn by love for their father, who found it hard to reconcile his own paternal feelings with the dictates of his conscience. To strain relations further, Tolstoy alternated between anguished celibacy ("I know for certain that copulation is an abomination") and boundless lust for his wife, who bore thirteen children (eight of whom lived) and wrote: "I am to gratify his pleasure and nurse his child, I am a piece of household furniture, a *woman*!"

Around the house

Although this psychodrama was played out over the twenty years that the Tolstoys lived in Khamovniki, the house-museum enshrines the notion of one big happy family. Its cheery ground-floor **dining room** has a table laid with English china, oilcloth wallpaper and a painting of their daughter Maria by her sister, Tatyana. Tatyana's own portrait (by Repin) hangs in the **corner room** that belonged to the older sons, Sergei, Ilya and Lev, where Tolstoy once wept with relief upon learning that Ilya was still a virgin at the age of twenty.

The **Tolstoys' bedroom** doubled as Sofia's salon and study, with a sofa for guests and a mahogany bureau where she made fair copies of his draft manuscripts; their walnut bed is hidden behind a screen. Down the corridor, their youngest, Vanichka, slept in a truckle bed with his rocking horse at hand, within earshot of his foreign governess and the scullery where the maids took tea. While Andrei and Mikhail leave little impression, **Tatyana's room** bespeaks a bright, artistic young woman who often chafed at Tolstoy's strictures. Hung with her paintings and sketches, it contains a table covered with black cloth that she got family and friends to sign, embroidering their signatures in coloured thread.

Upstairs in the **salon**, Scriabin, Rachmaninov and Rimsky-Korsakov played on the piano and Tolstoy read his latest works to Chekhov and Gorky (an early recording can be heard). The carpeted **drawing room** full of knick-knacks was favoured by Sofia Andreevna, who read Tolstoy's proofs by the window; her portrait (by Serov) hangs on the opposite wall. Conversely, **Maria's room** is low and Spartan, in keeping with her Tolstoyan ideals; she taught at the Yasnaya Polyana peasants' school every summer. Further down the passage are the tiny housekeeper's room (she was with them for thirty years), and the room of Tolstoy's valet, who cared devotedly for his ailing master but avoided other work as demeaning.

Tolstoy's study with its heavy desk and dark leather furniture fits his gloomy literary output in the 1880s. Here he penned *The Death of Ivan Ilyich* and *The Power of Darkness*; the moral treatises *On Life* and *What Then Are We to Do?*; and began his famous polemic against sex and marriage, *The Kreutzer Sonata* (which Sofia read aloud to the family without a blush). Next door is a small room devoted to Tolstoy's enthusiasms: weightlifting, boot-making and bicycling (which he took up at the age of 67). Tolstoy usually reached his study by the back stairs near the pickling-room.

The coach house in the courtyard has been converted into a **video hall** where documentaries and adaptations of Tolstoy's stories are shown (as advertised), and visitors can also wander around the spacious back **garden**.

At the far end of the street, a seated statue of Tolstoy broods beside a landscaped remnant of the Devichovo pole (Maidens' Field) near which he set the scene in *War and Peace* where Pierre Bezhukov witnesses the execution of prisoners by the French. Tolstoy's readers would have known that, centuries earlier, this was the spot where teenage girls were left as tribute to the Tatars – a shameful custom that prevailed for nearly two hundred years, symbolizing Moscow's submission to the Golden Horde and establishing the idea of women as chattels for long afterwards. Present-day Russian nationalists evoke historic memories of sexual slavery to whip up xenophobia; Glazunov's depiction of the rape of Slav women is lauded on White supremacist websites.

Novodevichie Convent

Where the Moskva River begins its loop around the marshy tongue of Luzhniki, a cluster of shining domes above a fortified rampart proclaims the presence of the **Novodevichie Convent** (Novodevichie monastyr; Mon & Wed–Sun 10am–5.30pm; R150). One of the loveliest monasteries in Moscow, the New Maidens' Convent was founded in 1524 to commemorate Vasily III's capture of Smolensk from the Poles a decade earlier. It was home to many high-born nuns and often played a role in politics – one of the sisters prevented the convent from being blown up by the French in 1812, by snuffing out the fuses. Here, Irina Godunova retired after the death of her imbecilic husband, Fyodor I, and her brother Boris Godunov was proclaimed Tsar. Ravaged during the Time of Troubles, the convent was rebuilt in the 1680s by the Regent Sofia, who was later confined here by Peter the Great, along with his unwanted first wife. Bequests made Novodevichie a major landowner with fifteen thousand serfs, but after the Revolution its churches were shut down and in 1922 the convent was turned into a museum, which spared it from a worse fate until the cathedral was returned to the Church in 1945 as a reward for backing the war effort. Restoration began in the 1960s and in 1988 an episcopal see was established here. Though still officially a museum, Novodevichie is once again a convent, whose nuns and novices keep a low profile.

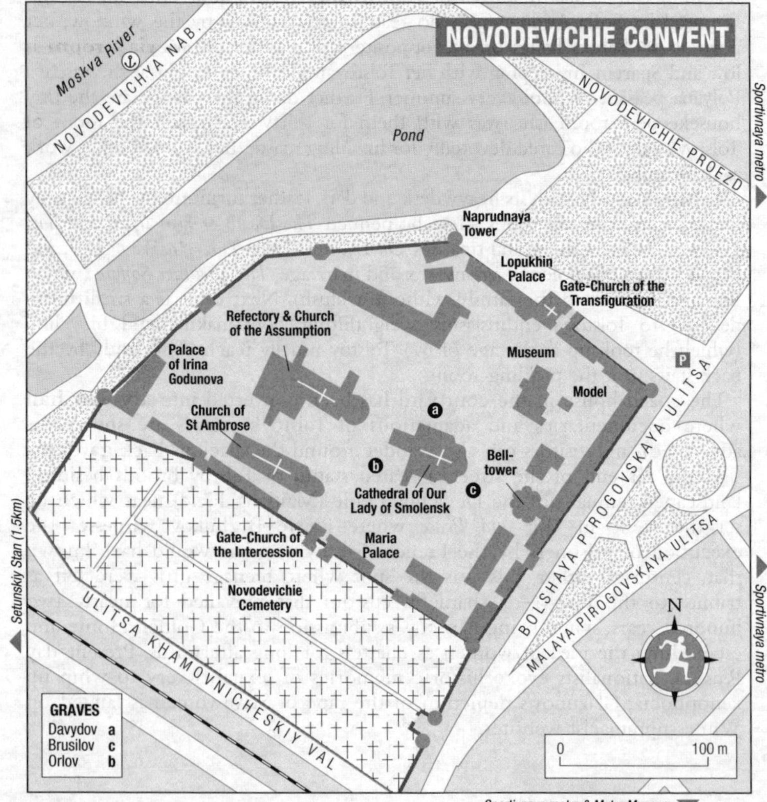

To get here, take the metro to Sportivnaya, exit at the rear of the train, turn right outside the station and walk to the far end of ulitsa Desyatletiya Oktyabr, where the convent's domes are visible. **Tickets** are sold from a kiosk within the grounds, but nobody checks them unless you enter temporary exhibitions in the former palaces. **Guided tours** in English (R1200 per group of 15 maximum) can be arranged by phoning ⓣ246 85 26. During Easter and other festivals like the **feast days** of the icons of Our Lady of Smolensk (Aug 10) and Tikhvin (July 9), tourists may not be allowed to enter the churches in the convent, and the main cathedral may be closed in wintertime.

Into the grounds

Surrounded by a massive brick wall with swallow-tailed crenellations and twelve bastions, the convent is entered via the **Gate-Church of the Transfiguration** (Preobrazhenskaya tserkov), a Moscow Baroque tower crowned by five gilded coronet-domes. Its shell-scallop gables and carved pilasters are of white stone, contrasting with the russet-hued stucco – a colour scheme repeated throughout the convent, enhanced by green roofs and gilded domes and softened by trees and ivy. The Gate-Church was built at the behest of the Regent Sofia in 1687–89, as was the **Lopukhin Palace** (Lopukhinskiy korpus) just inside the entrance, which now houses the Metropolitan (Archbishop) of Moscow and sports an attractively painted sundial. The palace's name recalls the involuntary sojourn of Yevdokiya Lopukhina, the pious first wife of Peter the Great, who was forced to enter a convent in Suzdal, and later confined to Novodevichie, after their marriage broke down and he wished to be free to wed again.

Near the ticket kiosk, down the path to the left as you enter the grounds, is a white building containing a **museum** of icons and manuscripts relating to the convent, while further along you'll find a **model** of the complex, detailing when each part was built. More arresting is Novodevichie's 72-metre-high **belltower** (Kokolnya), whose six decorative tiers culminate in a gilded onion dome on a slender drum, all so perfectly proportioned that many reckon it to be the finest belltower in Moscow. Unusually, it is situated near the east wall rather than on the western side, as was customary with Russian monasteries. The Futurist Tatlin is said to have retreated to this tower to design his famous articulated glider, *Letatlin*, which never flew.

The Cathedral of Our Lady of Smolensk

At the heart of the convent stands the white **Cathedral of Our Lady of Smolensk** (sobor Smolenskoy Bogomateri), whose tall *zakomary* gables give it a strong resemblance to the Cathedral of the Assumption in the Kremlin. Constructed in 1524–25 on the orders of Vasily III, its architects borrowed a device from the Kremlin's Church of the Deposition of the Robe, by sitting the cathedral on top of a high *podklet* or undercroft, to enhance its majesty. But what really make it impressive are the massed onion domes, added in the seventeenth century: the central one gilded and the others green with gold frills, supporting tall crosses that glitter in the sunlight.

The interior is worth seeing if you get the chance – which depends on its current renovation status. Its **frescoes** weren't painted until 1684 (reflecting the troubled century after the completion of the cathedral), executed in only three months by a team of 35 painters under Dmitri Grigorev of Yaroslavl. The enormous five-tiered **iconostasis** also dates from Petrine times, but was salvaged from the Church of the Assumption in Pokrovka, demolished in the Soviet era. Flowers and ribbons garland the icons of the Smolensk and Tikhvin Virgins on feast days. Notice the large copper font and wooden ciborium, dating from the latter half of the seventeenth century. Regent Sofia and the two other sisters of Peter the Great are buried in the (inaccessible) vaults underfoot.

Somewhat incongruously, Novodevichie is the burial place of Tsarist military heroes, whose **tombs** cluster around the cathedral. A bronze moustachioed bust honours **Denis Davydov**, a poet and Hussar slain battling the French in 1812, who was immortalized in verse by Pushkin, and by Tolstoy in *War and Peace*. **General Orlov**, who accepted the surrender of Paris from Napoleon, lies beneath a jet-black slab. Beside the grave of **General Brusilov** – the only successful Tsarist general of World War I, who later joined the Reds – is a plaque added by the far-right group Pamyat, dedicated to the generals of the Imperial Army and the "Russian Resistance" against Communism. Nearby you'll see a beautiful neo-Russian **mausoleum** whose stone base, carved with birds and flowers, rises in tiers of gilded wings like a Buddhist *stupa*.

Other sights

The red-and-white **Church of the Assumption** (Uspenskaya tserkov) and its adjacent **Refectory** were constructed at Sofia's behest in the 1680s. Its rows of vaulted windows interspersed with icons, and the gilded iconostasis fronted by tall candleholders, are almost as impressive as the cathedral. Lurking in a dell around the back is the lower, all-white **Church of St Ambrose**, which contains an exhibition of cloth-of-gold cassocks and eighteenth-century icons.

Further west stands the modest two-storey **Palace of Irina Godunova**, where the widow of the last of the Rurik monarchs retired in 1598. State business continued to be transacted in her monastic name of Alexandra until Patriarch Job and the clergy came en masse to the convent to implore her brother, Boris Godunov, to assume the vacant throne – a show of popular support that he had orchestrated himself.

The Regent Sofia

Tsarevna **Sofia** (1657–1704) was remarkable for ruling Russia at a time when noblewomen were restricted to the stultifying world of the *terem*. As a child, she persuaded her father Tsar Alexei to let her share lessons with her brother, the future Fyodor III, and from the age of nineteen attended the boyars' council. After Fyodor's death she feared being relegated by the Naryshkin relatives of the new heir, Peter, and manipulated the Streltsy revolt of 1682 in order to get another sibling, Ivan, recognized as co-tsar, and make herself **regent**. As Ivan was half-witted and Peter only ten years old, she prompted them by whispering from a grille behind their specially made double throne, and privately received ambassadors in person, seated on the Diamond Throne. The diplomat De Neuville noted that "though she has never read Machiavelli, nor learned anything about him, all his maxims come naturally to her".

Nonetheless, Sofia's regency was inevitably threatened as Peter came of age. In August 1689, rumours that she was about to depose him and crown herself empress impelled the 17-year-old tsar to flee to a monastery outside Moscow and rally supporters. By October, Sofia's allies had deserted her and she was ceremonially escorted to the convent. When the Streltsy rebelled again, nine years later, Peter was sure of her involvement but refrained from executing her through admiration, confessing: "What a pity that she persecuted me in my minority, and that I cannot repose any confidence in her, otherwise, when I am employed abroad, she might govern at home." She died of natural causes as the nun Susanna.

The southern wall of the convent is breached by the triple-domed **Gate-Church of the Intercession** (Pokrovskaya tserkov), whose red-and-white facade surmounts a gateway wide enough to drive a hearse into the adjacent Novodevichie Cemetery. Alongside stands the three-storey **Maria Palace** (Mariinskiy korpus) where Peter the Great confined his half-sister Sofia, after deposing her as Regent (see box opposite). Sofia was allowed no visitors except her aunts and sisters, but wasn't obliged to forego any comforts until after the Streltsy revolt of 1698, when she was forced to take religious vows, making her "dead" to the world. According to popular history, 195 rebels were hanged in full view of the palace, while three ringleaders who had petitioned her to join them were strung up outside her window and left hanging all winter. However, some maintain that Sofia actually lived in the green-roofed building by the **Naprudnaya Tower**, and the Streltsy were executed outside the city walls – visible from the tower but not so close as legend has it.

Novodevichie Cemetery

Beyond the convent's south wall lies the fascinating **Novodevichie Cemetery** (Novodovicheskoe kladbische; daily: summer 9am–7pm, winter 9am–6pm; free; Ⓦwww.novodevichye.narod.ru), where many famous writers, artists and politicians are buried – only burial in the Kremlin Wall is more prestigious. It seems fitting that Novodevichie was the site of Trotsky's last public speech in Russia, at the graveside of an Old Bolshevik who committed suicide in protest against Stalin's dictatorship. During the Brezhnev era, the disgraced former leader Khrushchev was buried here, after which the cemetery was closed to prevent any demonstrations at his grave. Now that visiting restrictions have been lifted, Russians of all ages come to grave-spot, laying flowers on the tombs of some, tutting or cursing over others.

The cemetery's division into three main sections, each composed of two or more plots with numerous rows of graves, can be confusing, but the route described below is as good a way as any of visiting the "top thirty" or so graves, distinguished by their occupants or funerary monuments.

Some notable graves

The highest concentration of famous dead is in the oldest part of the cemetery, reached by passing through a gap in the wall near an array of **Soviet generals**, who make rather incongruous company for **Rostropovich** – one of Russia's great conductors – and the late **Yuri Nikulin**, the circus clown and comedian who was the only man in the USSR allowed to openly make fun of its leaders in the old days.

In the first row beyond the wall is the boulder-like tomb of **Vladimir Gilyarovsky**, author of *Moscow and the Muscovites*, while further back lies the grave of **Nikolai Gogol**. When Soviet historians exhumed Gogol's grave they found claw marks inside the coffin, proving that he had been buried alive following a cataleptic fit. Two rows on, **Anton Chekhov** and his actress wife **Olga Knipper-Chekhova** lie near to **Konstantin Stanislavsky**, a proximity that reflects their fruitful collaboration at the Moscow Art Theatre; the novelist **Mikhail Bulgakov** lies directly opposite, beneath a stone inscribed "I shall make fun with bitter words". Further along are the graves of the painters **Valentin Serov** and **Isaak Levitan**, and the composer **Dmitri Shostakovich**.

An equally diverse bunch reposes in plot 1, where a poignant bust and pair of hands recall Stalin's wife, **Nadezhda Allileueva**, not far from the family plot of

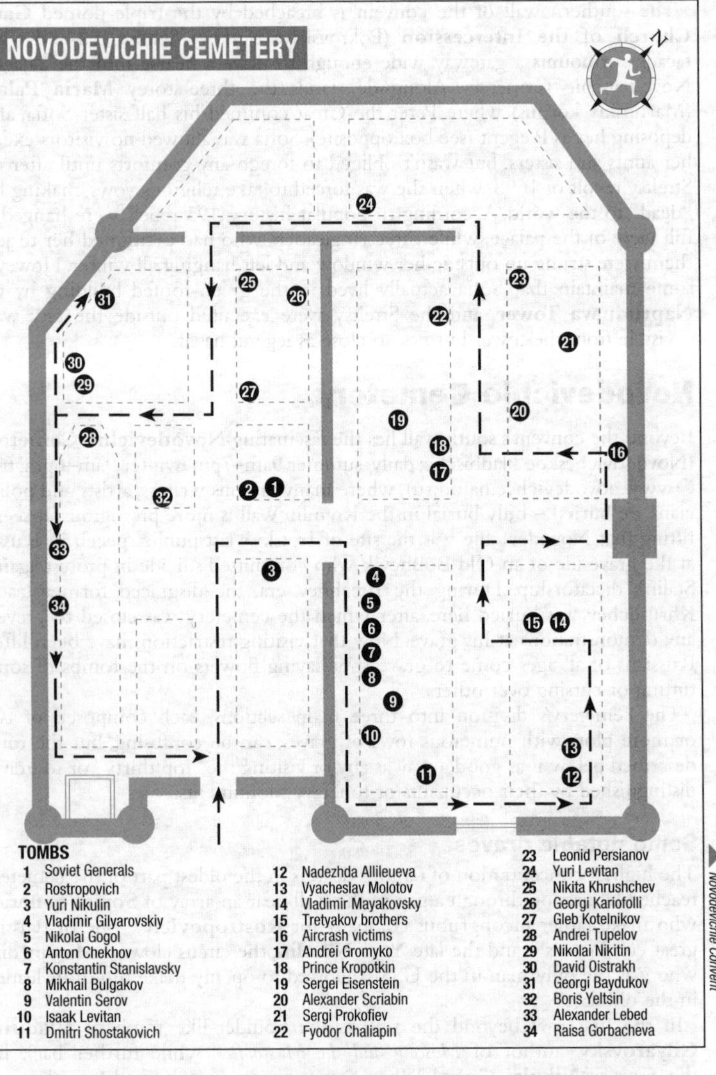

his Foreign Minister, **Vyacheslav Molotov** – who continued to serve Stalin even after his own wife had been sent to the Gulag – while the Futurist poet **Vladimir Mayakovsky** is buried near the philanthropist **Tretyakov brothers**, Pavel and Sergei.

On the wall adjacent to the convent, two huge sculpted plaques honour those who died in the **crashes** of the B-6 airship and the airliner *Maxim Gorky* in the 1930s, while plot 4 juxtaposes the grave of Soviet Foreign Minister **Andrei Gromyko** (suggestive of a graph of his career – rising and then dropping abruptly) with an obelisk commemorating the Anarchist **Prince Kropotkin** (which tactfully describes him as a geographer), before the tombs of the director

Sergei Eisenstein and the opera singer **Fyodor Chaliapin**, the latter bearing a life-size statue of him reclining in a languid pose. Across the way lie the composers **Alexander Scriabin** and **Sergei Prokofiev**, and an endearing statue of the pediatrician **Leonid Persianov**, cradling a newborn baby.

Heading through the northwestern part of the cemetery, past the tomb of the radio broadcaster **Yuri Levitan** – portrayed at the microphone – you arrive at the grave of **Nikita Khrushchev**, the Soviet leader who risked de-Stalinization and reform, was ousted by his colleagues and died in obscurity in 1971. (*Pravda* reported the death of "pensioner N.S. Khrushchev" in one line, 36 hours after the news broke.) The striking headstone was designed by Ernst Neizvestny,

▲ Yuri Nikulin's tomb

whom Khrushchev had once lambasted, but requested him in his will to create his memorial – a bronze cannonball headlocked between jagged white and black monoliths, symbolizing the good and bad in Khrushchev's life.

Other plots are devoted to inventors and designers, whose works adorn their tombstones, from the salvo of Katyusha rockets above **Georgi Kariofolli**'s bust to the billowing parachute on **Gleb Kotelnikov**'s grave, or the bird's wings and jet on the tomb of **Andrei Tupelov**, and the image of the Ostantinko TV Tower on the grave of **Nikolai Nikitin**. Near Tupelov is one of the newest graves, that of Russia's first president, **Boris Yeltsin**, who died in 2007. You'll also find a bust of **David Oistrakh** playing his violin, and the grave of the pilot **Georgi Baydukov**, with a model of the globe showing his trans-polar flight from Moscow to Vancouver in 1937.

On the way back to the exit are the graves of two figures associated with recent history. A larger-than-life statue of **Alexander Lebed**, in full dress uniform and medals, enthroned with a shield and sword beside him, honours the paratrooper general whom admirers once saw as Russia's saviour; he was killed in a helicopter crash in 2002. Nearby, a mournful female figure hunched over a slab commemorates **Raisa Gorbacheva**, who broke with the tradition of invisible Kremlin wives to accompany Gorbachev abroad as the "Soviet First Lady", promoted Russian culture and won the nation's sympathy with her battle against cancer, from which she died in 1999.

The Metro Museum and Luzhniki Sports Complex

Returning from Novodevichie you can use the other Sportivnaya metro pavilion exit and visit the intriguing **Metro Museum** (muzey Moskovskiy Metropolitan; Mon 11am–6pm, Tues & Fri 9am–4pm, ⓣ622 73 09; free), hidden away above the station's Militia post. To find it, enter the unmarked wooden door to the right of the exit (as you leave the station) and walk upstairs to the third floor.

Its exhibits are as old as the metro itself. Photos of the construction of the earliest lines in the 1930s highlight the role of Komsomol volunteers and gloss over that of slave-labourers, twenty thousand of whom perished so that the regime didn't have to import costly machinery after opting for the deep tunnelling method that caused less disruption on the surface and allowed deeper stations that could serve as bomb shelters. The project was led by Lazar Kaganovich, in honour of whom the whole metro system was named until 1957, when he was ousted from the Politburo by Khrushchev, who had been his deputy twenty years earlier and felt that his own contribution to the metro had never been acknowledged. History aside, you can check out a driver's cab and get a good idea of how the metro is controlled from various working models.

An underpass near Sportivnaya leads to the sprawling **Luzhniki Sports Complex**, laid out in the 1950s and modernized for the 1980 Olympics. Its parking lot hosts Moscow's annual **beer festival** and a daily **market** for fake-brand clothing, luggage and watches. The Lenin Central Stadium – now called **Luzhniki Stadium** – was one of the first assets in Moscow to be privatized. Its new owners refurbished it to meet UEFA standards and purchased the bankrupt club Torpedo to play there. The $200 million refit laid to rest the ghost of Europe's worst-ever stadium disaster, when, in 1982, 340 Spartak fans were crushed to death during a UEFA Cup match against Holland – though due to Soviet censorship details of the tragedy took seven years to emerge. Coincidentally, the company that got the contract to refurbish the seating is owned by the mayor's wife. See p.399 for details of football matches at Luzhniki and Moscow's other stadiums.

To the east of the stadium is the 13,000-seater **Sports Palace**, while on the far side of Komsomolskiy prospekt gleams the multi-purpose **Friendship Sporting Hall** that Muscovites nicknamed the "Golden Tortoise". From here you can see the enclosed bridge that carries the metro across the river towards the Sparrow Hills and Moscow University.

The Sparrow Hills and beyond

A wooded ridge overlooking the city, the former Lenin Hills have reverted to their Tsarist-era name, the **Sparrow Hills** (Vorobyovie gory), but still look quintessentially Soviet. The main reason is the Moscow State University (MGU), whose stupendous Stalin-Gothic skyscraper dominates the plateau, its formal gardens extending to the granite esplanade where newlyweds come to be photographed and rollerbladers risk their necks. Besides the university, the attraction is quite simply the **panoramic view of Moscow**, with Luzhniki Stadium and the Novodevichie Convent in the foreground, the White House and the Kremlin in the middle distance, six Stalin skyscrapers ranged across the city, and an outer ring of even taller megaliths that are under construction.

The most direct way of **getting here** is to travel to Universitet metro and exit near the back of the train; you'll see the University tower above the trees to the left, and the silvery dome of the Circus off to the right. MGU can also be reached from ploshchad Gagarina (see Chapter 6) by riding trolleybus #7 out along ulitsa Kosygina. To **get back** to the city centre from the Sparrow Hills, you can walk down through the woods to Vorobvovie Gory metro station, across the river from Luzhniki.

MGU

Moscow State University (Moskovskiy Gosudarstveniy Universitet) – known by its initials as **MGU** (pronounced "em-ge-oo") – occupies the largest of the city's skyscrapers. In 1947, the Supreme Soviet decreed that Moscow's skyline should be embellished by eight such buildings (of which seven were raised), grouped around the colossal (but never built) Palace of Soviets. Sixty trains were required to transport the building's steel frame from Dneiprpetrovsk, and thousands of free and slave workers toiled night and day from 1949 to 1953 – a construction period that almost matched the duration of the whole skyscraper programme, overseen by Beria from the half-built main hall of MGU.

The MGU building consists of a 36-storey teaching block flanked by four huge wings of student accommodation, said to have 33km of corridors. Wheatsheaf pinnacles cap the side towers, which bear giant clocks and temperature/humidity indicators, while the central tower is festooned with swags and statues, carved with the Soviet crest, and surmounted by a gilded spire that looks small and light but is actually 240m tall with a star that weighs twelve tonnes. The most impressive facade faces northeast towards the city, across a terrace with heroic statues of a male and female student gazing raptly into the future. Try to plead or bluff your way past the guard outside its massive columned portico, to see the fabulous green-marbled, colonnaded foyers lined with medallions of world-famous scientists, culminating in bronze figures of illustrious Soviet ones. As yet, there is no statue of Gorbachev, who graduated from MGU with a law degree in 1955.

The Circus and Children's Musical Theatre

Aside from students, the locality sees plenty of parents and kids, drawn to two long-established and much-loved institutions on the avenue that runs past MGU, within walking distance of Universitet metro.

The **Circus** on prospekt Vernadskovo is visible from the metro station, but rates a closer look for its silvery, wavy-edged cupola, resembling a giant jelly-mould. The glass curtain walls allow a glimpse of the ring, which has four interchangeable floors that can be switched in five minutes (including a pool for aquatic events and a rink for ice shows), with seating for 3400 spectators. Its opening in 1971 coincided with the closure (for refurbishment) of the original State Circus on Tsvetnoy bulvar.

Further up the prospekt stands the **Children's Musical Theatre**, named after its creator, the late Natalya Sats, who founded Moscow's Central Children's Theatre as a teenager, inspired Prokofiev to write *Peter and the Wolf* in 1936, and spent sixteen years in the Gulag after the execution of her husband, Marshal Tukhachevsky. Initially set up in a tiny hall in 1965, the company now enjoys a purpose-built theatre with a giant filigree birdcage and a Palekh Room painted with fairytale scenes, where actors costumed as animals mingle with the children before each performance.

For details of shows at both venues, see Chapter 14, "The Arts".

The Darwin and Paleontology museums

The vast arc of Moscow to the **east of Leninskiy prospekt** contains numerous institutes, student hostels and flats owned by scientists and academics – making it an apt setting for two science museums. Both are easily accessible from stations on the Kaluzhsko-Rizhskaya **metro** line, but if you're coming from MGU it's quicker to take a **taxi** to the Darwin Museum, 3–4km away, rather than travel back to the Circle line and then out again to Akademicheskaya metro.

From Akademicheskaya, it's about fifteen-minutes' walk to ulitsa Vavilova 7, where the **Darwin Museum** (Darvinovskiy muzey; 10am–6pm; closed Mon & the last Fri of each month; R80) extols the evolutionary vision that supposedly provided an underpinning for the Marxist-Leninist theory of history. Though you need to understand Russian to get the most out of it, there are displays such as a reconstruction of an alchemist's laboratory and Darwin's cabin aboard HMS *Beagle* that transcend the language barrier – not to mention automated dinosaurs, a section on urban ecology, and a collection of stuffed foxes, wolves, bears and tigers on the third floor.

Six stops on from Akademicheskaya to Tyopliy Stan metro you can catch any bus or trolleybus one stop back towards the centre to reach Moscow's **Paleontology Museum** (Paleontologicheskiy muzey imeni Yu. Orlova; Wed–Sun 10am–6pm; R100, photo permit R50, video permit R150) at Profsoyuznaya ulitsa 123. Named after the paleontologist Yuri Orlov, the museum is a stylishly designed 1970s showcase for some amazing fossils, such as **dinosaur skeletons** found near the Severnaya Dvina River in the late nineteenth century, including a six-metre-high Tardosaurus – a relative of Tyrannosaurus Rex dubbed the "Russian Godzilla". In *The Gulag Archipelago*, Solzhenitsyn cites a report in the Soviet journal *Nature* on the discovery of an ice lens on the Kolyma River containing frozen prehistoric fishes and salamanders – which famished Gulag prisoners thawed out and consumed "with relish" before any scientists could get there. Visitors should bear in mind that the museum closes for several weeks during the summer – phone ⓣ339 15 00 to check if it's open.

Streets and squares	
Bolshaya Dekabrskaya ulitsa	Большая Декабрьская улица
Bolshaya Dorogomilovskaya ulitsa	Большой Дорогомиловская улица
Bolshaya Filyovskaya ulitsa	Большая Филёвская улица
Bolshaya Gruzinskaya ulitsa	Большая Грузинская улица
Bolshoy Predtechenskiy pereulok	Большой Предтеченский переулок
Druzhinnikovskaya ulitsa	Дружинниковская улица
Komsomolskiy prospekt	Комсомольский проспект
Krasnopresnenskiy Zastavy ploshchad	Краснопресненский Заставы площадь
Kutuzovskiy prospekt	Кутузовский проспект
ulitsa Lva Tolstovo	улица Льва Толстого
prospekt Vernadskovo	проспект Вернадского
Timiryazevskaya alleya	Тимирязевская аллея
ulitsa 1905 goda	улица 1905 года
ulitsa Khamovnicheskiy val	улица Хамовнический вал
ulitsa Kosygina	улица Косыгина
ulitsa Krasnaya Presnya	улица Красная Пресня
Metro stations	
Akademicheskaya	Академическая
Bagrationovskaya	Багратионовская
Barrikadnaya	Баррикадная
Fili	Фили
Kievskaya	Киевская
Krasnopresnenskaya	Краснопресненская
Krylatskoe	Крылацкое
Kuntsevskaya	Кунцевская
Kutuzovskaya	Кутузовская
Molodezhnaya	Молодежная
Park Kultury	Парк Культуры
Park Pobedy	Парк Победы
Sportivnaya	Спортивная
Tyopliy Stan	Тёплы Стан
Ulitsa 1905 Goda	Улица 1905 года
Universitet	Университет
Museums	
Biological Museum	Биологический музей имени К.А. Тимирязева
Borodino Panorama Museum	музей-панорама Бородинска Битва
Museum of the Great Patriotic War	музей Великой Отечественной войны
Darwin Museum	Дарвиновский музей
Metro Museum	музей Московского Метрополитена
Paleontology Museum	Палеонтологический музей имени Ю. Орлова
Red Presnya Museum	музей Красная Пресня
Setunskiy Stan	Сетунский Стан
Tolstoy House-Museum	музей-усадьба Л.Н. Толстого

6

Zamoskvareche and the south

Zamoskvareche and the south are clearly defined by geography and history. The Zamoskvareche district dates back to medieval times and preserves a host of colourful **churches** and the mansions of civic-minded merchants. Some of them founded the **Tretyakov Gallery**, Moscow's pre-eminent gallery for Russian art, whose superlative collection of paintings is now divided between the gallery's "old" and "new" premises, a kilometre or so apart. In pre-Petrine times, Moscow ended at its earthen ramparts (now the Krymskiy and Vatsepskiy val), beyond which the fortified **Donskoy and Danilov monasteries** overlooked fields and orchards.

By the mid-eighteenth century, Moscow had expanded as far as the Kamerkollezhskiy boundary, drawn by the tsar's tax collectors; over the next century, slums and factories surrounded what had been suburban estates. In the Soviet era, these were collectivized into Gorky Park, vast new thoroughfares were laid out, and the city spread out past the magical summer retreats of **Kolomenskoe** and **Tsaritsyno**, to what is now the Moscow Ring Road.

Zamoskvareche

Zamoskvareche simply means "Across the Moskva River", a blunt designation in keeping with the character of its original inhabitants. As the part of Moscow most exposed to Tatar raids, it was once guarded by twenty companies of Streltsy, settled here with their families, and separated from the other, civilian, settlements by meadows and swamps. In the long term, these communities of skilled artisans and shrewd merchants did more for Zamoskvareche than the riotous Streltsy. The artisans erected the parish churches that are still its glory, while the merchants' lifestyle provided inspiration for the playwright Ostrovsky and the artist Tropinin in the nineteenth century. By the 1900s, Zamoskvareche had become a major industrial district, with a fifth of Moscow's factories and a third of its workers. Today, it is still defined by three long, narrow thoroughfares, lined with modest stuccoed houses and colourful churches.

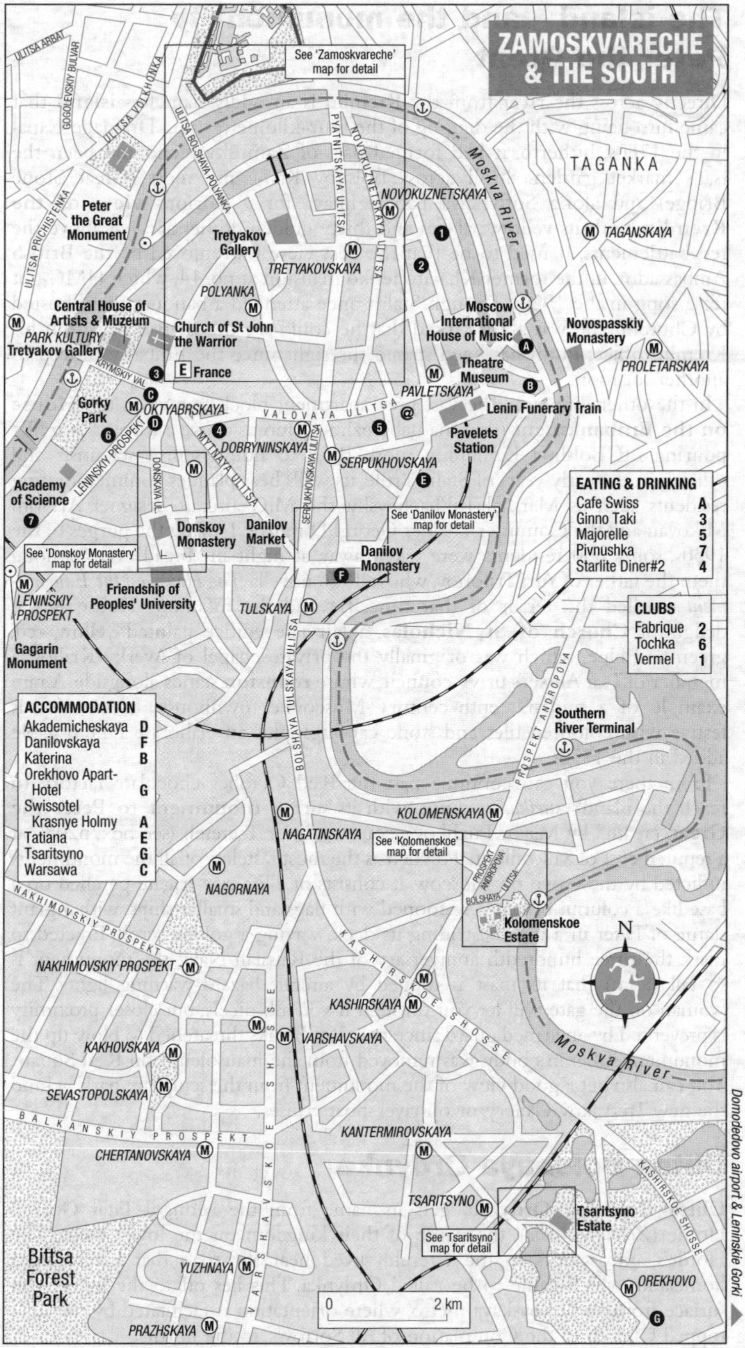

ZAMOSKVARECHE & THE SOUTH

EATING & DRINKING

Cafe Swiss	A
Ginno Taki	3
Majorelle	5
Pivnushka	7
Starlite Diner#2	4

CLUBS

Fabrique	2
Tochka	6
Vermel	1

ACCOMMODATION

Akademicheskaya	D
Danilovskaya	F
Katerina	B
Orekhovo Apart-Hotel	G
Swissotel Krasnye Holmy	A
Tatiana	E
Tsaritsyno	G
Warsawa	C

See 'Zamoskvareche' map for detail
See 'Danilov Monastery' map for detail
See 'Donskoy Monastery' map for detail
See 'Kolomenskoe' map for detail
See 'Tsaritsyno' map for detail

Ulitsa Arbat
Gogolevskiy Bulvar
Ulitsa Volkhonka
Ulitsa Prichistenka
Ulitsa Bolshaya Polyanka
Pyatnitskaya Ulitsa
Novokuznetskaya Ulitsa
Moskva River
Taganka
Novokuznetskaya
Taganskaya
Peter the Great Monument
Tretyakov Gallery
Tretyakovskaya
Polyanka
Central House of Artists & Muzeum
Church of St John the Warrior
Moscow International House of Music
Novospasskiy Monastery
Park Kultury
Tretyakov Gallery
Krymskiy Val
France
Theatre Museum
Proletarskaya
Pavletskaya
Gorky Park
Oktyabrskaya
Valovaya Ulitsa
Lenin Funerary Train
Pavelets Station
Leninskiy Prospekt
Mytnaya Ulitsa
Dobryninskaya
Serpukhovskaya Ulitsa
Serpukhovskaya
Donskaya Ul.
Academy of Science
Donskoy Monastery
Danilov Market
Danilov Monastery
Friendship of Peoples' University
Leninskiy Prospekt
Tulskaya
Gagarin Monument
Bolshaya Tulskaya Ulitsa
Prospekt Andropova
Southern River Terminal
Kolomenskaya
Nagatinskaya
Prospekt Andropova
Bolshaya Ulitsa
Nagornaya
Nakhimovskiy Prospekt
Kolomenskoe Estate
Kashirskoe Shosse
Nakhimovskiy Prospekt
Kashirskaya
Varshavskaya
Kakhovskaya
Moskva River
Sevastopolskaya
Balkanskiy Prospekt
Varshavskoe Shosse
Kantermirovskaya
Chertanovskaya
Kashirskoe Shosse
Tsaritsyno
Tsaritsyno Estate
Bittsa Forest Park
Yuzhnaya
Orekhovo
Prazhskaya
0 2 km
Domodedovo airport & Leninskie Gorki

6 ZAMOSKVARECHE AND THE SOUTH

The island – and the monument to Peter the Great

Directly across the river from the Kremlin is an oddly nameless **island** that came into being with the digging of the four-kilometre-long Drainage Canal in the 1780s; hitherto, it had formed part of Zamoskvareche and been the tsar's market garden. Stroll across Bolshoy Kamenniy most (Great Stone Bridge) and along Sofiyskaya naberezhnaya for a glorious **view of the Kremlin**, with its yellow palaces and thirty golden domes arrayed above the red battlements. It used to be that the best view was enjoyed by the British Ambassador, in the former Kharitonenko mansion at no. 14, which HMG got for a song in the 1920s. Though Stalin once attended a banquet there hosted by Churchill, he was always irked that he could see the British flag from his Kremlin office; Putin has been spared the sight since the Embassy moved to another location.

In the other direction, the vast grey apartment block known as the **House on the Embankment** (dom na naberezhnoy) looms above a torrent of traffic pouring off Bolshoy Kamenniy most. Built to house senior scientists and officials in the early years of Stalin's rule, its walls bear plaques commemorating residents such as Marshal Tukhachevsky, the MiG aircraft designer Artyom Mikoyan and the Comintern leader Georgi Dimitrov. During the purges of the 1930s, some 600 residents were taken away at night in "bread" vans, among them the father of Yuri Trifonov, whose 1976 novella *The House on the Embankment* recalled the terror of that time. Beyond the infamous House is the delightful **Church of St Nicholas**, a fairytale edifice painted yellow, red, green and blue, which was originally the private chapel of Averky Krillov, a member of Tsar Alexei's privy council, whose **mansion** stands alongside. A rare example of a mid-sixteenth-century Muscovite townhouse, its exterior is festive with coloured tiles and stone carvings, plus an elaborate Dutch gable added in the 1750s.

From there you can continue past the Red October chocolate factory to reach the island's *strelka*, or point, with its surreal **monument to Peter the Great**, created by Mayor Luzhkov's court sculptor, Tsereteli (see box, p208), at a reputed cost of $11 million. Reviled as the most tasteless of all the monuments inflicted by these two on Moscow, it consists of a life-size frigate perched on a base like a column of water, festooned with flags and smaller ships, with a giant statue of Peter in a toga bestriding its deck, waving a golden scroll. Erected to mark the three hundredth anniversary of the Russian Navy, the monument is so tall (95m) that its mast is topped by aircraft hazard-warning lights. The woman on the gate will let you through if you ask nicely, but closer proximity is prevented by an armed guard since neo-Bolsheviks threatened to blow up the monument if Lenin's body was removed from the mausoleum on Red Square. You can also get a good view of the monument from the sculpture park behind the new Tretyakov Gallery, or on river-boat cruises.

Ulitsa Bolshaya Ordynka

Ulitsa Bolshaya Ordynka gets its name from the Mongol-Tatar Golden Horde (*Zolotaya Orda*), the name of their kingdom on the lower Volga. The Horde's ambassadors to the Kremlin lived near the road that led to their homeland, which came to be called Ordynka. This lies off to the left as you surface from Tretyakovskaya metro, where orientation is facilitated by the gilt-topped Church of the Consolation of All Sorrows, to the north.

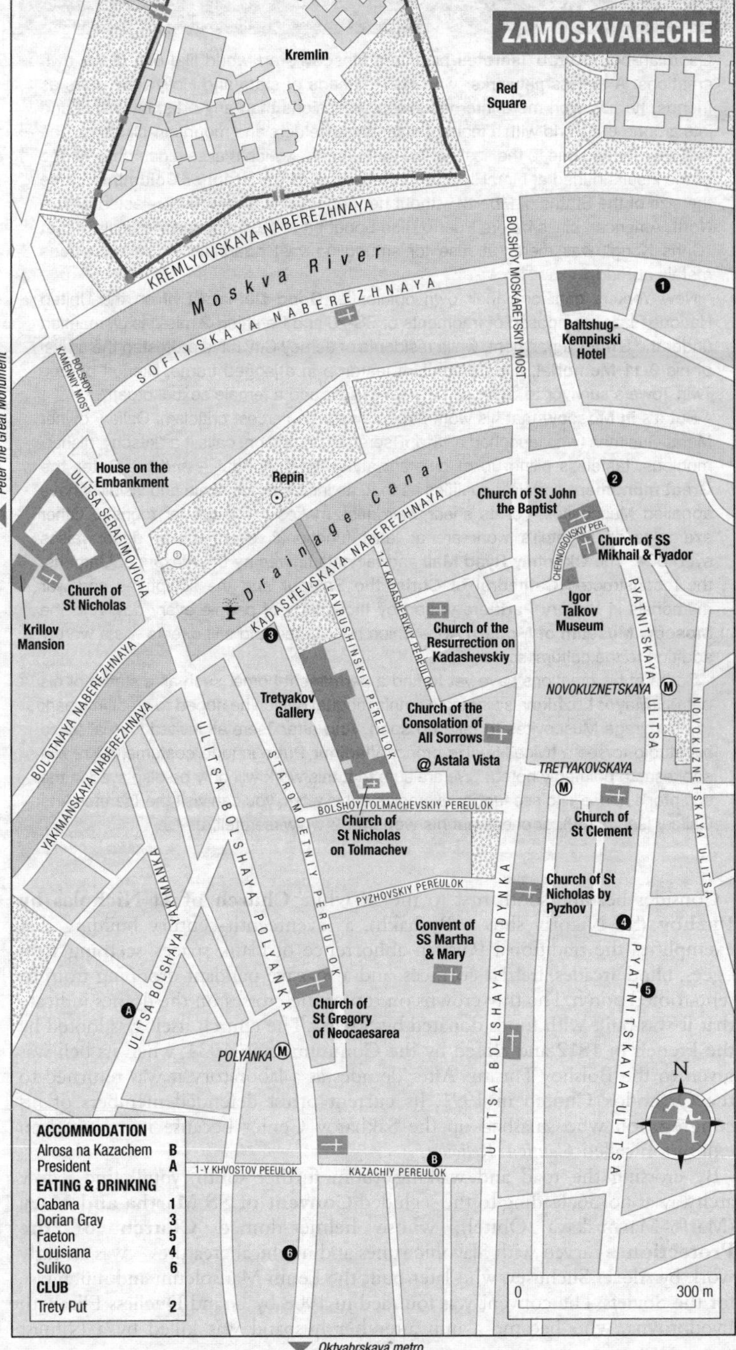

ZAMOSKVARECHE
Kremlin
Red Square
KREMLYOVSKAYA NABEREZHNAYA
Moskva River
SOFIYSKAYA NABEREZHNAYA
BOLSHOY MOSKARETSKIY MOST
BOLSHOY KAMENNIY MOST
Baltshug-Kempinski Hotel
Peter the Great Monument
House on the Embankment
Repin
Drainage Canal
ULITSA SERAFIMOVICHA
Church of St John the Baptist
CHERNOGIGOVSKIY PER.
Church of SS Mikhail & Fyador
Igor Talkov Museum
Church of St Nicholas
Krillov Mansion
KADASHEVSKAYA NABEREZHNAYA
LAVRUSHINSKIY PEREULOK
1-Y KADASHEVSKIY PEREULOK
Church of the Resurrection on Kadashevskiy
PYATNITSKAYA ULITSA
NOVOKUZNETSKAYA
BOLOTNAYA NABEREZHNAYA
YAKIMANSKAYA NABEREZHNAYA
Tretyakov Gallery
Church of the Consolation of All Sorrows
@ Astala Vista
TRETYAKOVSKAYA
NOVOKUZNETSKAYA ULITSA
ULITSA BOLSHAYA POLYANKA
STAROMONETNIY PEREULOK
BOLSHOY TOLMACHEVSKIY PEREULOK
Church of St Nicholas on Tolmachev
Church of St Clement
ULITSA BOLSHAYA YAKIMANKA
PYZHOVSKIY PEREULOK
Church of St Nicholas by Pyzhov
Convent of SS Martha & Mary
ULITSA BOLSHAYA ORDYNKA
Church of St Gregory of Neocaesarea
POLYANKA
N
ACCOMMODATION
Alrosa na Kazachem B
President A
EATING & DRINKING
Cabana 1
Dorian Gray 3
Faeton 5
Louisiana 4
Suliko 6
CLUB
Trety Put 2
1-Y KHVOSTOV PEEULOK
KAZACHIY PEREULOK
0 300 m
Oktyabrskaya metro

Zurab Tsereteli

Georgian-born **Zurab Tsereteli** bestrides Moscow's art world like one of his own creations. A tireless networker who claims heads of state and Hollywood stars as friends, he has won more international commissions than any artist in Russia and jets around the world with a team of engineers, welders and mountain-climbers. The last are required due to the scale of his monuments, which makes gigantomania one of the insults hurled at him. His 660-tonne **statue of Christopher Columbus** (twice the size of the Statue of Liberty without her pedestal) was famously rejected by five North American cities before Puerto Rico bought it in 1995; legend in Russia is that "Chris Kong" was merely a ruse for smuggling vast quantities of semi-precious metals abroad.

New Yorkers can form their own opinion of **Good Defeats Evil** on the United Nations Plaza, composed of fragments of SS-20 and Pershing-2 missiles dismantled under the START agreement, while residents of Jersey City have protested the arrival of his **9/11 Memorial**, a giant titanium teardrop in a jagged frame, likened by one Twin Towers survivor to "a cross between a scar and a female sexual organ".

But it's **in Moscow** that his work has aroused the fiercest criticism. Gallery owner Marat Guelman (who launched a "Stop Tsereteli" campaign) calls it a "kitschy, disharmonious, tasteless piling up of different styles and periods" – and the **Peter the Great monument** certainly qualifies as that. Its incongruous scale and visibility have appalled Muscovites, yet its sheer weirdness makes it a must for tourists. Other examples of Tsereteli's work are at least functional, even if their decor raises eyebrows. The **Okhotniy Ryad Mall** and fairytale figures by the Alexander Gardens, the reconstructed **Cathedral of Christ the Saviour** and the sculptures and war memorials in **Victory Park** are visited by thousands of people every day. And the **Moscow Museum of Modern Art** – which he initiated and still directs – is a worthy addition to the cultural scene.

Some of his creations have yet to find a permanent home, such as a statue of his patron, **Mayor Luzhkov**, swinging a tennis racquet, which he hoped to erect in a park to encourage Muscovites to take up sport. And after Tsereteli invited journalists to his studio to see a twice life-size bronze **Vladimir Putin** in judo costume, a Kremlin spokesman pointedly noted: "We are sure that this work will only be displayed in the sculptor's house". To see further examples of his work, you can visit the Tsereteli Arts Gallery (see p.169), or check out his **website**, Ⓦwww.tsereteli.ru.

Consider heading south first to the all-white **Church of St Nicholas by Pyzhov** (Sv. Nikolay shto v Pyzhakh), a seventeenth-century building that exemplifies the traditional Russian abhorrence of blank spaces, seething with ogees, blind arcades, fretted cornices, and a massive pendant drooping from its tent-roofed porch. The tiny crowns on top of the crosses on the domes indicate that it was built with funds donated by Streltsy. The church itself was looted by the French in 1812 and closed by the Communists in 1934, when its bell was given to the Bolshoy Theatre. After decades as a laboratory it was returned to the Orthodox Church in 1991. Its current priest defended members of his congregation who smashed up the Sakharov Center because it mounted an exhibition called *Caution: Religion*.

By crossing the road and walking 150m further south, you'll find a low archway at no. 36, leading to the secluded **Convent of SS Martha and Mary** (Marfo-Mariinskaya Obitel), whose helmet-domed **Church of the Protection** – carved with Slavonic runes and mythical creatures – was an early work by Alexei Shchusev, who later built the Lenin Mausoleum and much else for the Soviets. The convent was founded in 1908 by Grand Duchess Elizabeth Fyodorovna, who became a nun after her husband was killed by a Nihilist bomb, and devoted herself to charitable works. In 1917 she was captured by the Bolsheviks and thrown alive down a mineshaft; the convent and its hospices were closed down in 1926. In the early 1990s she was canonized as an Orthodox saint and the convent was revived, complete with a monument in her honour. To gain entry requires permission from an office down the street, but you can get a limited view through a crack in the gateway.

Alternatively, head north along Ordynka towards the Moskva River, where a yellow belltower heralds the **Church of the Consolation of All Sorrows**

▲ The Church of St Nicholas by Pyzhov

(tserkov Vsekh Skoryashchikh Radosti). This embodies the skills of two leading architects working in different styles: Bazhenov's Neoclassical porticoed refectory and pilastered belltower of the 1780s; and Bove's lusher Russian Empire-style rotunda (1828–33). The narthex contains more oil paintings than frescoes, while a ring of thick Ionic columns defines the pale blue, white and gold sanctuary, partly obscuring its iconostasis. The feast day of the church's sacred icon of the Madonna of Tenderness is on November 6.

Slightly further north, a lane on the left called 1-y Kadashevskiy pereulok provides a fine view of the awesome, derelict, viridian-domed **Church of the Resurrection on Kadashevskiy** (tserkov Voskresenie v Kadashakh). Built in 1687, in the Naryshkin Baroque style, it is rich in limestone ornamentation, with a fancy parapet instead of the usual pyramid of *kokoshniki*, while the belltower, added in 1695, rises from a ponderous base through delicate tiers emblazoned with flame-shaped mouldings. Although its name alludes to the Kadeshi quarter of barrel-makers that existed here in the fifteenth and sixteenth centuries, the church's construction was actually funded by factory workers in what had by then become a textile-producing quarter. In Soviet times it was turned into a workshop for a furniture factory (hence the steam pipes that cross the street to enter the compound) that refuses to vacate the building. "Since 1992 we have sought the return of the Church of the Resurrection on Kadashevskiy. Shame on you!" reads a sign, left by protesters.

By following 2-y Kadashevskiy pereulok eastwards, you can re-emerge on Bolshaya Ordynka opposite Chernigovskiy pereulok, leading through to Pyatnitskaya ulitsa (see below), with an unexpected **view** of the Kremlin towers and St Basil's Cathedral, to the north.

Pyatnitskaya ulitsa

Zamoskvareche's busiest thoroughfare and traditional marketplace, **Pyatnitskaya ulitsa** remains the heart of the neighbourhood, flushed with kiosks and shops in the vicinity of Novokuznetskaya metro – a palatial 1950s station smothered in bas-reliefs and murals of military heroes.

If you don't start there, the best approach is via the **Church of St Clement** (tserkov Klimenta), to the east of *McDonald's* near Tretyakovskaya metro. Looming above the stalls on Klimentovskiy pereulok, this was Moscow's last great monument of Baroque religious architecture, built sometime between 1740 and 1770. Corinthian pilasters and seraphim-topped windows rise from a lower level clad in fretted stucco to a parapet with flame-patterned railings. Its five black domes rest on sienna-red drums of equal height; the four corner ones are spangled with gold stars. Unfortunately the church is locked and derelict, so there's no need to linger.

Head northwards past Novokuznetskaya metro until you see the green-and-white belltower of the **Church of St John the Baptist** (tserkov Ioanna Predtechi) on the corner of Chernigovskiy pereulok. While this was raised in 1758, the church proper is exactly a century older, and less ambitious: a red-and-white refectory allied to a small sanctuary, nowadays lit by stainless-steel chandeliers from the time when it was a museum of glassware. The tiny, multi-domed **Church of SS Mikhail and Fyodor** (tserkov Mikhaila i Fyodora) directly across the street was built in 1675.

Around the bend is a maroon mansion housing a Slav Cultural Centre whose outbuildings harbour the **Igor Talkov Museum** (Tues–Sat noon–6pm, Sun 11am–5pm; free). Known for his sugary nationalistic pop songs during the last years of perestroika, Talkov achieved cult status when he was shot dead in 1991 by the bodyguard of another singer, during an argument over who should take precedence at a concert in Leningrad – though his right-wing fans blamed a "Jewish conspiracy". Talkov's Soviet army uniform takes pride of place amongst the memorabilia, and a crumbling effigy of the singer stands outside. Recordings of his songs are for sale.

Ulitsa Bolshaya Polyanka

Though fairly close to Ordynka, **ulitsa Bolshaya Polyanka** is awkward to reach from there, involving a zigzagging route through the backstreets, or two changes of line to get there by metro from Tretyakovskaya or Novokuznetskaya.

Emerging from Polyanka metro station, you can't miss the silvery domes and vividly coloured towers of the **Church of St Gregory of Neocaesarea** (tserkov Grigoriya Neokesariiskovo), built in 1667–69 by Peter the Great's father, Alexei. This lovely church is unusual on two counts: the porch at the base of its belfry straddles the pavement out to the kerb, while the main building is girdled by a broad frieze of dark blue, turquoise, brown and yellow tiles, whose floral motifs so resemble plumage that Muscovites dubbed the church "the Peacock's Eye". Even without the tiles, its facade would be striking: the walls are painted bright orange with a sky-blue trim, and the roofs turquoise.

The Tretyakov Gallery

Moscow's **Tretyakov Gallery** (Tretyakovskaya galereya, familiarly called the "Tretyakovka") has the world's largest collection of Russian art – over 100,000 pieces – and is a must-see for anyone. The gallery owes its existence to the financier Pavel Tretyakov (1832–98), who began collecting Russian art when he was 34, and in 1892 donated 2000 works to the city of Moscow, together with his own house and other buildings, united after his death by a neo-Russian facade designed by the artist Viktor Vasnetsov. Tretyakov's influence on Russian art was enormous, for without his patronage many artists might never have achieved success or created large pictures requiring many years' work. Nationalized after the Revolution, the gallery acquired a host of expropriated icons and paintings and went on to purchase Socialist Realist art, increasing its collection almost fivefold. Though its exhibition space was doubled in the 1930s, the lack of space remained acute until the construction of an entirely new building on the Krymskiy val, and the refurbishment of its original premises in Zamoskvareche.

The only **drawback** is that you have to visit *both* galleries to enjoy the entirety of Russian art – which means two journeys and double the expense of tickets. The account below covers the "old" Tretyakov Gallery in the heart of Zamoskvareche, which exhibits icons, portraits, academic and Symbolist artworks from medieval times up until the end of the nineteenth century, while the Tretyakov Gallery on Krymskiy val houses the Futurist and Social Realist art of the twentieth century (described on pp.222–225).

The "old" Tretyakov

The gallery is five-minutes' walk from Tretyakovskaya metro: turn left outside, cross the road, go straight on and bear right at the first turning to reach its ornate entrance on Lavrushinskiy pereulok. **Opening hours** (10am–7.30pm;

TRETYAKOV GALLERY

SECOND FLOOR

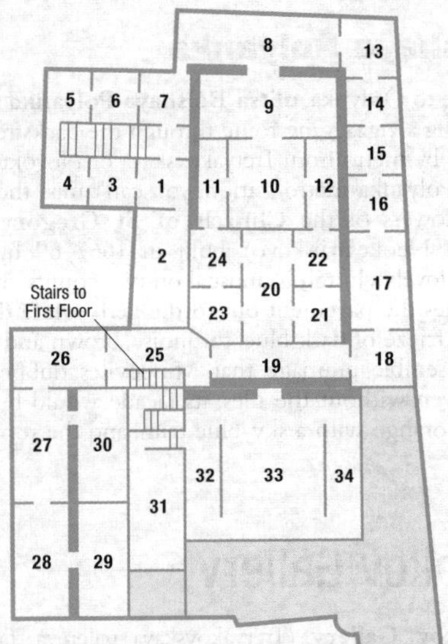

FIRST FLOOR

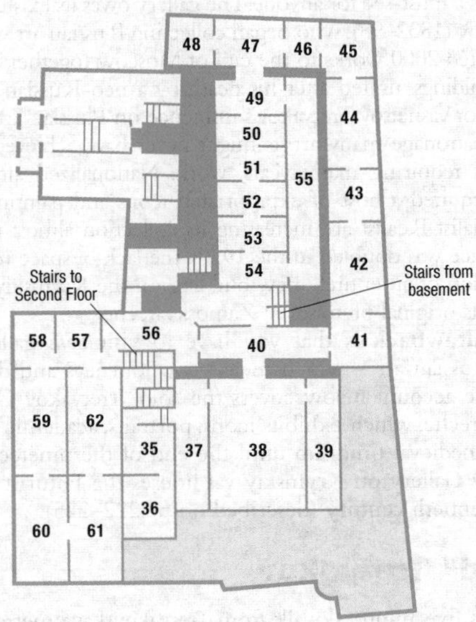

closed Mon) are straightforward, but ticket offices close at 6.30pm. **Tickets** (R250; students R150) are sold in the basement foyer, which has separate cloakrooms for coats and bags. Cameras must be stashed too, as **photography** is not allowed in the gallery. Wheelchairs are available if needed, and all of the floors are accessible by lift.

Though the floor plans opposite should help, the gallery's **layout** is confusing, as some of its thematic sections straddle two floors, while the medieval art section comes at the end of the recommended itinerary, which starts on the second floor and finishes on the floor below. Also bear in mind that the room numbers over the doorways refer to the room beyond rather than the one that you're in. Although the medieval art is labelled in Russian only, labelling in English (or French) is quite common for paintings of a later date.

One-and-a-half-hour **guided tours** in foreign languages may be booked in advance (Ⓣ953 52 23 or 238 20 54) for R1000–1500, or you can simply tag along behind a group for a free commentary. Alternatively, you can rent an **audioguide** for R300 (ID required as deposit), which gives a room-by-room rundown of the gallery, although it's slightly out of date. Our account differs from the Tretyakov's **itinerary** by covering medieval art first (rather than last), which gives a better sense of the development of Russian art and doesn't involve so much backtracking.

You'll find an exchange office, ATM, information desk, art shops and toilets in the basement. There's a chic, expensive café (10am–11pm; closed Mon) outside the main entrance, and several fast-food outlets just around the corner on the way to the metro station.

For a preview of some of the artworks in the Tretyakov's collection, visit its **website**, Ⓦwww.tretyakov.ru.

The Church of St Nicholas on Tolmachev

The gallery's southern wing partially encloses a seventeenth-century church on Tolmachev lane. In the 1990s, this was fitted with climate control and security features so that some of Russia's holiest icons could be moved to a house of God – as the Church wished – while the Tretyakov kept ownership and ensured their safety. The most revered icon is **Our Lady of Vladimir**, reputedly painted by St Luke but actually from the early twelfth century. Brought from Constantinople to Kiev, then to Vladimir and in 1395 to the Kremlin's Cathedral of the Assumption, it became a symbol of national unity and was credited with saving Moscow from the army of Timerlane. On the main iconostasis are seventeenth-century masterpieces from the Kremlin Armoury. The church is accessible by a **passage** and stairs from the gallery's basement or directly from the street – but you must have a ticket for the gallery to show the guards. It's best seen before the rest of the gallery, as it's only **open** from noon till 4pm.

Medieval Russian art (rooms 56–62)

The **medieval Russian art** section on the **first floor** is reached by a stairway on the right of the basement foyer, and expresses a different aesthetic to the rest of the Tretyakov's collection. For 600 years, almost the only form of pictorial art in Russia was religious art – mosaics, murals and, above all, icons. **Icons** (from the Greek *eikon*, "image") came to Russia from Byzantium, like Orthodox Christianity. Painted on wooden panels varnished with linseed oil and amber, their patina darkened by candle smoke, these holy images were mounted in tiers to form iconostases in churches, or hung in the *krasniy ugol* ("beautiful corner") of every Russian household. While generally venerated, those that failed to "perform" were sometimes beaten by their irate owners.

Icons were valued for their religious and spiritual content rather than artistic merit. One Russian critic argues that their visual flatness reflects a view of each human soul as the centre of the universe, unlike the spatial and moral distancing implied by Renaissance perspective. Anatomical realism was initially taboo as a reminder of mortal imperfections, but gradually became more accepted. The Tretyakov owns works from all of the main schools (see box opposite), including several that are deeply revered by believers, who pray before them.

Room 56 displays the **oldest examples** of Russian art, predating the thirteenth-century Mongol invasion. To the left as you enter are a mosaic of St Demetrius of Salonika and a fresco of St Nicholas from the Church of the Archangel Michael in Kiev, opposite a rare stone relief of two horsemen from the same church. A glass case displays the double-sided *Image of the Saviour Not Made by Human Hands*, relating to a legend that Christ imprinted his visage on a cloth to cure the ailments of the King of Edessa. At the far end of the room are life-sized panels of *St George* and the *Ustyug Annunciation*, the oldest icons (c.1130–40) extant from Novgorod.

Russia inherited from Byzantium six conventions for depicting the **Mother of God**, of which the two most popular were the Hodegetria, who sits serenely unrelated to the miniature adult in her lap; and the Eleousa, or Madonna of Tenderness, who lovingly embraces the Christ child. Russians have always preferred the latter, and referred to Mary as the Mother of God (*Bogomateri* or *Bogoroditsa*) rather than the Virgin. Since the icon of the *Mother of God of Vladimir* was transferred to the Tretyakov's chapel (see above), the most notable iconographic image in **Room 57** has been the *Our Lady Great Panagia*, representing her as the Heavenly Sovereign with Christ Emmanuel, which was discovered in the lumber room of a monastery in Yaroslavl in 1919.

Room 58 displays icons of the **Novgorod and Pskov schools** of the thirteenth to the fifteenth centuries. To the left of the door are *SS Boris and Gleb*, who let themselves be killed by their brother rather than fight for their inheritance, while on the right is the *Battle of the Men of Novgorod and Suzdal*, commemorating the siege of Novgorod (1170) and its deliverance by an icon of the Virgin of the Sign which, hit by an enemy arrow, recoiled, so outraging the Novgorodians that they stormed out of the city and routed the Suzdalians. Also notice the typically Pskovian icon of *St Paraskeva and the Three Hierarchs*, in white surplices emblazoned with black crosses.

One of many craftsmen and scholars who fled to Russia before the fall of Constantinople, **Theophanes the Greek** (c.1340–1405) has been justly called the "Russian El Greco". Though he is said to have decorated forty churches before coming to Moscow, all that survive *in situ* are his murals in the Church of the Transfiguration in Vladimir, and his icons in the Cathedral of the Annunciation in the Kremlin. **Room 59** exhibits his *Our Lady of the Don*, and attributes to the school of Theophanes the early fifteenth-century *Transfiguration*, showing Christ atop Mount Tabor, with unbelievers smitten by rays emanating from its summit. Another superb icon is the so-called "Blue" *Dormition* from Tver, featuring the apostles floating on clouds accompanied by angels (in the second tall case to the right).

Room 60 is devoted to the two greatest icon painters of medieval Russia. **Dionysius** (c.1440–1508) was the first famous lay painter, whose career coincided with a rising demand for icons, which spread from the noble and mercantile classes to the peasantry. His *Christ Enthroned* (framed by a red rhombus, a dark green oval and a red quadrangle, symbolizing Christ's glory,

A brief history of Russian icons

While it's true that much **icon painting** was done by monks and priests as a spiritual devotion, artels of decorators who specialized in churches and produced icons to order were equally active – if not more so.

Kiev, where Christianity took root in 988, was the main centre of icon production until its devastation by the Mongols in 1240. What little survives from this era shows a taste for figures in dark, earth colours, against a plain background, often of gold (representing the Holy Ghost). After Kiev's fall, other schools began to develop regional identities. **Novgorod** icons were painted in emerald green, vermilion and other bold colours, with figures defined by resolute, angular lines, their faces given character by highlighting and shading. The "Northern School" of **Vladimir-Suzdal**, **Yaroslavl** and **Pskov** combined bright colours and rhythmical patterning with simpler forms and more gestural symbolism, while **Tver** icon painters preferred paler, more delicate hues.

The **Moscow school** developed in the late fifteenth century after Ivan the Terrible ordered artists to reside and work in the Kremlin; only then did this style become the most prevalent. However, the Kremlin had been employing the finest artists ever since the dawn of the **golden age** of Russian icon painters such as Rublev and Theophanes, in the 1370s.

Theophanes the Greek made his mark in Novgorod sometime in the latter half of the fourteenth century, starting an illustrious career that overlapped with those of the earliest known native masters, **Andrei Rublev** and **Daniil Cherniy**. The torch was carried on by **Dionysius**, and handed down to **Simon Ushakov** in the seventeenth century, after which it never shone as brightly again. So far as is known, there were no women icon painters until the late nineteenth century.

his earthly and heavenly powers) was once the centrepiece of the Deisis tier in the Pavlovo-Obnorskiy Monastery, while the icons beside it were painted with the help of Dionysius's sons and belonged to the Deisis row of the Therapont Monastery.

The work of the monk **Andrei Rublev** (c.1360–1430) is more searching and mystical, its draughtsmanship at once bold and gossamer-fine. To contemporaries, the huge faces of *Our Saviour*, the *Archangel Michael* and the *Apostle Paul* that he painted for Zvenigorod Cathedral seemed "as though painted with smoke". Alongside are *The Descent into Hell*, *The Annunciation* and *The Assumption* from the festival tier of the Cathedral of the Assumption in Vladimir, where Rublev and **Daniil Cherniy** also created a Deisis tier of larger-than-life figures, including *Christ Enthroned*. The Tretyakov also owns Rublev's *Old Testament Trinity*, a later icon whose gold-and-blue angels seem "full of joy and brightness", as Rublev himself was said to be; he painted it at the request of the Trinity Monastery, where he had served his novitiate.

Room 61 contains sixteenth-century works of the **Moscow school** and northern Russia. The large horizontal icon *Blessed be the Host of the King of Heaven* celebrates Ivan the Terrible's capture of Kazan, with the tsar and his army returning from a burning fortress to the holy city of Jerusalem, symbolizing Moscow. Nearby hang two fine icons of *St George and the Dragon*, which was adopted as the emblem of the Muscovite state by Ivan III. Also notice the *Last Judgement* from Novgorod, showing Christ presiding over the weighing of souls and a green snake writhing down to a winged Satan and the child Antichrist.

The exhibition ends in **Room 62** with icons from the seventeenth century, when the appearance of lay figures in icons (such as the Stroganovs in *The Cherubic Hymn "We, the cherubim"*) and a stylized form of portraiture called the

parsuna (represented by an early one of the boyar Skopin-Shuisky) presaged the emergence of secular forms of art. Arguably the last great icon painter was **Simon Ushakov** (1626–86), who headed the icon-painting studio in the Kremlin Armoury, and was also a muralist and art theorist. His *Tree of the Muscovite State* at the far end of the room shows the Virgin of Vladimir conferring her protection on its rulers. Nearby hangs a rare icon of *St Basil the Blessed* by an unknown artist, depicting the holy man wandering naked outside the Kremlin walls.

Other icons can be seen in the Treasures section (room 55) on the same floor (see p.221).

Portraiture and the Academy: rooms 1–15

The **eighteenth century** was a great watershed in Russian art, as secular painting and sculpture supplanted icons, with **portraiture** leading the way. While Peter the Great was the first to collect foreign paintings and sent native artists to be trained in Europe, it was his daughter Elizabeth who established the **Academy** (1757) that was to dominate Russian art until the second half of the nineteenth century. Its curriculum was modelled on the French Academy's and further circumscribed by Tsarist censorship: artists were told to stick to Classical themes, safe genre scenes or flattering portraits. Since state commissions accounted for much of their earnings, most obliged – or worked abroad.

The official itinerary begins on the **second floor**, reached by a staircase from the basement signposted "Entrance" in English, a room listing the Tretyakov's sponsors, and then another flight of steps. **Room 1** displays work by foreign artists who worked in Russia and early native painters such as **Ivan Nikitin** (c.1680–1742), whose vivid portraits of Peter the Great's sister Natalya and Chancellor Golovkin didn't save him from being denounced as a traitor during the reign of Empress Anna. **Sculpture** was slower to develop, the first real Russian master being **Fedot Shubin** (1740–1805), whose busts of aristocrats appear in **Room 2**.

Alexei Antropov (1716–95) was a trained icon painter who turned to portraiture under the tutelage of the Italian Pietro Rotari. His flamboyant *Peter III*, in **room 3**, stands comparison with a portrait of Catherine the Great by another pupil of Rotari's, **Fyodor Rokotov** (1736–1808), whose later use of soft, indirect lighting and silvery olive hues has been likened to Gainsborough. Of the many serf artists trained at the expense of the Sheremetevs, the most talented was **Ivan Argunov** (1729–1802), whose *Unknown Woman in Russian Dress* (on the wall to the right as you enter **Room 4**) was said to embody the Russian ideal of feminine beauty.

A more ubiquitous subject was Catherine the Great, an enthusiastic patron of the arts whom the Ukrainian-born **Dmitri Levitsky** (1732–1822) depicted as the law-giver against a backdrop of drapery and smoke (**Room 5**). Typical of the state portraits that she gave as gifts to other monarchs, it's less revealing than the picture of the Empress walking her dog in a dressing gown, by Levitsky's pupil, **Vladimir Borovikovsky** (1735–1825), which hangs in **Room 7**. Of historical interest are the views of Red Square and the Neva in St Petersburg by **Fyodor Alexeev** (1753–1824), and the *Portrait of Paul I* by **Stepan Shchukin** (1762–1828) in **Room 6**.

Russia's first Romantic painter was **Orest Kiprensky** (1782–1836), the illegitimate son of a nobleman and a serf, who became involved with the Decembrists while painting his *Portrait of Pushkin* (on the wall to the right as you enter **Room 8**) and died in exile from tuberculosis. Two of his contemporaries who also spent many years in Italy but managed to become Academicians in

Russia were **Karl Bryullov** (1799–1852) and **Alexander Ivanov** (1806–58). Bryullov is best known for his *The Last Day of Pompeii*, in St Petersburg's Russian Museum, but his love of melodrama is apparent from the action-packed *Siege of Kiev* (**Room 9**). Ivanov's monumental *Christ Among the People*, which dominates **Room 10**, was the result of years of preparatory sketches, exhibited alongside mementos of his Italian sojourn such as *Apollo with Youths* and *Olive Trees at Albano* (others are in **Room 12**).

Room 13 exhibits sugary genre portraits by **Vasily Tropinin** (1776–1857), who trained as a confectioner before graduating from the Academy at the age of 48. More intriguing are the contemplative scenes of rural life by **Alexei Venetsianov** (1780–1847), who never studied at the Academy and found his subjects at a small estate that he bought in Tver province, where he portrayed the seasons of agriculture and human life in such works as *Ploughing in the Spring* and *Last Communion of a Dying Woman* (**Room 14**).

In **Room 15**, look out for three pictures by **Pavel Fedotov** (1815–52), who was censored and finally expelled by the Academy, went mad and died in an asylum. *The Major's Courtship* depicts a merchant's daughter recoiling from the attentions of a preening soldier, *The New Chevalier* a minor official exalting over a medal in his dressing gown, and *The Aristocrat's Breakfast*, a dissolute youth surprised by visitors.

Realists and Wanderers: rooms 16–31 and 35–37

The **second half of the nineteenth century** saw genre painting become increasingly infused with **realism** and concern for social issues, reflecting a growing civic consciousness in society. In 1863 fourteen of the Academy's most talented pupils refused to paint the mythological subject set by their examiners, and left to set up an artists' cooperative that was the genesis (1870) of the Society for Travelling Art Exhibitions, known as the **Wanderers** (peredvizhniki), which evaded censorship by exhibiting in the provinces, and heralded a wave of artistic movements that washed over Russia as the Revolution approached.

Room 16 suggests that the Tsarist censors tolerated criticism of society but not of autocracy itself. **Vasily Pukirev** (1832–90) could highlight the plight of a maiden forced to marry an old roué in *The Unequal Marriage*, and **Valery Yakobi** (1834–92) the brutality of the penal system in *A Halt for Convicts on the Road to Siberia*, whereas **Konstantin Flavitsky** (1830–66) took refuge in allegory by portraying Princess Tarakanova, drowning in her cell, as an innocent victim of state oppression (see p.254).

The Siberian **Vasily Perov** (1834–82) caused a furore with his *Village Easter Procession* – showing a drunken priest lurching from an inn (which seems to have been withdrawn from display) – but silenced critics with his penetrating *Portrait of Dostoyevsky* and large-scale historical works such as *The Dispute on Faith*, hung in **Room 17**.

Rooms 18 and 19 show the emergence of **landscape painting** as a lyrical genre. The leader of the Moscow school was **Alexei Savrasov** (1830–97), whose wintry *The Rooks Have Come* is to Russian landscape painting what Pushkin's *Yevgeny Onegin* is to Russian literature, while **Fyodor Vasiliev** (1850–73) was akin to Lermontov in his romanticization of the Crimea. **Ivan Aivazovsky** (1817–1900) captured the essence of storms in his *Black Sea* and *The Rainbow*; **Alexei Bogolyubov** (1824–96) made his name with views of St Petersburg; and the Crimean Greek **Arkhip Kuindzhi** (1842–1910) rendered Russia's rivers, islands and steppes (**Room 21**).

The moving spirit of the Wanderers was **Ivan Kramskoy** (1837–87), renowned for his portraits of Tolstoy, for a pert *Nameless Lady* who is thought to have been the model for Anna Karenina, and for a melancholy Slavic *Christ in the Wilderness* which Kramskoy painted because "The Italian Christ is handsome, one may say divine, but he is alien to me" (**Room 20**).

While most of the Wanderers agreed with the socialist Chernyshevsky that art is only valid if socially engaged, the Academy venerated the cult of beauty and antiquity, epitomized by the titillating *Sword Dance* and *An Orgy in Tiberius' Day* in **Room 22**, by **Genrikh Semiradsky** (1843–1902). Conversely, **Vasily Maximov** (1844–1911) quit the Academy to paint rural life, treating the twilight of the gentry (in *Everything in the Past*) as sympathetically as the plight of landless labourers (**Room 23**). Others focused on nature. **Ivan Shishkin** (1832–1898) was nicknamed the "Accountant of Leaves" for his meticulous depictions of foliage in such pictures as *Bears in a Pine Forest* and *Tree-Felling*, which hang in **Room 25**, near the stairway from room 56 on the floor below.

The 1860s and 1870s were a time of soul-searching over Russia's identity. **Viktor Vasnetsov** (1846–1926) was a founder of the neo-Russian style and avowed Russia's Slavic heritage in scenes like *Three Warriors* and *After the Battle of Igor and Svyatoslavich with the Polovtsians* (**Room 26**) – which some consider inferior to his later pictures inspired by Russian fairytales, exhibited at Vasnetsov's former house (covered on p.269).

Vasily Vereshchagin (1842–1904) joined several Russian campaigns as an official war artist yet professed pacifism and was enthralled by Central Asia before the "civilizing" rule of the Tsars (**Room 27**). Best known for *Apotheosis of War* and *Skobelev at Shipka* (in which he placed himself on the darker horse behind the general taking the salute), he perished with the Russian fleet at the disastrous battle of Tushima Bay.

Russia's foremost historical painter, **Vasily Surikov** (1846–1916), is represented by four canvases in **Room 28**. *The Morning of the Execution of the Streltsy on Red Square* and the *Boyaryna Morozova* being dragged away to meet her death for heresy both depict "martyrs" in the defence of traditional values. The *Tsarevna's Visit to a Monastery* alludes to the fate of princesses condemned to a nunnery, while *Menshikov in Berezovo* shows the disgraced ex-Prince brooding in a Siberian hut on his days of fortune under Peter the Great.

▲ The Tretyakov Gallery

Rooms 29 and 30 are devoted to the great realist **Ilya Repin** (1844–1930), whose populist sympathies were expressed in *A Religious Procession in Kurskaya Guberniya* and narrative works like *They Did Not Expect Him*, portraying a dissident's return from exile. His anguished Ivan the Terrible cradling his dying son still has the power to shock, while Repin's frank portrait of the alcoholic composer Mussorgsky is no longer shown.

Although **Nicholas Ge** (1831–94) reinterpreted biblical themes like Calvary and the Garden of Gethsemane in a strikingly original style that prefigured Expressionism, the public preferred his Academic historical works, particularly *Peter the Great Interrogating Tsarevich Alexei at Peterhof*, in **Room 31**.

From here it's easy to wander up a short flight of steps into the Vrubel hall (see next section), rather than descend a parallel staircase to view the remainder of the Wanderers **downstairs**. There, **Room 35** displays genre landscapes by **Vasily Polonev** (1884–1927), including his popular favourites *Moscow Courtyard*, *Grandmother's Garden* and *Christ Among the Teachers*. Look out for the portrait of Chekhov among the landscapes in **Room 36**. The Wanderers section concludes in **Room 37** with **Isaak Levitan** (1860–1900), the finest Russian landscapist of the nineteenth century, revered for his limpid rivers and soft light, in works like *The Evening Bells* and *Eternal Peace*.

Vrubel, Symbolism and the World of Art: rooms 32–34 and 38–48

Mikhail Vrubel (1856–1940) had an impact on Russian art akin to that of Cézanne in the West, emerging from the Abramtsevo artists' colony (p.298) to found the **Symbolist movement** that began the revolt against realism. Post-Impressionism, Symbolism, Art Nouveau and Expressionism reached Russia almost simultaneously, producing a heady brew whose ferment equalled that of Western European art, while coinciding with a political and social avalanche.

A lofty hall on the second floor (**Room 33**) exhibits huge panels commissioned for the mansions of wealthy Muscovites, such as the *Faust* series from Morozov's Gothic study at his home on ulitsa Spiridonovka. Vrubel's *Lilacs* are textured like coral reefs and as epic as Monet's *Water-lilies*, while *The Demon* is one of a series inspired by Lermontov's poem of the same name, which obsessed him to the point of madness. In 1902, on the eve of the opening of the fourth World of Art exhibition, Vrubel locked himself in the gallery with a bottle of champagne and totally repainted it; next morning he was found gibbering incoherently and committed to an asylum.

The adjacent **rooms 32 and 34** are devoted to **Nikolai Roerich** (1874–1947), for whom the Kievan Rus and Eastern civilizations were spiritual lodestars. Roerich's Varangian longships and citadels resemble illustrations from a child's history primer; his saturated-colour views of the Himalayas are found in student dormitories and cafés to this day. The Roerich Museum (see p.131) displays a whole lot more of his work.

Downstairs the focus shifts to a multitude of artists from different movements, starting in **Room 38**. Neo-Russian romanticism's exponents included **Apollinarius Vasnetsov** (1856–1927) – the brother of Victor Vasnetsov – and **Andrei Ryabushkin** (1861–1904), who both specialized in depicting seventeenth-century Muscovy. Early landscapes by **Konstantin Yuon** (1875–1958) give no hint of the fireworks he'd unleash later on (exhibited at the new Tretyakov Gallery), while **Filipp Malyavin** (1869–1940) progressed from tame society portraits to coruscating images of peasant women such as the crimson *Whirlwind* that dominates the room.

Mikhail Nesterov (1862–1942) of the Abramtsevo colony was inspired by Orthodox spirituality. *The Child Bartholomew's Vision* depicts the moment when St Sergei of Radonezh first felt the touch of God (see p.292), the life of the monks of Solovetsky Monastery is captured in *Silence* and *The Hermit*, while *The Soul of the People* embodies Nesterov's view of Russia as a spiritual ethos (**Room 39**).

Passing through room 40 (allowing access to the medieval art section) you'll find two rooms of pictures by **Valentin Serov** (1865–1911), an Abramtsevo artist who favoured Impressionism and prospered as a society portraitist. Among those portrayed in **rooms 41 & 42** are Rimsky-Korsakov, Chaliapin, Levitan, Surikov, various Morozovs, and the daughter of the colony's patron, Mamontov, in the much-reproduced *Girl with Peaches*.

Another Russian Impressionist and protégé of Mamontov's was **Konstantin Korovin** (1861–1939), whose journey with Serov around the Murmansk region where Mamontov was building a railway inspired such works as *Northern Idyll* – although Parisian street scenes and still lifes account for most of his *oeuvre* in **Room 43**. Korovin emigrated there after the Revolution and eventually starved to death in the gutters of Paris.

Most of the first wave of Symbolists belonged to the **World of Art** (Mir istkusstva) movement in St Petersburg, led by Diaghilev and Benois, the creators of the *Ballet Russe*. Many of its sets were designed by **Leon Bakst** (1866–1924) and **Alexander Golovin** (1863–1930), who applied the techniques of the stage to easel painting, as in Bakst's *Siamese Sacred Dance* and Golovin's portrait of Chaliapin in the role of Holofernes. While **Konstantin Somov** (1869–1939) was influenced by eighteenth-century French Mannerism, **Boris Kustodiev** (1878–1927) went in for brilliantly coloured "Russian" scenes, such as *Shrovetide Festival* and *Haymaking*. Another much loved picture in **Room 44** is the self-portrait *At the Dressing Table*, by **Zinaida Serebryakova** (1884–1967).

After Vrubel, the most influential Symbolist of the time was **Viktor Borissov-Mussatov** (1870–1905), who was crippled in childhood and secretly lusted after his sister; his *Phantoms*, *The Pool* and *Sleep of the Gods* are brooding meditations on young womanhood (**Room 45**). By the early 1900s Russian and Western art were evolving in tandem and mutually indebted, with Kandinsky and Chagall teaching in Munich and Paris, and international Symbolist exhibitions held in Moscow. The leading lights of Russia's Blue Rose movement of Symbolists were **Pavel Kuznetsov** (1878–1968) and the Armenian **Martiros Saryan** (1880–1972), whose mysterious, static landscapes influenced the German *Blaue Reiter* school (**Room 46**).

A room full of **sculptures** presages the end of the chronological exposition in **Room 47**, displaying early works by **Natalya Goncharova** (1881–1962) and **Mikhail Larionov** (1881–1964), which only hint at their subsequent Primitivist and Rayonist styles that catalyzed the avant-garde of the 1900s. Their later work – and that of the Futurists – can be seen in the Tretyakov Gallery on Krymskiy val.

Graphic art and treasures: rooms 49–55

The last two sections of the Tretyakov are usually overlooked by visitors unless they end up there by accident, but it's worth seeing what's there as some of it is top class. If you only have an hour to spend in the gallery, the **Graphic art** section (**rooms 49–54**) on the first floor offers a speeded-up *tour d'horizon* of Russian art, with engravings, drawings and watercolours by many of the artists whose oils hang in other rooms. Highlights include Levitan's *Autumn*, Surikov's

Spanish scenes, gouaches by Bakst, Lanceray and others from the World of Art, and studies from the folios of Chagall, Malevich, Kandinsky and Popova.

Room 54 gives access to the **Treasures** gallery, a single long room of showcases displaying pearl-embroidered veils that shrouded icons of the Virgin in the sixteenth century, the icon of St Nicholas of Mozhaisk that once stood above the Kremlin's St Nicholas Gate, and others set in magnificent silver frames. You can also see items of jewellery made by rival workshops to the House of Fabergé.

Krymskiy val to Pavelets Station

The southern arc of the Garden Ring lacks the epic architecture seen north of the river, but is redeemed by cultural attractions at both ends. Its western end – called Krymskiy val after the bygone Crimean Rampart of the Zemlyanoy Gorod – runs past Gorky Park, the new Tretyakov Gallery and the Central House of Artists. At Oktyabrskaya ploshchad you can make a detour to see the heroic Gagarin monument on Leninskiy prospekt, or witness the annual Communist march from Lenin's statue if you happen to be around in November. After that there's nothing till Lenin's funerary train, the Theatre Museum and the International House of Music near Pavelets Station.

To reach Gorky Park or the Tretyakov it's better to start from Park Kultury metro across the river rather than Oktyabrskaya, so that your appetite for Soviet culture is whetted by the bas-reliefs in Park Kultury station, and further aroused by the grand arch at the entrance to the park, as its architects intended. The Communist march kicks off by Oktyabrskaya metro, while the sights around Pavelets Station are accessible from Paveletskaya metro. All three stations are on the Circle line, whose decor alone is worth a journey.

Gorky Park (Park Kultury)

Moscow's riverside **Gorky Park** (daily 10am–10pm; R50) is known to Muscovites as Park Kultury and famous abroad due to Martin Cruz Smith's 1980s thriller, which opens with the discovery of three faceless corpses in snowbound Gorky Park. The reality is less sinister but still a bit creepy in another way, as Pepsi culture flourishes amid the relics of a totalitarian regime's fun side.

Inaugurated in 1928, the Soviet Union's first "Park of Culture and Rest" was formed by uniting an exhibition zone near Krymskiy val with the vast gardens of the Golitsyn Hospital and the Neskuchniy Palace, totalling 300 acres. In winter, recalled diplomat Fitzroy Mclean, "the whole of it was flooded, and on skates one could go skimming along for miles over brilliantly lighted frozen avenues to the strains of Vienna waltzes and Red Army marches".

Nowadays, three funfairs constitute the main attraction, though very few rides operate over winter. Thrill-seekers go for the funfair beside the river, with **bungee-jumping**, two **roller coasters** and a **water chute**, whose rides are more exciting than a "flight" in the *Buryan*, a retired Soviet **space shuttle** linked to a series of domes offering a "cosmic experience". The build-up to the ride is fun, but its gyroscopic chairs do a poor job of simulating zero gravity, so you basically pay to see thirty minutes of videos, and some spacesuits. It seems an ignominious end for the *Buryan*, which made a trial orbit of the earth under remote control in 1988 and might have carried cosmonauts into space, had not the Soviet space programme virtually collapsed a few years later. Today, a new suborbital shuttle is being developed at the Zhukovsky air base outside Moscow (see p.310).

In summer kids can enjoy the Wondertown and Fantastic Journey fun houses; the carousels and electronic games work all year; and rollerbladers turn out in force whenever the weather's fine. Nor does winter dampen spirits: the **ice disco** is jumping at weekends and most evenings, and in February the park hosts a **festival of ice sculptures**. However, **beware** of visiting on the days dedicated to Russia's Border Guards (May 28), Navy (last Sun in July) or Airborne Forces (first Sat in Aug), or whenever Luzhniki Stadium hosts a match between Spartak, Dinamo or TsKA, as the park is full of drunken servicemen or football fans, spoiling for a fight.

The Tretyakov Gallery on Krymskiy val

On the other side of Krymskiy val, Vuchetich's "Swords into Ploughshares" (a copy of the original sculpture presented to the UN in 1957) and other allegorical statues greet visitors to a riverside arts complex. Although you'll first encounter the Central House of Artists and the entrance to the sculpture park (see p.225), it's only a minute's walk to the entrance of the new **Tretyakov Gallery** (Tues–Sun 10am–7.30pm; R250, students R150) on the eastern side of the building. This takes up where the old Tretyakov left off, with a bravura display of **twentieth-century Russian art**, from dazzling Futurist designs to Socialist Realism and "nonconformist" art from Soviet times, exhibited on the fourth floor. Additionally, it holds regular **temporary exhibitions** of anything from European Cubism to masterpieces from the Russian Museum, on the second floor (for which a separate charge is levied).

Photography is not permitted; cameras must be left at the cloakroom. On your way upstairs, you'll pass a scale model of Tatlin's un-built *Monument to the Third International*, in the foyer on the second floor. The permanent exhibition fills some forty rooms; artworks are captioned in English, with an explanatory text in each room.

Primitivism, Futurism, Suprematism and Constructivism: rooms 1–9

Rooms 1 and 2 are devoted to **Primitivism** with sculptures and paintings by husband-and-wife team **Natalya Goncharova** (1881–1962) and **Mikhail Larionov** (1881–1964), as well as works by **Konenkov** (1874-1971) and Tatlin (see below). You'll also find three pictures by the Georgian artist **Niko Pirosmanashvili** (1863–1918), who pursued his own style of Primitivism and was so poor that he often painted on scraps of wood or tarpaulin. **Rooms 3–5** are focused on the **Jack of Diamonds** society, which existed from 1910 to 1916, whose influences were Cézanne, Matisse and Fauvism. Among the "Cézannists" were **Alexander Kuprin** (1880–1960), **Robert Falk** (1886–1958) and **Aristarkh Lentulov** (1882–1943). Their fellow "Jack", **Ilya Mashkov** (1881–1944), specialized in luscious pictures of food, which he had to imagine during the hungry years after 1917. Another major figure was **Pyotr Konchalovsky** (1876–1958) – the son-in-law of the historical painter Surikov – whose vibrant portrait of the theatre director Meyerhold lounging on a divan later helped restorers re-create his apartment.

Although works get rotated or sent abroad, in **rooms 6–9** you can be sure of finding something by nearly all the big names in Russian **Futurism** – a catch-all term for the explosion of artistic styles and theories between 1910 and 1920. Early Futurists, such as the Burlyuk brothers and Mayakovsky, were out to shock – the Futurist manifesto was entitled *A Slap in the Face of Public Taste.* More cerebral was **Kazimir Malevich** (1878–1935), whose Cubo-Futurism – influenced by the bold lines of icons and peasant woodcuts – evolved into what he termed **Suprematism**, the "art of pure sensation". Malevich's rival for ascendancy over the avant-garde movement was **Vladimir Tatlin** (1885–1953), who anticipated Dadaism with his junk collages and experimented with theatre design and the "Culture of Materials". What came to be called **Constructivism** owed much to his collaboration with Meyerhold and the painters **Lyubov Popova** (1889–1924) and **Nadezhda Udaltsova** (1885–1961). Much of their conceptual work was never realized: Tatlin's glider, *Letatlin*, never left the ground, while his *Monument to the Third International* – intended to be over 396m high and revolve on its axis – got a dusty response from Lenin.

While the Russian Museum owns more works by Malevich and Tatlin, the Tretyakov scores with designs by other artists, such as a decorative panel for the Central Children's Theatre by Kuprin, and sets and costumes for the operas *Tales of Hoffman*, *Romeo and Juliet* and the Futurist play *Victory Over the Sun*, by Lentulov, Alexander Exter and **El Lissitzky** (1896–1941), who dreamt of skyscrapers on stilts above the Boulevard Ring. Look out, too, for book illustrations by Goncharova and Larionov, textile designs by Popova, and scenes from Jewish life in Vitebsk by **Marc Chagall** (1887–1985), as well as his exquisite *Lilies of the Valley*. **Pavel Filonov** (1883–1943) developed a system of "analytical art" to reflect the atomic nature of reality, layering detail upon detail to create such kaleidoscopic masterpieces as *The First Shostakovich Symphony* and *Composition with Six Faces*.

Most of these works, including vibrant Constructivist pictures by Popova, Malevich, Anna Leporskaya, **Olga Rozanova** and Chagall, once belonged to **George Costakis** (1921–1990), a Russian-born Greek who began collecting Futurist art in the 1940s when it was all but forgotten in the Soviet Union, and amassed nearly 300 paintings which he exhibited in his flat as the climate thawed, and finally sold to the state.

Rooms 10 and 11 are devoted to an exhibition of twentieth-century **Graphics and Sculpture**, which continues in **rooms 18**, **19**, **24**, **29 and 34**, but the works displayed are rotated regularly from the gallery's collection.

Pre-Revolutionary works, agitprop and early realism: rooms 13–16

Works by **Kuzma Petrov-Vodkin** (1878–1939), a Symbolist who expressed the hopes and fears raised by the revolutions of 1917, can be found in **Room 13**. His *Petrograd 1918* – depicting a nursing mother overlooking a street where excited citizens discuss the latest events – was a proletarian reinterpretation of traditional icons of the Virgin and Child that came to be known as the "Petrograd Madonna". His other masterpiece, *Bathing the Red Horse*, is an allegory of revolutionary idealism, painted in 1912 before war, revolution and famine tore Russia apart. In the 1920s, he nourished his dream of socialism with scenes such as *By the Samovar* and *Housewarming: Working-class Leningrad*. Look out also for the panel *Flowers* by **Boris Grigoriev** (1886–1939) and a portrait of the ballerina Pavlova by **Alexander Yakovlev** (1887–1938) – both of whom emigrated after the Revolution.

Another pre-Revolutionary artistic grouping was the **Blue Rose**, so-called after the name of their first exhibition in 1907. Sharing a love of blue (symbolizing spirituality), dreams and the simplification of forms, they each sought a world of their own. **Pavel Kuznetsov** (1878–1968) found his ideal life with the Kyrgyz nomads whom he portrayed in soft blues and yellows, while **Martiros Sariyan** (1880–1968) rendered Armenia and the Near East in hues of yellow, red and indigo (**Room 14**).

Many Futurists threw themselves into the Revolution and produced what became known as **agitprop**, or "agitational propaganda" – particularly posters aimed at promoting public health, literacy or recruitment for the Red Army. However, vitriolic disputes between Proletkult, LEF and other groups, and the impracticality of the cerebral "laboratory art" espoused by Tatlin, led to a backlash in favour of easel painting, realism and simplicity. The Association of Artists of Revolutionary Russia (AKhRR) led the charge with didactic works such as Cheptsov's *Meeting of the Village Communist Cell* and Bogrodsky's *Sailors Ambushed*, while the decorative painter **Konstantin Yuon** (1875–1978) alternated between utopian visions and crowd scenes like *New Planet* and *Red Army Parade*. Look out, too, for a bronze worker's head from a series commissioned in 1922 for reproduction on Soviet banknotes, and the *Youth with a Star and Banner* for the Soviet pavilion at the 1939 New York Expo, both sculpted by Ivan Shadr.

The Society of Easel Painters (OST) shared AKhRR's aims but expressed them in a freer style (**Room 15**). **Alexander Deineka** (1899–1969) created stark, monochrome compositions depicting the heroism of the proletariat (*Defence of Petrograd*) and industrialization (*Building New Workshops*), and lyrical scenes of women playing ball games – themes echoed by the sexy women builders and valiant Red Guards depicted by **Alexander Samokhvalov** (1894–1971), the *Anti-Imperialist Meeting in New York* and *Get Heavy Industry Going!* by **Yuri Pimenov** (1903–77), and the ceramic tableau of Red Army soldiers, *On the Southern Front*, by **Isidor Frikh-Khar** (1893–1978). **Room 16** features a dynamic footballer sculpted by Iosif Chaikov, and a bronze *Peasant Woman* by **Vera Mukhina** (1889–1953), designer of the iconic Worker and Collective Farm Girl monument (see p.279). Throughout this section, look out also for works by the Makovets group – whose emphasis on spiritual values made them outcasts in the 1930s – with pictures by those who reached a *modus vivendi* with the authorities, such as **Alexander Tyshler** (1898–1980), whose *Shooting of the Baku Commissars* gives no hint of his later abstractionism.

Social Realism: rooms 20, 25, 26 and 28

Following the dissolution of all artistic groups in 1932, **Socialist Realism** became the only acceptable form of art. As articulated by Stalin's mouthpiece Zhdanov at the All-Union Congress of Writers, its principles were *partiinost*, *ideinost* and *naorodnost* (Party character, socialist content and national roots). Its academic style suited **Isaak Brodsky** (1884–1939), a pupil of Repin's who created such "Bolshevik masterpieces" as *Lenin in the Smolniy*, which shares **Room 25** with a giant bronze head of Dzerzhinsky, and the original casts for monuments at Leningrad and Kharkov and the statues in Ploshchad Revolyutsii metro station, by **Matvei Manizer** (1891–1966).

Many of the first generation of artists trained under the Soviet system were purged in the 1930s for being "Formalist". While **Alexander Drevin** (1889–1938) died in exile in the Altay region, his wife, Udaltsova, survived by destroying much of her early Futurist work. You can see why Party *apparatchiki* had it in for **Pavel Chelishchev** (1898–1937), whose vast *Phenomena* – full of transsexual figures, brains in globes, futuristic cities and interplanetary monsters – resembles a poster for a 1970s sci-fi movie (**Room 20**), or why the pre-Revolutionary Romantic Nesterov switched to "safe" portraits of fellow painters, the sculptor Mukhina and the scientist Pavlov (**Room 25**).

The apotheosis of Socialist Realism was attained by two ardently Stalinist presidents of the Artists' Union, showcased in **Room 26** – which affords a fantastic **view** of the Peter the Great monument (see p.206). While **Alexander Gerasimov** (1881–1963) glorified the Soviet leadership in the staff conference of the *First Cavalry Army* and his portrait of Stalin and defence minister Vorishilov on the ramparts of the Kremlin (it's said that Stalin ordered another version without Voroshilov, in case he was purged), his successor, **Boris Ioganson** (1893–1973), is remembered for *The Interrogation of the Communists* by decadent, brutish White Guards, whose subtext was the need for constant vigilance against the class enemy.

Arkady Plastov (1893–1972) idealized Collective Farms in saturated colours and later created a wartime propaganda masterpiece, *The Fascist Flies Past* – a country boy and cows lying in the grass, at first sight asleep, but actually riddled with bullets (**Room 28**).

Postwar works: rooms 30–33 and 35-37

During Khrushchev's "thaw" artistic controls were relaxed, but the limits of the permissible were drawn at the 1954 Manège exhibition, when he lambasted abstract works by Ernst Neizvestny as "dogshit". (Khrushchev later relented, and asked Neisvestny to design his tombstone) Yet the genie was out of the bottle, and throughout the Brezhnev years there was ambivalence in the regime's acknowledgment of an avant-garde tradition (with exhibitions of Constructivists, Falk and other artists shunned in the 1930s), its tolerance of stylistic variations that didn't impinge on ideology, and its repression of a dissident subculture typified by the bohemian **Mytki** – whose neo-Primitivist work is exhibited in **Room 32**. Other rooms feature an ever-changing array of works by living artists, from the neo-Expressionist Elii Belyutin (**Room 35**) to Op-Artist Sergei Bordcharov, who shares **Room 36** with "**Sots Art**" subverting the genre of Socialist Realism, such as Boris Orlov's *Avenue of Heroes* or the creepy bronze figures of Grisha Bruskin's *The Hero's Birth*. Also look out for work by the **Actionists** who mirrored the absurdities of the Yeltsin era with provocative stunts. Oleg Kulik was arrested for chaining himself naked to a kennel and sodomizing dogs, while Alexander Brener made headlines by spraying a dollar sign on a Malevich in protest against the commercialization of art – though cynics noted that he defaced one in Holland, where his crime rated some months in an open prison, rather than in Russia, where he would have been punished by fifteen years in a hard-labour camp.

The Central House of Artists and the Muzeon

Around the corner from the Tretyakov, the **Central House of Artists** (Tsentralniy dom Khudozhnikov, or TsDKh; Tues–Sun 11am–8pm; R100) is Moscow's showcase for visiting **exhibitions** and contemporary art from all over the former USSR, and the venue for Moscow's international **folk music festival** in October. Check the *Moscow Times* or *Pulse* to see what's on – or visit TsDKh's website, Ⓦ www.cha.ru.

Behind the Tretyakov lies the **Muzeon** or Park of Arts (daily 9am–9pm; free), known as the "sculpture park". This started out as a graveyard of Communist monuments that gave pride of place to the statue of "Iron Felix" Dzerzhinsky that stood outside the Lubyanka until it was toppled in 1991, but has since accrued over 600 contemporary sculptures, from caged heads representing the victims of repression, to sappy statues of Einstein and Niels Böhr. Tsereteli's *Peter the Great* towers in the background, spectacularly floodlit at night.

Oktyabrskaya ploshchad and Leninskiy prospekt

Oktyabrskaya ploshchad (October Square) is an urban showpiece from the Era of Stagnation: ugly blocks of once prestigious accommodation, flanking an arterial junction and the last **statue of Lenin** to be erected in Moscow (in 1985). Bestriding a plinth embossed with peasants and workers fired by his vision, he is cast as a Titan of world history – now reduced to insignificance by the giant satellite dishes and neon hoardings on Oktyabrskaya's skyline. On **November 7**, however, thousands rally here to **march** into the centre, led by brass bands and banners spanning the width of Krymskiy val. Many are old Communists wearing medals, marching and singing Soviet hymns with the precision of a lifetime's rallying. The youthful National Bolsheviks who make up the other contingent can't march at all, but bellow the name of their leader, Limonov, and carry effigies of Bush and international capitalism to burn. But the march is usually peaceful, and there are so many photographers and riot police present that you can watch from the sidelines or join in without drawing attention. It begins about 11am and ends up wherever the Kremlin permits about two hours later.

Following ulitsa Bolshaya Yakimanka, you reach the satellite-dish-festooned **French Embassy**, whose ambassador resides in the adjacent **Igumnov House**, a neo-Russian fantasy of peaked roofs and gables, pendant arches, coloured tiles and a blend of Gothic, Byzantine and Baroque decor, built for a rich merchant in 1893. While tales that Igumnov buried his mistress in one of the walls and the architect hanged himself in the hallway are probably untrue, the mansion did later contain the Institute of the Brain, where Lenin's brain was cut into thirty thousand slices and studied, with the aim of discovering the source of his genius – a procedure later applied to the brains of Stalin, Pavlov, Gorky, Eisenstein, Mayakovsky and Sakharov.

Directly opposite, the gaudily painted **Church of St John the Warrior** (tserkov Ivana Voina) is one of the few buildings erected in Moscow under Peter the Great, who is said to have personally chosen its site and even sketched out a plan. Its construction (1709–13) was entrusted to Ivan Zarudny, whose design married the configuration of a Moscow Baroque church with new European decorative forms. The interior is obviously European in its lavish use of sculptural mouldings, but holds such native treasures as the *Icon of the Saviour* that once hung above the Saviour Gate of the Kremlin. St John's became the custodian of all kinds of relics, as it was one of the few churches in Moscow to escape closure in the 1920–30s.

Leninskiy prospekt

From Oktyabrskaya, consider a detour by metro down **Leninskiy prospekt** – Moscow's longest avenue, running for 14km to the city's outer Ring Road. The initial stretch is flanked on one side by Stalinist blocks, and on the other by Gorky Park and two eighteenth-century palatial buildings. The **Golitsyn Hospital** was a charitable bequest from Russia's ambassador to Vienna and now contains an orphanage run by nuns, while the Neskuchniy Palace was once the mansion of the mining magnate Demidov and now houses the **Russian Academy of Science**.

Its main landmark is **ploshchad Gagarina**, where Leninskiy Prospekt metro exits behind a Stalinist **apartment block** with several towers, forming one half of a gigantic crescent defining the northern edge of the plaza, which used to be called Kaluga Gate Square. These flats for the postwar *nomenklatura* were constructed by German POWs and Russian convicts (including Solzhenitsyn); residents boasted of the workmanship of "their" German builders. Near the metro exit, the giant titanium **Gagarin Monument** resembles a muscular superhero braced to blast off on a column of energy. The square was renamed after tens of thousands of Muscovites turned out to welcome Gagarin as he arrived from Vnukovo Airport, following his sensational orbit around Earth in April 1961.

Around Pavelets Station

With its facade modelled on a Loire Valley chateau, its shuttle-link to Domodedovo airport, and several airline offices in the towering business centre alongside, **Pavelets Station** (Paveletskiy vokzal) seems more international than Moscow's other railway termini – though it's still a far cry from Eurostar. Behind a cluster of kiosks to the east of the station is a small park harbouring a pavilion containing the **Lenin Funerary Train**. When last seen, the pavilion wasn't open to the public, but its glass frontage allows a glimpse of the gleaming orange-and-black steam engine and wagon that brought Lenin's body to Moscow for his funeral on Red Square in 1924. A giant bust of Lenin gazes blindly from a flame-shaped aperture at the back of the hall, while the inscription on the wall outside the pavilion asserts: "The name of V.I. Lenin is immortal, like his ideas and his deeds."

A long underpass connects Pavelets Station to the northern exit of Paveletskaya metro, across the traffic-choked square. Nearby, on the corner of ulitsa Bakrushina, a lovely neo-Gothic mansion once owned by the pre-Revolutionary theatrical impresario Alexei Bakhrushin houses a **Theatre Museum** (teatralniy muzey imeni A.A. Bakrushina; Mon, Wed–Sun noon–7pm; closed last Mon of each month; R150) which bears his name. Downstairs are opera set designs for *Boris Godunov* and *Ivan the Terrible*, and costumes worn by Chaliapin in the title role of Boris. Upstairs there's a gorgeous puppet theatre; Nijinsky's dancing shoes; decadent gouache designs by Michael Fokine; and stage-models for Constructivist dramas like *Zori*, which involved architects and painters. Though poorly laid out and only captioned in Russian, the museum should appeal to aficionados of theatre history or design.

Music lovers have to walk a few hundred metres to reach the **Moscow International House of Music** (Moskovskiy Mezhdunarodniy dom Muzyki), a circular, glassy cultural centre with the most high-tech auditorium in Moscow, on the southern tip of the nameless island that enfolds Zamoskvareche, overlooking the Kosmodamianskaya embankment, across the river from the Novospasskiy Monastery.

The Donskoy and Danilov monasteries

Indisputably the main attractions in this part of Moscow, the Donskoy and Danilov monasteries originally stood a kilometre or so beyond the city ramparts, serving as defensive outposts and sanctuaries. While both are interesting, the

Donskoy is far more atmospheric, with a lovely cemetery. The Danilov's own cemetery lies further south, near the city's Muslim burial ground. The cemeteries are out here because of an Imperial edict following the last visitation of the Black Death in 1770–71. To combat its spread, a quarter of Moscow's houses were burnt and all the medieval cemeteries within the centre were dug up and removed – it was believed that "miasmas" emanating from corpses caused the plague. Seven large new Orthodox cemeteries were then prepared beyond the city limits, as the death toll soared. In Moscow province, a third of the population – over 200,000 people – died of plague that year.

The Donskoy Monastery and around

The massive red-brick walls of the **Donskoy Monastery** (Donskoy monastyr; daily 7.30am–7pm; free) call to mind the Red Fort at Agra or a Crusader castle in Palestine. Their height and thickness reflect a historic fear of Mongols shooting catapults and fire-arrows rather than of European armies fielding massed cannons – as do the dozen towers spaced at regular intervals. The monastic enclosure covers 42,000 square metres, with plenty of room for an old graveyard that shouldn't be confused with a newer cemetery down the road.

Although the monastery is open daily, parts are off limits on weekdays so it's best to come at the weekend. **Getting there** involves taking the metro to Shabolovskaya station and walking a few blocks from there. Depending on which route you take, a few other landmarks can be seen on the way to the monastery or back towards the metro.

Some history

The monastery dates back to 1591, when Boris Godunov routed the last Crimean Tatar raid on Moscow. His victory was attributed to the **icon of Our Lady of the Don**, which had accompanied Dmitri Donskoy to war against the Mongols and ensured his victory at Kulikovo in 1380. To hearten his own troops, Godunov paraded the icon around camp on the eve of the battle and, following a brief skirmish the next day, Khan Kazy-Gire's army fled. In thanksgiving, the Russians erected a church to house the icon and founded a monastery on the spot.

Robbed and abandoned in the Time of Troubles, the monastery was restored by tsars Fyodor and Alexei, but remained small and poor until renewed warfare against the Tatars prompted the Regent Sofia and her lover Prince Golitsyn to strengthen its defences. Continued by Peter the Great, this building programme (1684–1733) resulted in the existing fortifications and Great Cathedral. By the late eighteenth century the Donskoy had become not only prosperous, but a fashionable burial ground for Georgian and Golitsyn princes and cultural figures.

Soon after the Revolution the monastery was closed down by the Bolsheviks, though its monks continued to live there until 1929, when they were evicted to make way for a Museum of Atheism. It subsequently became a branch of the Shchusev Architectural Museum, collecting sculptures from demolished churches across Moscow.

The Nazi invasion obliged Stalin to enlist the Orthodox Church as an ally; to reward its support, services were resumed at the Old Cathedral in 1946. However, not until 1992 was **Patriarch Tikhon**'s sanctified body laid to rest there with due honours. Invested as Patriarch on the eve of the Revolution, he had been jailed by the Bolsheviks and buried in an unmarked grave within the monastery in 1925. Soon after his reburial a fire destroyed all the icons in the cathedral except *Our Lady of the Don*, and when restorers opened the tomb

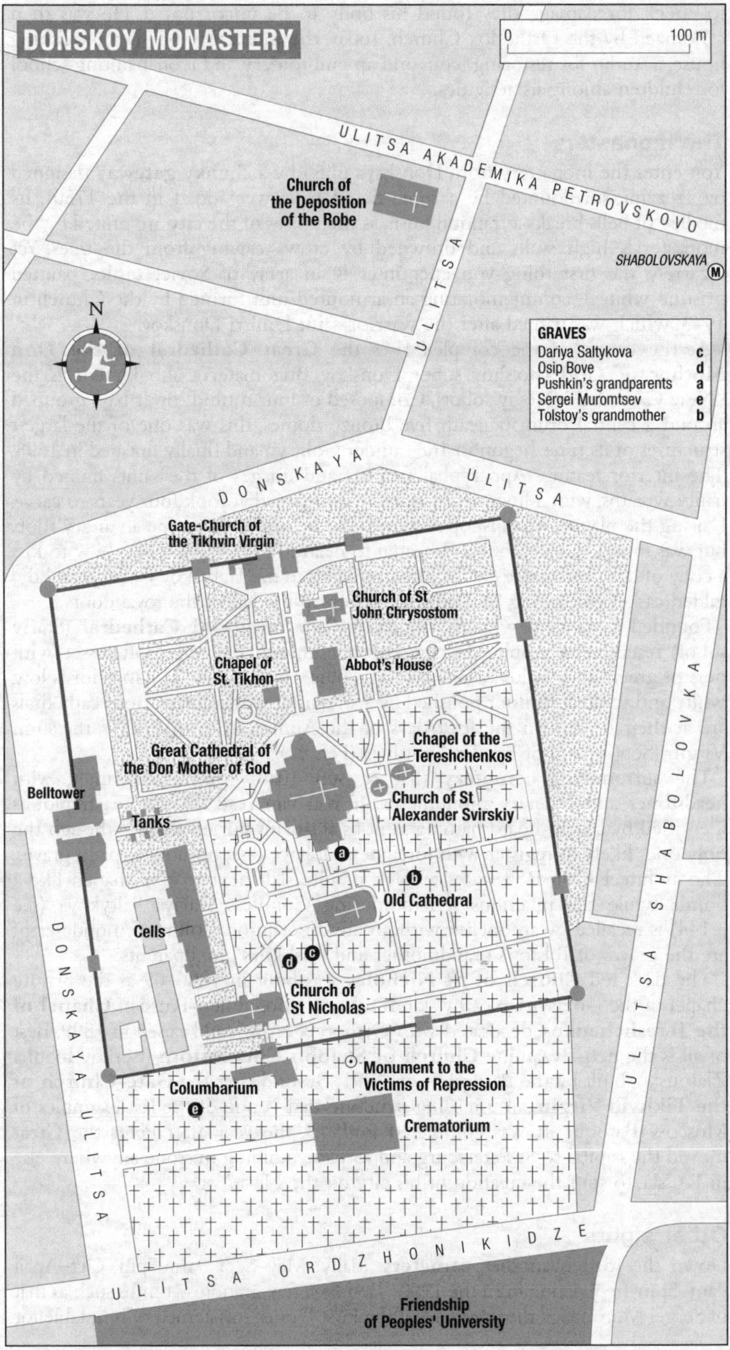

DONSKOY MONASTERY

0 100 m

ULITSA AKADEMIKA PETROVSKOVO

Church of the Deposition of the Robe

ULITSA

SHABOLOVSKAYA

N

Cominterm Radio Tower

GRAVES	
Dariya Saltykova	c
Osip Bove	d
Pushkin's grandparents	a
Sergei Muromtsev	e
Tolstoy's grandmother	b

DONSKAYA ULITSA

Gate-Church of the Tikhvin Virgin

Church of St John Chrysostom

Chapel of St. Tikhon

Abbot's House

Great Cathedral of the Don Mother of God

Chapel of the Tereshchenkos

Belltower

Church of St Alexander Svirskiy

Tanks

Old Cathedral

Cells

Church of St Nicholas

Monument to the Victims of Repression

Columbarium

Crematorium

ULITSA SHABOLOVKA

DONSKAYA ULITSA

Danilov Monastery (1.5km)

ULITSA ORDZHONIKIDZE

Friendship of Peoples' University

to check for damage they found his body to be uncorrupted. He was then canonized by the Orthodox Church. Today, the monastery boasts a publishing house, a studio for restoring icons and an embroidery and icon-painting school for children among its activities.

The monastery

You enter the monastery from Donskaya ulitsa by a chunky **gateway** designed by Trezzini, surmounted by a three-tiered belltower added in the 1750s. Its medley of bells breaks a tranquil hush, as the noises of the city are muted by the monastery's high walls and drowned by crows cawing from the trees. Yet bizarrely, the first thing you encounter is an array of Soviet **tanks**, painted pristine white – commemorating an armoured unit formed by the Church in 1943, which was named after the warrior-saint Dmitri Donskoy.

At the centre of the complex rises the **Great Cathedral of the Don Mother of God** (Bolshoy sobor Donskoy Bogomateri), also known as the "New Cathedral" (Noviy sobor). Composed of four rotund tower bays grouped around a central drum beneath five bronze domes, this was one of the largest structures of its time, begun in 1684 under Golitsyn and finally finished in 1698. The interior features Apocryphal frescoes and images of the saints framed by fruity wreaths, with a huge seven-tiered iconostasis that took four years to carve. During the plague, Archbishop Amvrosy hid behind it to escape an angry mob, but was found, dragged out and beaten to death. Today, worshippers bow to kiss a copy of the *Don Mother of God* (the original is in the Tretyakov Gallery) and the gilded casket enshrining **St Tikhon's relics**, to the left of the royal doors.

Founded in tandem with the monastery, the small **Old Cathedral** (Stariy sobor) resembles a simple Moscow Baroque church, painted a soft russet, with tiers of green-and-white *kokoshniki* and a blue onion dome. The interior is low, white and vaulted, its floor polished by a stream of worshippers. Both cathedrals are at their busiest on the feast-days of the Annunciation (April 7), the Don Virgin (Sept 1) and St Fyodor Stratilites (Feb 21).

The surrounding **cemetery** (Sat & Sun 10am–4pm) is crammed with headstones and funerary monuments. If you can read Cyrillic, each plot is identified by a map-board naming famous Russians buried there – though the only ones likely to register with foreigners all have disappointingly plain graves. The architect Osip Bove rates a black granite slab next to one shaped like a bomb, while the infamous serf-murdering Countess Dariya Saltykova (see p.144) is recalled by an obelisk without any inscription. Still more nondescript are the graves of Tolstoy's grandmother and Pushkin's grandparents.

The dark red **Church of St Nicholas** was built in 1806–09 as the private chapel of the Golitsyns. Nearby stands the tent-roofed neo-Russian **Chapel of the Tereshchenkos**, decorated with Orthodox crosses and raised in 1899. Best of all is the neo-Byzantine **Church of St John Chrysostom** (tserkov Ioanna Zlatousta), built by the Pervushins in 1891. Beyond rises the **Gate-Church of the Tikhvin Virgin**, an imposing structure that is one of the last examples of Moscow Baroque. It was completed in 1713, the year after Peter the Great moved the capital to St Petersburg and forbade building in stone anywhere else in Russia, to spur the creation of his city on the Neva.

Other sights

Down the road is another **cemetery** (daily: May–Sept 9am–7pm, Oct–April 9am–5pm; free) dating from the 1900s. Besides a few grandiose tombs such as that of Sergei Muromtsev, the president of the First Duma, this cemetery is notable for

▲ The Great Cathedral of the Don Mother of God

its **Monument to the Victims of Repression**, near the **Crematorium**. Originally the monastery's hospital before the Bolsheviks turned it into a crematorium to encourage secular burials, its ovens incinerated thousands of corpses delivered at night from the Lubyanka and Butyrka Prisons or the Military Collegium in the 1930s, whose ashes were shovelled into pits and asphalted over. While

Soviet victims are namelessly commemorated by a statue of a mourning woman, foreigners shot at Butyrka after 1945 are recalled by individual tablets erected by their relatives, including the wartime Hungarian prime minister Count Bethlen, a Polish cabinet minister and a dozen Japanese soldiers.

Depending on which route you take from the metro to the monastery you're sure to see at least one of a trio of landmarks. Look right leaving the station to sight the 160-metre-high **Comintern Radio Tower**, a red-and-white lattice-structure that looks straight out of Tintin. Erected in 1922 and named after the Communist International (Comintern) to whom it transmitted, the tower was also used for the first Soviet television broadcasts in 1945. Turning left from the metro into ulitsa Akademika Petrovskovo, and left again on to Donskaya ulitsa, you'll pass the stately **Church of the Deposition of the Robe** (tserkov Rizopolozheniya). Built in 1701, it combines the traditional forms of a Moscow parish church with the attenuated drums and domes of the early medieval Yaroslavl style. Its ornamentation is similar to the gate-churches of Novodevichiy Convent, with white scalloped gables, double-crested *nalichniki* and engaged columns with acanthus-leaf capitals against a maroon facade. The congregation is called to services by an amazingly deep **bell**, and a peal of smaller ones.

At the far end of Donskaya ulitsa, a gargantuan Stalin-style block houses several faculties of the **Friendship of Peoples University**. Founded in 1960 to train students from the Third World, it once bore the name of Patrice Lumumba, the murdered leader of the independence movement in the Belgian Congo, and was regarded by Western governments as a school for revolutionaries. Although Carlos "The Jackal" attended the university (and was expelled for rowdiness), the majority of its students bitched about the amount of time wasted studying Marxism-Leninism. More recently, safety and living conditions have been an issue; 36 students died and 197 were injured by a fire in a dilapidated dormitory in 2003.

From there, it's a twenty-minute **walk to the Danilov Monastery** if you're up for it. Simply cross the junction at the end of ulitsa Ordzhonikidze and walk along Serpukhovskiy val, whose central, wooded strip is decorated at either end by giant urns. Like the Khamovnicheskiy val near Novodevichiy Convent, it once delineated the city's customs boundary, where goods entering or leaving Moscow were taxed. Despite being termed a *val* (rampart), it had no defensive purpose. You'll know you're getting near when you reach the circular **Danilov Market** and catch sight of the blue-glass tower of the **Moscow Tax Inspectorate**.

The Danilov Monastery

As the official residence of the head of the Russian Orthodox Church, the **Danilov Monastery** (Danilovskiy monastyr; daily 8am–8pm; free) exudes modernity and purpose, reflecting the Patriarch's prestige and influence in Russia, where only four "traditional" religions enjoy constitutional protection (Orthodoxy, Islam, Judaism and Buddhism). Besides lobbying for restrictions on other religions, the Orthodox Church has been creative in its efforts to re-evangelize Russia: in 2000, Patriarch Alexei consecrated a "prayer train" to take the faith to remote communities where no churches existed – the second church on wheels in Russian history, following the example of one ordered by Nicholas II to take the state religion to the heathen heartland of Siberia.

The Danilov Monastery was founded in 1282 by **Prince Daniil** of Moscow (honoured by a statue near the market hall), and thereby claims to be the oldest in Moscow – though its monks and icons were moved into the Kremlin in 1330 by Ivan I, and only came back when Ivan the Terrible revived the original site 230 years later. In 1652 Prince Daniil was canonized and the monastery was renamed in his honour; expanded over decades behind a crenellated wall with ten bastions, it ultimately included an almshouse and a hospital.

Though officially closed soon after the Revolution, it somehow survived as the last working monastery in Russia until 1930, when the monks were expelled and a **borstal** was established here. Most of the inmates were children whose parents had been arrested or shot in the purges; they had to chant: "We are all indebted to our Motherland – we are in debt for the air we breathe." As a condition of being allowed to reclaim the premises in 1983, the Church was obliged to finance another borstal elsewhere.

Following the monastery's rededication ceremony, five years later it became the seat of the Patriarch and the Holy Synod, which had previously been at the Trinity Monastery of St Sergei, outside Moscow.

The easiest way of **getting there** is to catch the metro to Tulskaya station. Exiting at the back of the train, you'll emerge outside the Tax Inspectorate tower. Walk away from this towards a small gilt-domed chapel in a park and follow ulitsa Danilovskiy val until you reach the monastery, about 200m on.

The monastery

Visitors enter by the **Gate-Church of St Simeon the Stylite** (Nadvodyashiy tserkov Simeonia Stolpnika), which had to be entirely rebuilt since the original gate-tower was torn down in the 1920s and its bells sold to Harvard University. Painted a soft pink, with its archway framed by fat-bellied columns and an elaborate cornice, the gate is surmounted by a triple-tiered belltower inset with pictures of the saints, ending in a gold finial.

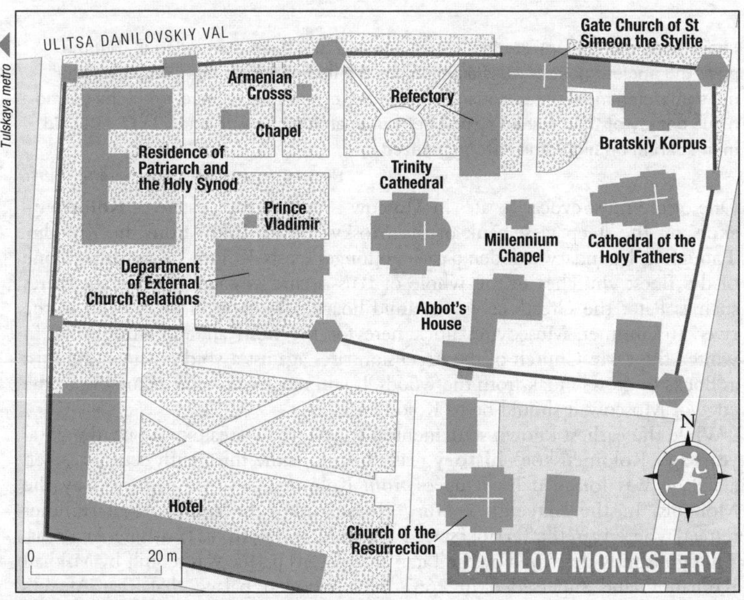

Inside the compound, you'll see some of the monastery's fifty monks putting the finishing touches to the administrative blocks and garden, while old women genuflect before the holy images on the walls of the churches – you may even spot a spurred and booted Cossack with a sabre, strutting across the yard (Cossacks provide security for the Patriarchate). Straight ahead stands the gold-domed **Millennium Chapel**, with a quadruple arch erected to mark the millennial anniversary of Russian Orthodoxy in 1988. The ornately carved stone *khachkar*, or **Armenian Cross**, near the monastery's north wall was a millennial gift from the Armenian Church.

A bronze **statue of Prince Vladimir** waves a crucifix near the turquoise building housing the **Department of External Church Relations**, while a huge gilded mosaic of the Saviour stares down from the modern **Residence of the Patriarch and the Holy Synod**, at the far end. The Patriarch is known to prefer living at the Trinity Monastery of Sergei or at his *dacha* in Peredelkino, outside Moscow, so is seldom in residence.

Relics of Prince Daniil are enshrined in two churches: the austerely Neoclassical **Trinity Cathedral** (Troitskiy sobor) built by Bove in the 1830s; and the seventeenth-century **Cathedral of the Holy Fathers** (khram vo imya Svyatykh Ottsov), with a deep porch and a refectory preceding two chapels, one dedicated to Daniil and the other to SS Boris and Gleb (feast day on Aug 6). Notice the sixteenth-century icons of *St Daniil* and *Our Lady of Vladimir*.

By passing through a gate in the rear wall, you'll find a luxurious **hotel** (see Chapter 11, "Accommodation"). Around the corner stands the **Church of the Resurrection**, a square-towered Neoclassical edifice.

Kolomenskoe

I have seen much in my life that I have admired and been astounded at, but the past, the ancient past of Russia which has left its imprint on this village, was for me something most miraculous ... Here in the mysterious silence, amid the harmonious beauty of the finished form, I beheld an architecture of a new kind. I beheld man soaring on high. And I stood amazed.

Hector Berlioz, recalling Kolomenskoe in 1847

One of the most evocative sites in Moscow is the old royal estate of **Kolomenskoe**, on the steep west bank of the Moskva River, 10km from the Kremlin. Though its legendary wooden palace no longer exists, Kolomenskoe still has one of the finest churches in the whole of Russia, and vintage wooden structures such as Peter the Great's cabin, set amid hoary oaks above a great bend in the river. In summer, Muscovites flock here for the fresh air and sunbathing; in winter, the eerie Church of the Ascension rises against a void of snow and mist as flocks of crows croak from the woods. If you make only one excursion to the edge of Moscow, it should be to Kolomenskoe.

While the earliest known settlement in the Moscow area existed nearby 2500 years ago, Kolomenskoe's **history** really begins in the thirteenth century, when a village was founded by refugees from Kolomna, a town destroyed by the Mongols. In the sixteenth century Kolomenskoe became a royal summer retreat, where Ivan the Terrible stayed as a child, and with his first wife, Anastasia. Though utterly destroyed by the Tatars in 1591, its palace was rebuilt by Mikhail Romanov, and superseded in 1667 by a wooden palace that Tsar Alexei's courtiers called the "eighth wonder of the world". As a child, Peter the Great took refuge there during the Streltsy revolt of 1682, and later held war games with his "toy" regiments on the estate.

Though Catherine the Great and Alexander I also built palaces, Kolomenskoe eventually reverted to being a mere village, whose fate was sealed after the Revolution. The cemetery was razed and the churches closed; then the

Festivals at Kolomenskoe

Exact dates may vary from year to year; confirm ahead by calling ☎499/615 27 68

New Year (Jan 1–2)
A kids' festival round a Christmas tree, with Ded Moroz (Grandfather Frost), Leshy (wood sprites), the witch Baba Yaga, and other characters from Russian fairytales.

Christmas and Svyatki (Jan 7–19)
Following the all-night Orthodox Christmas service (Jan 6/7), the festival of *Svyatki* traditionally lasted until *Kreshenie*, or Epiphany (Jan 19), but at Kolomenskoe the masquerades, puppet theatre, songs, games and merry-making usually finish on the nearest Sunday to that date, with bell-ringing and the blessing of the water.

Maslenitsa (Sat, one week before the beginning of Lent – usually in late Feb).
Based on the pagan spring festival that also marked the onset of Lent, it features performing bears, puppets, the building of snow forts and the burning of straw dolls, boxing matches, masquerades and giant swings. Everyone eats tonnes of pancakes, slathered in butter; the name *maslenitsa* comes from the Russian word for butter.

Easter Sunday
Orthodoxy's chief holy day is marked by a ritual procession and a service in the Church of the Ascension, followed by feasting, folk dancing and games.

My Moscow (May 1–2)
A May Day festival for residents of southern Moscow, with Orthodox music, and lots of handicrafts for sale.

Victory Day (May 9)
Military bands, a memorial service in the Church of the Icon of Our Lady of Kazan, and a fireworks display.

Peter the Great's Birthday (May 30)
A pageant based on Peter's life and achievements, staged around his cabin.

Troitsa (first Sun in June)
Rituals surrounding the day of the dead, when families picnicked in cemeteries and girls wove garlands and told fortunes beside rivers or lakes.

Festival of Orthodox Spiritual Music (June)
A series of concerts in the Church of the Ascension; space is limited, so you must book tickets in advance.

Under St Andrew's Flag (last Sun in July).
A pageant in honour of Peter the Great's creation of the Russian Navy, with a regatta on the Moskva River.

Spas Yablochni Medovi (Aug 30–Sept 2)
A traditional harvest festival, with folkloric displays and a big market selling honey, apples, nuts and pastries.

Moscow Day (Sept 6)
A pageant starring Ivan the Terrible, Alexei, Peter the Great and other figures from Kolomenskoe's history.

village was destroyed by collectivization. It was only thanks to the architect Baranovsky that the churches were saved from ruin and a Museum of Wooden Architecture was established in the grounds in 1925, providing the justification to later declare it a conservation zone and spare 400 hectares of ancient woodland from the encroachment of flats. In World War II, a barrage balloon unit was stationed there. More recently it has been added to UNESCO's World Heritage List and amply funded by Mayor Luzhkov, so the site is now well cared for.

Practicalities

Despite its distance from the centre, **getting there** is easy. From Teatralnaya metro, near the Bolshoy Theatre, it's only four stops to Kolomenskaya station. Take the exit near the front of the train; turn left in the underpass and then right at the end to surface at the correct spot. It's about ten-minutes' walk along prospekt Andropova to the main entrance to the grounds of Kolomenskoe.

Opening hours and admission fees vary. You can wander around the grounds (daily: April–Oct 8am–10pm; Nov–March 8am–9pm) free of charge, but **tickets** are required for the museums (all Tues–Sun 10am–6pm), the Treasures of Kolomenskoe Museum (R300), Peter's cabin (R100), the Water-Drawing Tower (R100), the 1825 Pavilion (R100) and the Church of the Ascension (May–Sept only; R100). The museum *kassa* sells tickets for all of them except the 1825 Pavilion, which you buy on the spot.

Kolomenskoe hosts a dozen free **festivals** celebrating folk traditions, holy days or historical events. Unfortunately, dates aren't posted on their clunky **website** (Ⓦwww.mgomz.ru) so you'll need to confirm them by phone (Ⓣ499 615 27 68) or email (Ⓔinfo@mgomz.ru) prior to the approximate date in the box on p.235. In addition, there are **programmes** for groups of ten or more people (for which one pays), ranging from crafts workshops to banquets and operatic performances. For details, ask the Excursion Bureau outside the main entrance. You can also arrange **private visits** to the Repository, which holds items that aren't displayed in the museum – the collection of Art Nouveau tiled stoves is especially remarkable.

On Saturdays and Sundays, visitors can enjoy a brief **horse-ride** around parts of the estate (adults R170; children R120). Alternatively, take a two-hour **cruise** on the Moskva River, sailing downriver past Kolomenskoe and Dyakovo before heading upstream for a brief view of the isolated Nikolo-Perevenskiy Monastery. Cruises run daily from mid-April to the end of October, with departures every fifty minutes till as late as 2am in midsummer. You can buy tickets (adults R250; children R100) at the boat landing stage.

Into the grounds

Beyond the *kokoshniki*-topped **Main Entrance** (the rear gate in olden days, when visitors approached by river), you're confronted by the **Church of the Icon of Our Lady of Kazan** (tserkov ikony Kazanskoy bogomateri), whose azure domes spangled with gold stars glint alluringly. Its box-like refectory and covered stairway are typical of churches from the reign of Alexei, who erected it in 1644 in memory of the struggle against the Poles during the Time of Troubles. In modern times the church became famous for an **icon** known as *Derzhavnaya* (The Majestic), which was found in its attic on the day of Nicholas II's abdication, by a woman who dreamt of being told that the divine power vested in the tsars had now returned to the Mother of God. It shows

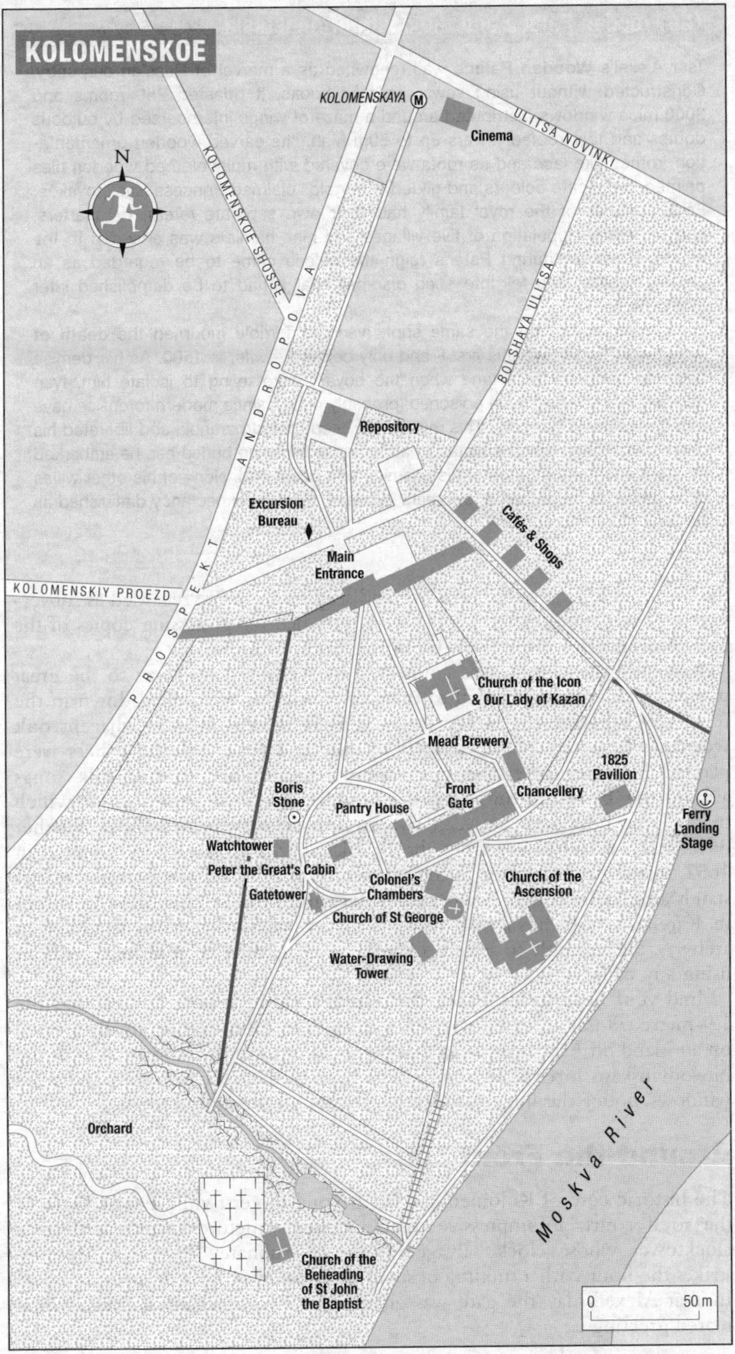

KOLOMENSKOE

KOLOMENSKAYA (M)
Cinema
ULITSA NOVINKI
KOLOMENSKOE SHOSSE
PROSPEKT ANDROPOVA
BOLSHAYA ULITSA
Repository
Excursion Bureau
Cafés & Shops
Main Entrance
KOLOMENSKIY PROEZD
Church of the Icon & Our Lady of Kazan
Mead Brewery
1825 Pavilion
Boris Stone
Front Gate
Chancellery
Pantry House
Ferry Landing Stage
Watchtower
Peter the Great's Cabin
Colonel's Chambers
Church of the Ascension
Gatetower
Church of St George
Water-Drawing Tower
Orchard
Moskva River
Church of the Beheading of St John the Baptist
0 50 m

The Wooden Palace and the death of Anastasia

Tsar Alexei's **Wooden Palace** was renowned as a marvel of Russian carpentry. Constructed without using saws, nails or hooks, it boasted 250 rooms and 3000 mica windows distributed around a maze of wings interspersed by bulbous domes and tent-roofed towers up to 50m high. "Its carved wooden ornamentation frothed like lace and its roofs were covered with multicoloured wooden tiles painted in delicate colours and gilded with gold" claimed Princess Shakhovskoe. Each member of the royal family had their own separate *terem*, or quarters, and the entire population of five villages and nine hamlets was enserfed to the estate. However, during Peter's reign the palace came to be regarded as an archaic liability, and fell into such disrepair that it had to be demolished later that century.

In an earlier age on the same spot, Ivan the Terrible mourned the **death of Anastasia Romanova**, his first – and only beloved – wife, in 1560. As her demise occurred suddenly at a time when the boyars were trying to isolate him, Ivan decided that she had been poisoned (probably rightly, since modern forensics have found mercury in her hair). This revived his deep-rooted paranoia and liberated his darkest impulses, which Anastasia had restrained. Having buried her, he embarked on a debauch and a purge of his enemies with equal zeal. None of his other wives ever lasted for more than a few years – indeed, their life expectancy diminished as he grew older and crazier.

the Virgin holding the Imperial orb and sceptre, an image regarded as subversive in Soviet times, when people were punished for possessing copies of the icon. November 4 is the feast-day of the Virgin of Kazan.

Originally, the church was connected by a covered walkway to the great wooden palace that sprawled to the west, until this was pulled down in the reign of Catherine the Great. Today, you are drawn into the adjacent **oak woods**, where one of the trees is six hundred years old and others were planted by Peter when he was young. Russians like to sing folk songs around the **Boris Stone**, a granite boulder inscribed with a cross, which marked the boundary between two twelfth-century principalities. Further on is a log **watchtower** from the Bratsk *ostrog*, a Cossack fort founded in 1652 on the Angara River in Siberia, which also served as a prison. Nearby stands an equally rough-hewn **gate-tower** from the St Nicholas Monastery in Karelia, whose hexagonal tower with its witch's-hat brim straddles an archway big enough to admit a wagon – all crafted to interlock without using any nails.

Mind your head inside **Peter the Great's cabin**, whose low ceilings the 1.9-metre tall tsar accepted without a qualm. The cabin was originally erected on an island off Arkhangelsk, so that he could observe the construction of the Novodvinskaya fortress. Its four rooms have tiled stoves, log walls and mica windows; notice the huge wooden beer-scoop in the dining room.

Around the Front Gate

The historic core of Kolomenskoe lies beyond the erstwhile **Front Gate** of the royal court, an impressive double-arched structure surmounted by a clocktower whose clock, salvaged from the Sukharev Tower in Moscow, strikes the hour with a tinkling of small **bells**, followed by a deep, brazen one. In Tsar Alexei's day the gate was guarded by two mechanical lions, which roared greetings.

Flanking the gateway are buildings originally devoted to the administration and provisioning of the palace, which now house the **Treasures of Kolomenskoe Museum**. Tickets are sold in the two-storey **Pantry House** (Sytniy dvor), whose lower floor displays a splendid collection of icons and woodcarvings, including a superb altar canopy from the Solovetsky Monastery in the White Sea. Upstairs you'll find royal portraits, decorative stove-tiles, and a ceramic frieze by Vrubel depicting the legend ofVolga and Mikula. Near the Pantry House are the restored **Frjazhsky Cellars**, once used for storing wine and nowadays for hosting banquets.

Once restoration work is finished visitors will also be able to enter the **Chancellery** (Prikaznye Palaty), to see a re-creation of the room where royal scribes worked at a long table covered in red cloth, wanly illuminated by mica windows and flickering candles. It is also planned to re-create the interior of the **Guardhouse** and allow visitors to see the mechanism inside the clocktower.

In the vicinity of the Chancellery are two separate, unrelated buildings. The **Mead Brewery** (Medovarnya) dates from the twelfth century and was one of the few wooden buildings to survive the Great Fire of 1812. It originally stood in the village of Preobrazhenskoe where Peter the Great spent much of his youth. Downhill lies the **1825 Pavilion**, a small Neoclassical edifice which is all that remains of the summer palace that Alexander I built at Kolomenskoe. It's worth the admission fee to see a lovely 1:40 **scale model** of Alexei's palace, executed in 1868 from sketches, using wood salvaged from the building.

The Church of the Ascension

Beyond the Front Gate the ground falls away towards the river and your eyes are drawn to the soaring **Church of the Ascension** (tserkov Vozneseniya), whose primeval grandeur rivals that of St Basil's Cathedral on Red Square. Though the two buildings look very different, they are related in that this church was commissioned by Vasily III in 1529 as a votive offering in the hope that he be granted an heir, who as Ivan the Terrible would later decree the creation of St Basil's; this feeling of ancestral kinship is almost palpable.

Aside from this, what makes the Ascension Church so remarkable is its stupendous **tent-roof**. Rising from an octagonal base culminating in tiers of *kokoshniki* resembling giant artichoke leaves, its facets are enhanced by limestone ribbing and rhomboid patterns, while a lantern, cupola and cross bring the total height to 70m. This was such a radical departure from the domed stone churches that then prevailed, that architectural historians decided it must have sprung from the separate tradition of wooden tower churches, until new evidence that the Italian Petrok Maly had supervised its design led some to argue that it represented a late development of the Romanesque pyramid-roofed tower.

Like a rocket clamped to its launch pad by gantries, the church is girdled at its base by an elevated **terrace** reached by three staircases, incorporating sharp turns that would have heightened the drama of ritual processions in olden days. When filming *Ivan the Terrible*, Eisenstein used this to frame the unforgettable scene in which Ivan watches a long column of people snaking over the snow-clad hills to beg him to return to rule them. On the river-facing side of the terrace are the remains of a stone throne, where Ivan used to sit and enjoy the view. The **interior** of the church is surprisingly light thanks to its double corner-windows, and remarkably small due to the thickness of the walls supporting the spire. The tsar and his family observed services from a gallery above the doorway; the original iconostasis hasn't survived, but services are once again held here on Sundays at 8pm.

On to Dyakovo

In the vicinity of the Ascension Church are two slender towers that form an integral part of the ensemble. The cylindrical **Church of St George** was designed to serve as Kolomenskoe's main belltower and dates from the mid-sixteenth century. In those days the courtyard was surrounded by huts and stables, while wagons rattled in through the gateway beneath the barrel-roofed **Water-Drawing Tower** (Vodovzvodnaya bashnya). Originally built as an eyrie for Alexei's hunting birds, it was adapted in 1675 by Bogdan Puchin, who constructed a mechanism to pump up water from the river and deliver it to the palace – it now features an exhibition on falconry. The nearby **Colonel's Chambers** were once the residence of the commander of the palace guards, and stand on the site of a cemetery where casualties of the epic battle of Kulikovo were buried.

The steps leading down towards the riverside bring you to two ponds formed by damming a stream flowing through the ravine that separates Kolomenskoe from what was once the village of Dyakovo. Although this area was inhabited as early as the first century BC, its only tangible relic is the hilltop **Church of the Beheading of St John the Baptist** (tserkov useknoveniya chestnya glavy Ioanna Predtechi), erected by Ivan the Terrible to celebrate his coronation in 1547, and to importune God to grant him an heir. Squatter and squarer than the Church of the Ascension, with four chapels around an octagonal core with a lofty onion dome, it was probably designed by the architect of St Basil's. The surrounding cemetery contains several **gravestones** from the sixteenth century, though most of the tombs are far more recent. Beyond the gate at the end of the path is an orchard where visitors gather apples in September, while the lovely view of the Moskva River attracts Sunday painters.

Tsaritsyno

The ruined palace of **Tsaritsyno** is an Imperial summer retreat that never was: a grandiose project that consumed resources for decades, only to be aborted as it neared fruition. Its history goes back to the sixteenth century, when Irina, the wife of Tsar Fyodor, had an estate here, which passed eventually from Peter the Great to the Moldavian Prince Dmitri Cantemir, whose writer son sold it back to Catherine the Great for 25,000 rubles in 1775. She changed its dismal name, "Black Dirt" (Chyornaya Gryaz), to "Empress's Village", and envisaged an estate to match her glorious summer palaces outside St Petersburg.

Catherine entrusted the building task to **Vasily Bazhenov**, perhaps as recompense for cancelling a scheme to rebuild the Kremlin, on which he had worked for years. His brief specified a park with pavilions in the Moorish-Gothic style that was fashionable in Europe, and adjoining palaces for the Empress and her son Paul. Ten years later she returned to inspect the nearly completed buildings – only to order that the main palace be torn down and built anew by Bazhenov's young colleague, **Matvei Kazakov**.

Some believe this was because Catherine objected to the **Masonic symbols** used as ornamentation; others that she could no longer bear the idea of living with Paul, who had grown to loathe her. In the event, Kazakov devoted over a decade to the project until its abrupt termination in 1797, owing to the drain on the treasury caused by a war with Turkey, and the ageing Empress's waning desire for an estate outside Moscow.

Thereafter Tsaritsyno was abandoned to the elements, barring a brief interlude as a museum under Stalin, and various schemes to turn it into a barracks, a champagne factory or a diplomatic residential colony. However, in 1984 it was decided to restore Tsaritsyno, and much of the grounds are now landscaped and the palaces renovated, including the Great Palace, making the estate Moscow's largest museum, occupying over 1700 acres.

Practicalities

Tsaritsyno is 3km south of Kolomenskoe and accessible by the same **metro** line. Alighting at Tsaritsyno station, use the exit at the front of the train, turn left and go on to the end of the underpass; bear right beneath two railway bridges past an electronics market and follow the road round to the right until you see the woods, then left along a road past two ponds. Alternatively, you can ride on to the next station, Orekhovo, exit near the rear of the train and turn left in the underpass, which brings you out directly opposite the far end of the avenue of lime trees on the eastern edge of Tsaritsyno park – a more attractive approach.

No tickets are required to enter the grounds, which are open day and night. **Opening hours** (Wed–Fri 11am–5pm; Sat & Sun 11am–9pm) apply to the Great Palace (Bolshoy Dvorets; R200) and the Bread House (Khlebniy Dom; R150), **tickets** for which are sold on the spot. For information call ⓣ322 68 43 or check ⓦwww.tsaritsyno-museum.ru.

Almost all the buildings at Tsaritsyno have been restored and the best time to arrive is the evening when the lights in the buildings and grounds turn the

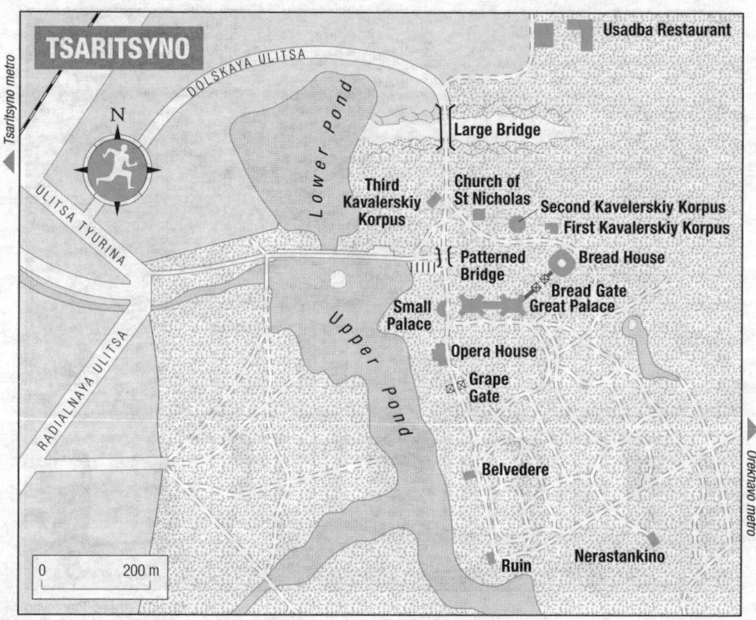

ponds and walkways into a magical wonderland. Russians come here to picnic, fish, hunt for mushrooms or go sledging, depending on the season – there are kids' bouncy castles in the summer – but beware of slippery slopes and frozen ponds in winter, or thick mud in spring. In summertime, *bliny* and hot-dog stalls on the lawn behind the Great Palace and a *shashlyk* and beer tent attached to the *Usadba* restaurant provide cheap **food**, but out of season there's only the extremely costly restaurant.

The estate

Coming from Tsaritsyno station, you approach the estate by a causeway across the **Tsaritsyno Ponds** to pass beneath the **Patterned Bridge** (Figurniy most), which spans a cleft in the hillside. Built of pinkish brick, it bristles with white stone pinnacles and Gothic arches, Rosicrucian blooms and Maltese Crosses – a combination that typifies all the buildings at Tsaritsyno.

The most imposing is the **Great Palace** (Bolshoy dvorets), whose twin wings stretch for 130m, replete with pilastered corner towers and rows of lofty pointed arches. After years as a ruin, the palace has finally been reconstructed, and it now looks pretty much as it would have done in the 1700s. Inside, it houses a **museum**, displaying some of Tsaritsyno's vast collection of antique tapestries, Russian and Central Asian folk art, contemporary glassware, ceramics and naive paintings.

By following a paved path back into the woods you'll reach the ornamental **Bread Gate** (Khlebniy vorota), leading into what was to have been the palace courtyard. Adjacent is the reconstructed **Bread House** (Khlebniy dom), an enormous oval structure that was meant to be the palace kitchens. Its name comes from the white-stone images of a loaf of bread and a salt cellar on its walls, and the building now houses art exhibitions and musical concerts.

▲ The Bread Gate at Tsaritsyno

Bazhenov's other service buildings were intended for courtiers or soldiers; the **First and Second Kavalerskiy Korpus** now house Tsaritsyno's administration and Excursions Bureau, while the Third is in the final stages of reconstruction and it is likely to house a new hotel when finished. Designed to lure strollers on to the **Large Bridge** across the ravine beyond, this route takes you past the eighteenth-century **Church of St Nicholas**, freshly restored with a pistachio-coloured exterior – the only building at Tsaritsyno that wasn't designed by Bazhenov.

Heading in the opposite direction from the Patterned Bridge you'll come to the semicircular **Small Palace** (Maliy dvorets), whose vaulted interior is wonderfully light and airy, and an ideal exhibition space. Just beyond is the **Opera House** (Operniy dom), its pediment crowned by a Tsarist eagle. Intended for operatic performances but never finished, its interior has now been completed using Bazhenov's plans. The beautifully proportioned hall is almost monastic in its simplicity, aside from four gold-and-red chandeliers, and hosts **concerts** of chamber music (Ⓣ321 63 66 for details). Temporary exhibitions are held upstairs; the stairway features lamp-brackets shaped like armoured fists.

Beyond the Opera House stands the **Grape Gate** (Vinogradiy vorota), named after the fruity pendant suspended from its archway. An avenue of lime trees continues southwards into the wooded, hilly park that surrounds Tsaritsyno, where you'll find a derelict **Belvedere** and an artificial **Ruin** such as was *de rigueur* for landscaped grounds in the late eighteenth century. The cryptically named **Nerastankino** is used by fantasy war gamers for **mock battles** at weekends, so don't be surprised to see teenagers whacking each other with fake battle-axes and swords, in the woods off the avenue of lime trees leading to the edge of the estate, near Orekhovo metro station.

Streets and squares

Chernigovskiy pereulok	Черниговский переулок
Bolshoy Kamenniy most	Большой Каменный мост
Donskaya ulitsa	Донская улица
1-y Kadashevskiy pereulok	1-й Када шевский переулок
Krymskiy val	Крымский вал
Leninskiy prospekt	Ленинский проспект
Oktyabrskaya ploshchad	Октябрьская площадь
ploshchad Gagarina	площадь Гагарина
prospekt Andropova	проспект Андропова
Pyatnitskaya ulitsa	Пятницкая улица
Sofiyskaya naberezhnaya	Софийская набережная
ulitsa Bakhrushina	улица Бакрушина
ulitsa Bolshaya Ordynka	улица Большая Ордынка
ulitsa Bolshaya Polyanka	улица Большая Полянка
ulitsa Bolshaya Yakimanka	улица Большая Якиманка
ulitsa Danilovskiy val	улица Даниловский вал
ulitsa Serpukhovskiy val	улица Серпуховский вал

Metro stations

Kolomenskaya	Коломенская
Novokuznetskaya	Новокузнецкая
Oktyabrskaya	Октябрьская
Orekhovo	Орехово
Park Kultury	Парк Культуры

Metro stations

Paveletskaya	Павелецкая
Polyanka	Полянка
Shabolovskaya	Шаболовская
Tretyakovskaya	Третьяковская
Tsaritsyno	Царицыно
Tulskaya	Тульская

Museums

Central House of Artists	Центральный дом художника
Igor Talkov Museum	музей Игоря Талькова
Kolomenskoe	музей-усадьба Коломенское
Theatre Museum	театральный музей им. А.А. Бакрушина
Tretyakov Gallery	Третьяковская галерея
Tsaritsyno	музей-усадьба Царицыно

Taganka and Zayauze

Taganka and Zayauze are the beachheads of Moscow's eastward expansion far beyond the Moskva and Yauza rivers, originally led by tsars and nobles who hunted in the forests and built country palaces that now stand marooned amid a tide of concrete. Eastern Moscow may be drab overall, but this area has enough sights and historical associations to justify a dozen forays into the hinterland.

A perennial draw is the **Izmaylovo Art Market**, whose glut of icons, handicrafts and Soviet kitsch offers the widest choice of souvenirs in Moscow. Nearby are the remains of the royal estate where Peter the Great spent his childhood, after which the district is named. Admirers of the tsar can track down other localities where he trained his "toy regiments" or roistered with the Drunken Synod – at Preobrazhenskoe and on the upper reaches of the River Yauza – but the finest historic monuments are situated in an arc around the Taganka district. There are picturesque backstreets to explore in the shadow of the Stalin skyscraper called the **Kotelnicheskaya Apartments** – a major landmark on the waterfront. Further out, the **Andronikov Monastery** is a must for icon-lovers due to its Museum of Early Russian Art, but others may prefer the more atmospheric **Novospasskiy Monastery**, the half-ruined **Simonov Monastery** or the **Old Believers' Commune**.

Another site that should please everyone is the palatial Sheremetev estate at **Kuskovo** – a gem of eighteenth-century architecture with a superb collection of ceramics. If you're especially keen on stately homes and their conservation, it's worth visiting another estate at **Kuzminki**; otherwise, the only attraction in the southeastern suburbs is the **Lomakov Museum of Antique Automobiles and Motorcycles**, boasting an array of vehicles once owned by Nazi or Soviet bigwigs.

Taganka

The history of **Taganka** is as colourful as its main square and avenues are drab. Originally a quarter inhabited by smiths who made cauldrons (*tagany*) for the Muscovite army, it later became a shelter area for thieves and various undesirables who were obliged to live beyond the city walls. It was well known for its prison, which was the inspiration for many *blatny pesny* or ballads of the criminal underworld: "Taganka I am yours forever. My power and my talent perished inside your walls." This subculture profoundly influenced Vysotsky's performances at the famous Taganka Theatre (see p.248).

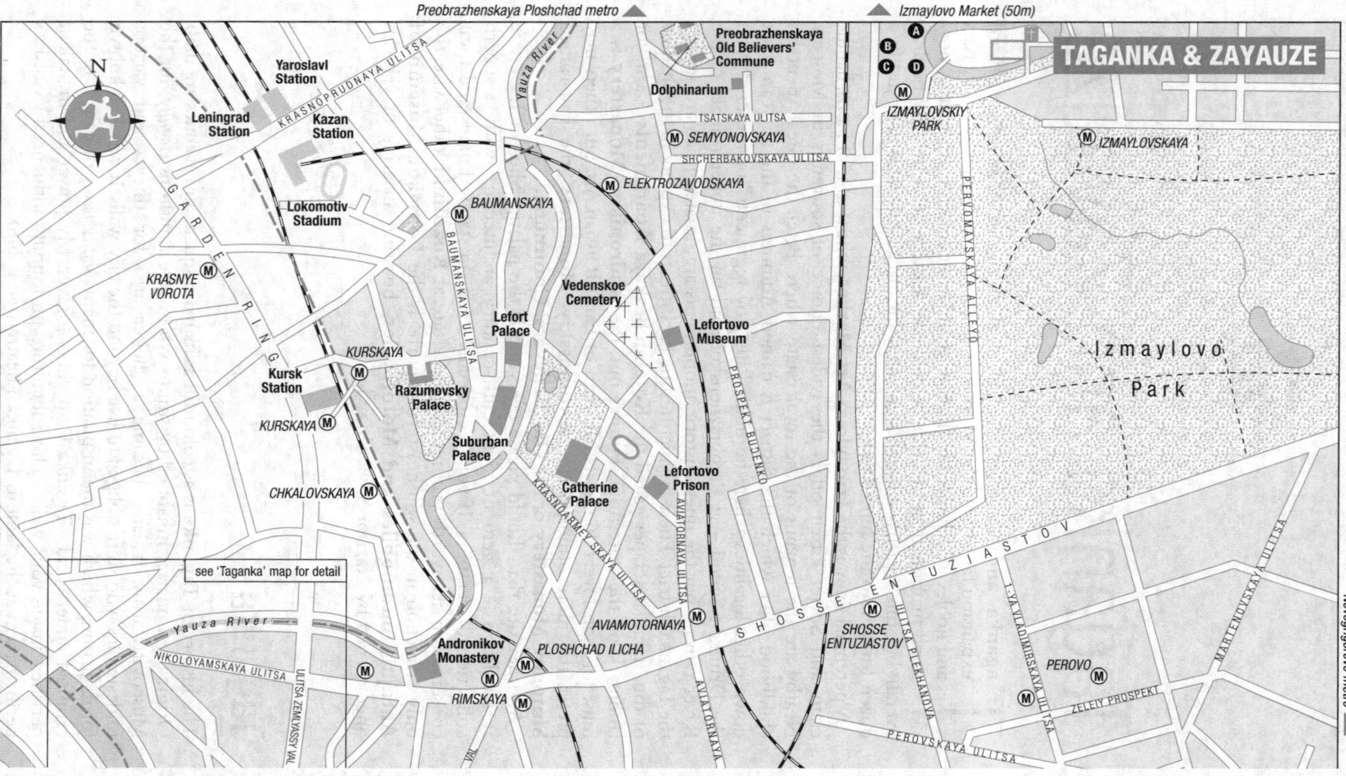
TAGANKA & ZAYAUZE
Preobrazhenskaya Ploshchad metro
Izmaylovo Market (50m)
Novogrigorevo metro
N
Yaroslavl Station
Leningrad Station
Kazan Station
KRASNOPRUDNAYA ULITSA
Lokomotiv Stadium
GARDEN RING
KRASNYE VOROTA
KURSKAYA
Kursk Station
KURSKAYA
CHKALOVSKAYA
Razumovsky Palace
BAUMANSKAYA
BAUMANSKAYA ULITSA
Lefort Palace
Suburban Palace
Yauza River
Preobrazhenskaya Old Believers' Commune
Dolphinarium
TSATSKAYA ULITSA
SEMYONOVSKAYA
SHCHERBAKOVSKAYA ULITSA
ELEKTROZAVODSKAYA
Vedenskoe Cemetery
Lefortovo Museum
Catherine Palace
Lefortovo Prison
KRASNDARMEY SKAYA ULITSA
AVIATORNAYA ULITSA
PROSPEKT BUDENKO
AVIAMOTORNAYA
PLOSHCHAD ILICHA
Andronikov Monastery
RIMSKAYA
see 'Taganka' map for detail
Yauza River
NIKOLOYAMSKAYA ULITSA
ULITSA ZEMLYASSY VAL
VAL
AVIATORNAYA
A
B
C
D
IZMAYLOVSKIY PARK
IZMAYLOVSKAYA
PERVOMAYSKAYA ALLEYO
Izmaylovo Park
SHOSSE ENTUZIASTOV
SHOSSE ENTUZIASTOV
ULITSA PLEKHANOVA
1-YA VLADIMIRSKAYA ULITSA
PEROVO
ZELEIY PROSPEKT
PEROVSKAYA ULITSA
MARTENOVSKAYA ULITSA

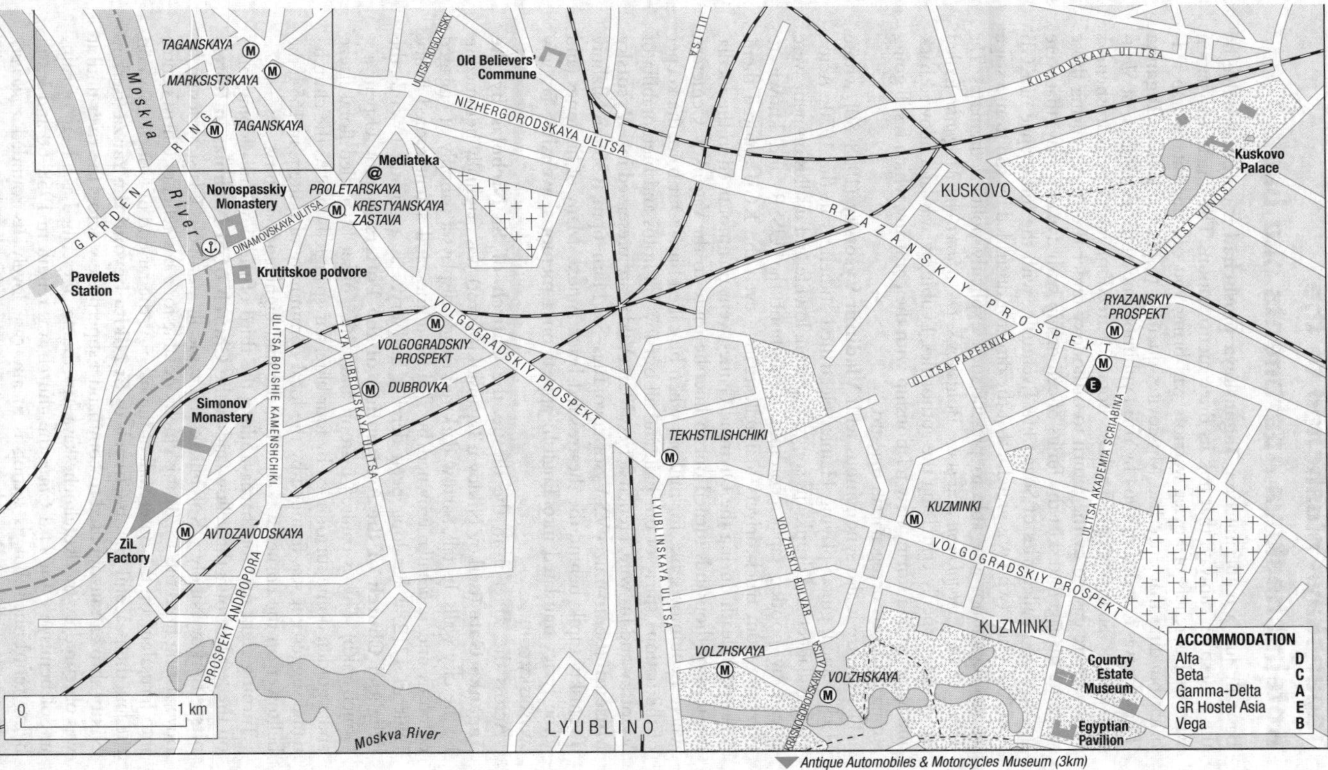

TAGANSKAYA
MARKSISTSKAYA
TAGANSKAYA
Moskva
River
GARDEN RING
ULITSA ROGOZHSKY
Old Believers' Commune
NIZHERGORODSKAYA ULITSA
ULITSA
KUSKOVSKAYA ULITSA
Kuskovo Palace
KUSKOVO
ULITSA YUNOSTI
Mediateka
Novospasskiy Monastery
PROLETARSKAYA
KRESTYANSKAYA ZASTAVA
DINAMOVSKAYA ULITSA
Krutitskoe podvore
Pavelets Station
RYAZANSKIY PROSPEKT
RYAZANSKIY PROSPEKT
ULITSA PAPERNIKA
ULITSA AKADEMIA SCRIABINA
VOLGOGRADSKIY PROSPEKT
VOLGOGRADSKIY PROSPEKT
ULITSA BOLSHIE KAMENSHCHIKI
-YA DUBROVSKAYA ULITSA
DUBROVKA
Simonov Monastery
TEKHSTILISHCHIKI
KUZMINKI
ZiL Factory
AVTOZAVODSKAYA
PROSPEKT ANDROPORA
LYUBLINSKAYA ULITSA
VOLZHSKIY BULVAR
KRASNOGORODSKAYA ULITSA
VOLZHSKAYA
VOLZHSKAYA
KUZMINKI
Country Estate Museum
Egyptian Pavilion
LYUBLINO
Moskva River
0
1 km
ACCOMMODATION
Alfa D
Beta C
Gamma-Delta A
GR Hostel Asia E
Vega B
Antique Automobiles & Motorcycles Museum (3km)

Taganskaya ploshchad to the Kotelnicheskaya Apartments and back

Basically just a traffic junction, **Taganskaya ploshchad** is only traversable by the pedestrian subways that link its three metro stations. The Circle line station with its bas-reliefs of Soviet warriors will bring you out opposite a drab red-brick building that once had Muscovites queuing to get inside. The **Taganka Theatre** was founded in 1964 by Yuri Lyubimov, one of the generation of *Shestidesyatniki* ("Sixties people") whose hopes of freedom raised by Khrushchev's "thaw" were dashed by the return to orthodoxy under Brezhnev. During those years, he managed to skirt the limits of censorship with dynamic plays that were understood as allegories of Soviet life. Eventually, with the indulgence of KGB boss Andropov (who was grateful that the director dissuaded his son from a stage career), Lyubimov was able to present such explicitly political drama as *The House on the Embankment* and stage Bulgakov's *The Master and Margarita*. Exiled in 1983 for openly criticizing the authorities, Lyubimov was later allowed back and underwent a stormy new relationship with the company, which is still going strong under its octogenarian maestro.

The theatre is also synonymous with **Vladimir Vysotsky** (1938–80), whose black-jeaned, guitar-playing Hamlet electrified audiences in the 1970s. Actor, poet, balladeer and drunk, his songs of prison, lowlife and disillusionment were spread by bootleg tape recordings throughout the USSR and known to everyone from truck drivers to intellectuals – even the KGB enjoyed them. Vysotsky's death during the Olympic Games went unannounced in the media, but tens of thousands turned out to line the route to the Vagankov Cemetery, where Lyubimov spoke for millions when he called him "Our bard, the keeper of the nation's spirit, of our pain and all our joys". Photos and memorabilia of Vysotsky and his wife, French actress Maria Valdai, are preserved in a **Vysotsky Museum** (tsentr-muzey V.S. Vysotskovo; Tues–Sat 11am–6pm; R35) on Nizhniy Taganskiy tupik, behind the theatre's red-brick annexe. Many of his songs (and some lyrics translated into English) appear on a memorial **website**, Ⓦ www.wysotsky.com.

Across the street from the theatre, the **Church of St Nicholas by the Taganka Gate** (tserkov Nikloy u Taganskikh vorot) was originally hemmed in by the city walls. Its tall, narrow, dark red facade displays a panoply of engaged columns and *nalichniki*, crowned by slender domes and a tent-roofed belfry. Built in 1712, it has long been derelict but serves as a pointer towards the delightful **Church of the Assumption of the Potters** (tserkov Uspeniya v Goncharakh). This is painted maroon and white, offset by a tiled floral frieze and a golden dome surrounded by four blue, star-spangled ones. As the church's name suggests, it was founded by the local community of potters, in 1654; the belltower on the corner was added in the mid-eighteenth century.

Turning right up Goncharnaya ulitsa, the third of the downhill-sloping lanes on the left harbours the yellow-and-white **Church of St Nicholas in Kotelnitsa** (tserkov Nikoly v Kotelnikakh). A typically pompous Classical design by Bove, dating from the 1820s, it is chiefly notable for a bas-relief of Christ's entry into Jerusalem, on the outer wall of the nave. At the far end of Goncharnaya on the left, the peaceful hilltop **Church of St Nikita beyond the Yauza** (tserkov Nikity shto za Yauzoy) used to command a superb view across the river until it was obscured by the Kotelnicheskaya Apartments. Described as a heap of ruins in Solzhenitsyn's *The First Circle*, the church was rebuilt in 1958–60 and is still being refurbished, but its setting is in any case lovely. Its rounded *zakomary* gables and small, cap-shaped cupola are typical of the churches erected in the

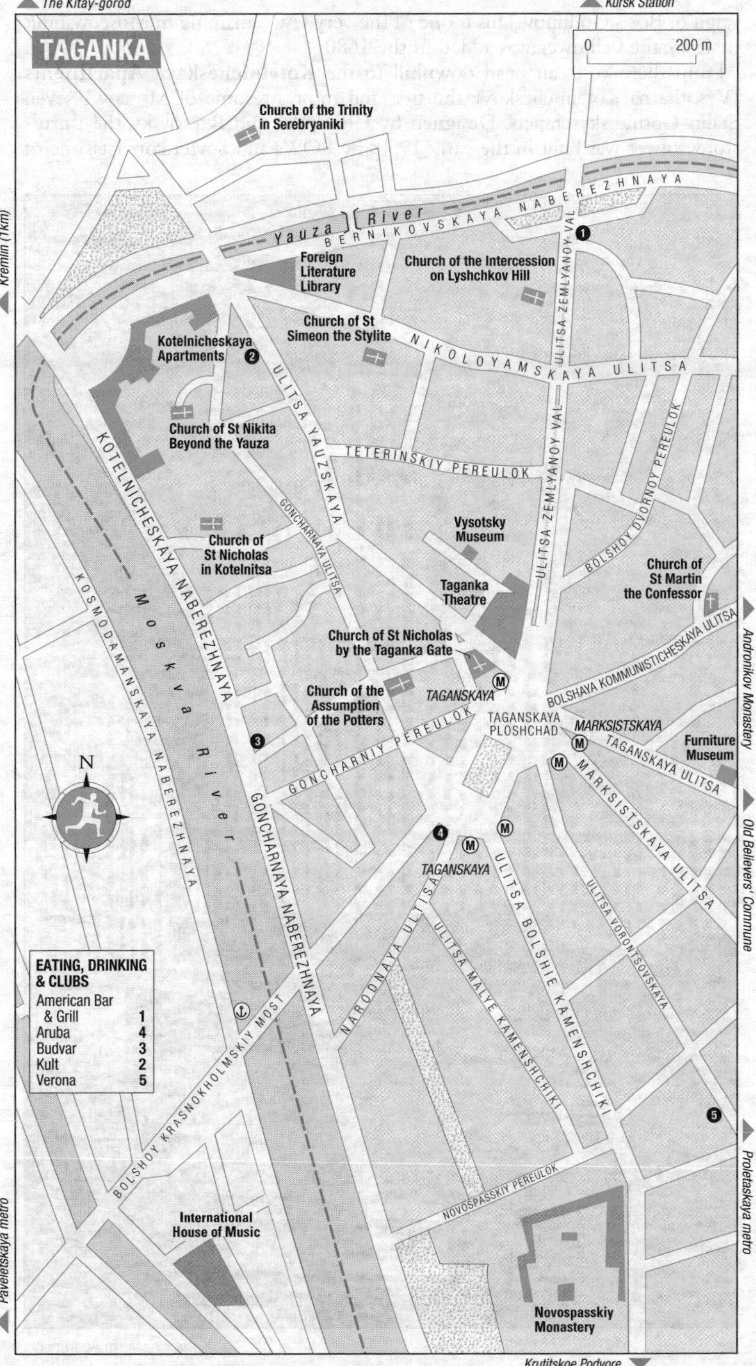

TAGANKA
The Kitay-gorod
Kursk Station
0
200 m
Kremlin (1km)
Church of the Trinity in Serebryaniki
Yauza River
BERNIKOVSKAYA NABEREZHNAYA
Foreign Literature Library
Church of the Intercession on Lyshchkov Hill
ULITSA ZEMLYANOY VAL
Church of St Simeon the Stylite
NIKOLOYAMSKAYA ULITSA
Kotelnicheskaya Apartments
Church of St Nikita Beyond the Yauza
ULITSA YAUZSKAYA
TETERINSKIY PEREULOK
BOLSHOY DVORNOY PEREULOK
GONCHARNAYA ULITSA
Vysotsky Museum
Church of St Nicholas in Kotelnitsa
Taganka Theatre
Church of St Martin the Confessor
KOTELNICHESKAYA NABEREZHNAYA
KOSMODAMANSKAYA NABEREZHNAYA
Moskva River
Church of St Nicholas by the Taganka Gate
BOLSHAYA KOMMUNISTICHESKAYA ULITSA
Church of the Assumption of the Potters
TAGANSKAYA
TAGANSKAYA PLOSHCHAD
MARKSISTSKAYA
GONCHARNIY PEREULOK
TAGANSKAYA ULITSA
Furniture Museum
Andronikov Monastery
N
MARKSISTSKAYA ULITSA
Old Believers' Commune
GONCHARNAYA NABEREZHNAYA
NARODNAYA ULITSA
ULITSA MALYE KAMENSHCHIKI
ULITSA BOLSHIE KAMENSHCHIKI
ULITSA VORONTSOVSKAYA
EATING, DRINKING & CLUBS
American Bar & Grill 1
Aruba 4
Budvar 3
Kult 2
Verona 5
BOLSHOY KRASNOKHOLMSKIY MOST
NOVOSPASSKIY PEREULOK
Proletaskaya metro
International House of Music
Paveletskaya metro
Novospasskiy Monastery
Krutitskoe Podvore

reign of Boris Godunov. This is one of the very few remaining in Moscow, built in 1595; the belltower was added in the 1680s.

From there you can head downhill to the **Kotelnicheskaya Apartments** (Vysotka na Kotelnicheskoy), the first and most awesome of Moscow's seven Stalin-Gothic skyscrapers. Designed by Chechulin and Rostovsky, the thirty-storey tower was built in the early 1950s by POWs and Soviet convicts, one of

▲ Kotelnicheskaya Apartments

whom is said to have emulated Icarus in a bid to escape, as workers who perished on the job were immured in the walls. This could explain why water oozes from the plug sockets fifty years later, to the chagrin of tenants who once belonged to the elite. For all that, the exterior is mightily impressive, clad in rusticated granite with furled banners and wheat-sheaves above its portals, and spires and statues on the heights.

To return to Taganka by a different route, head upriver past the humpback footbridge and into a housing estate built around the eighteenth-century **Church of the Intercession on Lyshchkov Hill** (tserkov Pokrova na Lyshchkovoy gore), whose plain white walls are counterpointed by a bizarre green-and-gold "pineapple", capped by an egg-shaped blue finial spangled with golden stars. The massive green cupola of the derelict **Church of St Simeon the Stylite** can be seen as one exits from the estate onto Nikoloyamskaya ulitsa, from which ulitsa Zemlyanoy val leads back to Taganskaya ploshchad.

Beyond Taganka

Radiating from Taganka are several avenues lined with two-storey ochre houses from the nineteenth century, or yellow-brick 1970s high-rises. Negotiating the underpasses to surface on a specific one can be awkward if you can't read Cyrillic, and the only useful landmark is the shopping centre at the start of Taganskaya ulitsa, which will set you on the right track for the **Furniture Museum** (muzey Mebely; Tues–Sat 11am–6pm, Sun 11am–5pm; R40) at no. 13, 300m along the street. Housed in the restored Arshenevsky mansion, it replicates a Russian aristocratic home, complete with living room, study and nursery, grandfather clocks and other period items. While Russian visitors want to see the small armchair bearing the fingerprints of Alexander I – who sat in it before the varnish had dried – foreigners are more interested in "Big Bill", a chair in the form of a giant wooden zipper dedicated to former president Clinton – or the stool shaped as Salvador Dalí's ear. Also look out for the Nostradamus chair with an elbow rest like a hand holding a magic ball and a raven perched on the back rest, and an equally Goth Bat Chair, by the deluxe-furniture firm that sponsors the museum – which includes a café and beer cellar next door.

The monasteries are further away but quite easy to reach; details of how to get there appear under the appropriate heading. All of the places described below are open daily, except for the Andronikov Monastery.

The Andronikov Monastery

As late as the eighteenth century, an arc of monasteries formed Moscow's outer line of defence against invaders. The southeast was historically the direction from which the Tartars came and thus most strongly defended. While the Novospasskiy and Simonov relied on the strength of their ramparts and bastions to hold flat terrain beside the Moskva River that was the final obstacle to sacking Zamoskvareche, the steep east bank of the Yauza River lent a natural advantage to the smaller **Andronikov Monastery** (Spaso-Andronikov monastyr; daily 8am–8pm, free). Founded in 1360 by Metropolitan Alexei, who vowed that, should he survive the stormy return sea journey from Constantinople, he would found a monastery and dedicate it to the saint whose feast day coincided with his safe return to Moscow – which turned out to be Our Saviour (Spas) – it got its present name after he was summoned to Crimea to treat the Khan's ailing wife and entrusted it to the monk Andronik, who became its first abbot. Its most famous monk was the great icon painter Andrei Rublev (see box opposite).

After the October Revolution the monastery was turned into a prison camp, then into housing for workers at the nearby Hammer and Sickle Factory, and finally scheduled for demolition – but reprieved by the postwar upsurge of patriotism. In 1960 it was formally reopened as the Andrei Rublev Museum of Early Russian Art, in honour of the 600th anniversary of his birth. Though still designated as a museum, several of the buildings are once more occupied by Orthodox monks and institutions, including a choristers' school (you might hear them practising).

To **get there** catch trolleybus #47 or #53 along Nikoloyamskaya ulitsa to Andronevskaya ploshchad. Another method is to travel by metro to Ploshchad Ilicha station, and then ride the same trolleybus in the other direction, to approach the monastery from the east. Alternatively, walk along Bolshaya Kommunisticheskaya ulitsa, lined with two-storey dwellings from the nineteenth century, where the prosperous Old Believers once lived.

The monastery

The monastery looks impressive from the outside but, except for the Refectory and the Archangel Michael church, not nearly so romantic once you're inside. Enclosed by white stone ramparts with rounded crenellations and chunky towers at three corners, the complex is entered by a **Holy Gate** (Svyatye vorota) flanked by turrets with conical wooden roofs, whose belltower was demolished in the 1930s. To the left of the gate stands the seventeenth-century **Abbot's Residence** (Nastoyatelskie Pokoi), decorated with ceramic insets; the **ticket office** and an early nineteenth-century **Seminary** (Dukhovnoe Uchilishche) lie off to the right.

The elaborate structure near the west wall was created over several centuries, starting with the two-storey tent-roofed **Refectory** (Trapeznaya palata) in 1504–06. A saw-toothed cornice integrates this with the Moscow Baroque **Church of the Archangel Michael** (tserkov Arkhangela Mikhaila) that rises alongside in variegated tiers. The church was commissioned in 1694 as a private chapel and burial vault for the family of Yevdokiya Lopukhina, Peter the Great's first wife. Four years later he forced her into a convent and exiled the Lopukhins to Siberia, whereupon the pace of construction slackened so much that the church wasn't finished until 1731.

The smaller **Cathedral of the Saviour** (Spasskiy sobor), in the centre of the grounds, was built in 1425–27 and decorated by Rublev. Although traces of his frescoes remain, the cathedral is closed for restoration, so you can only see its weathered stone facade, whose perspective-arch is surmounted by a relief of the Saviour. The helmet-shaped dome and triple apses reflect the influence of early medieval Vladimir architecture, while the pyramid of *zakomary* and *kokoshniki* are characteristic of the early Moscow style. Much altered over the centuries, it was restored to its original appearance during the 1950s. The feast day of Our Saviour falls on August 16.

The exhibitions

The **Rublev Museum**'s collection of icons is distributed around several buildings, some of which may be closed; your likeliest bets are the ground floor of the Refectory and the service block near the ticket office. Highlights include fifteenth-century icons by the school of Rublev (but none by the master himself),

Andrei Rublev

The monk **Andrei Rublev** (pronounced "Rubl*yov*") is revered as the greatest painter of medieval Russia, whose work remained a beacon throughout the dark centuries of the Tatar invasions and the Time of Troubles. The place of his birth is unknown and its date uncertain (possibly 1360), but he probably served his apprenticeship in the icon workshop of the Trinity Monastery of St Sergei, outside Moscow. Having painted the icons for Zvenigorod Cathedral, 40km northwest of Moscow, in 1400 Rublev worked on the Cathedral of the Assumption in the Kremlin, and its namesake in Vladimir (with Daniil Cherny). He painted his masterpiece, the *Old Testament Trinity*, in about 1411 or 1422, for the monastery where he had served his novitiate, before retiring to the Andronyevsky Monastery, where he is said to have died in 1430.

The Soviets honoured him as an artist, but delayed the release of Tarkovsky's superb film, *Andrei Rublev*, with its scenes of Christian faith and pagan nudity, until the early 1980s. In 1989, he was canonized by the Russian Orthodox Church and a **statue of Rublev** was erected in the park outside the monastery, which hosts an annual **celebration** in his honour on July 17.

seventeenth-century icons from Novgorod, and an eighteenth-century *Our Lady of Tikhvin* from the Donskoy Monastery – the collection, however, doesn't compare with that of the Tretyakov Gallery. A separate exhibition of applied art contains jewellery, goblets, coins, vestments and other artefacts, from medieval times onwards, and there is also an exhibition devoted to church bells.

The Novospasskiy Monastery and Krutitskoe podvore

The high-rise sprawl to the south of Taganka harbours two unexpected treats near the river: the Novospasskiy Monastery and the Krutitskoe podvore. **Getting there** from Taganskaya ploshchad entails walking 1km down ulitsa Bolshie Kamenshchiki, where the monastery's belltower soon becomes visible; you can reach the podvore afterwards by walking downhill from the monastery, crossing the highway and following Krutitskaya ulitsa uphill. Starting from Proletarskaya metro instead, you'll pass the podvore en route to the monastery; the distance is a bit shorter but the route is confusing at the outset. In summertime, you can also reach the Novospasskiy Monastery on a scenic river **cruise** past the Kremlin and the Novodevichiy Convent, to disembark at the Ustinskiy most landing stage, nearby.

The Novospasskiy Monastery

When you first see its walls from the river, or its golden-yellow belltower above the rooftops, the **Novospasskiy Monastery** (Novospasskiy monastyr; daily 8am–8pm; free) looks grander than the better-known Novodevichie or Donskoy monasteries. Indeed, it claims to be the oldest in Moscow, tracing its foundation back to the twelfth-century reign of Yuri Dolguruky, who established a monastery dedicated to the Saviour on the site of the present-day Danilov Monastery. In 1300, Ivan I transferred this to the Kremlin, whence Ivan III relocated it to its present site in 1490 – hence the appellation, "New Monastery of the Saviour". Subsequently razed by the Tatars, most of the existing complex dates from the seventeenth century, when the monastery was surrounded by a thick wall with seven bastions, which preserved it through the Time of Troubles and determined its grim role in modern times, when it was used as a concentration camp by the Bolsheviks, who imprisoned and shot their victims in the almshouse and hospital alongside the northern wall. It then became an orphanage, an NKVD archive, a furniture factory, and finally a drunk-tank. Returned to the Church in 1991, the buildings are slowly being restored, but the ravages of its past are still evident within its walls.

The entrance is through an archway to the left of its gigantic four-tiered **belltower**, whose gold finial was once visible from afar. As at all Orthodox monasteries, visitors must be suitably dressed (women are expected to wear a headscarf and a skirt, but they don't insist). Inside you'll be confronted with a muddle of sheds and chapels, where the main cathedral stands out as the focus of attention for monks and pilgrims alike, while novices and kids lurk around the fringes where a publishing house and a Sunday school occupy the outbuildings.

The **Cathedral of the Transfiguration of the Saviour** (sobor Spasa Preobrazheniya) is a medieval-style edifice with huge arched gables and helmet-shaped domes, erected on the site of the original cathedral in 1645. An image of the Saviour watches over the portal to the (locked) crypt that served as the family vault of the Romanov boyars until Mikhail Romanov's ascension to the throne in 1613. The cathedral's lofty nave is dominated by a massive gilt-framed **iconostasis** that includes the icons of the *Image of Christ* and *Our Lady of Smolensk*, a gift from Tsar Mikhail's mother, who became a nun in later life. On either side are shrines containing relics from Kiev, including a piece of the Virgin's robe, which was a wedding gift from the Byzantine empire to Ivan the Great. The walls are covered in frescoes representing the genealogy of the sovereigns of Russia from St Olga to Tsar Alexei, and the descent of the kings of Israel, while the refectory stairway is flanked by images of ancient Greek philosophers.

The begrimed orange **Church of the Sign**, around the back of the cathedral, contains the tomb of **Parasha Kovalyova**, whose marriage to Count Sheremetev amazed Moscow society. But the most curious story relates to the terracotta-coloured tent-roofed **chapel** nearby, where Princess Tarakanova is interred (see box below). Beyond the monastery's west wall lies a large pond that once supplied the monks with fish. During the mid-1930s, the NKVD used its steep bank as a burial ground for the bodies of foreign Communists secretly shot in the purges.

The legend of Princess Tarakanova

The chapel contains the remains of Sister Inokinya Dosieeya, better known to Russians as **Princess Tarakanova**. As the illegitimate child of Empress Elizabeth and Count Razumovsky (see p.264), she was sent abroad to be educated, enabling a Polish adventuress to claim her identity and the right to inherit the throne of Russia. Though this impostor was swiftly incarcerated (and died in prison), Catherine the Great decided to lure Tarakanova back home and confine her to a nunnery "for the good of Russia". **Legend** has it that the task was entrusted to Catherine's lover, Count Orlov, who seduced Tarakanova aboard a ship before locking her in their nuptial cabin as they approached St Petersburg. Though one version maintains that she was imprisoned in an underground cell of the Peter and Paul fortress and drowned during a flood, Tarakanova was actually confined in Moscow's Ivanovskiy Convent, where she remained for 25 years until Catherine's death, by which time she had come to accept her fate and chose to remain a nun.

The Krutitskoe podvore

Across the highway, lanes ascend to the **Krutitskoe podvore** (10am–5pm; closed Tues and the first Mon of each month; free), a picturesque "yard" (*podvore*) of seventeenth-century buildings named after the steep (*krutoy*) bank of the nearby Moskva River. Established as the seat of the Metropolitan of the Christian minority among the Tatar Golden Horde, it originally covered a much larger area, until Catherine the Great turned part of it into a military prison that's still visible around the back. Architecturally, the *podvore* is remarkable for being devoid of any Western influences, its tent-roofed chapels and walkways arranged in a seemingly haphazard fashion that's purely Muscovite, an impression enhanced by the wooden houses in the yard dating from the 1920s, when the complex became a workers' hostel.

Its centrepiece is a **Cathedral of the Assumption** (Uspenskiy sobor) constructed entirely of brick – onion domes included – connected by an overhead arcade to the **Metropolitan's Palace** in the far corner of the yard. The arcade passes through an impressive arched structure called the **Teremok**, one wall of which is decorated with turquoise tiles in colourful floral designs and has beautiful window frames carved like grapevines. Sadly, all the facades need a lot of restoration, and you can't enter the Teremok or Metropolitan's Palace.

While the cathedral's lower "winter" church is once again a place of worship, the upper "summer" church remains in the hands of a museum which uses it as a storeroom and refuses to hand it back. Otherwise, however, the *podvore* has been reclaimed by the Church, which has set up a printing house and holds meetings of Orthodox youth organizations here. If you turn up at the right time, a small subterranean **Museum of Pilgrimages** (muzey Palomnichestva no svyatim mestam; Sat 11am–5pm, Sun noon–5pm) can be visited – it's tucked away around the corner to the far right of the complex.

The Simonov Monastery

Of the trio of monasteries on this flank, the most embattled was the **Simonov Monastery** (Simonovskiy monastyr; daily 8am–dusk; free). Founded in 1371 by the monk Fyodor, a nephew of Sergei of Radonezh, it resisted many sieges before being sacked by the Poles in the Time of Troubles, but was rebuilt even stronger, as "Moscow's Sentinel". In Soviet times, however, its environs were considered an ideal site for a car factory, and much of the monastery was destroyed to make way for a football stadium and palace of culture. What remains attests both to its former strength and to the ravages that surpassed anything inflicted by foreign invaders; of all the city's monasteries, none is sadder-looking or more haunting – yet what its community of believers has accomplished is inspiring.

Getting there involves catching the Zamoskvoretskaya line to Avtozavodskaya metro station and exiting by the front of the train; as you come up the steps, you'll see one of the monastery's towers, 400m up the road ahead to the left.

The ruins

The most imposing aspect is a 250-metre-long section of **fortified wall** (which once totalled 655m in length), guarded by three massive stone towers. Fyodor Kon, who designed the walls of the Beliy Gorod, is thought to have created the **Dulo Tower** on the corner by the river, with its tiers of windows at staggered intervals; the archers' gallery and tent-roofed spire were added in the seventeenth century, when the towers of the Kremlin received similar additions. Nearer the road, the **Solevaya** and **Kuznechnaya towers** resemble giant mushrooms, their white stalks capped by brown spires.

Entering the grounds by a gate in the fence near the palace of culture you're confronted by industrial debris where nineteenth-century visitors were delighted by "gardens of marigolds and dahlias, and bees humming in hedges of spiraea". Ahead looms the huge **Refectory-Church of Our Lady of Tikhvin**, where services are once again held in the uppermost part, reached by a stairway on the far side. There used to be six churches (the oldest built in 1405), but in 1934 five of them were blown up in a single day. Since the Church regained ownership in 1994 volunteers have cleared tonnes of rubbish, set up a factory to recycle scrap metal, planted sunflowers in the grounds, and established a community of deaf people that's unique for holding Orthodox services with signing.

Other sights nearby

In its medieval heyday the Simonov owned twelve thousand "souls" and a score of villages, while its walls encompassed three times the present area – a measure of how much was destroyed to create the Torpedo Football Stadium and the **ZiL Palace of Culture**. The largest and most lavishly appointed of the workers' clubs built in the 1930s, the ZiL Palace was designed by the Vsenin brothers, the top Constructivist architects of their day. It is best viewed from the river-facing side, where an expansive curved gallery floods the interior with light. Otherwise, it has not aged well; like other Constructivist buildings, its design required better materials than were available at the time. As for the stadium, it has hardly been used since Torpedo decamped to Luzhniki Stadium after the club changed hands following the collapse of ZiL in the mid-1990s.

Previously, both the team and palace belonged to the **ZiL Motor Works** (Avtozavod imeni Likhachova), Russia's oldest car factory (founded in 1916), best known for producing the ZiL limousines used by Soviet leaders. In the

The Dubrovka Theatre siege

On October 23, 2002, Muscovites were stunned by news that forty Chechen terrorists had seized the audience and cast of the *Nord–Ost* musical at the **Dubrovka Theatre** and threatened to kill the 800–900 hostages unless Russian forces withdrew from Chechnya. Images of masked gunmen and women with explosives strapped to their bodies went round the world; some hostages were able to phone local radio stations and beg the government to negotiate. Yet it was clear that the Kremlin would never accede to the Chechens' demand, and after they killed a hostage on the second day, a violent end to the **siege** was inevitable. At 5.50am, October 26, Special Forces stormed the theatre, having pumped a paralyzing gas into the auditorium where the hostages and terrorists were gathered.

All the Chechens were shot dead and at least 129 hostages died – mostly from the effects of the **gas** (probably the anesthetic Fentanyl or Phentalin), which hospitals couldn't treat because its identity was classified. Their corpses were taken to different morgues, where relatives had to identify them from photo albums, raising fears that the real death toll was higher. Some relatives rejected the $3000 compensation offered by Moscow City Government and sued the authorities for failing to intercept "bus loads of criminals armed to the teeth riding around the city"; 26 families won lump sums before the City passed the financial onus to the Federal government. Yet no expense was spared to refurbish the theatre (about 1km from the Simonov Monastery) and reopen the musical on the first anniversary of the siege.

1990s ZiL barely averted bankruptcy by laying off thousands of workers and not paying others for months, before winning orders for a new limo. The half-moribund factory is a weird setting for the resurrected **Church of the Nativity of the Virgin in Old Simonov**, built in 1509. Previously used as a compressor shed, it now has a new iconostasis and a charming garden (services at 8am & 5pm). To have a look, enter the factory by the park gate facing the monastery's ramparts and follow the walkway – you can't go astray.

The Old Believers' Commune and Rogozhskoe Cemetery

The **Old Believers' Commune** (Staroobryadcheskaya Obshchinatserkoy'; daily 8am–dusk; free) is a relic of an Orthodox sect that once loomed large in Tsarist Russia – especially in Moscow, where many of the merchants and coachmen were Old Believers. Their Moscow commune was founded in the 1770s after Catherine the Great granted them limited rights and many returned from hiding in Siberia. Though Nicholas I reimposed discriminatory laws, the sect had become established enough to weather official disapproval until the onset of liberalization in 1905. After the October 1917 Revolution, however, they were doubly suspect for their piety and wealth, and suffered even more severe repression, which forced the sect underground for decades. Today, the commune is coming back to life, but their strict ethics effectively bar them from the cut-throat business world of New Russia.

To get there, catch trolleybus #16 or #63 from Taganskaya Metro station. Get off at the seventh stop, "Staroobryadcheskaya ulitsa", and look for a belltower on the far side of Nizhergorodskaya ulitsa. A path crossing the train tracks should bring you to the commune in less than ten minutes. Note that women visitors dressed in trousers or short skirts will not be allowed inside, and must cover their heads with a shawl.

The **belltower** is a soaring neo-Byzantine structure with elaborate blind arcades and Moorish arches, erected to celebrate the reopening of the commune's churches in 1905. Soon after the Revolution, the Bolsheviks closed them down again and turned the **Cathedral of the Intercession** (Pokrovskiy sobor) into a cobblers' workshop. Built in 1792 by Kazakov, its Neoclassical facade doesn't prepare you for the vastness and magnificence of the interior, whose arches and pillars are outlined in gold and covered with frescoes of saints and biblical events. *Murray's Handbook* (1875) warned visitors that "the singing will be found very peculiar . . . especially that of the women, who perform Divine service in a chapel apart from the men". By turning up at 5pm you can hear the liturgy and judge for yourself. Further north stands the attractive neo-Russian **Church of St Nicholas** (tserkov Nilolay), whose white walls are jazzed up by red, white and blue *kokoshniki*, sage-green pendentives and turquoise shingled onion domes.

By passing through the church's tent-roofed archway – originally the entrance to the commune – you'll find the **Rogozhskoe Cemetery** (daily: summer 9am–7pm, winter 9am–6pm), where Old Believers and Soviet functionaries are buried. The main path leads uphill past the headstone of **Admiral Gorshkov** (who headed the Soviet Navy under Brezhnev) to the **Morozov family** plot, beneath a wrought-iron canopy. A thrifty serf couple who sold their homespun cloth on the streets of Moscow after the great fire, the Morozovs bought their freedom and within thirty years owned a cotton mill which their son **Timofey** developed into a textiles empire. (It was at the Morozov mills in Orekhovo

The Old Believers

During the 1650s, Patriarch Nikon's reforms of Orthodox ritual were rejected by thousands of Russians who felt that only their traditional rites offered salvation. Calling themselves **Old Believers** (*Staroobryadtsy*) – others termed them *Raskolniki* (Dissenters) – they held that crossing oneself with three fingers instead of two was an infamy, and shaving a beard "a sin that even the blood of martyrs could not expiate". Opposition intensified under Peter the Great, whom they saw as the Antichrist for promoting tobacco, ordering men to cut their beards (which believers kept to be buried with them, lest they be barred from paradise), and imposing the Julian Calendar and a chronology dating from the birth of Christ, rather than Creation – thus perverting time itself.

To escape forced conversions, the Old Believers fled into the wilds; if cornered, they burned themselves to death, singing hymns. During generations in exile, they became divided into the less stringent *Popovtsy*, who dealt with Orthodox priests and were willing to drink to the tsar's health; and the *Bezpopovtsy* (Priestless), who totally rejected both Church and state. The latter included wilder sub-sects like the *Skoptsy* or "Mutilated Ones", who castrated themselves, and the *Khlisty* (Flagellants), whose orgies and lashings expressed their belief in salvation through sin (Rasputin was said to have been one).

Zuevo that football originated in Russia.) Alongside are buried Timofey's widow **Maria**, a fervent Old Believer who henceforth ran the show; their sons **Savva**, who sponsored the arts and left-wing causes before killing himself (see p.158), and **Aseny**, who died of a stupid prank.

Kuskovo and Kuzminki

It's a measure of Moscow's growth that the southeastern suburbs now incorporate what were country estates in the eighteenth and nineteenth centuries. Kuskovo and Kuzminki once embodied a way of life that amounted to a credo: the pursuit of pleasure and elegant refinement by an aristocracy that was no longer obliged to serve the state (as Peter the Great had insisted). The fate of Kuskovo and Kuzminki since the Revolution illustrates the Soviets' Janus-like view of Russia's aristocratic heritage, with one estate being preserved as a museum and the other being allowed to moulder away until Mayor Luzhkov took an interest in its fate. Although Kuskovo should please everyone, Kuzminki requires a real interest in stately homes and you may prefer the Museum of Antique Automobiles and Motorcycles in Lyublino. Getting there entails using a different metro line to the one serving the estates unless you come on a summer weekend, when there's a tourist bus from Kuzminki to Lyublino.

Kuskovo

The industrial suburb of **Kuskovo** takes its name from the former **Sheremetev estate** – Moscow's finest example of an eighteenth-century nobleman's country palace. Its **history** dates back to 1715, when Peter the Great awarded the village of Kuskovo to Boris Sheremetev, a general at the battle of Poltava, who built a summer residence there. Its present layout is owed to his son Pyotr, who devoted himself to managing the estate after inheriting some 200,000 serfs and marrying Varvara Cherkasskaya, whose dowry included the talented serf architects Fyodor Argunov and Alexei Mironov. In its heyday Kuskovo was known as the "Count's State" and included a zoo covering 230 acres, but after Pyotr's death it fell into disuse as his son Nikolai preferred his own palace at Ostankino (see p.282) – so, barring some repairs after Kuskovo was looted by French troops in 1812, its mid-eighteenth-century decor remained unchanged until it was nationalized by the Bolsheviks as a monument to "serf art".

Kuskovo is **open** from Wednesday to Sunday 10am–6pm (closed last Wed of each month), though it sometimes closes with no notice on very rainy days, and last tickets are sold an hour before closing time. Separate **tickets** for the palace

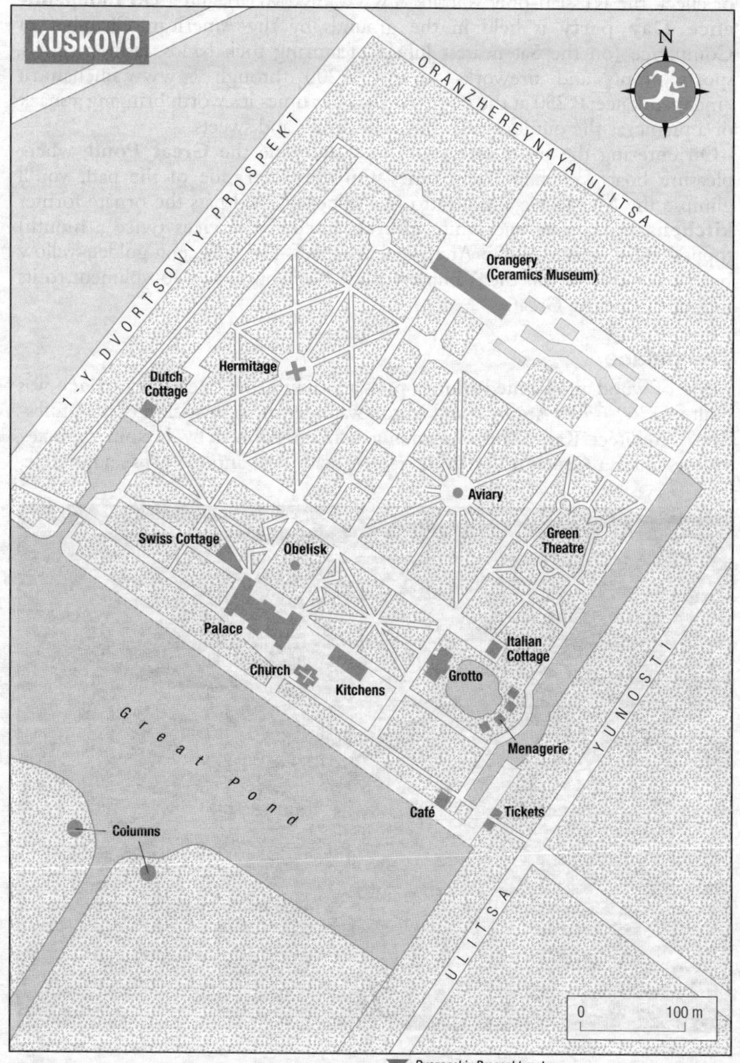

(R250), Orangery/Ceramics Museum (R200), grotto (R100), Dutch and Italian cottages (R100 each) are sold at the main gate to the estate.

Getting there is easier than it sounds. Take the metro from Taganskaya to Ryazanskiy Prospekt station and leave by the exit near the front of the train; then from the third bus stop on the right, ride bus #133 or #208 six stops to the main entrance, or alight one stop earlier to approach the palace through its stately park (created where the village of Kuskovo existed until 1977). Though best visited in summer, when its formal gardens are abloom, the grounds are also lovely in autumn, and the palace and the ceramics museum in the Orangery are worth seeing at any time.

Over summer **concerts** take place in the palace (for details, call ⓣ370 01 60 or check the Russian-only website ⓦwww.kuskovo.ru), and a **US Independence Day party** is held in the grounds by the American Chamber of Commerce (on the Sat nearest July 4), featuring rock bands, fashion shows, sports events and fireworks (tickets R200 through ⓦwww.amcham.ru/independence; R250 at the door). At all other times it's worth bringing a snack or a picnic, as the outdoor café only sells drinks and sweets.

On entering the main gate you'll pass alongside the **Great Pond**, where pleasure boats sailed in olden times. On the other side of the path you'll glimpse the Menagerie and Grotto (see opposite), and pass the ornate former **kitchens** and a grey-and-white **church** (used for services twice a month) topped by a statue of the Archangel Michael. The adjacent golden-yellow **belfry** is modelled on the Admiralty in St Petersburg, as a compliment to its founder Peter the Great.

The palace

Made of wood and painted salmon-pink and white, the one-storey **palace** was built in 1769–77 by Argunov and Mironov, under the supervision of the professional architect Karl Blank. Ascending a ramp flanked by buxom sphinxes, visitors enter a **Grecian Vestibule**, replete with fake antique urns and marble.

▲ Kuskovo Palace

The tour of the palace progresses through the silk-wallpapered **card room** and **billiard room** to the pink-and-white mirrored dining hall, and thence to the "informal" rooms in the west wing. These include a **tapestry room** hung with Flemish tapestries; a **mauve drawing room** upholstered in cerise and silver silk; a **state bedchamber** with an allegorical fresco, *Innocence Choosing Between Wisdom and Love*; and an oak-panelled **study**.

The highlight is the **ballroom**, dripping with gilt and chandeliers, whose fresco, *Apollo and the Muses*, glorifies the Sheremetevs. Relief panels on the walls depict the exploits of the ancient Roman hero Mucius Scaevola, who thrust his hand into fire to prove his indifference to pain, an image that resonated with the Russians at the time of the Napoleonic invasion.

The garden and pavilions

Behind the palace an obelisk introduces the **garden**, laid out in the geometrical French style; during winter its statues are encased in boxes to protect them from the cold. Off to the right you'll find the **Grotto** pavilion, with its prominent dome and ornate wrought-iron gates; the interior was decorated by the St Petersburg "Master of Grotto Work", Johannes Fokt, using shells, stones, textured stucco and porcelain. Nearby is the charming **Italian Cottage** (Italyanskiy domik), a miniature palace in its own right; if you're there on the hour, don't miss the melodious grandfather clock. The four cute little houses topped with urns, across the pond behind the Grotto, once housed a **Menagerie** of birds and animals.

Further on, beyond the lattice-work **Aviary** and the open-air **Green Theatre**, the old **Orangery** houses a **Ceramics Museum** displaying a superb collection of eighteenth-, nineteenth- and twentieth-century porcelain, ranging from the Egyptian dinner service of Alexander I to plates and vases commemorating the construction of the Moscow metro. On the way back, cast an eye over Blank's Baroque **Hermitage** pavilion, topped by a statue of the goddess Flora, before visiting the steep-roofed **Dutch Cottage**, built in 1749, which contains three rooms entirely covered in Delft tiles. Nearby stands an elaborately gabled **Swiss Cottage**, created by the St Petersburg stage designer Nikolai Benois, which is now the curator's residence.

Kuzminki

A few kilometres south of Kuskovo is an older estate that belonged to the Stroganovs before passing to the Golitsyn family in the nineteenth century. At the time of its last owner – Prince Sergei Golitsyn II – **Kuzminki** was a model estate with a hospital and school for its staff and their families, marred only by a fire that destroyed the main palace in 1915. After the Revolution Kuzminki was turned into a veterinary research institute, whose work on animal viruses was later directed towards biological warfare. While the Egyptian Pavilion was kept busy as a laboratory and administrative block, the surrounding service wings and stables and the pavilions in the park were left to rot. Restoration only began a few years back and still has a long way to go, but the Moscow History Museum has established a branch devoted to aristocratic country life and organizes themed walks and events when the weather allows.

It takes about an hour to **get there** from the centre or from Kuskovo, despite being on the same metro line, one stop nearer the centre. Exiting Kuzminki station at the front of the train, you want to be on the southern, even-numbered side of Volgogradskiy prospekt to catch bus #29 or minibus

#29-K in the right direction, which eventually terminates 200m from the main entrance to the grounds of the estate. On summer weekends and public holidays only, an hourly **tourist bus** running between the estate's Stables pavilion and Lyublino metro makes it possible to visit the Antique Automobiles Museum without the hassle of travelling back to the Proletarskaya/Krestyanskaya Zastava metro interchange and then out again on the Lyublinskaya line (or vice versa).

On public holidays and at fortnightly intervals over summer, Kuzminki's museum runs guided **walks** and historical re-enactments for children (Ⓣ377 94 57 for details). Their appeal to foreigners is limited by the fact that all are in Russian only, and the costumed **events** aren't nearly so elaborate as the ones at Kolomenskoe (see p.235). In wintertime, come for the solitude of the park – acres of birches, larch and spruce, and ruined follies covered in snow.

Exploring the park

At the end of the avenue through the woods, a domed **Golitsyn Mausoleum** and a **Church of the Virgin** with a gilt-crowned tower mark the start of the estate proper. Straight ahead is what you'd assume to be the Golitsyn mansion, but was in fact merely its **Egyptian Pavilion**. Built by Voronikhin in 1811, the faded Neoclassical edifice is hardly redolent of Egypt, but is handsomely set back behind a fence guarded by statues of fierce gryphons and dozy lions, augmented by a statue of Lenin up the drive. Still a veterinary research institute, it's not open to the public.

East of the church, tree-lined Tyoplovaya alleya (Warm Alley) runs past the erstwhile hospital, school and stables to the *Slobodka* or Servants' House that's now a **Country Estate Museum** (muzey russkoy Usadby; Tues–Sun 10am–6pm; closed the last Fri of each month; R200). If Empire furniture, porcelain and engravings are your thing, there's much to see; photos of the Golitsyns picnicking and playing tennis at Kuzminki in the 1900s strike a more personal note on the second floor.

Heading the other way, across a bridge over a weir between the **Upper and Lower Ponds**, you'll see the Classical mass of the **Stables** (Konniy dvor) on the far bank. Actually a grandiose music pavilion built in 1793 by Rodion Kazakov, its name comes from the huge sculpted **horses** that rear outside the entrance. It's here that the tourist bus to and from Lyublino turns around (a timetable should be posted somewhere). If you want more exercise, it's a little over a kilometre's walk past a chain of ponds till the end of the park and **Volzhskaya metro** station. As this is on the same line as Lyublino, you could use it as a way to reach the Antique Automobiles Museum when the tourist bus isn't in service.

The Antique Automobiles and Motorcycles Museum

The smoggy Lyublino district beyond Kuzminki is only worth a trip on the Lyublinskaya metro line to visit the **Lomakov Antique Automobiles and Motorcycles Museum** (Lomakovskiy muzey starinnykh avtomobiley i mototsiklov; daily 11am–7pm; R100; Ⓦwww.lomakovka.ru).

Sited on Lot #58 (vladenie 58) of an industrial zone off Krasnodarskaya ulitsa, 350m from Lyublino metro, this private collection of 85 historic cars, trucks and motorbikes was previously based in the Kashirskaya district. The pride of Dmitri Lomakov's collection are vehicles used by senior Nazis or Soviet figures, including Goering's Horch-853 roadster, a Mercedes Benz 540K driven by Goebbels, and a Mercedes Benz 320 from Bormann's garage; a Rolls-Royce used by Lenin after the Revolution, a 1949 ZiL limo presented by Stalin to Patriarch Alexei I and a later model bestowed on Patriarch Pimen by Brezhnev. Among the vintage motorbikes are a Peugeot abandoned by French troops at Arkhangelsk in 1917, and a 1942 US Army Harley-Davidson supplied to the Red Army under the Lend Lease programme, like the Studebaker trucks that were converted into rocket launchers (fondly known to Soviet troops as "Katyusha" and feared by the Germans as "Stalin Organs"), one of which can also be seen. Guided **tours**, and even night tours, can be arranged for R2800 on Ⓣ356 79 95, or Ⓔlomakov@rosmail.ru.

Zayauze and Izmaylovo

Strictly speaking, Zayauze refers to the entire east bank of the Yauza as far downstream as Taganka, but here it means both sides of the upper reaches of the river, taking in the Baumanskiy quarter behind Kursk Station and Lefortovo on the east bank – a backwater of the city with river-side palaces associated with Peter the Great and his successors, which is intriguing if you like exploring "unknown" Moscow, but hardly bursting with tourist attractions.

Izmaylovo is another matter. Its outdoor Art Market is a must for anyone seeking souvenirs – genuine or fake Soviet memorabilia, icons, cameras, antiques, or contemporary artwork and crafts. Nearby are the peaceful vestiges of the Izmaylovo royal estate where Peter the Great spent his childhood, the forested park of the same name, and a hotel complex offering decently priced accommodation (see p.332). Further west lies another childhood haunt of Peter's, Preobrazhenskoe, harbouring an Old Believers' Commune and a Dolphinarium.

Unless stated otherwise, all the places covered below are within walking distance of (if not close to) a metro station on the Arbatsko-Pokrovskaya line, which intersects with the Circle line at Kursk Station on the Garden Ring.

Baumanskiy to Lefortovo

Today's **Baumanskiy** district was once the so-called **German Suburb** (Nemetskaya sloboda), where foreigners were obliged to live by Tsar Alexei, so that their "heathen" churches and customs wouldn't outrage the xenophobic Muscovites. Ironically, what began as a form of quarantine ended up infecting Alexei's son – the future Peter the Great – with the very ideas and habits that traditionalists deplored. The suburb was a European oasis of brick houses and formal gardens, whose three thousand residents enjoyed mixed *soirées*, ballroom dancing and tobacco. In a society that mingled Dutch merchants, German architects and Scottish mercenaries, Peter not only enlarged his view of the world, but took a foreign mistress, **Anna Mons**. The daughter of a Westphalian wine merchant, Anna was encouraged to hope that she might become empress because of Peter's lavish gifts and obvious disenchantment with his wife Yevdokiya. Though their relationship lasted for twelve years, her ambition was ultimately fulfilled by her successor Catherine I, whose origins were even humbler than Anna's.

Surprisingly, the small **house** where Peter installed Anna at the start of their affair still stands at Starokirochniy pereulok 6, on a lane past the market on Baumanskaya ulitsa, as you walk southwards from Baumanskaya metro station. The lane emerges onto 2-ya Baumanskaya ulitsa opposite the **Lefort Palace** (Lefortovskiy dvorets) that Peter built in 1697 to host parties for his "Jolly Company". From this evolved the famous "Drunken Synod", dedicated to mockery of Church rituals, whose rule book stated that members were to "get drunk every day and never go to bed sober" – many died as a result. The palace's nominal owner was the Swiss mercenary Franz Lefort, who had introduced Peter to Anna in 1690. It was in the Lefort Palace that the tsar's heir Peter II died of smallpox at the age of fourteen, on his wedding day. The palace's full size can only be appreciated by peering through the gateway; it now houses photographic and military archives, and isn't open to the public – but some items from the palace are exhibited in the Lefortovo Museum (see opposite).

Further downhill stands the **Suburban Palace** (Slobodskiy dvorets) of Catherine the Great's chief minister, Prince Bezborodko, who responded to a remark by her successor, Paul, that the gardens would look better as a parade ground by having them flattened overnight and presenting the palace to the tsar as a gift the very next day. Decades later it became the Imperial Technical Academy, a hotbed of revolutionary activity where the Bolshevik Moscow Committee met in 1905; their local organizer, Nikolai Bauman, was beaten to death by ultra-rightists outside the building. As the Bauman Technical Academy, it was a training school for Soviet technocrats destined for high positions.

You can also get there from higher ground behind Kursk Station; one of the exits from Kurskaya metro brings you out on a street which switchbacks down the hillside past the **Razumovsky Palace**. This stately pile was built by Alexei Razumovsky, the lover of Empress Elizabeth, whose nickname was the "Night-time Emperor"; he outlived her and went on to serve Catherine the Great as a minister. Since the palace became a sports training institute, generations of athletes have left it so battered that hopes of restoring it as a museum were abandoned in the 1990s. Shortly after the palace the road joins ulitsa Radio, running down towards the Suburban Palace and a **bridge** across to Lefortovo.

Lefortovo – its prison, cemetery and museum

The **Lefortovo** district is named after Lefort, whose professional skills enabled Peter to turn his "toy regiments" into the nucleus of a European-style army, to replace the Streltsy. Lefort's own troops were garrisoned on what is now Krasnokursantskiy proezed (Red Cadets' Drive), running alongside the longest colonnade in Moscow, with sixteen columns set in the loggia of the **Catherine Palace** (Yekaterininskiy dvorets), which turns its back on a park and ponds that once belonged to the grounds of Lefort's palace. Built in the second half of the eighteenth century by three leading architects – Quarenghi, Rinaldi and Camporesi – the Catherine Palace was inherited by her soldier-mad son Paul, who turned it into a barracks. Owned by the military ever since, it now houses the Malinovsky Tank Academy.

If you don't turn back at this point, there are some other places of historic interest within twenty-minutes' walk of the Catherine Palace – not all of which are so picturesque. Strike out along Energeticheskaya ulitsa past a sports ground and at the next crossroads turn left into a lane behind a row of houses and you'll be confronted with the walls of **Lefortovo Prison**. Founded in

1881, it rivals Butyrka Prison (see p.275) for infamy but doesn't admit sightseers. During the 1930s, "enemies of the people" like Yevgenia Ginzburg waited here to be transferred to camps in Siberia, as did Brezhnev-era dissidents such as Anatoly Sharansky and Father Gleb Yakunin. Under Gorbachev, the German flyer Matthias Rust spent eighteen months here for his escapade (see p.70), while Yeltsin's foes were bundled into Lefortovo after the storming of the White House, only to be amnestied by parliament a few months later. As the FSB's holding and interrogation centre, it is often in the news for its high-profile prisoners.

For those truly into local history, there's the overgrown **Vedenskoe Cemetery** (Vedenskoe kladbishe; daily: summer 9am–7pm, winter 9am–6pm; free) where residents of the German Suburb were buried. Some are featured in the nearby **Lefortovo Museum** (Lefortovskiy muzey; Tues–Sun 10am–6pm; R200) at Kryukovskaya ulitsa 23, a branch of the Moscow History Museum displaying engravings, uniforms and documents related to Peter's revels in the Lefort Palace and his reforms of Russian institutions and society. Though guided tours are available, nobody speaks any English so you might as well just drop in and look around if you're interested. The museum is about fifteen-minutes' walk from the prison, or you can catch tram #32, #46 or #50 from Semyonovskaya metro to the "Ukhtomskaya" stop.

Izmaylovo and Preobrazhenskoe

Further east, the 750-acre **Izmaylovo Park** is named after the estate where Peter the Great grew up, and nowadays known for its art market. Take the metro to Izmaylovskiy Park station, whose decor commemorates the Great Patriotic War (notice the PPSh machine-gun motifs on the pillars, and the statues of Partisan heroine Zoya Kosmodemskaya at the top of the stairs). Stepping outside, you'll see the five high-rise blocks of the hotel complex that was built for the 1980 Olympics, and a stream of shoppers heading for the **Izmaylovo Market** (Izmaylovskiy rynok or Vernissazh; daily 10am–5pm). One of Moscow's top tourist attractions, its stock ranges from *matryoshka* dolls and officers' caps to prewar cameras, busts of Lenin, woodcarvings, paintings, ceramics, carpets, quilts and even wolfskins for sale. The widest selection is on Saturdays and Sundays, when there may be buskers strumming away on the stage-set medieval **wooden palace** just inside the entrance to the market.

On the far side of the fenced path to the market, a few-minutes' walk past a sports ground will bring you to an island that was once the heart of the **Izmaylovo Royal Estate**. Owned by the Romanov boyars since the sixteenth century, it was Tsar Alexei's favourite retreat and Peter's home during the regency of Sofia (see p.196). In 1688 Peter discovered a small boat of Western design abandoned on the Yauza, and insisted on being taught how to sail by a Dutchman – the birth of his passion for the sea, which led to the creation of the Russian Navy and vistas of maritime power for what had previously been a landlocked nation.

During his childhood, a wooden palace stood amidst the enclosure of two-storey brick buildings, entered by a **Ceremonial Gate** with a tent-roof and three archways barred by oaken grilles. Emerging on the far side of the enclosure, a statue of Peter with his foot on a coil of rope and his hand resting on an anchor adorns a park outside the **Cathedral of the Intercession** (Pokrovskiy sobor). This regal Moscow Baroque edifice is overhung by five massive domes, clustered so closely that they almost touch, resting on drums decorated with majolica tiles in the peacock's-eye motif. Behind this stands the **Bridge Tower** that once guarded the way to the estate. Like Kolomenskoe, Izmaylovo fell into disuse after St Petersburg became the capital, and Peter's successors built more modern palaces for themselves in Moscow, if they bothered to stay there at all.

Preobrazhenskoe

The other location associated with Peter's youth was the village of **Preobrazhenskoe**, 1km or so west of Izmaylovo. Here, his war games gradually evolved into serious manoeuvres using real weapons from the Kremlin Armoury. Playmates and servants were drilled by experts from the German Suburb; Peter insisted on being treated like a common soldier and on mastering every skill himself (he loved drumming in the band). Eventually, there were two companies, each 300 strong, which formed the nucleus of the first units of the Imperial Guard – the Preobrazhenskiy and Semyonovskiy regiments. Russians who mocked Peter's "**toy**" **regiments** were obliged to revise their opinion after the Guards crushed the Streltsy revolt of 1689, and subsequently won honours at Poltava and other battles, against the renowned Swedish army.

Though nothing remains of their former stamping grounds, you might care to visit the **Preobrazhenskaya Old Believers' Commune**, founded in the late eighteenth century by *Bezpopovtsy* (Priestless) sectarians. Several of their churches and dormitories remain at no. 17 ulitsa Preobrazhenskiy val, which runs past the local cemetery, midway between Preobrazhenskaya Ploshchad and Semyonovskaya metro stations. Moscow's **Dolphinarium** (see p.373 for details) is also in this part of town.

Streets and squares

Andronevskaya ploshchad	Андроньевская площадь
Baumanskaya ulitsa	Бауманская улица
Bolshaya Kalitnikovskaya ulitsa	Большая Калитниковская улица
Bolshaya Kommunisticheskaya ulitsa	Большая Коммунистическая улица
Energeticheskaya ulitsa	нергетическая улица
Goncharnaya ulitsa	Гончарная улица
Krasnokazarmennaya ulitsa	Краснoказарменная улица
Krutitskaya ulitsa	Крутитская улица
Kryukovskaya ulitsa	Крюковская улица
Nikoloyamskaya ulitsa	Николоямская улица
Nizhergorodskaya ulitsa	Нижергородская улица
Nizhniy Taganskiy tupik	Нижний Таганский тупик
Starokirochniy pereulok	Старокирочний переулок
Taganskaya ploshchad	Таганская площадь
Taganskaya ulitsa	Таганская улица
ulitsa Bolshie Kamenshchiki	улица Большие Каменщики
ulitsa Lefortovskiy val	улица Лефортовский вал
ulitsa Preobrazhenskiy val	улица Преображенский вал
ulitsa Radio	улица Радио
ulitsa Vostochnaya	улица Восточная
ulitsa Zemlyanoy val	улица Земляной вал

Metro stations

Aviamotornaya	Авиамоторная
Avtozavodskaya	Автозаводская
Baumanskaya	Бауманская

Metro stations

Izmaylovskiy Park	Измайловский парк
Kuskovo	Кусково
Kuzminki	Кузьминки
Marksistskaya	Марксистская
Preobrazhenskaya Ploshchad	Преображенская площадь
Proletarskaya	Пролетарская
Rimskaya	Римская
Ryazanskiy Prospekt	Рязанский проспект
Semyonovskaya	Семёновская
Taganskaya	Таганская

Museums

Andrei Rublev Museum of Early Russian Art	музей древне русской культуры им. Андрея Рублева
Antique Automobiles and Motorcycles Museum	Ломоковский музей старинных автомобилей и мотосиклов
Ceramics Museum	музей керамики
Country Estate Museum	музей русской Усадбы
Kuskovo	музей-усадьба Кусково
Kuzminki	Кузьминки
Lefortovo Museum	музей Лефортово
Museum of Furniture	музей Мебели

8

The Northern Suburbs

Moscow's **northern suburbs** lack the eclectic charm of the inner city, and even if you wanted to wander about, the distances are too vast. Instead, they have a scattering of interesting museums and sights that call for a targeted approach, relying on the metro to get you within striking distance of each attraction.

Foremost among them is the **VVTs**, a huge exhibition park that has been likened to a Stalinist Disney World, near the iconic Space Obelisk and Worker and Collective Farm Girl monument. The eighteenth-century **Ostankino Palace** – a shrine to aristocratic romanticism – stands not far away, as do Moscow's **Botanical Gardens** and **TV Tower**.

Nearer the centre of town, an odd assortment of museums and theatres merits a few sorties beyond the Garden Ring. The arts are represented by the **Museum of Musical Culture**, the fairytale **Vasnetsov House** and **Dostoyevsky's childhood home**; the **Durov Animal Theatre** offers one of Moscow's weirdest performances; and the Armed Forces Museum is a Mecca for armchair militarists. Also in this part of town are the **Lubavitch Synagogue** and the notorious **Butyrka Prison**.

Further west, you can see football or ice-hockey matches at the **Dinamo** or **TsKA** stadiums, or watch trotting-races at the **Hippodrome**. When the weather is fine, Muscovites come to swim, sunbathe and party at **Serebraniy bor**, a chain of lakes fringed by pine woods and *dacha* colonies.

Near the Garden Ring

There are two fascinating museums a few blocks **beyond the Garden Ring**: one within ten-minutes' walk of Triumfalnaya ploshchad (see p.153); the other further from Tsvetnoy Bulvar metro (see p.171). To visit them both, it's best to start with the Museum of Musical Culture, and then catch a trolleybus б further round the Ring to Sadovaya-Samotyochnaya ploshchad, for the Vasnetsov House.

The Museum of Musical Culture

Two blocks north of Sadovaya-Triumfalnaya ulitsa, at ulitsa Fadeeva 4, the composer Glinka lends his name to the **Museum of Musical Culture** (muzey muzykalnoy kultury imeni M.I. Glinki; Tues–Sun 11am–7pm; closed last day of each month; R50). It exhibits all kinds of beautifully crafted instruments from around the world. You can hear recordings of some of them being played if you book a foreign-language tour beforehand (price negotiable). The museum also hosts concerts, lectures and temporary exhibitions, and has an archive of scores by Glinka, Tchaikovsky, Rachmaninov and Prokofiev. Visit Ⓦwww.museum.ru/glinka for details.

The instruments are grouped according to their origins in colour-coded rooms, starting with pianos, guitars, zither-lyre hybrids and a rare crystal flute in the red Western European section. Dragon-embossed Buryat horns and Shamen's skin drums from Yakutia are found in the green hall, along with a nineteenth-century 22-piece silver horn band from western Russia. The yellow room brings together Moldavian hurdy-gurdies, gorgeously inlaid Caucasian stringed instruments and a huge bowl-shaped contrabass from Khirgizia. Casting its net still wider, the blue hall displays Eastern European and Oriental instruments, such as Polish bagpipes, Chinese drums and a horse-headed Korean *morinkhuur*. Look out for the **Termenvox**, one of the first electrophonic instruments, whose inventor, Lev Termen, demonstrated its sound to Lenin in the early 1920s. There's also a small **memorial room** devoted to the Russian conductor and violinist David Ostrakh, whose seventeenth-century Stradivarius viola was stolen from the museum in 1996, but recovered by the police in Sochi the following year.

The street on which the museum stands is named after Alexander Fadeev, a Stalinist literary bureaucrat who went on a drinking binge and shot himself after hearing Khrushchev's "Secret Speech" – overcome with remorse for the scores of writers who'd been shot or sent to the camps after his denunciations.

The Vasnetsov House

The **Viktor Vasnetsov House** (dom-muzey V.M. Vasnetsova; Wed–Sun 10am–5.30pm; closed last Thurs of each month; R160) is a delightfully archaic anomaly amid the tower blocks across the Ring from Tsvetnoy bulvar. To find it, cross beneath the flyover and head up the grass slope into a housing estate, turning left 50m later; the house at the far end of pereulok Vasnetsova is instantly recognizable by its timbered upper floor, with a *terem*-style belvedere above the entrance door. Its former owner was a key figure in the Russian revival style, who believed that "a true work of art expresses everything about a people … It conveys the past, the present and, perhaps, the future of the nation" and sought to express this in his own work. An architect as well as a painter, he designed the facade of the Tretyakov Gallery, a church for the artists' colony at Abramtsevo, and the wooden house in Moscow where he lived for 32 years until his death in 1926.

Its ground-floor rooms are furnished with tiled stoves, chairs and cabinets, designed by Vasnetsov himself. The pieces are massive but so delicately carved as to be fit for a boyar's palace. Echoes of medieval Russia abound, from pictures of processions to a chain-mail tunic, fixed to the spiral staircase leading to his studio. Its cathedral-like space is filled by huge paintings of warriors confronting monsters, and various Russian fairytales. One wall is dominated

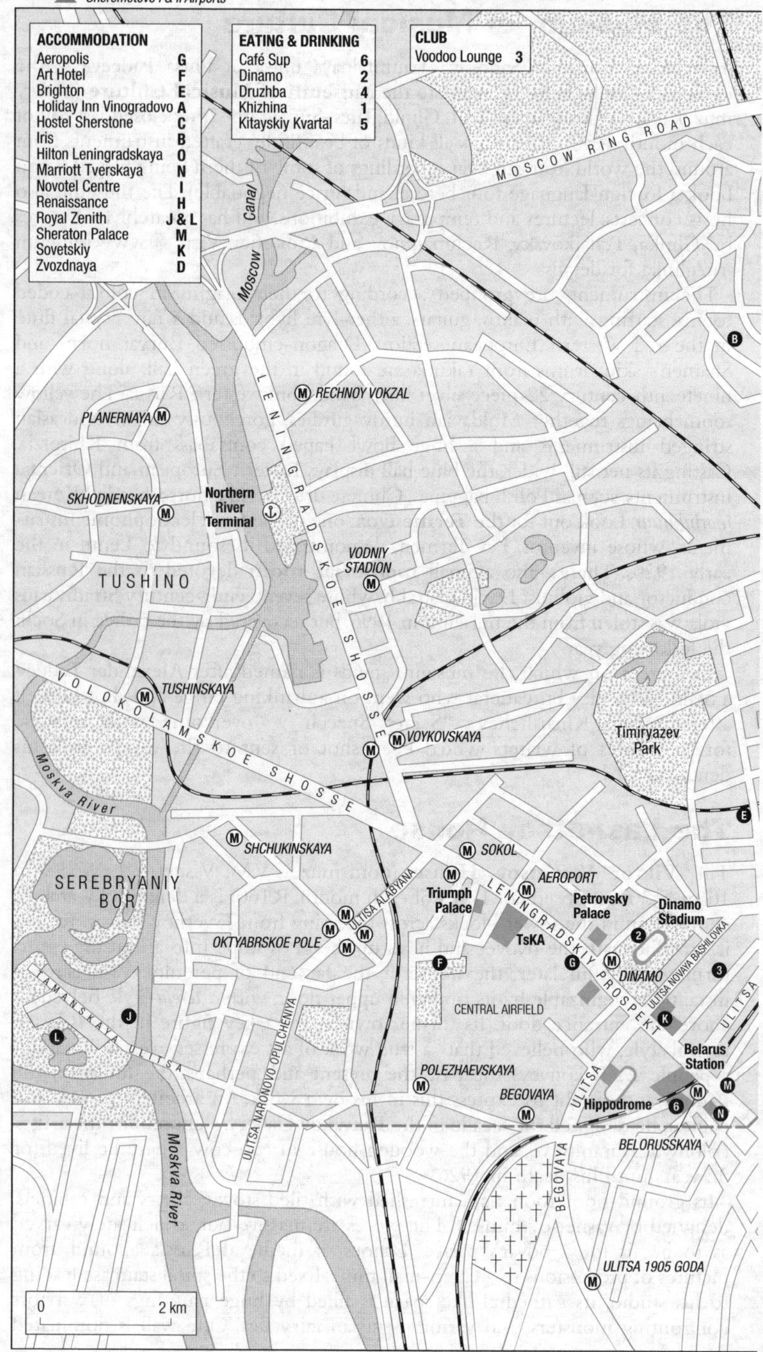
Sheremetevo I & II Airports
ACCOMMODATION
Aeropolis G
Art Hotel F
Brighton E
Holiday Inn Vinogradovo A
Hostel Sherstone C
Iris B
Hilton Leningradskaya O
Marriott Tverskaya N
Novotel Centre I
Renaissance H
Royal Zenith J & L
Sheraton Palace M
Sovetskiy K
Zvozdnaya D
EATING & DRINKING
Café Sup 6
Dinamo 2
Druzhba 4
Khizhina 1
Kitayskiy Kvartal 5
CLUB
Voodoo Lounge 3
MOSCOW RING ROAD
Canal
Moscow
RECHNOY VOKZAL
PLANERNAYA
LENINGRADSKOE SHOSSE
SKHODNENSKAYA
Northern River Terminal
VODNIY STADION
TUSHINO
TUSHINSKAYA
VOLOKOLAMSKOE SHOSSE
VOYKOVSKAYA
Timiryazev Park
Moskva River
SHCHUKINSKAYA
SOKOL
AEROPORT
SEREBRYANIY BOR
Triumph Palace
LENINGRADSKIY PROSPEKT
Petrovsky Palace
Dinamo Stadium
ULITSA ALABYANA
TsKA
OKTYABRSKOE POLE
DINAMO
ULITSA NOVAYA BASHILOVKA
CENTRAL AIRFIELD
TAMANSKAYA ULITSA
ULITSA
ULITSA NARONOVO OPULCHENIYA
Belarus Station
POLEZHAEVSKAYA
BEGOVAYA
ULITSA
Hippodrome
BELORUSSKAYA
Moskva River
BEGOVAYA
ULITSA 1905 GODA
0
2 km

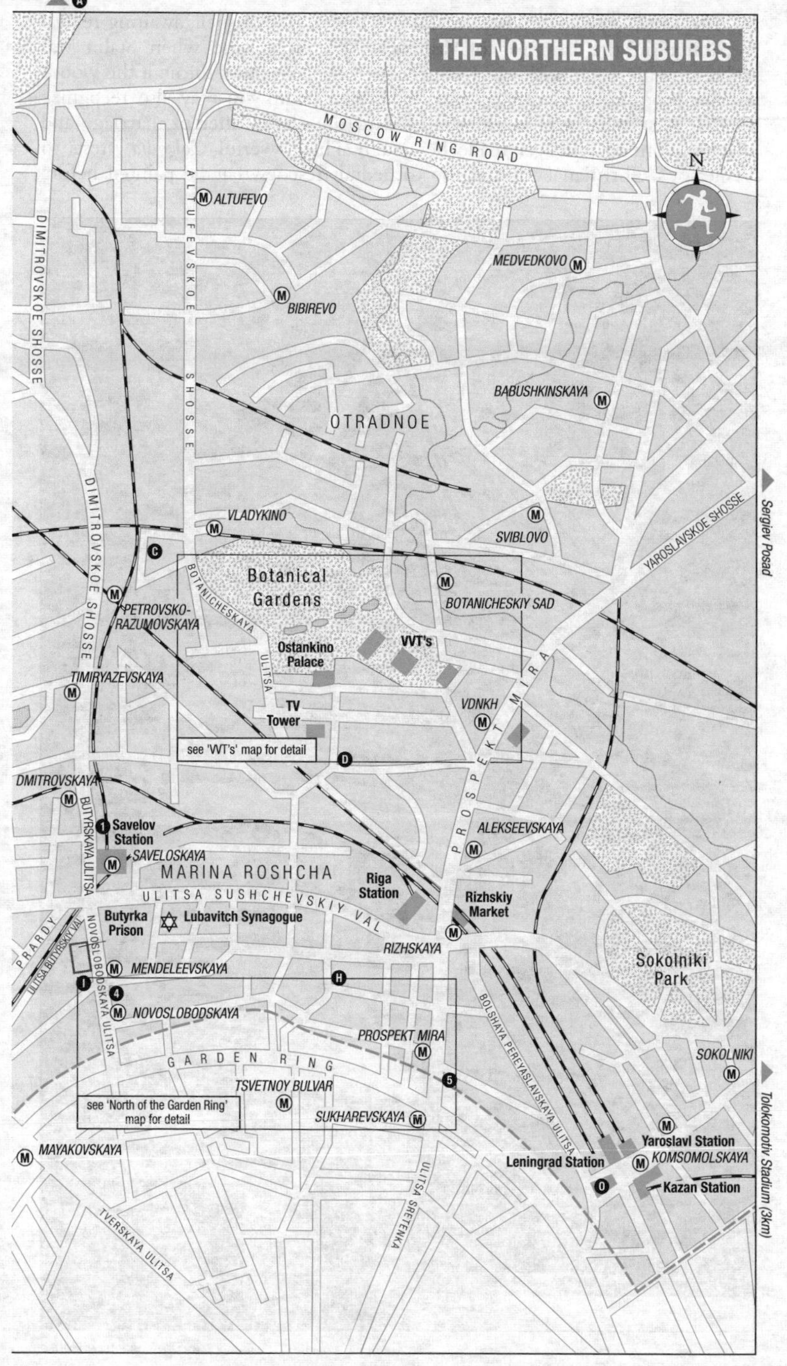
THE NORTHERN SUBURBS
MOSCOW RING ROAD
N
ALTUFEVO
ALTUFEVSKOE SHOSSE
DIMITROVSKOE SHOSSE
MEDVEDKOVO
BIBIREVO
BABUSHKINSKAYA
OTRADNOE
VLADYKINO
SVIBLOVO
YAROSLAVSKOE SHOSSE
Sergiev Posad
Botanical Gardens
BOTANICHESKAYA
BOTANICHESKIY SAD
PETROVSKO-RAZUMOVSKAYA
Ostankino Palace
VVT's
ULITSA
TIMIRYAZEVSKAYA
TV Tower
VDNKH
PROSPEKT MIRA
see 'VVT's' map for detail
DMITROVSKAYA
BUTYRSKAYA ULITSA
Savelov Station
SAVELOSKAYA
ALEKSEEVSKAYA
MARINA ROSHCHA
Riga Station
Rizhskiy Market
ULITSA SUSHCHEVSKIY VAL
Butyrka Prison
Lubavitch Synagogue
RIZHSKAYA
PRARDY
ULITSA BUTYRSKIY VAL
NOVOSLOBODSKAYA ULITSA
MENDELEEVSKAYA
NOVOSLOBODSKAYA
Sokolniki Park
BOLSHAYA PEREYASLAVSKAYA ULITSA
PROSPEKT MIRA
GARDEN RING
SOKOLNIKI
Tolokomotiv Stadium (3km)
TSVETNOY BULVAR
see 'North of the Garden Ring' map for detail
SUKHAREVSKAYA
MAYAKOVSKAYA
Yaroslavl Station
Leningrad Station
KOMSOMOLSKAYA
Kazan Station
ULITSA SRETENKA
TVERSKAYA ULITSA

by *The Sleeping Princess*, whose realm lies under an evil spell, awaiting revival – painted in the last year of Vasnetsov's life, at a time when Stalin was tightening his grip on Russia. In the corner, *Baba Yaga* flies through the woods on her broomstick, clasping a terrified stolen child; you may also recognize *Princess Nesmeyana*, whose glumness led to the classic offer of marriage and the kingdom to whoever made her laugh. The powerful *Golgotha* attests to Vasnetsov's Christian faith and the cathedral frescoes that he painted before

▲ The Vasnetsov House

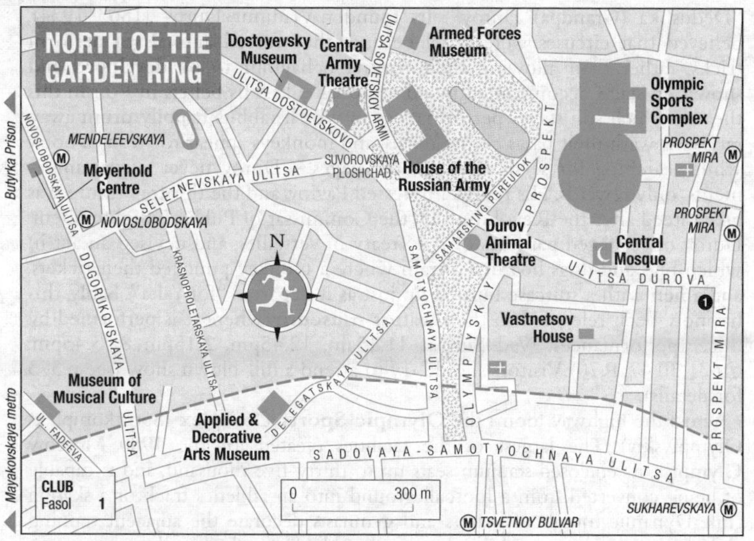

the Revolution (supposedly faithful copies of which can be seen in the reconstructed Cathedral of Christ the Saviour).

Around Suvorovskaya ploshchad

Other sights form a constellation around **Suvorovskaya ploshchad**, a conjunction of thoroughfares and parks named after the Tsarist General Alexander Suvorov, honoured by Russians for his triumphs over the Turks and Napoleon, and reviled by the Poles for crushing their revolt in 1830. To avoid offending their Warsaw Pact allies, the Soviet leadership didn't authorize a monument to Suvorov until 1982, when the declaration of martial law in Poland made such niceties irrelevant. Among the many local buildings connected with the army is the giant **Central Army Theatre**, whose star-shaped form is utterly unrelated to its function, and only apparent from the air. It's said that the design was the idea of the Moscow Party boss Lazar Kaganovich, doodling around his five-pointed inkpot. Completed in 1940, its facade combines aspects of the Colosseum and the Acropolis, while its Great Hall has a stage designed to allow battle scenes using real artillery and armoured cars, and a ceiling fresco of Olympian warriors and athletes.

Until the completion of two new stations in the vicinity (the date keeps slipping), **getting there** entails walking from Prospekt Mira or Novoslobodskaya metro station (worth seeing for its stained-glass panels) or the Vasnetsov House, which takes about fifteen minutes. Or you can take a #69 trolleybus directly from Novoslobodskaya metro to the Armed Forces Museum.

The Durov Animal Theatre, the Olympic Sports Complex and Central Mosque

The oddest sight is the bunker-like **Durov Animal Theatre** (teatr Zvery imeni Durova), a unique institution known to generations of Muscovites as

"Dedushka (Grandpa) Durov". Its founder, Vladimir Durov (1863–1934), believed that circuses were cruel because they forced animals to perform tricks, rather than allowing their natural behaviour to be developed and shown on stage, accompanied by educational talks. His beliefs live on in this theatre, which still stages performances in which rabbits happily drum away, raccoons wash their paws before meals, and monkeys appear to "read" a book while searching for seeds between the pages – Durov never used punishments, only rewards. His results impressed Pavlov, and the theatre's future was guaranteed after the Revolution by the Commissar of Public Enlightenment. Durov once staged parodies of the Treaty of Versailles, and devised an act in which pigs and dogs boarded a train where a monkey punched their tickets, and a hen with a suitcase bustled up just as it departed "for Yalta". Sadly, this has now been relegated to the theatre's **museum**, where it is performed by mice (performances: Wed–Sun at 11.15am, 12.45pm, 2.15pm & 3.45pm; ⓣ631 30 47; R70). Visitors should try to attend a full-blown show (see p.373 for details).

Across the highway looms the **Olympic Sports Complex** (Sportkompleks Olympiyskiy). The largest of the facilities created for the 1980 Moscow Olympics, its enclosed stadium seats up to thirty-five thousand, and is capable of being converted from a football ground into an athletics track or a skating rink. Dynamic murals of skaters and gymnasts decorate the adjacent training rink and gymnasium, while the smaller block to the north contains an Olympic-sized pool (see "Sports", p.395).

In the shadow of the stadium stands a neo-Russian edifice that's only recognizable as the **Central Mosque** (Tsentralniy mechet) by the Islamic crescents atop its domes. Such discretion is understandable given the fate of another mosque in Moscow whose Imam was shot on the premises by the NKVD, though this one was cynically permitted to continue working as "proof" that religious freedom existed in the USSR. Today, its Imam is spiritual head of the (mainly Sunni) Muslim communities of Moscow, Yaroslavl and Tver.

The Dostoyevsky Museum

The **Dostoyevsky Museum** (muzey-kvartira F.M. Dostoevskovo; Wed & Fri 2–7pm, Thurs, Sat & Sun 11am–6pm; closed last day of each month; R40) occupies a small, gloomy house in the grounds of the Mariya Hospital for the Poor, granted to Dostoyevsky's physician father when he worked here. As his salary wasn't enough to maintain the standards expected of them, the family was dogged by financial worries, compounded by the doctor's alcoholism and violence (he was eventually murdered by his own serfs). After Dostoyevsky himself died in St Petersburg in 1881, his widow and brother preserved many of his possessions as the foundation of the memorial museum opened in 1928, which now features a reconstruction of his childhood home, based on Dostoyevsky's own diaries and descriptions of his youth.

He and his brother shared a tiny room filled by steel trunks and a tiled stove where they played with toy soldiers and a hobby horse, and had their lessons at the card table in the living room. A drawing room was so crucial to the family's social standing that their parents were prepared to sleep in a narrow bed behind a screen, jammed beside a washstand and a baby's crib. The museum also exhibits the parish ledger recording Dostoyevsky's birth in 1821, and his quill pen and signature preserved under glass. If you're particularly interested in his life, it's possible to arrange a **guided tour** in English (R1200 group rate) by phoning a day or two ahead (ⓣ681 10 85).

The Armed Forces Museum

Off in the other direction from Suvorovskaya ploshchad, at ulitsa Sovetskoy Armii 2, the **Armed Forces Museum** (muzey Vooruzhennykh sil; Wed–Sun 10am–5pm; R70) is instantly recognizable by the T-34 tank and ballistic missile mounted out front, archetypal assertions of Soviet power that give no indication of how this bastion of ideological rectitude was shaken by the fall of Communism. One result is a sympathetic exhibition on the White Army, centred on a diorama of trench warfare in Eastern Siberia. Upstairs is devoted to the Great Patriotic War and features such emotive juxtapositions as a replica partisan hide-out, human hair and tattooed skin from Majdanek concentration camp, and a poster of a woman prisoner entitled *All hopes are on you, Red forces*. Victory is represented by a shattered bronze eagle from the Reichstag and the Nazi banners that were cast down before the Lenin Mausoleum in 1945 – as depicted in a huge painting.

The upbeat postwar section proudly displays the wreckage of an American U-2 spy-plane shot down over the Urals in 1960 (hall 20), and barely mentions the invasions of Hungary and Czechoslovakia. In the two rooms on Afghanistan, evidence of casualties and atrocities is confined to photo albums, easily overlooked beside the huge booster-stage of an SS-16 missile, which the Soviets agreed to scrap under SALT II. Don't miss the gleeful picture of the burning of Hitler's corpse, at the top of the stairs.

Parked around the sides and back of the museum is an array of hardware that includes an **armoured train** such as carried Trotsky into battle during the Civil War, and a **helicopter gunship** and an **Su-25** of the type used to slaughter Afghans in the name of Internationalism. If you're especially interested in military matters, it's worth pre-arranging a guided tour in English (R1500 group rate; ⓣ681 63 03).

Novoslobodskaya, Butyrka and Marina Roshcha

The **Novoslobodskaya** (New Settlement) district is going up in the world, with a *Novotel* and high-rise offices forming a new financial district, whose **Meyerhold Centre** sanctifies corporate leases with the inclusion of a venue for the performing arts, named after the great director killed during the purges (see p.117). Another locus is the **Russian State University for Humanities** (RGGU) on Miusskaya ploshchad, the country's first privately funded university – which distanced itself from its main donor, Khodorkovsky, after he was arrested in 2003. In the RGGU building at ulitsa Chayanova 15 is an exhibition of Moscow "underground" art of the 1950s and 1960s, collected by Leonid Talochkin, entitled the **Other Art Museum** (muzey Drugoe Iskusstvo; Wed–Sun 10am–5pm; R25). Elsewhere, Novoslobodskaya remains a sprawl of freight-yards and factories, whose high walls and watch-towers make them hard to distinguish from the prison with which Muscovites associate this part of the city.

Butyrka Prison

A grim huddle of blocks at Novoslobodskaya ulitsa 45, **Butyrka Prison** was founded by Catherine the Great as the point of departure for prisoners bound for hard labour in Siberia, who walked there in fetters along the Vladimir Road (named after the next prison en route). Muscovites always came to give them food and clothing and distribute alms at Easter. Before 1905, political prisoners were so rare that staff apologized to a Bolshevik who disliked the food. Later, Dzerzhinksy was lauded for being one of the few revolutionaries to escape from Butyrka – but as it was just after the fall of Tsarism he probably bribed a guard to let him walk out. There was no such laxity under Soviet rule when over 100,000 prisoners a year passed through Butyrka: a feat achieved by cramming 140 into a cell meant for 25, and 2000 men into the prison church. The demand for slave labour meant that most were fed into the maw of the camps, but the writer Babel was shot there in 1940, while the scientist Termen was lucky enough to end up in a *sharashka* (secret research centre) where survival was relatively easy.

Today, Butyrka is a pre-trial detention centre, or SIZO, like St Petersburg's Kresty Prison, where multi-drug-resistant tuberculosis and HIV are equally rife. Butyrka's facilities got a $2.5 million overhaul in 2002, and some progress has been made in reducing its inmates from 7000 to 3700 (the prison was designed for 2190), but prisoners are still packed 120–150 to a cell, where the temperature in summer reaches 50°C and their skin peels off because of the humidity. Inmates may have to wait up to five years before they receive a trial; some plead guilty to be sent to a camp where conditions are better. While public opinion has been inured to the need for penal reform by decades of rough justice and rampant criminality, the Justice Ministry has gone some way to meeting the agenda of NGOs in Russia and abroad, with assistance from the European Union. The prison has also stopped running its voyeuristic tours, and is no longer open to the public.

Marina Roshcha and the Lubavitch Synagogue

A couple of kilometres from Butyrka, **Marina Roshcha** was once a labyrinth of shacks where only the locals knew their way around and the police seldom ventured; where pious Jews rubbed shoulders with denizens of the *Blatnoi mir* (Thieves' World). A tale is attached to every grave in the local cemetery, such as the one that belonged to a youth who unknowingly impregnated his own mother and then married his daughter (whom he believed to be his adopted sister), inscribed: "Here lies father and daughter, brother and sister, husband and wife". Although the hovels were replaced by blocks of flats in the 1960s and its criminal subculture faded away, Marina Roshcha's Jewish heritage has endured in the form of the **Lubavitch Synagogue** (Mon–Fri: winter 10am–3pm; summer 10am–6pm). The only synagogue in the country built during the Soviet era (in 1926), the original wooden building was destroyed by arsonists in 1993 and the brick one that replaced it was bombed in 1996 – yet it continues to grow as a place of worship, with a community centre and dining room attached. Visitors are welcome during opening hours, but services (Wed–Fri 9am) are for worshippers. The synagogue is sited on 2-y Vysheslavtsev pereulok, a backstreet off ulitsa Sushchevkiy val, 15–20-minutes' walk from Mendeleevskaya or Savelovskaya metro station.

The VVTs and Ostankino

The star attraction of the northern suburbs is the All-Russia Exhibition Centre or **VVTs** (Vserossiyskiy Vystavochniy Tsentr) and its supporting cast of **iconic monuments** to Space, Industry and Collective Agriculture, their symbolism subverted by the collapse of the system they glorified and the triumph of capitalism. Grandiose Stalinist pavilions that once showcased Soviet products or technology are now full of imported toasters and televisions. Space exploration was once the USSR's trump card, and you shouldn't miss the Museum of Cosmonautics even if you forgo visiting the former home of the nation's top rocketry scientist, a time capsule of early 1960s interior decor.

When snow or rain isn't forecast, you can also enjoy the lovely **Ostankino Palace**, with its antique theatre and landscaped grounds, or wander through the groves and flowerbeds of Moscow's **Botanical Gardens**. While in the vicinity, you can't miss the giant **TV Tower** and Centre that were once headline news.

Getting there is easy. The VVTs, Space Obelisk, Cosmonautics Museum and Worker and Collective Farm Girl are all a few-minutes' walk from VDNKh **metro** station. From there, tram #11 and trolleybus #9 run along ulitsa Akademika Koroleva to the palace, which can also be reached by exiting the VVTs near the Outdoor Theatre and walking through Ostankino Park. There's also a well-marked pedestrian route from the VVTs to the Botanical Gardens further north.

The Space Obelisk and Cosmonautics museums

One of the boldest Soviet monuments, the **Space Obelisk** consists of a rocket blasting nearly 100m aloft on a stylized plume of energy clad in shining titanium. Unveiled in 1964, three years after Gagarin orbited the earth, this unabashed expression of pride in a unique feat rises from a base featuring tableaux of engineers and scientists striving to put a cosmonaut into his rocket, and Lenin leading the masses into space, as a woman offers her baby to the sun. In summertime, Moscow youths gather here to strum guitars.

Beneath the monument, a **Memorial Museum of Cosmonautics** (Memorialniy muzey Kosmonavtiki; currently closed for renovation) traces the history of rocketry and space exploration from the 1920s to the present day. Exhibits include the first rocket engine, created by Tsander and tested in 1931; models of missiles, satellites and moon-walkers; genuine spacesuits and space meals; photos of cosmonauts learning the art of working and eating in zero gravity at Star City, outside Moscow; and a fantastic collection of Soviet space posters.

Beyond the obelisk, a **statue of Konstantin Tsiolkovsky** (1837–1935), the "father of rocketry", gazes over an **Alley of Cosmonauts** flanked by bronze busts of space voyagers, while a humbler relic of the heroic era of Soviet space travel stands near the perimeter of the VVTs ten-minutes' walk away, at 6-y Ostantkinskiy pereulok 2/28. Only accessible on tours, the **Korolev House-Museum** (dom-muzey akademika S.P. Koroleva; Wed–Sun 11am–4pm; closed last Fri of each month; hourly tours; R600 group rate for up to 10 people) preserves the domicile awarded to the man who put Tsiolkovsky's theories into practice. Sergei Korolev began working on rockets in his early twenties and, like most of the early Soviet rocket scientists, was arrested in 1937–38. He continued his work in a *sharashka* and won his first state award the year he was released. During the heyday of Sputnik, Korolev was known to the public only as the Chief Designer, and his

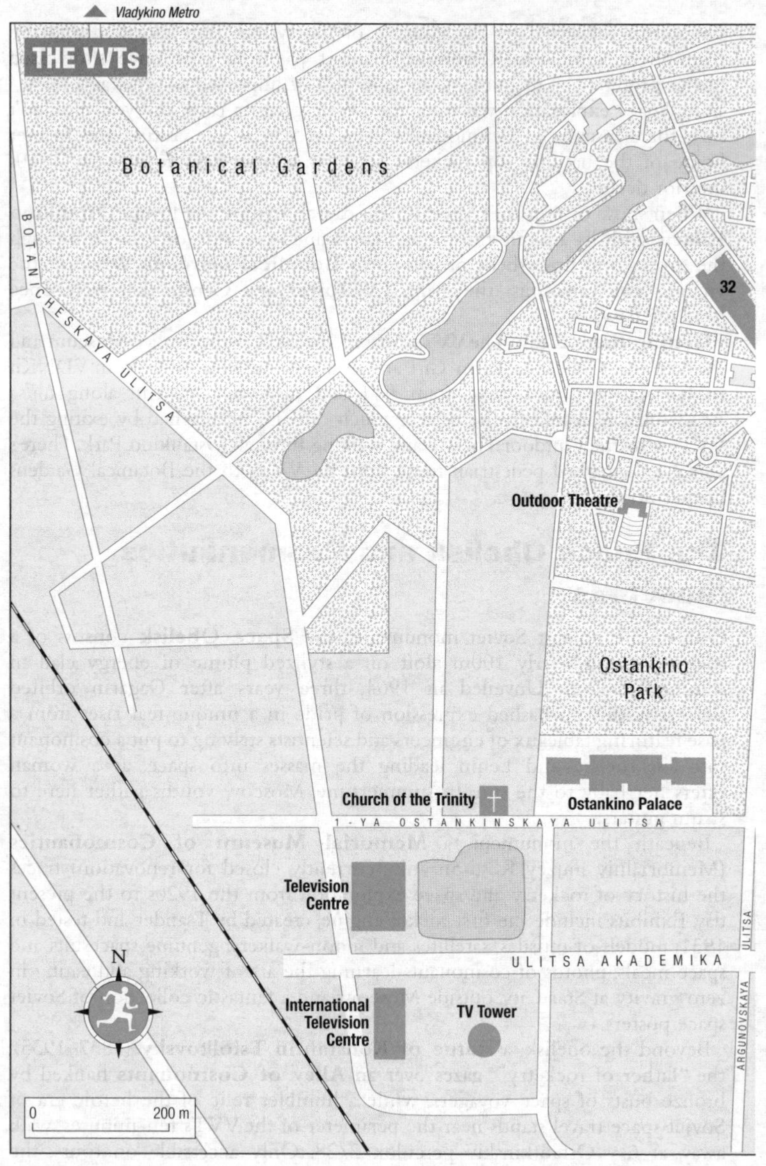

leadership wasn't widely acknowledged until after his death. On the sideboard in his living room stand models of spacecraft designs and a "medal tree" given to him by his co-workers, to display all his decorations. The multiple telephones – with direct links to the Kremlin, Star City and the Zhukovsky air base – are another sign of the status he enjoyed within the Soviet system.

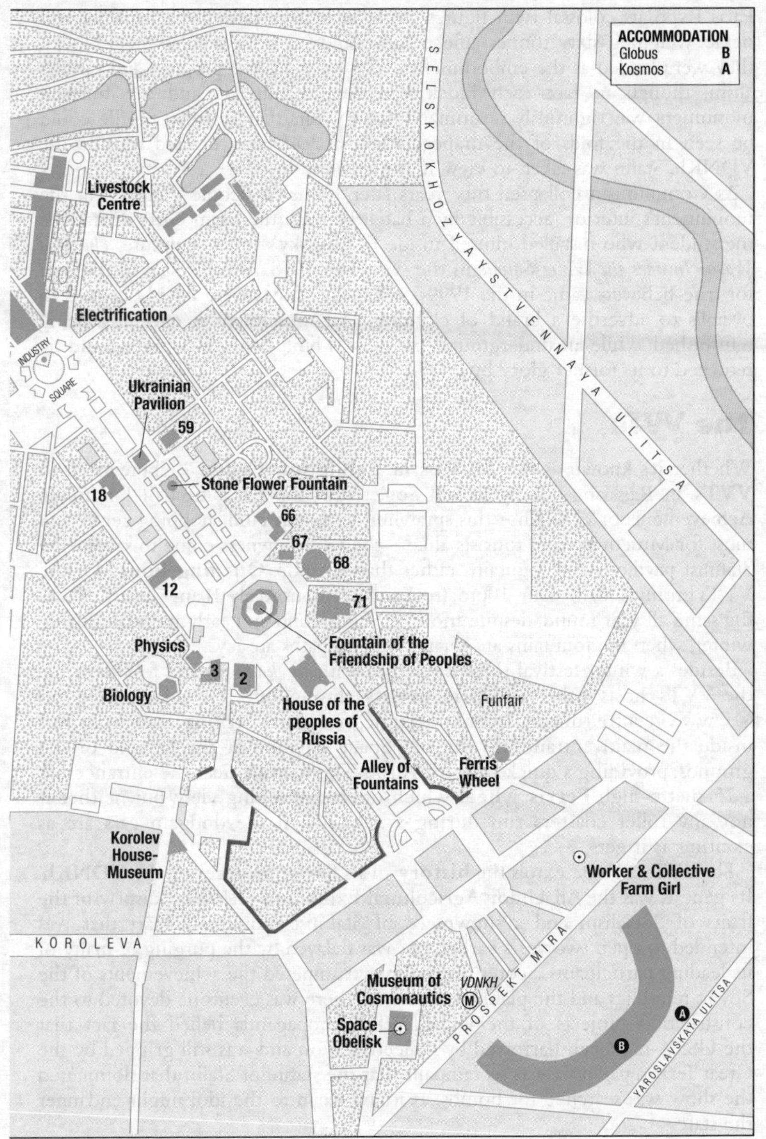

The Worker and Collective Farm Girl monument

In the other direction, past the main entrance to the VVTs, stands an even more iconic monument, the **Worker and Collective Farm Girl** (Rabochy i kolkhoznitsa). Designed by Vera Mukhina for the Soviet pavilion at the 1937

Paris Expo, its colossal twin figures stride in unison, raising the hammer and sickle. Weighing sixty tonnes apiece and fashioned from stainless-steel blocks, they were lauded as the embodiment of Soviet industrial progress and rationalism, though in fact each block had been handmade and the finished monument was rigorously scrutinized due to fears that Trotsky's profile could be seen in the folds of the drapery. Once it had been erected outside the VDNKh, Stalin was taken to view it at night, and loved it.

As Communism collapsed fifty years later, homeless people sheltered in the monument's interior (accessible by a hatch beneath the Farm Girl's skirts) like the student who installed himself inside El Lissitsky's street-sculpture *The Red Wedge Invades the White Square* in the winter of 1918. Another slap in the face for true-believers came in the 1990s, when the statues were illicitly dressed in overalls to advertise a brand of clothing. The monument is currently being refurbished, while an underground car park is built beneath it, and should be returned to its former glory by 2009.

The VVTs

Whether it's known as the **All-Russia Exhibition Centre** – abbreviated to **VVTs** in Russian – or by its old Soviet title, the Exhibition of Economic Achievements or VDNKh – this sprawling trade-fair cum shopping centre is a must for Muscovites and tourists alike – though foreigners come to savour the Stalinist pavilions and fountains rather than to shop. **Opening hours** for the VVTs grounds (daily 8am–10pm; free) and pavilions (daily 10am–7pm; free) are the same all year round, despite snow on the ground and early nightfall during winter, when the fountains are turned off and paths are icy.

Besides a winter festival (Dec 25–Jan 5) with *troyka* rides and folk dancing, the VVTs hosts other folkloric **events** throughout the year, posted on Ⓦwww.vvcentre.ru/eng. In summertime, miniature "**trains**" run from just inside the main entrance to the old Space Pavilion at the far end of the grounds, providing a quick tour for R100. The **funfair** near the entrance has a 75-metre-high **Ferris wheel** which offers a stunning view, but neither it nor any roller coasters run during winter, when the dodgem cars are as exciting as it gets.

The VVTs website extols the **history** of its Soviet predecessor, the **VDNKh**. Its genesis was the All-Union Agricultural Exhibition of 1939, a display of the fruits of Socialism and a showpiece of Stalinist monumental art that was intended to open two years earlier, but was delayed by the purging of many of its leading participants. Scores of pavilions trumpeted the achievements of the Soviet republics and the planned economy; there was even one devoted to the construction projects of the Gulag. While propaganda belied the fact that the USSR had been harrowed by collectivization and was still gripped by the Great Terror, paranoia was so rampant that the statue of Stalin that dominated the show was searched for bombs, as if any harm to the idol might endanger the state.

In the event, the exhibition was so successful that it was revived on a permanent basis in 1954, with some eighty pavilions over 578 acres. During Brezhnev's time, a tour of its pig farm was mandatory for every schoolchild, while canny Muscovites flocked to the Consumer Goods pavilion, previewing things they might hope to find in the future. By the 1980s Western goods were starting to appear and the Soviet pavilions lost whatever conviction they might once have possessed; in 1990 state funding ceased and the newly renamed VVTs was left to fend for itself. Historic spacecraft were sold to foreign museums and the animals in its livestock pavilions almost starved to death before the VVTs clawed its way to profitability in the new millennium.

The pavilions

A triumphal Soviet arch surmounted by smaller statues of a tractor driver and farm girl brandishing wheat-sheaves, the main entrance of the VVTs sets the scale for the avenue of fountains that follows, flanked by pavilions which used to have descriptive names that related to their contents, but are now identified by numbers. Don't bother stopping till you reach the **House of the Peoples of Russia**, a renamed Stalinist wedding-cake culminating in a 35-metre spire, reminiscent of the Admiralty in St Petersburg. Its interior once featured a huge illuminated map of the USSR, and dioramas of Lenin's home town and a hydroelectric power station in Siberia, but is now divided up into booths selling electrical goods and cosmetics, with a lame exhibition of folk art (R30 admission), and pictorial vestiges of workers and peasants upstairs. A **statue of Lenin** still beckons imperatively in front of the building – a photo opportunity if ever there was one.

Beyond lies an octagonal square focused on the **Fountain of the Friendship of Peoples**, whose gilded statues of maidens in the national costumes of the sixteen Soviet republics demurely encircle a golden wheat sheaf. When operating, the basin erupts into 800 jets of water sprayed 24m into the air, illuminated at night by 525 spotlights.

Of the nine pavilions here, most are monuments to Soviet science which have been denuded of their original exhibits and filled with goods for sale. **Pavilion #71** once held a small working atomic pile, whose rods glowed underwater; its portico fresco depicts women and babes picking fruit, promising Eden rather than Chernobyl. The fruit-laden facade of the former Coal Industry exhibition barely finds room beneath its pediment for a miner and a teacher, and is now **Pavilion #68**, where you can sample Armenian wines and cognacs for R150–400 a glass.

▲ Fountain of the Friendship of Peoples

A splendid wooden frieze of lumberjacks and farmers toiling in the wilderness fronts the old Press building, now full of Karelian furniture and numbered as **Pavilion #67**. Even finer is **Pavilion #66** (still nominally dedicated to Culture), fronted by a star-like pagoda and tiled arabesques derived from the mosques of Central Asia. Architects felt encouraged to draw on ethnic motifs by Stalin's pronouncement that art should be "national in form, socialist in content". His own homeland, Georgia, is represented in **Pavilion #2** by a lavish range of wines and brandies, while the facade of **Pavilion #3** is patterned like a Caucasian rug.

The Soviet taste for mineral extravagance runs riot with the mosaic-encrusted **Stone Flower Fountain**, flanked by spouting geese and fish, like a fountain at one of the Imperial palaces outside St Petersburg. Even wilder are the pavilions beyond. The columns of **Pavilion #18** are wreathed in mosaic ribbons of Soviet heraldry, giving no clue that it was once devoted to Electrotechnology, while the Agriculture building, crenellated with ears of corn and crowned by a rotunda with a gilded spire, has reverted to being the **Ukrainian pavilion**, as it was in 1939, when it boasted of abundance while Ukraine was still depopulated and half-starved after collectivization. On either side of its fruit-heavy portal, statues of husky peasants enthuse over the harvest and Stalin's wisdom. Similar motifs adorn the entrance to **Pavilion #59**, formerly dedicated to Grain and now selling gold jewellery.

At the far end of the avenue, two Soviet **passenger airliners** are open for inspection in the summer, but the scene is stolen by a **Vostok rocket** of the type that carried Gagarin into orbit, suspended from an enormous gantry outside the former Space Pavilion. Once the VDNKh's glory but now merely **Pavilion #32**, its hangar-like interior echoes with the sound of trolleys laden with imported TVs, and not a trace remains of the spacecraft or the giant portrait of Gagarin that once wowed visitors. Retired cosmonauts still live in *dachas* beside Ostankino Park.

Ostankino Palace

Moscow's **Ostankino Palace** (Ostankinskiy dvorets; May–Sept Wed–Sun 11am–7pm except on very rainy days; R80) is inseparably linked to the story of Count Nikolai Sheremetev, his love of the theatre and Parasha Kovalyova, a serf girl on his Kuskovo estate whom he first set eyes on as she was leading a cow home from the woods. Tutored in the dramatic arts, she became a gifted opera singer with the stage name of "Zhemchugova" (from the Russian word for "pearl"), and the prima donna at Ostankino, a palace specially built for staging performances. Its grandeur and theatricality were epitomized by a reception staged for Tsar Paul in 1795. As he rode through the woods, dozens of pre-sawn trees suddenly fell aside to reveal the palace in all its glory. Remarkably, the whole palace is made of wood, disguised beneath a stucco veneer; for fear of fire, it has never been electrified or centrally heated – which is why the palace is only open five months of the year.

Guided tours in Russian (R150) run every thirty minutes, starting with an exhibition on the Sheremetev family, which owned three million acres and 300,000 serfs and preserved its fortune by bequeathing the lot to the eldest son instead of dividing it between several heirs – a custom maintained until Nikolai's grandsons agreed to take equal shares. On the left of the columned hall beyond is a portrait of Parasha, visibly pregnant with Count Nikolai's child; she died twenty days after giving birth, whereupon he revealed that they had secretly married three years earlier, after fourteen years of living together out of wedlock.

Beyond the hall lies the **Italian Pavilion**, a large room sumptuously decorated with Classical motifs made from tiny pieces of paper glued together, with fake marble columns and bronze sconces, and a superb parquet floor of mahogany, birch and ebony. A vaulted **Gallery** awash with fake malachite and gilded sphinxes provides a suitably dramatic approach to Ostankino's *pièce de résistance* – the **Theatre** where the Count staged performances by 200 serf actors, trained since the age of seven. As it stands today the hall is configured as a ballroom, but was designed so that the floor could be lowered and the chandelier lifted into the ceiling, where a copper sheet reflected its light onto the stage; the columns could be moved around, and there were ingenious devices for simulating the sound of rain and thunder (which still work) and lightning flashes. **Concerts** of classical music are held here three times a week in June, July and August (Ⓣ683 46 45 for details).

Visitors may also see the **Egyptian Pavilion**, with its pseudo-Pharaonic statues, but the rest of the upper floor is still being restored, having been occupied and looted by one of Napoleon's generals in 1812, and last inhabited in 1856. The palace was subsequently allowed to decay until Soviet times, when it was opened as a Museum of Serf Art in recognition of the fact that it was designed and built by serf artisans. Finally, you can roam the formal **gardens** behind the palace, featuring a Hill of Parnassus and numerous copies of antique statues.

Beside the road in front of the palace stands the **Church of the Trinity** (tserkov Troitskiy), whose elaborate *nalichniki*, *kokoshniki*, and blue-and-gold ceramic insets are typical of the Moscow Baroque style of the 1680s. Commissioned by the Cherkassky family which owned this land before the Sheremetevs, the church was at one time connected to the palace by a covered walkway, and served as its private chapel.

What really happened at Ostankino?

Nobody who was in Moscow at the time can forget the **battle of Ostankino** on the night of October 3/4, 1993, when a mob of parliamentary supporters tried to seize the TV Centre. The national news channel announced "We're under attack" and then went off the air, leaving millions of Russians convinced that it had fallen to Yeltsin's enemies in a *coup d'état*. Only those with access to CNN were aware that it remained in government hands despite an eight-hour battle in which over sixty people died, till the army moved in to crush the rebels in the White House the next day – an action justified as a legitimate response to the attack on Ostankino.

Though this scenario was widely accepted then, a more sinister one has emerged. Contrary to initial reports, the TV Centre was defended by 450 elite troops and six armoured vehicles, while the attackers had only twenty Kalashnikovs and one grenade launcher between them. Of the 65 fatalities (including TV cameramen and pensioners), only one was inside the building – all the rest died outside. The cessation of transmissions was ordered by the Kremlin, to heighten the sense of crisis. When one also considers the mysterious lack of OMON on the streets, how easily the rebels seized a fleet of trucks with ignition keys, and that their column was escorted to Ostankino by Special Forces' armoured cars, it becomes clear that they were lured into a trap, giving Yeltsin the pretext to crush parliament while posing as a champion of democracy. Even then, some commanders baulked at being used in what they saw as a political fight, and in units that obeyed his order, soldiers were briefed that Chechens were attacking parliament and policemen were being hanged from lampposts.

The TV Centre and Tower

Across the road from the Church of the Trinity, a large ornamental pond and vistas of concrete surround the glassy **Ostankino Television Centre**, a complex of studios at the base of a **TV Tower** (Telibashnya) whose 35,000 tonnes of ferroconcrete taper from 50m in diameter at the base, to a needle-like shaft 540m high – making it the tallest freestanding structure in Europe. Heralded as proof of Soviet technological prowess when it was constructed in 1967, the TV Tower became yet another symbol of Russia's decline when it caught **fire** in August 2000. Fire-fighting efforts were hindered by the discovery that the central part of the tower was not linked to the automatic fire extinguisher system, as the architects' plans had specified. As a result, Russia was briefly without a national television system, and the choice of channels for Muscovites was severely restricted for months. It also deprived tourists of the bird's-eye view of the VVTs and Moscow from 337m up, formerly provided by an observation deck and the revolving restaurant *Seventh Heaven*. Prior to its "towering inferno" notoriety, Ostankino was best known abroad for its role in the 1993 battle between Yeltsin and parliament (see box, p.283).

The Botanical Gardens

As an alternative to Ostankino, you could walk from the VVTs past the aptly named Golden Spike amid a chain of ornamental lakes named after the plant scientist Michurin, into Moscow's tranquil **Botanical Gardens** (Botanicheskiy sad; May–Oct daily 10am–8pm; Nov–April 10am till dusk; R30). Laid out in 1945 as part of the postwar beautification of Moscow, the 860-acre park is centred on groves of birches and 200-year-old oaks to delight the Russian soul, and rose gardens planted with sixteen thousand varieties of blooms. Access to its tropical Orangerie, Japanese Garden and Dendarium is by individual ticket (R40), or on hourly **guided tours** in Russian (40min; R100). The Botanical Gardens originally boasted of the pseudo-scientific triumphs of the notorious Stalinist agricultural biologist, Trofim Lysenko, whose theory that "environmental characteristics" were inheritable distorted Soviet biology for over twenty years.

Other locations

The appeal of most of the Northern Suburbs' other locations depends on the weather or your interest in sports. The **beaches** at Serebraniy bor are the place to relax or party in summertime, Sokolniki Park is fun for **winter sports**, and you can watch **premier-league matches** on Leningradskiy prospekt or horse-racing at the Hippodrome any season. Alternatively, if **Stalinist monuments** are your thing, Komsomolskaya ploshchad, near Krasnye vorota, or the Moskva Canal upriver from Serebraniy bor, could be just the ticket.

Komsomolskaya ploshchad

Despite its earnest name, **Komsomolskaya ploshchad** (Young Communists Square) is one of Moscow's grungiest localities, dominated by three main-line stations swarming with provincial visitors, hustlers and drunks.

From being merely disreputable in Soviet times, it has sunk to a level of squalor akin to the notorious pre-Revolutionary Kalchanovka Market that used to exist on what was then "Three Stations Square". Yet it's worth coming here just to see the majolica decor of the vestibules and surface pavilion of **Komsomolskaya metro** station, opened in 1935 – even if you don't set foot on the square.

The pavilion stands between two railway termini. **Yaroslavl Station** (Yaroslavskiy vokzal), built in 1902–04, is a bizarre Style Moderne structure with Tatar echoes, whose hooded arch sags with reliefs of Arctic fishermen and Soviet crests. In 1994, it was here that Solzhenitsyn arrived back in Moscow twenty years after his deportation from the USSR, and promptly denounced the post-Soviet Babylon outside. Further west is **Leningrad Station** (Leningradskiy vokzal), a yellow-and-white Neoclassical edifice with a modern annexe around the back.

Directly opposite, the spectacular **Kazan Station** (Kazanskiy vokzal) was designed by Shchusev in 1912 but only completed in 1926. Its seventy-metre spired tower (based on the citadel in the old Tatar capital of Kazan), faceted facade and blue-and-gold astrological clock have led many a yokel stumbling off the train to ask if this was the Kremlin.

At the end of the square nearest the Garden Ring looms the Gothic-spired **Leningradskaya Hotel**, a pocket-sized Stalin skyscraper that represents the functional nadir of Soviet architecture, utilizing only 22 percent of its space. After Stalin's death, architectural excess came in for criticism, and in 1955 the architects of the hotel were deprived of their Stalin Prizes. The lobby is well worth a peek but you won't want to stay there (see p.333).

Sokolniki Park

After Komsomolskaya ploshchad, **Sokolniki Park**, several kilometres to the north, comes as light relief. Laid out in 1930–31, as Moscow's second "Park of Culture and Rest", it used to welcome citizens with martial music blaring from loudspeakers at the entrance, but was nevertheless cherished for its "emerald paths" through the old Sokolniki Woods, named after the royal falconers (*sokolniki*) who lived here in the seventeenth century. Nowadays the park swarms with Muscovites bound for the cash-and-carry warehouses at one end, but people also come to go jogging or enjoy more traditional pleasures. Off behind the cafés facing the *Étoile*, pensioners meet in a glade for outdoor ballroom **dancing** on Sunday afternoons (weather permitting); while in the woods near the central pavilions is a special **chess** corner, where matches are played against the clock. In winter you can go **ice-skating** or cross-country **skiing**; gear is rented on the spot. The Exhibition Pavilions are used for international trade fairs; at the first US–Soviet exhibition in 1959, Khrushchev and the then Vice-President Nixon had a famous, impromptu "washing machine debate" over the superiority of their respective systems.

Leningradskiy prospekt

Leningradskiy prospekt is one of Moscow's major arteries, leading to Sheremetevo Airport. Before the Revolution it was the road to the Imperial capital of St Petersburg, subsequently renamed Leningrad. After World War II, the avenue was transformed into an eight-lane motorway flanked by monumental apartment blocks, superseded by humbler "*Khrushchoby*" flats and newer, high-rise estates further out. Beside the highway at Khimiki, a monument in the form of giant anti-tank "hedgehogs" marks the spot where the Nazi advance on Moscow was halted.

A continuation of 1-ya Tverskaya-Yamskaya ulitsa, the prospekt begins at ploshchad Belorusskovo Vokzala, named after **Belarus Station** (Belorusskiy vokzal) on the western side of the square. If you happen to be in the area, it's worth crossing the square to take a look at the **Armenian Church** on the corner of ulitsa Butyrskiy val. Its golden dome and giant mosaic *Image of the Saviour not Made by Human Hands* are offset by white walls and severe lines reminiscent of Pskovian architecture; the murals and icons inside are Armenian in spirit, reflecting the fact that the church was built for Old Believers in 1914, it was never used as such due to war and revolution, until Moscow's Armenian community made it their own in the 1990s.

The Hippodrome

Moscow's **Hippodrome** (Ippodrom) racecourse is a world unto itself. Its monumental Stalinist grandstand is as down-at-heel as the spectators at its *troyka* races – a killjoy Soviet substitute for "bourgeois" flat-racing, with jockeys riding light gigs instead of horses. Yet *troyka* racing still has a devoted following; the illegal betting, race fixing and doping that made it so raffish in Soviet times now seem quaint compared to the murders that have afflicted Russian football clubs in the post-Communist era. You don't have to enjoy racing to find it interesting; anyone studying Russian can vastly improve their knowledge of *mat* (obscenities) by spending an hour here. To get into the spirit, buy a plastic cup of vodka before heading up the backstairs to the highest tier of the stands. In 2004, they were sanitized for the inaugural race for the Prize of the President of Russia, an event based on the Tsar's Prize last staged for Nicholas II in 1916. Competing for the $100,000 purse were horses entered by the presidents of Armenia, Azerbaijan, Georgia, Kazakhstan, Kyrgyzstan and Ukraine, and Russia's regional governors. A strict dress code and tickets costing $660 kept out the hoi polloi. The race is now an annual fixture on the first weekend in June. Regular racing events are detailed under "Sports" (p.395).

The hippodrome is located 500m down **Begovaya ulitsa** (Running St), a turning off Leningradskiy prospekt 1km beyond Belarus Station. Catch any bus from there in the right direction, alighting just after another side street flanked by twin statues of horses. Some buses turn off Begovaya ulitsa near the **Botkin Hospital**, where Lenin underwent an operation in 1922 to remove a bullet that had remained in his body since an assassination attempt in 1918.

Between Dinamo and Aeroport metro

The 1500-metre stretch of Leningradskiy prospekt between Dinamo and Aeroport metro stations is interspersed by sporting venues. **Dinamo Stadium** is home to Russia's oldest football club (founded in 1887), which was renamed Dinamo by Dzerzhinsky and later patronized by Beria, becoming the model for postwar secret police teams throughout the Eastern bloc. To learn more about the club, visit the **Dinamo Museum** (Mon–Thurs 10am–1pm & 2–6pm, Fri 10am–4pm; R40) in front of the north stand, which has some Dzerzhinsky exhibits on the first floor and a display about the great 1960s goalie Lev Yashin upstairs, plus a **shop** selling Dinamo strips and memorabilia. A fantastic Georgian **restaurant** patronized by football-mad oligarchs can be found near Gate #10 (see p.357).

Further from the metro stands the **Petrovsky Palace**, founded by Catherine the Great as a rest house for travelling royalty, which was a refuge for Napoleon at the height of the fire of 1812. An early work by Kazakov, the U-shaped palace is enclosed by crenellated walls and outbuildings; its red brick and white masonry prefigure his design for Catherine's Gothic summer palace at Tsaritsyno. During the nineteenth century it was fashionable for the rich to show off their carriages or *troykas* here, while bourgeois families picnicked on the grass with samovars. Until a few years ago it housed the Zhukovsky Air Academy, whose alumni include the aircraft designers Mikoyan and Ilyushin and the cosmonauts Gagarin and Tereshkova: a deluxe **hotel** is under construction here, due to open in 2010.

Nicholas II was the last monarch to stay at the palace for his ill-fated coronation in May 1896, when disaster struck on **Khodynka Field** across the road, which had been chosen as the site for the traditional distribution of gifts. The arrival of the beer wagons coincided with a rumour that the souvenir mugs were running out, causing a stampede in which more than 1500 people were trampled to death. In Soviet times, Khodynka Field became Moscow's first civilian airport, the **Central Airfield**, which is nowadays used by sports flyers.

Further on towards Aeroport metro, the sprawling grounds of the **Central Army Sports Club** – or **TsKA** – are synonymous with the soccer and ice-hockey teams better known abroad as CSKA. The football club remains in the premier division as it has for decades, but the ice-hockey club has slipped so far down the league that its bosses recently resorted to the old Soviet method of conscripting talented players into the army and transferring them to the Moscow team. Their former club, Omsk, was especially annoyed that TsKA waited until their three desired players were in Moscow for a match, and thereby saved the expense of transporting them to the capital.

Beyond TsKA and further off the highway, the colossal **Triumph Palace** is one of several new skyscrapers to echo Stalin's "Seven Sisters", and casts a whole neighbourhood of the city into perpetual shadow.

The Moscow Canal and Serebryaniy bor

Further out past the Khimkinskoe Reservoir, the **Northern River Terminal** (Severniy rechnoy vokzal) is the point of departure for ships to St Petersburg and the Volga cities. The spired terminus – fifteen-minutes' walk from Rechnoy Vokzal metro – was inaugurated upon the completion of the 128-kilometre-long **Moscow Canal** joining the Moskva and Okha rivers to the Volga, constructed (1932–37) shortly after another canal joining Leningrad to the White Sea set the precedent for using mass forced labour. Mostly peasants convicted of being *kulaks*, or rich exploiters, they toiled all winter in thin jackets, using only hand tools and wheelbarrows; up to 500,000 died from cold and exhaustion. Needless to say, the two colossal **statues of workers** that ennoble the canal banks near Vodniy Stadion metro look well fed and pleased with themselves. **Khimiki Hospital #1** on the northern shore of the canal is thought by Bulgakov scholars to be the model for Stravinsky's clinic, where the Master is confined.

The final leg of the canal drops through two locks to join the Moskva River just upstream of **Serebryaniy bor**, a recreation area named after its giant silver pines, some of which are over two hundred years old. Besides these there are colonies of wooden *dachas* and various bathing and fishing lakes, with a **nudist beach** that gets more gay-friendly as you move towards the end of the peninsula. In summer the area is inundated with visitors at weekends, and in June, when it stays light till 11pm, there are daily beach parties and discos. From May to October **motorboats** ply the river between the Strogino and Serebryaniy bor-4 landing stages, calling at several points en route, including the village of Troitse-Lykovo, where **Solzhenitsyn** lived after returning to Russia and died in August 2008.

To reach Serebryaniy bor, take the metro to Sokol station and then trolleybus #65 to Serebryaniy bor-2 landing stage, at the end of the line.

Streets and squares	
Begovaya ulitsa	Беговая улица
Komsomolskaya ploshchad	Комсомольская площадь
Leningradskiy prospekt	Ленинградский проспект
pereulok Vasnetsova	переулок Васнецова
prospekt Mira	проспект Мира
Sadovaya-Triumfalnaya ulitsa	Садовая-Триумфальная улица
Seleznevskaya ulitsa	Селезневская улица
Suvorovskaya ploshchad	Суворовская площадь
ulitsa Fadeeva	улица Фадеева
2-y Vysheslavtsev pereulok	2-й Вышеславцев переулок
Metro stations	
Belorusskaya	Белорусская
Cherkizovskaya	Черкизовская
Dinamo	Динамо
Komsomolskaya	Комсомольская
Novoslobodskaya	Новослободская
Polezhaevskaya	Полежаевская
Prospekt Mira	Проспект Мира
Rechnoy Vokzal	Речной вокзал
Rizhskaya	Рижская
Shchukinskaya	Щукинская
Sokolniki	Сокольники
Tsvetnoy Bulvar	Цветной булвар
Tushinskaya	Тушинская
VDNKh	ВДНХ
Museums	
Armed Forces Museum	музей Вооруженных Сил
Dinamo Museum	музей Динамо
Dostoyevsky Museum	музей-квартира Ф.М. Достоевского
Memorial Museum of Cosmonautics	Мемориальный музей космонавтики
Museum of Musical Culture	музей музыкальной культуры им. М.И. Глинки
Ostankino Palace	Останкирский дворец
Viktor Vasnetsov House	дом-музей В.М. Васнецова

Out of the City

Out of the City

Outside Moscow

Beyond Moscow's outer Ring Road, forests of birch trees or conifers are interspersed by colonies of gaily painted *dachas* – the clapboard cottages where Muscovites relax at weekends or rusticate over summer – juxtaposed with the pretentious villas of the nouveaux riches, and run-down villages where cows roam the muddy lanes. By venturing out of the city, you'll glimpse the vast gulf between Moscow and its ramshackle hinterland, a disparity that underlies the duality of life in Russia and the national psyche – without which, neither can be understood. The chief reason to venture to the city's outer reaches is the glorious **Trinity Monastery of St Sergei**, a Kremlin-like citadel better known in the West as "Zagorsk", after the Soviet-era name of the town in which it is located, 75km northeast of Moscow. A bit closer to the capital is the former artists' colony of **Abramtsevo**, a lovely estate, where most of the big names of late nineteenth-century Russian art painted the local landscape and created fairytale buildings that still stand. While both can be enjoyed by anyone, the appeal of the other sites is more particular. If stately homes and parks are your thing, there is the romantic, half-ruinous **Arkhangelskoe** estate, and Lenin's country retreat at **Gorki Leninskie**. Lovers of the arts will be drawn to Tchaikovsky's home in **Klin** or Pasternak's *dacha* in **Peredelkino**, while those into military history can tread the famous battlefield of **Borodino**, and even see the battle re-enacted in September.

Practicalities

It's possible to visit all the places in this chapter as **day-trips**, using **public transport** or an organized tour. Getting there yourself costs very little, but requires patience and some knowledge of the language. Many of the sites are accessible by a suburban line (*prigorodnye poezda* or *elektrichka*) train from one of the big main-line stations in Moscow, some of which have separate ticket offices and platforms for these services. Their frequency varies from every forty minutes to two hours, with longer intervals in the afternoon, so it's easy to waste time hanging around. This is also a problem with sites that are accessible by bus from an outlying district of the city. If you don't speak Russian, get somebody to write your destination in Cyrillic to show to ticket-sellers and fellow passengers. Foreigners with a car will find that the highway junctions on the Moscow Ring Road (MKAD) are clearly numbered, but side turnings off the main roads can be hard to identify.

To avoid such hassles, check out the **excursions** offered by Patriarshy Dom Tours (see p.46), whose monthly programme covers all the main sites, as scheduled in leaflets distributed at the *Starlite Diner*, *American Bar & Grill* and elsewhere; bookings should be made 48 hours in advance (Ⓣ&Ⓕ795 09 27, Ⓔalanskaya@co.ru). Note that most tours are fairly infrequent (once a

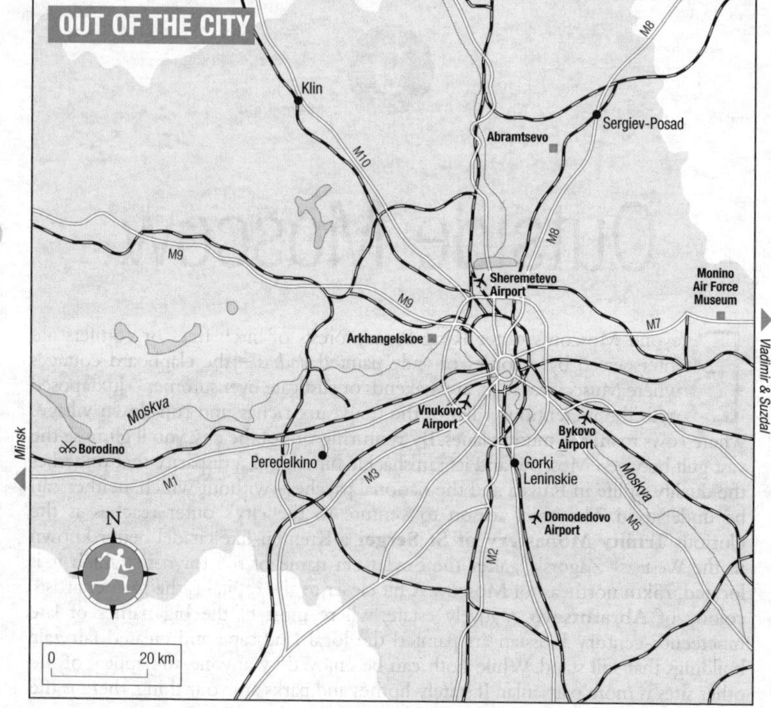

month or so), although the popular excursion to the Trinity Monastery runs every fortnight.

The range of places to eat outside Moscow is limited, or nonexistent at some locations, so it's wise to bring a snack.

The Trinity Monastery of St Sergei

Of all the monasteries in Russia, none is holier than the **Trinity Monastery of St Sergei** (Troitse-Sergeeva lavra), a bastion of Orthodoxy that was a place of pilgrimage for tsars and peasants alike. Even Stalin recognized its spiritual potency by allowing the monastery to reopen in 1946 as a reward for the Church's support in wartime; for decades afterwards it was one of the few surviving vestiges of Holy Russia in an avowedly atheist state.

The monastery is named after **St Sergei of Radonezh** (c.1321–91), who is said to have cried from his mother's womb while in church, refused to consume milk on Wednesdays or meat on Fridays as a baby, and had a vision of a hooded figure who explained the Bible to him as a child (depicted in a famous painting by Nesterov in the Tretyakov Gallery; see p.220). Forsaking a diplomatic career to become a hermit in the forest with his brother, he later urged Prince Dmitri Donskoy to fight the Tatars at Kulikovo, blessing his army as it left Moscow.

After Sergei's death the Tatars sacked the monastery, but his body miraculously survived to become the focus of a cult, resulting in his canonization in 1422 and the reconstruction of the monastery.

In 1552, Abbot Bassyan persuaded Ivan the Terrible to mount a last assault on the Tatar stronghold of Kazan, succeeding where seven attempts had failed. In the **Time of Troubles** the monastery was besieged for sixteen months by thirty thousand Poles, whose cannonballs bounced off its walls. Later, it was here that young tsars Peter and Ivan hid from the Streltsy in 1685; and where the seventeen-year-old Peter again sought refuge during his struggle with the Regent Sofia.

In recognition of his debt Peter showered the monastery with gifts, while his daughter Elizabeth awarded it the title of *lavra* – the highest rank of Orthodox monasticism, held by only three other monasteries in the Tsarist empire. Though Catherine the Great was also keen on pilgrimages to the Trinity Monastery, she had no qualms about confiscating its huge estates in 1763, reproving the clergy with the words: "You are the successors of the Apostles, who were very poor men." Nevertheless, it was the centre of Holy Russia until 1920, when the Bolsheviks closed it down and sent the monks to the Gulag. To add insult to injury, the surrounding **town** of Sergeiovo was renamed **Zagorsk** in 1930, after the Bolshevik "martyr" Vladimir Zagorsky – the name it bore until 1991, when it was changed to **Sergiev Posad** (Sergei's Settlement). Despite having grown into an industrial town of over 100,000 people, the centre is still dominated by the *lavra*, whose panoply of towers and domes rivals the Kremlin's.

Visiting the monastery

Traditionally, rulers on **pilgrimages** took six or seven days to get to the monastery, resting at palaces and hunting on the way. Tsar Alexei's party was preceded by two hundred messengers, with a dozen horses pulling the tsaritsa's carriage, followed by a smaller gold one containing the infant Peter – while the pious Alexei chose to emulate ordinary pilgrims by walking to the monastery, which was believed to purify one's spirit. Though few Russians go to such lengths today, many old folk arrive with nothing to sustain them but a hunk of bread, and even day-trippers often fast or abstain from sex beforehand.

Without a car, the easiest way of **getting there** is a Patriarshy Dom **tour** (R1040, plus admission charges), usually scheduled twice a month on Fridays, which spends about three hours at the monastery. To stay longer or pay less, catch one of the buses to Sergiev Posad that leave from Metro Station VDNkH (every 30min 8.30am–7.30pm; 40min), bus #388, or a train from the Yaroslavsky train station (every 30min) – the fastest is the "Fyodor Chizhov" train (40min). Be sure to retain your ticket to be able to leave the station upon your return. Arriving in Sergiev Posad, it's 10–15-minutes' walk from the bus or train station to the monastery.

The monastery is **open** daily from 10am to 6pm (free), though its churches are closed to the public at weekends, and its museums on Monday. Inside the gate is a kiosk selling photo permits (R200). You'll need separate tickets to visit the museum and sacristy, and these are sold on the spot; don't feel obliged to do so, however, as neither compares with the monastery itself. Visitors must dress decorously (no shorts), and are forbidden to take photos inside the museums and churches, or smoke in the grounds. **Guided tours** of the grounds by English-speaking monks cost R550 per person, and don't cover the museums.

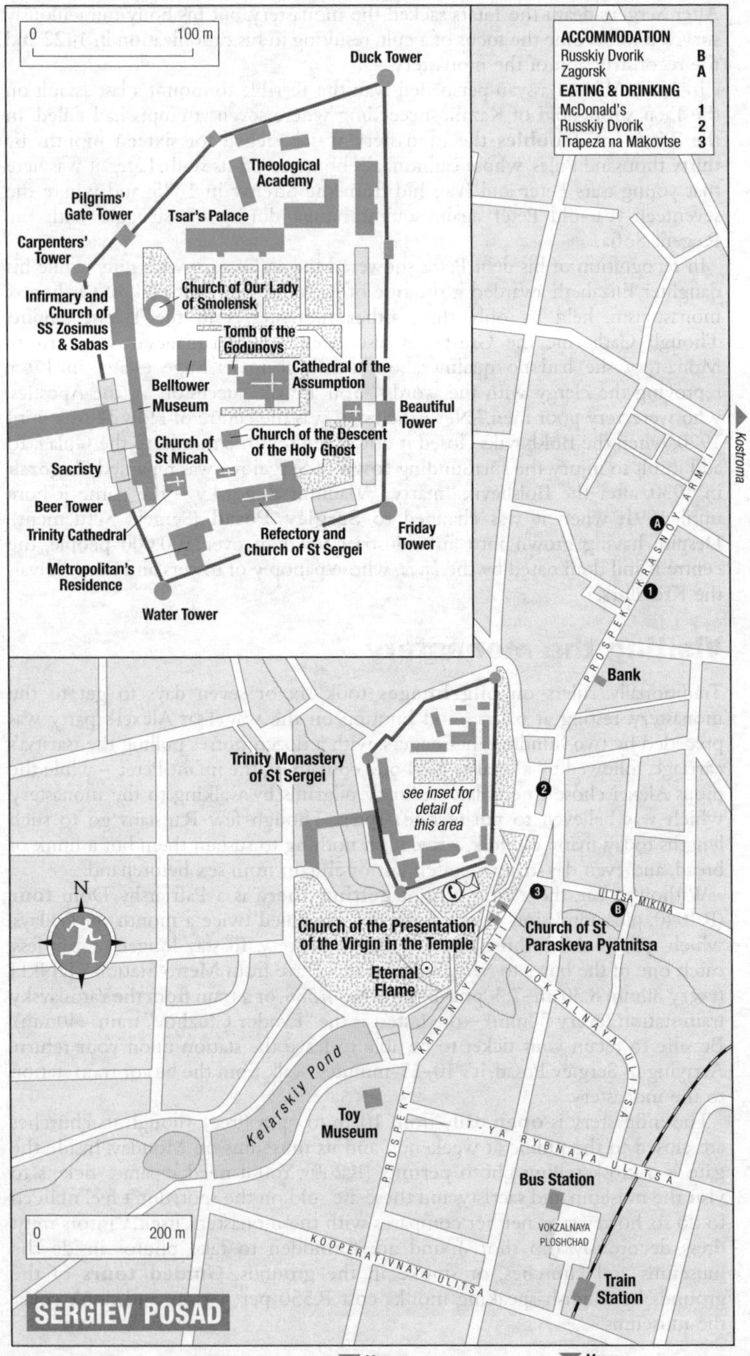

0
100 m
ACCOMMODATION
Russkiy Dvorik B
Zagorsk A
EATING & DRINKING
McDonald's 1
Russkiy Dvorik 2
Trapeza na Makovtse 3
Duck Tower
Theological Academy
Pilgrims' Gate Tower
Tsar's Palace
Carpenters' Tower
Church of Our Lady of Smolensk
Infirmary and Church of SS Zosimus & Sabas
Tomb of the Godunovs
Cathedral of the Assumption
Belltower Museum
Beautiful Tower
Church of the Descent of the Holy Ghost
Church of St Micah
Sacristy
Beer Tower
Trinity Cathedral
Refectory and Church of St Sergei
Friday Tower
Metropolitan's Residence
Water Tower
Kostroma
PROSPEKT KRASNOY ARMII
Bank
Trinity Monastery of St Sergei
see inset for detail of this area
N
ULITSA MIKINA
Church of the Presentation of the Virgin in the Temple
Church of St Paraskeva Pyatnitsa
Eternal Flame
VOKZALNAYA ULITSA
Kelarskiy Pond
Toy Museum
1-YA RYBNAYA ULITSA
Bus Station
0
200 m
VOKZALNAYA PLOSHCHAD
KOOPERATIVNAYA ULITSA
Train Station
SERGIEV POSAD
Moscow
Moscow

Prospekt Krasnoy Armii is the place to head for **food**, where you can choose from *McDonald's*, at no. 194, or two tourist-oriented restaurants nearer the monastery: *Russkiy Dvorik*, at no. 134 (Ⓣ49 654 451 14), is often full of groups, while *Trapeza na Makovtse*, further down (Ⓣ49 654 411 01; daily 11am–9pm), has a fine view of the monastery's walls from its outside tables but slightly higher prices (around R1000 for a full meal). If you want **to stay**, the small, comfy, rustic-style *Russkiy Dvorik* at ulitsa Mitkina 14/2 (Ⓣ49 654 753 92, Ⓕ753 91, Ⓔrus_dvornik@conternet.ru; R4800) is far better than the soulless *Zagorsk Hotel* (Ⓣ49 654 242 26; R4200) at Krasnoy Armii prospekt 171. There's a post

▲ The Refectory at the Trinity Monastery of St Sergei

and **telephone** office near the south wall of the monastery; you can change **money** at *Bank Moskyi* (Mon–Sat 9.30am–5pm), Krasnoy Armii 190, or at the exchange office in the *Zagorsk Hotel*.

The lavra complex

The *lavra* is enclosed by brick **walls** 1.6km in circumference, which replaced the original wooden ramparts in 1540–50 and were doubled in height a century later, when tent-roofed spires were added to six of the twelve towers (as happened to the Kremlin around the same time). A gate in the bronze-mantled **Beautiful Tower** and a tunnel painted with scenes of Sergei creating his hermitage in the wilderness bring you out below the **Gate-Church of St John the Baptist**. Built by the Stroganov boyars in 1693, its terracotta walls, Venetian scallops and gilded domes pale before the glorious buildings ahead, whose harmony belies their "picturesque carelessness of arrangement".

The **Refectory** (Trapeznaya), just inside the gates, resembles a gaudy version of the Faceted Palace in the Kremlin, with painted red, orange, pistachio and grey facets, and slender columns entwined in carved vines. In the late nineteenth century the British traveller Augustus Hare found four hundred monks dining in its vaulted hall, glittering with gold and "smelling terribly of the cabbage they adore". These days the hall is only used for ceremonies and is often locked.

The cathedrals

Across from the Refectory looms the majestic **Cathedral of the Assumption** (Uspenskiy sobor), similar in shape to its namesake in the Kremlin, but with four azure onion domes clustered around a huge gilded one. Begun by Ivan the Terrible to honour the fall of Kazan, it was completed in 1585 by his imbecile son Fyodor – a cat's paw of the regent, Boris Godunov, who succeeded him as tsar. It's indicative of their bad name that the **tomb of the Godunovs** is half-sunk into the ground outside the church, while dozens of Golitsyns, Trubetskoys and other nobles are entombed inside.

In the nave, a Tsarist eagle commemorates the moment in 1685 when the Streltsy found Peter's mother and her two sons hiding behind the iconostasis, and were about to kill them when a mutineer shouted "Comrades, not before the altar!" and loyal cavalry arrived to rescue them.

Downhill stands the **Church of the Descent of the Holy Ghost** (Dykhovskaya tserkov), whose walls are girdled by a band of intricate fretwork, tapering into a belltower with a blue-and-gold, star-spangled dome. Built by craftsmen from Pskov in 1476–77, it is unusual for having its bells in the base of the tower, which was used as a lookout post in the days when the monastery walls were much lower.

Before the walls were raised in the sixteenth century, the white stone **Trinity Cathedral** (Troitskiy sobor), near the southwest corner, was the tallest structure in the monastery. Erected in 1422–23, it pioneered the use of *kokoshniki* – the leitmotif of Muscovite church architecture – and inspired the "gold-topped" Cathedral of the Assumption in the Kremlin. The nave is astir with believers queuing up to kiss a silver shrine containing the **relics of St Sergei**, and tourists jostling to see the **iconostasis**, three rows of which were painted by Andrei Rublev, Daniil Cherny and their artel. The copy of the *Old Testament Trinity* that replaces the original (now in the Tretyakov Gallery) was donated to the monastery by Ivan the Terrible. In the southeast corner is the Chapel of St Nikon, built over the tomb of Sergei's successor, Nikon of Radonezh.

Behind the cathedral is an eighteenth-century Metropolitan's Residence that served as the home of the Patriarch of All Russia from 1946 until 1988, when the Danilov Monastery (p.232) became the Patriarchal seat.

Chapels, towers and museums

Between the cathedrals, you can't miss the small octagonal **Chapel over the Well** (Nakladeznaya chasovnya), whose pillars and *nalichniki* are carved with flowers and vines, offset by blue arabesques and white seraphim. The chapel was built over a spring discovered by the monks in 1644, and today its interior (daily 8.30am–5pm) is packed with people filling bottles with holy water, and murals of divine miracles. You can also drink from a fountain beneath a pillared **pavilion**, outside.

Building continued into the late eighteenth century, when Prince Ukhtomsky erected an 88-metre **Belltower** (Kolokolnitsa), whose five turquoise-and-white tiers are equal in height to the surrounding churches, and which once boasted fifty bells – the largest weighing 65 tonnes. Ukhtomsky also built the rounded Baroque **Church of Our Lady of Smolensk**, with its pilastered facade and gold finial, to house an icon of the same name. Off to the left stand the former **Infirmary** and **Church of SS Zosimus and Sabas**, dating from the 1630s; this church is the only one in the monastery with a tent-roofed spire.

En route to SS Zosimus and Sabas you'll pass the ticket office for the **History Museum** (10am–6pm; closed Mon & the last Tues of each month; R200). The best of the many icons on the ground floor is Simon Ushakov's *Venerable Nikon of Radonezh*, painted in the 1670s. Upstairs is more interesting, with two English coaches belonging to former metropolitans; some arresting royal portraits (notice Peter's first wife Yevdokiya to the right as you enter); and a surfeit of gold plate, pearl-encrusted mitres and robes. More of the same can be seen in the monastery's **sacristy** (riznitsa), now described as an **Art Museum** (10am–6pm; closed Mon & the last Wed of each month; R200).

From June to August, visitors can enjoy exploring the **ramparts** between the **Beer Tower** and the **Carpenters' Tower** – except on Tuesdays and Wednesdays. Otherwise, bear right at the green-spired **Pilgrims' Gate Tower** to reach the former **Tsar's Palace** (Tsarskie Chertogi). Constructed in the late seventeenth century for Tsar Alexei and his entourage of 500, its elongated facade is patterned with red-and-mauve facets and crested *nalichniki*. It is now a seminary, which includes an offshoot for young women bent on marrying priests, where they're taught housekeeping. The ceiling of the main hall bears a fresco of the triumphs of Peter the Great, who, while sheltering here in 1685, relaxed by shooting fowl from what was henceforth called the **Duck Tower**, and decorated with a bronze duck.

Other sights

The square outside the monastery hosts a lively market in religious artefacts and handicrafts. Off to the right downhill are the gold-domed **Church of St Paraskeva Pyatnitsa** – dedicated to the "Friday Saint" revered in Orthodox countries – and the **Church of the Presentation of the Virgin in the Temple**, likewise built in 1547. Further along, past an Eternal Flame to the dead of World War II, the Kelarskiy Pond is rimmed by garden walls, offering splendid views of the monastery, and frequented by artists in summer. On the far side of the pond, in a red-brick edifice at pr. Krasnoy Armii 15, the **Toy Museum** (muzey Igrushki; 10am–5pm; closed Mon, Tues & the last Fri of each month; R100) boasts a fine collection of historic toys. It was a local artist who invented the ubiquitous *matryoshka* doll, and there's still a tradition of toy making in the town. You can buy all kinds in the market or the souvenir section of the museum.

Abramtsevo

If the Trinity Monastery redeemed Russia's soul in medieval times, the **Abramtsevo** estate helped define it during the nineteenth century, when disputes between Slavophiles and Westernizers dominated cultural life. Indeed, Abramtsevo was acquired by the devout Slavophile writer Aksakov because of its proximity to the *lavra*, which made it an apt meeting place for like-minded, devoutly Orthodox intellectuals. The estate's next owner, the millionaire Mamontov, was equally passionate about Russian culture, supporting an **artists' colony** that gave rise to Russia's modern art movement. Many of the works in the Tretyakov Gallery – by Repin, Serov, Vrubel and the Vasnetsov brothers – reflect their shared interest in medieval architecture, folk art and mythology – as do the fairytale buildings on the Abramtsevo estate, whose rolling woodlands have been depicted on canvas more than any other landscape in Russia. And on a humbler but more pervasive note, it was at their Children's Education Workshop that Sergei Malyutin produced the first *matryoshka* doll, in 1890.

Practicalities

Abramtsevo lies about 6km south of Sergiev Posad; the turn-off is clearly signposted. By **car**, follow the road to Khotkovo and bear left before the Convent of the Intercession (where St Sergei's parents are buried). En route to the estate you'll pass a big pond; the entrance to the grounds is further uphill. Most (but not all) **trains** from Yaroslavl Station to Sergiev Posad stop at Abramtsevo en route; from the station, it's a pleasant twenty-minute country walk to the estate. There are regular **buses** from Sergiev Posad to Abramtsevo (20min).

To avoid a wasted journey, phone ahead (Ⓣ254/324 70) to verify that the estate is **open** (10am–5pm; closed Mon, Tues & the last Fri of each month; R150), as it sometimes shuts in April and October. The charm of the estate is best appreciated by wandering around the outbuildings constructed by the artists, which lead you away from the main house. Summer or autumn are the best times to visit. Bring a picnic.

The main house

Knowing that Chekhov used the main **house** as a model for the manor in his play *The Cherry Orchard* raises your expectations of the plain, grey-and-white clapboard building. The interior (which can still be visited) is a vivid reflection of its former owners: **Sergei Aksakov** (1791–1859) was a friend of Gogol (who wrote part of *Dead Souls* here) and a foe of Westernizers such as Herzen, who mocked him for wearing "a dress so national that people in the street took him for a Persian". In 1870, the house was bought by the railroad tycoon **Savva Mamontov** (1841–1918) and his wife Elizabeth, who vowed to continue its traditions and preserved half of the house as Aksakov had left it – hence the different decors in each wing. While the Slavophile Aksakov shared the mid-nineteenth-century gentry's taste for French Empire, the worldlier Mamontovs preferred neo-Russian and Style Moderne.

Across the way is a larger white building housing an **exhibition** of modernist paintings by Aristakh Lentulov, Robert Falk and other artists of the Soviet era who also worked at Abramtsevo, with graphics such as Alimov's illustrations for *Dead Souls* and *The Master and Margarita* upstairs.

The outbuildings

More alluring is the tiny wooden **studio**, with its fretwork roof, where the painters Serov and Vrubel tried their hands at ceramics. The small Egyptian and Russian figures on display here presage Vrubel's bas-relief for the *Metropol Hotel* in Moscow, while the tiled stove epitomizes the colony's interest in old Russian applied arts. Peasant crafts were a major source of inspiration: the kitchen now displays part of their collection of artefacts (including cake moulds and ironing boards) as a **Museum of Folk Art**.

Their vision of an ideal cottage was realized in the **Teremok**, or guest house, whose steep roof and gable call to mind the *podvore* of medieval Muscovy. It is

▲ Church of the Saviour Not Made by Human Hand, Abramtsevo

furnished with heavy, carved furniture, like the Mamontovs' section of the main house. Further into the woods you'll come upon the **House on Chicken Legs**, built by the Vasnetsov brothers for the estate's children to play in. A tiny hut on chunky stilts, the house is based on the fairytale cottage of Baba Yaga, which shuffled around to face trespassing kids who uttered the words "*Izbushka, izbushka, povernis k mne peredom, a k lesy zadom*" ("Little House, Little House, turn around to face me with your back to the woods") – just before she flew out and threatened to eat them.

The whole colony collaborated on the **Church of the Saviour Not Made by Human Hand**, a diminutive structure based on medieval churches at Novgorod, whose strong lines and whitewashed walls are softened by curvaceous ogees and tiled friezes. The icons were painted by Repin, Polonev, Nesterov and Apollinarius Vasnetsov, whose brother Viktor designed and laid the mosaic floor in the form of a spreading flower, while Vrubel made the tiled stove, and the pulpit was painted by Andrei Mamontov, who died as a child and was buried in a vault to the left of the nave.

The **woods** beyond are a quintessentially Russian mixture of birch, fir, oak, larch, elder and hazel, with sedge creeks and ponds marking the course of the Vorya River.

Arkhangelskoe

During the heyday of the Russian aristocracy in the late eighteenth and early nineteenth centuries, the epicurean ideal of enjoying life to the hilt reached its apotheosis at **Arkhangelskoe**, the suburban estate of **Prince Nikolai Yusupov** (1751–1831). So rich that he was unable to count all his properties without the aid of a notebook, Yusupov collected art, dabbled in science, discussed philosophy with Voltaire and poetry with Pushkin, and kept a harem at Arkhangelskoe. Herzen recalls the 80-year-old Prince "sitting in splendour, surrounded by beauty in marble and colour, and also in flesh and blood". He opened his art collection and grounds to the public, but his private theatrical performances reputedly included nude dancing.

Arkhangelskoe's allure for visitors has waned since the palace was closed for repairs in 1989, and its appeal now lies mainly in the beauty of the park, dotted with pavilions and statues – best seen in summer, when its roses are blooming; in winter, the statues are encased in boxes to prevent them from cracking in the cold. Although a wing of the palace has now been opened to the public, the rest is only partially accessible on guided tours, or to those attending private conferences (which is how the museum is raising money for further repairs).

Practicalities

Arkhangelskoe is 22km west of central Moscow. **Getting there** entails taking the metro to Tushkinskaya station, and then a half-hour journey by bus #549 to the "Arkhangelskoe" stop, or minibus #151 to the "Sanatorium" stop. Drivers should follow Leningradskiy prospekt to Sokol, turn onto Volokolamskoe shosse and follow this out beyond the Moscow Ring Road, before heading left along Ilyinskoe shosse, which runs alongside the western edge of the estate.

Before travelling, it's worth checking that Arkhangelskoe is **open** (Ⓣ363 13 75; Ⓦwww.arkhangelskoe.ru; summer 10am–6pm; winter 10am–4pm; closed Mon, Tues & the last Fri of each month; R170), in case a conference is

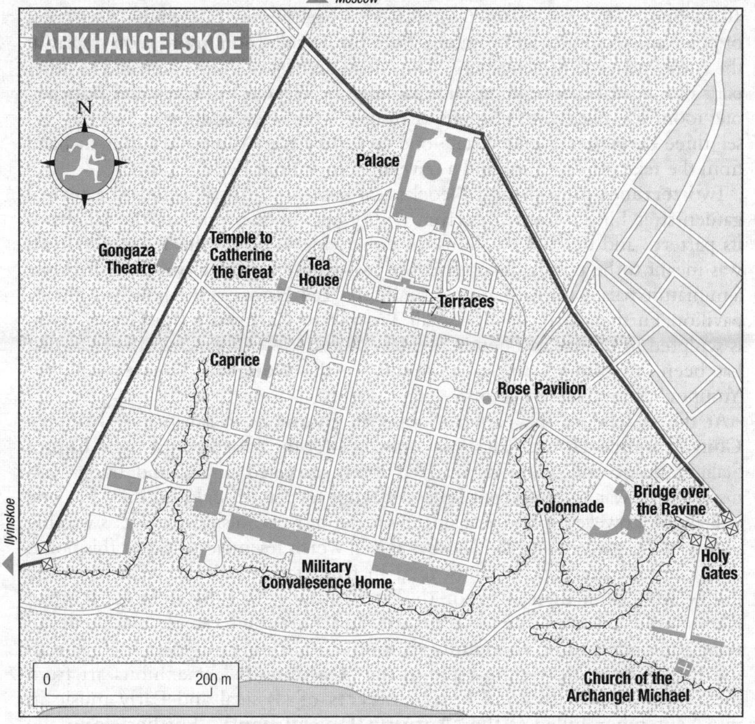

scheduled. The grounds are accessible by gates at the southwest and southeast corners, where *kassa* sell tickets for the palace (see below). The museum offers several guided **excursions**, some of which visit otherwise off-limits parts of the palace – but the group rate (up to fifteen people) for foreigners is exorbitant (R3300 for a tour in Russian; R4000 in English or German).

Around the estate

Although the estate dates back to the 1670s, its features recall the era of Catherine the Great, who put Prince Nikolai Golitsyn in charge of the building project. When Golitsyn died in 1809, his heirs sold the estate to Yusupov, who continued with the project undaunted by a serf riot in 1812 and a fire in 1820. Embodying five decades of Neoclassical architecture and interior design, the palace and pavilions were near to completion when Yusupov himself died in 1831, whereupon the estate was neglected until the early years of the twentieth century, when it had a brief revival. In 1919, the Bolsheviks decreed Arkhangelskoe a public museum; a military convalescence home was built in the grounds after World War II.

Today the estate stands on shaky ground, for although a protected reserve, the land belongs to the Ministry of Defence, which has granted developers leases on tracts of woodland, where trees have been felled to build luxury houses. Meanwhile, the museum depends on corporate sponsors to fund the restoration of the long-neglected **Palace**. So far, only the **Kontorsky Wing** (Kontorskiy fligel; Wed–Fri

10am–5pm, Sat & Sun 10am–6pm; R50) has been restored to exhibit a selection of porcelain, sculptures and paintings from his art collection (more is on display at the family palace in St Petersburg). The wing's decor is nothing compared to other parts of the palace, once hung with paintings by Tiepolo, Van Dyck and Boucher; one room was filled with portraits of Yusupov's mistresses and lovers. You can also see three **carriages**: a gilded state one owned by Irina Yusupova, a four-in-hand from the reign of Tsar Paul, and a travelling coach from Pushkin's time.

Two **terraces** topped with Neoclassical busts and urns descend to a formal garden stretching towards the river, with grape arbours running the length of its parterre and derelict pavilions on either side. Whereas the **Rose Pavilion** was meant to be purely decorative, the two-storey **Caprice** was furnished like a miniature palace for garden soirées, and the **Tea House** started out as a library pavilion. Further north stands a small **Temple to Catherine the Great** – who is sculpted in bronze as Themis, goddess of justice – while across the road that has been cut through the estate you'll see the **Gongaza Theatre** built for Yusupov's troupe of serf actors.

At the far end of the parterre looms an enormous Palladian-style **Military Convalescence Home** that's easily mistaken for the palace at first sight. Fans of Stalinist decor will adore its marbled foyers, carpeted in red and hung with inspirational war paintings, but keep a lookout for the *babushka* on duty. No one will mind, however, if you just linger on the terrace outside, with its sweeping **views** of the gardens and the Moskva River, which resembles a lake at this point.

The rest of the park is landscaped in true Italian fashion, with romantic follies. To honour their ancestor, the later Yusupovs had the architect Roman Klein build an imposing rose granite and limestone temple with curved wings, intended to be the family mausoleum but never used as such due to the Revolution. Now signposted as the "**Colonnade**", it exhibits art from the Yusupov collection and hosts **concerts** of classical and Early music in mid-September, billed as the "**Autumn Divertimenti**". Further along, the older, Gothic-style **Bridge over the Ravine** is followed by the Corinthian-columned **Holy Gates**, framing the path to the **Church of the Archangel Michael**. A tiny whitewashed edifice with a shingled dome atop a pyramid of *kokoshniki*, the church was built as early as 1667, and subsequently gave its name to the estate. The white stone **grave** outside is reputedly that of a Yusupov daughter who flung herself off a cliff after being denied permission to marry her beloved.

Klin

By the mid-fourteenth century, the Grand Duchy of Muscovy encompassed a ring of towns straddling the rivers that were Russia's chief lines of communication. **Klin** was founded on the banks of the Sestra (a tributary of the Volga) in 1318, with a Kremlin as its nucleus. In 1570, Ivan the Terrible massacred the entire population for no apparent reason, and the town took nearly a century to recover. As an overland route to Novgorod (and later St Petersburg) grew, Klin became more of a stopover than an *entrepôt*, and eventually found favour with Tchaikovsky, who had spent his summers in the region since 1885, avowing: "I can't imagine myself living anywhere else. I find no words to express how much I feel the charm of the Russian countryside, the Russian landscape and the quiet that I need more than anything else."

Today, he would turn in his grave at the town, with its suburbs of wooden hovels interspersed with the crenellated *kottezhi* of local mafiosi. There isn't much in the way of sights, but Tchaikovsky lovers can visit his former residence on a Patriarshy Dom **excursion** (R1040), or **by train** from Leningrad Station (1hr 30min), and then a fifteen-minute ride on bus #5, #14, #15 or #16 within Klin. Travelling **by car**, Klin is about 80km from Moscow on the Leningradskoe shosse (M10); both the town and the house are well signposted. To avoid a wasted journey, **phone** (Ⓣ539 81 96) in advance to verify that the house is open – it might close for renovation at some point in the future.

Tchaikovsky's house

A few years before his death in 1893, Tchaikovsky rented a house in the woods below town, telling his brother Modeste, "What a blessing it is to know that no one will come, no one will interrupt neither work, reading nor strolling" – before writing *The Sleeping Beauty*, *The Nutcracker Suite* and his Fifth and Sixth symphonies. At his death, Modeste inherited the property and converted it into a **Tchaikovsky Memorial House**, ulitsa Chaykovskovo 48 (dom-muzey P.I. Tchaikovskovo; Tues & Fri–Sun 10am–6pm; R150), which has been preserved ever since – surviving the Bolshevik Revolution and World War II (when the Nazis stored fuel and parked motorbikes in the drawing room) – but is slowly succumbing to post-Soviet decline.

Painted a soft blue-grey with a white trim, the house has a veranda opening onto the back garden, where Tchaikovsky strolled with his dogs. The interior is warm and cosy, with flesh-toned stucco or wood-panelled walls hung with portraits of composers and relatives. On the composer's birthday, May 7, the winners of the international Tchaikovsky Competition have the honour of playing his Becker **grand piano** in the sitting room where he wrote his Sixth Symphony. While the library, with its jigsaw ceiling, verges on baronial grandeur, the bedroom is simple and homely, with his slippers placed beside the bed. In 1964 a concert hall was built in the grounds, where visitors can hear recordings and watch **films** about the composer – Ken Russell's *The Music Lovers* not being among them. The museum's **archives** remain off limits, as Russia is loath to acknowledge Tchaikovsky's homosexuality – and his death in St Petersburg is still controversial. Some biographers reject the official verdict that he died of cholera after drinking contaminated water, on the grounds that his fellow composer Borodin (a doctor) said that a cholera victim's body would never have been displayed in an open coffin – while others refute the theory that Tchaikovsky was sentenced to death by a secret court, on the basis that homosexuality was tacitly tolerated in Russian aristocratic society.

Peredelkino

Southwest of Moscow the forested countryside harbours numerous *dacha* colonies, including the famous writers' village of **Peredelkino**, where the poet and novelist **Boris Pasternak** is buried. In the Brezhnev era a visit to Pasternak's grave on the anniversary of his death (May 30) was a kind of rite of passage for the Muscovite intelligentsia, while foreign journalists found weekend house parties at Peredelkino the best source of gossip about the Kremlin and Moscow's cultural life. Today, Peredelkino has less significance, if only because its best-known living residents have either left or are now regarded as has-beens – except for the Orthodox Patriarch Alexei II, who has a villa here. In 1990, after decades of official hostility towards the writer and his memory, Pasternak's *dacha* was opened as a museum.

As with other sites, a Patriarshy Dom excursion (R1040) will save you the trouble of **getting there** by Kaluga II line *elektrichka* from Kiev Station (20min), or driving, which involves following Kutuzovskiy prospekt/Mozhayskoe shosse to the outer Ring Road, then the M1 highway (Minskoe shosse), and turning left at the 21km marker. It's advisable to phone (☎934 51 75) to confirm that the *dacha* is open, before undertaking the journey.

Pasternak's dacha

Pasternak's dacha (dom-muzey Pasternaka; Thurs–Sun 11am–4pm; R200), at ulitsa Pavlenko 3, is hard to locate without asking locals for directions (*Izviníte, pozhálsta, kak praíti k dómu Pasternáka?*). Painted dark brown with a white trim, its main feature is an oblong veranda wing covered by windows, which juts into the garden. Built by his artist father Leonid in 1937, the house became Pasternak's refuge after he was forced to decline the Nobel Prize for Literature which he was due to receive for his novel *Doctor Zhivago* in 1953. Vilified by the Soviet media and the Writers' Union, Pasternak spent his final years gardening, writing poetry and entertaining friends at the *dacha*, where he died of lung cancer in 1960 at the age of seventy. Despite being officially disgraced, thousands of people attended his funeral.

The **dining room** is filled with sketches and portraits by his father, including a large oil painting of Tolstoy, a family friend. It also contains Pasternak's collection of Georgian ceramics and a huge television set that he never watched, preferring to hear news only from visitors. His favourite place was the glassed-in **veranda**, with its wicker furniture and antique samovar. Notice the bucket filled with glass clubs, a "winter bouquet" given as a gift by a crystal factory. Visitors are led upstairs to his **study-bedroom**, covering most of the top floor. His coat and boots are where he last placed them, next to a bookshelf lined with Russian encyclopedias and novels by Virginia Woolf in English. Pasternak knew the language well, having translated Shakespeare into Russian during the Terror years, when translations were a safer way of earning a living than writing poetry or novels.

The village **cemetery** (kladbische) where Pasternak is buried can be found by walking up the main road from the train station to the church at the top of the hill, and then following the path on the right-hand side towards the back. **Pasternak's grave** lies beside those of four other members of the family, in a pine grove. His headstone – bearing his signature and a faint portrait – is always laid with flowers by admirers. The fifteenth-century **Church of the Transfiguration** above the graveyard conducted religious services throughout the Soviet era.

Gorki Leninskie

South of Moscow the country estate of **Gorki Leninskie**, where Lenin died, used to be a place of pilgrimage for the faithful, employing two hundred guides to handle the bus-loads of visitors. Attendances plummeted after the fall of Communism, and the estate-museum's future looked seriously doubtful for some years, but the threat of closure has now receded, leaving it as a fascinating example of the kind of idolatry that was ubiquitous in Soviet times but became almost extinct during the 1990s. While Yeltsin never managed to remove Lenin's body from the mausoleum, he rid the Kremlin of Lenin's quarters and statue, which have been rebuilt here. Putin, however, had closer links with the estate; his own grandfather cooked for Lenin at Gorki Leninskie, as well as for Stalin at the "Near Dacha" (see box, p.190).

Practicalities

As the estate is 32km south of the Kremlin, it's worth taking a Patriarshy Dom excursion (R900) to avoid the hassle of **getting there** by public transport. This involves taking the metro to Domodedovskaya station and then a twenty-minute journey on bus #439, leaving every half hour; ask to be dropped at the Gorki Leninskie stop, right outside the estate. There are buses back to Moscow till about 4pm. To get there by car, take the Kashirskoe shosse (M4); 11km beyond the Moscow Ring Road, the turn-off is indicated by a small sign 200m before the bronze statue of Lenin that strides away from the gates of another (locked) entrance to the grounds. Although it's wise to phone (Ⓣ548 93 09) to check, the estate should be **open** from 10am to 4pm, except on Tuesdays and the last Monday of each month. There are separate admission charges for the museum (closed Mon and the last Fri of each month; R40), the mansion (R25) and Lenin's quarters in the Kremlin (R25), and a decent **café** in the grounds.

The museum

In sight of the gates is a monstrously ugly block with a quasi-pharaonic portico, containing the last Lenin Museum opened in the USSR (in 1987), now blandly entitled the **Museum of the Political History of Russia and the Beginning of the Twentieth Century**. Built of black-and-white marble and furnished with bronze fittings and ruched curtains, its opulence would have appalled Lenin. Visitors are greeted at the top of the stairs by a giant effigy of the leader, seated against a billowing scarlet backdrop in an enclosure paved with cobblestones taken from Moscow's "Red" Presnya district, hallowed for its part in the 1905 and 1917 revolutions.

With its auto-controlled tedious video-montages accompanied by portentous music, the exhibition manages to be dull despite its technical wizardry. As the guide's spiel (in Russian) is of post-glasnost vintage, visitors who ask probing questions are rewarded with the sight of some pages from Lenin's Testament (see opposite), and told that the attempt to assassinate him in August 1918 may not have been carried out by Fanya Kaplan, the Left SR who was executed for the deed. The attack left Lenin with a bullet lodged in his body and led to his first period of convalescence at Gorki (as it was then called), where he later suffered a series of incapacitating strokes.

The mansion

The real attraction is the elegant yellow-and-white stucco **mansion**, ten minutes' walk through the forest of blue firs. Previously owned by the Borodino hero General Pisarov and Zinaidia Morozova, the widow of Savva Morozov (see p.158), the estate was expropriated in 1918 to become a sanatorium for Party leaders. Lenin only agreed to convalesce there because it had a phone line to Moscow – a vital consideration during the Civil War.

Initially Lenin resided with his wife Krupskaya in the small, detached **northern wing**, above his doctors and bodyguards on the floor below. They shared their meals in a dining room with walnut furniture in striped dust covers, where his sister Maria (a *Pravda* journalist) often slept. Their austere separate bedrooms were softened only by wolf-skin rugs; the largest room, with a tiled stove, was reserved for guests such as Lenin's other siblings, Dmitri and Anna, who lived here after his death. Lenin was moved into the main house after a stroke in May 1922 left him half-paralyzed, temporarily unable to speak, and suicidal. Though he recovered enough to return to work, a second stroke that year enabled Stalin to isolate him from events, and a third left him speechless for the last ten months of his life.

Entering the **main house** via its glassed-in veranda, you'll see a telephone room with three direct lines to the Kremlin, off a hallway where the clock has been stopped at the moment of Lenin's death, and his jacket, boots and hunting gear are preserved in glass cases. The **library** contains four thousand books (Lenin had a working knowledge of nine foreign languages) and a desk set carved with worker and peasant figures, made for the first VDNKh. Next door is a sunny, palmy **conservatory** with a projector for showing silent films and a piano for singsongs in the evening. Notice the flies embroidered on the curtains, and the special mechanized wheelchair at the foot of the stairs. It was a gift from factory workers, who never knew that he was paralyzed on his right side and made the wheelchair's controls right-handed, so it was never used.

Upstairs, the dining room displays a large map of Germany, in expectation of the next outbreak of revolution in Europe. While he was still able, Lenin worked in a pretty **study-bedroom**, dictating by phone to a stenographer next door. His secretaries secretly divulged all to Stalin, including Lenin's so-called Testament (written over New Year 1923), which advised dismissing Stalin from the post of General Secretary. After Lenin's death, Stalin brushed it aside as the delusion of "a sick man surrounded by womenfolk", and the postscript was suppressed.

Lenin's final hours on January 21, 1924, were spent in a small, gilded room, where he expired shortly before 7pm. His body was laid out in the **salon**, whose mirrors and chandeliers were draped in black according to Russian custom, while the sculptor Merkurov made a death mask and casts of Lenin's hands (the right one clenched into a fist). Next day, his coffin was taken to Moscow by train (see p.227). Visitors can peer into a shrouded aperture to see a life-sized photo of the body, surrounded by wreaths. In contrast, the last room you enter is richly decorated and crammed with porcelain objects, as it was when inhabited by Morozova.

Following that, you're taken to the garage to view **Lenin's Rolls-Royce**. One of two expropriated Rollers used by the Soviet leader (the other is in a private collection; see p.262), this vehicle was fitted with caterpillar tracks and skis for travelling across country in winter, and converted to run on pure alcohol, which was easier to obtain than petrol during the Civil War. Large enough to seat six bodyguards, it had a top speed of forty kilometres an hour.

To complete the feast of Leninalia, an outbuilding contains a reconstruction of **Lenin's quarters in the Kremlin**, which existed in the Senate Palace until Yeltsin had the contents packed off to Gorki Leninskie in 1998. Visitors can feel a frisson at the sight of Lenin's desk with its famous statuette of a monkey pondering a human skull (a gift from Armand Hammer), and wall-maps that place Russia at the centre of the world Revolution. Next door is a mock-up of the simple kitchen where he and Krupskaya ate in their spartan quarters – and guides can point you in the direction of a **statue** of Lenin that formerly sat in the grounds of the Kremlin.

Borodino

The bloodiest battle in the Patriotic War took place in rolling countryside 120km west of Moscow, at **Borodino** (pronounced "Barodin-*o*"). On August 26 (Sept 7 by today's calendar), 1812, Napoleon's multinational *Grande Armée* of 135,000 men and 600 cannons fought a 121,000-strong Russian host led by Mikhail Kutuzov. In fifteen hours the Russians lost 40,000 men and the French 30,000; Napoleon considered it the "most terrible" of all his battles. Though the Russians withdrew next day – allowing the French to claim victory and continue advancing – Kutuzov's decision to sacrifice Moscow to preserve his army, and to burn the city to deny the French shelter, was vindicated by events – so Russians see Borodino as a defeat for the French, if not the turning point of the Patriotic War.

A thanksgiving memorial was erected as soon as the invaders had fled, and other monuments on the first, tenth, fiftieth and centenary anniversaries of the battle. In October 1941 war came to Borodino again, as the Soviet Fifth Army held the *Wehrmacht* for six days in what Marshal Zhukov called "the most difficult battle for Moscow". The Soviet Union built monuments to its own heroes on the site hallowed by their Tsarist predecessors, and wove both into a patriotic threnody that all citizens could identify with. In 1812, a Georgian general in the Tsarist army was the hero of the day and Zaporodzhe Cossacks harried the remnants of the *Grande Armée*. In the Great Patriotic War of 1941–45, it was winter-trained Siberian divisions that halted the Nazis, and soldiers from every corner of the USSR that eventually slew the Fascist beast.

The **Borodino Military History Museum-Reserve** (Borodinskiy voenno-istoricheskiy muzey-zapovednik) covers 110 square kilometres of untilled fields or hills with dug-in redoubts (*ravelin*), dotted with monuments or plaques to the regiments or commanders involved. A **Museum** (10am–5pm; closed Mon & the last Fri of each month; R50) midway between Semyonovskoe and Borodino – the two villages at the epicentre – presents an overview, with models, dioramas and relics such as Napoleon's field cot.

The **front line** ran roughly along the four-kilometre road from Borodino village to the train station. Attacking from the southwest (**Napoleon's command post** was above Shevardino village), the *Grande Armée* concentrated on the troops of the Georgian Prince Bagration, dug in at Semyonovskoe and the **Ravetskiy Ravelin** to the northeast. The redoubts around **Semyonovskoe** changed hands eight times during the battle, with a ferocity that prefigured the fighting at Stalingrad, 140 years later. **Bagration's grave**, 400m east of the museum, attests that he was mortally wounded, and an obelisk with a pineapple finial honours the defenders of the Ravetskiy battery. Some historians reckon that Bagration's Second Army was sacrificed to preserve the larger First Army, positioned around **Kutuzov's headquarters** in the village of Gorki (now marked by an obelisk).

For more insights into the battle, visit the ex-**Convent of the Saviour of Borodino** (Spaso-Borodinskovo monastyr; same hours; R50), on the south-western edge of Semyonovskoe. Founded by Countess Tyucheva, who became a nun after her husband was slain at Borodino, this served as a Soviet field hospital in 1941 and now hosts exhibitions of artefacts from both conflicts, as well as a jaunty display of **model soldiers**. The blue-and-white former domicile of Abbess Maria (as Countess Tucheva became) stands nearby, containing exhibits relating her life and times. Also in the vicinity is the former pilgrims' hostel, where **Tolstoy** stayed when researching his novel *War and Peace*; the history and notebooks he used are preserved there (same hours; R25).

A scaled-down **re-enactment of the battle** is held every year on the first Sunday of September, starting at noon, when hundreds of military enthusiasts in period costume mount cavalry charges, skirmish with muskets and fire cannons. After two hours the field is obscured by smoke, and solemn music rises from the loudspeakers as a voice intones the names of the Russian regiments, to a chorus of *Vechnaya Slava!* (Immortal Glory!). If you enjoy such spectacles, this is definitely the time to visit. The event kicks off with a religious service by the Ravetskiy battery.

Borodino is on the road (M1) and railway to Minsk; hourly trains from Belarus Station in Moscow take about two hours to **get there**. A few trains return to Moscow in the evening, but you're likely to have to wait a while, and it might be better to catch a bus to Mozhaysk, 13km away, whence there are regular buses and trains to the capital. The battlefield can also be reached on a Patriarshy Dom **excursion** (R1550), run on the anniversary day only.

Places

Abramtsevo	Абрамцево
Arkhangelskoe	Архангельское
Borodino	Бородино
Gorki Leninskie	Горки Ленинские
Khotovo	Хотово
Klin	Клин
Peredelkino	Переделкино
Sergiev Posad	Сергиев Посад

Vladimir and Suzdal

In the heyday of Intourist and the USSR, coach-loads of foreign tourists circled the "Golden Ring" of historic towns to the northeast of Moscow, trying to get their tongues around such names as Yaroslavl and Pereslavl-Zalesskiy. Today, relatively few groups venture out beyond Sergiev Posad, and those that do focus almost exclusively on **Vladimir** (pronounced "Vla-*dee*-mir") and **Suzdal** ("*Sooz*-dahl") – two ancient settlements that once surpassed Moscow in importance. Vladimir is an industrial city that doesn't rate a visit on its own, but is an essential staging post for Suzdal – a real gem of a place that's ideal for chilling out after the stress of Moscow.

The two are historically linked as the nexus of a northern Russian polity that arose as the Kievan Rus crumbled due to dissension and invasions, and peasants and boyars abandoned the Dnieper basin for the security of the *zalesskiy* region of the upper Volga, whose fertile soil, abundant timber, stone and waterways provided the essentials for towns and trade to develop – the same conditions that later favoured Moscow as the nucleus of the future Russian state.

Due to the inconvenience of public **transport from Moscow** (see "Practicalities" under Vladimir), anyone short on time should consider a **day-excursion**: Patriarshy Dom Tours (see p.46) runs one once a month (possibly twice a month in the summer) for R2020 per person, while the *G&R Asia* or *Sherstone* hostels (see Chapter 11) can organize trips at your convenience for R5800 for one person, R6300 for two, or R7800 for three people. These rates include the cost of admission to local museums and other sights.

Another, unrelated, attraction is the **Air Force Museum** at **Monino**, off the M7 highway to Vladimir. Russia's equivalent of the RAF Museum at Hendon outside London, or Wright-Patterson Air Force Base in Ohio, this is a must for anyone interested in aviation. In a similar vein, there's the biennial **MAKS Air Show** at the otherwise off-limits Zhukovsky air base, where Russia's latest aircraft and space vehicles are tested. See the box below for details of both, and how to get there.

Vladimir

Had it not been for the Mongols who devastated the city in 1238, **Vladimir** might be Russia's capital and Moscow a mere provincial town – Vladimir having risen so high and contributed so much to Russian culture within a few generations. Its sublime **cathedrals** are among the few surviving from the time before the Mongol invasion, which inspired Russian architecture and art for centuries to come – and the reason why Vladimir deserves any attention. Although factories

Monino Air Force Museum and the MAKS Air Show

For those interested in aviation, another reason to come is the **Air Force Museum** (muzey Voenno-Vozdushnykh Sil) at **Monino**, on the road to Vladimir. Sited on a mothballed air base, the museum was founded in 1958 but not opened to foreigners till forty years later. Its huge collection spans nearly a century (the oldest plane dates from 1909) and includes Russian civilian as well as military aircraft, arrayed on the runway. Many are impressive simply for their size, such as the intercontinental bombers that once probed NATO's air defences over the Atlantic (manufactured by reverse-engineering a US B-29 bomber that crash-landed on Soviet territory in 1945), or the Mi-12 helicopter, created in 1969, whose heavy-lifting capacity is still unrivalled today. For a preview, check out the English-language **website** ⓦwww.moninoaviation.com.

Patriarshy Dom runs occasional excursions to the museum, or you can visit independently. To **visit** the museum (Mon, Tues, Thurs & Fri 9.30am–1.30pm & 2.15–5pm, Sat 9am–2pm), foreigners must phone (ⓣ526 33 27) a day or two ahead and submit their passport details (as must anyone bringing a car onto the base). By car, follow the M7 out of Moscow to KM 37.5 and look for the signpost. Alternatively, you can **get there** by taking a #322 bus from Izmaylovskiy Park metro to the "VVA imeni Yu. Gagarina" stop on the highway, near the air base,

Another Mecca for aviation buffs is the **Zhukovsky air base**, 20km southeast of Moscow. This highly restricted facility is home to the Gromov Flight Research Institute, which tests most of Russia's aviation projects and part of its space programme. Other than spending a fortune to become a "space tourist" (see box, p.26), outsiders can only visit the base during the **MAKS Air Show** (ⓦwww.airshow.ru), held in mid-August on odd-numbered years. This arms fair of aircraft, helicopters, rockets and other hardware from different countries attracts crowds of visitors with awesome **flying manoeuvres** by Russian, US, French and Italian teams.

To **get there** from Moscow, catch a train from Kazan Station to the "Otdykh" or "KM 42" halt near the town of Zhukovsky, from which there are shuttle-buses to MAKS. Alternatively, minibus #424 from Vykhino metro station, or bus #478 or #525 from Kuzminki metro, will drop you at ploshchad Gromova in the town, from where there's also a shuttle-bus. Driving from Moscow, it's necessary to park at one of the shuttle-bus termini, as cars aren't allowed onto the base.

and freight yards mar the panorama above the Klyazma River, it is sufficiently grand to make you wonder what Vladimir looked like in its glory days.

Founded in 1108 by Prince Vladimir of Kiev, it became a power base for his son Yuri Dolgoruky (the founder of Moscow), and even more so for Dolgoruky's son, who made Vladimir his capital in 1169. Despite being called "the God-loving", **Andrei Bogolyubsky** (1157–1174) stole a holy icon to enshrine it in Vladimir, warred with Kiev and Novgorod and was so hated that his own wife joined in his murder, which caused universal rejoicing – yet he left his successors a mighty principality and a city whose churches and gates gleamed with gold and silver. Its heyday lasted seven decades, until a 150,000-strong Mongol horde under Genghis Khan's grandson Batu besieged the city and massacred its inhabitants. Although Vladimir rose again, its power inexorably ebbed towards Moscow, the future capital. In Soviet times, Vladimir became an industrial centre specializing in textiles, mechanical engineering and chemicals.

The sights

Arriving at the train station, you can see the gilded domes of Vladimir's cathedrals rising from a ridge that was once enclosed by ramparts nearly 8km long. A steep lane behind the bus terminal leads up to the lower end of Bolshaya

Moskovskaya ulitsa – the main street running uphill towards the centre. If you're not pushed for time, it's worth walking around the walls of the old **Monastery of the Nativity** that used to be part of the city's defences and still provides a fine view of the river; otherwise, catch a bus (#20, #52) or trolleybus (#1, #4 or #5) or keep on walking up towards **Sobornaya ploshchad**, where two magnificent cathedrals stand in a wooded park.

The **Cathedral of the Assumption** (Uspenskiy sobor; Tues–Sun 1–5pm; R100) would be easily recognizable as the model for its namesake in the Kremlin, were it not for a colossal belltower erected in the nineteenth century,

▲ Stone carvings on the Cathedral of St Demetrius

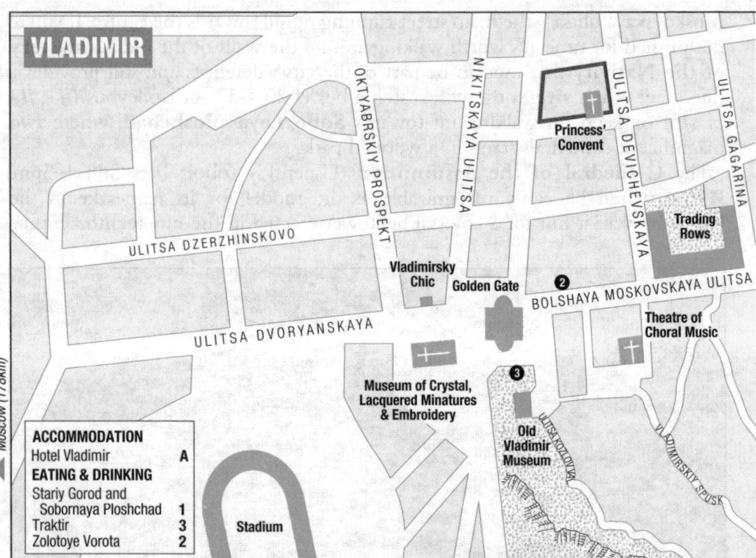

whose fussy neo-Medievalism jars with the majestic simplicity of the cathedral. Constructed between 1158 and 1160 by "master craftsmen from all countries" hired by Prince Bogolyubsky, it was damaged by fire and rebuilt in the 1180s, by which time the Russians were skilled enough to dispense with foreign experts and enlarge the cathedral by raising three new outer walls and broadening the altar apse to support a configuration of five domes instead of the original three.

Its **exterior** is notable for its Romanesque appearance, with blind arcades of pilasters that create a "drooping" effect around the apses and drums of the cupolas, echoed by the curves of the windows and gilt-frilled gables. Scholars disagree over the extent to which these forms owed to German, Polish or Byzantine influences or to Russian inventiveness. Symbolically, the cathedral expressed Bogolyubsky's ambition to unify the Russian princedoms, since the Assumption is the name given to the time when the twelve Apostles returned from the ends of the earth to gather round the Virgin's death bed – but as fate had it, the wife and children of Vladimir's last prince were burned alive there by the Mongols.

If the cathedral is open, you can see how the original walls were knocked through to create aisles behind the new external walls; in one of the niches are the **sarcophagi** of Bogolyubsky and his successor Vsevolod III, who rebuilt the cathedral. More significantly, there are remains of **frescoes** painted in 1408 by Andrei Rublev and Daniil Cherniy (the only ones authenticated by contemporary documents as being the work of their artel), the best-preserved being the *Last Judgement* beneath the choir gallery. The 25-metre-high **iconostasis** once contained the revered twelfth-century Byzantine icon *Our Lady of Tenderness*, which Bogolyubsky took from Kiev for his new capital; subsequently called *Our Lady of Vladimir*, it was removed to Moscow in 1395 and is now in the Tretyakov Gallery.

A little way downhill stands the smaller **Cathedral of St Demetrius** (Dmitrievskiy sobor), built of the same local limestone in the 1190s by Vsevolod

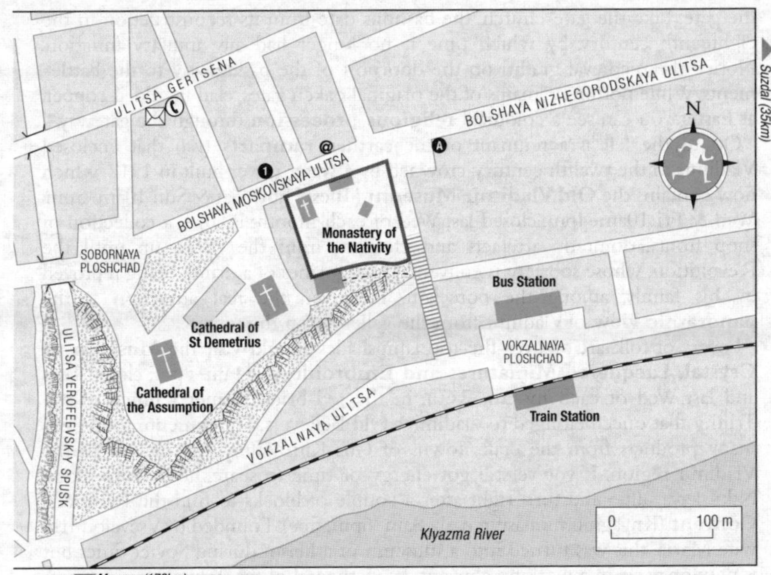

III "Big Nest" – a sobriquet that referred to his many sons. St Demetrius is famous for its **stone carvings**, with rows of saints and mythical creatures on the blind arcades and large compositions beneath the *zakomary*, where Vsevolod and his brood are associated with the biblical David, angels and chimeras, and the ascension to heaven of Alexander the Great. The carvings were originally painted in bright colours, like ancient Greek temples, and it's debated whether their symbolism is pagan or Christian. Its interior boasts a fine *Last Judgement* by artists of the Constantinople school, but, as with the Cathedral of the Assumption, you'll be lucky to find it open.

The Golden Gate and beyond

Beyond Sobornaya ploshchad the avenue widens as it approaches the town centre. On the northern side of the street you'll see the **Trading Rows**, a nineteenth-century shopping arcade with many small shops in the vicinity. Across the road, you can follow a narrow, winding side street with antique lampposts to find the **Theatre of Choral Music** housed in the former Church of St George, where **concerts** are usually held on Saturdays and Sundays from September to May.

Sticking to the main drag, you'll reach the **Golden Gate** (Zolotye vorota) bestriding Vladimir's main square, which has sunk 1.5m into the ground over the centuries due to its weight. Completed in 1164, it was once the western entrance to Bogolyubsky's walled city, modelled on the gates of Kiev (themselves copied from Constantinople's), which featured a church above the gateway for divine protection. Vladimir might have withstood the Mongol siege had not the young Prince Yuri lost his nerve and ventured forth carrying gifts, hoping that Batu Khan would spare his life – but "Batu, like a wild beast, ordered that he be slaughtered before him" and launched a final assault on the city's walls – as depicted by a diorama in the **Military History Museum** (10am–6pm; closed Tues & last Fri of each month; R60) in one of the bastions at the foot of the gate. Like the gate-church, the bastions date from its reconstruction in the eighteenth century, by which time it no longer had any military function. Notice the medieval graffiti on the doorpost of the passageway to the battlements. While nothing remains of the original oaken gates, clad in gilded copper, at Easter you can see a colourful **religious procession** through the gateway.

Off to the left is a remnant of the earthen **ramparts** (*val*) that enclosed Vladimir in the twelfth century, crowned by a water tower built in 1912, which now contains the **Old Vladimir Museum** (Tues, Thurs, Sat & Sun 10am–5pm, Wed & Fri 10am–4pm; closed last Wed of each month; R60) – a collection of shop fronts, domestic artefacts and clothing from the 1860s up until the Revolution, whose sobriety is enlivened by figurines of a drunk being reproved by his family, among the porcelain. However, the real attraction is the **panoramic view** of Vladimir from the gallery atop the tower.

Lovers of folk art or over-the-top lampshades should visit the **Museum of Crystal, Lacquered Miniatures and Embroidery** (11am–7pm; closed Tues and last Wed of each month; R60), in the red-brick former Church of the Trinity that once belonged to Vladimir's Old Believers. The museum showcases many products from the crafts towns of Gus-Khrustalniy and Palekh, in the Vladimir region. If you've still got energy or time to spare, head north along Nikitskaya ulitsa and turn right after a couple of blocks to find the **Princess' Convent** (Knyagnin monastyr; daily 8am–6pm; free). Founded by Vsevelod III's wife Maria, this was turned into a museum of atheism during Soviet times but is now once again a working convent. Its Cathedral of the Assumption contains some well-preserved frescoes from the 1640s.

Vladimir Prison

Though it's not on the tourist trail, no account would be complete without mentioning **Vladimir Central Prison** (Vladimirskiy tsentral). Founded by Catherine the Great in 1783, this famous gaol was the first halt on the long convict trail to Siberia known as the Vladimir Road; later, Lenin and other Bolsheviks spent time within its walls. In 1929 it became an *Izolator* for the incarceration of prisoners whom the NKVD wished to keep apart from the rest. Some were foreigners charged with spying, from British engineers working on the Moscow Metro to postwar inmates like Raoul Wallenberg, the "Swedish Schindler", and Gary Powers, the pilot of an American spy plane shot down over the Urals in 1960. Others were Soviet VIPs such as the idolized singer Lidya Ruslanova or the film star Zoya Fedorova, who was sentenced to 25 years for "terrorism" but amnestied after Stalin's death. Subsequently, Stalin's alcoholic son, Vasily, spent six months there in 1958, as one of the "numbered" prisoners whose identity was only known to senior officials. If you're curious to see the prison from the outside, it's located at Bolshaya Nizhgorodskaya ulitsa 69, on the eastern side of town.

Practicalities

Public **transport from Moscow** is patchy. Suburban **trains** from Kursk Station leave every hour or so but can take up to five hours, unless you go for the late-afternoon express (2hr 30min). Some Russians prefer using privately run buses or **minibuses**, leaving from Kursk and Kazan stations (3hr), which don't run to a timetable but leave once they've filled up. Alternatively, **buses** from Moscow's Central Bus Station depart from platform #3 or #4 at 7.45am (daily), 1.40pm (Mon only), 7.45pm (Mon–Wed) and 8.30pm (daily), arriving about three-and-a-quarter hours later. If you are heading straight on

to Suzdal you can get a **bus** from the bus terminal behind the train station at roughly hourly intervals, or hire a **taxi** (R500), which will get there in 30–40 minutes instead of an hour.

If you are **staying** in Vladimir, your best bet is the *Hotel Vladimir* (Ⓣ4922/ 32 44 47 or 32 30 42, Ⓔtour@gtk.elcom.ru; R3200), at Bolshaya Moskovskaya ulitsa 74, whose "first category" rooms with private bathrooms are comfy and cheerful (the cheaper rooms with shared bathrooms less so), with a superbly kitsch floor lounge. You can also **eat** well in Vladimir for a fraction of what you'd pay in Moscow: try the fancy *Stariy Gorod* at Bolshaya Moskovskaya ulitsa 41 (Ⓣ4922/32 51 01; daily 11am–2am), or the more bar-like *Sobornaya Ploshchad* (daily 11am–midnight) next door. Tour groups are usually taken to the *Zolotoye Vorota* (Ⓣ4922/32 34 35; daily noon–midnight) near the Golden Gate, while locals patronize the folksy *Traktir* (daily 11am–1am) in a wooden cabin near the Old Vladimir Museum. Service at all of these places is leisurely, so don't bank on a quick meal.

You can change **money** at banks near the Trading Rows, or use the ATM in the *Hotel Vladimir*. There's an **Internet** café (Mon–Fri noon–10pm; R50 per hr) at Bolshaya Moskovskaya ulitsa 51; the **post and telephone** office (Mon–Fri 8am–8pm) is a block or two north on ulitsa Gertsena.

Vladimir is a good place to shop for **souvenirs**: head to Vladimirskiy Chic, in the former Troitskaya church at Dvoryanskaya ulitsa 2 (10am–6pm, closed Tues and last Fri of each month), for jewellery, paintings, porcelain and traditional Russian souvenirs at far lower prices than antique shops in Moscow.

Suzdal

Unlike Vladimir, **Suzdal**'s glorious architectural legacy is unmarred by factories and in total harmony with its surroundings, a Russian fairytale vision of onion domes above meadows and woods beside the meandering Kamenka River, spanned by wooden footbridges, and green with reeds and lilies in summertime. It looks gorgeous whatever the season, but especially in winter, blanketed with snow. Most of the houses are of the traditional wood-and-stone kind, with kitchen gardens; grazing cows and sheep add a pastoral touch, and even tourism doesn't ruffle its tranquillity. The lack of litter or drunks on the streets suggests that the town's self-esteem is still intact, despite its economic woes – perhaps due to its illustrious past.

Suzdal's **history** is entwined with Vladimir's, for it was the princely capital during Dolgoruky's reign – when the court resided at Kideshka, 5km outside Suzdal on the River Nerl – until his successor moved it to Vladimir. Even so, Suzdal became the religious centre of medieval Rus, with monasteries associated with SS Boris and Gleb and Alexander Nevsky, which later princes and tsars lavishly funded in return for using it as a dumping ground for unwanted wives, ensuring that the town prospered during the sixteenth and seventeenth centuries, when a spate of church building saw the emergence of a distinctive Suzdal style. In its heyday, Suzdal had fifty churches, monasteries and cathedrals, forming a unique architectural ensemble – and although the Soviets closed down the religious orders and wantonly destroyed twelve churches and ten monasteries, they preserved others as monuments and declared the whole town a protected museum reserve. It's easy to see why Russian film directors have used it as a location for historical epics – most notably Tarkovsky's masterpiece *Andrei Rublev*.

If you're going to stay it's essential to **reserve accommodation** over Christmas, New Year and during local **festivals**. *Kupava*, in early June, is a pagan celebration where teenage girls in white robes gather ferns and bathe in the river and both sexes jump over bonfires after dark; this is followed in mid-July by the Cucumber Festival, with food and drink tasting, dancing and jollity at the Museum of Wooden Architecture.

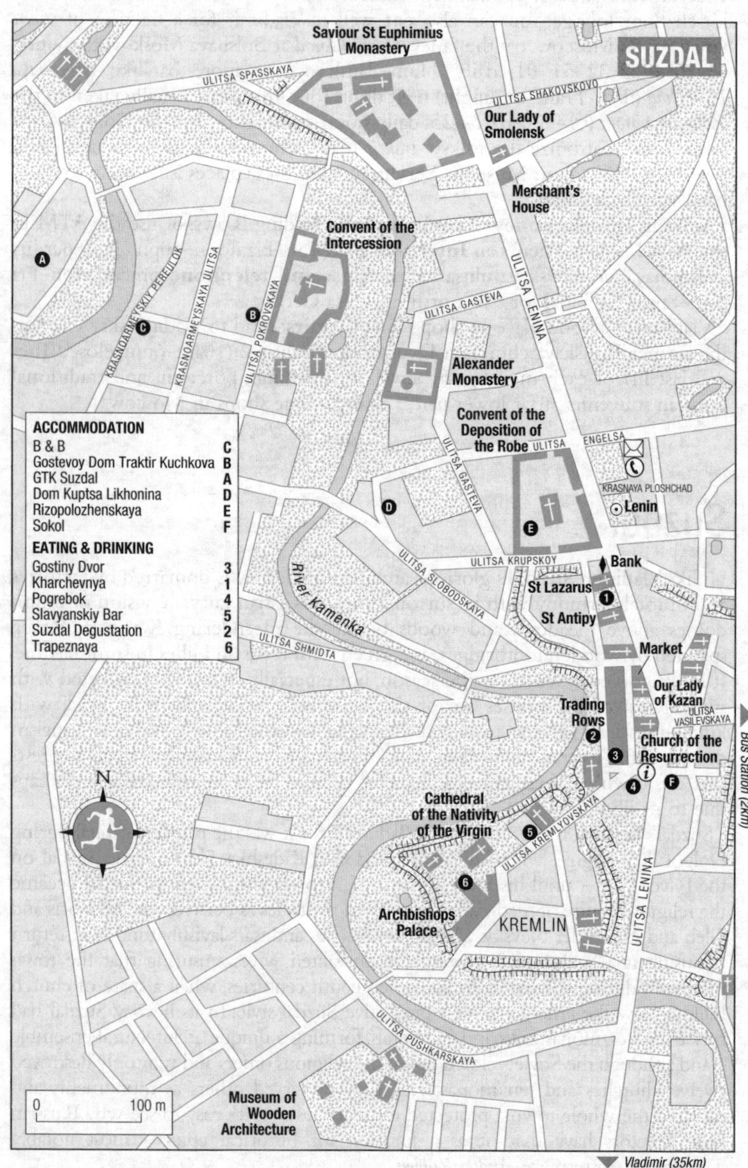

As the town covers only seven square kilometres you can comfortably explore it on foot, but there's a lot worth seeing, so a couple of hours isn't really enough. The **itinerary** described here can take the best part of a day if you don't hurry. Whether you start or finish with the Convent of the Intercession is likely to depend on whether you're staying at the *GTK* on the edge of town or somewhere more central. A torch will be useful if you go out for a meal in the evening, as the streets are unlit.

The Convent of the Intercession

Nestled in an oxbow of the river, the white-and-gold **Convent of the Intercession** (Pokrovskiy monastyr; daily 7am–7pm; free) is a monument to the length that tsars would go to rid themselves of unwanted spouses. The convent's cathedral was built by Vasily III in the hope of curing his wife Solomonia's infertility; when divine intercession failed to produce an heir, she was browbeaten into taking the veil – only to become pregnant at the last moment and give birth to a boy in the convent, whereupon she faked his death and had him secretly adopted. The practice was continued by Vasily's son Ivan the Terrible and grandson Ivan (who disposed of two wives this way), while later victims included Boris Godunov's daughter Xenia, and Peter the Great's wife Yevdokiya (who was later exiled to a remoter convent for plotting against Peter and taking a lover).

Today, this grim history is at odds with the convent's manicured beauty; its elegant cathedral, bell tower and refectory form a single conjoined entity in a delightful garden created by a new generation of nuns, surrounded by the log cabins of the *Pokrovskaya Hotel*, installed in Soviet times. There's also a small **museum** (currently closed) re-creating the *Prikaz* (administration) that controlled the land and serfs owned by the convent until Catherine the Great took them away, whereupon the redundant building was used for storing salt.

To see the rest of Suzdal, cross the river by footbridge and head uphill towards the Saviour-St Euphimius Monastery.

The Saviour-St Euphimius Monastery

Built atop the steep east bank, enclosed by a fortified wall 1200m in length, the **Saviour-St Euphimius Monastery** (Spaso-Yevfimiev monastyr; Tues–Sun 10am–6pm; closed last Thurs of each month; R400) is easily mistaken for Suzdal's Kremlin, and once doubled as a fortress. Although founded as early as 1352, by abbot Euphimius (after whom it is named), most of what you find today dates from the sixteenth and seventeenth centuries, when the patronage of Vasily III and Prince Pozharsky made it one of the richest monasteries in Russia. To cut it down to size, Catherine the Great established a prison there in 1766, which remained until 1905; during World War II the monastery served as a POW camp for Nazi generals, before being restored in peacetime and turned into a series of museums highlighting different facets of its history.

Try to time your visit to hear the **bells** at 11am: a fifteen-minute symphony performed by one of Suzdal's master bell-ringers, Yuri Yurev or Vladimir Gagarin – whose playing can best be seen from a vantage point on the eastern side of the belltower, which was erected to mark the birth of the future Ivan the Terrible. Beyond rises the **Cathedral of the Transfiguration**, created in 1594 to replace an earlier, single-domed church built over the tomb of St Euphimius, which was turned into a side-chapel. Its interior is decorated with bold, naturalistic frescoes in vivid blues, ochre, turquoise and yellow, and was once the burial place of **Prince Pozharsky**, who led the army that rid Moscow of the Poles and Lithuanians in 1612. He was later reburied beneath a pavilion to the east of the cathedral, where signs direct visitors towards a museum in his memory, in a former church.

Tucked away at the back is the low, linear **Prison Wing** that once held the ringleaders of the Pugachev Revolt, the civil servant Gavril Popov (gaoled for writing "Man is born free" in his diary), and the Decembrist Prince Shakovsky (who died on hunger strike). After 1829 it was used exclusively for clerics, sentenced by the Church authorities – as related in an exhibition that includes a re-creation of a prisoner's cell.

A **Museum of Treasures** in the monastery infirmary contains some fine icons (notably a *Saviour* "with the Wet Beard") and lapis lazuli-inlaid jewellery, while the **Museum of Naïve Art** in the ex-Church of the Annunciation features scenes of village and town life by artists born in the 1920s and 1930s. Finally, there are two exhibitions in the archimandrite's house. **Book Treasures of Six Centuries** displays rare volumes such as Fyodorov's *The Apostle* (1564), the first illustrated *Primer* (1694) and a silver-chased Gospel, presented to the monastery by Prince Pozharsky, which is the largest book in Russia. The other exhibition examines the fate of POWs, including the commanders of the German Sixth Army captured at Stalingrad, who were held here in 1943 and suborned into backing the "National Committee for Free Germany".

The Posad

Suzdal's layout is typical of medieval Russian towns, with a Kremlin and monasteries interspersed by a **posad** (trading quarter) and satellite settlements, each with their own parish church built of wood. In the seventeenth century these were replaced by stone ones, often erected in pairs: a high-vaulted church for summer worship, and a lower one where the candles and lamps created an illusion of warmth during winter. Over time their design grew lighter, with facades whose decoratively framed symmetrical windows are visually akin to the embroidered white cloths in peasant households. Architecture buffs can find dozens of examples, but most visitors will be content to see the ones along **ulitsa Lenina**, en route to the Kremlin.

Near the St Euphimius Monastery, the "summer" **Church of Our Lady of Smolensk** has lost its winter counterpart but acquired a tall, freestanding bell-tower. Across the road is a whitewashed dwelling with a wooden roof, which once belonged to the religious dissenter Nikita Pustosvyat, who was executed on Red Square in 1682. It is now furnished like a **Merchant's House** (Posadsky dom; summer 10am–6pm; closed Mon, Fri & last Thurs of each month; R100) from the eighteenth century, when its owner was engaged in baking *kalachi* (bagels) and ran a tavern. Vendors outside sell homebrewed mead, a traditional local speciality.

Further down ulitsa Lenina, a gate beside no. 101 opens onto a path to the **Alexander Monastery** (Aleksandrovskiy monastyr; daily 8am–6pm; free), high above the river. Founded in 1240 by the warrior-saint Alexander Nevsky for soldiers' widows, it held the rank of Great *Lavra* until it was usurped by the Alexander Nevsky Monastery in St Petersburg, established by Peter the Great – whose mother, Natalya Naryshkina, had financed the **Cathedral of the Ascension** in Suzdal's monastery twenty years earlier. Today the complex is in a poor state, but worth a detour for the lovely **view** of the Convent of the Intercession across the river.

Back on ulitsa Lenina, the only blot on the landscape is an ugly telephone office and municipal block fronted by an archetypal **Lenin statue** on Krasnaya ploshchad. Lenin appears to be haranguing Suzdal's tallest landmark, a 72-metre-high **bell tower** erected by the townsfolk to celebrate Russia's victory in 1812. Its gaping archway is an invitation to enter the **Convent of Deposition of the Veil** (Rizopolozhenskiy monastyr; daily 8am–midnight; free), another decrepit walled complex whose origins go back to 1207, which was renowned for the deeds of a nun called Euphrosinia. Its **Cathedral of the Deposition** is unusual for its helmet domes on tall drums, like minarets, and was financed by the boyar who coerced Vasily's wife into a nunnery. The interior is all but gutted, since after the convent was dissolved it was turned into a hostel and workshops, only mentioned in Soviet guidebooks for its chunky sixteenth-century **Holy Gate**.

Further south, **churches** sprout like mushrooms on verges. **St Lazarus**, built in 1667, was one of the first churches where the formerly functional *zakomary* (arched gables) became purely decorative, due to new construction techniques. Its lowly neighbour **St Antipy**, erected eight decades later, has an adjacent belfry painted maroon, cream and white, with an unusual concave tent-roof. While the winter church was invariably built later, the interval varied greatly; only seven years separates the **Church of the Resurrection** from the **Church of Our Lady of Kazan**. The former is a typical Suzdal parish church, shaped like a truncated cube and almost devoid of decoration, bar a frieze of *kokoshniki* beneath the roof. Across the road lie the **Trading Rows**, an early nineteenth-century shopping arcade with another church behind it, and two more on the way to the Kremlin.

The Kremlin

Founded in the twelfth century by Vladimir of Kiev, Suzdal's **Kremlin** has been ravaged and rebuilt many times since – and lost its stone ramparts in the eighteenth century – but its archaic grandeur still captivates. The star-spangled onion domes of its cathedral make it the visual focus of the whole town, which at close quarters becomes a melange of extraordinary buildings, where it's easy to imagine boyars strolling across the yard and livestock grazing between the wooden houses that stood here in medieval times. The **grounds** of the Kremlin are open daily 24 hours, while its **museums** – the Interior (R100), the Cross Chamber (R60), the Children's Museum Centre (R30) and the Old Russian Painting (R60) – are all open 10am–6pm (closed Tues & the last Fri of each month).

The **Cathedral of the Nativity** (Rozhdestvennskiy sobor) is a majestic hybrid of early thirteenth- and sixteenth-century architecture. A band of blind arcading delineates the lower half, built of limestone by Prince Yuri Vsevolodovich, from the upper portion, rebuilt with five domes instead of three, as was required by canonical law by the 1530s. While you can admire the carved stonework around its portals, the cathedral is rarely open – which is a real shame, as its frescoes are superb, with ultramarine and orange as the dominant colours and more ancient portions in softer hues – not to mention a chandelier bestowed by the brother of Tsar Vasily Shuysky, and the magnificent Golden Gates (see p.313).

Happily, there's plenty to see in the **Metropolitan's Palace**, a huge, rambling complex built over the course of two hundred years, completed in the eighteenth century by Metropolitan Hilarion. Having bought a strip of tickets, your first stop is the **Cross Chamber** (Krestovaya palata) that he built for official

▲ The Metropolitan's Palace in the Kremlin

receptions, which is over twice as large as its namesake in Moscow's Kremlin, and likewise unsupported by pillars. Furnished with tiled stoves, a long table covered in red cloth, and portraits of tsars and clerics, it makes a superb setting for performances of Russian church music by the **Blagovest male choir**, coinciding with visits by tour groups.

Afterwards, cross the yard and climb the stairs to the Metropolitan's living quarters, now a **Historical Museum**. Among its prized exhibits is one of the two pairs of **Golden Gates** from the cathedral. These huge bronze doors are the earliest example in Russia of the technique known as fired gilding, producing images in gold on a black background: episodes from the Gospels, and homely scenes such as an angel teaching a man to use a spade. The giant candleholders and urn for dispensing holy water are also memorable, and a model of medieval Suzdal shows how its topography has changed. Don't overlook the sixteenth-century crucifix so finely carved that it needs a magnifying glass to reveal its details, the child's silk tunic, nor the portrait of Vasily's wife, Solomonia Saburova.

Upon exiting you'll find yourself facing the seventeenth-century **Church of St Nicholas**, a simple log edifice whose beetling roof and hanging gallery make it an arresting sight. It was moved here from the village of Glotovo in 1950, as the first of the exhibits in the Museum of Wooden Architecture that was later sited across the river.

The Museum of Wooden Architecture

A short walk from the Kremlin via a footbridge, you'll find a series of diverse buildings that might otherwise have rotted in their native villages gathered together to form a **Museum of Wooden Architecture** (muzey Dereyannovo Zodchestva; May–Oct Fri–Mon 10am–5pm, Tues 9am–7pm, Thurs 10am–5pm; grounds open year-round daily 9am–7pm; R200). The **Church of the Transfiguration** from Kozlyatevo (1756) has a hexagonal tower, shingled roofs and domes, and a covered porch and galleries; its interior features a folk-Baroque iconostasis, and saints painted on the raw plank ceiling. Nearby are two nineteenth-century **farmsteads** furnished with artefacts and overseen by guides in folk costume; authenticity extends to the visitors' toilet – an earth closet out back. The "winter" **Church of the Resurrection** from Pobshino (1776) and two nineteenth-century **windmills** from Drachevo are more rough-hewn structures; a **waterwheel** and poultry sheds complete the ensemble. There's also a **shop** in one of the houses selling attractive handmade quilts and tea cosies.

Practicalities

Suzdal's **tourist office** (Wed–Sun 10am–6pm ☎49231/216 99 or 229 72), at ulitsa Lenina 63A, isn't always open as advertised, but, when it is, can help with hotel reservations, transport and excursions. You can **change money** at the *GTK* (see "Accommodation") or *Sberbank* (Mon–Fri 8am–4.30pm) on ulitsa Lenina, but neither has an ATM. The **post and telephone** office on Krasnaya ploshchad is open 24 hours for phone calls, and there's a **pharmacy** across the road from *Sberbank*.

When leaving Suzdal, bear in mind that the **bus station** is 15–20-minutes' walk from the town centre; buses run there from Krasnaya ploshchad (#1 & #4) and the *GTK* (#3) at irregular times, and local motorists aren't inclined to act as unofficial taxis. **Taxis** wait outside the *GTK*.

Accommodation

If you fancy staying with a local family, there's a pleasant **B&B** at Krasnoarmeyskiy pereulok 11 (☎49231/202 60), 300m from the Convent of the Intercession. A standard room costs R2500, a deluxe room with a fireplace R4000, and guests can enjoy a wood-fired *banya* (R800 per person). Hosts Boris and Svetlana are friendly and helpful, but only speak Russian. They advise reserving a week or two ahead and confirming nearer the time. Otherwise, take your pick of the local **hotels** – bearing in mind the advisability of reserving in advance.

Dom Kuptsa Likhonina **ul. Slobodskaya 34 ☎49231/219 01, ⓔaksenova-museum@mt.vladimir.ru.** Charming nineteenth-century house in the centre of town with four rooms with folk decor and furnishings and a lovely garden. Reservations essential. R2400.

Gostevoy Dom Traktir **Kuchkova ul. Pokrovskaya 35 ☎49231/202 52.** Comfortable modern guesthouse facing the Convent of the Intercession. Rooms have double beds, TV and mini-bar, and there's a sauna and pool table. Breakfast included. R3000.

GTK Suzdal **ul. Korovniki 45 ☎49231/209 08, or 215 33, ⓔgtk@suzdaltour.ru** This sprawling 1980s complex on the edge of town, with a pool and sauna, has recently been refurbished. Its regular rooms have bathrooms; ones in the Rizalit wing have superior decor, fridge and TV, while the detached motel has two-room apartments above private garages. Breakfast included. R2460.

Sokol **Torgovaya ploshchad, 2A ☎49231/209 87 or 200 88.** In the historical centre of the town, facing the Trading Rows, with modern rooms with TV and telephone. There's a good restaurant on the ground floor. R2460.

Rizopolozhenskaya **Kommunalniy gorodok 9 ☎49231/207 06.** A hostel in all but name, in the decrepit Convent of the Deposition of the Robe. Singles with washbasins, doubles with bathrooms, and triple rooms with sofas, some refurbished, others very dingy – ask for a *lyuks* one. R1700, *lyuks* R3600.

Eating, drinking and nightlife

While Suzdal hasn't a big choice of places **to eat**, you can't complain about the prices – even if you go wild, it's difficult to spend over R350–450 a head. Home-made cheeses, pickles and vodkas can be sampled at the Cucumber

Festival in mid-July, while at any time of year you can try the local speciality **honey mead** (*medovukha*), served at restaurants and sold by the bottle by street traders (who usually allow you to taste before buying) – it doesn't keep for longer than a week. **Nightlife** boils down to a teenagers' disco on Krasnaya ploshchad, and the bar in the *GTK*, with pool tables and hookers.

Gostiny Dvor **ul. Lenina 63A ☎49231/211 90.** A beautiful old-style restaurant in the Trading Rows serving Russian cuisine at fairly high prices: expect to pay around R1500 for a meal. Tues–Sat noon–11pm.

Kharchevnya **ul. Lenina 73 ☎ 49231/ 207 22.** A good place for a simple lunch in the centre of the town. Quick service and good-quality meals at average prices (around R700). Tues–Sun 9am–9pm.

Pogrebok (Pickle Cellar) **ul. Kremlyovskaya 5 ☎49231/217 32.** Across the street from the Trading Rows, this pine-panelled basement has a wide selection of Russian cuisine at slightly higher prices than *Kharchevnya*. Wed–Sun 11am–8pm.

Slavyanskiy Bar (Slav Bar) **ul. Kremlyovskaya.** A simple café-bar on the way to the Kremlin serving soup, sandwiches, salads, beer and spirits – all at low prices. Wed–Sun noon–7pm.

Trapeznaya **ul. Kremlyovskaya ☎49231/217 63.** A medieval refectory, in the Kremlin's Archbishop's Palace. Guests are seated in a vast whitewashed hall with long trestle tables, once the small room is full. Try *kuritsa pod sloyke*: chicken cooked in an earthenware pot with a mushroom-shaped cap of puff pastry, which is sliced off to form a bowl from which you eat. Daily 9am–10pm.

Suzdal degustation **ul. Lenina 63a ☎49231/208 03.** A good place to sample numerous kinds of *medovukha* made by the local mead brewery and served with snacks, such as pickled fish, and cabbage and carrot salads: expect to pay around R700. Wed–Sat noon–8pm.

Suzdal	Суздаль
Krasnaya ploshchad	Красная площадь
ulitsa Lenina	улица Ленина
Vladimir	Владимир
Bolshaya	Большая-
Moskovskaya ulitsa	Москов ская улица
Nizhgorodskaya ulitsa	Нижгородская улица
Sobornaya ploshchad	Соборная площадь

Listings

Listings

11

Accommodation

There has long been a shortage of good, inexpensive to middle-range places in Moscow and **accommodation** is likely to be by far the largest chunk of your daily expenditure, with most half-decent hotels charging R8000 upwards for a double room. In addition, complicated new registration procedures have made things even more difficult for budget travellers. The **registration process** for foreigners is getting ever more complex and difficult for hotels, especially the cheaper ones, leading them to adopt a "no foreign guests" policy. This effectively bars foreigners from low-cost accommodation, so always check before you book with any of the cheaper hotels. On the plus side, visitors can now compare rates on hotel websites with those being quoted by accommodation agencies (see p.326), and the range of accommodation is opening up, with ever more apartments available for rent, and many of the old Soviet-style two-star dumps being refurbished to offer much better value.

While the supply of accommodation has improved, it can still fall short of demand at any time of year, making **reservations** advisable. Many hotels charge more in **high season**, but what constitutes high season varies from place to place, although October to mid-December and late January to the end of April is widely reckoned low season. You may be able to get a peak-period **discount** by booking in winter or spring. The acceptability of credit cards in listings below is indicated by the abbreviations: Amex = American Express; DC = Diners Club; EC = EuroCard; JCB = Japanese Credit Bank; MC = MasterCard. Russia's central bank levies a three-percent surcharge on card transactions initiated abroad, and some mini-hotels or landlords prefer bank transfers instead.

Visas and registration

While **visas and registration** (see pp.30–33) are taken care of for package tourists, independent travellers require visa support and must be registered once in Moscow. **Hotels** must register guests for the duration of their hotel stay, however they obtained their visa. Visa support is also available online, for tourists booking hotel rooms and maybe also **homestay or flat rental**. In the case of the last two, only the company that issued your visa invitation is legally allowed to register you, so it's vital that they have an office (or accredited partner) in Moscow. Similarly, **hostels** may only register guests who got their visa support from the hostel (or its partner). Beware of staying somewhere that can do neither, as this will leave you liable to a hefty fine if you can't find somebody to register you. In this fix, the *Zvozdnaya* (p.334) hotel might register "**virtual guests**" for a week or two, for the price of a night's room rental (you don't have to stay there), though it is unlikely as the regulations are currently being rigorously enforced. The Way to Russia website (ⓦwww.waytorussia.net) spells out the **current regulations** in all their Kafkaesque complexity.

The **cost of visa support** cited for accommodation agencies or individual hotels listed below refers to visa support for a single person for a regular tourist visa, unless specified otherwise.

Accommodation agencies

Accommodation agencies and the internet are revolutionizing the market, allowing tourists to shop around for **discounts** at hotels, far below their walk-in rack rates. This applies equally to deluxe hotels like the *Metropol*, old Soviet behemoths, and smaller hotels opened in recent years. As a rule, the prices in our listings refer to rack rates, and you should be able to save anything from R500–5000 by booking through an agency rather than the hotel itself. Other agencies specialize in homestay, flat rental or sharing; some are just an individual with a few rooms to rent. Check references if available, as there are some dodgy agencies about, and the consequences of a foul-up are potentially worse than not being happy with the room – such as spending days trying to sort out your registration.

All Hotels in Russia ⓦ**www.all-hotels.ru.** One of Russia's leading online agencies, offering discounts at forty hotels in Moscow.

All Russia Hotels ⓦ**www.allrussianhotels.com.** Besides discounts on hotels, this online agency offers one-bedroom flats to rent on Noviy Arbat or Tverskaya ulitsa.

Apartment Accommodation in Moscow ⓦ**www.moscow-apartment.com.** A landlord with a Euro-standard one- or two-person flat in Zayauze to rent (R2500 a night; long-term negotiable). Payment by Amex, MC, Visa.

Astor Apartments ⓦ**www.astor-apartments.com.** Serviced apartments near the US Embassy, from €95–210 per night. Only accepts booking online or by phone and in euros.

At Home in Moscow ⓦ**http://uk.geocities.com/at_home_in_moscow.** A landlord with a comfortable serviced flat in a tower block near Serpukhovskaya metro, which sleeps up to three and costs €75 a night. Only accepts payment in euros.

FlatMates.Ru ⓦ**www.flatmates.ru.** This site puts you in touch with landlords and tenants wanting to rent or share apartments in Moscow. You negotiate the cost between yourselves. The information can be sometimes slightly out of date but it's a great place to meet flatmates.

Go Russia ⓦ**www.justgorussia.co.uk.** UK-based company offering hotel reservations, visa support and tours both in Moscow and around Russia.

Host Families Accommodation (HOFA) ⓦ**www.hofa.ru.** Reliable St Petersburg-based company that can arrange homestay B&B in Moscow. Also transfers, tours, excursions and language tuition. Visa support and registration. Payment by bank transfer, MC, Visa or Western Union.

Lodging.ru ⓦ**www.lodging.ru.** Russian online agency offering discounts at a dozen or so three- and four-star hotels in Moscow, and similarly in many other cities. No visa support, but registration isn't problematical for hotel guests.

Ost-West Kontaktservice ⓦ**www.ostwest.com.** Established St Petersburg-based agency offering discounts at seven hotels in Moscow and visa support.

Rick's Apartments ⓦ**www.enjoymoscow.com.** Run by an American living in Moscow, this reliable agency specializes in renting apartments, and provides great support in both English and Russian. Visa support, transfers and other services available.

Russian Guide Network ⓦ**www.russianguidenetwork.com.** This site features links to several local hotel and apartment booking agencies, with visa support and registration, but is chiefly notable for its warts-and-all reviews of over 130 hotels in Moscow.

Uncle Pasha ⓦwww.cheap-moscow.com. An idiosyncratic site offering cheap homestay, a basement backpacker den, and flats to rent. Also lets out a *dacha* outside Moscow on the Volga River.

Way to Russia ⓦwww.waytorussia.net. Russia-based information portal with hotel discounts, visa support and registration, plus all kinds of useful practical information including a regularly updated section on the rules governing visas and registration.

Hotels

Moscow has heaps of deluxe **hotels** catering to business travellers and Russia's mega-rich, but barely enough for **budget** travellers. While some places charge over R20,000 for a double room, you're unlikely to find much in the city centre for much less than R8000 a night. To get a decent room for that kind of figure, you have to look far out in the high-rise suburbs. This isn't as bad as it could be, since some of the best locations are near places you'd want to visit anyway – the Izmaylovo art market, the VVTs exhibition grounds or Tsaritsyno – and are never more than 30 minutes from the centre by metro. Overall, though, low-budget travellers face a trade-off between cost, location and standards.

The Russian system of **rating** hotels with stars should be taken with a pinch of salt. When a hotel was built (or last refurbished) is more important. Whereas two-star hotels are 1950s low-rises or Stalinist tenements, sometimes lacking en-suite facilities, three-star hotels may be recently refitted 1970s complexes with restaurants and nightclubs, or brand-new mini-hotels that can be as stylish as four- and five-star hotels, which come closest to matching the standards of their Western counterparts. While the cheapest rooms at old hotels may lack en-suite **bathrooms**, these are mandatory for three-stars upwards.

Decor is age-related, too; places basically unchanged since Soviet times (described in our reviews by the shorthand *sovok*, a slang term for Soviet that literally means "dustpan") have ugly wallpaper, stained carpets, shoddy fittings and cramped beds. Many of these hotels have **refurbished** a floor or two and designated the rooms as "business class" or "lux" (there's also a "half-lux" category). This should mean that the bathroom, bed, carpet and paint job are recent, but the overall effect may still be neo-*sovok* – or something quite special: it depends on the hotel. Even otherwise *sovok* places might have one fancy room with a jacuzzi. At many hotels, foreigners are automatically offered the refurbished, higher-priced rooms and staff may try to hide the existence of inferior, cheaper ones.

Proximity to a **metro** station is important, especially beyond the Garden Ring, where city blocks are on a huge scale, and bus stops and pedestrian crossings few and far between. Conversely, a few hotels in the centre are relatively far from a metro while still being within **walking** distance of sights such as Red Square. Anywhere in the city, rooms overlooking main roads will suffer from traffic **noise** unless they have sound-proofing or are at least four floors above street level, and from **air pollution** if you have to open the windows to cope with the sultry heat of summer. At this time of year, **mosquitoes** are a pest near rivers or ponds, making **air conditioning** (a/c) a real plus. If it doesn't exist, the room's *fortochka* (small ventilation window) should be screened to keep mosquitoes out (if not, buy an Ezalo device, see p.35).

Another consideration is **security**. Most hotels have guards and/or CCTV – but you also need to consider the neighbourhood. Having an embassy, government building or mall nearby is a good sign. Staying at the end of a long, poorly lit road in a remote suburb is unwise if you're going to be returning late at

Accommodation prices

The accommodation lists below are divided according to area; within each section the lists are arranged alphabetically. All prices quoted are for the **cheapest double room available in high season**, which may mean without a private bath or shower in the cheapest places. For a single room, expect to pay around two-thirds of the price. Some hotels also offer "lux" or "half-lux" rooms with a lounge and/or kitchen, suited to several people self-catering. The prices given in this guide include 18 percent VAT (НДС in Cyrillic) and four percent city tax. The acceptability of credit cards is specified in the hotel listings.

At many hotels, **weekend rates** can be half-price or even less, as most places are aimed principally at business travellers – the earlier in the week the higher the price. If you can start and end your trip at the weekend, you will usually get charged the weekend rate for your whole stay. The best rates are generally available through booking agencies rather than direct with the hotel.

With inflation in Russia running at fifteen percent, the soaring cost of energy, combined with the imminent removal of price controls on many commodities in Russia, means that **prices are rising** very quickly. The rates listed here are accurate at the time of printing, but make sure you check the current price before booking.

night – especially for anyone dark-skinned. At larger hotels you'll receive a **guest card** (*propusk*) that enables you to pass the guards and claim your room key – don't lose it. Top hotels have electronic card keys for improved security. Most big hotels have a **service bureau**, which can obtain theatre tickets and suchlike. In older hotels, each floor is monitored by a **concierge** or *dezhurnaya*, who will keep your key while you're away and can arrange to have your laundry done. A small gift to her upon arrival should help any ensuing problems to be resolved, but her presence is no guarantee of security. Though relatively few hotels still include **breakfast** in the price, it does no harm to ask; indeed, in low-rated places there may not be anywhere to eat at all.

Central Moscow

We've taken this to mean hotels within the Garden Ring, plus a few places out towards Belarus Station, or directly across the river from the Kremlin. High prices prevail, but even at the deluxe end you can save R3000 or more by shopping around or staying at weekends rather than midweek. Each hotel is marked on the chapter map of the area where it's located (as specified below).

Ararat Park Hyatt Neglinnaya ul. 4 ⓣ783 12 34, ⓕ783 12 35, ⓦwww.moscow.park.hyatt.com; 5min walk from Teatralnaya metro. See map, p.112–113. The city's latest elite hotel occupies a converted Stalinist ministry near the Bolshoy. Luxurious to a fault, its health club has a Roman bath, and guests a choice of Armenian, Japanese and European cuisine. R17,553.

Arbat Plotnikov per. 12 ⓣ244 76 35, ⓕ244 00 93, ⓦwww.president-hotel.ru/arbat, ⓔreservation-arbat@president-hotel.net; 5min walk from Arbatskaya metro. See map, pp.150–151. Just off the Arbat, this three-star hotel was built for visiting Party functionaries and once played host to Fidel Castro. Mostly refurbished, it has a lovely garden with a fountain. Reserve direct by email; bookings made through websites often go amiss. Free visa support. Amex, DC, MC, Visa. R11,000, including breakfast.

Baltschug Kempinski ul. Balchug 1 ⓣ230 65 00, ⓕ230 65 00, toll free ⓣ0800/86 8588 (from UK), ⓣ800-426 3155 (from US & Canada), ⓦwww.kempinski-moscow.ru; 15min walk from Kitay-Gorod or Novokuznetskaya metro. See map, pp.68–69. In walking range of Red Square, across the river, with amazing views from its corner rooms, this stylishly modernized pile is all you'd expect from a deluxe hotel boasting such guests as David Bowie, Michael Jackson and Chuck Norris. Amex, DC, JCB, MC, Visa. R23,000.

Belgrad (Belgrade) Smolenskaya ul. 8 ⓣ248 26 92, ⓕ248 28 14, ⓦwww.hotel-belgrad.ru; near Smolenskaya metro. See map, pp.150–151. Just across the Garden Ring from the Arbat, this three-star twin block to the *Zolotoe Koltso* (see p.330) offers a choice of *sovok* or refurbished a/c rooms and suites. Amex, DC, EC, Maestro, MC, Visa. R5900.

Budapest Petrovskie Linii 2/18 ⓣ621 10 60, ⓕ621 52 90, ⓦwww.hotel-budapest.ru; 10min walk from Teatralnaya or Kuznetskiy Most metro. See map, pp.112–113. Recently refurbished, this atmospheric pre-Revolutionary hotel between the Bolshoy and the Sandunovskiy Baths is a good-value option. Amex, Visa, MC, DC, JCB. R9912, including breakfast.

East-West Tverskoy bul. 14, str. 4 ⓣ232 28 57, ⓕ956 30 27, ⓦwww.eastwesthotel.ru; 10min walk from Tverskaya/Pushkinskaya metro. See map, pp.112–113. This modernized nineteenth-century mansion on the Boulevard Ring has individually styled rooms ranging from minimalist chic to Madame de Pompadour. Sauna; laundry service. Reserve two or three weeks ahead. No credit cards. R14,500.

Golden Apple Hotel Str. m. Dmitrovka 11 ⓣ980 70 00, ⓕ980 70 01, ⓦwww.goldenapple.ru. See map, pp.150–151. Billed as Moscow's only boutique hotel, the *Golden Apple* is a bit like a cross between a New York boutique hotel and a funky nightclub. Great location, with a very decent breakfast, the food is better during the week when there are more business travellers. R18,000.

Marco Polo Presnya Spiridonovskiy per. 9 ⓣ244 36 31, ⓕ926 54 02, ⓦwww.presnja.ru; 10min walk from Mayakovskaya or Pushkinskaya metro. See map, pp.150–151. A discreet, modern, a/c four-star hotel in a quiet side street near the Patriarch's Ponds. Solarium, sauna, gym and jacuzzi. Amex, DC, MC, Visa. R15,850.

Marriott Aurora ul. Petrovka 11/20 ⓣ937 10 00, ⓕ937 08 01, ⓦwww.marriotthotels.com/mowdt; 10min walk from Teatralnaya or Tverskaya metro. See map, pp.112–113. One of several Marriotts in Moscow, this five-star hotel a few blocks from the Bolshoy Theatre has all the facilities you'd expect, including a pool and health club. All major cards. R27,140.

Marriott Grand Tverskaya ul. 26 ⓣ937 00 00, ⓕ937 00 01, ⓦwww.marriott.com; 10min walk from Tverskaya, Pushkinskaya or Mayakovskaya metro. See map, pp.150–151. The five-star flagship of the Marriott fleet has modems in every room and a suite on each floor designed for wheelchair users, yet costs less than the Aurora. Amex, DC, MC, Visa. R15,000–21,000.

Metropol Teatralniy proezd 1/4 ⓣ927 60 00, ⓕ927 60 10, ⓦwww.metropol-moscow.ru; near Teatralnaya, Ploshchad Revolyutsii and Okhotniy Ryad metros. See map, p.102. Luxuriant Art Nouveau edifice on the edge of the Kitay-gorod, whose list of guests has included Tolstoy, Chaliapin, Shaw and JFK. Amex, DC, JCB, MC, Visa. R19,000.

▲ The Art Nouveau exterior of the Metropol hotel

National Okhotniy ryad 14/1 ⓣ258 70 00, ⓕ258 71 00, ⓦwww.national.ru; near Okhotniy Ryad and Teatralnaya metros. See map, pp.112–113. A historic Art Nouveau-Eclectic hotel with terrific views of the Kremlin. Rooms are furnished with antique furniture and have hardwood floors; rooms start at R18,762, but the finest suite costs R81,900. Gym, pool and sauna. Part of the Meridien chain. Amex, DC, JCB, MC, Visa.

Pekin (Beijing) ul. Bolshaya-Sadovaya 5/1 ⓣ777 19 38, ⓦwww.pekinn.ru; near Mayakovskaya metro. See map, pp.150–151. This Stalin-Gothic pile on the Garden Ring was meant to be a postwar HQ for the secret police, and staff act like they've trained at the Lubyanka. Renovated rooms are quite decent though the old *sovok* ones (meant to be interrogation rooms) are pretty dismal. This kitsch monument to the era of Sino-Soviet friendship needs a good purge if it's ever to fulfil its potential. Amex, EC, MC, Visa. R12,300.

Savoy ul. Rozhdestvenka 3 Ⓣ258 41 00, Ⓕ929 86 65, Ⓦwww.savoy.ru; near Kuznetskiy Most metro. See map, pp.112–113. Member of Small Luxury Hotels of the World, this historic four-star hotel has gorgeous, recently updated rooms and a splendid Art Nouveau/Baroque restaurant with a fountain. It also has a business centre, sauna, gym, pool and art gallery. Amex, DC, EC, JCB, MC, Visa. R24,854, including buffet breakfast.

Sretenskaya ul. Sretenka 15 Ⓣ933 55 44, Ⓦwww.hotel-sretenskaya.ru; 5min walk from Sukharevskaya metro. See map, pp.150–151. An attractive new mini-hotel between the Boulevard and Garden Ring, whose folksy decor is themed on *The Scarlet Flower* (the Russian version of *Beauty and the Beast*). Health club, billiards and secure parking. All major cards. R11,220.

Sverchkov 8 Sverchkov per. 8 Ⓣ925 49 78, Ⓕ925 44 36, Ⓔsvertchkov8@mail.ru. See map, pp.112–113. A quirky, old-fashioned place in the quiet backstreets near the Boulevard Ring (in the wing on the left as you enter the yard). Clean rooms with baths, phone and TV; "lux" ones carpeted, with several rooms. Little English spoken but staff are friendly. A pet owl flies around the lobby at night. Reserve in advance as it is popular. No cards. R9700, including breakfast.

Tiflis (Tiblisi) ul. Ostozhenka 32 Ⓣ733 90 70, Ⓦwww.hoteltiflis.com; 10min walk from Park Kultury or Kropotkinskaya metro. See map, pp.150–151. A fantastic option if you can afford it, this deluxe mini-hotel beside a Georgian restaurant combines all mod cons with traditional Caucasian features. Some rooms have balconies overlooking a courtyard with a fountain, while for R16,000 there are two-storey apartments with jacuzzis (one has a sauna, too). R12,040, including breakfast.

Zolotoe Koltso (Golden Ring) Smolenskaya ul. 5 Ⓣ725 01 00, Ⓕ725 01 01, Ⓦwww.hotel-goldenring.ru; near Smolenskaya metro. See map, pp.150–151. Just beyond the Arbat, this recently renovated tower-block is comfortable and well managed, with a winter garden and restaurant with panoramic views on the 22nd and 23rd floors. All major cards. R19,383.

Krasnaya Presnya, Fili and the southwest

Though these are rated good areas to live by Muscovites and expatriates, visitors should keep transport in mind. The *Radisson Slavyanskaya*, and *Yunost* are easily reached; the *Mezhdunarodnaya* is awkward, while the *Sputnik* and *Tsentralniy Dom Turistov* are way out, but accessible by metro. All hotels are marked on the map on p.178.

Mezhdunarodnaya (International, aka "the Mezh") Krasnopresnenskaya nab. 12 Ⓣ253 21 22, Ⓕ253 20 51, Ⓦwww.wtcmoscow.ru/eng/hotel; 20min walk from Krasnopresnenskaya metro. Hard to reach except by taxi, this corporate haven has an atrium, mall, pool, gym and solarium. Its smallish, sterile rooms overlook the business district upriver from the White House. Rates are higher during trade fairs. Breakfast included. All major cards. R11,900.

Radisson Slavyanskaya Berezhovskaya nab. 2 Ⓣ941 80 20, Ⓕ941 80 00, Ⓦwww.radissonSAS.com; near Kievskaya metro. Moscow's only US-managed hotel has a great view of the Crystal Bridge, is within a 20min walk of the Arbat, and claims Bill Clinton as a past guest. It contains an excellent mall and copying centre, a gym, pool and sauna. It also has free wi-fi, though it doesn't always work straight away. Amex, DC, JCB, MC, Visa. R9500.

Sputnik Leninskiy pr. 38 Ⓣ930 22 87, Ⓕ930 63 83; 10min walk from Leninskiy Prospekt metro. An ugly 1970s hotel with a machine-gun toting cop at the door and a "Gentlemen's Club" on the top floor. Rooms *sovok* but clean; only the tenth floor has been renovated. Its saving grace is the *Darbar* Indian restaurant – but you don't have to check in to enjoy it (see p.356). No cards. R7000.

Tsentralniy Dom Turistov (Central House of Tourists, or CDT) Leninskiy pr. 146 Ⓣ434 94 67, Ⓕ438 77 56, Ⓦwww.cdt-hotel.ru; 10min walk from Yugo-Zapadnaya metro (25min ride

from the centre). Further out than the Sputnik, but clean and safe, this 34-storey block's facilities include bowling, a swimming pool, sauna and billiards; all rooms have a fridge, TV and bathroom. Breakfast included. All cards except Amex. R4600.

Yunost (Youth) ul. Khamovnicheskiy val 34 ⓣ242 48 61, ⓕ242 02 84; near Sportivnaya metro. Popular with Russian tourists from the provinces, this 1960s hotel 10min walk from the Novodevichiy Convent has *sovok* rooms with baths, and refurbished doubles on the eighth floor (R1550). No English spoken. MC, Visa. R3400.

Zamoskvareche and the south

This corresponds to the area covered by Chapter 6, minus the riverbank opposite the Kremlin. Hotels in the Zamoskvareche quarter with its famous Tretyakov Gallery and waterfront views (see map on p.207) are predictably costlier than those out in high-rise land, 15–30 minutes by metro from the centre. All hotels listed below are marked on the map on p.205, unless otherwise stated.

Akademicheskaya Leninskiy pr. 1/2 ⓣ959 81 57, ⓕ238 25 39; near Oktyabrskaya metro. Once reserved for guests of the Academy of Sciences, this block just off Oktyabrskaya ploshchad now takes anyone. The old rooms (R3590) are really *sovok*, refurbished ones cost an extra R2200, and the only amenity is a café. Only really worth trying if the nearby *Warsawa* (see p.332) is full. No English spoken; MC, Visa.

Alrosa na Kazachem 1-iy Kazachiy per. 4 ⓣ745 21 90, ⓕ745 77 63, ⓦwww.alrosa-hotel.ru; 10min walk from Polyanka metro. See map, p.207. A comfortable mini-hotel on a quiet street off Bolshaya Ordynka, with a pool, gym and sauna – all very nice but a bit overpriced, compared to the *Katerina* or *Tatiana* (see below & p.332). All major cards. R6900.

Danilovskaya Bolshoy Stariy Danilovskiy per. 5 ⓣ954 04 51, ⓕ954 07 50, ⓦwww.hotel-danilovskaya.da.ru; 10min walk from Tulskaya metro. Built alongside the Danilov Monastery to lodge Patriarchal guests, but open to anyone if they book ahead. Upholding the maxim that cleanliness is next to godliness, the hotel features a pool with a waterfall, a *banya* and laundry, plus icons, a Bible and a portrait of Patriarch Alexei in every room. There's also an internet café. Buffet breakfast included. Amex, DC, MC, Visa. R3900.

Katerina Shlyuzovaya nab. 6, str. 1 ⓣ933 04 01, ⓦwww.katerina.msk.ru; 10min walk from Paveletskaya metro. Named after its owner's daughter, this classy Russo-Swedish "city hotel" opposite the International House of Music and the Riverside Towers financial district is an amalgam of a nineteenth-century mansion and Scandinavian chic, with a/c rooms, Turkish and Finnish saunas, a gym and jacuzzi. Buffet breakfast included. DC, JCB, MC, Visa. R5500.

Orekhovo Apart-Hotel Shipilovskiy proezd 47 ⓣ392 33 27; ⓦwww.reisebuero-welt.com; 10min walk from Orekhovo metro (30min from the centre). In the fresh-air zone near Tsaritsyno, it looks like any shabby block of flats from outside, but its rooms are spanking new. Guests can take a room on a "block" of four sharing a bathroom and kitchen (R6600), or rent a four-roomed apartment for just over R8700. Staff are friendly and eager to please. No cards. R6600–R8700.

President ul. Bolshaya Yakimanka 24 ⓣ239 38 00, ⓕ230 23 18, ⓦwww.president-hotel.ru; 10min from Polyanka metro. See map, p.207. Weird, time-warped 1980s hotel once reserved for foreign Communist leaders and still owned by the Kremlin. Guests are frisked incessantly and the bathrooms are *sovok* – don't be fooled by website photos. Swimming pool, billiards and sauna. Amex, DC, EC, MC, Visa. R5400.

Swissotel Krasnye Holmy Moscow Kosmodamianskaya nab. 52, bld. 6 ⓣ495 221 53 67, ⓕ495 787 98 98. ⓦwww.swissotel.com. A 5min walk from Pavletskaya metro station in the same complex as the House of Music concert hall, this fantastic hotel has great views of the city, and offers free shuttles to the centre. The tall space-age tower is crowned by an inverted cone which houses a cocktail bar, with the best views and serving great drinks. R16,900.

Tatiana Stremyanniy per. 11 ⓣ721 25 02, ⓕ721 25 01; 10min walk from Paveletskaya metro. This newer, smaller sister hotel to the *Katerina* (see p.331) has the same stylish Swedish decor and attentive service, with a fitness club and sauna, but rooms cost a third less and the location isn't so good. Breakfast included. DC, JCB, MC, Visa. R12,500.

Tsaritsyno Shipilovskiy proezd 47, korpus 1 ⓣ343 43 43, ⓦwww.all-hotels.ru/moscow/tsaritsino; 10min walk from Orekhovo metro (30min from the centre). Inferior to the nearby *Orekhevo Apart-Hotel* (see above), this tower block has 1-to 4-room flats with TV, phone and kitchenette, furnished to Russian or "Euro" standard. For R14,800 you can get an apartment with a sauna, jacuzzi, kitchen and dining room, while the standard rooms start at R5600. No English spoken.

Warsawa (Warsaw) Leninskiy pr. 2/1 ⓣ238 41 01; ⓦwww.moscow-hotel.ru; near Oktyabrskaya metro. This outwardly gloomy 1950s block on the corner of Krymskiy val has freshly renovated rooms with a/c, attractive bathrooms, hairdryers and even wall-safes. R5990.

Taganka and Zayauze

If you don't mind a twenty-minute metro ride into the centre, one of the best cheap locations to stay is by the souvenir market at Izmaylovo, where six 28-storey blocks built for the 1980 Olympics now function as four hotels, whose standards and prices vary – though all of their rooms have bathrooms and are uniformly box-like. All accommodation listed below is marked on the map on pp.246–247.

Alfa Izmaylovskoe shosse 71 ⓣ166 01 63, ⓕ166 03 63, ⓦwww.english.alpha-hotel.ru, near Izmalovskiy Park metro. The best of the four, its regular (R4400) and "lux" (R6600) rooms have all been attractively refurbished, and there's a sauna on almost every floor of the hotel, which also has an internet café. MC, Visa.

Beta ⓣ792 99 11, ⓣ792 99 12, ⓦwww.beta.all-hotels.ru. Its *sovok* "economy" rooms (R3800) are as cheap as you'll get at Izmaylovo, as are the "business" (R4400) and "first-class" (R5900) rooms. DC, JCB, Maestro, MC, Visa.

Gamma-Delta ⓣ166 41 27, ⓦwww.izmailovo.ru. These two blocks offer a choice of decent *sovok* (R3800) or refurbished "business class" (R6600) rooms, some on non-smoking floors. That, and the pleasant shared lobby, makes *Gamma-Delta* the best option after *Alfa*.

Vega ⓣ956 06 42, ⓦwww.hotel-vega.ru. Its *sovok* rooms (R8900) are dearer than *Gamma-Delta*'s but in no way superior, and for the cost of a "lux" room (R15,600) on the 14th floor (with free internet access) you could stay somewhere fancier nearer the centre. Maestro, MC, Visa.

Northern suburbs

This vast area is a grab-bag of locations within one to five stops (5–20min) by metro from the Circle line and the city centre. Serebryanjy bor is lovely but remote; places on or off Leningradskiy prospekt run the gamut from Stalinist class to overpriced *sovok*; mid- to low-budget hotels cluster around the VVTs; and there are deluxe hotels nearer the Garden Ring. The *Sovietskiy*, *Kosmos*, *Royal Zenith*, and *Zvozdnaya* are all bargains in their respective price ranges. All hotels listed below are marked on the map on pp.270–271 unless otherwise stated

Aeropolis Leningradskiy pr. 37, korpus 5 ⓣ151 04 42, ⓕ151 75 43, ⓦwww.moscow-hotel.ru; 15min walk from Dinamo or Aeroport metro. An ex-Aeroflot staff hotel beside the former Air Terminal. Rather *sovok*, as you'd expect, though "business-lux" rooms on the twelfth floor have new furnishings and a/c. Buffet breakfast included. DC, JCB, MC, Visa. R7000.

Art Hotel 3-ya Peschanaya ul. 2 ⓣ725 09 05, ⓦwww.arthotel.ru; 15–20min walk from Sokol or Polezhaevskaya metro. If you don't mind its distance from a metro station, this Best Western hotel in a quiet neighbourhood on the edge of the TsKA offers guests satellite TV, gym, sauna, access to tennis courts and even accommodation for pets. Amex, DC, EC, JCB, MC, Visa. R7950.

Brighton Petrovskovo-Razumovskiy proezd 29 ⓣ&ⓕ214 93 32, ⓦwww.brh.ru; 20min walk from Dinamo or Dmitrovskaya metro. Named after the upstate New York Russian colony of Brighton Beach, this nice mini-hotel has a pool, sauna, solarium and massage, with a paying-playground next door that makes it especially good for those with kids – but is difficult to reach without a car. R6800, including breakfast.

Globus (Globe) **Yaroslavskaya ul. 17 ⓣ286 41 89, ⓕ286 46 16, ⓦwww.hotelglobus.ru; 10min walk from VDNKh metro. See map, pp.278–279** On the same street as the metro station, this 1950s block has OK *sovok* rooms with bathrooms, fridge, phone, cable TV and electric kettle; rooms #115 and #116 have nicer decor and a jacuzzi, for R600 more. There's also a sauna on the premises. R6750.

Hilton Hotel Leningradskaya (Leningrad) **Kalanchovskaya ul. 21/40 ⓣ495 627 55 50 ⓕ495 627 55 51, ⓦwww1.hilton.com; near Komsomolskaya metro.** A pint-sized Stalin skyscraper at the end of Komsomolskaya ploshchad, off the Garden Ring (see p.285), it has been completely renovated and offers very high standard rooms in a historic building. Amex, Visa, MC. R18,000.

Holiday Inn Vinogradovo Dmitrovskoe shosse 171 ⓣ937 06 70, ⓕ937 06 71, ⓦwww.moscow-vinogradovo.holiday-inn.com; free shuttle bus from Sheremetevo-2 and the centre, or bus #685 from Altufevo metro. Aimed at those who crave a respite from Moscow, this upscale *Holiday Inn* has a pool, gym, sauna and full business facilities, by a lake just beyond the outer ring road. Amex, Visa, DC, MC. R7490.

Iris Korovinskoe shosse 10 ⓣ933 05 33, ⓦwww.iris-hotel.ru; shuttle-bus to the centre (7.30am–midnight). Built at the same time as a nearby eye hospital, in the shape of an eye, this a/c four-star hotel has a pool, gym and sauna and is set in a park with other facilities, in a remote district that's great for fresh air but hopeless for sightseeing. R8100.

Kosmos (Cosmos) **pr. Mira 150 ⓣ234 10 00 or 234 12 06, ⓕ215 88 80, ⓦwww.hotelcosmos.ru; 5min walk from VDNKh metro. See map, pp.278–279** This revamped 1970s colossus facing the Space Obelisk has a large pool with a tube slide, a panoramic view of the VVTs from its 25th-floor restaurant, a casino and bowling. Rooms with cable TV and minibar. Tight security. Amex, MC, Visa. R7990, including breakfast.

Marriott Tverskaya 1-ya Tverskaya Yamskaya ul. 34 ⓣ258 30 00, ⓕ258 30 99, ⓦwww.marriott.com; 10min from Belorusskaya metro. Smaller than its siblings, with only four stars, but nonetheless popular with business travellers due to its location near the Garden Ring, Belarus Station and the Novoslobodskaya financial district. Free gym and sauna. Amex, DC, MC, Visa. R13,500–19,000.

Novotel Centre Novoslobodskaya ul. 23 ⓣ780 40 00, ⓕ780 40 01, ⓦwww.novotel.com; near Mendeleevskaya metro. On the Circle line, so easily accessible, this new, classy four-star high-rise has pleasant a/c rooms and fab views from its 18th-floor café/bar, *The Top*. Buffet breakfast included. Amex, DC, MC, Visa. R12,450.

Renaissance Olympiyskiy pr. 18/1 ⓣ931 90 00, ⓕ931 90 76, ⓦwww.marriott.com/hotels/travel/mowrn-renaissance-moscow-hotel; 15min walk from Prospekt Mira metro. Refurbished to the highest standards, this four-star Marriott near the Olympic Sports Complex has shuttle buses into the centre and to the Izmaylovo market, plus a 22m pool, large gym, and English-language cinema on the premises. Amex, DC, JCB, MC, Visa. R13,400.

Royal Zenith I Tamanskaya ul. 49b ⓣ119 15 11, ⓕ119 81 01; and II 1-ya liniyia ul. Khoroshevskovo 10T ⓣ721 900, ⓕ199 14 36, ⓦwww.royal-zenith.ru; trolleybus #20, #21, #65 or #86 from Polezhaevskaya metro. If you don't mind being far from the centre (1hr by public transport), these two delightful hotels in the woods of Serebryaniy bor are an ideal retreat. The first has just twelve rooms, each with a stereo and jacuzzi; the main hotel (10min walk away) has a 20m pool, gym, sauna and two large freshwater aquariums. Breakfast included. Amex, DC, JCB, Maestro, MC, Visa. R17,900.

Sheraton Palace 1-ya Tverskaya Yamskaya ul. 19 ⓣ931 97 00, ⓕ931 97 04, ⓦwww.sheratonpalace.ru; 10min from Mayakovskaya metro. Modern a/c five-star hotel only 500m beyond the Garden Ring. All rooms have king-size beds and fax machines; some rooms are for non-smoking or disabled guests, and there's a VIP floor. Gym, jacuzzi and sauna, and a fine seafood restaurant. Its prices vary depending on the day of the week, starting at R19,000 at the beginning of the week, R12,000 at the end of the week, and going down to a bargain R6990 at the weekend. Amex, Visa, DC, MC, JCB.

Sovetskiy (Soviet) **Leningradskiy pr. 32/2 ⓣ960 20 00, ⓕ250 80 03, ⓦwww.sovietsky.ru; 5min walk from Dinamo metro.** Its marble lobby, high-ceilinged rooms and attentive service make this the best of the "Stalin" hotels. Celeb guests include Margaret Thatcher, King Juan Carlos, Indira Gandhi and Arnold Schwarzenegger (to open the hotel's Planet Fitness). Its historic *Yar* restaurant is named after a famous haunt of Tolstoy, Chekhov and Rasputin; guests can see its floor show for free. Amex, Visa, MC. R16,900.

Zolotoy Kolos (Golden Wheatsheaf) Yaroslavskaya ul. 15, str. 1 ⓣ217 6666, ⓦwww.zkolos.ru; 10min walk from VDNKh metro. This 1950s building has a modern lobby and some attractive renovated rooms, but the older, half-price ones can be musty. No cards. R8300.

Zvozdnaya (Starry) Argunovskaya ul. 2 ⓣ215 42 83; VDNKh metro, then any bus or minibus along Zvozdniy bulvar. Slightly over 1km from the Ostankino Palace, this refurbished tower block is a bit remote, but deserves consideration for its clean rooms (R5800) and wild themed suites (R13,200) – Arabian, Japanese or honeymoon, the latter with a jacuzzi. No cards.

Homestay accommodation

Unlike St Petersburg, the capital has no walk-in **agencies** where visitors can arrange a room on the spot, and only a few **online** offer homestay in Moscow. Host Families Association (ⓦwww.hofa.ru) has flats in different parts of the city starting at R1200 per person upwards, while Uncle Pasha (ⓦwww.cheap-moscow.com) offers lodgings from €15–40, if you pay in advance from abroad, or R1500–3500 if you pay on arrival. Companies abroad (see "Getting there" in *Basics*) may charge up to €50 a head per night. Try to ascertain the exact location, and weigh up if it's worth the price. Booking through an agency or tour company that also provides visa support, your **registration** should be handled automatically – but be sure to verify that this is so. There have been instances where agencies failed to follow through with the paperwork, landing their clients in a bureaucratic nightmare.

Staying with a Russian family, you should be well looked after and experience the cosy domesticity that is the obverse of brusque public life. Your introduction to this homely world will be a pair of *tapochki* – the slippers which Russians wear indoors to avoid tramping in mud – followed by a cup of tea or a shot of vodka. Your room will be clean and comfortable, though it can be disconcerting to discover, in small apartments, that it belongs to one of the family, who will sleep elsewhere for the duration of your stay.

Another, more disagreeable, surprise might be that the district **hot-water** supply has been cut off, as happens for up to two weeks during the summer, so that the utilities company can clean the water mains. Don't blame your hosts should this happen – it's not their fault. All you can do is put up with it, or move to another district of the city that isn't affected at the time. The water company gives only a week's notice that supplies will be cut off, so a flat with its own boiler is highly desirable.

This being Russia, there's also an **unregulated alternative** – namely people touting for guests at railway terminals. Most are genuine widows or pensioners with a room or flat to let, but inevitably there are tricksters too. You'll have to depend on your instincts as to whom to trust, and shouldn't agree to anything without them showing you the flat's location on a map – let alone part with cash before seeing it. They're extremely unlikely to be able to register you, so anyone using this option faces a registration problem if they stay more than three days. Rates for "unofficial" B&B can be R500 a day or less.

Flat rental

If you're going to be in town longer than a week, or are coming as a group of friends or a family, you should consider renting a self-contained **apartment** (*kvartira*) to save money and enjoy more privacy than a hotel or homestay allows. This can be done before you arrive through **online** agencies such as Rick's Apartments, HOFA, Astor Apartments, Apartment Accommodation in Moscow, Uncle Pasha or Flatmates.Ru (see p.326). With the exception of the last two, a fixer's **fee** is built into the price, which is higher with locally based agencies catering to business travellers that advertise in the *Moscow Times* and *Moscow Journal*. If you're settling here, time spent investigating the **direct rental** market is a wise investment – local trade papers like *Tovary i Tseni* (Goods and Prices) and *Ruk v Ruki* (Hand to Hand) are full of adverts for flats without the cost of an intermediary. It's worth hiring an interpreter to ring around and translate in negotiations. Dealing directly with the landlord, the monthly rent for a standard *sovok* **flat** outside the centre should be about R15,000 for a one-room "studio", R20,000 for a two-room flat or R30,000 for an apartment with two bedrooms. Anywhere within the Garden Ring or any of the new business districts will be at least a third more expensive (from R20,000/R30,000/R45,000 for a studio, one- or two-bedroom flat), while if the flat has been refurbished the rent is likely to be well above R45,000. Conversely, if the flat is way out from the centre and quite far from a metro station, the benchmark *sovok* price may drop by a third. Another option is renting a **room** in someone's apartment; here, it's usual to pay 20–30 percent of the monthly rent bill.

Aside from the price, location and decor, the things to look for are a **boiler** (*kolonka*), so you won't be deprived of hot water if the district supply is cut off, a **bed** that's long enough to be comfortable, and a **door** that provides good security. Many apartments have a sturdy outer door, whose lock is operated by pushing in and then retracting a notched metal strip; the inner door is unlocked by conventional keys, while the door from the apartment building onto the street or yard may be locked by a device which requires you to punch in a code. **Door codes** usually consist of three digits; you have to push all three buttons simultaneously to make it work; alternatively, if there's a metal ring, press the numbers in order and pull upwards. In some blocks, tenants open the street door with electronic touch keys.

Hostels

Ever since the Russian Youth Hostel Association (RYHA) and the first international hostel were set up by a Californian and his Russian partners in 1992, Moscow's **hostels** have faced the dilemma that not enough backpackers visit the city to balance their books without raising prices so high that their clientele decides that homestay or cheapo hotels offer better value for money. Another constraint is that, by law, hostels may register only guests who've obtained their visa support through the hostel or its partner agency – which means that guests who didn't and stay longer than three days risk being in breach of registration rules (see p.33). In fact, many hostels are currently considering closing because of the new registration laws which make it almost impossible for them to be profitable. Really, the main advantage of staying at a hostel is the chance to meet fellow backpackers and access information and internet in English – which you won't find in a cheap hotel.

The two **official places** listed below are both in far-flung suburbs and keep a low profile, with no prominent identifying signs on the buildings in which they're located. Both can provide visa support and have OK security on the premises; airport or station transfers, city tours and excursions can be arranged.

There are no age or membership restrictions, but a Hostelling International (HI), RYHA or ISIC student card may get you a few dollars' discount. Decor is basic and shared bathrooms none too clean, but hot water can usually be relied upon.

Without endorsing it, we'd be remiss not to mention a cheaper **unofficial hostel**. It can't register you, but prices are rock-bottom for the city centre: *Galina's Flat* (ul. Chapygina 8, flat #35 ⓣ921 60 38, ⓔgalinas.flat@mtu-net.ru), on a backstreet off the Boulevard Ring within walking distance of Chistye Prudy metro, has a couple of rooms with bunks (R500 a bed), a kitchen, internet, and lots of cats.

G&R Hostel Asia Zelenodolskaya ul. 3/2 ⓣ378 00 01, ⓕ378 28 66, ⓦwww.hostels.ru; near Ryazanskiy Prospekt metro. See map, pp.246–247. Occupying the top three floors of a fifteen-storey block, 20min ride from the centre (exit at the front of the train) or a short bus ride from Kuskovo Palace, this hostel has single (R1200) and double (R2100) rooms with shared bathrooms, and a few en-suite doubles (R2800). English-speaking staff and information board; internet. Visa support; transfers and excursions.

Hostel Sherstone Gostininichniy proezd str. 1 ⓣ&ⓕ797 80 75, ⓦwww.sherstone.ru; 15min walk from Vladykino metro. See map, pp.270–271. An offshoot of the *Asia*, in a grungy part of the northern suburbs (20min by metro; R1000 transfer from Sheremetevo airport), this third-floor hostel has en-suite facilities, cable TV, fridge and phone in all its dorms (€22–60). Only accepts payment in euros. Visa, MC or Western Union.

The Moscow metro

As well as being the best way to get around the city, the Moscow metro makes a fascinating sight in itself. From the ornate older stations – often decorated with fixtures stolen from palaces or churches – to the later Style Moderne stops, the entire metro system has been built on an impressively grand scale. All the station halls are huge, so that even with well over nine million people using the metro each day there is space to stop and appreciate the art and architecture around you.

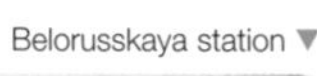

Arbatskaya station ▲

Belorusskaya station ▼

Kievskaya station ▼

Stations not to miss

Arbatskaya: Arbatsko–Pokrovskaya #3, Koltseveaya #5, Serpukhovsko–Timiryazevskaya #90 and Filyovskaya #4 lines. The platforms on the Arbatsko–Pokrovskaya line, opened in 1953, share a vestibule whose arches rise from red marble seat-plinths to vaults dripping with ceramic flowers and hanging bronze lamps. Look out for the arched wall at the top of the escalator to street level with its mural of Stalin smoking a pipe.

Belorusskaya: Circle and Zamoskvaretskaya #2 lines. The lower Circle line station, opened in 1952, has a stuccoed, coffered hall with a tessellated floor in a Belarus rug pattern. Look out, too, for the mosaic panels of flower-bedecked citizens in national dress enjoying a peaceful life, won by the sacrifices of the muscular partisan figures in the transit hall between the two levels.

Kievskaya: Filyovskaya # 4, Arbatsko–Pokrovskaya #3 and Circle lines. The Circle line station was completed shortly after Belorusskaya, and likewise has an ethnic slant. Mosaic vignettes from the history of Russo-Ukrainian amity, in stucco frames imitating lace, unfold under the benign gaze of Lenin.

Komsomolskaya: Sokolnicheskaya #1 and Circle lines. Dedicated to the Communist Youth activists whose work on the first line in 1935 is depicted on majolica panels in the rose marble columned hall on the upper level. A ceiling awash with gold-encrusted mosaics ennobles the Circle line station, opened in 1952. The mosaic of the parade in Red Square was retouched as the Soviet leadership changed, with Beria and Stalin being effaced in the mid-1950s, and Khrushchev in 1964.

Mayakovskaya: Zamoskvaretskaya #2 line. Part of the second line, completed in 1938; its magnificent design – by Alexei Dushkin – won the Grand Prix at the World Fair that year. The station is spacious and stylish, with ribbed steel and red and black marble columns, lit by 36 oval cupolas decorated with mosaic panels on the theme of sports and aviation. Stalin spoke here during the dark days of 1941 (see p.154).

Novokuznetskaya: Zamoskvaretskaya #2 line. Built and opened during wartime, this station's pale marble hall (designed by Vladimir Gelfreykh and Igor Rozhin) is decorated with a bas-relief frieze of military heroes, and mosaic ceiling panels showing athletic youths garlanded in flowers.

Park Kultury: Sokolnicheskaya #1 and Circle lines. Originally the end station of the Sokolnicheskaya line, its barrel-vaulted main hall (by Rozhin) is clad in marble to head height, with niches displaying bas-relief medallions of workers skating, dancing, playing chess and reading poetry (by Sergei Ryabushkin).

Ploshchad Revolyutsii: Arbatsko–Pokrovskaya #3 line. Opened as part of the third line, which employed the most renowned Soviet architects of the late 1930s. Dushkin designed the red marble central hall, flanked by 36 life-sized crouching bronze statues (by Matvei Manizer) personifying the defence of Soviet power and its achievements, interspersed with Art Nouveau sheaves of corn and circular lamps.

Taganskaya: Circle and Tagansko–Krasnopresnenskaya #7 lines. Its Circle line station is themed on the Great Patriotic War, with marble archways bearing pale blue and white ceramic cameos of partisans, pilots, tank drivers and munitions workers, in tulip-shaped frames.

▲ Mayakovskaya station

▼ Ploschad Revolyutsii station

▼ Taganskaya station

Rush hour on the Moscow metro ▲

Statue at Ploschad Revolyutsii station ▼

Navigating the metro

The **least crowded** times of day to explore the metro are between 10am and 3pm or 9pm and midnight. The evening tends to be less busy, though more people will be drunk and there's a higher police presence: you'll also need to take care not to miss the last train back (they stop running at 1am, but the intersections close at 12.30am). During the **rush hours**, both the escalators and the trains themselves suffer from traffic jams – while everyone is generally very stoic and invariably polite, it's not for the claustrophobic.

All the signs are in Cyrillic, but if you can't read them, listen to the **tannoy announcements** – if the voice is a woman you are heading out of the centre, if it is a man you are heading into the centre. All the lines are **colour coded** and numbered; many Moscow residents know their line by its colour, rather than its name. On the wall across the tracks from each platform are route descriptions showing every station and highlighting the intersections. When you exit the train the signs directing you to the intersecting station are colour-coded too.

Cultural customs

You can see that over the years, the older stations have developed certain cultural superstitions. In **Ploshchad Revolyutsii**, for example, there is a row of statues, with a dog about three quarters of the way down the platform. Check out the dog's nose – touching it is meant to bring you luck and at exam times students from the nearby university queue up to do so. Over the years the statue has developed a noticeably shiny snout.

12

Eating and drinking

When I eat pork at a meal, give me the whole pig; when mutton, give the whole sheep; when goose, the whole bird. Two dishes are better than a thousand provided a fellow can devour as much of them as he wants.

Dead Souls, Gogol

As the above quotation suggests, quantity rather than variety has long characterized the Russian appetite. Especially under Communism, when haute cuisine was wiped out, citizens made a virtue of the slow service that was the norm in Soviet restaurants by drinking, talking and dancing for hours. The Western notion of a quick meal was unthinkable.

Nowadays, the **gastronomic scene** has improved enormously, with hundreds of new cafés and restaurants offering all kinds of cuisine and surroundings, aimed at anyone with a disposable income – from mega-rich New Russians and expense-account expatriates to fashion-conscious wealthy teenagers. While some places at the top end of the market can rightfully boast of their haute cuisine, there are lots whose decor and pretensions surpass their cooking, where the clientele's main aim seems to be to flash their money around.

While all bars, cafés and restaurants take payment in rubles, more tourist-oriented places may list prices on their menus in so-called "Standard" or "**Conditional Units**" (using the Cyrillic abbreviation УЕ), equivalent to US dollars, euros, or some point between the two currencies, converted into rubles at the current central bank rate or the rate of exchange advertised on the premises (which may be less favourable). It's often (though not invariably) true that a menu in dollars is an indication that the establishment is overpriced by local standards.

Credit cards are accepted by most top-range or foreign-managed restaurants – we've indicated in our listings which ones are accepted using the relevant abbreviations (Amex = American Express, DC = Diners Club, EC = Eurocard MC = Mastercard, JCB = Japanese Credit Bank) – but you shouldn't take it for granted. As for paying with traveller's cheques, forget it.

Breakfast, bakeries and snacks

At home, most Russians take **breakfast** (*zavtrak*) very seriously, tucking into calorific dishes such as pancakes (bliny) or buckwheat porridge (*kasha*), with curd cheese (*tvorog*) and sour cream (*smetana*), although some settle simply for a cup of tea and a slice of bread. Hotels will serve an approximation of the "Continental" breakfast, probably just a fried egg, bread, butter and jam; the flashier joints, however, provide a Shvedskiy stol, or "Swedish table", a sort of smorgasbord – and may feature a slap-up Sunday brunch.

Pastries (*pirozhnoe*) are available from cake shops (*konditerskaya*) and some grocers (*gastronom*). Savoury pies (*pirozhki*) are often sold on the streets from late morning; the best are filled with cabbage, curd cheese or rice. It's advisable to steer clear of the meat ones unless you're buying from a reputable outlet.

Bread (*khleb*), available from bakeries (*bulochnaya*), is one of the country's culinary strong points. "Black" bread (known as *chorniy* or *rzhanoy*) is the traditional variety: a dense rye bread with a distinctive sourdough flavour and amazing longevity. *Karelskiy* is similar but with fruit; *surozhniy* is a lighter version, made with a mixture of wheat and rye. French-style baguettes (baton) – white, mixed-grain or plaited with poppy seeds – are also popular. For wholegrain, focaccia or fruit breads, check out the Baltic Bread chain of bakeries.

Like other Eastern Europeans, the Russians are very fond of **cakes** (*tort*). The Sladkoezhka chain of patisseries sells all kinds of freshly made fruit or chocolate gateaux, while supermarkets stock various cakes whose main ingredients are sponge dough, honey and a distinctive spice like cinnamon or ginger or lots of cream and jam. Whatever the season, Russians are always happy to have an **ice cream** (*morozhenoe*), available from kiosks all over town. Much of the locally produced ice cream is cheaper and of better quality than the imported brands; try the popular crème-brûlée or eskimo, a sort of choc-ice. Alternatively, there are a few Baskin-Robbins outlets around town.

Department stores, theatres and major museums feature a stand-up **buffet**, offering open sandwiches with salami, caviar or boiled egg as well as other nibbles. Less appealing buffets can be found in train and bus stations, and around metro stations and markets.

Zakuski

Despite the popularity of Western fast food, Russian culinary traditions are still strong, especially with regard to bliny (pancakes), one of the best-loved of Russian **zakuski** – small dishes or hors d'oeuvres, which are often a meal in themselves. Zakuski traditionally form the basis of the famous *Russkiy stol*, or "Russian table", a feast of awesome proportions, in which the table groans under the weight of the numerous dishes while the samovar steams away. Among the upper classes in Tsarist times, *zakuski* were merely the prelude to the main meal, as foreign guests would discover to their dismay after gorging themselves on these delights. Salted fish, like sprats or herrings, are a firm favourite, as are gherkins, assorted cold meats and salads. Hard-boiled eggs and bliny, both served with **caviar** (*ikra*), are also available. Caviar is no longer as cheap as during Brezhnev's era, when people tired of eating so much of it, but it's still cheaper than in the West. There are two basic types: red (*krasnaya*) and black (*chornaya*), with the latter having smaller eggs and being more expensive.

Meals

Russians usually eat their main meal at lunchtime (*obed*), between 1pm and 4pm, and traditionally have only *zakuski* or salad and tea for supper (*uzhin*). Restaurants, on the other hand, make much more of the evening, though many now offer a set-price business lunch to attract extra customers.

Menus are usually written in Russian only, although more and more places offer a short English version. But beware: the Russian menu is usually typed up every day, whereas the English version will give only a general idea of what might be available. In such cases, you'd probably be better off asking what they recommend (*shto-by vy po rekomendovali?*), which can elicit some surprisingly frank replies.

If your main concern is price, you'll need to stick to fast-food outlets or cafés, the latter providing some of the best **ethnic food** in the city, including Armenian (*Armyanskiy*), Georgian (*Gruzinskiy*) and Korean (*Koreyskiy*), as well as traditional Russian cooking.

Russian cuisine owes many debts to Jewish, Ukrainian and Caucasian cooking, but remains firmly tied to its peasant origins. In former times, the staple diet of black bread, potatoes, cabbages, cucumber and onions made for bland eating – *Shchi da kasha, pishcha nasha* ("cabbage soup and porridge are our food"), as one saying goes – with flavourings limited to sour cream, garlic, vinegar, dill and a few other fresh herbs. These strong tastes and textures – salty, sweet, sour, pickled – remained the norm, even among the aristocracy, until Peter the Great introduced French chefs to his court in the early eighteenth century.

Most menus start with a choice of soup or *zakuski*. **Soup** (*sup*) has long played an important role in Russian cuisine (the spoon appeared on the Russian table over four hundred years before the fork). Cabbage soup, or *shchi*, has been the principal Russian dish for the last thousand years, served with a generous dollop of sour cream; beetroot soup, or borsch, originally from Ukraine, is equally ubiquitous. Soups, however, are often only available at lunchtime and Russians do not consider even the large meaty soups to be a main meal; they will expect you to indulge in a main course afterwards. Chilled soups (*okroshki*) are popular during the summer, made from whatever's available.

Main courses are overwhelmingly based on meat (*myaso*), usually beef, mutton or pork, and sometimes accompanied by a simple sauce (mushroom or cheese). Meat may also make its way into *pelmeni*, a Russian version of ravioli, usually served in a broth. As far as regional meat dishes go, the most common are Georgian barbecued kebabs (*shashlyk*), or pilau-style Uzbek rice dishes called plov.

A wide variety of **fish and seafood** is available in Moscow. Pickled fish is a popular starter (try *selyodka pod shuboy*, herring in a "fur coat" of beetroot, carrot, egg and mayonnaise), while fresh fish often appears as a main course – salmon, sturgeon and cod are the most common choices, though upmarket restaurants may boast lobster and oysters as well.

In cafés most main courses are served with boiled potatoes and/or sliced fresh tomatoes, but more expensive restaurants will serve a full selection of accompanying **vegetables**. These are called *garnir* and often have to be ordered and paid for separately. Where the meat is accompanied by vegetables, you may see an entry on the menu along the lines of 100/25/100g, which refers to the respective weight in grams of the meat (or fish) portion, and its accompanying servings of rice/potatoes and vegetable *garnir*. In ethnic restaurants, meat is almost always served on its own. Other vegetables are generally served boiled or pickled, but seldom appear separately on the menu.

Desserts (*sladkoe*) are not a strong feature of Russian cuisine. Ice cream, fruit, apple pie (*yablochniy pirog*) and jam pancakes (*blinchikiy s varenyem*) are restaurant perennials, while in Caucasian restaurants you may get the flaky pastry and honey dessert, *pakhlava* (like Greek or Turkish baklava).

Ethnic food

The influence of diverse culinary traditions on Russian food is epitomized by *pelmeni* (ravioli). Originating as dim sum in pork-eating China, they spread as *manty* to the mutton-eating cultures along the Silk Road and westwards with the Tatars to Crimea, before being adopted by Russian peasants in Siberia – whence the recipe spread to European Russia. Closer to home, Jewish, Russian and Ukrainian cooking were so entwined that the only dishes not claimed by all three traditions are ones using pork. The cuisines of the Caucasus were also a lasting influence; most Russian restaurants have *shashlyk*, the Georgian kebab, or *dolma*, Armenian stuffed vineleaves, on the menu. Yet each ethnic cuisine is distinctive and deserves to be experienced in a proper "national" restaurant.

In Soviet times **Georgian** restaurants were the most esteemed, and Caucasian entrepreneurs supplied Russian cities with fruit, wine and flowers. Georgians have a legend that God took a meal break from Creation, tripped over the Caucasus range and spilled his food onto the land below – their cuisine was "scraps from Heaven's table". Its distinctive ingredients include ground walnuts and walnut-oil for cooking; condiments like *khmeli-suneli* (dried coriander, chilli, garlic, pepper and marigold petals), *adzhika* (tomato, red pepper and chilli sauce) and *tkemali* (plum sauce); and lashings of fresh dill, coriander, parsley and cilantro, which are also eaten raw, to cleanse the palate between courses, and used to garnish cheeses made from sheep's or goat's milk. Traditionally, dishes of aubergines, tomatoes, garlic and beans were the staple diet, but feast days were marked by banquets of meaty soups, stews and kebabs, with repeated toasts in wine or brandy, orchestrated by a *tamada* (toast master). Favourites include *satsivi*, a cold dish of chicken in walnut sauce; *chikhirtmi*, lemon-flavoured chicken soup; *kharcho*, spicy beef soup; and *khinkali*, dumplings stuffed with lamb or a mixture of pork and beef. *Khachapuri*, a delicious, cheesy soft bread that's served hot, is a filling starter.

Armenian and Azerbaijani cuisine is closer to Middle Eastern cooking (with the addition of dried nuts, saffron and ginger), while Uzbek features *khinkali* (a spicier kind of *pelmeni*) and sausages made from pony meat (*kazy*). Ginger and garlic also feature prominently in **Korean** food, originally introduced by Korean railway workers exiled to Kazakhstan in the 1930s. Marinaded beef dishes like *bulkogi* are fried at your table, accompanied by raw vegetables and hot pickled garlic relish (*kimichi*). One dish often found even in non-Korean eateries is spicy carrot salad (*morkov po-koreyskiy*). More recently, Russians have fallen in love with **Japanese** food – though arguably sushi and sashimi aren't far removed from smoked fish *zakuski*, or the salmon and crab diet of Russia's Far Northern peoples. **Thai** and fusion food are also currently chic, while a decade's exposure to **Indian and Chinese** cuisine has acclimatized sophisticated locals to curries and spicy dishes that were previously toned down to suit Russian tastes.

Vegetarian food

Although the situation for **vegetarians** has improved a lot with the spread of salad bars and health (or at least weight-watching) awareness, meat still takes pride of place in the nation's cuisine. While fish eaters will find plenty to sustain them, strict vegetarians often have to fall back on bliny stuffed with mushrooms or cabbage, *griby so smetanoy* (mushrooms cooked with onions and sour cream), or the cold summer soup *okroshka*, if there aren't any vegetarian dishes from other ethnic cuisines, such as Korean carrot salad, Caucasian aubergine purée or the Georgian bean dish *lobio*. You could also try asking for *postniy shchi* (meatless, literally "fasting", *shchi*, or cabbage soup) or *ovoschnoy plov* (vegetable pilaf). If obliged to spell things out, the crucial phrases are *ya vegetarianets/vegetarianka*, meaning I'm a vegetarian (masculine/feminine), and *Kakiye u vas yest blyuda bez myasa ili ryby?* (Is there anything without meat or fish?). For emphasis you could add *ya ne yem myasnovo ili rybnovo* (I don't eat meat or fish). Ham or salami are often not considered to be "real" meat, so check that it's free from those too.

In general, ethnic restaurants (Georgian, Lebanese, Korean, Indian, Japanese or Chinese) have the most interesting vegetarian options, though many pizzerias run to veggie pizzas and salad bars. For those **self-catering**, fresh vegetables are widely available in markets (see p.382) and on the streets, and many supermarkets sell beans, grains and pulses. Locally produced fruit and vegetables are available only from June to October; at other times of the year everything is imported and therefore pricier.

Drinking

The story goes that the tenth-century Russian prince Vladimir, when pondering which religion to adopt for his state, rejected Judaism because its adherents were seen as weak and scattered; Catholicism because the pope claimed precedence over sovereigns; and Islam because "Drinking is the joy of the Russians. We cannot live without it."

A thousand years on, **alcohol** remains a central part of Russian life, and the prime cause of falling life expectancy of Russian males. It's a sobering experience to visit provincial towns where almost every man is stumbling drunk by midday, or villages where dozens have died from toxic hooch. In Moscow, alcoholics congregate in parks and around kiosks; virtually all cafés serve alcohol, and it seems as if every fourth pedestrian is swigging from a bottle of beer. As the price of drinks in cafés and bars is at least double that charged by the street kiosks, many Russians still prefer to buy booze from them and drink it at home, or on the nearest bench. Partly due to the prevalence of bootlegging, the City Government prohibits the sale of spirits from kiosks, though many continue to sell vodka under the counter, and cans of ready-mixed gin and tonic or vodka and cranberry don't count as spirits anyway. It is illegal to drink spirits on the streets or in parks (though the law is flouted by alcoholics), but beer drinking is not an offence.

Drinking spirits in a bar, the usual measures are 50 or 100 grams (*pyatdesyat/sto gram*), which for those used to British pub measures seem extremely generous. If invited to eat with Russians, it can be difficult to avoid drinking a succession of toasts in vodka, each glass tossed back *do dna* – to the end – as refusal may cause offence. The only ironclad excuse is to pretend that you have a liver problem, or suffer from alcoholism. If you do submit to a drinking session, be sure to eat something after each shot – Russians say that even the smell of a crust of bread is better than nothing.

Vodka and other spirits

Vodka is the national drink – its name means something like "a little drop of water". Normally served chilled, vodka is drunk neat in one gulp, followed by a mouthful of food, such as pickled herring, cucumber or mushrooms; many people inhale deeply before tossing the liquor down their throats. Drinking small amounts at a time, and eating as you go, it's possible to consume an awful lot without passing out – though you

▲ Vodka, the national drink

soon reach a plateau of inebriated exhilaration.

Taste isn't a prime consideration; what counts is that the vodka isn't **bootleg liquor** (*poddelnaya, falshivaya* or *levaya* in Russian). At best, this means that customers find themselves drinking something weaker than they bargained for; at worst, they're imbibing diluted methanol, which can cause blindness or even death. To minimize the risk, familiarize yourself with the price of a few brands in the shops; if you see a bottle at well below the usual price it's almost certainly bootleg stuff. Among the hundreds of legitimate **native brands** on the market, Nemiroff, Russkiy Standart, Putinka and the varieties produced under the Liviz and Dovgan labels are probably the best, though many drinkers regard **imported vodkas** such as Absolut, Finlandia or Smirnoff as more prestigious. Always check that the bottle's seal and tax label are intact, and don't hesitate to pour its contents away if it smells or tastes strange. A litre of decent vodka costs about R300 in the shops.

In addition to standard vodka you'll also see **flavoured vodkas** such as *pertsovka* (hot pepper vodka), *limonnaya* (lemon vodka), *okhotnichaya* (hunter's vodka with juniper berries, ginger and cloves), *starka* (apple and pear-leaf vodka) and *zubrovka* (bison-grass vodka). Some Russians make these and other variants at home by infusing berries or herbs in regular vodka.

Other domestic liquors include **cognac** (*konyak*), which is pretty rough compared to French brandy, but easy enough to acquire a taste for. Traditionally, the best brands hail from Armenia (Ararat) and Moldova (Beliy Aist), but as both states now export these for hard currency, bottles sold in Russia are often fakes. More commonly, you'll find Georgian or Dagestani versions, which are all right if they're the genuine article, but extremely rough if they're not. Otherwise, you can find imported spirits such as **whisky**, **gin** and **tequila** in many bars and shops, along with Irish Cream, Amaretto and sickly Austrian fruit brandies.

Beer, wine and champagne

Beer (*pivo*) is the preferred drink of younger Russians if only because it's widely available – and consumed – at

Vodka folklore

Russians have a wealth of phrases and gestures to signify **drinking vodka**, the most common one being to tap the side of your chin or windpipe. The story goes that there was once a peasant who saved the life of Peter the Great and was rewarded with the right to drink as much vodka as he liked from any distillery. Fearing that a written *ukaz* would be stolen while he was drunk, the man begged the Tsar to stamp the Imperial seal on his throat – the origin of the gesture.

Fittingly, the Russian word for drunk – *pyany* – comes from an incident where two columns of drunken soldiers advancing on either side of the Pyany River mistook each other for the enemy and opened fire. Given its long and disreputable role in Russian warfare, it's ironic that the Tsarist government's prohibition of vodka for the duration of World War I did more harm than good, by depriving the state of a third of its revenue and stoking class hatred of the aristocracy, whose consumption of cognac and champagne continued unabated. Stalin knew better during World War II, when soldiers received a large shot of vodka before going into battle.

In Soviet society, vodka was the preferred form of payment for any kind of work outside the official economy and the nexus for encounters between strangers needing to "go three" on a bottle – a half-litre bottle shared between three people was reckoned to be the cheapest and most companionable way to get a bit drunk. Whereas rationing vodka was the most unpopular thing that Gorbachev ever did, Yeltsin's budgets categorized it as an essential commodity like bread or milk. Yet despite Yeltsin's notorious fondness for vodka, one would rather not believe Shevardnadze's claim to have found him lying dead drunk in the White House during the 1991 putsch, though at the time Shevardnadze told the crowd outside that "I have met the President and he is standing firm in defence of democracy." At least Yeltsin never lent his name and face to his own brand of vodka – unlike Zhirinovsky (who professes not to drink the stuff) – while Putin is well known to prefer beer.

any time of day or night, and hardly regarded as alcohol, but simply as a refreshing drink. (A clinic for child alcoholics opened in Moscow in 2004.) Most of Russia's best-selling beers come from St Petersburg breweries. **Baltika beers** come in 50cl bottles, numbered from 1 to 12 (mainly in order of their strength). The most popular are #3, "Classic" lager (ask for Troika), #4, "Original" brown ale, and #5, "Porter" stout; #6 and #7 are often found on tap in pool bars and discos; #9 is the strongest; #10 has an aroma of almond and basil, and Medovoe supposedly tastes of honey. **Stepan Razin** (named after the peasant rebel hero) produces eleven different beers, including Spetsialnoe (only 3.6 percent alcohol), the light pilsner Admiralteyskoe, the potent Kalinkin (7 percent), and Zolotoe, with a fine aroma of malt and hops. The **Vena brewery** is best known for Nevskoe Originalnoe (which won second prize at a beer festival in Britain) and Porter (which got a gold medal in Denmark); it also makes Svetloe, a light beer, and Kronverk, without alcohol. More recent newcomers are **Bochkarev**, whose Svetloe (light) and Tyomnoe (dark) are very popular, and **Tinkoff**, which bottles some of the unfiltered beers available on tap at its micro-brewery in Moscow (see p.350). **Other Russian brands** worth trying include Afanasy, a mild ale brewed in Nizhniy Novgorod; Sibirskaya Korona (Siberian Crown) lager; Sokol; Zolotaya bochka; and Okhota. You're bound to find some of these on tap (*razlivnoe*) in bars, together with foreign imports such as Tuborg, Carlsberg, Holsten, or Guinness, which may also come in bottles or cans in shops.

The **wine** (*vino*) on sale in Moscow is either imported from the European Union or California, or from the vineyards of Moldova, Georgia and Crimea, Russia's traditional source of wine. **Georgian and Moldovan wines** are made from varieties of grapes that are almost unknown abroad, so it would be a shame not to sample them, but since the cheapest generic brands in shops are either bootlegs or simply disgusting, you should stick to the dearer versions (R200 and upwards). The ones to look out for are the dry reds *Mukuzani* and *Saperavi*, or the sweeter full-bodied reds *Kindzmarauli* and *Khvanchkara*, drunk by Stalin. Georgia also produces some fine white wines, like the dry *Gurdzhani* and *Tsinandali* (traditionally served at room temperature), as well as the fortified wines *Portvini* (port) and Masala, which are also produced in the Crimea and known in Russian as *baramatukha* or "babbling juice", the equivalent of Thunderbird in the US.

Despite notice from France that Russia's concession to use the word **champagne** has expired (it was granted after World War II in gratitude to the Soviet Union), not all local manufacturers have relabelled their product "Soviet Sparkling" (*Sovietskoe Igristoe*), and consumers still request "Soviet champagne" (*Sovetskoe shampanskoe*, or *shampanskoe* for short). Besides being far cheaper than the French variety, some of it is really pretty good if properly chilled. The two types to go for are *sukhoe* and *bryut*, which are both reasonably dry; *polusukhoe* or "medium dry" is actually very sweet, and *sladkoe* is like connecting yourself to a glucose drip. It's indicative of Russian taste that the last two are the most popular.

Tea, coffee and soft drinks

Traditionally, Russian **tea** (*chay*) was brewed and stewed for hours, and topped up with boiling water from an ornate tea urn, or samovar, but nowadays even the more run-of-the-mill cafés use imported teabags. Quite a few places also offer herbal or fruit-flavoured teas, which were traditionally prepared at home using herbs and leaves from the forest (*travyanoy chay*), or ginseng and ginger from the east. Most Russians drink tea without milk, and you need to ask for it in cafés. Milk (*moloko*) itself is sold in stores alongside *kefir*, a sour milk drink that's something of an acquired taste for foreigners. There are full-cream and low-fat versions of both.

Coffee (*kofe*) is sold all over the place and varies enormously in quality. Kiosks and cheap cafés use vile powdered stuff; avoid places with automats and look for a proper coffee maker on the premises. Seattle-style coffee houses are all the rage in Moscow, with chains like Coffee Bean and Coffee House offering espresso, cappuccino, lattes, mocca, flavoured coffees and alcoholic coffee cocktails. A few old-fashioned cafés prepare Turkish or Arabic coffee by heating it in hot sand, a method used in Soviet times.

Pepsi and Coca-Cola jostle for sales with cheaper brands of **fizzy drinks** imported from Eastern Europe, or manufactured in Russia. Besides generic colas, lemonades and orangeades, you'll see such distinctly Russian drinks as **kvas**, an unusual but delicious thirst-quencher made from fermented rye bread; **myod**, or honey-mead, which is seen as a soft drink but contains alcohol; and **tarkhun**, a bright green, sickly sweet drink made from tarragon – all of which have made a comeback since they fell out of fashion with the demise of the Soviet Union.

The days when the only **mineral water** (*mineralnaya voda*) available was Narzan and Borzhomi from the Caucasus (both a bit salty and sulphurous for most Western tastes, but worth persevering with) are long over. Kiosks and shops are full of Evian, Vittel and Perrier, and diverse Russian brands of spring water, which may be carbonated (*gazirovanaya voda*) or without gas (*negazirovanaya*). The brand *Svyatoi Istochnik* (Sacred Spring) even comes with a blessing from the Orthodox Patriarch.

Fast-food chains

Fast-food chains have become hugely popular in Moscow and St Petersburg, offering a variety of food and standards of hygiene and service infinitely superior to the grimy *stolovaya* (canteens) that were the lot of generations of citizens during Soviet times, but which younger Russians now take for granted. Besides such worldwide giants as *McDonald's*, *Pizza Hut* and *KFC*, there's the Italian pizza chain *Sbarro*, and various homegrown chains serving Russian or Ukrainian food – bliny (pancakes), salads, *zakuski* – or modelled on *Starbucks*. The outlets listed in the box on pp.346–347 are reliable, but not reviewed under cafés or included on maps in this book.

Cafés and bars

Cafés and bars in Moscow run the gamut from humble eateries to chic watering holes, and since most places serve alcohol (beer, if not spirits too) the distinction between them is often a fine one. With some exceptions (mostly places in top-class hotels) cafés are generally cheaper than fully fledged restaurants, making them popular with Russians who have some disposable income, but don't ride around in a Mercedes.

Though all cafés are private ventures nowadays, some retain the surly habits of Soviet days, when customers counted themselves lucky if they got served at all, and even where they aim to please, you sometimes find inexplicable lapses in

The chain gang

Coffee Bean *Sells the best coffee and cakes of all the Seattle-style chains, and wine by the glass. No smoking. MC, Visa.* Ul. Pokrovka 18/3, Kitay-Gorod or Chistye Prudy metro (daily 8am–11pm); Pyatnitskaya ul. 5, Novokuznetskaya metro (Mon–Sat 8am–11pm, Sun 9am–10pm); Tverskaya ul. 10, Pushkinskaya metro (Mon–Sat 8am–11pm, Sun 9am–11pm); ul. Sretenka 22/1, Sukharevskaya metro (daily 8am–11pm); Leningradsky prospect 56, Aeroport metro (daily 8am–11pm); ul. Khachaturyana 16, Otradnoye metro (Mon–Fri 8am–11pm, Sat & Sun 9am–10pm).

Coffee House *Moscow's largest coffee chain. Smoking allowed. No cards.* Ul. Arbat 1, Arbatskaya metro (daily 24hr); Tverskaya ul. 17 str. 1, Pushkinskaya metro (daily 24hr); ul. Chayanova 12, Novoslobodskaya metro (daily 8am–11pm); Gogolevskiy bul. 2/3/1, Kropotkinskaya metro (daily 24hr); ul. Maroseyka 6–8, str. 1, Kitay-gorod metro (daily 24hr); ul. Nikolskaya 12/1/2, str. 1, Lubyanka metro (daily 8am–11pm); ul. Pokrovka 38, Kurskaya metro, (daily 8am–11pm); and many other locations, including most shopping centres.

Coffee Mania *Almost as good as Coffee Bean, particularly the Conservatory branch, which also serves hot meals and cocktails. Smoking allowed. No cards.* Corner of ul. Rozhdesvenka and ul. Pushechnaya, Lubyanka metro (daily 8am–11pm); Bolshaya Nikitskaya ulitsa 13 (beside the Conservatory), Okhotniy Ryad or Arbatskaya metros (daily 24hr); Kudrinskaya pl. 46/54, Barrikadnaya metro (daily 24hr); Komsomolsky prospect, 21/2, Frunzenskaya metro (daily 8am–midnight); Sadovnicheskaya st., 82/2, Paveletskaya metro (daily 8am–11pm), Bagrationovsky proezd, 7/2, Bagationovskaya metro (daily 8am–10pm).

Kroshka Kartoshka *Outdoor kiosks selling filled jacket potatoes (R45–50) and salads. No cards. Daily 9am–11pm.* Lubyanka, Tverskaya; Kuznetskiy Most, Teatralnaya, Arbat; and many other locations, mostly near metro stations or in shopping centres.

McDonald's *The cleanest toilets in Moscow. No smoking; no cards.* Manezhnaya ploshchad 1, str. 2, Okhotniy Ryad metro (daily 7am–midnight); ul. Arbat 50/52, Smolenskaya metro (daily 8am–11.30pm); Bolshaya Bronnaya ul. 29/corner of Tverskaya ul., Tverskaya metro (daily 7am–11.30pm); Bolshaya Dorogomilovskaya ul. 8, Kievskaya metro (daily 7am–midnight); ul. Maroseyka 9/2, str. 1, Kitay-gorod metro (daily 7am–11.30pm); Bolshaya Serpukhovskaya ul. 4, Tulskaya metro (daily 7am–midnight); Gazetniy per. 17/corner of Tverskaya ul. Okhotniy Ryad metro, and other locations.

Mi Piace *A chain of Italian pizzerias decorated mainly with black and white photos of girls devouring macaroni. Prices are moderate (around R900 per person), though portions are rather small. Also offers Italian delicacies and pizza delivery. All cards. All branches Mon–Fri 11am–midnight, Sat & Sun noon–midnight. Ⓦwww.mipiace.ru.* Ul. Chayanova 22 Ⓣ250 08 93, Novoslobodskaya metro; ul. Bolshaya Ordynka 13/9 Ⓣ951 52 50 or 953 96 65, Novokuznetskaya metro; ul. Tverskaya 20 Ⓣ650 75 75, Tverskaya/Pushkinskaya metro; ul. Sadovaya-Samotechnaya 20 Ⓣ694 00 01, Tsvetnoy Bulvar metro; ul. Pokrovka 16/16 Ⓣ623 44 11, Tsvetnoy Bulvar metro; ul. 1st Tverskaya-Yamskaya 7 Ⓣ970 11 29; Mayakovskaya metro.

Nyam-Nyam *Kiosks selling sausage rolls and flaky pastries with various sweet or savoury fillings (R50). Daily 9am–11pm.* Found in metro stations and pedestrian underpasses also on the Arbat facing *McDonald's*.

Il Patio *Thin-crust wood-oven pizzas, salad bar, alcohol. Child-friendly. Visa, MC, JCB. Daily noon–midnight unless stated otherwise.* Ul. Volkhonka 13a, Kropotkinskaya metro; 1-ya Tverskaya-Yamskaya ul. 2, Mayakovskaya metro; Leninskiy pr. 68/10, Universitet metro; pr. Mira 33, Prospekt Mira metro (8am–midnight); Smolenskaya ul. 3, Smolenskaya metro (11am–11pm); ul. Narodnovo Opulcheniya 46, str. 1, Ulitsa 1905 Goda metro; Taganskaya ul. 1 str. 2, Marksistskaya metro (24hr); ul. Udaltsolva 40a, Prospekt Vernadskovo metro (10am–midnight); ul. Akademika Koroleva, 8a, VDNKh metro.

Planet Sushi *Affordable sushi, Thai and Chinese; set lunch R200–300; all-you-can-eat sushi buffet (price varies from branch to branch). Amex, DC, MC, Visa. Daily* *noon–midnight unless stated otherwise.* Manezhnaya ploshchad 1, str. 2, Okhotniy Ryad metro (24hr); Nikolskaya ul. 10, Lubyanka metro; Leninskiy pr. 1/2 Oktyabrskaya metro; ul. Narodnovo Opolcheniya 46, Oktyabrskaya metro; Taganskaya ul. 1, Marksistskaya metro; 1-ya Tverskaya-Yamskaya ul. 2, Mayakovskaya metro; ul. Udaltsova 40, Prospekt Vernadskovo metro; ul. Garibaldi 23, Novye Cheremushki metro; ul. Akademika Koroleva, 8a, VDNKh metro.

Rostik's-KFC *Chicken, fries, doughnuts, milkshakes. No cards.* GUM, Nikolskaya ul., Ploshchad Revolyutsii metro (daily 9am–9pm); Leninskiy pr. 68/10, Universitet metro (daily 10am–11pm); pr. Mira 92 str. 3, Rizhskaya metro (daily 9am–11pm); 1-ya Tverskaya-Yamskaya ul. 2/1, Mayakovskaya metro (daily 9am–midnight); also in most shopping centres.

Russkoe Bistro *Endorsed (and co-owned) by Mayor Luzhkov, this chain sells* pirozhki *(pies), bliny, salads, herbal teas and* kvas*; some branches sell vodka. No cards. Daily 5.30am–12.30am.* Bolshaya Gruzinskaya ul. 50, Belorusskaya metro; ul. Varvarka 14, Kitay-gorod metro; pl. Kurskovo vokzala, Kurskaya metro; Manezhnaya ploshchad 1, Okhotniy Ryad metro; ul Rusakovskaya 22, Sokolniki metro; ul. Energeticheskaya, 18, Aviamotornaya metro.

Sbarro *Self-service pizza and salad chain that does deliveries (☎741 77 55). Amex, MC, Visa.* Manezhnaya ploshchad 1, str. 2, Okhotniy Ryad metro (daily 10am–midnight); Krasnoprudnaya ul. 1, Komsomolskaya metro (daily 10am–11pm); Tverskaya ul. 10, Pushkinskaya metro (daily 10am–midnight); Sheremetevskaya ul. 60A, Maryina Roshcha metro (daily 10am–11pm); ul. Arbat 21 str.1, Arbatskaya metro.

Taras Bulba Korchma *Rustic-style inns named after the legendary Cossack warrior, which serve tasty Ukrainian borsch,* vareniki *(dumplings) and gorilka vodka. Amex, DC, Maestro, Visa.* Ul. Petrovka 30/7, Chekhovskaya metro (daily noon–midnight); Leninskiy pr. 37, Leninskiy Prospekt metro (daily 11am–midnight); Pyatnitskaya ul. 14, Tretyakovskaya metro (daily noon–2am); Sadovaya-Samotechnaya ul. 13, Tsvetnoy Bulvar metro (daily 24hr); Smolenskiy bul. 12, Smolenskaya metro (daily 24hr); Leningradsdkiy prospect 64, Aeroport metro (daily noon–2am).

Teremok *Freshly made Russian bliny (pancakes) with sweet or savoury fillings, including caviar (R50–150). No cards. Daily 9am–11pm.* Ul. Tverskaya 6, Okhotniy Ryad metro; ul. Ostozhenka 44, Park Kultury metro; ul Neglinnaya 29, Tsvetnoi Bulvar metro; and many other locations outdoors and in shopping centres.

T.G.I. Friday's *Burgers, cajun chicken, Caesar salad, ribs, and cocktails mixed by juggling bartenders. Amex, DC, MC, Visa. Mon–Fri noon–1am.* Kodak Kinomir, Tverskaya ul. 18/2, Pushkinskaya/Tverskaya metro; Atrium Mall, ul. Zemlyanoy val 33, Kurskaya metro; ul. Garibaldi 23, Novye Cheremushki metro; Komsomolskiy prospect 28, Frunzenskaya metro; ul. Noviy Arbat 14 str. 1, Arbatskaya metro; ul. Novoslobodskaya 3, Novoslobodskaya metro.

Yakitoriya *A superior Japanese chain to* Planet Sushi, *they insist on reservations. Go for the sushi, seaweed salads, miso and kento soups, with Fuji cake or bean pastila for dessert. MC, JCB, Visa. Daily 11am–6am.* Ul. Noviy Arbat 10, ☎290 43 11, Arbatskaya metro; 1-ya Tverskaya-Yamskaya ul. 29, str. 1 ☎250 53 85, Belorusskaya metro; ul. Novoslobodskaya 20, ☎973 20 14, Mendeleyevskaya metro.

Yolki Palki (Fiddlesticks) *The inspiration for* Taras Bulba*, these self-service taverns do a tasty buffet of Russian* zakuski *(the branch on Tverskaya also has a Mongolian stir-fry), and sell vodka and home-made* kvas*. No cards. Daily 11am–11pm unless stated otherwise.* Neglinnaya ul. 8/10, Kuznetskiy Most metro (10am–midnight); Klimentovskiy per. 14, str. 1, Tretyakovskaya metro (10am–9pm); ul. Arbat 16/2 str. 3, Arbatskaya metro; ul. Sadovaya-Triumfalnaya 18/20, Mayakovskaya metro; ul. Solyanka 1/2 str. 1, Kitay-gorod metro (10am–11pm); Bolshaya Dorogmilovskaya ul. 12A, Kievskaya metro; pr. Mira 118, Alekseevskaya metro; Bolshaya Serpukhovskaya ul. 17 str. 1, Serpukhovskaya metro.

standards or decorum. However, you can also find some delicious meals and friendly watering holes if you know where to look, and the number of acceptable places is rising all the time.

The following selection is listed in alphabetical order under area headings corresponding to the chapters in the guide section. We've provided phone numbers for bars and cafés where it's advisable to phone ahead and reserve a table, particularly if you are planning to eat in the evening.

Red Square and the Kitay-gorod

Besides the places listed below, there are branches of *Rostik's-KFC*, *Sbarro* and *McDonald's* in the Manezh mall, and another *Rostik's* in GUM.

Café Prosto Lubyanskiy proezd 25, str. 2; Kitay-Gorod metro. See map, p.102. Prosto means "simple" and this basement café near the Cyril and Methodius statue on Staraya ploshchad is certainly that – but warm and friendly, with tasty *solyanka* and *pelmeni* on the menu. No cards. Daily noon–midnight.

Drova Nikolskaya ul. 3; Ploshchad Revolyutsii metro. See map, pp.68–69. Unbeatable value for its location just off Red Square, *Drova* offers a healthy breakfast (7–11am; R90), a filling three-course lunch (Mon–Fri 11am–5pm; R190) and an all-you-can-eat buffet of Russian, Caucasian and Uzbek delicacies (R490). Try to get a table by the window. No cards. Daily 24hr.

Loft Nautilus Trade House, Teatralniy proezd 25 ⓣ933 77 13; Lubyanka metro. See map, p.102. You'll need to get past the guards in the lobby to reach this chic sixth-floor "health café" with a view of the Lubyanka and a summer balcony. Its salads, fresh juices and tiger shrimps in garlic sauce are winners, and on weekdays they serve breakfast (9am–noon) and English tea (5–7pm). A full meal costs about R1500. Daily 9am–midnight.

Beliy gorod

Besides the places below (marked on the map on pp.112–113), there are branches of *Yolki Palki*, *Sbarro*, *Coffee House* and *Yakitoriya* on or around Tverskaya ulitsa and Kuznetskiy most.

Annushka (Annie) Chistoprudniy bulvar; near Chistye Prudy metro. *Annushka* is a tram that's been converted into a café-bar, which circles Chistye Prudy boulevard – you can board it near Griboedov's statue. There's more to drink than there is to eat and the karaoke may deter some. Daily 11am–10pm.

Café Manner Berlin House, ul. Petrovka 5; 10min walk from Teatralnaya or Kuznetskiy most metro. A classy lounge café with a summer patio that produces "smart fusion" cuisine using high-quality ingredients. Their horseradish vodka and *wasabi* mustard are the hottest in Moscow. All major cards. Daily 10am–midnight.

Café Sindbad Bolshaya Nikitskaya ul. 23/9 (entrance on Nikolskiy bul.); 15min walk from Arbatskaya metro. This authentic, cramped Lebanese café serves a R180 lunch of soup, spicy *kofta*, *tabouli* salad and fries, and has hookahs for smoking apple-, pomegranate- or coffee-flavoured tobacco. No cards. Daily noon–midnight.

Drevniy Kitay (Chinese Village) Kamergerskiy per. 5/6; 10min walk from Teatralnaya or Kuznetskiy Most metro. Eat before 5pm for a cut-price choice of any soup (R70), cold appetizer (R70) or hot dish with rice (R165), rather than in the evening, when you'll pay more for what is really just takeaway chow. DC, JCB, Maestro, MC, Visa. Daily noon–midnight.

Drova Myasnitskaya ul. 24; 5min walk from Chistye Prudy/Turgenevskaya metro. Offering the same buffet and lunch deals as *Drova* on Nikolskaya (see above), this branch is more atmospheric in the evening, with candles and recorded birdsongs (cable TV and music later on), and an outdoor tented area for smoking hookahs. No cards. Daily 24hr.

Eat and Talk Café ul. Mokhovaya 7 ⓣ495 720 18 23. Popular with young Moscovites from the nearby university, this fantastic café-restaurant offers great breakfast and lunch buffets (R350), has free wi-fi and very friendly staff, many of whom speak English. Its mojitos, made by Cuban bartenders, are the best in Moscow. MC, DC, Visa. Daily 24hrs.

Galereya (Gallery) ul. Bolshaya Lubyanka 15; 10min walk from Lubyanka metro. Up the hill from Shchit i Mecht and Varcha Traktir (see below), this cosy, inexpensive café serves fabulous cakes, ice cream, tiramisu and freshly squeezed juices, and features an ever-changing display of contemporary art. MC, Visa. Daily 9am–11pm.

Jagannath (Juggernaut) ul. Kuznetskiy most 11 ⓦ www.jagannath.ru; 5min walk from Kuznetskiy Most metro. Moscow's funkiest vegetarian café-restaurant shop features lots of tasty dishes, a salad bar and a R370 set lunch, enlivened by Bollywood pop in the daytime, belly-dancing and live music in the evening, and a chill-out party (Fri & Sat from 11pm; R1000–1500). No smoking or alcohol. No cards. Sun–Thurs 10am–11pm, Fri & Sat 10am–midnight.

La Cantina Tverskaya ul. 5; near Okhotniy Ryad metro. A popular pick-up spot and watering hole for foreigners and hookers, featuring live music from 9pm. Good for a beer or a cocktail, though the Tex-Mex food is pretty average. Daily 8am–midnight.

Shchit i Metch (Shield and Sword) ul. Bolshaya Lubyanka 13; 10min walk from Lubyanka metro. KGB-themed canteen attached to the MVD social club across the road from the Museum of the Security Service (see p.139). Serves cheap *pelmeni*, *borsch* and other Soviet favourites for lunch, and has a bar with a "Miss KGB" barmaid to warm things up for the evening crowd. Mon–Sat noon–midnight.

Varcha Traktir (Varcha Tavern) ul. Bolshaya Lubyanka 13; 10min walk from Lubyanka metro. This café beside *Shchit i Metch* serves cheap Georgian food, with a set lunch from 11am–3pm. Live music after 6pm. No cards. Daily 11am–11pm.

Zemlyanoy gorod

The listings in this section are marked on the map on pp.150–151.

American Bar & Grill Tverskaya-Yamskaya ul. 2 str.1; near Mayakovskaya metro. Slightly pretentious and overpriced diner for shy expats and aspiring Russians, with burgers, pizzas, baked potatoes and ribs, plus hash browns for breakfast. All major cards. Daily 24hr.

Bookafe Sadovaya-Samotochnaya ul. 13; 15min walk from Tsvetnoy Bulvar metro. A luxuriously austere coffee house for people featured in *Afisha* – or who dream of being so. Costly coffee-table books of photography or art provide an excuse for conversation with *kulturniy* strangers. The place is quiet by day but perks up at night. All major cards. Daily 24hr.

Café Margarita Malaya Bronnaya ul. 28; 10min walk from Mayakovskaya metro. Named after the heroine of *The Master and Margarita* and sited just across from Patriarch's Ponds where the novel begins, this perestroika-era art café is a meeting place for musicians from opera theatres, who jam here. Daily 8pm–midnight.

Mu-Mu (Moo-Moo) ul. Arbat 45/24; 5min walk from Smolenskaya metro. A life-size spotted cow welcomes diners to this decorative self-service bistro, whose cheap Russian salads, soups and stews hit the spot with tourists and locals alike. *Mu-Mu* also sells *kvas*, beer and vodka. No cards. Daily 10am–11pm.

The Real McCoy Kudrinskaya pl. 1 (in the Stalin Skyscraper) ⓦ www.mccoy.ru; near Barrikadnaya/ Krasnopresnenskaya metro. Themed on a Prohibition speakeasy and popular with staff from the US Embassy, this bar-restaurant does great baguettes, steaks and cocktails. Breakfast (5am–noon; R90); business lunch (noon–5pm; R250); happy hours (daily midnight–noon & 5–8pm), where you get a double drink for the price of a single. Live jazz or boogie music (Wed–Sun 8–11pm) and a disco (Thurs–Sat from midnight). Amex, DC, EC, MC, Visa. Daily 24hr.

Starlite Diner #1 Bolshaya Sadovaya ul. 16; near Mayakovskaya metro. This American eatery at the back of the Aquarium Gardens has a glass conservatory that's fun in winter time. Go for the breakfast special (till 11am), chilli cheese fries, or spicy Thai wraps. Amex, Electron, Maestro, MC, Visa. Daily 24hr.

Krasnaya Presnya, Fili and the southwest

Besides the places below (marked on the map on p.178), there are *McDonald's* near Barrikadnaya and Ulitsa 1905 Goda metro stations.

Bavarius Komsomolskiy pr. 21/10 ⓦ www.bavarius.ru; 5min walk from Frunzenskaya metro. A German Biergarten and restaurant with ten draught beers and fourteen bottled ones on the menu. A Weisswurst with sweet mustard and a pretzel washed down with a Weissbier is the archetypal Bavarian snack. MC, Visa. Daily noon–midnight.

Mu-Mu (Moo-Moo) Komsomolskiy pr. 26; near Frunzenskaya metro. An offshoot of the popular self-service bistro on the Arbat, with its bovine decor. No cards. Daily 10am–11pm.

Ogonyok (Little Fire) ul. Krasnaya Presnya 36 str. 1; 10min walk from Ulitsa 1905 Goda metro. This café has tasty Russian food at reasonable prices, and attentive table service. No cards. Daily noon–11pm.

Tinkoff Protochniy per. 11 ⓣ777 33 00, ⓦwww.tinkoff.ru; 15min walk from Smolenskaya metro. Oleg Tinkov became a household name by founding Russia's first microbrewery in St Petersburg. Its Moscow offshoot likewise has industrial decor, ten varieties of unfiltered beer (R130–480), sushi or European cuisine (set lunch R300), and live acid jazz or funk in the lounge (Thurs & Fri after 9pm) – plus a children's room with a clown (Sat 1–6pm). Reserve a table if you want to eat in the evening. All major cards. Mon–Sat noon–2am.

Zamoskvareche and the south

Besides the following, there are *McDonald's* and *Russkoe Bistro* (between Tretyakovskaya metro and the Tretyakov Gallery), *Coffee Bean* and *Taras Bulba Korchma* (on Pyatnitskaya ulitsa).

Faeton Pyatnitskaya ul. 37; 10min walk from Tretyakovskaya or Novokuznetskaya metro. **See map, p.207.** Handy if you're exploring Zamoskvareche, this Georgian café serves tasty shashlyks (including a veggie version) and other Caucasian staples. No cards. Daily 11am–midnight.

Pivnushka (Beer-hall) Leninskiy pr. 28; 10min walk from Leninskiy Prospekt metro. **See map, p.205.** A split-level Bierkeller with an Austrian chef and Bavarian dishes – try the fried breaded camembert with currant jam. They stock twelve kinds of draught beer, French, Italian and German wines. No cards. Daily noon–11pm.

Starlite Diner #2 ul. Koroviy val 9; 10min walk from Oktyabryskaya/Dobryninskaya metro. **See map, p.205.** Good-value American food day or night; the weekday breakfast special, chilli cheese fries and the broccoli and cheese omelettes are the best in Moscow. Amex, MC, Visa. Daily 24hr.

Taganka and Zayauzye

Besides the listings below (marked on the Taganka map on p.249), there are branches of *Il Patio* and *Planet Sushi* on Taganskaya ploshchad and lots of fast-food kiosks around the metro stations.

American Bar & Grill ul. Zemlyanoy val 59; 10min walk from Taganskaya metro. Another branch of the US diner, with a summer patio for BBQs. Pizzas, baked potatoes, ribs and "kickin' chicken", plus a big choice of R225–325 combos (noon–4pm). Amex, MC, Visa. Daily noon–2am.

Aruba Narodnaya ul.4; 5min walk from Taganskaya metro. This Cuban bar-restaurant does great margaritas and filling Cuban dishes, accompanied by salsa music. Visa. Daily noon–5am.

Northern Suburbs

Besides the following (marked on the map on pp.270–271), there are branches of *Yakitoriya* and *Il Patio* on 1-ya Tverskaya Yamskaya ulitsa, and a *Rostik's-KFC* on prospekt Mira.

Café Sup (Soup Café) 1-ya Brestskaya ul. 62/25 str. 3; 10min walk from Belorusskaya metro. This larger-than-you'd-expect candle-lit basement café serves over twenty different soups (from salmon *ukha* to meaty *solyanka*) and a smaller choice of entrées, with beer, vodka, herbal teas or flavoured coffees. Try to get a table in the quilted backroom. No cards. 24hr.

Druzhba (Friendship) Novoslobodskaya ul. 4; near Novoslobodskaya metro. An authentic Cantonese greasy spoon in the Chinese market beyond McDonald's. You can't lose with dumplings or noodles; the dearer dishes aren't so reliable. No cards. Daily 11am–11pm.

Khizina Butyrskaya ul. 8; 5min walk from Savyolovskaya metro. Caucasian food lovers take note: *khichiny* are like *khachapuri*, only made of potato instead of flour, and can be found nowhere else in Moscow but at this café, whose *suluguni* cheese starters, meat pies and *adzhapsandali* all go well with Georgian wine from a barrel. No cards. Daily noon–midnight.

Kitayskiy Kvartal (Chinese Quarter) pr. Mira 12; 5min walk from Sukharevskaya or Prospekt

Mira metro. Another, slightly fancier, Cantonese chow place, with hefty-sized portions. You need to order extra-spicy to get dishes cooked moderately spicy, but for a cheap meal at any time you can't complain. No cards. Daily 24hr.

Restaurants

Moscow's **restaurants** are as diverse as the food they serve. At the top end of the scale, you'll probably feel uncomfortable if you're not dressed to the hilt – though not many places impose a formal dress code (a jacket and tie for men, a dress for women). At present, relatively few places include a service charge in the bill, so you can tip (or not) as you like. Some places feature **floor shows** consisting of "folk music" (or belly dancing) and maybe some kind of striptease act (which Russians regard with equanimity), for which there may or may not be a surcharge. At most restaurants it's customary to consign your coat to the garderobe on arrival; if helped to put it back on later, a small tip is warranted.

More and more places offer set **business lunches** at lower prices than you'd pay dining à la carte. Such deals are advertised by signboards outside with the Cyrillic words, бизнес ланьч (pronounced biznes lanch), and in the city's foreign-language press, where you may also find details of food festivals being held at the city's better hotels. To keep abreast of the culinary scene, compare the restaurant reviews on websites such as ⓦwww.expat.ru, ⓦwww.go-magazine.ru, ⓦwww.exile.ru and ⓦwww.waytorussia.net.

We've given telephone numbers for all the restaurants listed, as **reserving in advance** is always a good idea, particularly to eat after 9pm. Most places now have at least one member of staff with a rudimentary grasp of English. If not, a useful phrase to get your tongue around is *Ya khochu zakazat stol na … cheloveka sevodnya na … chasov* (I want to reserve a table for … people for … o'clock today).

Red Square and the Kitay-gorod

Expensive

1 Krasnaya Ploshchad in the Historical Museum ⓣ925 36 00, ⓦwww.redsquare.ru; 5min walk from Ploshchad Revolyutsii/Okhotniy Ryad metro. See map, pp.68–69. As central as you can get, with excellent Tsarist-era dishes served in a cosy setting. There's a business lunch (noon–4pm; R470), and nightly jazz or music from a trio of psaltery, flute and zither (from 7pm). Amex, DC, EC, MC, Union, Visa. Daily noon–midnight.

Boyarskiy Zal (Boyar's Hall) Metropol Hotel, fourth floor ⓣ927 60 00; 5min walk from Ploshchad Revolyutsii, Okhotniy Ryad and

The restaurant listings are divided into geographical areas that correspond to the chapters, and into price categories, too – cheap, inexpensive, moderate, expensive and very expensive. You should be able to get a soup, a main course, a dessert plus a couple of beers or vodkas in the price bracket indicated:
Cheap up to R500 a head.
Inexpensive R500–1000 a head.
Moderate R1000–2000 a head.
Expensive R2000–3000 a head.
Very expensive over R3000 a head.

These categorizations refer to dining à la carte, but many restaurants offer a business lunch or Sunday brunch that costs a lot less than this. Generally, beer and vodka are cheap enough to drink a lot without hugely increasing the final bill – but wine or imported liquors are another matter, especially in restaurants with deluxe cellars. Never order wine without verifying the price.

Teatralnaya metros. See map, p.102. Princely Russian cuisine and folk music (from 8pm) in a room decorated in the style of a sixteenth-century boyar's palace. Amex, DC, EC, MC, Visa. Daily 7pm–midnight.

Beliy Gorod

The listings in this section are marked on the map on pp.112–113.

Inexpensive

Amarcord ul. Pokrovka 6 ⓣ923 09 32; 15min walk Chistye Prudy metro. This Trattoria-style establishment serves delicious salmon carpaccio, decent antipasti and cheap thin-crust pizzas – though the desserts and chianti are overpriced. Amex, DC, MC, Visa. Daily 11am until the last person leaves.

Eat and Talk Bar and Restaurant ul. Mokhovaya, 7 ⓣ495 720 18 23. An Irish-styled pub and restaurant connected to the *Eat and Talk Café* (see p.348). Serves a wide selection of food, ranging from Asian Fusion to Kazak/Georgian dishes as well as Western-style sandwiches. It also serves an even wider range of beers, including cold Guinness. MC, DC, VISA. Daily 24hr.

Ginno Taki Tverskaya ul. 6 ⓣ692 53 50; 10min walk from Teatralnaya or Okhotniy Ryad metro. This trendy sushi place seems to enjoy making customers queue (you can't reserve a table) before giving them a menu that lists the calorific value of every dish. That said, its tempura, Dragon rolls, cocktails and sundaes will mellow you out enough to make a return visit seem a good idea. Set lunch (Mon–Fri 11am–4pm; R780); deliveries to regular clients. No cards. Daily 11am–6am.

Mos–Bombay Glinishchevskiy per. 3 ⓣ292 93 75; 5min walk from Pushkinskaya/Tverskaya metro. One of the earliest joint ventures in perestroika times, this Indian restaurant has had its ups and downs but is currently almost as good as the perennial Indian favourite *Darbar* (see p.356). Lots of vegetarian options and a business lunch (R390) till 3pm – good service, too. There's also live music (Thurs & Fri 8.30–10.30pm) and oriental dancing (Fri 8.30–9.30pm). Amex, DC, MC, Visa. Daily 11am–11pm.

Tamada (Toastmaster) Maliy Gnezdnikovskiy per. 12/27 ⓣ229 66 88; 10min walk from Pushkinskaya/Tverskaya metro. Situated on a side street off Tverskaya ulitsa, this Georgian restaurant serves fantastic *khachapuri* (R270), *shashlyk* (from R480), *satsivi* (R320) and *tolma* (R200), but the house wine is over-sweet. No cards. Mon–Sat noon–10pm.

The Tunnel Lubyanskiy proezd 7 ⓣ937 41 01; 5min walk from Lubyanka or Kitay-Gorod metro. Boasts Indian, Tex-Mex and European cusine, steaks and sushi – in that order of how good they are. The Indian food never disappoints and their nachos score highly, as do the mango milkshakes. Deafening MTV. No cards. Daily 24hr.

Tibet Himalaya ul. Pokrovka 19 ⓣ917 39 85, ⓦwww.tibethimalaya.menu.ru; 10min walk from Kitay-Gorod or Chistye Prudy/Turgenevskaya metro. You can't go wrong with the *momo* dumplings, egg-fried noodles, aubergine with garlic sauce, or the set lunch (noon–5pm; R760) – but their meat dishes could be spicier. Customers can chill out with a hookah. Amex, DC, MC, Visa. Daily noon–midnight.

Tibet Kitchen Kamergerskiy per. 5/6 ⓣ923 24 22; 10min walk from Okhotniy Ryad metro. One of several ethnic eateries along this fashionable street, its spring rolls, garlic noodles and sweet-and-sour chicken rock – though the set lunch doesn't. No cards. Daily noon–11pm.

Yaposhka ul. Tverskaya, 20/1 ⓣ650 58 92 or 650 59 18; Tverskaya/Pushkinskaya metro. The first Moscow branch of this St. Petersburg chain of sushi-bars has casual decor and surprisingly low prices. As well as sushi, it also offers Russian *vareniki* (dumplings) with mashed potatoes. Maestro, MC, Visa. 24hr.

Moderate

Beijing Duck ul. Tverskaya, 24 ⓣ755 84 01, Tverskaya/Pushkinskaya metro. As well as the house speciality, authentic Beijing Duck, they serve a variety of Chinese dishes, including handmade Chinese *pelmeni*, carp in sweet-and-sour sauce, pork with pineapple, and apples baked in caramel for dessert. Amex, DC, EC, Maestro, MC, UC, Visa. Daily noon–midnight.

Dzhonka (The Junk) Tverskoy bul. 22 (on Shvedskiy tupik around the side of MKhAT) ⓣ203 94 20; 5min walk from Tverskaya or Pushkinskaya metro. Relaxed Chinese restaurant styled like a junk. Try the sweet-and-sour carp or Gonbo chicken, but give the dim sum a miss. There's a lunch menu (noon–4pm) and a 20 percent reduction for takeouts. Billiards. DC, JCB, MC, Visa. Daily noon–midnight.

Goa Myasnitskaya ul. 8/2 ⓣ504 40 31; 5min walk from Lubyanka metro. Only in Moscow would you find a restaurant offering Indian and French cuisine, sushi and cocktails. You can't go wrong with the chicken tikka masala and lamb samosas, a warm duck-breast salad, or the cocktails. Goa is quite exclusive and insists that guests make reservations at the weekend. No cards. Mon–Sat noon–10pm.

Goodman Ul. Tverskaya 23 ⓣ937 56 79; Tverskaya/Pushkinskaya metro. Also has branches at Kievskiy Vokzal pl. 2, Evropeiskiy Mall ⓣ229 17 18, Kievskaya metro; and Novinskiy Bulvar. 31, Novinskiy Mall, ⓣ981 49 41, Krasnopresnenskaya metro. ⓦwww.goodman-steak.ru. A solid group of steak houses specializing in high-quality grilled meat. Leather sofas with high backs are arranged around each table and the enormous business lunch is excellent value at R380. Amex, Maestro, MC and Visa. All branches daily from noon till the last diner leaves.

Marharaja ul. Pokrovka 2/1 (entrance on Starosadskiy per) ⓣ921 98 44, ⓦwww.maharaja.ru; Kitay-Gorod metro. The decor and service are fine, but *Maharaja's* Mogul, Punjabi and vegetarian dishes are on the bland side (and can be made without spices if required). Also does takeaways. Amex, DC, MC, Visa. Daily noon–11pm.

Moskva-Roma Stoleshnikov per. 12 ⓣ229 57 02; 10min walk from Teatralnaya, Okhotniy Ryad or Chekhovskaya metro. As classy as the street on which it's located, this Euro/Russian restaurant serves fantastic salads (R320–600), pasta dishes (R590) and grilled sea bass (R920), but the soups are less to write home about and it's hard to get a table outside when the weather's fine. Major cards. Daily 24hr.

Noev Kovcheg (Noah's Ark) Maliy Ivanovskiy per. 9 ⓣ917 07 17, ⓦwww.noevkovcheg.ru; 10min walk from Kitay-Gorod metro. This faux-posh Armenian restaurant near the Ivanovskiy Convent has reasonably priced home-made cheese plates, *basturma* with peppers and diverse *shashlyks* that encourage splurging on their fine wines and brandies. Eat before 3pm for a 15 percent discount, while US citizens get 25 percent discount any time. Amex, DC, EC, MC, Visa. Daily noon till the last customer leaves.

Expensive

Beloe Solntse Pustyni (White Sun of the Desert) ul. Neglinnaya 29/14 ⓣ209 75 25, ⓦwww.bsp-rest.ru; 10–15min walk from Tsvetnoy Bulvar, Kuznetskiy Most or Teatralnaya metro. Themed on a classic Soviet "western" film (think: *The Good, the Bad and the Ugly* set in 1920s Uzbekistan), the restaurant ritually spit-roasts a lamb (Thurs & Fri 8.30pm) and has belly dancing, live music and filmic "events" after 8pm. All cards. Daily noon–3am.

Café Pushkin Tverskoy bul. 26A ⓣ229 55 90; 5min walk from Tverskaya/Pushkinskaya metro. Pushkin would have felt at home in this lovely nineteenth-century mansion with a sumptuously decorated library, a rooftop summer café, and waiters in period costume. Its haute Russian cuisine is nearly faultless; order bliny with black caviar if you can afford to. Amex, DC, EC, MC, Visa. Daily 24hr.

Limpopo Varsonofievskiy per. 1, off ul. Rozhdestvenka ⓣ925 69 90; 10min walk from Kuznetskiy Most metro. Shamelessly pandering to stereotypes, this tribal hut-style African restaurant serves grilled crocodile, baked tortoise, kangaroo and impala steaks, plus South African wine and beer, and cocktails with zoomorphic swizzle-sticks. MC, Visa. Daily noon–midnight.

Savoy *Savoy Hotel*, ul. Rozhdestvenka 3 ⓣ929 86 00, ⓦwww.savoy.ru; near Kuznetskiy Most metro. One of Moscow's classiest restaurants, with magnificent Rococo decor, French, Russian and Scandinavian haute cuisine and top-class service – enjoy it for less with a business lunch (noon–4pm; R1200). Live music from 8pm. Amex, DC, EC, MC, Visa. Daily noon–midnight.

Very expensive

Bulvar (Boulevard) ul. Petrovka 30/7 ⓣ209 68 87, ⓦwww.boulevard.ru; 10min walk from Chekhovskaya metro. Smart dress and reservations are essential for this high-class French/fusion restaurant on the Boulevard Ring. It has a seafood display for guests to select their own fish, and a vintage wine list. Free secure parking. Amex, DC, EC, Visa. Daily noon till the last customer leaves.

Vannil (Vanilla) Ostozhenka ul. 1/9 ⓣ202 33 41; near Kropotkinskaya metro. If you've money to burn, this ultra-exclusive restaurant with a superb view of the Cathedral of Christ the Saviour serves the finest French/fusion cuisine in Moscow and boasts a VIP guest list as long as Leninskiy prospekt. Reservations and smart dress required; strict face control. Amex, DC, EC, JCB, MC, Visa. Daily noon–midnight.

Zemlyanoy gorod

The listings in this section are marked on the map on pp.150–151.

Cheap

Dioskuriya Nikitskiy bul. 5, str. 1 ⓣ291 37 59; near Arbatskaya metro. Head through the post office arch off Noviy Arbat to find this Georgian restaurant, featuring a trio of singers at weekends. The Mingrelian-style *khachapuri* (with an egg in the middle), *tolma* and sturgeon *shashlyk* with pomegranate sauce are sublime – but the choice gets limited as evening wears on, and they hate people arriving after 10.30pm. No cards. Daily noon–midnight.

Genatsvale (Friend) ul. Ostozhenka 12/1 ⓣ203 12 43; 5min walk from Kropotkinskaya metro. Another great, low-priced Georgian place – the *shashlyks* are especially good value, or try the *matsoni* (*kefir* with honey and nuts). Eat during the day to avoid the loud band and toasting in the evenings. All major cards. Daily 11am–midnight.

Karetniy dvor (Carriage House) Povarskaya ul. 52 ⓣ291 63 76; 10min walk from Barrikadnaya metro. You can tell this is an authentic Azerbaijani/Caucasian restaurant because its clientele comes from there and it has a row of chalet-style dining rooms for private parties, like restaurants in Baku or Tiblisi. The food is spot-on and cheap: *shashlyk* (R360), *kharcho* soup (R270) and barbecued rack of lamb (R560), but sadly no *khachapuri* or *lobio*. No cards. Daily 24hr.

Pilsner ul. 1st Tverskaya-Yamskaya 1 ⓣ251 20 23, Mayakovskaya metro. Located in a former ministerial dining room, this Czech beer hall has a high ceiling and a booming echo. The beer is home-brewed, but the point of coming is for the snacks – huge portions of chicken wings, sausage, salads and ribs – and it is all very cheap. Amex, Maestro, MC, Visa. Daily noon–1am.

Vostochniy Kvartal (Eastern Quarter) ul. Arbat 45/24 ⓣ241 38 03; near Smolenskaya metro. Directly opposite Bosfor on Plotnikov pereulok (see below), this colourfully decorated Uzbek restaurant wows visitors with its tasty soups and *lagman* (the Uzbek version of *pelmeni*) and attentive service. Reservations are rarely needed and you can eat well for R1000. No cards. Daily noon–11pm.

Inexpensive

Bosfor (Bosporus) ul. Arbat 47/23 ⓣ241 93 20; near Arbatskaya/Smolenskaya metro. Turkish-Caucasian restaurant on Plotnikov pereulok, just off the Arbat, serving *tolma*, *shashlyk*, plus a few fancier dishes like baked trout in wine sauce, with Georgian, Italian or Spanish wines. Business lunch (R540). Daily 11am–midnight.

Bungalo Bar ul. Zemlyanoy val 6 ⓣ916 24 32; 10min walk from Kurskaya metro. This friendly, funky restaurant on the Garden Ring is the hub of Moscow's Ethiopian community. Lots of spicy veggie choices; omnivores should order the *firmenaya bluda* – a little bit of everything on a platter of *enjira* (sourdough bread). Business lunch (R380); fantastic spiced coffee. Maestro, MC, Union, Visa. Daily 10am–midnight.

Cutty Sark Novinskiy bul. 12 ⓣ202 13 12, ⓦwww.cuttysark.inforos.ru; 15min walk from Smolenskaya or Barrikadnaya metro. Decorated like a luxurious Edwardian yacht, with an aquarium of live lobsters and a sushi bar. Set lunch R780; princely choice of vintage wines and whiskies. All major cards. Daily noon until the last customer leaves.

Mama Zoya Sechenovskiy per. 8 ⓣ201 77 43; 10min walk from Kropotkinskaya metro. Although the quality of its food has declined and the cost of wine has soared, this Georgian restaurant is still packed out with tourists and expats by 9pm. The decor is engagingly kitsch, and there's schmaltzy music; children welcome in the afternoon when it's not so crowded. No cards. Daily noon–11pm.

Mehana Bansko (Bansko Tavern) Smolenskaya pl. 9/1 ⓣ244 73 87; 5min walk from Smolenskaya metro. Very agreeable Bulgarian taverna with staff in national costume and live folk music after 6pm. Ask for the lamb dish that arrives on fire. Its four-course lunch (noon–4pm; R490) includes a glass of beer or wine. It even does deliveries. No cards. Mon–Thurs & Sun noon–midnight, Fri & Sat noon–2am.

TRAM ul. Malaya Dmitrovka 6 ⓣ299 07 70; near Chekhovskaya metro. A showbiz basement hang-out beside the Lenkom Theatre: the interior is smoky and intimate; tables on the street less glamorous. Russian, European and vaguely Asian dishes are named after plays or theatrical genres – try the *Kabuki* (set lunch R600). They show Tom and Jerry cartoons or Chaplin movies, and have a pianist in the evenings. No cards. Daily 24hr.

Moderate

El Gaucho Bolshoy Kozlovskiy per. 3/2 ⓣ923 10 98; 5min walk from Krasnye Vorota metro. Top-quality grills prepared by an Argentine chef, accompanied by French wines. Cholesterol-watchers and vegetarians needn't bother. All major cards. Daily noon–11pm.

La Grotta Bolshaya Bronnaya ul. 27/4 ⓣ200 30 57; near Tverskaya/Pushkinskaya metro. Reservations are mandatory for this minimalist Italian restaurant, whose delicious tomato soup, penne gorgonzola, chicken alla Nicoise and pizzas are far better value for money than at other Italian places in Moscow. Business lunch (Mon–Fri noon–4pm; R460). No cards. Noon till last customer leaves.

Pyat Spetsii (Five Spices) per. Sivtsev Vrazhek 3/18, on the corner of Gogolevskiy bul. ⓣ203 12 83, ⓦwww.5spice.menu.ru; 5min walk from Kroptokinskaya metro. One of those Moscow hybrids: an Indian-run Chinese restaurant serving yummy Thai prawn soup, vegetable spring rolls, honey-glazed ribs, stir-fry noodles, king prawns in oyster sauce, and barbecue chicken in hot black bean sauce. Business lunch (R550) noon–4pm. Amex, JCB, MC, Visa. Daily noon–4pm.

Rybniy Bazar (Fish Market) Troykhprudy per. 10/2 ⓣ209 54 44; 10min walk from Pushkinskaya metro. Pick your own seafood from the selection on ice in this cool restaurant on the first floor of an old mansion near Patriarch's Ponds (set lunch from R380). Downstairs is a jigger room stocking over 30 brands of vodka and home-made liquors (noon–midnight); secure parking. Amex, MC, Visa. Daily noon until the last customer leaves.

Scandinavia Maliy Palashovskiy per. 7 ⓣ937 56 30, ⓦwww.scandinavia.ru; near Tverskaya metro. A Swedish restaurant that scours the world to deliver mouthwatering coconut soup with crayfish dumplings, tuna fillet with Kamchatka crab risotto, T-bone steaks and a prawn-packed Caesar salad (lunch from R550). Its bar (till 1am) mixes the best cocktails in Moscow, and the vodka bar made from ice on the patio is also a hit during their Christmas and New Year parties. Major cards. Daily noon–midnight.

Tandoor Tverskaya ul. 30/2 ⓣ699 80 62 or 699 89 62, ⓦwww.tandoor.ru; near Mayakovskaya metro. Probably the best of the three Indian restaurants in the centre, with a fabulous business lunch (R440). Ordering à la carte, you can't go wrong with the coconut soup, garlic nan, the kebab platter or an aubergine (*baklazhan*) dish that's not on the menu. Amex, Visa. Daily noon–11pm.

011 Sadovaya-Triumfulnaya ul. 10/3 ⓣ699 09 63; near Mayakovskaya metro. A Yugoslav restaurant that started life as a nightclub and retains an air of intrigue, it's ideal for a candlelit tête-à-tête or a raucous meal with a bunch of friends. Fish dominates the menu. Amex, DC, EC, JCB, MC, Visa. Daily 10am–11pm.

Expensive

TsDL (House of Writers) Povarskaya ul. 50 ⓣ291 15 15; 10min walk from Barrikadnaya metro. Reserved for members of the Writers' Union in Soviet times – when it served food rarely seen elsewhere – its high-ceilinged Oak Hall serves fine Russian cuisine (entrees R1000–1500), has a princely wine list (from R1000–10,000) and may close in respect to deceased authors. Also on the premises is the slightly less expensive *Zapisky Okhotnika* (Hunter's Sketches) dining room, named after the stuffed animals and graffiti on the walls. Reservations for both are essential. Amex, DC, MC, Visa. Daily noon–midnight.

Krasnaya Presnya, Fili and the southwest

All the listings below are marked on the map on p.178.

Inexpensive

Da Cicco Profsoyuznaya ul. 13/12 ⓣ125 11 96, ⓦwww.da-cicco.menu.ru; 5min walk from Profsoyuznaya metro. Attractively furnished trattoria-pizzeria, with tables outside in the summer. Over 50 kinds of thin-crust pizzas, delicious pasta dishes and calzone, plus a salad bar. All cards accepted. Daily 11am–11pm.

Moderate

Baan Thai Bolshaya Dorogomilovskaya ul. 11 ⓣ499 240 05 97, ⓦwww.baanthai.ru; 10min

walk from Kievskaya metro. Moscow's best-value Thai restaurant, its satay, spicy noodle soups and duck curry are perfect, and the service attentive. Business lunch (R560); takeouts; free deliveries. Amex, DC, EC, MC, Visa. Daily noon–midnight.

Darbar ***Sputnik Hotel*****, Leninskiy pr. 38 ⓣ930 29 25, ⓦwww.darbar.ru; 5min walk from Leninskiy Prospekt metro.** Worth the trip to eat the finest Indian food in Moscow, but be sure to reserve a table. Live Indian music nightly. Business lunch (noon–4pm; R550), takeouts and free deliveries. Amex, DC, EC, MC, Visa. Daily noon–midnight.

Expensive

Bochka (Barrel) ul. 1905 goda 2 ⓣ252 30 41; 10min walk from Ulitsa 1905 Goda metro. Opposite the *Mezh*, this fancy rustic-style place does fine Russian food with a Caucasian twist; try the *golubtsy* (stuffed cabbage) with sour cream, or the turkey *shashlyk* (not listed on the menu). Amex, DC, EC, MC, Visa. Daily 24hr.

Shinok (Farm) ul. 1905 goda 2 ⓣ255 02 04; 10min walk from Ulitsa 1905 Goda metro. Faux-Ukrainian tavern with a captive cow and milkmaid for diners to gawp at. The menu lists two kinds of *borsch*, four varieties of *vareniki* (dumplings) and five types of *salo* (lard) as starters, with suckling pig, chicken or rabbit to follow, accompanied by *gorilka* (Ukrainian vodka) and folk music after 7pm. Amex, DC, MC, Visa. Daily noon–midnight.

Very expensive

Uley (Hive) ul. Gadeshka 7 ⓣ095 797 43 33; 10min walk from Mayakovskaya metro. Moscow's first Fusion restaurant is still trendy, but its food has declined since chef Correa departed. Try the monkfish with absinthe pork, the smoked duck or the red pepper bisque. They also sell absinthe and even distil grappa at your table. The sofa lounge for smoking hookahs and playing backgammon is spoilt by loud music and poor ventilation. Secure parking. All major cards. Mon–Fri noon–2am, Sat & Sun noon till the last guest leaves.

Zamoskvareche and the south

The listings in this section are marked on the map on p.205, unless otherwise stated.

Inexpensive

Ginno Taki ul. Bolshaya Yakimanka 58/2 ⓣ238 95 33; near Oktyabrskaya metro. Similar to its namesake on Tverskaya ulitsa regarding queuing, food and drink (see p.352), but even more cramped, with loud MTV and all-night karaoke, encouraging diners to eat up and leave. All cards. Daily 11am–6am.

Majorelle ul. Zatsepa 19/2 ⓣ959 78 82; 10min walk from Paveletskaya metro. An unexpected delight on a backstreet to the west of Paveletsk Station: decorative tents pitched in a grove of trees, with hookahs, Arab music, mint tea and Moroccan food. The mixed *mezze* appetizers are superb but the soups could be spicier. Business lunch R350. No cards. Daily noon–10pm.

Moderate

Cabana Raushskaya nab. 4 ⓣ239 30 45; 15min walk from Novokuznetskaya metro. See map, p.207. Conveniently close if you're staying at the *Baltschug-Kempinski* Hotel, the eclectic menu includes plentiful salads, black-bean soup, seafood dishes and lunchtime special deals. See also Nightlife, p.359. All major cards. Daily 6pm–6am.

Louisiana Pyatnitskaya ul. 30, str. 4 ⓣ951 42 44; near Novokuznetskaya metro. See map, p.207. American steakhouse with southern flavour. If you're not up for the gigantic T-bone steaks (R650), go for the chicken and seafood jambalaya. There's also a children's menu, Californian wines, cheap drinks for women (7–8pm), and family discounts on Sun. Amex, DC, EC, JCB, Maestro, Visa. Daily 11am–11pm.

Suliko ul. Bolshaya Polyanka 42/2 ⓣ238 25 86; 10min walk from Polyanka metro. See map, p.207. This small Georgian restaurant does fantastic *khachapuri*, *lobio* and other appetizers. Go for a set lunch (R650) with a glass of wine or the evening buffet (R2300). No cards. Daily noon–6am.

Expensive

Café Swiss ***Swissotel Kraysnye Holmy Moscow Hotel*****, 52 Kosmodamianskaya nab., Bldg 6 ⓣ787 98 00; 10min walk from Paveletskaya metro.** Serves good-quality French fare; it's overpriced, but worth it for the fantastic views of the city. High in the sky above the House of Music, it's a good place for lunch or dinner on a clear day. All cards. Daily 7am–11pm.

Very expensive

Dorian Gray Kadashevskaya nab. 6/1 ⓣ 238 64 01; 10min walk from Tretyakovskaya or Polyanka metro. See map, p.207. A classy Italian restaurant beloved of Russian film moguls and starlets, with a view of the Kremlin and the Moskva River embankment. Try the shrimp salad with rucola, the veal fillet with mushroom sauce or the sautéed seafood, followed by a tiramisu. Secure parking. Amex, Visa, DC, EC, MC, JCB. Daily noon–midnight.

Taganka and Zayauze

The listings in this section are marked on the map on p.249.

Inexpensive

Verona Vorontsovskaya ul. 32/36 ⓣ 912 06 32; 10min from Proletarskaya metro. Excellent-value Italian restaurant, with fabulous prosciutto, *penne arrabbiata* and garlicky pizzas. On the downside it gets overcrowded and the wine list is paltry. No cards. Daily 11am–11pm.

Moderate

Budvar Kotelnicheskaya nab. 33 ⓣ 915 15 98; 10min from Tanganskaya metro. Huge portions of rich Central European food washed down with draught Czech and German beer or Russian *kvas*. Try the crackled duck, smoked venison or crawfish. MC, Visa. Daily noon–midnight.

Northern Suburbs

The listings in this section are marked on the map on pp.270–271.

Inexpensive

Bega Tokyo ***Bega Hotel*****, Begovaya alleya 11 ⓣ 946 17 33; 15min walk from Dinamo metro.** A long walk but worth it, this eighth-floor restaurant is home from home for Japanese businessmen, who have their own individual bottles of whisky behind the bar, and Japanese TV to watch. Noodle dishes, beef, seafood and tempura to die for, but the menu is difficult to decipher – ask the staff for advice.

Moderate

Dinamo Leningradskiy pr. 36 ⓣ 495 613 42 74; 5min walk from Dinamo metro. Another place for cognoscenti, tucked away by gate #10 of Dinamo Stadium. VIP guests like Pele, Abramovich and Chubais reserve the hall off the foyer; ordinary mortals are guided past the toilet through a door, into a kind of chalet with a carp pool. The Georgian food is heavenly and it's easy to over-order (they'll box up any leftovers). Quite affordable, providing you drink beer instead of wine. No cards. Daily 1–11pm.

Expensive

Yar (Wayside Halt) ***Sovetskiy Hotel*****, Leningradskiy pr. 32/2 ⓣ 960 20 04, ⓦ www.yar-restaurant.ru; 10min walk from Dinamo metro.** A re-creation of the famous pre-Revolutionary restaurant where Rasputin once caused a scandal by exposing himself, the *Yar* features aristocratic dishes like Tsar's sterlet, venison steak or stuffed quail, and a Gypsy variety show from 9pm (R650 surcharge). Buffet breakfast (R450) till noon in the Green Bar. Amex, MC, Visa. Daily 7.30am till the last guest leaves.

13

Nightlife

Moscow isn't a city that goes to bed early. With alcohol on sale 24-hours, Russian youths wander the streets from one *tusovka* (event) to another, playing guitars in the parks and underpasses on the Boulevard Ring. Winter may force parties indoors, but there's no let-up on the club scene. Whether it's jazz-fusion, trance, grunge, S&M or gender bending, there are **clubs** for any taste. Local DJs and foreign guests perform at most of these, and there are lots of one-off raves and theme parties (advertised by flyers). Many also double as **live music venues**, hosting indigenous acts, spanning the range of tastes from Russian reggae to thrash, plus alternative and world music bands from abroad – big-name acts are likely to stage concerts in one of the city's sports palaces or stadiums.

The term *klub* can cover anything from an arthouse café with a spot of live music to a dance warehouse, or a fancy nightclub with a restaurant and casino. Most cater to a certain crowd, whether it's creative professionals, students, shell-suited flatheads or designer-draped models. While formal dress codes are rare, **face control** (*feys kontrol*) is widespread. Russians distinguish between "democratic" face control (aimed at keeping out hooligans and bandits) and the kind that favours the rich (never mind how they behave). It's unwise to rile club security staff, however rude they might be. If you end up in a club full of **flatheads**, be careful not to flash your money around but don't be too nervous; they are out for a good time and unlikely to be looking for trouble. Men should be aware that most of the tourist-oriented clubs are full of **prostitutes**, for whom dancing with guys is just a prelude to business – though there are also lots of girls simply out for a good time, which can lead to misunderstandings. Striptease or pole-dancing acts are a feature of quite a few clubs and generally not regarded as sleazy by Russians – and cabaret shows can be even raunchier.

Admission charges and **drinks** prices are modest in most places, but some clubs are seriously pricey on both counts – see the reviews below. To find out the latest on up-and-coming events, check the **listings** sections in the Friday edition of the *Moscow Times*, the current month's issue of *Pulse* or *Afisha* (see p.48), or the online **club reviews** at Ⓦwww.expat.ru, Ⓦwww.go-magazine.ru and Ⓦwww.waytorussia.net.

Pop, dance, rock and world music

Russian pop music is something of a joke to foreigners. The only act to get worldwide fame in recent years was the "lesbian" duo TaTu, while before them, the only performer that anyone outside Russia could identify was Alla Pugachova, who resembles a contestant in a drag ball. MTV-Russia is dominated by bland boy bands and Britney wannabes like Zemfira and Glucosa, while glamorous girl bands, such as Viagra, whose name speaks for itself, and numerous graduates of the annual TV show *Star Factory* flood Russian pop music; the only indie bands to get any exposure are Mumiy Troll from Vladivostok (led by the androgynous, intellectual Ilya Lagutenko), and the multi-instrumental Chizh (whose fusion of Celtic, Russian and Soviet roots music fits the prevailing mood of retro-patriotism). However, a far wider range of bands plays in Moscow's clubs, particularly during **festivals**. The main events are **SKIF** – a gathering of DJs, **indie** bands and performance artists from Russia and abroad, in mid-April; the **ethnic** music festival in the Hermitage Garden in early July; and the international **rock** and folk festivals at Luzhniki Sports Complex and the Central House of Artists (mid- or late Oct). A DJ **lounge** music festival takes place most years (late March to mid-April), and there are sporadic mini-festivals of **Celtic/Slavic** pop, rock or folk (signposted on Ⓦwww.celtic.ru).

Russian **bands** to look out for include hard rockers Leningrad (banned by Mayor Luzhkov, but defiantly playing surprise gigs); Dva Samolota and Tequilajazz (reggae/fusion); Markschneider Kunst (techno-trance); Ariya (whose audio-visual onslaught is like Pink Floyd); Iva Nova (Slavic folk punk) and Jah Division (reggae). Recent foreign acts have included George Michael, Elton John, Madonna, Scorpions, Kiss, Kylie Minogue and Lenny Kravitz. Otherwise, dance music rules and the big names at clubs are **DJs** Ivan Rudyk, Fonar, Suhov, List, Smash, Katrin Vesna, Pilot and Sanchez – often joined by foreign DJs such as Paul Oakenfold, West Bam, Svan Vath, Paul Van Dyk, John Digweed, Danny Tenaglia and Sasha.

B2 Bolshaya Sadovaya ul. 8 Ⓣ650 99 18; Ⓦwww.b2club.ru; 5min walk from Mayakovskaya metro. **See map, pp.150–151.** One of Moscow's most popular clubs, this modish five-floor labyrinth has a restaurant, sushi-bar plus seven other bars under one roof. Access to the 4th level, where DJs or bands perform, may involve a separate cover charge, depending on who's playing. Daily noon–6am; R400–3000.

Cabana Raushskaya nab. 4/5 str. 1 Ⓣ238 50 06, Ⓦwww.cabana.ru; 15min walk from Novokuznetskaya metro. **See map, p.207.** Famed for its black stripper, Dillon, who once outraged Duma deputies with his "livened up" dance to the national anthem. He performs on Tues, when women are plied with free champagne and vodka to fuel a near-orgy. Daily 6pm–6am; R300.

Che Nikolskaya ul. 10/2 Ⓣ621 74 77 1960s; 5min walk from Lubyanka or Ploshchad Revolyutsii metro. **See map, p.102.** Ay, Commandante! A dance club in the Kitay-Gorod with 1960s guerilla decor, Cuban/Latin music that sizzles, the best mojito cocktails in town (2-4-1 at weekends), and a sweat-lodge dance floor. Face control. Daily 24hr; free.

Club na Brestskoy (Club on Brestskaya) 2-ya Brestskaya ul. 6 (entrance from 1-ya Brestskaya) Ⓣ694 09 36; 10min walk from Mayakovskaya metro. **See map, pp.150–151.** This unpretentious basement den often books great alternative bands such as the Romanian folk-punk group Spitalul de Urgenta. Daily noon until the last customer leaves; free.

Fabrique Kosmodamianskaya nab. 2 Ⓣ953 65 76, Ⓦwww.fabrique.ru; 15–20min walk from Novokuznetskaya metro. **See map, p.205.** A huge split-level basement club in the University of Design and Technology, throwing parties hosted by Saltykov, Fashion, Fenix, Cat and other visiting DJs. Face control. Daily 11pm–7am.

Fasol pr. Mira 28 (entrance down an alley) Ⓣ680 28 33; 5min walk from Prospekt Mira metro. **See map, p.273.** A dining club for forty-something socialites, that hosts retro parties on Thurs. Face control; table reservation advised. Sun–Wed noon–midnight, Thurs noon–2am, Fri & Sat noon–4am; free.

Garazh (Garage) Tverskaya ul. 16, str. 2 Ⓣ650 18 48; near Pushkinskaya/Tverskaya/Chekhovskaya metro. **See map, pp.150–151.** Hip-hop and R&B night (Wed) attracts African expats and Russian students, but at other times you're likelier to find off-duty girls from *Night Flight* and their flathead boyfriends. Capricious face control. Daily 24hr; free.

Golodnaya Utka (Hungry Duck) ul. Pushechnaya 9/6 ☎517 01 99; beside the pedestrian tunnel from Kuznetskiy Most metro. See map, pp.112–113. Once denounced in the Duma for debauching Russian youth, the former *Hungry Duck* is tamer nowadays, but still the kind of dive where groping somebody counts as an introduction. In winter daily 7pm–6am; in summer Fri & Sat 10pm–6am; women R100; men R350.

Hot Dog's Bar ul. Zemlyanoy val 26 ☎917 01 50, ⓦwww.hotdogsbar.ru; near Kurskaya metro. See map, pp.150–151. A certified pick-up spot for expatriates and hookers, with a disco or rockabilly bands, theme parties, pool tables and sports TV. Daily 24hr; free, except when special bands are playing.

Karma-Bar Pushechnaya ul. 3 ☎624 56 33, ⓦwww.karma-bar.ru; 5min walk from Kuznetskiy Most or Lubyanka metro. See map, pp.112-113. Originally called the Buddha bar, but renamed after local Buddhists threatened to curse it; they've kept the statue of Buddha on the dance floor and added a pair of bronze breasts. DJ Carlos Tico's Latin parties (Thurs & Fri), Latina dance classes (Fri & Sat 9–11.30pm), and Porno Parties (Thurs) are the most popular nights. Liberal face control. All major cards. Thurs–Sun 9pm–6am; R200–300.

Kitayskiy Lyotchik Dzhao Da (Chinese Pilot Dzhao Da) Lubyanskiy proezd 25 ☎623 28 96, ⓦwww.jao-da.ru; near Kitay-Gorod metro. See map, pp.112–113. Set up by Irina Papernaya, the doyenne of the Boho club scene, this basement club/restaurant themed on a mythical airman hosts gigs by the likes of Leningrad, Markschneider Kunst or Prepinaki – plus a disco most nights. Cheap drinks; tasty Russian food. Daily 24hr; R300–400 on gig nights.

Kult (Cult) Yauzskaya ul. 5 ☎917 57 06; 15–20min walk from Kitay-Gorod or Taganskaya metro. See map, p.249. A hangout for designers, artists and trendsetters, with an African restaurant, cushion-lounge, art gallery, and Euro movies on the monitors. Plays jazz, mood or ethnic music in the week, and funk and disco at weekends. Dress code and face control. Mon & Tues noon–midnight, Wed noon–2am, Thurs & Fri noon–6am; Sat 2pm–6am, Sun 2pm–midnight; free, or cover charge, depending on events.

Metelitsa (Snowfall) ul. Noviy Arbat 21 ☎291 11 70, ⓦwww.metelitsa.ru; 10min walk from Arbatskaya metro. See map, p.150–151. The club that epitomized the nouveaux-riche 1990s, with its swanky casino and whores primed to relieve bigshots and flatheads of their surplus cash. Worth trying once, if you've got the money. Live entertainment; Western-style kitchen. Smart dress; strict face control. DC, MC, Visa. Wed & Thurs 9pm–5am, Fri & Sat 9pm–6am; R2400, which is exchanged for counters that you can use at the casino or to pay for drinks and snacks.

Ministerstvo (Ministry) Malaya Nikitskaya ul. 24 ☎222 01 58; 10min walk from Barrikadnaya metro. See map, pp.150–151. Housed in a wing of the Ministry of Broadcasting, this elite club's decor is Stalinist Empire, with gilded statues, lofty ceilings and doors. Technic, Spyder and guest DJs play techno and house to a coked-out crowd with money to burn. Fascist face control. Thurs & Sat 11pm–6am; free.

Night Flight Tverskaya ul. 17 ☎629 41 65, ⓦwww.nightflight.ru; 5min walk from Tverskaya metro. See map, pp.150–151. Visiting execs are assured of finding a deluxe hooker on the tiny dance floor of this split-level bar restaurant, serving top-notch Euro cuisine under tolerant Swedish management. Disco from 11pm. Amex, DC, EC, MC, Visa. Daily restaurant 6pm–4am; club 8pm–5am; R900.

Papa John's Myasnitskaya ul. 22 (below *Johnny's*) ☎755 95 54; ⓦwww.papas.ru; 5min from walk Chistye Prudy/Turgenevskaya metro. See map, pp.112–113. Alcoholism and lechery rule at this successor to the infamous *Hungry Duck* (see *Golodnaya Utka* above). Wet T-shirt contests, audience strips, cockfights, turtle races and brawls. Cuban bartenders in nappies serve a wide range of pricey drinks (happy hour 6–9pm). Tues are Latin nights. Daily 6pm–6am; Fri & Sat women R200, men R300.

Parizhskaya Zhizn (Parisian Life) ul. Karetniy ryad 3, str. 1 (in the Hermitage Gardens) ☎209 45 24; 10min walk from Tsvetnoy bulvar metro. See map, pp.150–151. Flatheads and *Sex and the City* babes fight and smooch around the dance floor and pool tables, if not diverted by a band playing upstairs. Face control. EC, MC, Visa. Daily: bar/restaurant 11am–7am; disco 7pm–7am; Mon–Wed free, Thurs R200, Fri & Sat R300.

Piramida (Pyramid) Tverskaya ul. 18a ☎694 36 03, ⓦwww.piramida-cafebar.com (in Russian only); near Tverskaya/Pushkinskaya

metro. See map, pp.150–151. An ultra-hip, glass-walled club across the road from *McDonald's*, featuring a seated Pharaonic colossus, space-suited waiters, and DJs Ostap, Mike and Misha Bear playing trip hop, fusion or broken beat, with a party the last Thurs each month. Great for people-watching, even if you don't want to dance. Daily 8am–5am; free.

Proekt OGI (Project OGI) Potapovskiy per. 8/12, str. 2 ⓣ627 53 66, 10min walk from Chistye Prudy metro; Nikolskaya ul. 19/21 ⓣ621 58 27, 5min walk from Lubyanka or Ploshchad Revolyutsii metro See map, p.102. An evolving project by a publishing company, these two basement book cafés offer trance and lounge music, poetry readings, kids' events and gigs by indie bands. The first *OGI* is hidden in a courtyard (turn right at the end and look for a black door); the second, by the fashion mall on Tretyakovskiy proezd. Both serve good food at bargain prices. No cards. Daily 24hr; free.

Propaganda Bolshoy Zlatoustinskiy per. 7 ⓣ624 57 32, ⓦwww.propagandamoscow.com; near Kitay-Gorod or Lubyanka metro. See map, p.102. Relaxed bar-club with a mix of students, gays and expats, grooving to mood music (Tues), garage, house and jungle spun by Sanchez (Thurs) or guest DJs, or at the China-Town gay party (Sun). Tasty food served until 10–11pm, when tables are cleared for dancing. Democratic face control. Daily noon–6am; free.

Shestnadsat Tonn (Sixteen Tons) ul. Presnenskiy val 6, str. 1 ⓣ253 53 00, ⓦwww.16tons.ru; near Ulitsa 1905 Goda metro. See map, p.178. An English-style pub with a microbrewery and a disco that often features rockabilly bands upstairs. Lots of singles action, but it's not obligatory. All major cards. Daily: bar 11am–6am, club 6pm–6am; Wed-Sat R300–800.

Sorry, Babushka Slavyanskaya ploshchad, 2/1 ⓣ495 788 06 15, ⓦwww.sorrybabushka.ru; Kitay-gorod metro. See map, p.102. Popular with students from Moscow University, this funky dance club plays an eclectic mix of music from the 1960s to modern techno. Noon–6am; free.

Tabula Rasa Komsomolskiy prospekt 28 ⓣ248 66 88, ⓦwww.tabulaclub.ru; Frunzenskaya metro. See map, p.178. Acoustic or alternative gigs are usually better than the DJs' sets, and there's a striptease on Wed, so check what's on before coming. Food is quite pricey and the service sucks. Daily noon–6am; R200–400.

Tinkoff Protochniy per. 11 ⓣ777 33 00, ⓦwww.tinkoff.ru; 15min walk from Smolenskaya metro. See map, pp.150–151. A snazzy microbrewery-restaurant (see p.350) with live acid jazz or funk in the lounge (Thurs–Fri after 9pm); its range of unfiltered beers costs R130–480, but the sushi is reasonably priced. All major cards. Mon–Sat noon–2am; free.

Tochka (Dot) Leninskiy prospect 6 ⓣ737 76 66; Oktyabrskaya metro. See map, p.205. Although *tochka* is slang for a flat used by prostitutes, this isn't that kind of place at all. A stark factory conversion, with two bars, pool tables, a restaurant, a decent-sized dance floor and concerts at weekends, its Celtic affiliations extend to hosting a St Patrick's Day party (late Feb) and mock-battles by Sword 'n' Sorcery troupes. Face control. DC, MC, Visa. Daily 6pm till the last guest leaves; R250–1200.

Trety Put (Third Way) ul. Pyatnitskaya 4 ⓣ951 87 34, ⓦwww.thirdway.ru; 5min walk from Novokuznetskaya metro. See map, p.207. Far from being a coven of Blairites, this is a genuinely bohemian club with chess tables, cheap beer, penurious regulars and occasional gigs. Bohemian face control. Mon–Sat 10pm–5am; free.

Vermel (Vermicelli) Raushkaya nab. 4 ⓣ959 33 03, ⓦwww.vermel.ru; 15min walk from Novokuznetskaya metro. See map, p.205. From the same stable as *Kitayskiy Lyotchik*, with a young student crowd dancing to diverse sounds. Free projects Mon; Celtomania on Tues; live music Wed & Thurs; retro-parties Fri & Sat; rockabilly Sun. Affordable drinks. Beware of the low doorways. Mon–Thurs noon–5am, Fri–Sun noon–6am; R100–350.

Voodoo Lounge Sredniy Tishinskiy per. 5/7 ⓣ253 23 23; ⓦwww.vlclub.ru, 10min walk from Belorusskaya metro. See map, p.270–271. One of Moscow's punchier pick-up spots, with a summer patio, Latin music and a Mexican restaurant. Try the Macchiato cocktail with mint leaves, rum and sugar. Tues–Sat 6pm–6am; Tues–Thurs free; Fri & Sat R200–300.

Zapasnik (Art Garbage) Starosadskiy per. 5 ⓣ628 87 45, ⓦwww.art-garbage.ru; 10min walk from Kitay-Gorod metro. See map, p.112–113. More of a restaurant-hangout than a club, its dance hall comes to life on Fri nights, or whenever bands play, but otherwise there's just people chilling out or dining on the patio. Good-value drinks and meals. Daily noon–6am; Thurs–Sun R100–300.

Zhiguli ul. Noviy Arbat 11, str. 1 ⓣ291 41 44; 5min walk from Arbatskaya metro. See map, p.150–151. Brezhnev-era Retro rules at this refitted Soviet beer hall with its own micro-brewery. The beer dispensers resemble mineral water automats and the beer mugs are authentically lumpy. Former beer-hall waiters now in their fifties sometimes drop in to recall the old days, and there are Soviet singsongs in the evenings. A beer costs only R120. Daily 9am–4am; free.

Occasional live venues

The following places are sometimes used for concerts by major Russian pop stars or foreign bands, as advertised in the *Moscow Times*, *Pulse* and *Russia Journal*, and by posters around the city. Tickets can be obtained through booking agencies (see Chapter 14, "The Arts").

Central House of Artists (TsDKh) ul. Krymskiy val 10 ⓣ238 96 34, ⓦwww.cha.ru, 10min walk from Park Kultury metro. Hosts an international folk festival in the second half of Oct.

D/K Gorbunova ul. Novozavodskaya 27 ⓣ145 80 98; ⓦwww.dkgorbunova.ru; 15min from Bagrationovskaya metro. This ex-Soviet House of Culture near the Gorbunov CD mall was once Moscow's main "alternative" venue for rock and punk bands (Nick Cave and the Smashing Pumpkins played here), but don't bother coming if nothing is advertised. Box office Mon–Fri 11am–7pm, Sat & Sun 11am–5pm; R500–3000.

Luzhniki Stadium Luzhnetskaya nab. 24 ⓣ785 97 17; ⓦwww.luzhniki.ru; 10min walk from Sportivnaya metro, or trolleybus #28 from Park Kultury metro. Moscow's largest stadium has hosted concerts by Michael Jackson, Whitesnake and Motorhead.

Luzhniki Sports Palace Luzhnetskaya nab. 24 ⓣ637 04 20; directions as above. A smaller indoor venue near the stadium, where Robbie Williams and Metallica have played.

Moscow International House of Music (MMDM) Kosmodamianskaya nab. 52, str. 8 ⓣ730 10 11, ⓦwww.mmdm.ru; 10min walk from Paveletskaya metro. A prestigious high-tech venue with Moscow's best audio-visual facilities, more often used for concerts by the likes of avant-garde composer Philip Glass or the opera soprano Jessye Norman.

Olympic Sports Complex pr. Mira 16 ⓣ688 53 22; ⓦwww.olimpik.ru, 10min walk from Prospekt Mira metro. Another indoor sporting venue that has staged concerts by Deep Purple and Russian pop stars like Zemfira. Ticket office daily 10am–2pm & 3–7pm.

Rossiya Concert Hall Moskvoretskaya nab. 1 ⓣ637 04 20, ⓦwww.rossia-hall.ru; 10min from Kitay-Gorod metro, on the embankment side of the *Rossiya Hotel*. Currently closed for renovation, but due to reopen late 2009, this venue has hosted gala concerts by Alla Pugachova and other Russian stars, with rare visitations by Placido Domingo, Prodigy, Elton John and Cliff Richard.

State Kremlin Palace in the Kremlin ⓣ628 52 32, ⓦwww.gkd.ru; near Biblioteka Imeni Lenina and Aleksandrovskiy Sad metros. Cesaria Evora, Bowie, Sting, Tina Turner and Diana Ross are among those who have played in this hall where Communist Party congresses were once held. The booking office is beside one of the exits from Aleksandrovskiy Sad metro.

Gay and lesbian nightlife

Although homosexuality is no longer illegal in Russia, society remains extremely homophobic. Most local gays are still in the closet, and while Moscow's club scene is more tolerant than society at large, only gay clubs are reliable havens. In recent years several well-known clubs have gone straight or folded after trouble – one had the misfortune to be right behind the Dubrovka Theatre in the 2002 siege; commandos blew a hole in the wall to burst into the theatre. For changes in the future, check the **website** ⓦwww.gay.ru, which is full of advice and **listings**, as well as links to gay and lesbian organizations, legal rights and much else. Currently, Sunday's the night for gay-friendly **parties** at the popular straight club *Propaganda* (see p.361).

Baza (Base) Milyutinskiy per. 6 ⓣ927 31 93; 10 min walk from Turgenevskaya or Lubyanka metro. To find this basement drag bar, look for the "Business Klass-Audit" sign, go through the gate to the back and turn left. Its staff and regulars are as picturesque as the show (from 1am), and drinks are cheap. Daily 8pm–6am; free.

Dary Morya (Gifts of the Sea) Maliy Gnezdnikovskiy per. 9 str. 6; 10min walk from Tverskaya/Pushkinskaya metro. A seedy rough-trade bar with rent boys, reached by an anonymous dark brown door on the left-hand side of the first right turning off the pereulok, if approached from Tverskaya ulitsa. Daily 10pm–midnight; free.

Samovolka (AWOL) Novaya Basmannaya ul. 9, str. 2 ⓣ261 78 44; 10min walk from Komsomolskaya or Krasnye Vorota metro. To Russian conscripts *samovolka* signifies freedom, booze and sex. The club's decor is military themed and its staff wear fatigues, though the drinks are expensive. Thurs–Sat 10pm–5.30am; free.

Tri Obezyany (Three Monkeys) Nastavnicheskiy per. 11, str. 1 ⓣ916 35 55, ⓦwww.gaycentral.ru; Chkalovskaya metro. This long-established club is Moscow's only place that runs lesbian nights (Thurs 7pm–midnight). It has pool tables, a tiny dance floor and unisex toilets. Amex, EC, MC, Visa. Daily 7pm–7am; Sun–Wed free; Thurs–Sat R250.

Jazz and blues

Moscow has an indigenous jazz tradition going back to the 1930s, and its clubs lure talent from across Russia and the Baltic States, plus elsewhere during **festivals**. The most prestigious is **Jazz at the Hermitage Garden** in late August, an outdoor feast of ethno-jazz and rock fusion (ⓣ299 99 52, Ⓔmgreen@home.relline.ru), closely followed by the acclaimed vocalists' festival **Jazz Voices** (*Dzhazovye Golosa*) in December, at the Central House of Artists (see p.225) and the Jazz Art Club (see below). Besides the clubs listed here there's a 24-hour **jazz cruise** on the Moscow Canal in late July, sailing from the Northern River Terminal (see p.287). Bring a swimming costume and wine to enjoy chilling out at the Pirogovskoe Reservoir: for information, call the Jazz Art Club (ⓣ499 191 83 20). **Blues**, Cuban, flamenco and *fado* music also have their admirers. Two useful **websites** with audio links are "Jazz in Russia" (ⓦwww.jazz.ru) – whose text in English includes a section on festivals – and "Blues" (ⓦwww.blues.ru).

Jazz Art Club Olimpiyskiy prospekt, 16, str. 1, in the café "Olympiad-80" (Olympic stadium) ⓣ4991 91 83 20; Prospekt Mira metro. Only open on Wed and closed throughout June, this joint, decorated with abstract paintings and models of flying birds hanging from the ceiling, is a venue for the Jazz Voices festival in Dec. Live music till 11pm. Cheap drinks and snacks. Wed 7.30–11pm; R 100–200.

Pivnaya Galereya (Beer Gallery) Novoslobodskaya ul. 14/19, str. 7 ⓣ499 978 23 19, ⓦwww.jvlclub.ru; near Novoslobodskaya metro. Has an eclectic programme, with jazz, classical or folk music every night, mini-shows by actors, 1920s retro dances, and maybe film screenings. Sun–Thurs noon–midnight; Fri & Sat noon–3am; the entrance fee depends on the event and varies from free to R750.

Sezon (Season) Ulanskiy per. 16 ⓣ632 92 64; Chistiye Prudy metro. Popular jazz club run by saxophonist Igor Butman. Russian musicians at weekends and holidays; guest artists have included Gary Burton, Joe Lock and Kenny Garret. Daily 7.30pm–midnight; concerts R1000.

FAQ Café Gazetny per. 9, str. 2 ⓣ629 08 27, ⓦwww.faqcafe.ru. Art workshop holding concerts, exhibitions, body-art parties, discussions and performance. Jazz concerts on Sundays. Daily noon–6am; R200–300.

Sinaya Ptitsa (Blue Bird) ul. Malaya Dmitrovka. 23/15 ⓣ209 30 27; 10min walk from Mayakovskaya or Chekhovskaya metro. Currently closed for renovation, but due to reopen in late 2009, this forty-year-old jazz restaurant (dining from R1000 per head) hosts live bands, including music of the 1920s and 1930s, jazz improvisations, and Sergei Manukyan's jazz ensemble. Also has karaoke, pool tables, bar and videos. Amex, EC, MC, Union, Visa. Daily 24hr; free.

Bard music

Russian **Bard music** is associated with the *shestidesyatniki* or "Sixties people" who came of age under Khrushchev and Brezhnev, when Bulat Okudzhava, Alexander Gallich and the gravel-voiced Vladimir Vysotsky moved millions with their bittersweet, satirical or savage ballads, skirting or straying well over the edges of what was officially permissible. Four decades on, Vysotsky remains almost as popular as ever and new generations of Bards have attracted a devoted following, even if it's not on the scale of their predecessors' appeal. If you're interested in hearing how the genre has developed, visit the website ⓦwww.Bard-Cafe.komkon.org, or reserve a table at *Gnezdo Glukharya*.

Gnezdo Glukharya (The Widgeon's Nest) Bolshaya Nikitskaya ul. 22 ⓣ291 93 88, ⓦwww.gnezdogluharya.ru;10–15min walk from Arbatskaya, Pushkinskaya or Okhotniy Ryad metro. Down a lane across the road from the *Helikon Opera*, this is Moscow's most accessible Bards venue, but table reservations are essential. The Russian food is inexpensive but distinctly average. Daily noon–11pm; R300–1000, depending on the concert.

Chalet Bard Cub Elektrolitny proezd, 7 str. 2 ⓣ499 317 61 01, ⓦwww.shale.ru. Restaurant serving alpine cuisine, with billiards tables and a sauna. Hosts bards concerts on Tues & Wed at 7pm (from Sept till May). R150–500.

14

The Arts

For well over a century, Moscow has been one of the world's great centres of **classical music, opera and ballet**, most famously represented by the Bolshoy Theatre but also by its orchestras and choirs. Although many suffered from the withdrawal of state funding and the exodus of talented artists in the early 1990s, new orchestras and ensembles have emerged. **Theatre**, too, has bounced back, with local audiences returning in droves, and directors competing to scandalize or delight. Some productions are exciting enough to surmount the language barrier for foreigners, and **circus** and **puppetry** require little or no knowledge of Russian. Moscow's **film** industry and annual international film festival dwarf St Petersburg's, but at other times most cinemas screen Hollywood blockbusters. However, the **visual arts** are thriving, with dozens of exhibitions, multi-media and performance events every month – though they're not always widely advertised.

If you're lucky (or you've planned ahead), you'll be able to catch specific **festivals** or events. These are detailed under the appropriate heading (eg, "Drama"); for a seasonal overview of Moscow festivals, see the box on pp.50–51 in "Basics".

Tickets and information

For most concerts and theatrical performances you can buy **tickets** from the venue's box office (*kassa*), or from the many theatre-ticket kiosks (*Teatralnaya kassa*) on the streets and in metro stations. However, these latter vendors can add whatever mark-up they choose, so unwary buyers may be overcharged. Other than buying directly from the venue's *kassa*, it's best to use reputable ticket **agencies** such as Parter (Ⓣ258 00 00, Ⓦwww.parter.ru) or Kontramarka (Ⓣ933 32 00, Ⓦwww.kontramarka.ru), which also has a walk-in office at Bolshaya Dmitrovka ul. 1 (Ⓣ692 05 32; Mon–Fri 9am–8.30pm, Sat & Sun 10am–7pm), opposite the exit of Teatralnaya metro, near the Bolshoy Theatre. Both agencies levy 10 percent commission, and will deliver tickets to your address for R200 within Moscow, R350 in the suburbs. Don't buy from **touts** lurking outside the Bolshoy; you might be fobbed off with out-of-date tickets. The *Traveller's Yellow Pages* features **seating plans** for major theatres and concert halls.

Music lovers planning to be in town for some time might buy **abonimenty**, batches of tickets to about ten concerts – by a specific composer, or in a genre such as chamber music – performed at one concert hall or different venues over the course of a month or two. There are various *abonimenty* available, and besides saving you money they can also save you the hassle of queuing for popular

theatre	театр	beletazh (1st tier above the dress circle)	белэтаж
cinema	кино-театр	dress circle	кресла
theatre-ticket kiosk	театральная касса	stalls	партер
box office	касса	seat	место
box	ложа	row	ряд
balcony	ъалккон	tier	ярус

concerts if you choose them carefully beforehand. At any performance where there's an **intermission**, be sure to keep your ticket if you leave the auditorium, or you may not be allowed back in for the second half.

The *Russia Journal* and the Friday edition of the *Moscow Times* carry extensive arts **listings in English**, while the magazine *Where Moscow* highlights events for the month ahead. Besides the websites of the *Russia Journal* and *Moscow Times*, there are **reviews** on Ⓦwww.waytorussia.net and Ⓦwww.expat.ru.

Ballet, opera and classical music

Russians are justifiably proud of their classical music tradition, and the composers, conductors, musicians, opera singers, ballet dancers and choreographers who have made their name in Moscow are legion. Moscow audiences are among the world's most discerning; unsparing in their criticism, but ready to embrace artists with a passion. Some years ago, concertgoers complained that the removal of two urns spoiled a hall's acoustics, while fans' devotion was epitomized by the thousands who attended the funeral of the ballerina Ulanova, forty years after she left the stage where she had captivated the public during Stalin's time.

Ballet is what Moscow is famed for, and while the Bolshoy is going through uncertain times, few would deny themselves the chance to see this legendary company. However, they're not the only show in town, and visitors who've never seen any Russian classics before might be happy with the Kremlin Ballet Theatre. Dancers from St Petersburg's Mariinskiy (better known abroad as the Kirov) Theatre appear during Moscow's Easter Festival (see pp.50–51), and companies from New York, London and Copenhagen have visited in recent years. For news, see Ⓦwww.for-ballet-lovers-only.com (devoted to the Bolshoy and Mariinskiy) and Ⓦwww.bolshoi.org (an internet journal of Russian dance). Moscow is also gaining a name for **modern dance**, due to its New Ballet and Kinetic troupes, and the talent that attends the international **Dance Inversion** which is held every two years, and the **TsEKh Festival** in late November/early December (Ⓦwww.tsekh.ru). The latter is a great opportunity to see companies from the Urals that rarely tour abroad, such as the award-winning Chelyabinsk Theatre of Contemporary Dance, directed by Olga Pona.

While the Bolshoy is also synonymous with **opera**, other companies whose names are less familiar are more adventurous in their staging. If you've never seen any modern opera, Moscow offers the perfect opportunity to see classics reinterpreted at the Helikon-Opera Theatre, the Kamerniy Musical Theatre, the Stanislavsky and Nemirovich-Danchenko Musical Theatre, or the New Opera.

Classical concerts take place throughout the year, but especially during **festivals**. Christmas at the Kremlin is a series of chamber concerts during the run-up to the Western Christmas and the first weeks of January. Around the time of the Orthodox Easter, soloists from the Mariinskiy Theatre and guests invited by its maestro Gergiev take centre stage at the Bolshoy, the Conservatory and International House of Music, in a stellar **Easter Festival** (Ⓦwww.easterfestival.ru) that also features Orthodox choirs and bell-ringing at cathedrals in Moscow and towns on the Golden Ring. Another mega-fest of home-grown and international talent is **Moscow Stars** in May, at the Conservatory, the Tchaikovsky Concert Hall and International House of Music – also venues for festivals of **French, Japanese and Spanish music** in October and November, which segue into the **December Evenings** at the Pushkin Museum of Fine Arts. Music lovers should also pencil into their diaries the world-class **Tchaikovsky Competition** (Ⓦwww.tchaikovsky.org.ru) at the Conservatory. Prizes are awarded to cellists, violinists and singers during the three years between the quadrennial piano competitions (next scheduled for 2011). New music is showcased at two international festivals – **Moscow Forum** in April, hosted by the Conservatory's Centre for Contemporary Music (Ⓦwww.mosconsv.ru), and the **Long Arms** festival in May – which might include the famous Theremin Ensemble – while the **Autumn Divertimenti** concerts at Arkhangelskoe are devoted to Early music.

You should definitely try to hear some **Russian Orthodox Church music**, which is solely choral and wonderfully in keeping with the rituals of the faith. The Divine Liturgy can be heard at any church or monastery in the city (see p.57); musically speaking, the best services are those on Saturday evening and Sunday morning. Russia's finest Orthodox choirs and bell-ringers appear at annual **festivals**, over Easter (at monasteries and cathedrals around the city) and in June (at Kolomenskoe, see p.235). At other times, look out for concerts by the Moscow-based Akafist Choir (Ⓦwww.aha.ru/%7Eakafist).

Military bands are also worth hearing; you're sure to find them at the Tomb of the Unknown Soldier on Defenders of the Motherland Day (Feb 23), Victory Park on Victory Day (May 9), and Red Square on Russian Independence Day (June 12). Look out, too, for the outdoor **summer concerts** held in the Gorky, Izmaylovo and Sokolniki parks, as advertised.

Arkhangelskoe outside Moscow ⓣ797 54 09 (concert department), Ⓦwww.arkhangelsoe.ru; minibus #151, buses #541 or #549 from Tushinskaya metro. Autumn Divertimenti concerts by the Early Music Academy Ensemble in the grounds of the estate (see p.300) in mid-Sept.

Apparatus Theatre Groupe Ⓦwww.apparatus.dance-net.ru. Performing at a variety of venues throughout Moscow and abroad, this innovative contemporary dance company continues and develops the ideas of the experimental "Kinetic Theater". Led by the choreographer Gordeyeva, it's known for its shows *Mixed Doubles*, *Nails* and *Swan Lake*.

Bolshoy Theatre (Bolshoy teatr) Teatralnaya pl. 1 ⓣ250 73 17 (information: daily 10am–7pm) or 250 73 17 (bookings: daily 11am–8pm), Ⓦwww.bolshoi.ru; near Teatralnaya metro. The theatre is currently being renovated, so until Nov 2009 all performances will be held on the New Stage, which may lack the beauty of the old one but still hosts equally impressive performances.

You can order tickets by phone (payment on delivery), through the Bolshoy website (by credit card), or buy them in person. The Central Bolshoy box office (daily 11am–2pm

▲ Moscow's renowned ballet company, the Bolshoy

& 3–7pm) beside the Russian Academic Youth Theatre sells tickets for both the New Stage and the old or "Main" theatre, whose box office (daily 11am–3pm & 4pm–8pm) is just a hatch in the wall and only sells tickets for its own shows. However, large blocks of tickets are allocated to Parter or Kontramarka – so if the Bolshoy says everything is sold, try them. If you can afford to, it's worth paying more for a seat in the stalls (R500–8000) rather than the balcony, where the dress circle affords a good view, but binoculars are needed from the second tier upwards and anyone who suffers from vertigo should avoid the third and fourth tiers. Tickets for ballet are 15 percent dearer than for opera, and productions at the old theatre cost half as much again as on the New Stage; some operas and ballets are staged at both venues.

Chaliapin House-Museum Novinskiy bul. 25 ⓣ205 62 36; 5min from Barrikadnaya metro. Throughout Sept there are solo operatic renditions in the White Hall of the maestro's mansion (see p.154).

English Court ul. Varvarka 4a ⓣ698 39 52; 10min from Kitay-Gorod metro. Although the vaulted hall of this sixteenth-century embassy (see p.106) is an ideal venue for monthly concerts of medieval English and Russian music, they seldom live up to expectations.

Helikon-Opera Bolshaya Nikitskaya ul. 19/16, ⓦwww.helikon.ru. The building is currently being renovated and, until its completion at the end of 2009, all performances are held at Noviy Arbat 11-2 (information ⓣ290 65 92; bookings daily noon–7pm on ⓣ202 65 84). Dmitri Bertman has delighted and outraged spectators and critics with his bold and bawdy productions of *La Traviata*, *Yevgeny Onegin*, *Mazeppa* and other classic operas, and his *Lulu* and *Lady Macbeth of Mtensk* scooped Golden Mask awards.

The Bolshoy's repertoire and stars

The company is now in the hands of Alexei Ratmansky – formerly male lead soloist at the Toronto and Copenhagen ballets – who was once told by a previous director "We'll make sure you never dance here", but nominated by the legendary ballerina Plisetskaya to rescue the sinking ship. The *enfant terrible* of Russian ballet, Ratmansky's tactics of introducing new steps influenced by Martha Graham and Thala Thorp, and inviting foreigners to rework old classics caused great controversy but ultimately proved a huge success.

Critics savaged the choreography of *Romeo and Juliet*, directed by Declan Donnellan, praised Pierre Lacotte's reworking of *The Pharaoh's Daughter* (featuring a live horse) and gave mixed reviews to *Don Quixote* and *Swan Lake*. Choreography and staging changes are ongoing, making it hard to say which productions to catch. However, Nina Ananiashvili and Nina Semirechenskaya are great in almost anything; Nadezhda Gracheva and Galina Stepanenko shine in *La Bayadère*, Svetlana Zakharova in *Swan Lake*, Yuliana Malkhasyants in *Don Quixote* and Dmitri Belogolovtsev in *Spartacus*.

The operatic repertoire hasn't changed (yet), and Russian classics such as *Ivan Susanin* or *Boris Godunov* are magnificent, especially in the rare event of a performance by Vladimir Matorin. Otherwise, look out for Vasily Kirnos in the role of Malyuta-Skuratov or Khan Konchak, Vladimir Redkin (in anything), Lev Kuznetsov (*The Queen of Spades*, *Tosca*, *Prince Igor*), Pavel Chernykh (*Yevgeny Onegin*, *Mazeppa*), Nina Terenteva (*The Tsar's Bride*, *Aida*) and Larisa Rudakova (in anything).

While opera is good any time, the ballet company is usually abroad over summer and sometimes also in the autumn, leaving the junior corps de ballet to entertain visitors – although star dancers are certain to be in Moscow for the opening of the new season in September. During the season, evening performances start at 7pm, and Saturday and Sunday matinees at noon; there are no shows on Monday. You can see what's on currently and for a few months ahead on the Bolshoy's website – although the English version sometimes lags behind the Russian one, and if there's any contradiction this will be the correct one. For reviews of recent productions, see ⓦwww.bolshoi.org and ⓦwww.for-ballet-lovers-only.com.

Online booking exclusively through Ⓦ www.parter.ru. Tickets R120–3500.

Kamerniy Musical Theatre Nikolskaya ul. 17 Ⓣ 620 13 26; near Ploshchad Revolyutsii metro. Ⓦ www.opera-pokrovsky.ru/, If you can't see the Helikon, try a chamber opera here instead. They perform *Cosi fan Tutte*, *The Barber of Seville* (Piazelli's version, not Rossini's), Monteverdi's *Coronation of Pappea*, and several Russian/Soviet classics rarely seen outside the country – notably a Soviet rendition of Shostakovich's *The Nose* (based on Gogol's story of the same name).

Kremlin Ballet Theatre State Kremlin Palace Ⓣ 628 52 32, Ⓦ www.kremlin-gkd.ru; near Aleksandrovskiy Sad metro. Balletomanes may sneer, but visitors who aren't so discerning can enjoy performances of *Swan Lake*, *The Nutcracker*, Prokofiev's *Romeo and Juliet* or *Cinderella* for a fraction of what they'd pay to see the Bolshoy – and tickets are always obtainable. The 6000-seat hall (built for Communist Party congresses) has a fine view of the stage but suffers from poor acoustics. The box office is at Vozdvigenka 1, and tickets cost R30–800.

Kremlin Chamber Orchestra Ⓣ 755 77 95, Ⓦ www.chamberorchestrakremlin.ru; near Aleksandrovskiy Sad metro. The orchestra's Christmas at the Kremlin season of concerts in the Armoury Hall and Patriarch's Palace features Western classical music before New Year and Orthodox music in the second half of Jan.

Moscow Conservatory Bolshaya Nikitskaya ul. 13/6, information Ⓣ 629 94 01; bookings Ⓣ 629 81 83 or 629 74 12, Ⓦ www.mosconsv.ru; 10min from Okhotniy Ryad, Aleksandrovskiy Sad/Biblioteka Imeni Lenina or Arbatskaya metros. Box office noon–3pm & 4–7pm. Varied programmes of top-quality concerts in the Great Hall (venue for the Tchaikovsky Competition, see p.367), the Small Hall, and the Rachmaninov Hall next door at no. 11 (where purists complained that the removal of two urns from the hall's niches spoilt its acoustics). The Small and Rachmaninov halls have a separate box office (11am–8pm; closed Tues Ⓣ 629 81 83).

Moscow Contemporary Music Ensemble Bryusov per. 8/10 Ⓣ 629 71 87, Ⓦ www.mcme.theremin.ru; 10min from Okhotniy Ryad metro. Better known as the Theremin Ensemble, its mission is to popularize twentieth-century Russian music abroad, and contemporary Western music in Russia – for instance avant-garde music of the 1920s and 30s by Nikolai Roslavets and Alexander Mosolev, or works by Schnitke and Edison Denisov.

Moscow International House of Music (Moskovskiy Mezhdunarodniy dom Mukzyka, or MMDM) Kosmodamianskaya nab. 52, str. 8 Ⓣ 730 18 65 or 988 76 55; 10min from Paveletskaya metro. This prestigious venue hosts the Boheme Jazz Festival, the opening and closing nights of the Easter Festival, and concerts by visiting artistes throughout the year – which its acoustics don't always suit.

Moscow Operetta Theatre (Moskovskaya Operetta) Bolshaya Dmitrovka ul. 6 Ⓣ 692 12 37 or 540 30 00, Ⓦ www.mosoperetta.ru; near Teatralnaya metro. Performs Strauss's *Die Fledermaus*, Lehar's *The Merry Widow*, Offenbach's *Prima Donna* and Kalman's *The Queen of Csardas* in a slightly "over-milked" style, for a doting audience of fans. They also do runs of musicals, such as *Metro* (a Muscovite *Madame Butterfly*) or *Notre-Dame de Paris* (a reworking of the Hunchback tale). Tickets R1000–1700.

Moskva Russian Chamber Ballet Theatre Novoryazanskaya ul. 16 Ⓣ 261 63 54 or 741 49 22, Ⓦ www.balletmoskva.ru; near Krasniye vorota metro. Small experimental group founded in 1991, which fuses traditional ballet with modern dance in such classics as *Giselle*, *Les Sylphides* and *The Rite of Spring*, as well as contemporary works like *Where from and Where to?*

Museum of Musical Culture ul. Fadeeva 4 Ⓣ 739 62 26. Ⓦ www.museum.ru/glinka; 10min from Mayakovskaya metro. Interesting programmes of classical, avant-garde and ethnic music. For details of the museum, see p.269.

New Ballet (Noviy Ballet) Novaya Basmannaya ul. 25/2, str. 2 Ⓣ 632 19 63 or 632 29 11, Ⓦ www.new-ballet.ru; 5min from Krasnye Vorota metro. Modern dance company directed by Aida Chernova, whose repertoire includes *The Café "Stray Dog"*, *Moment of the Eternity* and *Thumbelina*. It sometimes performs at the Moscow International House of Music.

New Opera (Novaya Opera) Hermitage Gardens, ul. Karetniy Ryad 3 str. 2 Ⓣ 694 08 68, Ⓦ www.novayaopera.ru; 10min from Mayakovskaya or Tsvetnoy Bulvar metro. Its repertoire includes Mussorgsky's *Boris Godunov*, Tchaikovsky's *Yevgeny Onegin*, Rubinstein's *Demon* and a potpourri of Mozart, Salieri and Rimsky-Korsakov, entitled *Oh, Mozart! Mozart!* One production that's definitely worth seeing is their punk-style staging of *Pagliacci*. Tickets R100–2000.

Ostankino Palace 1-ya Ostankinskaya ul 5 ⓣ683 46 45; trolleybus #11 from VDNKh metro. Box office Wed–Sun 11am–6pm. Count Sheremetev's private theatre (see p.283) makes a wonderful setting for thrice-weekly concerts in June, July and Aug.

Pokrovsky Chamber Musical Theatre Nikolskaya ul. 17 ⓣ620 13 26 or 620 13 20, ⓦwww.opera-pokrovsky.ru; Lubyanka or Ploshchad Revolyutsii metro. Director Boris Pokrovsky stages one-act operas by Puccini (*The Cloak*) and Mozart (*Bastien and Bastienne* and *The Impressario*), pitched at children as well as adults. Tickets R80–300.

Pushkin Museum of Fine Arts ul. Volkhonka 12 ⓣ203 79 98, or 203 95 78, ⓦwww.museum.ru/gmii near Kropotkinskaya metro. Tickets (R150–300) from entrance; Tues–Sun 10am–7pm. Besides its programme of concerts during the "December Evenings", the museum hosts French and Spanish music festivals – mostly classics, but sometimes also modern composers. Admission free.

Russian National Orchestra (RNO) ul. Garibaldi 19 ⓣ504 07 85, ⓦwww.rno.ru; 10min from Novye Cheremushki metro. Since its foundation by Mikhail Pletnev in 1991, lavish private funding has enabled the RNO to cherry-pick the best players from other orchestras. Renowned for its recordings of Rachmaninov's *Second Symphony* and Prokofiev's *Cinderella*, the RNO nowadays spends most of the year abroad. When it is in Moscow, it performs at the Great Hall of the Conservatory, the Tchaikovsky Concert Hall or at Arkhangelskoe (see p.300).

Scriabin House-Museum Bolshoy Nikolopeskovskiy per. 11 ⓣ241 19 01; 10min from Smolenskaya or Arbatskaya metro. Hosts chamber concerts (tickets R150) of atonal music, with some pieces by Scriabin featuring the *son et lumière* apparatus that he created (see p.165).

Stanislavsky & Nemirovich-Danchenko Musical Theatre Bolshaya Dmitrovka ul. 17 ⓣ629 72 74 (information), 629 28 35 (box office), ⓦwww.stanislavskymusic.ru; 5min from Chekhovskaya metro. Maestro Wolf Gerelik elicits performances across an enormous repertoire of ballet (quite good), opera (excellent) and musicals, including *Swan Lake*, *The Nutcracker*, Shostakovich's *May Night*, Prokofiev's *Cinderella*, Rimsky-Korsakov's *Tale of Tsar Sultan*, Rossini's *Barber of Seville*, Bizet's *Carmen* and their award-winning *La Bohème*. Tickets R250–1500.

Tchaikovsky Concert Hall (Konsertniy zal imeni P.I. Chaykovskovo) Triumfalnaya pl. 4/31 ⓣ699 06 58, ⓦwww.classicalmusic.ru; near Mayakovskaya metro. Box office daily 10am–8pm. Tickets R150–3000. The home of the Moscow State Academic Philharmonia also hosts concerts by the Moscow Symphony Orchestra, and is a venue for several music festivals.

The Art of Goodness Charity Fund Malaya Gruzinskaya ul. 27/13 ⓣ252 40 51, ⓦwww.artbene.ru; 10min from Krasnopresnenskaya metro. Organ recitals (Bach, Mendelssohn, Vivaldi and Handel), and Mozart's *Requiem* performed by the State Academic Choir and the Russian Radio and TV Symphony Orchestra, in Nov.

Tolstoy Museum ul. Prechistenka 11 ⓣ637 74 10, ⓦwww.tolstoymuseum.ru; 10min from Kropotkinskaya metro. The Egyptian Hall of the Lopukhin mansion (see p.168) is sometimes used for chamber concerts.

Tsaritsyno Dolskaya ul. 1 ⓣ321 63 66, 321 80 39 or 321 07 43 (information); ⓦwww.tsaritsyno-museum.ru; 10–15min from Orekhovo or Tsaritsyno metros. Box office Wed–Sun 11am–6pm. The Opera House at Catherine the Great's Tsaritsyno palace (see p.243) makes a fine venue for concerts.

Yermolova House Museum Tverskoy bul. 11 ⓣ290 54 16 or 290 49 01, ⓦwww.museum.ru/M311; 5min from Tverskaya/Pushkinskaya metro. The White Hall of this theatrical mansion (see p.121) is another venue for chamber music concerts.

Drama

Traditionally, **theatre** (*teatr*) has had a special place in Russian culture as an outlet for veiled criticism under autocratic regimes. In Soviet times it was both nurtured and controlled, so that audiences came to expect top-class acting (due to extensive training based on Stanislavsky's "Method") in conservatively staged, often mediocre plays – the few theatres that dared stage bold dramas attracted queues stretching round the block. Nowadays there are no taboos, and most theatres have learned to woo audiences by offering popular favourites or carving a niche for themselves with controversial productions. If you understand some Russian, Moscow has as much to offer drama-lovers as London or New York does – at far lower prices.

Directors and companies to watch out for include Pyotr Fomenko (Fomenko Workshop Theatre), Konstantin Raykin (Satirikon Theatre), Vladimir Miroev (Stanislavsky Drama Theatre), Genrietta Yanovskaya and Kama Glinkas (Theatre of Young Spectators), Sergei Prokhanov (Luni Theatre) and Valery Fokin (as guest director) – nearly all of whom made their names in the 1960s or 1970s. New playwrights and directors are most often seen at the Debut Centre. The website Ⓦwww.theatre.ru is the best source of **news** from Moscow's stage world.

Spring and autumn are the time for festivals. In late February/early March, the **Golden Mask** competition (Ⓦwww.zolotaya.maska.ru) to choose the best of the previous year's drama, dance, opera and puppetry in Russia, sees dozens of shows over two weeks, culminating in a gala awards ceremony. Its rules specify that each entrant must have performed in Moscow. International talent is celebrated at **Solomon Mykhoels Festival** (Ⓦwww.festival.gluz.ru) in late September and **NET** (New European Theatre) in mid-November, followed by the **Baltic House Festival** of drama from northern Russia and the Baltic States, running into December. At the triennial **Chekhov Festival** (Ⓦwww.chekhovfest.ru), diverse companies perform the master's plays, dramas by other writers, and operettas. The next event is scheduled for some time between May and August in 2009.

Debut Centre House of Actors, ul. Stary Arbat 35 Ⓣ248 91 06, Ⓦwww.theatre.ru/debut/; near Arbatskaya/Smolenskaya metro. Moscow's main showcase for new talent has garnered mixed reviews since its foundation in 1996, but remains committed to taking chances. Located on the seventh floor of the block opposite the Vakhtangov Theatre, it's reached via Kaloshin pereulok.

Fomenko Workshop Theatre (Masterskaya Pyotra Formenko) Kutuzovskiy pr. 30/32 Ⓣ499 249 19 21, Ⓦwww.fomenko.theatre.ru; near Kutuzovskaya metro. This troupe of young actors under the veteran director Pyotr Fomenko is definitely worth checking out. Fomenko often directs at other venues, with or without his protégés (all of whom he once taught at the Russian Academy of Theatre Arts).

Lenkom Theatre Malaya Dmitrovka ul. 6 Ⓣ699 07 08, 699 96 68, Ⓦwww.lenkom.ru; near Chekhovskaya metro. Colourful drama and musicals directed by Mark Zakharov, who introduced lasers and rock to the Soviet stage. *Juno and Avos* and *Madame Juliy* can be enjoyed without much knowledge of Russian – though not Chekhov's *The Seagull* or Turgenev's *Two Women*. Tickets R100–2500.

Lime Light Theatre Galina Vishnevskaya Opera Centre, ul. Ostozhenka 25 str. 1 Ⓣ637 77 03 or 637 75 96, Ⓦwww.opera-centre.ru; 10min from Kropotkinskaya metro. This semi-professional company performs in English, twice a month. Its repertoire includes Shakespeare's *Twelfth Night* and *All's Well that Ends Well*, and Chekhov's *The Bear*.

Luna Theatre ul. Malaya Ordynka 31 Ⓣ953 13 17, Ⓦwww.lunatheatre.ru; Tretyakovskaya metro. Director Sergei Prokhanov specializes in modern drama, such as *Charlie Cha …* (a fictionalized account of Chaplin's life) and *Lips* (Nabokov's *Lolita* reworked as a musical). Tickets R50–1000.

Malaya Bronnaya Theatre (teatr na Maloy Bronnoy) Malaya Bronnaya ul. 4 Ⓣ290 40 93, Ⓦhttp://mbronnaya.theatre.ru; 15min from Tverskaya or Arbatskaya metro. Box office daily noon–3pm & 4–7pm. Good actors and a fine tradition, but it hasn't made waves for years. Its repertoire includes Molière's *Georges Dandin*, Coward's *Blithe Spirit*, Petrov's cabbalistic satire *A Yid in the City of Peter*, and the Agatha Christie mystery, *An Unexpected Guest*. Tickets R300–1500.

Maly Theatre (Maliy Akademicheskiy teatr Rossii) Teatralnaya pl. 1/6 Ⓣ623 26 21,

Ⓦ www.maly.ru; near Teatralnaya metro.** Old-fashioned productions of mostly nineteenth-century Russian plays (many of which were premiered here), plus new historical dramas such as A.K. Tolstoy's *Tsar Boris*. They also have an affiliate stage in Zamoskvareche, at ul. Bolshaya Ordynka 69 (Ⓣ 237 31 81).

Meyerhold Centre Novoslobodskaya ul. 23 Ⓣ 363 10 48, Ⓦ www.theatre.ru/meyerholdcentre; near Mendeleevskaya metro. Aside from being the main venue for the Solomon Mykhoels festival in late Sept, and hosting some events in the TsEKh dance festival (see p.366) this arts and business centre named after the murdered Soviet director (see p.177) has less happening culturally than you'd think.

Moscow Art Theatre (MKhAT imeni Chekhova) Kamergerskiy per. 3 Ⓣ 692 53 70, Ⓦ www.theatre.ru/mhat/; 5min from Okhotniy Ryad or Teatralnaya metros. The old MKhAT (named after Chekhov) was the birthplace of modern drama and the Method, but isn't rated so highly nowadays, despite the efforts of director Oleg Yefremov. Its repertoire includes works by Chekhov, Gogol and Dostoyevsky, *A Midsummer Night's Dream* and Tennessee Williams's *The Rose Tattoo*.

Moscow Art Theatre (MKhAT imeni Gorkovo) Tverskoy bul. 22 Ⓣ 203 87 73; 5min from Tverskaya/Pushkinskaya metro. Box office noon–3pm & 4–7pm. The new MKhAT (named after Gorky) specializes in plays by its namesake, and has two stages.

Mossovet Theatre Aquarium Garden, Bolshaya Sadovaya ul. 16 Ⓣ 699 20 35; near Mayakovskaya metro. Box office noon–3pm & 4–7pm. Its repertoire of farces, popular classics and musicals includes Molière, Bulgakov's *The White Guard* and Russian interpretations of *On Golden Pond* and *Jesus Christ Superstar*.

Russian Academic Youth Theatre (RAMT) Teatralnaya pl. 2 Ⓣ 692 00 69, Ⓦ www.ramt.ru; near Teatralnaya metro. Formerly the Central Children's Theatre, it now aims at an older audience with short seasons of plays, ballet, or stand-up performances by Russian actors or entertainers. Located beside the Bolshoy's New Stage.

Satirikon Theatre (Satirikon imeni A.I. Raykina) Sheremetevskaya ul. 8 Ⓣ 689 78 44, Ⓦ www.satirikon.ru; trolleybus #18 or #42 from Rizhskaya metro. Besides directing *Romeo and Juliet*, Konstantin Raykin plays the lead role in scintillating productions by guest directors – Fokin's *Metamorphosis*, Fomenko's *The Magnificent Cuckold* and Robert Sturua's *Hamlet* – which are keenly awaited by drama lovers. The theatre is named after Raykin's father, a famous Soviet comedian.

Shalom (Moskovskiy yevreyskiy teatr Shalom) Varshavskoe shosse 71, information Ⓣ 499 613 27 53, bookings Ⓣ 499 610 37 58; bus #147 from Varshavskaya metro. Russia's only professional Jewish theatre, staging plays about topical issues, and musicals for children or adults, in Russian and Yiddish with simultaneous translation into English.

Sovremennik Theatre Chistoprudniy bul. 19 Ⓣ 621 64 73, Ⓦ www.sovremennik.ru; 5min from Chistye Prudy metro. Box office noon–3pm & 4–7pm. Famous 1960s theatre, enjoying a new lease of life under director Galina Volchek. Productions include Shakespeare's *The Merry Wives of Windsor*, Shaw's *Pygmalion*, Chekhov's *The Cherry Orchard* and the 1930s German musical *Three Comrades*.

Sphere Drama Theatre Hermitage Garden, ul. Karetniy ryad 3 str. 6 Ⓣ 699 96 45; 10min from Chekhovskaya or Tsvetnoy Bulvar metro. Named after its round stage where adaptations of Nabokov's *Lolita* and *Laughter in the Dark*, Pinter's *The Lover* and *She She*, comedies by Zoshchenko and the musical *West Side Story* are performed.

Stanislavsky Drama Theatre (Moskovskiy Dramaticheskiy teatr imeni K.S. Stanislavskovo) Tverskaya ul. 23 Ⓣ 699 72 24; near Okhotniy Ryad metro. Regularly stages Vladimir Miroev's controversial avant-garde productions of *The Government Inspector*, *Twelfth Night* and *Amphitryon*. Also recently hosted sell-out one-man shows by Pyotr Mamonov of Zvuki Mu, entitled *Chocolate Pushkin* and *Is there Life on Mars?*. Not to be confused with the Stanislavsky & Nemirovich-Danchenko Musical Theatre. Tickets R300–1000.

Tabakov Theatre (teatr p/r O. Tabakova) ul. Chaplygina 1a Ⓣ 628 96 85, Ⓦ www.tabakov.ru; 10min from Chistye Prudy/Turgenevskaya metro. Box office daily noon–7pm. Crowd-pleasing playhouse under actor-director Oleg Tabakov, whose repertoire includes Gorky's *The Lower Depths* and Thomas Mann's *The Confessions of Felix Krull, Confidence Man*. Tickets R300–2500.

Taganka Theatre (teatr na Taganke) ul. Zemlyanoy val 76/21 Ⓣ 915 12 17,

Ⓦ www.taganka.org; near Taganskaya metro. Box office noon–8pm. A breath of fresh air during the Era of Stagnation, this famous theatre's productions include *The Master and Margarita*, Pushkin's *Yevgeny Onegin* and a dramatization of Solzhenitsyn's *The First Circle*.

Theatre of Young Spectators (teatr Yunovo Zritelya, or MTYuZ), Mamonovskiy per. 10 Ⓣ 699 53 60; near Pushkinskaya/Tverskaya metro. Box office daily noon–3pm & 4–7pm. MTYuz owes its reputation for bold, innovative drama to Genrietta Yanovskaya's productions of *The Heart of a Dog* and *The Storm*, her husband Kama Glinkas's internationally renowned *KI from Crime* (based on the story of Katerina Ivanovna in *Crime and Punishment*), and guest directors such as Mirzoev, whose zany *Amphitryon* was premiered here.

Theatre on Yugo-Zapad (teatr na Yugo-Zapade), pr. Vernadskovo 125 Ⓣ 433 11 91, Ⓦ www.teatr-uz.ru; 5min from Yugo-Zapadnaya metro. Box office daily 2–8pm. Intense amateurs (its star, Avilov, used to be a truck driver) in a tiny theatre beneath a tower block. Repertoire includes Chekhov, Gogol, *Hamlet*, Ionesco's *Rhinoceros* and a five-hour-long adaptation of Bulgakov's *The Master and Margarita*.

Vakhtangov Theatre (Akademicheskiy teatr imeni E. Vakhtangova) ul. Arbat 26 Ⓣ 241 07 28; 5min from Smolenskaya metro. One of the old heavyweights of Soviet drama, which last wowed audiences with Olga Mukhina's acclaimed *Tanya-Tanya*. Its Stalin-era building stands opposite the House of Actors on the Arbat.

Puppetry, circus and musicals

Puppet theatre (*kukolniy teatr*) has a long tradition in Russia, and there are several theatres devoted to the art in Moscow – the oldest lends its name to the **Obraztsov International Puppet Festival**, in mid-October. Abroad, however, Moscow is best known for its **circus** (*tsirk*), especially acts involving animals – whose training has been brought to a fine art at the House of Cats and the Durov Animal Theatre. Should it come to Moscow, it's worth catching the **All-Russian Festival of Circus Arts** (held in a different city each year in mid-Sept). **Musicals** are another entertainment that can be enjoyed without knowing the language. Some productions are adapted from foreign musicals; others are entirely Russian.

Children's Musical Theatre pr. Vernadskovo 5 Ⓣ 930 70 21; 5min from Universitet metro. A wonderful playhouse (see p.202) whose repertoire includes Prokofiev's *Peter and the Wolf* and *Cinderella*, Rubin's anti-capitalist fantasy *Three Fat Men*, Ravel's *Bolero, Snow White, The Little Match Girl, Winnie the Pooh* and *The Wizard of Oz*. Its charm is enhanced by the costumed actors mingling with the audience before performances. There are usually two shows daily.

Circus on prospekt Vernadskovo pr. Vernadskovo 7 Ⓣ 939 45 47, 930 03 00 or 930 28 15 (information), Ⓦ www.bolshoicircus.ru; near Universitet metro. One half of the world-renowned Moscow State Circus (the other being the Nikulin Circus, see p.171). Its show with a story, *Two Doves*, was a hit; otherwise, animal acts and clowns are its forte. Box office daily 10.30am–7pm; tickets R100–1000.

Dolphinarium Mironovskaya ul. 27 Ⓣ 369 79 66, Ⓦ www.delfinarium.ru; trolleybus #22 or bus #22, #24 from Semyonovskaya metro. A 50min show by cetaceans and sea lions (with which kids can be photographed). Adults may be dismayed by the conditions. Performances: Wed noon, 4pm & 6pm; Thurs 4pm & 6pm, Fri noon, 4pm & 6pm; Sat & Sun noon, 2pm, 4pm & 6pm. Box office daily 11am–6pm. Tickets R180–300, under 6s free.

Durov Animal Theatre (teatr zverey imeni V.L. Durova) ul. Durova 4 Ⓣ 631 30 47, Ⓦ www.ugolokdurova.ru; tram #7 from Tsvetnoy Bulvar metro. A unique institution loved by generations of kids, with some surreal acts (see p.273). Not recommended for anyone with allergies. Shows on the large stage involve elephants, monkeys, tigers and a hippopotamus; rodents appear on the small stage. Large stage: Fri noon; Sat & Sun noon & 3pm. Small stage: Wed & Thurs 11am; Sat & Sun 11am & 2pm. Tickets R150–600.

Estrada Theatre Bersenevskaya nab. 20/2 ⓣ959 05 50; 15min from Borovitskaya or Polyanka metro. This Constructivist variety theatre beside the infamous House on the Embankment (see p.206) hosts musicals, such as the Queen homage, *We Will Rock You!*

Green Theatre Gorky Park; 15min from Park Kultury metro. An outdoor summer-only venue staging unbelievably awful productions of *Grease, Hair* and *Jesus Christ Superstar*, by old rocker Stas Namin.

House of Cats Kutuzovskiy pr. 25 ⓣ249 29 07, ⓦwww.kuklachev.ru; bus #174 from Kievskaya metro. An exclusively feline version of the Durov Theatre, in a small hall with a family ambience, where cats push prams, among other tricks imparted by the animal trainer and clown, Yuri Kuklachev. During the summer they also do shows at the Zoopark. Box office daily 11am–6pm. Performances Mon–Fri at noon, 4pm & 6pm, Sat at 3pm, Sun at 3pm. Tickets R200–700.

Moscow Palace of Youth (MDM) Komsomolskiy pr. 28 ⓣ788 46 46 (bookings), ⓣ782 88 22 (information), ⓦwww.mdmpalace.ru; near Frunzenskaya metro. A venue for contemporary musicals, currently staging *Mamma Mia* and *Beauty and the Beast*. Tickets R500–4000.

Moscow Puppet Theatre Spartakovskaya ul. 26/30 ⓣ267 42 88; Baumanskaya metro. Aimed at 5–8-year-olds, their repertoire includes *Masha and the Bear, Aybolit* (Chukovsky's adaptation of Dr Doolittle), *The Rhinoceros and the Giraffe*, and *The Trunk-less Baby Elephant*. Box office daily 11am–7pm; performances Sat & Sun at noon. Tickets R150–300.

Nikulin Circus (Moskovskiy Tsirk Nikulina) Tsvetnoy bul. 13 ⓣ621 14 03, ⓦwww.circusnikulin.ru; near Tsvetnoy Bulvar metro. Trapeze artists, tightrope walkers, jugglers, illusionists, performing lions, tigers, bears, dogs, pigs and even crocodiles. Box office Mon–Fri 11am–2pm & 3–7pm, Sat & Sun 11am–12.30pm & 1.30–7pm. Schedules vary, but there are usually shows at 2.30pm & 7pm. Tickets R250–1500.

Obraztsov Puppet Theatre Sadovaya-Samotyechnaya ul. 3 ⓣ699 59 79 or 699 53 73, ⓦwww.puppet.ru; 10min from Tsvetnoy Bulvar metro. One of the world's oldest and best puppet theatres – founded by Sergei Obraztsov in 1931 – it still features some of his productions, such as *The Divine Comedy*, which were once innovative for injecting adult themes into an art form regarded as children's entertainment. Matinees are fun for kids of all ages, and include puppet versions of *Maugli* (the Jungle Book) and *Buratino* (the Russian Pinocchio); evening performances are more adult-oriented. The theatre contains a winter garden and aquarium. Box office daily 11am–4.30pm & 3.30–7pm. Tickets R150–700.

Shadow Theatre (teatr Teney) Izmaylovskiy bul. 60/10 ⓣ465 65 92 or 465 50 70; 15min from Pervomayskaya metro. Its repertoire of 22 productions draws on Hindu mythology and Russian fairytales, using a combination of flat and 3D shadow puppets and live actors to create beguiling effects. Performances Sat & Sun at 11am. Box office Mon–Fri noon–7pm, Sat & Sun 10am–3.30pm. Tickets R150.

Studio Theatre of Cinema Actors (teatr Kinoaktyora) Povarskaya ul. 33 ⓣ290 28 11 ⓦwww.teatrkinoaktera.ru; 10min from Barrikadnaya metro. Current repertoire of musicals and other shows includes Durochka, Korsikanka, Morozko, Russian chanson, etc. Tickets R100–1200.

Theatre of Clown Art under the direction of Tereza Durova (teatr klounady Terezy Durovoy) Pavlovskaya ul. 6 ⓣ958 59 50; ⓦwww.durova.ru Serpukhovskaya metro. Founded by a descendant of the Durov family of animal trainers, this theatre's repertoire includes shows aimed at adults rather than kids, and others for all ages. Box office Mon–Fri 11am–7pm. Tickets R150–2500.

Cinema

Since Russian **cinema** (*kino*) imploded in the early 1990s, a handful of directors have managed to produce box-office hits to challenge Hollywood on the home market, which have also been praised abroad. Alas, the biggest recipient of state and private funding has been Nikita Mikhalkov, whose epic

The Barber of Siberia provoked mass walkouts at Cannes but won its director the place of honour at the Moscow 2000 Film Festival, attended by Putin (who went on to restore the Soviet anthem, whose words had been written by Mikhalkov's father).

Meanwhile, the public remain in love with Hollywood, whose films account for ninety percent of what's on in Moscow's cinemas. Though most have now been modernized to Western standards, few of them accept credit-card bookings. Aside from a handful of places that show films in their original language, most foreign movies are dubbed (*dublirovanniy;* дублированный) into Russian – hopefully by several people doing the speaking parts, rather than just one or two – or have Russian subtitles (*subtitry;* субтитеры).

The *Russia Journal* and the Friday edition of the *Moscow Times* list films in English and Russian currently showing. As you'd expect, the widest choice of Russian and (subtitled) foreign films is during the **Moscow International Film Festival** or MIFF (Ⓦwww.moscowfilmfestival.ru), for two weeks in June, July or August. Fans surround the Pushkin Hall to watch the stars arrive, and many other cinemas host their own events. **Experimental** films may get their own festival in June (depending on funding) and are shown at the outdoor **Art Klyazma** (Ⓦwww.artkliazma.ru) in early or mid-September. Other specialized events are the Vertical festival (Ⓦwww.8848.ru/eng/) of mountaineering and extreme **sports** films (mid-April) and the Goldfish Festival of **animation** films for children (late Aug or early Sept). New **video-art** is showcased at the two-day open-air Pusto festival (Ⓦwww.winzavod.ru/pusto/) near the old Tretyakov Gallery in late August.

Cinema Centre on Krasnaya Presnyna (Kinotsentr na Krasnoy Presne), Druzhinnikovskaya ul. 15 Ⓣ255 92 37 Ⓦwww.kinocenter.ru; near Krasnopresnenskaya metro. The Muscovite film buff's mecca, with three halls screening classic and new Russian and foreign films (dubbed into Russian); also holds lectures. You can even book tickets online. Tickets R50–250.

Cinema Museum (muzey kino) Druzhinnikovskaya ul. 15 Ⓣ255 90 57, Ⓦwww.muzeikino.ru. near Krasnopresnenskaya metro. In the same complex as the above, this four-screen cinema shows films in their original languages, without subtitles. It's worth buying tickets the day before if the film is especially popular. Closed in Aug. Tickets R70–100.

Dome Cinema (Pod Kuplom) *Renaissance Hotel*, **Olympiyskiy pr. 18/1 Ⓣ931 98 73 (recorded information in Russian only), Ⓦwww.domecinema.ru; 10min from Prospekt Mira metro.** Located in a small building outside the hotel, this 300-seat hall with a Dolby Surround system screens US movies with Russian translation by headphone.

Five Stars (Pyat Zvyozd) ul. Bakrushina 25 Ⓣ916 91 79 (bookings), Ⓦwww.5zvezd.ru; 5min from Paveletskaya metro. An attractive new cinema whose five halls are named after cinematic greats, with roomy seating and a fancy lobby. Mostly foreign films dubbed into Russian. Tickets R50–400.

Illusion (Ilyuzion) Kotelnicheskaya nab. 1/15 Ⓣ915 43 53; trolleybus #63 & #45 from Kitay-Gorod metro, or trolleybus #16 & #63 from Tanganskaya metro. Located in a wing of the Stalin-Gothic Kotelnicheskaya Apartments, this well-loved art-house cinema shows Soviet classics, and foreign films in the original language (English on second Tues of the month, starting at 7pm; French on third Mon, starting at 7.30pm). Dolby sound. Tickets R20–120.

Karo Film Sheremetevskaya ul. 60a Ⓣ545 05 05, Ⓦwww.karofilm.ru; trolleybus #18 or #42 from Rizhskaya metro. This four-screen multiplex on the third floor of a Ramstore shopping centre is a hassle to reach if you don't live in the area. Tickets R130–270.

Khudozhvestnniy (Art) Arbatskaya ploshchad 14 Ⓣ291 96 24 (recorded information in English), 291 02 47 (bookings), Ⓦwww.arbat-moskino.ru; near Arbatskaya metro. Screens non-mainstream Russian films, and some foreign ones in their original languages. Tickets R50–220.

Kinomir Nastasinskiy per. 2 Ⓣ221 52 21 (information), Ⓣ650 25 28 (bookings), Ⓦwww.kinomax.ru; near Pushkinskaya/Tverskaya metro.

Popular US-style movie theatre just off Tverskaya, complete with popcorn, a video shop, bar and café. Tickets R70–280.

Mir Tsvetnoy bul. 11, str. 2 ⓣ624 96 47; near Tsvetnoy Bulvar metro. Widescreen cinema with 1050 seats and Dolby Surround, which sometimes shows foreign art movies. Tickets R120–200.

Nescafe-IMAX Pravoerezhnaya ul. 16 ⓣ775 77 79. Russia's first IMAX cinema is located in a Ramstore mall way out in Khmiki, and impossible to reach without a car. Tickets R200–550; discount for under 12s.

Pushkin Hall (Pushkinskiy zal) Pushkinskaya pl. 2 ⓣ545 05 05, ⓦwww.karofilm.ru; near Pushkinskaya metro. Moscow's largest cinema (2350 seats) is regularly used for glitzy premieres of new Russian films and foreign blockbusters, and hosts the annual international film festival. Dolby sound. Foreign films dubbed into Russian. Tickets R100–250.

35 MM ul. Pokrovka 47/24 ⓣ917 18 83, ⓦwww.kino35mm.ru; 10min from Kurskaya or Krasnye Vorota metro. Only in Moscow would you find a cinema with double-sized divans instead of seats, showing one or two movies around the clock – thrillers or art-house erotica, usually. Foreign films subtitled in Russian. Tickets R70–300.

The visual arts

Moscow has dozens of art galleries and exhibition halls, in addition to the temporary displays on show in its museums and major galleries. Listed below are some of the best-known galleries, where you can be fairly sure of finding something interesting at most times of the year. Most have works for sale; a few levy a small admission charge. **Festivals** come and go, but you can probably depend on some in future years. Moscow's **Photo-Biennial** occurs in May on even-numbered years (there's a Fashion Photography festival on odd-numbered ones), at the House of Photography, the Centre for Arts and other venues. **Pusto** (meaning "empty") is an exciting open-air **video-art** festival held at Dom-Kommuna (Leninskiy prospect metro), over two or three days (starts at 8pm) in late August (ⓣ900 30 07, ⓦwww.winzavod.ru/pusto for information). Another "alternative" event is the week-long **Art Klyazma** festival of **contemporary art** – also featuring films, live music and fireworks – beside the Klyazminskoe Reservoir, 20km north of Moscow, in early or mid-September (ⓣ588 88 10 or ⓦwww.artkliazma.ru for details). To get there, take the metro to Medvedkovo station and exit at the rear of the train; then bus or minibus #438 to Klyazminskoe Vodokhranitshche Posyolok, beside the reservoir.

Central House of Artists (TsDKh) ul. Krymskiy val 10 ⓣ238 98 43 (recorded information), ⓣ238 19 55 (bookings), ⓦwww.cha.ru; 10min from Park Kultury metro. Besides mounting its own exhibitions, this complex contains commercial outlets such as the Elizium Gallery (ⓣ230 00 77) of avant-garde paintings and graphics of the 1930s, and Alla Bulyanskaya's collection of contemporary art (ⓣ238 25 89, ⓦwww.allabulgallery.com), plus the Moscow Gallery of Old and New Art (ⓣ 238 86 69). Closed Mon; R50–100 for major exhibitions.

Dar ul. Malaya Polyanka 7/7, str. 5 ⓣ238 65 54; trolleybus #4 from Polyanka metro. One of two galleries in the same building, *Dar* specializes in Naïve art. Thurs–Sun 2–5pm.

Guelman Gallery 4 Siromyatnichesky per. 1 str. 6 ⓣ228 11 59 or 917 46 46, ⓦwww.guelman.ru; Chkalovskaya metro. In the Winzavod complex (see below), this gallery of contemporary art is owned by Marat Guelman, the organizer of the "Stop Tsereteli" campaign (see p.208). Noon–8pm, closed Mon.

Manège Exhibition Hall Manezhnaya pl. 1 ⓣ540 28 28; near Okhotniy Ryad, Biblioteka Imeni Lenina and Aleksandrovskiy Sad metros. Fully restored after burning down due to an "electrical fault" in 2004, this space hosts all sorts of exhibitions from fine art auctions to flower shows.

M'Ars Pushkarev per. 5 ⓣ623 56 10; Trubnaya/ Tsvetnoy bulvar metro. ⓦwww.marsgallery.ru. The city's first private art gallery when it opened in the perestroika era, organized by once underground artists like the Mitki. Tues–Sun noon–8pm.

Moscow Centre of Arts Neglinnaya ul. 14 ⓣ624 89 74; 10min from Tsvetnoy Bulvar metro. Paintings and graphics by Soviet and contemporary artists, plus a photographic gallery that's one of several venues during the Photo-Biennial. Tues–Sun 11am–8.30pm.

Moscow Fine Art Bolshaya Sadovaya ul. 3, korpus 10 ⓣ251 76 49, ⓦwww.galleryfineart.ru; near Mayakovskaya metro. Contemporary oil paintings, watercolours, graphics and photos. Mon–Fri 11am–6pm, Sat noon–5pm.

Moscow House of Photography (MDF) ul. Sushchevskaya 14 ⓣ231 33 25 or 737 66 47, ⓦwww.mdf.ru; 10min from Mendeleevskaya metro. The main venue for the Biennial, this stylish exhibition centre has 2–3 shows at any time. Prints by contemporary photographers are sold at the Glaz (Eye) gallery. Tues–Sun 11am–8pm; R50.

Roza Azora Nikitskiy bul. 12a ⓣ291 45 79, ⓦwww.rozaazora.ru; 5min from Arbatskaya metro. Contemporary work, from multimedia installations to portraits; also dolls, antiques and ceramics. Mon–Sat 11am–7pm.

Shishkin Gallery Neglinnaya ul. 29/14 ⓣ694 35 10, ⓦwww.shishkin-gallery.ru; 10min from Tsvetnoy Bulvar metro. Specializes in postwar Soviet Impressionism and Socialist Realist painting. Mon–Fri 11am–8pm, Sat noon–6pm.

Stella Art Gallery Skaryatinskiy per. 7 ⓣ291 34 07, ⓦwww.stella-art.ru; Arbatskaya metro. Russia's first gallery specializing in American Pop Art, with works by Warhol, Jean-Michel Basquiat, Tom Wesselman and others, for $100,000 upwards. Daily noon–6pm.

Winzavod 4 Siromyatnichesky per. 1 str. ⓣ495 917 46 46, ⓦwww.winzavod.com. This former wine warehouse is home to a collection of galleries, design stores and artists' and architects' studios, where many new designers and artists first get their break. Also hosts performances of indie bands from both Russia and abroad. Daily 10am–8pm.

15

Shopping

Older Russians conditioned by decades of queuing and carrying an *avoska* ("just in case" bag) find the notion of **shopping** for pleasure strange, but those with money revel in the diversity of products and today's teenagers are as label-conscious and shopping-happy as any in Europe. Mall-culture is big in Moscow, not just in the centre but in the suburbs, thanks to Ramstore and Ikea. For visitors, it's never been easier to buy foodstuffs, souvenirs and gifts; the main bargains are CDs, porcelain, lacquerware, Soviet memorabilia, caviar and vodka. Shop assistants in Soviet times were famously rude, and it's still unusual to be treated courteously unless you're a big-spender in a ritzy salon. Some former state stores still insist on the infuriating system where customers pay at the *kassa* before collecting their goods, which entails queuing at least twice, but most new shops use the one-stop system.

Antiques and icons

Antiques are loosely defined in Russia; anything pre-1960 can be deemed part of the national heritage and needs an **export licence** from the Ministry of Culture (see p.33). Lovely as they are, bronze and silver **samovars** (tea urns) are probably not worth the hassle of exporting legally (you can find them in flea markets abroad), and impossible to get past the scanners at the airport. The same goes for **icons** – although contemporary icons, which can look as fine as antiques, aren't yet subject to controls, and are sold at *lavka* (church shops) in the Novodevichiy, Andronikov and Novospasskiy monasteries and various churches in the city. Antique shops are known as *antikvar* in Russian.

Aktsiya (Action) Bolshaya Nikitsaya ul. 21/18 ☎290 54 13 (Pushkinskaya or Arbatskaya metro); Bryusov per. 2/14 ☎629 06 10 (Okhotniy Ryad/Teatralnaya metro). Two shops offering a mixture of pre-Revolutionary and Soviet *objets*; paintings, china and bronzes. The first stocks over 50,000 items (not including books) and holds regular auctions; the second specializes in antique furniture and lighting. Both Mon–Sat 11am–7pm, Sun noon–7pm.

Antikvar na Myasnitskoy Myasnitskaya ul. 13 str. 3 ☎628 67 57; 5min from Turgenevskaya metro. Timepieces, silver, porcelain, coins, icons, samovars and second-hand art books. Mon–Fri 11am–7pm, Sat 11am–6pm.

Antique butik Taganskaya pl. 86/1, second floor ☎915 70 21; Taganskaya metro. A good place to search for Commie kitsch, statuettes, antique silver, porcelain or icons. Mon–Fri 10am–6pm, Sat 11am–4pm.

Vernisazh v Izmaylovo Izmailovskoe shosse, Vladenie 73, 5min from Izmaylovskiy Park metro. Antique (and fake) icons, pre-Revolutionary and Soviet timepieces, cameras, jewellery and militaria are sold alongside contemporary handicrafts and souvenirs at this vast outdoor market that's open daily but offers the biggest choice at weekends. Beware of pickpockets. Daily 10am–5pm.

Books, maps and prints

Books about Moscow, the Kremlin and the Tretyakov Gallery are widely available in English and other languages (the Russian version of the same book is usually cheaper). If you can read Russian, bookshops offer a feast of literature and non-fiction at low prices (hardbacks especially), whereas the selection of imported books in other languages (on Russian history and society, or foreign fiction) is inevitably limited. The same is true of **maps**; locally produced ones in Cyrillic script are far more up to date than foreign maps. Glossy **calendars** featuring views of the city or the Kremlin, Russian icons or Old Masters, cost R300–500, and reproduction posters and **prints** (on Soviet themes or historic lithographs of the city) even less. An original litho or etching will set you back anything from R800 upwards. Legally, a **licence** is required to take books or prints more than twenty years old out of the country (see p.33). Bibliophiles can visit the **Book Fair** (Tues–Fri 9am–2pm, Sat & Sun 10am–3pm) in the Olympic Sports Complex on prospekt Mira – whose stock is overwhelmingly in Russian. For books in foreign languages see the outlets below.

Angliya (British bookshop) Vorotnikovskiy per. 6/11; near Mayakovskaya metro; ⓣ699 77 66, ⓦwww.anglophile.ru. Russia's largest British bookshop sells everything from *Rough Guides* to romances, and hosts literary evenings. Amex, MC, Visa. Mon–Fri 10am–7pm, Sat 10am–6pm, Sun 10am–5pm.

Biblio-Globus ul. Myasnitskaya 6/3 str. 1 ⓣ781 19 00, ⓦwww.biblio-globus.ru; near Lubyanka metro. A huge range of Russian books plus some foreign-language art tomes and pulp fiction, spread around two floors beneath the FSB's computer centre (see p.136). Major cards. Mon–Fri 9am–10pm, Sat 10am–9pm, Sun 10am–8pm.

Bookberry Nikitskiy bul. 17 str. 1 ⓣ202 66 79, ⓦwww.bookberry.ru; Arbatskaya metro. The downtown outlet of a chain of book-cafés with a range of English classics, art books, posters and all kinds of literature and reference books in Russian. Maestro, MC, Union, Visa. Daily 24hr.

Dom innostranoy knigi (House of Foreign Books) ul. Kuznetskiy most 18/7 ⓣ628 20 21; near Kuznetskiy Most metro. Moscow's most central foreign bookshop has a good range of US and British books. Maestro, MC, Visa. Mon–Fri 9am–9pm, Sat 10am–9pm, Sun 10am–8pm.

Dom knigi (House of Books) ul. Noviy Arbat 8 ⓣ789 35 91, ⓦwww.mdk-arbat.ru; Arbatskaya metro. Souvenir posters, postcards, reference books and a fair selection of English-language novels. MC, Visa. Mon–Fri 9am–11pm, Sat & Sun 10am–11pm.

John Parson's Bookshop Myasnitskaya ul. 20 str. 1 ⓣ628 29 60; Lubyanka or Chistye Prudy metro. Up the road from *Biblio-Globus*, this English-language academic bookshop has a good selection of travel and history books related to Russia.
Mon–Fri 10am–8pm, Sat 10am–6pm.

Moscow book house ul. Arbat 8 ⓣ789 35 91; 5min from Arbatskaya metro. Has the largest collection of art books, postcards and poster reproductions of pictures by foreign and Russian artists, plus Socialist Realist statuettes, but not propaganda posters. Mon–Fri 9am–11pm, Sat & Sun 10am–11pm.

Pangloss Bolshoi Cherkassky per. 13/14 str. 4; ⓣ625 58 19 or 628 04 65, ⓦwww.pangloss.ru. Kitay-gorod metro. Foreign books, newspapers and magazines (English, French, Spanish, Italian). Mon–Fri 10am–8pm, Sat 10am–7pm.

Shakespeare & Co 1-y Novokuznetsiy per. 5/7 ⓣ951 93 60; Novokuznetskaya or Paveletskaya metro. Small, friendly store selling bestsellers from the *New York Times* list, with a secondhand book exchange, coffee, and occasional literary evenings. MC, Visa. Mon–Sat 10am–7.30pm.

Clothing and accessories

While Moscow is awash with stores selling Italian, French and US designer clothing, prices are higher than abroad, and Russians with money to travel often restock their wardrobes in Paris or London. For visitors, the main bargains are Russian **linen** and **fur** hats and coats (if you've no moral scruples about fur), and brightly patterned merino-wool **shawls** from Pavlovskiy-Posad. Fake fur **hats** are a popular souvenir, but if you're going to wear a real fur *ushanka* here, avoid cheap rabbit-fur versions, as Russians look down on people wearing "road kill". Those with money to burn or an interest in fashion should check out some boutiques devoted to Russian designers.

Bolshoy Theatre Shop ul. Petrovka 3 ⓣ692 04 94; Teatralnaya metro. Ballet shoes, tights and tops, wigs, masks, make-up, videos of the great artistes, ballet books, magazines and Bolshoy T-shirts. Mon–Sat 10am–8pm.

Na' sh Fashion ul.Chertanovskaya 1, 12th floor ⓣ738 29 60; near Chertanovskaya metro. Irina Lesina specializes in ethnic designs using environmentally-friendly materials, and her cosy shop sells cushions and curtains as well as clothing. Daily 11am–9pm.

Platforma Mak Altufevo metro, then bus or minibus #685 to the "Platforma Mak" stop. A weekend flea market for secondhand clothing and bric-a-brac – Soviet stuff from the 1970s and 1980s, and more recent kitsch. Sat & Sun 8am–noon.

Shivrot-navyvorot (Inside Out) Begovaya ul. 6, str. 3 ⓣ946 01 59; Begovaya metro. From time to time this store has unusual sales – anything you can fit into a standard-sized parcel for R200. Mon–Fri 10am–8pm, Sun 11am–8pm.

Sport Express ul. Krasina 9, korpus 3; Mayakovskaya metro. A Portakabin subsidiary of the Russian sports paper of the same name, selling strips and pennants in the colours of all Moscow's football and ice hockey teams, and some clubs from the provinces. Mon–Sat 9am–7pm.

Visit ul. Prishvina 1/2 ⓣ407 19 29; Novokuznetskaya or Tretyakovskaya metro. If you're curious to see what Russian-made footwear is like, this shop stocks the entire range of products from the Paris Commune shoe factory. Daily 9am–8pm.

Vtore Dykhainie (Second Wind) Pyatnitskaya ul. 2 ⓣ951 31 61; Tretyakovskaya metro. You're invited to *Zeppelin* and haven't got anything to wear? This boutique sells second-hand Versace, Moschino, Kenzo and other designer clothes; blouses cost R3000 upwards, dresses R2000–7000, but items unsold after a month are marked down dramatically. Mon–Sat 11am–8pm, Sun noon–6pm.

Department stores and malls

The last fifteen years have seen the habit of shopping for pleasure firmly established in Moscow, as department stores and malls have burgeoned. While the earlier downtown ones were quite exclusive, the newer suburban ones have no such elite pretensions.

Atrium ul. Zemlyanoy val 33 ⓣ970 15 55, ⓦwww.atrium.su; 5min from Kurskaya metro. This multi-level mall near Kursk Station features Adidas, Benetton, Nike, Yves Rocher and Swatch outlets, restaurants, cafés, a sushi-bar and a 24hr supermarket (reached by a separate entrance when the mall is closed). Daily 11am–11pm.

Auchan Khimki Khimkinskiy area mcrn Ikea 4 ⓣ981 49 97, ⓦwww.auchan.ru; 20min by minibuses #443 or #662 from Recnoi vokzal metro or #43k from Voikovskaya metro. A huge shopping mall with two bookshops, ten accessories stores, four cafés, currency exchanges and a travel agency. Daily 8.30am–10pm.

Galereya Aktyor (Actor Gallery) Tverskaya ul. 16/2 ⓣ935 83 74 or 690 98 32; near Pushkinskaya/Tverskaya metro. Discreetly located on the corner of Tverskaya and Strastnoy bulvar, this black marble and chromed mall with a central fountain contains a score of designer outlets, of which the least expensive are NafNaf and Levi's. Some take cards. Mon–Sat 11am–9pm, Sun noon–9pm.

GUM Krasnaya pl. 3 ⓣ788 43 43, ⓦwww.gum.ru; near Ploshchad Revolyutsii metro. Although Benetton and their ilk have colonized the lower floor of this historic emporium (see p.73), a few Soviet-style shops can still be found upstairs, selling just about everything. Most outlets take major cards. Daily 10am–10pm.

Ikea Khimiki, Mikrorayon 8, str. 1 ⓣ737 53 29, ⓦwww.ikea.ru (in Russian only); 20min by minibus "Mega" from Rechnoy Vokzal or Planernaya metro. If you're settling in Moscow, Ikea is a godsend for equipping flats with furniture, kitchenware or other bits and pieces. There's a free shuttle between the store and the metro. Daily 10am–11pm.

Kalinka-Stockmann Smolenskiy Passazh, Smolenskaya pl. 3 ⓣ974 01 22, ⓦwww.stockmann.ru; near Smolenskaya metro. A huge department store with imported clothes and household goods, a supermarket and deli, marking the apotheosis of Stockmann's presence in Moscow, which dates back to the 1970s. MC, Visa. There is also a Stockmann department store at Mega mall Teply Stan, 41st km MKAD at the junction of ulitsas MKAD and Profsojusnaya (ⓣ980 82 82). Both daily 10am–10pm.

Okhotniy Ryad (aka Manezh Mall) Manezhnaya pl. 1 str. 2; T737 84 49, ⓦwww.oxotniy.ru; near Okhotniy Ryad/Ploshchad Revolyutsii metro. Created by Mayor Luzhkov and his court artist Tsereteli, this triple-level subterranean mall contains outlets for Benetton, Calvin Klein, Estee Lauder, Geiger, Mothercare and Speedo; an internet café (p.59) and a couple of cool bars opening onto the Alexander Gardens, which remain open when the boutiques are closed. Most shops take major credit cards. Daily 11am–10pm.

Petrovskiy Passazh ul. Petrovka 10 ⓣ628 50 12 or 623 70 80; 5min from Okhotniy Ryad or Kuznetsky most metro. Chic arcade of mostly Italian designer labels such as Bambino, Uomo, Nina Ricci and Bosco Scarpa. All major cards. Mon–Sat 10am–10pm, Sun 10am–8pm.

Ramstore Krasnaya Presnya ul. 23b/1 ⓣ255 54 12 (Ulitsa 1905 Goda metro) and in 16 suburban locations ⓦwww.ramstore.ru. Moscow's equivalent of Wal-Mart, selling everything from frozen food to tins of paint or boxer shorts. The Krasnaya Presnya store and many of the outlying branches are open daily 24hr.

TsUM ul. Petrovka 2 T933 73 00, ⓦwww.tsum.ru; near Teatralnaya metro. Moscow's oldest department store (see p.135), stocking Russian and imported clothing, household goods and toys, with a CD store on the top floor. MC, Visa. Mon–Sat 10am–10pm, Sun 11am–10pm.

Tyan Ke Lun ul. Noviy Arbat 21, str. 1 ⓣ202 65 61; near Smolenskaya metro. No wonder Russian economists despair of the trade deficit with China: this store stocks over 10,000 brands of Chinese products – from foodstuffs to home appliances, clothing to toys – and it's hard to imagine a Russian equivalent in Beijing. Amex. Daily 10am–10pm.

Lacquered boxes and tableware

After *matryoshka* dolls (see "Toys") the commonest souvenirs are **lacquered boxes**, varying in size and shape from pillboxes to jewellery caskets. Traditionally they were produced by four villages where the poor soil made handicrafts a better source of income than agriculture, each of which developed their own style, but nowadays imitations are widely produced and only connoisseurs know the differences between the Palekh, Fedoskino, Kholuy and Mstera styles – which most people would lump together as lush, minutely detailed depictions of Russian fairytales, medieval cities or rural scenes. A smudgy machine-printed "Palekh" box costs from R100–300, depending on the vendor or shop; quality hand-painted boxes start at R400 and can exceed R3000 for large compositions. Another "folk" product sold all over is birch-wood **bowls**, **spoons** and **platters** from Khokhloma, painted with floral patterns in red, black and gold. Finally there are objects made from supple **birch-bark** – purses, handbags, slippers, lampshades, table mats, coasters and fruit baskets – manufactured in Novgorod. All are widely available at wildly differing prices – shop around. The Izmaylovo Art Market (see p.265) is as good a place as any.

Markets and food and drink stores

While local groceries stock a range of Russian and foreign products, the freshest produce is found at **markets** (*rynok*), where vendors tempt buyers with nibbles of fruit, cheese, sour cream, ham, pickles and other home-made delights. Although large stores may accept credit cards, it's wiser to assume that you'll need to pay cash. Shopping for gifts, the best buys are **caviar** and **vodka**. Caviar should be bought in a delicatessen or supermarket rather than a market, where the stuff on sale is almost certainly of illicit origin and may be unsafe to eat. You can take out as much red caviar as you wish, but no more than 250 grams of black. To avoid any risk of bootleg liquor, vodka and other spirits are best purchased in a major supermarket such as Sedmoy kontinent.

Specialist food and drink stores

Armeniya VVC Pavillion 68; near VDNH metro. Well stocked with Caucasian and Russian foodstuffs and delicacies, including paper-thin *lavash* bread and vintage Georgian and Armenian wines and beer. Mon–Fri 10am–7pm, Sat & Sun 10am–8pm.

Diabetes shop Volgogradskiy prospect 46/15 ⓣ179 69 03; near Tekstilshiki metro. Sells food and drink formulated for diabetics. Daily 8am–9pm.

Honey Shop Prospect Vernadskogo 41 str. 3; ⓣ969 31 30 or 978 37 22, near Pr. Vernadskogo metro or VDNH metro. Sells honey from all over Russia, including linden, raspberry, chestnut and even buckwheat honey, plus gingerbread, honey-cakes, and honey-based skincare products. Honey can be delivered to any address within Moscow for R200. Daily 10am–8pm.

Indian Spices Shop ul. Sretenka 36/2, ⓣ607 16 21, near Sukharevskaya metro; also ul. Miklukho-Maklaya 5/2, ⓣ956 24 03, near Belyayevo metro. Stocks a wide range of Indian spices and condiments, Basmati rice, beans and pulses, and high-class Indian and Ceylon teas. Both daily 9am–9pm.

Novoarbatskiy ul. Noviy Arbat 11 str. 1 ⓣ202 46 97; 10min from Arbatskaya or Smolenskaya metro. Well-stocked Russian supermarket with an excellent bakery, a deli, coffee shop and snack bar. Major cards. Daily 10am–10pm.

Sedmoy kontinent ul. Arbat 54/2 (Smolenskaya metro); Manejnaya pl. 1 (Okhotniy Ryad metro); Bolshaya Gruzinskaya 63 str. 1 (Belorusskaya metro); Festivalnaya 8 str. 1 (Rechnoi vokzal metro); ⓣ777 77 79, ⓦwww.7cont.ru. This chain of supermarkets stocks high-quality Russian and imported food and booze – and even vegetarian *pelmeni*. Major cards. Daily 24hr.

Slastena-M ul. Petrovka 21/2 ⓣ621 00 75; Pushkinskaya or Chekhovskaya metro. A downtown outlet for confectionery from the Red October chocolate factory near the monument to Peter the Great. Mon–Fri 9am–2pm & 3–7pm.

U Yara Leningradskiy pr. 33, str. 4 ⓣ945 31 68; Dinamo metro. This liquor store has a big choice of Georgian and New World wines – from inexpensive ones up to vintages costing R77,000 – and sometimes tasting sessions. Daily 10am–10pm.

Yeliseev's Tverskaya ul. 14 T650 46 43, ⓦwww.eliseevskiy.ru; near Pushkinskaya/Tverskaya metro. Worth a visit purely for its fabulous decor (see p.119), but it also stocks a wide range of gourmet foods plus Baskin Robbins ice cream. All major cards. Daily 24hr.

Markets

Danilovskiy ul. Mytnaya 74 ⓣ954 34 66; near Tulskaya metro. One of the best markets in the city, selling everything from eggs to fur hats to car parts. Mon–Sat 8am–7pm, Sun 8am–6pm.

Rizhskiy pr. Mira 88; near Rizhskaya metro; ⓣ631 42 95. Like the Danilovskiy, this market has been a fixture in Moscow for generations and sells everything you'll need for daily life. At both markets, bargaining in Russian or much pantomime will help. Mon–Sat 7am–7.30pm, Sun 7am–5.30pm.

Music, videos and CD-ROMs

Hollywood and Microsoft may fume, but Russia remains the world's largest market for **pirate** CDs, DVDs, videos, cassettes and CD-ROMs. Kiosks in the Pushkinskaya ploshchad underpasses and in metro stations all over town sell bootlegs, while chain stores stock them alongside licensed products – and will happily tell you which is which. The quality of pirated products varies from abysmal to indistinguishable from the real thing, but prices are so much lower (R100–150 for a CD, R300–500 for a CD-ROM) that Russians are willing to risk the odd dud – especially when they can buy the entire recorded works of almost any top artist on a single CD-ROM. The same goes for computer games and software – even though it's said that three out of four programs have some kind of defect or virus.

Gorbushkin dvor Bagrationovskiy per. 7/1 ⓣ737 74 74, ⓦwww.shop.rubi.ru (in Russian only); 15min from Bagrationovskaya metro. Successor to the collector's fair at *D/K Gorbunova*, this factory-sized mart for CDs, DVDs, CD-ROMs, cassettes, second-hand LPs, video cameras and audio equipment, is the largest and cheapest in the city. No cards. Daily 10am–9pm.

Nastroenie Ladojskaya 4/6 str. 5 ⓣ267 71 35; near Baumanskaya metro. Over 2000 CDs, audio and video cassettes. Major cards. Daily 10am–10pm

Purple Legion Novokuznetskaya ul. 1 ⓣ225 13 86, ⓦwww.plegion.ru (in Russian only); Novokuznetskaya metro. More than 45,000 titles of CDs and DVDs. All major cards. Mon 10am–9pm, Tues–Sun 10am–10pm.

Soyuz Strastnoi bulvar 8A ⓣ694 45 71, near Tverskaya metro; GUM, Krasnaya ploshad 3 ⓣ620 33 44, near Ploshad Revolutsii metro, ⓦwww.soyuz.ru. Strastnoi bulvar is the flagship branch of a chain selling legit CDs (from R149) and DVDs (from R99). Maestro, MC, Visa. Daily 10am–10pm.

Transilvania Tverskaya ul. 6/1, str. 5 ⓣ629 87 86; Okhotniy Ryad or Teatralnaya metro. A downtown store stocking over 50,000 different CDs and audiotapes. Major cards. Daily 11am–10pm.

Videoboom ⓦwww.videoboom (in Russian only). This chain of 54 outlets has a vast stock of Russian and dubbed foreign movies and cartoons; the branch at ul. Usachova 29/6 (Sportivnaya metro) has a few shelves of films in their original languages (or dubbed into English). Rental R50 a day for blockbusters, R40 for three days to a week for classics. Daily 10am–10pm.

Porcelain, glass and crystal

Moscow has a long tradition of manufacturing **porcelain** (*farfor*), glass and crystal ware; most of the factories producing them today were founded to supply the Court and nobility with settings for their banquets. Russian Futurists leapt at the chance to turn these status symbols into utensils for the masses – the first Soviet ceramics bore the Romanov seal, overpainted with revolutionary imagery. Today, such porcelain is highly prized and requires an export licence (as does anything pre-Revolutionary), but high-quality reproductions are easily found and freely exportable. Among the most popular are Empire Style blue, gold and white patterns from Gzhel, Tver and Novgorod; Constructivist motifs from the 1920s, and sets celebrating the Moscow metro or Soviet feats in space. You can buy a single cup and saucer for R300–500, a dinner plate for R500–700, a teapot for R500–1000, and a full tea or dinner service for R5000 upwards (the more gilding the dearer). Gzhel porcelain figurines aren't nearly such good value: a lot of what's on offer is rubbish, or wildly overpriced (like the novelty figures of New Russians at play). Cut **glass** (*steklo*) or **crystal** (*khrustal*) glasses, bowls, ornamental vases and knick-knacks are a feature of most Russian homes, but the designs tend to be very 1970s – which may or may not be to your taste.

Dom Farfora (House of Porcelain) Leninskiy pr. 36 ⓣ137 60 23; trolleybus #33 or #62 from Leninskiy Prospekt metro. Stocks a huge range of china, glass and crystal tableware, made by different Russian factories – worth checking out if you're serious about buying. Mon–Sun 10am–9pm.

Slavyanskiy dom (Slavic House) Goncharnaya nab. 5 ⓣ915 68 31; Taganskaya metro. This store offers a big choice of vases, statuettes and tableware made by various porcelain or crystal factories. A set of tea cups and saucers costs from R4800 upwards. Mon–Sat 10am–7pm.

Soviet memorabilia

Soviet memorabilia is as popular with tourists as it was when the USSR still existed, but most of the posters, uniforms and watches on sale today are **reproductions** rather than originals; vintage posters fetch around R2300 at auctions, and embroidered banners are heading that way. About the only genuine items that are ubiquitous are **lapel pins** (*znachki*). In Soviet times, every sports club, factory or hobby society had its own and collectors traded them – *Pravda* once rebuked the Plumbers' Union for producing a badge shaped like a toilet. Nowadays, *znachki* made of semi-precious metals, or featuring Trotsky or Beria, are rare enough to be valuable – but there are still millions of enamelled alloy or plastic badges around. Repro **posters** (R50–150) are sold in many bookshops (see p.379) and are currently popular with Russians who never experienced Soviet life – whereas CCCP T-shirts, military fur hats, peaked caps or pointy felt Budyonny hats (named after the Civil War cavalry commander) are strictly for tourists. They're sold at street stalls on the Arbat and at the Izmaylovo Art Market (see p.265).

Main Post Office Myasnitskaya ul. 26 ⓣ623 41 63; near Chistye Prudy/Turgenevskaya metro. Cosmonauts, collective farms, Marxism, and Leninism are among the themes celebrated by Soviet commemorative stamps, sold at the philately booth. Many of the designs are exquisite, and stamps cost only R5. No cards. Mon–Fri 8am–8pm, Sat & Sun 9am–6.30pm.

Museum in the Museum of Modern History, Tverskaya ul. 21 ⓣ699 54 58, 699 52 17, ⓦwww.sovr.ru; near Tverskaya/Pushkinskaya metro. Authentic posters, postcards, badges and bric-a-brac from the Soviet era, some items at collectors' prices, others real bargains. Tues, Wed & Fri 10am–6pm, Thurs & Sat 11am–7pm, Sun 10am–5pm.

Sports equipment

Hunting and fishing are widely popular in Russia (obliging every cabinet minister to claim that their summer vacation was spent doing one or the other), while the younger generation is into in-line skating, skateboarding or martial arts. For visitors invited to go camping in the wilderness – or spend a weekend at someone's *dacha* – the following specialist stores may prove useful.

Bike 'n' Roll **Bolshaya Tatarskaya ul. 21 ⓣ959 31 29; Novokuznetskaya metro.** Staffed by ex-professional bikers, this is one of the most knowledgeable outlets. Major cards. Mon–Fri 10am–9pm, Sat 10am–6pm.

BikeMaster **Sokolnicheskaya pl. 4, k.1 ⓣ775 14 06; Sokolniki metro.** Housed in the same building as Moscow's weekend bike market, this trendy shop sells state-of-the-art cruiser and mountain bikes, and will customize them for clients. Expert staff. Mon–Sat 10am–8pm, Sun 10am–7pm.

Skif **ul. Krylatskaya 2 ⓣ499/140 95 39, ⓦwww.skif-sport.ru (in Russian only); Krylatskaya metro.** Located in the same suburb as the Olympic velodrome and rowing canal, this store stocks alpine and cross-country skis, ice skates and bicycles. Tues–Sun 11am–7pm.

Sportmaster **Bolshaya Sadovaya ul. 1, Mayakovskaya metro, and other locations; ⓣ777 77 71, ⓦwww.sportmaster.ru.** A chain of stores selling sports clothes, trainers, roller skates, tennis racquets, skis and accessories. Daily 10am–10pm.

Sport Service **Nagorniy bul. 39a ⓣ121 21 00, ⓔfond148@online.ru; bus #191 or #282 from Nagornaya metro.** Imported bikes, spare parts and repairs. Major cards. Mon–Sat 10am–7pm.

Vysshaya Liga **Olympiyskiy pr. 16 str. 1 ⓣ937 78 84; Prospekt Mira metro.** Swimwear, camping equipment, tennis racquets, boxing gloves, sports clothing and footwear. Major cards. Mon–Sat 10am–8pm, Sun 11am–6pm.

Toys

Nesting dolls, or *matryoshky*, are a cliché souvenir and symbol of Russia. Invented in 1890 at the children's workshop of the Abramtsevo artists' colony, the original design of a headscarfed peasant woman was subverted during perestroika, when Gorby, Lenin *et al* appeared – since followed by Putin, Medvedev, Bush and Bin Laden. A recent version panders to Islamophobia with Bin Laden, Arafat, a Chechen suicide bomber and a miniature Koran. You may also see traditional wooden toys from Novgorod, such as **dancing bears** and **bears on a see-saw**, which are also produced in joke forms such as two bears taking it in turns to work on a computer, or one bear spanking the other with a broom.

Detskiy Mir **(Children's World) Teatralniy proezd 5 ⓣ781 09 50; near Lubyanka metro.** Moscow's largest toyshop has a carousel in the main hall, three levels of shops, and an internet café and games centre on the top floor. Also sells sportswear, lingerie and domestic appliances. Major cards. Mon–Fri 9am–10pm, Sat & Sun 10am–8pm.

Malenkiy Genii **(Little Genius) Bolshoy Kozikhinskiy per. 6 str. 1 ⓣ291 21 47; Pushkinskaya/Tverskaya metro.** Imported and Russian educational toys, audiotapes, cartoon books and board games. Mon–Sat 10am–8pm, Sun 11am–6pm.

Bananamama **Svobodi 44, Petrozavodskaya 13, k.1 ⓣ725 55 55, ⓦwww.bananamama.ru (in Russian only); near Rechnoi vokzal metro.** Great variety of clothes, shoes and toys for children. Daily 10am–10pm.

▲ Detskiy Mir, Russia's largest toy shop

16

Children's Moscow

Although Russians dote on **children**, Moscow is not a child-friendly environment, especially for toddlers: traffic is heavy and unpredictable; parks and playgrounds are littered with broken glass, and slides and swings are often unsafe. However, in compensation, there are many attractions for kids to see and enjoy. Circuses, puppet shows or musicals are an obvious choice. Russians have high expectations of their children's attention span and behaviour; you'll see six-year-olds sitting through three-hour ballets at the Bolshoy Theatre (where the minimum age is five for matinees, ten for evening performances). Aside from bowling alleys and roller-dromes, sports facilities aren't so readily accessible to visitors, but children are welcome to accompany adults to the *banya* (bathhouse), a football or ice hockey match – and anyone with a skateboard will find lots of company (see Chapter 17 "Sports"). For toys and souvenirs, see "Shopping" (Chapter 15).

Children up to the age of seven ride free on all public **transport** (including minibuses, if they sit on a parent's lap). Baby food and disposable nappies are available at most supermarkets and pharmacies, though you may wish to bring a small supply to tide you over. Russians regard breastfeeding in public as something that "only Gypsies do". Outside of summer, Russians **dress** their children in hats, scarves and layers of clothing when foreign parents might simply pop a sweater on – and do their best to ensure that their kids never sit on the ground, for fear of catching cold, or developing maladies in later life. Russian grannies feel free to admonish strangers who allow their own kids to go "undressed".

Attractions

Museums that might interest children of all ages are the Kremlin Armoury (p.95), the Palace of the Romanov Boyars in Zaryade (p.107), the Vasnetsov House (p.269), the Museum of Cosmonautics near the VVTs (p.277), and the animatronic dinosaurs in the Darwin Museum (p.202). Boys going through a bellicose stage might also enjoy the Armed Forces Museum (p.275) or Central Museum of the Great Patriotic War (p.187), while young girls are more likely to enjoy the Museum of Unique Dolls (p.143). Moscow has nothing to rival St Petersburg's Imperial **palaces**, but Kuskovo (p.258) and Ostankino (p.282) can be recommended if your kids can tolerate a tour in Russian, while Kolomenskoe (p.234) and Tsaritsyno (p.240) are great for exploring and running about. Another sure-fire hit is the **VVTs**, with its fab statues and pavilions, and a funfair with a Ferris wheel (see p.280).

The **Izmaylovo art market** is great for souvenir-hunting (see p.265) and will keep kids intrigued for hours. In the Yeltsin years, another attraction was

▲ The VVTs is a sure-fire hit for children

the **pet market** near Taganka – but since being relocated outside the city, getting there entails catching a #79 or #655 bus from Kuntsevskaya metro station to the "Belaya Dacha" stop and isn't really worth the effort unless you're aiming to buy. However, Moscow's **Zoopark** (p.179) is an ideal place to spend an afternoon. The children's section (reached by a footbridge over Bolshaya Gruzinskaya ulitsa) has feeding-time shows and touchy-feely encounters, while the main part of the zoo contains such endangered species as Przewalski's horse, Siberian tigers and snow leopards, and spectacled bears. Don't miss the animalistic art in the monkey house or the African Pavilions. Admission is free for under-eighteens.

To expose your kids to **ballet**, try a performance by the Kremlin Ballet Theatre before lashing out on tickets for the Bolshoy (see p.368), or head for Moscow's wonderful Children's Musical Theatre (see p.373). Unless your kids are fervent animal-libbers, a visit to the **circus** is a must, and children are usually enthralled by the House of Cats or the Durov Animal Theatre (detailed on p.273). Younger children should go for **puppet theatre** (there are shows for older kids, too), and **musicals** may also prove a winner (see p.373 for details). Or you can catch the latest action film at a **cinema** that screens movies in English (see p.375). Under-sixes may be happy to watch Russian cartoons (*multiki*) like Kot Leopold, Karlson or Vinni Pukh (Winnie the Pooh); some cinemas run children's matinees.

Older kids can get their adrenalin flowing at **roller-dromes** (see p.393), or play **paintball**. Paintland, at Novoslobodskaya ul. 50/52 (Ⓣ772 88 83, Ⓦwww.paintland.ru), takes players on a first-come-first-served basis at weekends, or by pre-arrangement on weekdays for a minimum of six people. The cost per person (entrance and equipment rental: adults R600, children R300) depends on how many paintballs you buy (minimum R2700 a box), and includes lunch. The only snag is its distance from Mendeleevskaya metro station – you'll need to take a taxi from there.

Children's clubs

If your kids are hankering to play with others, a visit to a **children's club** (*detskiy klub*) should make them happy. Unlike the hobby and sports-centred Pioneers' clubs of Soviet days, these have play zones and entertainments, food and drink – and you needn't be a member. Expatriate execs with families have long cherished the *Radisson-Slavyanskaya*'s weekly **brunch** (see below) as a chance to socialize while their kids are fed and entertained.

Jungles Children's Club Chertanovskaya ul. Vladenie 9/8 ⓣ314 75 43, ⓦwww.jungleclub.ru (in Russian only); Chertanovskaya metro. This two-storey play centre for 1–13-year-olds has a split-level labyrinth of crawl tubes, soft cubes, balloons, a burger bar, animated shows and a clown by arrangement (R2000 p/hr). Adults R50, children R300.

Sunny Arlekino Club Verkhnaya Radishchevskaya ul. 19/3, str. 1 ⓣ915 11 07, ⓦwww.arlecino.com (in Russian only); Taganskaya metro. This club has a trampoline, a rope ladder and other play equipment, and offers kids unlimited free sweets and soda water. There is also a restaurant with adult and children's menus. Mon–Fri 1–10pm, Sat & Sun noon–10pm. Entry Mon–Thurs children R400, adult R50; Fri–Sun children R600, adult R50.

Viking Club Ship on the river opposite Berezhkovskaya nab 8 ⓣ499 240 46 89, ⓦwww.ship-viking.ru (in Russian only); Kievskaya metro. Five hours of dancing, entertainers, jugglers, magicians, clowns and exotic animals are included in the entry price, though cakes and chocolate cocktails are extra. Sat & Sun 1–6pm; adults and children R400.

Eating

Kids demanding to eat something familiar can be pacified with a visit to *McDonald's*, *Pizza Hut* or *Patio Pizza* – the *Patio Pizza* opposite the Pushkin Museum of Fine Arts supplies crayons and high chairs and is conveniently near the Cathedral of Christ the Saviour. But it would be a shame not to give Russian food a try. Pancakes (bliny) usually go down well with kids, once they've found a filling to their taste: salted fish is probably a no-no, but pancakes with condensed milk (*bliny so sgushchenkoy*) go down a treat. You can get bliny at almost any Russian café or restaurant, or the fast-food chain *Russkoe Bistro* (see box, pp.346–347). A good place to try other dishes is *Mu Mu*, with its groovy spotted cow decor (see p.349). For a slap-up feed and entertainments, take your progeny to the *Radisson-Slavyanskaya*'s Sunday brunch (see p.331).

Parks, playgrounds and rides

Moscow is conspicuously short of parks in the centre: the Alexander Garden, Patriarch's Ponds, a few grassy verges and the strip of trees and lawns around the Boulevard Ring, are all there is north of the river, while staying within the Garden Ring. On the south bank, **Gorky Park** (daily 10am–10pm; adults R80, children R20) rules for funfairs. Its Luna Park (ⓣ237 07 20) has carousels, dodgems and bouncy castles, all covered by a single ticket (R500/R600 for 1hr/2hr unlimited rides or R800 for the whole day). In the section for older children and adults there are two roller coasters and a water chute (R140–150 per ride), giant carousels (R150), bungee-jumping and a virtual ride on a space shuttle (see p.221). Over winter the roller coasters and water chute don't operate, but there's a popular **ice disco** at weekends and most evenings, and in

February the park hosts a festival of ice sculptures. The funfair at the **VVTs** has carousels, dodgems and Europe's largest **Ferris wheel**, offering a fantastic view of the exhibition grounds and its environs.

Other rides are fun, too. The **metro** is an obvious choice for its palatial stations – especially on the Circle line and at Ploshchad Revolyutsii near Red Square – you can avoid the crowds by travelling between 11am–noon and 2–4pm on weekdays or in the morning at weekends. See the *Moscow Metro* colour section for a list of decorative stations. Above ground, kids are sure to enjoy a ride on **Annushka**, a converted tram that circles Chistoprudniy bulvar with karaoke on board. Riding the **escalators** up and down the Crystal Bridge at ploshchad Yevropy, the glass elevators of the Atrium mall (p.174) or the high-speed **lifts** at the *Mezhdunarodnaya Hotel* should also please them.

Street entertainment and spectacles

There are **buskers and street performers** the length of the Arbat, where it's possible to **have your portrait drawn** (R800–1500) or **be photographed** with a cut-out Putin or Homer Simpson. On Red Square, you can have your picture taken with a Lenin lookalike or somebody in medieval Russian costume or nineteenth-century court dress. The former royal estate of Kolomenskoe hosts **historical pageants** and **folkloric events** throughout the year (see box, p.234 for details), while in Izmaylovo Park there's a winter festival with folk music, **troika rides** and traditional games like "Taking the Ice Fortress". Another medieval entertainment still popular in Russia is **performing bears**, which appear at Izmaylovo's art market on weekends all year round.

Aside from the **carnival** parade along Tverskaya ulitsa on City Day (Sept 6) and events on some national holidays (see pp.50–51), the main spectacles are **marathons** (on City Day and May 9) and the amusing **Police Relay-Race** (Sun nearest Oct 24), both detailed under "Sports" (p.397). Teenage rebels might thrill to the Red flags and revolutionary songs of the **Communists' march** from Oktyabrskaya ploshchad into the centre of town, on November 7. Although Yeltsin got rid of the guard of honour outside Lenin's Mausoleum, the **changing of the guard** at the Tomb of the Unknown Soldier in the Alexander Gardens involves the same ritual of goose-stepping, saluting and presenting arms (every hour on the hour; half hourly in winter). Occasional wreath-laying ceremonies are accompanied by a military band with bell-jingling standards.

Sports

In Soviet times, **sport** was accorded high status: a carefully nurtured elite of Olympic medal-winning sportsmen and women were heralded as proof of Communism's superiority, while ordinary citizens were exhorted to pursue sporting activities to make them "ready for labour and defence". Consequently, there's no shortage of sports facilities in Moscow, though most are for club members only; visitors can try striking some kind of deal with the staff, or settle for paying higher rates to use hotel facilities.

For the slothful majority of Muscovites, however, the most popular activity remains visiting the **bathhouse**, or *banya*. Russian bathhouses are a world unto themselves, and are the preferred cure for the complaint known locally as "feeling heavy" – which encompasses everything from having flu to feeling depressed. For a truly Russian experience, a visit to the *banya* is a must.

Baseball and basketball

It's widely believed in Russia that **baseball** (*beysbol*) derives from the ancient Russian game of *lapta* – which might explain the success of the national team on the European circuit, and the excellence of local teams such as Balashikha Tornado (Russian Championship winners in 2006 and 2007) and TsKA. The majority of matches are played in the Olympic training sport centre, Planernaya (Ⓣ571 45 37); take bus #817 or #154 from Planernaya metro to the "Sportivnaya Baza" stop. The season runs from April to October, with the Russian Championship in July.

Basketball was widely popular in Soviet times and Russia still performs well on the European stage. For news and match details, see the Russian Basketball Federation website Ⓦwww.basket.ru, or the TsKA team site Ⓦwww.cskabasket.com (which features more info in English).

Bathhouses

The Russian **banya** is as much a national institution as the sauna in Finland. Traditionally, peasants stoked up the village bathhouse and washed away the week's grime on Fridays; Saturdays were for drinking and Sundays for church – "a *banya* for the soul". Townspeople were equally devoted to the *banya*: the wealthy had private ones, while others visited public bathhouses, favoured as much for their ambience as the quality of their hot room. In Russia's favourite romantic comedy, *Irony of Fate*, the hero gets so drunk at the *banya* celebrating his stag night in Moscow that he ends up in Leningrad by mistake, and meets his true love there.

So here's the procedure when **visiting a banya**. Some have separate floors for men and women, while others operate on different days for each sex, but whatever the set-up, there's no mixed bathing, except in the section available for private rental (where anything goes). The only thing the *banya* will definitely provide (for a modest price) is a sheet in which to wrap yourself. You should **bring** a towel, shampoo, some plastic sandals and possibly a hat to protect your head (towels, flip-flops and weird mushroom-shaped felt hats can be rented at some *banyas*). At the entrance, you can buy a *venik* – a leafy bunch of birch twigs (or prickly juniper twigs for the really hardy) – with which bathers fan and flail themselves (and each other) in the steam room, to open up the skin's pores and enhance blood circulation. This isn't obligatory, but it feels great afterwards.

Hand your coat and valuables to the cloakroom attendant before going into the changing rooms. Beyond these lies a washroom with a **cold plunge pool** (*basseyn*); the metal basins are for soaking your *venik* to make it supple. Finally you enter the **hot room** – or *parilka* – with its tiers of wooden benches: the higher up you go, the hotter it gets. Unlike in a Finnish sauna, it's a damp heat, as from time to time water is thrown onto the stove to produce steam. Five to seven minutes is as long as novices should attempt in the *parilka*. After a dunk in the cold bath and a rest, you can return to the *parilka* for more heat torture, before cooling off again – a process repeated several times, with breaks for tea and conversation. Two hours is the usual time allowed in the public baths and the rental period for **private sections** (*individualny nomer*) – though you can reserve a *nomer* for longer if desired.

Many *banya*-goers cover their heads with hats to protect them from the heat, while others take advantage of traditional health cures and beauty treatments: men rub salt over their bodies in order to sweat more copiously, and women coat themselves with honey, to make their skin softer – you can also throw beer on the stove for a wonderful yeasty aroma. As *banya*-going is a dehydrating experience, it's advisable not to go drunk, with a bad hangover or on a full stomach. Beer is usually on sale in the men's section, but women should bring their own drinks. Pregnant women should forego the *banya* experience. The traditional farewell salutation to fellow bathers is "*S lyogkim parom*" – "May the steam be with you".

Lastly, a word of **warning**: Russian mobsters love partying at the *banya*. They usually rent a private section and bring their girlfriends or call girls along; drunken quarrels may occur, followed by murders the next day (so Militia detectives say). This tends to happen on Thursday nights, at baths that stay open late. By day, the clientele is far more respectable as a rule – and this is the time to bring kids along. It is also worth noting that Russian bathhouses are more associated with heterosexual than gay sexuality.

Astrakhanskie Astrakhanskiy per. 5/9 ⓣ680 43 29; Prospekt Mira metro. Hidden behind an apartment block, this pre-Revolutionary bathhouse is scruffy, but the quality of its steam is savoured by those who can't afford ritzier places. Tues–Sun 8am–10pm (*kassa* till 8pm): public baths R150; private section Tues–Fri R1000, Sat & Sun R1500.

Bani na Presne Stolyarniy per. 7 str. 1 ⓣ255 53 06 (men's baths) or 255 01 15 (women's baths); 10min from Ulitsa 1905 Goda metro. Built for the 1980 Olympics, this well-equipped *banya* is frequented by film stars, footballers and Mafiosi (in 1994, a Godfather was killed by a sniper as he left the baths). The women's *parilka* is dominated by regulars who boss strangers around. Gym, bar and restaurant. Amex, DC, MC, Visa. Mon & Sun 8am–10pm, Tues noon–10pm; Mon–Fri R700, Sat & Sun R800.

Russkaya Banya Pevchevskiy per. 6 ⓣ775 60 75, ⓦwww.expedicia.ru; Kitay-Gorod metro. Intimate, upmarket three-person *banya* combining traditional Russian steam-room practices with the latest spa technology. Customers can choose between birch, oak, juniper or eucalyptus *veniki* and indulge in a honey or foam massage, followed by herbal teas or balsams from the Altay mountains. MC, Visa. Daily 10am–10pm; Belaya banya (like a sauna) R12,900.

O-Furo Zubovskiy pr. 2 ☎246 44 24; near Park Kultury metro. Japanese-style baths with geisha girls, classical and erotic massage, acupuncture, aromatherapy, karaoke, Japanese tea room and restaurant. Reservation required. Amex, MC, Visa. Daily 24hr. R1600–5000.

Sandunovskiy Neglinnaya ul. 14 str. 3–7 ☎625 46 31, ⓦwww.sanduny.ru; 10min from Kuznetskiy Most metro. Historic *banya*, restored to its original grandeur. If you can afford it, go for the *VIP #1* section (R3200) on the top floor, with its columned swimming pool; *VIP #2* (R2500) on the floor below is well appointed, but not nearly so spectacular. The wing behind (☎628 46 33) contains private baths for up twelve people, rented by the hour (R4000–6000 group rate). Amex, DC, JCB, MC, Visa. Daily 8am–10pm.

Seleznevskie Seleznevskaya ul. 15 ☎499 978 84 91; Novoslobodskaya metro. A coterie of devotees banishes everyone from the *parilka* until they've fanned the air to achieve the desired super-hot "soft" steam. Between 8am–2pm on weekdays, 7–12-year-olds get a fifty percent discount and under-7s go free. Tues–Sun 8am–10pm (*kassa* till 8.30pm). R3500–4700.

Boating and yachting

In fine weather, **riverboat cruises** are an enjoyable way to see Moscow while getting some sun and fresh air. The Moskva River is navigable from the last week in April until the end of September or later (weather permitting). Sightseeing boats (*kater*) depart every 20 minutes (Mon–Fri 9am–8pm; Sat & Sun 10am–6pm) **from ploshchad Yevropy** near Kiev Station (Kievskaya metro), calling at piers near the Novodevichie Convent, at the foot of the Sparrow Hills, Gorky Park and the Kremlin, before terminating near the Novospasskiy Monastery (1hr 30min). Tickets cost R350 for adults and R150 for children (aged 6–11). On national holidays you can also catch a hydrofoil **from Gorky Park**, downriver past Novodevichie and the Kremlin, to the Novospasskiy Bridge (30min). And from late April to August smaller motorboats ply the beaches of **Serebryaniy bor** (see p.287); you can reach one of the piers by trolleybus #21 from Polezhaevskaya metro.

Chartering a **yacht** is a popular way for rich Russians to enjoy themselves, but their interest in sailing is summed up by the club that boasts of its "girls, sauna, bar and yachts". Most establishments are members-only, but outsiders can rent yachts, motorboats and **jet-skis** at the Avrora Yacht Club (☎576 83 66) or the Vodnik Sea Club (☎408 04 13), both on the Klyazma Reservoir, 7km out along the Dmitrovskoe shosse. Phone ahead to reserve, as members get first call on facilities.

Alternatively, you can rent **skiffs** in Gorky Park or **rowing boats** at Serebryaniy bor by the hour.

Bowling and billiards

Ten-pin **bowling** (sometimes known by its German name, *kegelbahn*) is very popular, and there are many well-equipped bowling alleys where you can rent a lane for R420–720 an hour. Even more widespread is **billiards**, which was introduced to Russia from Holland by Peter the Great. Though some places specialize in American pool or British snooker, most offer Russian billiards (R150–300/hr, depending on the venue and the time of day or night). With this, the table and balls are larger, the pockets smaller, and you can only score points by straightforward shots – there are no cannons. Some Russians prefer a more dynamic version called *Amerikanka*. Russian billiards can be played by two, three or even four players.

Apelsin Malaya Gruzinskaya ul. 15 ⓣ253 02 53; 10min from Krasnopresnenskaya metro. Thirty lanes, pool and ping pong, plus a games arcade and free disco. Daily noon–5am.

Champion Leningradskoe shosse 16 ⓣ747 50 00, ⓦwww.champion.ru; near Voykovskaya metro. A huge complex with 20 Brunswick lanes, 29 pool and 3 snooker tables, plus karaoke, big-screen TVs, internet, sushi and a load of bars. Mon–Fri 3pm–6am, Sat & Sun noon–6am.

Cosmik Vernadskogo Prospect 6 ⓣ644 42 32, ⓦwww.cosmik.ru (Russian only); near Universitet metro. Twenty-two Brunswick lanes, four virtual lanes for children and 21 pool tables. Euro cuisine and sushi, slot machines, bouncy castle and clown shows for children. Big-screen TV sports; free guarded parking. Daily 10am–5am.

Samolyot (Jet) ul. Presnenskiy val 14, str. 1 ⓣ234 18 18; Ulitsa 1905 Goda metro. This complex has 34 Brunswick lanes, American pool and Russian billiards, a go-karting track and restaurants serving steaks, sushi or Euro cuisine. Daily noon–6am.

Chess

Once the Soviet sport par excellence, **chess** (*shakhmaty*) no longer has such a high profile in Russia, but amateur chess still thrives, with games in every courtyard and park over summer (Sokolniki, Izmaylovskiy and Gorky parks have special "chess corners" for matches timed against the clock), where a foreign challenger will always be welcomed.

Russian Central Chess Federation Gogolevskiy bul. 14 ⓣ291 06 41; Arbatskaya metro. For serious players, this is the nerve centre of the sport throughout Russia, with information on tournaments, lectures and other events. Mon–Fri 10am–6pm.

Cycling, rollerblading and go-karting

Cycling for pleasure is trendy among affluent, health-conscious under-30s. While the city centre is a virtual no-go zone, there are some fine cycling spots in the suburbs. The slopes and rolling terrain of Bittsa Forest Park (see "Horseriding and racing") are perfect for novices and experts alike, and you can even rent bikes there. Filovskiy Park requires advanced riding skills, while Sokolniki is best for inexperienced bikers and is the site of a weekend bicycle market. The Neskuchniy sad near Gorky Park has many kilometers of cycle paths, while the Olympic cycling course at Krylatskoe features hilly, challenging terrain, closed to traffic. Serebryaniy bor (see p.287) has a network of dirt and paved tracks, and mountain-bike trails through the forest. Bike shops and repairs are detailed under "Shopping" (p.378).

Rollerblading (inline skating) is widely popular among Russian youth. Victory Park with its 4km of paths, plazas and ramps, and the sprawling VVTs exhibition grounds with their Stalinist pavilions, are the hottest sites. Full-on bladers should head for the wide pavements of ulitsa Kosygina, between ploshchad Gagarina and the Sparrow Hills; head uphill from Gagarina for a workout, or downhill from MGU if you've got the skill for the steep descent. **Roller-skating** and **skateboarding** can be practised at one of the city rollerdromes (see below).

Or you can say nuts to the environment and head for the Ten Inches **go-karting** club, Skladochnaya ul. 1, str. 6 ⓣ745 00 25, ⓦwww.kartingclub.ru (Savelyovskaya metro). No experience is required to drive around the 350-metre indoor track, and helmets and overalls are supplied. The club also features sports TV and a restaurant (MC, Visa; Mon–Fri 2pm–2am, Sat & Sun noon till the last customer leaves). There's another, smaller, go-karting track at the Samolyot bowling club (see p.393).

Centre Kholodilniy per. 3 ⓣ954 01 58, ⓦwww.rollholl.ru (Russian only); Tulskaya metro. Central it's not, but this large roller-drome has good facilities for adults and children, rents skates (though only small sizes are usually available), and has a tube-labyrinth and soft-foam Play City for younger kids upstairs (R200/hr). Daily 11am–11pm; Mon–Fri R180; Sat, Sun & national holidays R200.

Roller Club Shop ul. 1905 goda 14 ⓣ253 86 41; Ulitsa 1905 Goda metro. The most centrally located of the city's roller-blade shops. Mon–Fri 10am–9pm, Sat & Sun 10am–8pm.

Skate Park Adrenalin Chermyansky proezd, 1 ⓣ473 00 05; ⓦwww.skatepark.ru (Russian only); 20min from Medvekovo metro. Europe's largest facility has a 1000-square-metre skate park and a 2000-square-metre rollerdrome, with a bar, café and restaurant. Daily 11am–11pm.

Gyms and swimming pools

Fitness clubs in Moscow can be as much about socializing or status as anything, and membership fees far beyond the pockets of many. The listings below are a cross-section of gyms and pools – some in hotels, others not. If you're going to be around long enough to make it worth joining a club, always ask about introductory rates or special offers – there's stiff competition to sign up clients, so they might cut you a deal. While some public swimming baths maintain the Soviet rule that bathers must have a health certificate (*spravka*) from a doctor, this isn't the case with hotel pools or the new breed of aqua-centres.

Aurora Health Club *Marriott Aurora Hotel* ul. Petrovka, 11 ⓣ937 10 00 ext.1238; 10min from Teatralnaya metro. Gym, jacuzzi, wet and dry sauna, small swimming pool. Non-hotel guests can buy a monthly membership giving unlimited entrance for R5600–11,200. Open daily 24hr.

Fit & Fun Chistoprudniy bul. 12, str. 1 ⓣ924 11 21; near Chistye Prudy metro. Private club with several categories of membership, from R10,000 per month to R85,000 a year. Gym, pool, saunas, jacuzzis, aerobics and aqua-aerobics, beauty parlour and restaurant. Amex, DC, MC, Visa. Mon–Fri 7am–11pm, Sat & Sun 9am–10pm.

Fit Olimpix Olimpiyskiy pr. 16 str. 2 ⓣ688 20 88; 10min from Prospekt Mira metro. Decorated with Soviet murals of athletes, this club in the Olympic Sports Complex has a gym with aerobics and aqua-aerobics courses; monthly membership R4300/R5800 with/without use of the pool next door. No cards. Daily 8am–10pm.

Kimberly Land Azovskaya ul. 24 ⓣ310 04 01, ⓦwww.kimberlyland.ru (Russian only); Sevastapolskaya metro. Moscow's sole aqua-park, it has four garishly decorated pools, aqua-aerobics, hydro-massage, a sauna, body-building and shaping classes. Annual membership R78,740. All credit cards. Daily 7am–midnight.

Kosmos Fitness Centre *Kosmos Hotel*, pr. Mira 150 ⓣ234 14 11; near VDNKh metro. The hotel's 240-metre pool has fun chutes and a nice café area; the gym is decent-sized for Moscow and the aerobics hall has a "floating" floor to protect against stress injuries. A one-day pass costs R3700, with three-month membership R20,500. Daily 7am–11pm.

Marco Polo Health Club *Marco Polo Hotel*, Spiridonevskiy per. 9 ⓣ202 60 61; 10min from Pushkinskaya metro. Non-hotel guests pay R5000/R16,000 for one/three months' membership, to use the sauna, solarium, gym and whirlpool for two hours daily. All major cards. Daily noon–midnight.

Moscow Health & Swim Club ***Radisson-Slavyanskaya Hotel*, Evropi pl. 2 ⓣ941 80 20 ext. 3260; near Kievskaya metro.** Pool, sauna, gym and aerobics. Monthly membership R10,000 with no restrictions; annual membership R68,000. Amex, DC, Maestro, MC, Visa. Daily 6.30am–10.30pm.

Olympic Sports Complex **Olimpiyskiy pr. 16, str. 1 ⓣ755 65 22; 10min from Prospekt Mira metro.** An Olympic-sized pool, built in the late 1970s. No swimming between 3–6pm. A day pass costs R2230, with annual membership R91,000. All major cards. Daily 7am–1am.

Planet Fitness **ul. Pravdy 21, str. 2 ⓣ933 45 99, ⓦwww.fitness.ru; 10min from Belorusskaya metro.** Located in the former premises of the Communist Party daily *Pravda*, this club has a 25-metre pool, sauna, gym and solarium, and classes in step aerobics, karate and yoga. Annual membership R38,000–46,000. All major cards. Mon–Fri 7am–midnight, Sat & Sun 9am–10pm.

Horseriding and racing

Though it's possible to trot around Kolomenskoe on summer weekends (R1200 buys a few minutes in the saddle), opportunities for serious **horseriding** are restricted to the places listed below, of which Bittsa Forest Park (*Bittsevskiy Lesopark*), bordering the Moscow Ring Road, offers by far the most agreeable environment. However, if you're seriously into real nature and don't mind roughing it, you can't beat Uncle Pasha's *izba* outside Moscow (see below).

Horse-racing is a year-round event at Moscow's **Hippodrome**, Begovaya ul. 22 k.1 (ⓣ945 04 37; bus #27 or trolleybus #20 or #86 from Begovaya metro, or tram #23 from Dinamo metro). Though merely trotting races, they are taken as seriously as the Kentucky Derby by the drunken crowd. Bets (*stavki*) are placed on pairs (*parniy*) or combinations (*kombinatsiya*) of winners in each race (*zaezd*). From May to September races start at 6pm from Wednesday to Friday and at 1pm on Sunday; from October to April at noon on Saturday and Sunday only. Normal schedules are suspended on the first weekend in June, for the exclusive Prize of the President of Russia race.

Bittsa Horseback Riding Complex **Balaklavskiy pr. 33 ⓣ318 57 44; bus #28, #163, #624 or #671 from Chertanovskaya or Kaluzhskaya metro.** By far the most agreeable environment for riding within the city limits, this wooded park near the Moscow Ring Road has a riding school offering lessons at different levels (R600–800/hr), plus a gym, pool and shooting galleries, baseball, volleyball and badminton courts. Mon–Fri 9am–9pm, Sat & Sun 9am–5pm.

Matador Riding Club **Podyomnaya 7 str. 2 ⓣ507 08 07, ⓦwww.kskmatador.ru (Russian only); Marksistskaya metro.** Riding lessons in English by arrangement; contact Sergei Nikulin (mobile ⓣ926 228 12 23). Mon–Fri 7am–9pm, Sat & Sun 9am–9pm.

Rossiya Sport Riding Club **Svobodi ul. vladenie 103 ⓣ494 01 11; near Planernaya metro.** Charges R1000 per hour both for adults and for kids. Daily 9am–9pm.

TsKA Horseback Riding Complex **ul. Dybenko 5 ⓣ451 61 06; bus #673, #739 or #745 from Rechnoy Vokzal metro.** Daily 9am–8pm.

Uncle Pasha's Rural Rides **Staritsa, Tver region, mobile ⓣ8916 117 15 27, ⓦwww.russian-horse-rides.com.** Besides offering cheap lodgings in Moscow (see p.327), Uncle Pasha has an *izba* (log cottage) at Staritsa, near Tver on the River Volga, where you can enjoy unlimited riding in rolling terrain, and basic bed and board for only R750–1500 per day – a genuine Russian experience. There are also opportunities for caving or rafting in the area. Staritsa is a 4hr journey from Moscow: there's a daily bus from Tushino metro at 10.20am (buy tickets in advance), or you can take a train from Leningrad Station to Tver and then a bus to Staritsa (see the website for directions).

Ice hockey

Ice hockey is Russia's second most popular sport and Moscow is a major venue on the national and international circuit. Though the season runs from September to April, the highlights of the calendar for many fans are the Spartak Cup in August – a pre-season tournament featuring the Russian All-Stars – and the World Championship in July. Since the legendary TsKA team split into two clubs in 1997, the RHL "pro" league has been dominated by provincial

▲ Ice hockey is Russia's second most popular sport

hotshots, and Muscovites' hopes of victory have depended on TsKA's old rivals, Spartak and Dinamo. For a real grudge match, watch TsKA versus its sibling offshoot, HC (Hockey Club) TsKA. Matches are held at a number of so-called ice palaces (*ledovy dvorets*).

Besides the sports pages of the *Moscow Times*, you can find match details on Ⓦwww.nhl.ru (though the English-language link is hard to find and doesn't always work) or Ⓦwww.eurohockey.com/Russia/ (for general information); but there's far more in Russian on the Russian Hockey Federation site Ⓦwww.fhr.ru and the homepages of Dinamo (Ⓦwww.dynamo.ru), Spartak (Ⓦwww.spartak.ru) and TsKA (Ⓦwww.cska-hockey.ru).

Dinamo Ice Palace Leningradskiy pr. 36, str. 21 Ⓣ613 22 01; near Dinamo metro. Although the team more often plays at Luzhniki, this remains the official home ground of the "blue-and-whites".

Krilya Sovetov Ice Palace ul. Tolbukhina 10, k.4 Ⓣ448 87 77; bus #178 from Kuntsevskaya metro. Far-flung home ground of the Krilya Sovetov (Soviet Wings) club, which has overtaken Spartak and Dinamo. The rink is open all year round and trains professional sportsmen, and child skaters. Daily 7am–11pm.

Luzhniki Sports Palace Luzhnetskaya nab. 24 Ⓣ637 02 18; 10min walk from Sportivnaya metro, or trolleybus #28 from Park Kultury metro. The home of Spartak.

Sokolniki Palace of Sports ul. Sokolnicheskiy val 1b Ⓣ223 64 25; 10min from Sokolniki metro. Home of the Spartak hockey club, this is also a frequent venue for outsiders to play.

TsKA Ice Palace Leningradskiy pr. 39 Ⓣ613 71 63; tram #23 from Aeroport or Dinamo metro. Used by both TsKAs, and for major league games and international events.

Marathons and the Relay-Race

Victory Day (May 9) and City Day (Sept 6) both occasion **marathons** which start and finish at Gorky Park, following the Moskva embankment around to the Sparrow Hills before doubling back; the full marathon entails two laps of this circuit. The hills afford the best view of the course, and soon separate the well-trained from the dilettantes. The nearest metro station is Vorobovy Gory.

A more amusing event for spectators is the annual **Police Relay-Race**, when Moscow's Militia, traffic cops and fire brigade field teams which race around the Garden Ring. Starting from Triumfalnaya ploshchad at noon, runners, skiers and dogs carry the baton as far as Krasnye vorota; bikers take over at Pavelets Station; firemen drag hoses over an obstacle course near Park Kultury; policewomen sprint up Zubovskiy bulvar; squad cars manoeuvre outside the US Embassy; and cops in parade uniforms race to the finishing line. The event is usually scheduled for the Sunday nearest Police Day (Oct 24), but may be moved if the weather is bad.

Martial arts and yoga

Martial arts have been popular in Russia since the 1980s, and despite their association with criminal gangs any serious practitioner will be welcomed at Moscow's clubs. Wing Chun is the dominant style, but there are also clubs specializing in kendo or ancient Slavic combat with cold steel. Anyone who enjoyed the movie *Fight Club* should love the gory, no-rules **Mixed Fight World Championships** at Luzhniki Sports Complex in mid-October.

Although **yoga** is a more recent fashion, there's a long tradition of Russian scholars studying Tibetan Buddhism, Indian yoga and the shamanistic spirituality of Siberia and Central Asia, while faith healing and divination have deep roots in Russian folk culture – creating a heady brew of New Age beliefs and therapies.

Ashtanga Yoga Centre Stariy Tomachevskiy per. 7, mobile ☎926 000 01 08, Ⓦwww.yoga108.com; Novokuznetskayta metro. Four classes daily in Russian; a two-hour session costs R300; a month's classes R1500.

BKS Iyengar Yoga Centre Pyantnitskaya ul. 43, str. 5 ☎953 64 10, Ⓦwww.yoga.ru; Novokuznetskaya metro. Moscow's largest centre has classes at all levels, some in English (Mon–Fri 7am–8pm, Sat & Sun 9.30am–6.30pm); R400 session.

INBI pl. Borby 13a, str. 1 ☎684 41 17, Ⓦwww.inbi.ru; Mendeleevskaya metro. Classes in kung-fu, tai chi, the Brazilian dance/martial art capoeira, and ethnic drumming. Most instructors speak English. The first session is free; a month's course costs R2400. To get there, follow Novoslobodskaya ul. northwards and turn right along ul. Palikha; any tram will take you the rest of the way to pl. Borby.

Patanjala Yoga Centre ul. Bakrushina 24, str. 1 ☎220 95 09, Ⓦwww.pyogai.com (English link only works sporadically); 10min from Paveletskaya metro.

Wing Chun Club Kievskaya ul. 2 ☎240 52 25; near Kievskaya metro. Classes in Wing Chun, tai-chi, yoga and oriental dance.

Skiing, ice-skating, sledging and snowboarding

During winter, Russians dig out their ice skates or skis and revel in the snow. There are outdoor **ice-skating** rinks at Gorky, Sokolniki and Izmaylovo parks, and there might be a temporary rink on Red Square for a few days either side of New Year. You can rent skates at Gorky Park or Sokolniki for about R100 an hour (plus cash or passport as deposit); Sokolniki has the best gear. The ideal temperature for outdoor skating is between –8°C and –1°C. Indoor and outdoor rinks where you can skate all year round are listed below.

The steepest hills for **sledging** are at Kolomenskoe (see p.234) and near the ski runs at Krylatskoe, but you needn't go further than the Alexander Gardens beside the Kremlin to find shorter slopes where young children can enjoy themselves. Although Russia's terrain dictates that cross-country rather than downhill **skiing** is the norm, there are pistes at Krylatskoe (Krylatskaya metro) and large new ramps at Planernaya, outside the city (one stop by suburban train from Leningrad Station). The best place for cross-country skiing is Losiniy Ostrov in northeast Moscow, which is named after the elks (*los*) that roam its 110 square kilometres of deciduous and evergreen forest (accessible from Shcholkovskaya metro). There's a purpose-built facility for **snowboarding** near Nagornaya metro.

Olympic Sports Complex Olimpiyskiy pr. 16, str. 1 ☎688 15 33; 10min from Prospekt Mira metro. The complex's skating rink is mostly reserved for training, but the public can use it on Thurs (1.30–2.30pm) and Sun (5–6pm & 6.15–7pm); R180 (adults), R100 (children).

Pingvin Ice Palace Bulatnikovskaya ul. 2b ☎383 87 38; bus #296 from Prazhskaya metro to the "Apteka" stop. This all-year rink in the southern part of the city is reserved for teaching children ice hockey or figure skating during the day, but allows anyone in for a few hours at weekends (Sat 8–9pm & Sun 9–10pm); R70.

TsKA Skating Rink Leningradskiy pr. 39 ☎613 71 63; minibus #18 from Dinamo metro. Used for ice-hockey as well as figure skating. Daily 7am–11pm.

Sokolniki Palace of Sports ul. Sokolnicheskiy val 16 ☎645 20 65; 10min from Sokolniki metro. Three indoor rinks, off to the left of the main avenue as you enter the park. Daily 24hr.

Young Pioneers Sports Centre Leningradskiy pr. 31 ☎213 46 42; near Dinamo metro. An outdoor rink, floodlit at night. Daily 10am–midnight.

Soccer

After suffering years of under-funding, under-performance, corruption and violence, Russian **soccer** (*futbol*) is finally on the up. In the last few years, its national team has received millions of dollars from the National Football Academy, partly bankrolled by Chelsea owner Roman Abramovich, which has paid for new training facilities, players' fees and a new Dutch coach Gus Hiddinck. The investment has so far paid off, with Russia confounding expectations in the Euro 2008 competition to reach the semi-finals.

Moscow's clubs embody the best and worst of Russian football, with a history as colourful as any in Europe. **Dinamo** is Russia's oldest club (founded by British factory managers in 1887) and was sponsored by the secret police in Soviet times – though fans prefer to recall its legendary goalie, Lev Yashin, the hero of postwar Soviet soccer. Their chief rival, **TsKA** (known abroad as CSKA), was founded as the Red Army team, giving both clubs first call on young players by conscripting them, while **Lokomotiv** and Torpedo were affiliated to the railway workers and the ZiL auto factory. By contrast, **Spartak** lacked a powerful institutional base, but was widely popular with Muscovites as a maverick challenger. Today, Torpedo has shed its industrial affiliation to become **Torpedo Moskva** (sponsored by the City Government) and launched a long overdue campaign to tackle racism among fans. TsKA is bankrolled by the oil giant Sibneft and has been slugging it out with Spartak for supremacy in the premier league (*vyshaya liga*) in recent years.

There are two national tournaments, running concurrently. The **Russian Championship** starts in March and ends in November, while the **Russian Cup** starts in the summer and ends in the summer of the following year. Due to the number of teams participating, preliminary rounds for the Russian Cup occur just before the previous year's cup final in May. A third major competition is the indoor **CIS Cup** in January, featuring teams from all the former Soviet republics.

Russian-speakers can get tons of **information** from *Sport Express* (ⓦwww.sport-express.ru), the websites of the national team (ⓦwww.rfs.ru) and domestic league (ⓦwww.pfl.ru) and the homepages of Dinamo (ⓦwww.fcdinamo.ru), Lokomotiv (ⓦwww.lokomotiv.ru) and Torpedo Moskva (ⓦwww.torpedo.ru); the only sites with English-language versions belong to TsKA (ⓦwww.cska-football.ru) and Spartak (ⓦwww.spartak.com) – and only TsKA's is up to date. Nearer the time, match details may also appear in the *Moscow Times* or *Russia Journal*.

Matches usually begin at 6pm. **Tickets** are easy to obtain on the spot or from PATEK-express **kiosks** in Kurskaya, Borovitskaya, Kievskaya and other (mostly far-flung) metro stations. Prices range from R100–3000 in the stands to R30,000 for a VIP seat at a major international match, such as TsKA versus Chelsea.

Dinamo Stadium Leningradskiy pr. 36 ⓣ612 70 92; near Dinamo metro. Dinamo's home ground has a capacity of 36,800 and is also used for Russian Championship and Cup matches; look out for the Dinamo Museum and the *Dinamo* restaurant. There's also a smaller arena with tennis courts and a skating rink.

Luzhniki Stadium Luzhnetskaya nab. 24 ⓣ637 05 01; near Vorobyovi gori metro. Moscow's largest stadium (80,000 seats), refurbished to UEFA standards, it hosts Russian Cup and Championship and international matches, and is the home ground of Torpedo, the "black-and-whites".

Lokomotiv Stadium Bolshaya Cherkizovskaya ul., vladenie 125a ⓣ500 30 40; near Cherkizovskaya metro. Dating from Stalin's time and decorated with train motifs, this recently refurbished 24,000-seat stadium is being shared by Lokomotiv and Spartak until the latter's own grounds are completed, and is also used for international matches.

TsKA Stadium Leningradskiy pr. 39 ⓣ612 07 80; minibus #18 from Dinamo metro. Covered arena used for Russian and CIS Cup and international matches, plus athletics and basketball. Home of TsKA, the "red-and-blues".

Tennis

As a keen **tennis** player, Yeltsin did much to promote the sport in Russia, which became chic in a way that would have been inconceivable in Soviet times – while the photogenic Anna Kournikova raised the country's sporting profile abroad. The international **Kremlin Cup** tournament lures top players with over $2.5 million in prize money; in October 2004, home audiences had the pleasure of seeing Russia's Nikolai Davydenko and Anastasia Myskina win both the men's and women's singles. The tournament is held in October at the indoor Olympic Stadium on Olimpiyskiy prospekt; regular tickets cost R20–3000, VIP seats R5000–65,000; phone ⓣ925 77 77, or check ⓦwww.kremlincup.ru for full details in English, though its booking facility is in Russian only.

Unfortunately for visitors who might want to play, many former public courts have become private clubs, and rates have rocketed – not that this bothers its nouveau-riche devotees.

Chaika Korobeinikov per. 1/2 ⓣ202 04 74; 10min from Park Kultury metro. Six indoor courts. Mon–Sat 7am–10pm, Sun 8.45am–8pm.

Dinamo ul. Petrovka 26, str. 9 ⓣ625 58 38; Okhotniy Ryad or Teatralnaya metro. This absurdly expensive downtown club has six outdoor and six indoor courts, and offers lessons. It costs R600 (outdoor courts) and R800 (indoor courts) for one hour. Daily 7am–11pm.

Dinamo Sports Palace ul. Lavochkina 32 ⓣ454 95 41; bus #188 or #233 from Rechnoy Vokzal metro. Indoor tennis courts, ping-pong tables and coaching in both sports. Daily 9am–10pm.

Drujba Luznetzkaya nab. 24 str. 5, Universal Sports Arena ⓣ785 97 17; near1 Vorobyovi gori metro. Besides seven outdoor and indoor courts for hire (R750–1200/hr) there is a sauna (R1200), gym, solarium and swimming pool. No cards. Daily 7am–11pm.

Multisport Luzniki 24, str. 10 ⓣ788 16 98, ⓦwww.multisport.ru; 10min from Sportivnaya metro. This sports club has six covered tennis courts, six outdoor tennis courts, plus squash, aerobics, boxing and bowling. An hour's hire costs R3000 (covered court), R2800 (outdoor court). Daily 7am–11pm.

Contexts

Contexts

History

Moscow's turbulent history can be divided into three phases. The first saw it rise from a minor principality to the capital of a unified Russian state, and the birth of the Romanov dynasty. During the second – from the reign of Peter the Great onwards – Moscow was eclipsed by the new Imperial capital, St Petersburg, and played a secondary role in Russian history until the collapse of Tsarism in 1917. Then, after a year that saw the October Revolution in Petrograd (as St Petersburg was then called), the Bolsheviks returned the seat of government to the Kremlin, and Moscow's modern era began. The city celebrated its 850th birthday in 1997.

Beginnings

Despite evidence of human settlement as early as 500 BC, the first recorded mention was in 1147 AD, when Prince **Yuri Dolgoruky** of Rostov and Suzdal invited Svyatoslav of Novgorod and his boyars (nobles) to feast at Dolgoruky's hunting lodge, on a hill above the rivers Moskva and Neglina. Enlarged over the years and fortified with wooden walls and towers in 1156, this *Kreml* or **Kremlin** was the seed of a township named "Moskva", after the river. Though some claim this is a corruption of the Finnish word for "bear", it is more likely to derive from the Russian *mozgliy*, meaning "marshy". In any event, the town was conveniently located on the River Moskva that linked the great waterways of the Volga and the Okha – a major factor in its eventual rise to power.

Moscow's infancy coincided with two momentous events in Russian history. Early in the twelfth century, the great medieval civilization of the **Kievan Rus** collapsed amid internecine strife and invasions from the east and west. Much of the population fled northwards to the *zalesskiy* (beyond the woods) area of the Okha basin and the upper Volga, where Prince Andrei Bogolyubsky established the new capital, **Vladimir**, in 1169.

Barely fifty years later, the Mongols surged across the Russian steppes, laying waste to villages and towns – including Moscow. The **Mongol invasion** (1237–40) seemed like the end of the world foretold in the Bible, but in fact heralded two centuries of submission to their **Tatar allies**, who demanded tribute in gold, furs and slaves. The princes of Vladimir and other towns were only allowed to rule with the Tatar Khan's *yarlyk* (authority), which was auctioned off to the highest bidder. Their chief concerns were to squeeze as much wealth as possible from their fiefdoms, and to remain in favour with the Khan.

The Moscow princes of the **Rurik dynasty** were no exception to this rule. The town was first recognized as a principality under **Daniil** (1263–1303), the youngest son of Grand Prince Alexander Nevsky of Novgorod, who defeated the Teutonic Knights in a famous battle on Lake Peipus. His grandson, **Ivan "Kalita"** (1325–41), earned his nickname "Moneybags" for his skill at extracting taxes and expanding his influence over other principalities, proving so adept as "the Tatar's hangman, sycophant and slave-in-chief" (as Marx put it) that he got to marry the Khan's daughter and become Great Prince of Vladimir. In recognition of his power, the seat of the **Russian Orthodox Church** was moved from Vladimir to Moscow in 1326. That same year, work began on strengthening the Kremlin with higher oak ramparts, completed in time for the accession of **Simeon the Proud** (1341–53).

The rise of Muscovy

The **rise of Muscovy** (as the principality was named) owed to more than mere servility. An underlying factor was its location in the *mezhdureche* (between the rivers) area at the crossroads of Russia's trade routes, roughly equidistant from the Tatar Khanate on the lower Volga, the Lithuanian-Polish empire to the west, and the powerful city-state of Novgorod to the north. Another was its prestige as the seat of the Russian Orthodox Church, which would assume messianic significance after the fall of Constantinople in the fifteenth century. Moreover, during the 1350s, the Mongol-Tatar Golden Horde was weakened by power struggles within its vast empire, and would later be battered by another force of nomadic invaders, under Timerlane. Meanwhile, the Kremlin was strengthened by the building of limestone walls, from 1367 onwards.

In 1380, Simeon's grandson Dmitri dared to argue over the annual tribute to the Tatars, and, when Khan Mamai responded with a punitive invasion, Dmitri led a Russian army to confront the Horde at Kulikovo near the River Don. The **battle of Kulikovo** was the Russians' first victory in nearly a century and a half: a historic event commemorated by the foundation of the Donskoy Monastery on the site where his departing army had prayed for victory, while Dmitri himself assumed the title **Dmitri Donskoy**.

However, the Horde remained a formidable threat, and his successors, Vasily I and Vasily the Dark, paid tribute as normal. It was during this period that Russian **icon painting** and frescoes reached their zenith at the hands of Theophanes the Greek, Andrei Rublev and Daniil Cherniy (all of whom worked in Moscow), and that the Byzantine capital, Constantinople, fell to the Turks, in 1453.

Ivan the Great

The Tatar yoke was finally thrown off in the reign of Ivan III (1462–1505), known as **Ivan the Great** (*Ivan Veliki*). His boldness stemmed from a politically shrewd marriage to Sofia Paléologue of Byzantium, and his claim to rule the Eastern and Western Roman Empires was symbolized by the double-headed eagle that he adopted as his emblem. Having gained power over Yaroslavl, Rostov, Tver and Pskov before his marriage, Ivan waited eight years before tearing up the Khan's *yarlyk* in the Cathedral of the Assumption, in 1480. By the end of his reign the Lithuanians had been pushed back to the headwaters of the Dnieper and Dvina, and even proudly independent Novgorod had submitted, giving Muscovy control of a huge area as far north as the White Sea. This fourfold **territorial expansion** earned Ivan the titles "Gatherer of the Russian Lands" and "Autocrat of All the Russias".

Moscow – and the Kremlin in particular – were aggrandized to reflect this. In Sofia's wake came **Italian architects** who supervised the construction of the Kremlin's brick walls and two of its finest stone cathedrals. They also began work on a belltower intended to be the tallest building in Russia, later named after Ivan. The building programme was completed by his successor, who extended it to the Beliy Gorod, where stone parish churches were erected. However, stone buildings were still rare, and Moscow would remain a predominantly wooden city for three centuries, making **fires** a greater threat than Tatar raids. Yet Moscow thrived, its population rising to 100,000 by the mid-sixteenth century, when it was one of the largest cities in Europe.

Ivan the Great's successor, **Vasily III** (1505–33), is mainly remembered for clearing what is now Red Square, and siring the future Ivan the Terrible in 1530 – the moment of birth apparently coincided with a clap of thunder and lightning striking the Kremlin, which was held to signify the child's future greatness. Of equal importance to Moscow's destiny was a **prophecy** by the monk Philotey of Pskov, who told Vasily that "two Romes have already fallen but the third remains standing and a fourth there will not be". This belief that Moscow was the "third Rome" and the heir of Byzantium's sovereignty over Orthodox Christendom would inspire Russia's rulers for generations.

Ivan the Terrible

Despite his infamous deeds, Russians have always had a soft spot for **Ivan the Terrible** (*Ivan Grozny*). In modern times this can partly be attributed to Eisenstein's superb film, which portrays the tsar as a tortured soul driven to cruelty by the imperatives of power – a view that was personally dictated by Stalin, who felt that his own life and Ivan's had much in common. Historians have also pointed out that the title *Grozniy* (usually translated as "Terrible", but really closer to "Awesome" or "Formidable") was first adopted by his grandfather, Ivan the Great. Nevertheless, his life richly deserves the epithet "Terrible".

Ivan's **childhood** was spent in fear of the boyars, whose struggles for power after Vasily's death (when Ivan was three) worsened after his mother was poisoned five years later. Ivan only survived as the heir to the throne because no one could agree on an alternative figurehead. His chief pleasure was killing birds and dogs, followed by hunting and reading the Bible. In 1547, aged seventeen, Ivan assumed the Crown of Monomakh and insisted on being proclaimed **Tsar** (Caesar) instead of Grand Duke. However, he left affairs of state to the **Glinskys** until a rival family of boyars, the **Shyuskys**, succeeded in blaming them for a spate of fires in Moscow, inciting a riot. Ivan dismissed the Glinskys and publicly confessed his failings on Red Square, vowing to God to rule better in the future.

Foreign invaders were a major concern – particularly the Tatars, who made frequent incursions into Russia from Kazan on the lower Volga. After many attempts, Ivan's army captured **Kazan** in October 1552 and, to celebrate, St Basil's Cathedral was built. **Astrakhan** on the Caspian Sea fell to the Russians two years later. With the Tatars at bay, Ivan then turned to raid the Grand Duchy of **Livonia** to the west, ignoring protests from Poland and Sweden.

In 1560 his triumphs turned to ashes when his beloved wife **Anastasia** died shortly after a fire in Moscow. This seemed to Ivan a betrayal of his contract with God, and aroused all his latent suspicions of the boyars. As once-favoured courtiers were exiled or met worse fates, others fled abroad, confirming his fear of traitors – until in the winter of 1564 Ivan abruptly quit Moscow, leaving the populace agog. A month later, they received word that he had **abdicated** in protest at the boyars' lack of patriotism. Mobs besieged the Kremlin, demanding that the traitors be identified, until a delegation of clerics went to beg his forgiveness and implore him to rule them again.

The Oprichniki

In return, Ivan demanded that Russia be divided into two spheres: the *oprichnina* – constituting his personal domain – and the *zemshchina*, comprising the rest. The power of the boyars was broken by exiling 12,000 families to distant, inhospitable regions of the *zemshchina*, an act of expropriation carried out by a new militia, hand-picked by Ivan and devoted to his orders: the **Oprichniki**. As a symbol of their mission to hunt down and sweep away his enemies, they bore a dog's head and a broom on their saddles. Enjoying total licence to kill, loot, burn and torture, they took their cue from **Malyuta-Skuratov**, the most depraved of Ivan's favourites.

Initially quartered in the Oprichniy dvor (on the site of old Moscow University), they later moved with Ivan to the **Alexandrovskaya Sloboda**, a moated palace north ofVladimir whose interior reflected the different aspects of the tsar's personality. Some rooms were luxurious, some crammed with books, while others had a monastic bareness; torture chambers lay beneath them. To demonstrate Ivan's piety, the palace was transformed into a "monastery" where the Oprichniki attended services from 3am until 8pm, after which nightly orgies commenced.

Another bizarre story was his **wooing of Queen Elizabeth** of England, which preoccupied Ivan from 1567 to 1569. Besides the prospect of uniting their two nations, Ivan was excited by reports of this Virgin Queen, having tired of his fourth, Circassian, wife. Tactful evasions angered him into placing the English ambassador under house arrest in the Kitay-gorod, but he later forgave the offender. Not so those boyars whom Ivan suspected of treason, who were fed to dogs or raped to death. The atrocious climax was the **massacre of Novgorod** in 1569, when up to 60,000 citizens were tortured to death for supposedly plotting to side with Poland, and 200 more met a similar fate on Red Square.

Ivan's final years

In 1571 the Tatars made a devastating raid on Moscow, burning the city and carrying off thousands of citizens as slaves. Ivan fled to Yaroslavl, only returning once they had left. The last decade of his reign was given over to scheming to gain the throne of **Poland**, which twice rebuffed his overtures. Ivan then invaded Livonia, whereupon **Stephen Bathory** led a Polish army into Russia, in conjunction with a Swedish assault further north. Facing defeat, Ivan asked the Vatican to mediate and conceded Livonia to the Poles in 1582.

The previous year the tsar had killed his heir, **Tsarevich Ivan**, by striking him with an iron staff in a fit of rage. This left his dynastic hopes resting on his eldest son **Fyodor** – an imbecile – and a sickly infant, **Dmitri**. In the last year of his life Ivan compiled a register of all those he had killed, and paid monasteries to recite prayers for their souls. His guts putrefied and his testicles swelled; his only solace was fondling the gems in his treasury. When astrologers foretold the **tsar's death** on March 18, 1584, he swore to have them burned alive if they were wrong. On that day he collapsed over a game of chess and expired on the spot. In accordance with Ivan's wishes, he was buried as a monk.

Boris Godunov and the Time of Troubles

News of Ivan's death was released to the populace only after the details of the succession had been agreed by a Council of Regents. Fyodor reluctantly became tsar, but the power behind the throne was **Boris Godunov**, the brother of Fyodor's wife Irina. During his regency stone walls were built around the Beliy Gorod and the Trinity Monastery of St Sergei. Despised by the other boyars for his Tatar origins, Godunov was later suspected of having arranged the mysterious **death of Dmitri**, at Uglich in 1591 – though all that is certain is that he rewarded one of the Tsarevich's servants afterwards. The official explanation was that Dmitri fatally stabbed himself during an epileptic fit.

Whatever the truth, Godunov deftly staged his own **accession to the throne** after Fyodor died in 1598, bringing the Rurik dynasty to an end. At the instigation of his agents, a crowd of clerics and commoners went to the Novodevichie Convent to beg Fyodor's widow to bless her brother as the heir. However, even his devious statecraft was powerless against a run of **disasters** which occurred after 1601. Famine and plague beggared the towns, and rural areas fell into brigandage, while Godunov was compelled to raise taxes to combat disorder. Under such conditions it was relatively easy for him to be challenged by an impostor claiming descent from the Ruriks – even one who identified himself as Ivan the Terrible's son Dmitri, miraculously saved from his killers at Uglich.

The False Dmitris

The **first False Dmitri** was a minor official's son named Grigory Otrepiev, who fled to Poland and pressed his claim with the aid of the Jesuits. His small invasion force was helped by Cossacks and robber bands, but above all by Boris Godunov's timely death in April 1605. Though popularly acclaimed as tsar, Dmitri soon alienated Muscovites with his Polish ways and advisers, his unseemly beardlessness and habit of walking in the streets with foreigners, rather than being awesomely remote like a proper ruler. The final straw was his wedding to a Polish bride in May 1606, at which the Poles sat on holy relics and lounged against the iconostasis in the Cathedral of the Ascension, and his betrothed, Marina Mnishekh, kissed an icon of the Virgin on its mouth (not on its hand, as Russians did), arousing indignation among all classes.

A week later the boyar **Vasily Shyusky** led a force of conspirators into the Kremlin while supporters roused the city with cries of "The Poles are killing the tsar". Inside the citadel, Shyusky had a different war cry: "Death to the heretics! Death to the impostor!" As the mob ransacked his palace, Dmitri leapt from the walls to escape and broke his leg. Captured by the Streltsy, he protested his sincerity till he was torn to pieces; his remains were fired from the Tsar Cannon in the direction of Poland. The Shyusky clan took power, but their writ barely extended beyond Moscow.

In 1607 a **second False Dmitri** entered Russia backed by a Polish-Lithuanian army, and ensconced himself at Tushino, outside Moscow, to await the fall of the Shyuskys. However, the "Scoundrel of Tushino" dallied too long, and early in 1610 the Shyuskys drove him out, later bribing his servants to murder him. Soon afterwards, however, Tsar Vasily-Shyuysky himself was overthrown following the defeat of his army by a Polish force a tenth the size, consisting mainly of Scottish mercenaries. Thereafter, Russia was ravaged by feuding boyars, serf and Cossack revolts, and Swedish and Polish invasions. This **Time of Troubles** (*Smutnoe vreme*) was branded on the national psyche for generations afterwards, with the added humiliation that, in 1610, "Holy Mother" Moscow succumbed to the Poles for the second time.

Then, when all seemed lost, Russia demonstrated the astonishing powers of recovery that would save it at other critical moments in history. Abbot Palitsyn of the Trinity Monastery of St Sergei declared a holy war and vowed to excommunicate anyone who failed to support it. The **liberation of Moscow** was accomplished by a volunteer army under **Prince Pozharsky** of Suzdal and a butcher, **Kosma Minin** of Nizhniy Novgorod, who ensured that the latter's merchants did their duty and financed the campaign by holding all their womenfolk hostage till the money was paid. Having recaptured Moscow in 1612, they went on to expel the Poles from Russian soil by the year's end.

The early Romanovs

In the aftermath of the war, dissension arose again among the boyars over who should be elected tsar. To resolve the impasse, Abbot Palitsyn proposed **Mikhail Romanov**, the brother of Ivan the Terrible's first wife, whose accession in 1613 marked the end of the Time of Troubles and the beginning of the Romanov dynasty. Moscow made a dramatic recovery, with a spate of new stone churches in the tent-roofed style symbolizing the close cooperation between church and state, which reached its zenith under Mikhail's successor, **Alexei II** (1645–76), known as "The Quiet" for his piety and love of books. It was during his reign that the **German Suburb** (*Nemetskaya Sloboda*) was established to house foreign soldiers, doctors, engineers, and others with professional skills that Russia lacked, due to its backwardness and conservatism.

In 1669 the tsar's wife Maria Miloslavskaya died during childbirth, leaving two young sons to continue the dynasty: the frail Fyodor and his imbecilic younger brother Ivan. Within a year Tsar Alexei took another wife, Natalya Naryshkina, whose Naryshkin relatives promptly displaced his former wife's kinsfolk at court, and congratulated themselves on their future prospects following the birth of a healthy son named Peter – subsequently known to history as Peter the Great.

Peter the Great

Peter the Great (*Pyotr Veliki*) ranks alongside Ivan the Terrible and Stalin in the pantheon of despots who lashed Russia through a series of fundamental transformations. His greatest monument is St Petersburg, the capital city that he created from nothing – to replace Moscow, which represented all that he detested and reminded him of his traumatic youth. His energy was as extraordinary as his physique: Peter was 1.9m tall, with a disproportionately small head.

When Peter was three his father's demise made him an unwanted offspring. His sickly half-brother Fyodor became tsar, and the Miloslavsky boyars returned to court, banishing Peter's Naryshkin relatives. Peter continued to live uneventfully at Kolomenskoe until 1682, when the death of Fyodor left him the heir to the throne at the age of ten. The Miloslavskys retaliated by organizing a **Streltsy revolt**, during which several Naryshkins were butchered in front of Peter in the Kremlin. The upshot was that his retarded sibling **Ivan** was recognized as co-tsar, and his scheming half-sister **Sofia** became **Regent**.

While Sofia ruled from the Kremlin, Peter pursued his boyish enthusiasms at Preobrazhenskoe, staging war games with his "toy regiments" and learning how to sail. However, conflict was inevitable as he came of age, and in August 1689 Sofia ordered the Streltsy to mobilize, spurring Peter to flee to the Trinity Monastery of St Sergei. Safe within its walls, his party issued appeals for loyalty, and were heartened by the defection of the Patriarch from Sofia's camp. By October her support had collapsed and she was confined to the Novodevichie Convent.

Initially Peter left affairs of state to his Naryshkin elders, preferring to dally in the German Suburb, imbibing foreign ways with cronies like Lefort and Menshikov. His first serious venture was an attempt to capture the Turkish fort of **Azov**, which failed in 1695, but was pursued the following year until the city fell. It was the first Russian victory since Alexei's reign, and served notice that Russia could no longer be trifled with. Soon afterwards Peter announced plans to colonize Azov and construct a fleet, followed by the astounding news that he intended to tour Europe with a "**Great Embassy**".

Never before had a tsar travelled abroad; even stranger, Peter chose to go "incognito", to be free to study shipbuilding in Holland and England, where he mastered the skills by working in the dockyards. He also met monarchs and conversed with learned figures of the age. Peter was gripped by it all, and became determined to drag his nation into the modern world. During his homeward journey in 1698 the Streltsy rebelled again, but were crushed by his foreign-officered Guards regiments. Peter later participated in the mass execution of the rebels on Red Square.

Peter's reforms

Following his tour, Peter embarked upon the forced **westernization** of his backward homeland. He changed the country's name from Muscovy to Russia and invited foreigners to settle there. His courtiers were ordered to wear Hungarian or German dress instead of their familiar kaftans, and the tsar personally cut off their flowing beards – a symbol of pride for Orthodox believers, whose religion held that only the unshorn had a chance to enter heaven. When Peter extended the ban on beards throughout society and decreed the substitution of the "Popish" Julian calendar for the Orthodox one, he was denounced as the Antichrist for imperiling Russians' salvation and perverting time itself. In response, he replaced the self-governing Patriarchate with a Holy Synod (essentially a secular ministry of religion subordinate to the tsar), but permitted devout believers to keep their beards, providing they paid a "beard tax".

Of more lasting import was Peter's creation of the Table of Ranks, or *chin*. This abolished the hereditary nobility and recast a new aristocracy based on service to the state, extending across the civil service and the armed forces to include engineers and specialists at every level. In theory, promotion was based on merit rather than birth, and the system was meant to dissolve snobbish distinctions between those who served the greater good of the nation. It did see able men of humble origin elevated to the highest ranks of the state – such as **Mikhail Shafirov**, a Jew who became Peter's foreign secretary – but in practice, the *chin* soon became a self-interested bureaucracy. The *chinovnik*, or bureaucrat, would be a stock character in the plays of Gogol and Chekhov a century and a half later.

To enforce such changes Peter relied on traditional methods of repression, and invented new ones that his Tsarist and Communist successors would exploit to the hilt. He introduced the internal passport system and organized forced labour gangs to build his grand projects. Faced with opposition, he was ruthless, overseeing the torture and death of his own son, Alexei, whom he suspected of conspiring against him. Many of his reforms were simply intended to improve Russia's strength during the long **Northern War** against **Sweden** (1700–21), which began with their youthful monarch Charles XII putting the Russians to flight at **Narva**. However, Charles failed to press his advantage by marching on Moscow, concentrating on subduing the rebellious Poles instead.

St Petersburg

This lull in the war enabled Peter to strengthen Russia's hold on the Gulf of Finland, and fulfil the quest for a seaport and a navy that had long dominated his thinking. According to Pushkin's poetic account of its foundation in 1703, the tsar cut two lengths of turf, laid them crossways, and declaimed: "By nature we are fated here to cut a window through to Europe." As a place to found a city, it was hardly ideal: a fetid marshland prone to flooding, with few natural or human resources.

The **creation of St Petersburg** was accomplished by forced labour, under terrible conditions. Thousands died of starvation, cold, disease and exhaustion. Basic tools were so scarce that earth had to be carried in the workers' clothing. In the summer of 1706, with the city barely on the map, Charles XII invaded from Poland and again came within an ace of victory before making the fateful decision to concentrate his efforts on Ukraine, culminating in his defeat at Poltava in 1709. The Northern War dragged on for another twelve years but, as Peter put it, "Now the final stone has been laid on the foundation of St Petersburg."

In 1710 the Imperial family moved there together with all government offices, and in 1712 St Petersburg was declared the **capital**. To populate the city, landowners and nobles were obliged to resettle there and finance the building of their own houses. The tsar drafted in 40,000 workmen a year from the provinces, and overcame a shortage of stonemasons by prohibiting building in stone elsewhere in Russia. In Moscow church building ceased, and wealthy citizens complained of having to establish new households far from home at vast expense. Though they hated St Petersburg and returned to Moscow whenever possible, the lure of the court would eventually ensure that the old capital was eclipsed by its new rival.

Peter's successors

Having killed his only natural heir, Peter was forced to issue a decree claiming the right to nominate his successor, but when he died in 1725, he was so ill that he was unable to speak. Initially his wife, **Catherine I** (1725–27), was hailed as tsaritsa, but she died after a reign of less than two years. Peter's grandson, **Peter II** (1727–30), then became tsar and moved the capital and the court back to Moscow in 1728, leaving St Petersburg in decline.

Peter II's sudden death from smallpox in 1730 left the throne wide open. In desperation, the Supreme Privy Council turned to a German-born niece of Peter the Great. Empress **Anna Ivanova** (1730–40) re-established St Petersburg as the capital and brought with her an entourage of unpopular German courtiers. Her ten-year reign was characterized by cruelty and decadence; affairs of state were handled by her favourite, Ernst-Johann Buhren, a Baltic German baron who executed or exiled thousands of alleged opponents – a reign of terror known as the *Bironovshchina*, after his Russified name, Biron.

Anna died childless in 1740, leaving the crown to her great-nephew, **Ivan VI**, who – because of his youth – was put under the regency of his mother, Anna **Leopoldovna**. However, real power remained in the hands of the hated Biron, until a coup, backed by the Preobrazhenskiy Guards and financed with French money, elevated Peter the Great's daughter Elizabeth to the throne, whereupon Biron and Ivan were imprisoned.

Elizabeth and Peter III

Like her father, **Empress** Elizabeth (1741–61) was stubborn, quick-tempered and devoted to Russia, but, unlike him, she detested serious occupations and "abandoned herself to every excess of intemperance and lubricity". Elizabeth was almost illiterate and her court favourite, Razumovsky (a Cossack shepherd turned chorister whom she secretly married), couldn't write at all. She liked dancing and hunting, often stayed up all night, spent hours preening herself and lived in chaotic apartments, the wardrobes stacked with over fifteen thousand dresses, the floors littered with unpaid bills. Her peregrinations from palace to palace and from hunting parties to monasteries resulted in a budget deficit of eight million rubles by 1761.

Although Elizabeth hated the sight of blood, she would order torture at the slightest offence – or throw her slipper in the offender's face. Yet she abolished the death penalty and was sensible enough to retain as one of her principal advisors the enlightened Count Shuvalov, who encouraged her in the foundation of Moscow University, under the direction of **Mikhail Lomonosov** (1711–65), a polymath known as the "Russian Leonardo". In fact, the cultural achievements of Catherine the Great were based more than Catherine liked to admit on the foundations laid in Elizabeth's reign. In foreign affairs, Elizabeth displayed a determined hostility towards Prussia, participating in both the War of Austrian Succession (1740–48) and the Seven Years' War (1756–63), during which Russian troops occupied Berlin.

On Elizabeth's death in 1761, the new tsar – her nephew, **Peter III** – adopted a strongly pro-Prussian policy, forcing the army into Prussian uniforms and offending the clergy by sticking to the Lutheran faith of his Holstein homeland. The one concession to the nobility during his six-month reign was the abolition of the compulsory 25-year state service. It was a decree of great consequence, for it created a large, privileged leisured class, hitherto unknown in Russia. Childish, moody and impotent, Peter was no match for his intelligent, sophisticated wife, Sophia of Anhalt-Zerbst, who ingratiated herself with her subjects by joining the Orthodox Church, changing her name to Catherine in the process. Their marriage was a sham, and in June 1762 she and her favourite, Grigori Orlov, orchestrated a successful **coup** with the backing of the Imperial Guards. Peter was imprisoned outside St Petersburg and soon murdered by Orlov.

Catherine the Great

The reign of **Catherine the Great** spanned four decades (1762–96) and saw the emergence of Russia as a truly great European power. Catherine was a woman of considerable culture and learning and a great patron of the arts. Inevitably, however, she is best known for her private life. Her most prominent courtier – and lover – Prince Potemkin, oversaw one of the greatest territorial gains of her reign, the annexation of the Crimea (1783), which secured the Black Sea coast for Russia.

After consolidating her position as an autocrat – she had no legitimate claim to the throne – Catherine enjoyed a brief honeymoon as a liberal. French became the language of the court, and with it came the ideas of the **Enlightenment**. Catherine herself conducted a lengthy correspondence with Voltaire, while Lomonosov was encouraged to standardize the Russian language. However, the lofty intentions of her reforms were watered down by her advisers to little more than a reassertion of "benevolent" despotism. When it came to the vital question of the emancipation of the serfs, the issue was swept under the carpet. And when writers like **Alexander Radishchev** began to take her at her word and publish critical works, she responded by exiling them to Siberia.

Catherine's liberal leanings were given a severe jolt by the **Pugachev revolt**, which broke out east of the River Volga in 1773, under the leadership of a Don Cossack named Pugachev. It was the most serious peasant revolt in the entire 300-year rule of the Romanovs. Encouraged by the hope that, since the nobility had been freed from state service, the serfs would likewise be emancipated, thousands responded to Pugachev's call for freedom from the landowners and division of their estates. For two years Pugachev's forces conducted a guerrilla campaign from Perm in the Urals to Tsaritsyn on the Volga, before being crushed by the army. The French Revolution killed off what was left of Catherine's benevolence, and in her later years she relied ever more heavily on the powers of unbridled despotism.

Paul and Alexander I

On Catherine's death in 1796 (the story that she was crushed while attempting to copulate with a stallion was fabricated by Prussian propagandists), her son **Paul** became tsar. Not without reason, he detested his mother, and immediately set about reversing most of her policies: his first act was to give his father, Peter III, a decent burial. Like his father, Paul was a moody and militarily obsessed man, who worshipped everything Prussian. He offended the army by forcing the Guards back into Prussian uniform, earned the enmity of the nobility by attempting to curtail some of the privileges they had enjoyed under Catherine, and reintroduced the idea of male hereditary succession that had been abandoned by Peter the Great.

In March 1801 Paul was strangled to death in St Petersburg, in a palace coup that had the tacit approval of his son, **Alexander I** (1801–25). Alexander shared Catherine's penchant for the ideas of the Enlightenment, but also exhibited a strong streak of religious conservatism. His reign was, in any case, dominated by foreign affairs and, in particular, conflict with Napoleon. Initially, Alexander sought to contain France by an alliance with Austria and Prussia, but when this failed he signed the Treaty of Tilsit (1807) with Napoleon, in a hut moored on the River Niemen, which separated their domains. Like the pact between Stalin and Hitler 132 years later, this *volte-face* was intended to buy time to prepare for war, which seemed inevitable.

The Patriotic War and the burning of Moscow

In June 1812 **Napoleon** crossed the Niemen and invaded Russia with his *Grande Armée* of 600,000 – twice the size of any force the Russians could muster. The Russians employed "scorched earth" tactics and harassed the French flanks with partisans, but public opinion demanded a stand. Against his wishes, **Marshal Kutuzov** was obliged to fight a pitched battle, despite being outnumbered. The **Battle of Borodino** (Sept 7) killed 70,000 on both sides and left Kutuzov's forces so weak that defending Moscow seemed impossible. To save his troops, Kutuzov withdrew northwards, allowing Napoleon to advance on Moscow, which started a frenzied exodus of civilians.

Having waited in vain for a delegation of nobles to offer him the keys to the city, Napoleon entered Moscow on September 14 to find that over 100,000 inhabitants had fled. That same night agents of the Tsarist governor started fires in the Kitay-gorod, which a powerful wind the next day fanned into a conflagration. The following day Napoleon was obliged to flee to a palace outside Moscow, as the Kremlin was engulfed in smoke and cinders, while his troops abandoned fire-fighting in favour of looting. **Moscow burned** for six days, until three-quarters of its buildings were reduced to ashes.

Though the French lived off neighbouring estates and villages as best they could, staying for long was hardly feasible, and Tsar Alexander refused to surrender. With winter approaching and Russian forces mustering to the north, Napoleon had no choice but to begin the long **retreat** home. Harassed by Cossacks and partisans, and unprepared for the ferocity of the Russian winter, the *Grande Armée* had shrunk to a mere 30,000 men when it finally reached Poland. The Russians didn't stop there but pursued Napoleon all the way back to Paris, which they occupied in 1814. At the Congress of Vienna the following year, Russia was assured of its share in the carve-up of Europe.

The reconstruction of Moscow and the Decembrist revolt

Within months of the fire, a commission for the **reconstruction of Moscow** was formed, and submitted its proposals to Tsar Alexander. The plan involved creating new squares where Moscow's radial avenues met the Beliy and Zemlyanoy Gorod walls, which were levelled and turned into boulevards. Private houses were swiftly rebuilt, and within five years Moscow had almost replaced its residential quarters (chiefly with wooden dwellings, which still accounted for over half the buildings in the city forty years later). The architect Bove was alone responsible for about 500 buildings, many in the Russian Empire style that reflected the widespread mood of patriotic pride.

Another result of the war was that it exposed thousands of Russians to life in other countries. The aristocracy and gentry noted parliaments and constitutional monarchies, while peasant foot soldiers saw how much better their lot could be without serfdom. As the tsar and his chief minister, Count Akracheev, were sure that any reforms would endanger autocracy, opposition festered underground. Guards officers and liberal aristocrats formed innocuously named groups such as the "Southern Society", under the leadership of Colonel Pavel Pestel, whose aim was to establish a classless utopia; and the "Northern Society", which favoured a constitutional monarchy. Both conducted secret propaganda and recruitment from 1823 onwards, and planned to assassinate the tsar.

When Alexander died in November 1825 without leaving a male heir, the plotters sought to take advantage of the dynastic crisis that ensued. The Guards initially swore allegiance to Alexander's brother Konstantin, who was next in line for the throne, but who had secretly relinquished the succession. A coup was hurriedly devised, to be staged in St Petersburg on the day that troops were to swear a new oath of allegiance to Alexander's younger brother Nicholas. Word got out about the **Decembrists**, as they became known, and on the day, their nerve failed. Rebels and loyalist troops faced one another across Senate Square for six hours, both unwilling to shoot. As dusk fell, Nicholas gave the order to clear the square: two hours later the revolt was crushed and hundreds of corpses were tipped into the River Neva.

Nicholas I

In the aftermath of the revolt, **Nicholas I** (1825–55) personally interrogated many of the plotters. Five ringleaders were executed and more than a hundred exiled to Siberia. Though no mention of this "horrible and extraordinary plot" (as he called it) was allowed in public, the fate of so many aristocrats inevitably resulted in gossip – especially when Countess Volkonskaya followed her husband into exile, inspiring other wives to do likewise. Although the Decembrists themselves failed, their example would be upheld by future generations of Russian revolutionaries.

Nicholas's reign was epitomized by the slogan "Orthodoxy, Autocracy, Nationality", coined by one of his ministers. The status quo was to be maintained at all costs: censorship increased, as did police surveillance, carried out by the infamous **Third Section** of the tsar's personal Chancellery. A uniformed gendarmerie was created and organized along military lines, while an elaborate network of spies and informers kept a close watch on all potential subversives. The most intractable problem, as ever, was **serfdom**, "the powder-magazine under the state", as his police chief put it. Serfs accounted for four-fifths of the population, and during the late 1820s there were several abortive serf rebellions, though none approached the scale of the Pugachev revolt (see p.412). The economic position of Russia's serfs remained more or less stagnant throughout Nicholas's reign, and hampered the industrialization of the country, which was mostly confined to developments in the cotton and beet-sugar industries.

Perhaps the greatest social change in Russia took place in the upper echelons of society. In the 1840s, the deferential admiration in which the educated classes normally held the tsar was replaced by scorn and dissent. The writer Dostoyevsky was among those drawn to the clandestine **Petrashevsky Circle** of utopian socialists, who dreamt of a peasant rebellion. In 1849, over a hundred of them were arrested as Nicholas clamped down in the wake of revolutions in

▲ The Great Kremlin Palace epitomized Nicholas I's reactionary views of architecture

Poland and Hungary, which his armies suppressed, earning him the nickname the "Gendarme of Europe" abroad. (At home, he was known as Palkin, or "The Stick".) His reactionary views also applied to **architecture**, where he promoted a neo-Byzantine style harking back to pre-Petrine Russia, epitomized by the Great Kremlin Palace, built by his favourite architect, Ton.

In early 1854, the **Crimean War** broke out and Russia found itself at war with Britain, France and Turkey. The war went badly for the Russians and served to highlight the flaws and inadequacies inherent in the Tsarist empire: Russian troops defending Sebastopol faced rifles with muskets; Russian sailing ships had to do battle with enemy steamers; and the lack of rail-lines meant that Russian soldiers were no better supplied than their Allied counterparts, who were thousands of kilometres from home. The Allied capture of Sebastopol in 1855 almost certainly helped to accelerate the death of the despondent Nicholas, whose last words of advice to his son and successor were "Hold on to everything!"

The Great Reforms

In fact, the new tsar, **Alexander II** (1855–81), had to sue for peace and initiate changes. The surviving Decembrists and Petrashevsky exiles were released, police surveillance eased and many of the censorship restrictions lifted. The most significant of the so-called **Great Reforms** was the **emancipation of the serfs**, which earned him the soubriquet of "Tsar Liberator". Although two-thirds of the land worked by serfs was handed over to village communes, the ex-serfs were saddled with "redemption payments" to the former landowners over 49 years, and neither side was happy with the deal. Other reforms were more successful. Obligatory military service for peasants was reduced from twenty-five years to six; appointed regional *zemstva* (assemblies) marked the beginning of limited local self-government; trial by jury and a trained judiciary were instituted; and Jews were allowed to live outside the Pale of Settlement.

Yet Alexander baulked at any major constitutional shift from autocracy, disappointing those who had hoped for a "revolution from above". The 1860s saw an upsurge in peasant unrest and a radicalization of the opposition movements coalescing among the educated elite. From the ranks of the disaffected intelligentsia came the amorphous **Populist** (Narodnik) movement, which gathered momentum throughout the late 1860s and early 1870s. Its chief ideologue, **Nikolai Chernyshevsky**, was committed to establishing a socialist society based on the peasant commune, without the intervening stage of capitalism – but there were widely differing views on how to do this. Initially, the **Nihilists** – as the writer Turgenev dubbed them in his novel *Fathers and Sons* (1862) – led the charge, most famously with the first attempt on the tsar's life, carried out in April 1866 by the clandestine organization, "Hell".

The other school of thought believed in taking the Populist message to the people. This proselytizing campaign climaxed in the "**crazy summer**" of 1874, when thousands of students, dressed as simple folk, roamed the countryside attempting to convert the peasantry to their cause. Most of these exhortations fell on deaf ears, for although the peasants were fed up with their lot, they distrusted townspeople and remained loyal to the tsar. The state was nevertheless sufficiently nervous to make mass arrests, which culminated in the much publicized trials of "the 50" and "the 193", held in St Petersburg in 1877–78.

Following what was probably Russia's first political demonstration, outside St Petersburg's Kazan Cathedral in 1876, a new organization was founded, called **Land and Liberty**, which soon split over the use of violence. Land redistribution was the major aim of the "Black Partition", one of whose leaders, Plekhanov, went on to found the first Russian Marxist political grouping, while the **People's Will** (Narodnaya Volya) believed that revolution could be hastened by spectacular terrorist acts – "propaganda of the deed" – culminating in the **assassination** of the tsar himself in St Petersburg (March 1881).

Reaction and industrialization

But regicide failed to stir the masses to revolution, and the new tsar, **Alexander III** (1881–94), was even less inclined than his father to institute political change. Assisted by his ultra-reactionary chancellor, Pobedonostsev, the tsar shelved all constitutional reforms, increased police surveillance and cut back the powers of the *zemstva*. The police stood by during a wave of **pogroms** in 1881–82, Pobedonostsev subsequently promulgating anti-Semitic laws that reversed the emancipation of the Jews instituted by Alexander II. Though hated by Russian liberals, the regime succeeded in uprooting the terrorist underground, which wouldn't pose a danger until a decade hence.

Yet despite turning the clock back in many ways, social and economic change was inexorable. The emancipation of the serfs had led to ever more peasants seeking work in the cities. **Industrialization** increased with breakneck speed – Russia's rate of growth outstripped that of all the other European powers, and foreign investment more than doubled during Alexander III's reign. In Moscow, huge factories sprang up in the suburbs, where the harsh conditions and exposure to new ideas and ways of life gradually forged an urban working class. Ministers were keenly aware that the urban poor were a potential threat to the regime, but industrialization was essential if Russia was to compete with other European powers, and legislating factory conditions seemed a slippery slope to wider reforms. Meanwhile, the nouveau riche **Kuptsy**, whose ancestors had toiled as serfs, displayed their wealth by commissioning architects like Shekhtel to build them fabulous Style Moderne mansions, and sponsored endeavours such as the Tretyakov Gallery and the Moscow Art Theatre.

One problem that nobody anticipated was the death of Alexander III, at the age of 49, in October 1894. Immensely strong (he used to bend steel pokers for fun, and once held up the roof of a carriage which had derailed), he had been expected to reign for at least another decade. His heir, Nicholas, had barely begun to be initiated into the business of government and was "nothing but a boy, whose judgements are childish" (as Alexander described him).

The gathering storm

If ever there was a ruler unfit to reign at a critical time (1894–1917), it was **Nicholas II**. Obsessed by trivia, he hated delegating authority yet was chronically indecisive, consulting "grandparents, aunts, mummy and anyone else" and adopting "the view of the last person to whom he talks". His wife, the German-born princess Alexandra of Hesse, was a fervent convert to Orthodoxy who shared his belief in divinely ordained autocracy and a mystic bond between tsar and peasantry. Painfully shy at receptions and appalled by the lax morals of high society, she was scorned by the aristocracy and urged Nicholas to "stand up" to his ministers. At their Moscow coronation in May 1896, 1300 people were killed in a stampede on Khodynka Field (see p.287) – an inauspicious start to a doomed reign.

By rejecting the constitutional reforms proposed by the *zemstvo* of Tver as "senseless dreams", Nicholas dismayed liberals and turned moderate Populists into militants. The late 1890s saw a resurgence of underground activity by the **Socialist Revolutionary Party**, or SRs, whose terrorist wing, the SR Fighting Section, assassinated the interior minister, and the tsar's chief minister, Plehve, but still failed to attract the mass of the peasantry to its cause. Meanwhile, some of the intelligentsia had shifted its ideological stance towards **Marxism**, which pinned its hopes on the urban proletariat as the future agent of revolution. A Russian Marxist organization was founded as early as 1883 by ex-Populist exiles in Switzerland, but its membership was so tiny that, when out boating on Lake Geneva, the "father of Russian Marxism", **Georgy Plekhanov**, once joked, "Be careful: if this boat sinks, it's the end of Russian Marxism."

Yet its ideas spread back home, disseminated by study groups and underground newspapers. In 1898 Plekhanov was joined by Vladimir Ilyich Ulyanov – better known as **Lenin** – and founded the Russian Social Democratic Labour Party (RSDLP). At its 1902 congress in Brussels, the RSDLP split into two factions, over the nature of the party and its membership. Lenin wanted it restricted to active militants, obeying orders from the leadership, while his rival Martov desired a looser, mass membership. Adroitly, Lenin provoked half of Martov's supporters to walk out, thereby claiming for his own faction the description **Bolsheviks** ("majority") and casting his opponents as **Mensheviks** ("minority").

In Russia, meanwhile, the tsar continued to ignore pleas from the *zemstvo* and business groups to legalize moderate parties and establish a parliamentary system and civil rights. This failure to broaden his base of support and bring new talent into government while Russia was relatively stable would leave the regime perilously isolated when events took a turn for the worse.

The 1905 Revolution

In 1900, Russia's economic boom ended. Unemployed workers streamed back to their villages, where land-hunger and poverty fuelled unrest. The interior minister, Plevhe, organized anti-Semitic pogroms to "drown the revolution in Jewish blood", and urged a "short victorious war" with Japan. But the **Russo-Japanese War** soon led to disaster at Port Arthur, sending shockwaves across Russia. In St Petersburg, a strike broke out at the giant Putilov engineering plant and quickly spread to other factories that encircled the capital.

On January 9, 1905 – **Bloody Sunday** – 150,000 strikers and their families converged on the Winter Palace in St Petersburg to hand a petition to the tsar, demanding civil rights and labour laws. Led by Father Gapon, the head of a police-sponsored union, the crowd marched peacefully from different parts of the city, carrying portraits of the tsar and singing hymns. In a series of separate incidents, the Imperial Guards fired on the crowd to disperse the protestors, killing as many as one thousand demonstrators and wounding several thousand others. For the rest of his reign, the tsar would never quite shake off his reputation as "Bloody Nicholas".

When the first wave of strikes petered out, the tsar clung to the hope that a reversal of fortune in the Far East would ease his troubles. However, the destruction of the Baltic Fleet at **Tsushima Bay** in May 1905, and the mutiny of the crew of the battleship *Potemkin*, forced the reluctant tsar to make peace with Japan and concede the establishment of a consultative assembly – the **Duma** (from the Russian word **dumat**, "to think"). However, this last-minute concession was insufficient to prevent a printers' strike in St Petersburg in late September from developing into an all-out general strike. Further mutinies occurred among the troops and the countryside slid into anarchy.

By the middle of October, Nicholas had little choice but to grant further concessions. In the **October Manifesto**, he gave a future Duma the power of veto over any laws, promised basic civil liberties and appointed Count Witte as Russia's first prime minister. Meanwhile, in the capital, the workers seized the initiative and created the **St Petersburg Soviet**, made up of some 500 delegates elected by over 200,000 workers (Soviet meaning "council" in Russian). Under the co-chairmanship of **Leon Trotsky** (who had yet to join the Bolsheviks), the Soviet pursued a moderate policy, criticizing the proposed Duma, but not calling for an armed uprising – but still the middle classes took fright.

With the opposition divided over the issue of participation in the Duma, Nicholas seized the chance to arrest the leaders of the Soviet in December. In **Moscow** local Bolsheviks misjudged the situation and led radical workers in a vain attempt to seize power. Having failed to break through into the centre of town, they barricaded themselves into the **Presnya** district. The government used artillery to smash the barricades, and then sent in cavalry and machine-gun units to crush any remaining resistance. In the aftermath hundreds were summarily executed by field tribunals or exiled to Siberia. During 1906, there were further mutinies in the army and navy, and mayhem in the countryside, but the high point of the revolution had passed. Notwithstanding isolated terrorist successes by the SR Fighting Section, the workers' movement began to decline, while the revolutionary elite languished in prison or, like Lenin, were forced into an impotent exile in Europe.

The only joy for Nicholas and Alexandra during these years was the birth of a son, **Alexei** – and even this soon became a source of pain, for the tsarevich was afflicted by haemophilia, an incurable condition that put him at constant risk of death, which they dared not admit to the nation.

The Duma

Of the parties formed in the wake of the October Manifesto, the largest was the Constitutional Democratic, or Kadet, Party, founded by Professor Milyukov to represent Russia's liberal bourgeoisie, whose aims were shared by many of Nicholas's officials. Although the first nationwide elections in Russian history (on a broad-based franchise, though far from universal suffrage) propelled the Kadets to the forefront, the inauguration of the First Duma at the Tauride Palace in St Petersburg (May 10, 1906) saw an unprecedented confrontation of courtiers and peasants' and workers' deputies in overalls and muddy boots. After ten weeks of debate, the issue of land distribution reared its head, prompting the tsar to surround the palace with troops and dissolve the Duma. The succeeding Second Duma suffered a similar fate.

Witte's successor as prime minister, **Pyotr Stolypin**, sent nearly 60,000 political detainees to Siberia or the gallows (nicknamed "Stolypin's necktie"), but knew that repression alone was not enough. The **Third Duma**, elected on a much narrower franchise, duly ratified a package of reforms that let peasants leave the village communes to farm privately. Stolypin envisaged a new class of rural entrepreneurs as a bulwark against revolution, so that the state could wager its security "not on the needy and the drunken, but on the sturdy and the strong". However, vested interests and the peasants' reluctance to leave the security of the commune ensured that this new class grew far slower than he had hoped. Stolypin was also frustrated by Nicholas and Alexandra's increasing dependence on the debauched "holy man", **Rasputin**, whom they believed held the key to the survival of their son, Alexei. Stolypin's assassination by a secret police double agent in 1911 deprived Nicholas of his ablest statesman only a few years before the regime would face its sternest test.

The most positive post-Revolutionary repercussions took place within **the arts**. From 1905 to 1914, Moscow (and St Petersburg) experienced an extraordinary outburst of artistic energy: Diaghilev's Ballets Russes dazzled Europe; Chekhov premiered his works at the Moscow Art Theatre; poets and writers held Symbolist seances in city salons, while Mayakovsky and other self-proclaimed Futurists toured the country, shocking the general public with their statements on art.

World War I

By 1914, Europe's Great Powers were enmeshed in alliances that made war almost inevitable, once the fuse had been lit. The assassination of the Habsburg Archduke Ferdinand in Sarajevo, Austria-Hungary's ultimatum to Serbia and German mobilization left Russian public opinion baying for war in defence of its "Slav brothers". In the patriotic fervour accompanying the outbreak of **World War I**, the name of the capital, St Petersburg, was deemed too Germanic and replaced by the more Russian-sounding **Petrograd**. Yet grave deficiencies in the structure of army and military production were barely acknowledged, let alone tackled. The first Russian offensive ended in defeat at Tannenberg in August 1914, with estimated casualties of 170,000. From then onwards, there was rarely any good news from the front; in the first year alone, around four million soldiers lost their lives. In an attempt to prove that everything was under control, the tsar foolishly assumed supreme command of the armed forces – a post for which he was totally unqualified – and left his wife in charge of the home front.

By 1916, even devout monarchists were angry. Empress Alexandra, the "German woman", was openly accused of treason, and Rasputin was assassinated by a group of aristocrats desperate to force a change of policy. Ensconced with his son in the General Staff headquarters at Mogilev, Nicholas refused to be moved. As inflation spiralled and food shortages worsened, strikes began to break out once more in the capital. By the beginning of 1917, everyone from generals to peasants talked of an imminent uprising.

The February Revolution

On February 22, there was a lockout of workers at the Putilov works in Petrograd: the **February Revolution** had begun. The following day (International Women's Day) thousands of women and workers thronged the streets attacking bread shops, singing the *Marseillaise* and calling for the overthrow of the tsar. On February 27, prisons were stormed and the Duma was surrounded by demonstrators and mutinous troops, while Trotsky and the Mensheviks re-established the Soviet. On March 2, en route to the capital, the tsar was persuaded to **abdicate** in favour of his brother, who gave up his own claim the following day, bringing the Romanov dynasty to an end.

Out of the revolutionary ferment a state of "**dual power**" (*dvoevlastie*) arose. The **Provisional Government** under the liberal Count Lvov attempted to assert itself as the legitimate successor to autocracy by decreeing freedom of speech and an amnesty. There were to be elections for a Constituent Assembly, but no end to the war. This pacified the generals, who might otherwise have tried to suppress the revolution, but eroded the government's popularity. The other power base was the Menshevik-dominated **Petrograd Soviet**, which was prepared to give qualified support to the "bourgeois revolution" until the time was ripe for the establishment of socialism. Their "Order No. 1", calling for the formation of Soviets throughout the army, soon subverted military discipline.

After ditching some of its right-wing elements, the Provisional Government cooperated more closely with the Petrograd Soviet. **Alexander Kerensky** became the Minister of War and toured the front calling for a fresh offensive against the Germans. The attack began well but soon turned into a retreat, while discontent in Petrograd peaked again in a wave of violent protests known as the **July Days**. Lenin, who had returned from exile, felt that the time was not right for a coup and, indeed, loyalist troops soon restored order. Trotsky and others were arrested, Lenin was accused of being a German spy and forced once more into exile, and the Bolsheviks as a whole were branded as traitors.

Kerensky used the opportunity to tighten his grip on the Provisional Government, taking over as leader from Count Lvov. In late August the army commander-in-chief, General Kornilov, attempted to march on Petrograd and crush Bolshevism once and for all. Whether he had been encouraged by Kerensky remains uncertain, but in the event Kerensky decided to turn on

Kornilov, denouncing the coup and calling on the Bolsheviks and workers' militia to defend the capital. Kerensky duly appointed himself commander-in-chief, but it was the Left who were now in the ascendant.

The October Revolution

During September Russia slid into chaos: soldiers deserted the front in ever-greater numbers and the countryside was in turmoil, while the "Bolshevization" of the Soviets continued apace. By October Lenin had managed to persuade his colleagues that the time to seize power was nigh. Bolshevik Red Guards were trained and armed under the aegis of the **Military Revolutionary Committee**, based in the former Smolniy Institute for Ladies.

The **October Revolution** began in the early hours of the 25th (Nov 7 by today's calendar), with the occupation of key points in Petrograd. Posters announcing the overthrow of the Provisional Government appeared on the streets at 10am, though it wasn't until 2am the following morning that the Cabinet was arrested in the Winter Palace. In contrast to the almost bloodless coup in Petrograd, Moscow witnessed a week of fierce battles between Red Guards and loyalist troops holed up in the Kremlin and the *Metropol Hotel*.

The coup had been planned to coincide with the Second All-Russian Congress of Soviets, at which the Bolsheviks' majority was enhanced when the Mensheviks and right-wing SRs walked out in protest. Lenin delivered his famous decrees calling for an end to the war and approving the seizure of land by the peasants. An all-Bolshevik **Council of People's Commissars** was established, and issued a spate of decrees nationalizing banks and financial organizations and instituting an eight-hour working day.

Conditions in Petrograd and Moscow worsened. Food was scarcer than ever, while rumours of anti-Bolshevik plots abounded. In December 1917 Lenin created the "All-Russian Extraordinary Commission for Struggle against Counter-Revolution, Speculation and Sabotage", or Cheka for short (meaning "linchpin" in Russian). Although the Bolsheviks had reluctantly agreed to abolish the death penalty in October, the **Cheka**, under "Iron" **Felix Dzerzhinsky**, reserved the right to "have recourse to a firing squad when it becomes obvious that there is no other way".

Following elections, the long-awaited **Constituent Assembly** met for the first and only time on January 5, 1918, in the Tauride Palace. As the first Russian parliament elected by universal suffrage, this was meant to be "the crowning jewel in Russian democratic life", but Lenin regarded it as "an old fairytale which there is no reason to carry on further". Having received only a quarter of the vote, the Bolsheviks surrounded the premises the next day, preventing many delegates from entering; Red Guards eventually dismissed those inside with the words, "Push off. We want to go home."

Civil War: 1918–20

More pressing than the internecine feuds of the socialist parties was the outcome of the peace negotiations with Germany. In mid-February of 1918, talks broke down and the Germans launched a fresh offensive in Russia, which met little effective resistance. Eventually, on March 3, Trotsky signed the **Treaty of Brest-Litovsk**, which handed over Poland, Finland, Belarus, the Baltics and – most painfully of all – Ukraine, Russia's bread basket. But German artillery remained within range of Petrograd, and renewed hostilities seemed likely, so in March 1918 the Bolshevik government moved to **Moscow**, and proclaimed it the **capital** of the fledgling Soviet state. Lenin stayed at the *National Hotel* before moving into the Kremlin, while the Cheka took over the Rossiya Insurance Company building on Lubyanka Square.

At the Seventh Party Congress, held in the Bolshoy Theatre, the RSDLP was renamed the **Communist Party**, and the Left-SRs quit in protest at the Brest-Litovsk treaty. On July 6–7, the assassination of the German ambassador heralded an **abortive Left-SR coup** in Moscow, during which Dzerzhinsky was held hostage at SR headquarters. In August they struck again, with the murder of the Petrograd Cheka chief, and an unsuccessful attempt on Lenin's life at the Michelson factory in Moscow. The Bolsheviks responded with a wave of repression known as the **Red Terror**. Thousands of hostages were imprisoned and shot. Dzerzhinsky's deputy pronounced that one look at a suspect's hands would suffice to determine his class allegiance.

By this time a **Civil War** was raging across Russia, fuelled by **foreign intervention**. In a vain attempt to force Russia back into the war against Germany, but also from fear of Bolshevism spreading, the Western powers sent troops to fight the Reds. A Czech Legion seized control of the Trans-Siberian Railway; British troops landed in Murmansk and Baku; US, Japanese, French and Italian forces seized Vladivostok, while the Germans controlled the vast tracts of land given to them under the Brest-Litovsk treaty. Fearing that they would be freed from captivity in Yekaterinburg, Lenin and Sverdlov ordered the **execution of the Imperial family**, which was carried out by local Bolsheviks on July 16–17.

The victory of the Soviet regime owed as much to the failings of its enemies as to the tenacity of the Bolsheviks. The anti-Communist forces – or **Whites** – represented every strand of politics from monarchists to SRs, but their bias towards the propertied classes made it impossible for them to accept the land seizures endorsed by the Bolsheviks, thereby alienating the peasantry, whose support was vital. Moreover, their forces were dispersed over a vast area, with no centralized command and little coordination between them. By contrast, the Reds were united by their ideology and ruthless leaders, with a platform that appealed to peasants and workers. Militarily, they had the advantage of controlling the **railways** emanating from Moscow, which enabled them to switch resources from one battle front to another, while Trotsky solved the infant Red Army's lack of expertise by compelling ex-Tsarist officers to serve under the vigilant eye of Bolshevik commissars, as he ranged across the Russian heartland in his armoured train, shooting commanders who disobeyed orders to hold ground at all costs. However, both sides were evenly matched in numbers, and rivalled each other in ferocity when it came to exacting revenge on collaborators.

Besides costing well over a million lives, the Civil War promoted the militarization of Soviet society, under the rubric of "**War Communism**". Workers' control in the factories and the nationalization of land had plunged the Soviet economy into chaos just as the Civil War broke out. In an attempt to cope, the Bolsheviks introduced labour discipline of a kind not seen since the pre-trade union days of Tsarism. With money almost worthless, peasants had no incentive to sell their scarce produce in the cities, so Red Guards were sent into the countryside to seize food, and "committees of the poor" were set up to stimulate class war against the richer peasantry, or *kulaks*.

The Kronstadt revolt and the NEP

By 1921, Russia was economically devastated – in Petrograd alone, the population shrank by two-thirds. The Communists found themselves confronted with worker unrest and, for the first time, serious divisions appeared within the Party. The most outspoken faction was the **Workers' Opposition**, led by Alexandra Kollontai and Alexander Shlyapnikov, whose main demands were the separation of the trade unions from the Party and fewer wage differentials. In February 1921, even the Kronstadt sailors – who had been among the Bolsheviks' staunchest supporters – turned against the party. The **Kronstadt sailors' revolt** precipitated a general strike in Petrograd when troops once more refused to fire on the crowds. Rejecting calls for negotiations, the Bolsheviks accused the Kronstadt sailors of acting under the orders of a White general and, after a bloody battle, succeeded in crushing the rebellion.

Meanwhile, Lenin was presiding over the **Tenth Party Congress**, at which he banned factions and declared a virtual end to democratic debate. Those SRs still at large were rounded up and either exiled or subjected to the first Soviet show trial, in 1922. From now on, real power was in the hands of the emerging party bureaucracy, or **Secretariat**, whose first General Secretary was the Georgian Communist, **Iosif Stalin**.

At the congress, Lenin unveiled his **New Economic Policy** (NEP), a step back from the all-out confrontation with the peasantry that had been the hallmark of War Communism. The state maintained control of the "commanding heights" of the economy, but restored a limited free market for agricultural produce and consumer goods, giving peasants an incentive to increase productivity, and stimulating trade. It was a formula that favoured the peasantry (who still formed the majority of the population) and speculators of all kinds (known as "Nepmen") rather than the urban working class, who dubbed the NEP the "New Exploitation of the Proletariat".

Stalin and Collectivization

Lenin's death on January 24, 1924 inaugurated an all-out power struggle. Trotsky, the hero of the Civil War, and Bukharin, the chief exponent of the NEP, were by far the most popular figures in the Party, but it was **Stalin**, as head of the Secretariat, who held the aces. Stalin organized Lenin's funeral and was the chief architect in his deification, which began with the renaming of Petrograd as **Leningrad**. Using classic divide-and-rule tactics, Stalin picked off his rivals one by one, beginning with the exile of Trotsky in 1925, followed by the neutralization of Zinoviev, the Leningrad Party boss, and Bukharin in 1929.

Abandoning the NEP, in the first Five-Year Plan (1928–32) Stalin ordered the forced **collectivization** of agriculture and industrialization on an unprecedented scale. Declaring its aim to be "the elimination of the kulak as a class", the Party waged open war on a peasantry who were overwhelmingly hostile to collectivization. This conflict has been dubbed the "Third Revolution" – for it transformed Russian society more than any of the country's previous revolutions. The peasants' passive resistance, the destruction of livestock and the ensuing chaos all contributed to the **famine of 1932–33**, which resulted in the death of as many as five million people from starvation and disease. Party control of the media and communications ensured that it was largely kept a secret from the urban population.

In Moscow, many took pride in the achievements of Soviet power. Workers' families who had lived in shacks before the Revolution were now housed in subdivided apartments once owned by their social superiors, or even brand-new flats in the apartment blocks that were rising across town. Future developments were laid out in the **General Plan for the Reconstruction of Moscow**, produced by a committee under Stalin and Kaganovich. Its aim was to transform Moscow into the showcase capital of the world's first Socialist state; a city of grand boulevards and public buildings, converging on a ring of skyscrapers and the Palace of Soviets (see p.132). Its most ambitious aspect was the **metro** (an idea that had been rejected as blasphemous when it was mooted in 1902). The first shaft was sunk in 1931, and the first line (with thirteen stations) opened in May 1935. *Pravda* lauded the efforts of Komsomol volunteers and drew a veil over the forced labourers who also built the metro.

It was in this climate that the Seventeenth Party "**Congress of Victors**" met in 1934. Stalin declared that the Party had triumphed, pronouncing "Life has become better, Comrades. Life has become gayer." While the 2000-plus delegates cheered, there were many who privately thought that, with Soviet power assured, Stalin should make way for a new General Secretary and a return to collegial decision-making. The likeliest candidate was the Leningrad Party boss, **Sergei Kirov**, who had popular appeal, yet lacked the urge to dominate his colleagues.

The Great Terror

Whether there was ever a chance of unseating Stalin is among the many "what ifs" of Russian history. In reality, **Kirov's assassination** at Party headquarters in Leningrad (December 1, 1934) gave Stalin the pretext for a purge of the city that saw 30,000–40,000 citizens arrested in the spring of 1935 alone, and perhaps as many as a quarter of the population within a year – the majority destined for the **Gulag**, or "Corrective Labour Camps and Labour Settlements".

This was merely the prelude to a nationwide frenzy of fear and denunciation. In the summer of 1936 the first of the great **show trials** was held in Moscow's House of Unions. Lenin's old comrades, Kamenev and Zinoviev, "confessed" to Kirov's murder and were shot along with fourteen others (Zinoviev begged, "For God's sake, tell Stalin … he'll say it's all a dreadful mistake!"). In early 1937, the head of the NKVD (secret police), Genrikh Yagoda, was arrested and succeeded by the dwarfish Nikolai Yezhov, who presided over the darkest period in Russian history, the *Yezhovshchina*, or **Great Terror**, of 1937–38. Exact figures are impossible to ascertain, but the total number of people arrested during the purges is thought to have been in the region of eight million, of whom at least a million were executed, while countless others died in the camps. Besides the lives lost or blighted, the loss of engineers, scientists and skilled workers wreaked havoc on industry, research and the railways – there came a point beyond which terror was self-defeating, even for the most ruthless regime. So in December 1938 Yezhov was replaced by **Lavrenty Beria** – a signal from Stalin that the worst was over, for the time being.

Few realized that purges within the Red Army had left it gravely weakened. From the defence minister Marshal Tukhackevsky downwards, the majority of senior officers had been either shot or sent to camps, and their hastily promoted successors were under-qualified and afraid to display any initiative. This was known to Hitler (whose secret service fed Stalin's paranoia about spies within the High Command), and figured in his calculations about the European balance of power. As Anglo-French appeasement allowed Nazi Germany to invade Austria and Czechoslovakia, and to set its sights on Poland, Stalin feared that the USSR would be next on its *Drang nach Osten* (Drive to the East) and authorized Foreign Minister Molotov to negotiate with his Nazi counterpart. The Molotov-Ribbentrop pact of August 1939 bound both parties to non-aggression, and the Soviets to supply food and raw materials to the Nazis. It also contained secret clauses relating to the division of Poland and the Soviet occupation of the Baltic States, which was put into practice in the first weeks of World War II. In October, Stalin demanded the moving of the Finnish frontier further from Leningrad, and in November attacked the Karelian Isthmus. But the Winter War (1939–1940) exposed the flaws of the Red Army, and although it eventually prevailed – taking Karelia – Stalin's act ensured that Finland would join the Nazi invasion to recover its lost territory.

The Great Patriotic War

Despite advance warnings from his agents in Germany and Japan, Stalin refused to believe that Hitler would break the pact, and was stunned by the Nazi invasion on June 22, 1941, which began what Russians call the **Great Patriotic War**. He is thought to have had a nervous breakdown and to have withdrawn to his *dacha* outside Moscow, while his subordinates attempted to grapple with the crisis. When Stalin returned to the Kremlin he reputedly told them, "Lenin left us a great inheritance, and we, his heirs, have fucked it all up." Not until July 3 did he address the nation by radio, in a speech that began: "Brothers and sisters! I turn to you, my friends . . .".

In the first weeks of the war over 1000 Soviet aircraft were destroyed on the ground; whole armies were encircled and captured; and local officials fled from the advancing *Wehrmacht*. Stalin had four army commanders shot and put two incompetent "cavalry generals" – Voroshilov and Budyonny – in charge of the western front (they were dismissed two months later).

By mid-October the Nazis were almost on the outskirts of **Moscow**; an advance patrol even reached a suburban metro station. Four hundred and fifty thousand Muscovites were mobilized to dig trenches. On October 16, a decree on the evacuation of the government caused **panic**: the streets were choked with refugees and soot from burning archives. But Marshal Zhukov promised that Moscow could be held, so Stalin opted to stay and ordered that the traditional November parade should go ahead. The troops proceeded directly from Red Square to the battle front, which was reinforced by fresh divisions from Siberia, equipped for winter warfare – unlike the Germans, clad in summer uniforms, with guns that jammed when the temperature sank to below –30°C. The front held, and Moscow was saved.

During four years of war, western Russia, Ukraine and Belarus were devastated, and 27 million Soviet citizens were killed. Their sacrifices broke the back of Hitler's forces and brought the Red Army into the heart of Europe, determining the fate of those nations that subsequently formed the Eastern Bloc. On May 9, 1945, cannons and fireworks exploded above the Kremlin, to mark the end of war in Europe, and delirious crowds thronged the streets. At the great **victory parade** on Red Square on June 24, Nazi banners were cast down before the Lenin Mausoleum, and trampled by stallions ridden by Soviet marshals in magnificent uniforms. (There's a picture of the event in the Armed Forces Museum; see p.275.)

Stalin's final years

In the immediate postwar years, Moscow was transformed by huge **construction projects**, using POWs and Soviet convicts as slave labour. The widening of the Garden Ring, the Kaluga Gates and the initial stages of Leninskiy and Kutuzovskiy prospekts were all completed at this time, as were several of the famous **Stalin skyscrapers**. Moscow was the mecca of world Communism, whose domain stretched from Berlin to the newly proclaimed People's Republic of China – at least for the years of Sino-Soviet cooperation, symbolized by the *Pekin Hotel*. In 1949 Stalin's seventieth birthday occasioned a deluge of tributes, and his image was projected onto the clouds above the Kremlin, like a demigod's.

After the enormous sacrifices of the war, people longed for a peaceful, freer life. But any liberalization was anathema to Stalin, whose suspicion of rivals and subversive trends was stronger than ever. It seems likely that he planned to purge the Politburo of all those who had served him since the 1930s, and install a new generation of lackeys. As ever, he used others to pick off his victims and script the show trials. Beria and Malenkov united against **Andrei Zhdanov**, who had been promoted to the Politburo for leading Leningrad through its wartime siege. Criticized for a "lack of ideological vigilance" in his home city, Zhdanov responded with a crackdown on "anti-patriotic elements" among the intelligentsia.

When Zhdanov died (or was poisoned) in 1948, Beria fabricated the "**Leningrad Affair**", in which Zhdanov's closest allies were accused of trying to seize power and were executed. Thousands of Leningraders fell victim to the witch-hunt that followed and wound up in the Gulag. Stalin's final show trial was the notorious "**Doctors' Plot**", where eminent physicians "confessed" to murdering Zhdanov and plotting to kill others in the Politburo. It was "no coincidence" (a phrase beloved of Stalin) that the doctors were mostly Jewish, nor that the list of their intended victims omitted Beria. The stage was being set for a nationwide pogrom and the deportation of all Jews to a remote region of Siberia for "their own protection", while Beria would be cast as the villain in future show trials. Thankfully, two months into the charade, the **death of Stalin** (March 5, 1953) brought an end to proceedings and charges were later dropped.

Stalin's death occasioned a nationwide outpouring of grief, which was largely genuine. Nobody knows how many mourners were crushed to death outside the House of Unions, where his body lay in state in the Columned Hall where the show trials had been held. After decades of submission to the "Wise Father of all the Peoples", many citizens couldn't imagine how they could continue without him.

Khrushchev

Stalin's successors jockeyed for power. The odious Beria was the first to be arrested and executed, in July 1953; Malenkov lasted until 1955, before he was forced to resign; Molotov hung on until 1957. The man who emerged as the next Soviet leader was **Nikita Khrushchev**, who, in 1956, when his position was by no means unassailable, gave a "**Secret Speech**" to the Twentieth Party Congress, in which Stalin's name was for the first time officially linked with Kirov's murder and the sufferings of millions during the Great Terror. So traumatic was the revelation that many delegates had heart attacks on the spot. In the same year, thousands were rehabilitated and returned from the camps. Yet for all its courage, Khrushchev's **de-Stalinization** was strictly limited in scope – after all, he himself had earned the nickname "Butcher of the Ukraine" during the *Yezhovshchina*.

The cultural thaw that followed Khrushchev's speech was equally selective, allowing the publication of Solzhenitsyn's account of the Gulag, *One Day in the Life of Ivan Denisovich*, but rejecting Pasternak's *Doctor Zhivago*. Khrushchev emptied the camps, only to send dissidents to psychiatric hospitals. In **foreign affairs**, he was not one to shy away from confrontation, either. Soviet tanks spilled blood on the streets of Budapest in 1956, while Khrushchev oversaw the building of the Berlin Wall and, in October 1962, took the world to the edge of the nuclear precipice during the Cuban Missile Crisis. He also boasted that the Soviet Union would surpass the West in the production of consumer goods within twenty years, and pinned the nation's hopes on developing the so-called "Virgin Lands" of Siberia and Kazakhstan.

By 1964, Khrushchev had managed to alienate all the main interest groups in the Soviet hierarchy. His emphasis on nuclear rather than conventional weapons lost him the support of the military; his de-Stalinization was unpopular with the KGB; and his administrative reforms struck at the heart of the Party apparatus. As the Virgin Lands turned into a dust bowl, his economic boasts rang hollow and the Soviet public was deeply embarrassed by his boorish behaviour at the United Nations, where Khrushchev interrupted a speech by banging on the table with his shoe. In October 1964, his enemies took advantage of his vacation at the Black Sea to mount a bloodless coup, and on his return to Moscow, Khrushchev was presented with his resignation "for reasons of health". It was a sign of the changes since Stalin's death that he was the first disgraced Soviet leader to be allowed to live on in obscurity, rather than being shot.

Brezhnev and the Era of Stagnation

Khrushchev's ultimate successor, **Leonid Brezhnev**, made an about-turn. Military expenditure rose, attacks on Stalin ceased and the subject of the Great Terror became taboo again. The show trial of the writers Sinyavsky and Daniel in February 1966 marked the end of the thaw and was followed by a wave of repression in major cities, while the crushing of the Prague Spring in August 1968 showed that the new Soviet leaders were as ruthless as their predecessors in stamping out dissent abroad. At home, a tiny protest demonstration on Red Square was crushed within minutes by the KGB. Due to press censorship and public indifference, most Russians knew little of **Alexander Solzhenitsyn** when he was exiled to the West in 1974, and even less of **Andrei Sakharov**, the nuclear physicist sentenced to internal exile for his human-rights campaigns.

Despite Party and KGB control of society, the Brezhnev era is now remembered in Russia as a rare period of peace and stability. With many goods subsidized, citizens could bask in the knowledge that meat and bread cost the same as they had done in 1950 (even if you did have to queue for them), while those with money had recourse to the burgeoning black market. However, the new-found security of the Party cadres (subject to fewer purges than at any time since the Soviet system began) led to unprecedented corruption. As sclerosis set in across the board, industrial and agricultural output declined to new lows. By 1970, the average age of the Politburo was over seventy – embodying the geriatric nature of Soviet politics in what would later be called the **Era of Stagnation** (*zastoy*).

Brezhnev died in November 1982 and was succeeded by **Yuri Andropov**, the former KGB boss, who had hardly begun an anti-corruption campaign when he too expired (February 1984). Brezhnev's clique took fright at the prospect of yet more change and elected the 73-year-old **Konstantin Chernenko** as General Secretary, but when he also died barely a year later, it was clear that the post required some new blood.

The Gorbachev years

Mikhail Gorbachev – at 53, the youngest of the Politburo – was chosen with a brief to "get things moving". The first of his policies to send shock waves through society – a campaign against alcohol – was the most unpopular, abortive initiative of his career, followed shortly afterwards by the coining of the two famous buzz words of the Gorbachev era: **glasnost** (openness) and **perestroika** (restructuring). The first took a battering when, in April 1986, the world's worst nuclear disaster – at **Chernobyl** – was hushed up for a full three days, before the Swedes forced an admission out of the Soviet authorities. Muscovites realized that something was amiss when train-loads of evacuated children began arriving at Kiev Station. Similarly, Gorbachev denied the existence of political prisoners right up until Sakharov's release from exile in the "closed" city of Gorky, in December 1986. Sakharov returned to Moscow to a hero's welcome, and vowed to fight for the freedom of all.

Gorbachev pressed on, shaking up the bureaucracy and launching investigations into officials who had abused their positions in the Brezhnev era. One of the most energetic campaigners against corruption was the new Moscow Party chief, **Boris Yeltsin**, whose populist antics, such as exposing black-market dealings within the *apparat*, infuriated the old guard. In October 1987, Yeltsin openly attacked Gorbachev and the hardline ideologist, Yegor Ligachev, and then dramatically resigned from the Politburo; shortly afterwards, he was sacked as Moscow Party leader.

Yeltsin's fate was a foretaste of things to come, as Gorbachev abandoned his balancing act and realigned himself with the hardliners. In the summer of 1988, radicals within the Party formed the **Democratic Union**, the first organized opposition movement to emerge since 1921. Gorbachev promptly banned its meetings and created a new security force – the **OMON** – while in the Baltic republics, nationalist **Popular Fronts** emerged, instantly attracting a mass membership. Estonia was the first to make the break, declaring sovereignty in November 1988 and raising the national flag in place of the hammer and sickle in February the following year.

1989 and all that

In the elections for the Congress of People's Deputies of March 1989, Soviet voters were, for the first time in decades, allowed to choose from more than one candidate, some of whom were not even Party members. Despite the heavily rigged selection process, radicals – including Yeltsin and Sakharov – managed to get elected. At the congress in May, a Latvian deputy started the proceedings with a call for an enquiry into events in Georgia, where Soviet troops had recently killed 21 protestors. When Sakharov urged an end to one-party rule, his microphone was switched off – a futile gesture by Gorbachev, since the sessions were being broadcast live on Russian TV.

Gorbachev's next crisis came with the **miners' strike** in July, when thousands walked out in protest at shortages, safety standards and poor wages. Gorbachev managed to entice them back to work with various promises, but the myth of the Soviet Union as a workers' state had been shattered for ever. The events which swept across the satellite states in Eastern Europe throughout 1989, culminating with the **fall of the Berlin Wall** and the Velvet Revolution in Czechoslovakia, were another blow to the old guard, but Gorbachev was more concerned about holding together the Soviet Union itself. That Communism now faced its greatest crisis at home was humiliatingly made plain by unprecedented counter-demonstrations during the October Revolution celebrations on November 7, 1989: one of the banners read: "Workers of the World – we're sorry".

1990 proved no better for Gorbachev or the Party. On January 19, Soviet tanks rolled into the Azerbaijani capital, Baku, to crush the independence movement there – more than a hundred people were killed that night. In February, Moscow witnessed the largest **demonstration** since 1917, calling for an end to one-party rule and protesting against the rising anti-Semitic violence that had resulted in several murders in Leningrad. Gorbachev attempted to seize the initiative by agreeing to end one-party rule and simultaneously electing himself president, with increased powers to deal with the escalating crisis in the republics.

The voters registered their disgust with the Party at the March **local elections**. In the republics, nationalists swept the board and declarations of independence soon followed, while in Russia itself, the new radical alliance, **Democratic Platform**, gained majorities in the powerful city councils of Moscow and Leningrad. Economist **Gavril Popov** became chairman of the Moscow council, while the equally reformist Anatoly Sobchak was elected to the post in Leningrad. May Day was another humiliation for Gorbachev, who was jeered by sections of the crowd in Red Square. By the end of the month Yeltsin secured his election as chairman of the Russian parliament and, two weeks later, in imitation of the Baltic States, declared **Russian independence** from the Soviet Union (June 12, 1990).

In July, the Soviet Communist Party held its last ever congress. Yeltsin tore up his Party card in full view of the cameras – two million had done the same by the end of the year. The economic crisis, spiralling crime and chronic food shortages put Gorbachev under renewed pressure from Party hardliners. The first ominous signs came as winter set in, with a series of leadership reshuffles that gave the Interior Ministry and control of the media back to the conservatives. On December 20, the liberal Soviet foreign minister, Edvard Shevardnadze, resigned, warning that "dictatorship is coming".

The effects of Gorbachev's reshuffle became clear on January 13, 1991, when thirteen Lithuanians were killed by Soviet troops as they defended – unarmed – the national TV centre. Yeltsin immediately flew there and signed a joint declaration condemning the violence. A week later in Latvia, the OMON stormed the Latvian Interior Ministry in Riga, killing five people. Hours before this attack, Moscow witnessed its largest ever demonstration – 250,000 people came out to protest against the killings. The Russian press had a field day, going further than ever before, mocking Gorbachev and backing the Balts. Gorbachev responded by threatening to suspend the liberal press laws, while adding more hardliners to the Politburo and giving wider powers to the security forces.

In June, the citizens of Leningrad narrowly voted in a referendum to rename the city **St Petersburg**, to the fury of Gorbachev, who refused to countenance it (the decision was only ratified by parliament after the putsch). At the same time, both Moscow and St Petersburg voted in new radical mayors (Popov and Sobchak) to run the reorganized city administrations.

The end of the USSR

On Monday August 19, 1991, the Soviet Union awoke to the soothing sounds of Chopin on the radio and *Swan Lake* on television. A **state of emergency** had been declared, Gorbachev had resigned "for health reasons" and the country was now ruled by a self-appointed "State Committee for the State of Emergency in the USSR". Its members included many of Gorbachev's recently appointed colleagues, under the nominal leadership of Gennady Yenayev, whose election as vice-president Gorbachev had obtained only after threatening his own resignation. Gorbachev himself, then on holiday in the Crimea, had been asked to back the coup the previous night, but had refused (to the surprise of the conspirators) and was consequently under house arrest. So began what Russians call the **Putsch**.

In **Moscow**, tanks appeared on the streets from mid-morning onwards, stationing themselves at key points, including the Russian parliament building, known as the **White House**. Here, a small group of protestors gathered, including Yeltsin, who had narrowly escaped arrest that morning. When the first tank approached, he leapt aboard, shook hands with its commander and appealed to the crowd (and accompanying radio and TV crews): "You can erect a throne using bayonets, but you cannot sit on bayonets for long." The Afghan war hero, Alexander Rutskoy, turned up and started organizing the defence of the building, making it harder for regular troops to contemplate attacking it. Actually, the role of storming the White House had been allocated to the crack KGB Alpha Force, but, for reasons unknown, they never went into action. News of the standoff – and Yeltsin's appeal to soldiers not to "let yourselves be turned into blind weapons" – was broadcast around the world and beamed back to millions of Russians via the BBC and the Voice of America.

On Tuesday, the defenders of the White House were heartened by the news that one of the coup leaders had resigned due to "high blood pressure" (he had been

▲ The White House, scene of the 1991 coup that began the downfall of the Soviet Union

drinking continuously) and the crowd grew to 100,000 in defiance of a curfew order. Around midnight, an advancing armoured column was stopped and fire-bombed on the Garden Ring and three civilians were shot dead. Next morning it was announced that several military units had decamped to Yeltsin's side and on Wednesday afternoon the putsch collapsed as its leaders bolted. One group flew to the Crimea in the hope of obtaining Gorbachev's pardon and was arrested on arrival. Yenayev drank himself into a stupor and several others committed suicide.

Gorbachev flew back to Moscow, not realizing that everything had changed. At his first press conference, he pledged continuing support for the Communist Party and Marxist-Leninism, and openly admitted that he had trusted the conspirators as men of "culture and dialogue". He was, by now, totally estranged from the mood of the country and marooned by the tide of history. The same day, jubilant crowds toppled the giant statue of Dzerzhinsky that stood outside the Lubyanka in Moscow. On Friday, Gorbachev appeared before parliament and was publicly humiliated by Yeltsin in front of the television cameras. Yeltsin then decreed the Russian Communist Party an illegal organization, announced the suspension of pro-coup newspapers such as *Pravda* and had the Central Committee headquarters in Moscow sealed up.

The failure of the putsch spelt the **end of Communist rule** and the **break-up of the Soviet Union**. Any possibility of a Slav core remaining united was torpedoed by loose talk of re-drawing the border between Russia and Ukraine, and the new-found goodwill between Russia and its former satellites quickly evaporated. In December, Ukraine voted overwhelmingly for independence; a week later the leaders of Russia, Belarus and Ukraine formally replaced the USSR with a **Commonwealth of Independent States** (CIS), whose nominal capital would be Minsk; the Central Asian republics declared their intention of joining. On December 25, Gorbachev resigned as president of a state which no longer existed; that evening the Soviet flag was lowered over the Kremlin and replaced by the Russian tricolour.

New Russia

On January 2, 1992, Russians faced their New Year hangovers and the harsh reality of massive price rises, following a decree by Yeltsin that lifted controls on a broad range of products. The cost of food rose by up to 500 percent and queues disappeared almost overnight. According to the Western advisers shaping Russia's new economic policy, this would stimulate domestic production and promote the growth of capitalism in the shortest possible time. Initially **inflation** was limited by keeping a tight rein on state spending, in accordance with the monetarist strategy of Prime Minister **Yegor Gaidar**, but despite Yeltsin's defence of his painful and unpopular measures the policy soon came unstuck after the Central Bank began printing vast amounts of rubles to cover credits issued to state industries on the verge of bankruptcy. Inflation soared.

By the autumn of 1992, Russia's economic policy was in dire straits and Yeltsin was forced to replace Gaidar with the veteran technocrat **Viktor Chernomyrdin**, in December 1992. He surprised parliament by immediately reneging on earlier promises to increase subsidies to industry and to restore them for vital foodstuffs (including vodka). Then in March 1993, Congress reneged on its promise to hold a **referendum** on a new constitution. Yeltsin declared that he would hold an opinion poll anyway, which he hoped would provide evidence of popular support for himself, although it would have no legal force. On March 20, Yeltsin appeared on TV to announce the introduction of a special rule suspending the power of Congress and called for new elections. In the meantime, there was a nationwide vote of confidence in the president and vice-president, **Alexander Rutskoy**, plus a referendum on the draft constitution, and new electoral laws were passed. At this point Congress and Rutskoy attempted to impeach Yeltsin. The impeachment was narrowly avoided and a referendum was held. Yeltsin claimed to have been vindicated by 55 percent of those who voted (32 percent of the electorate), but the count took place in secret and the ballot papers were incinerated afterwards, so his opponents saw no reason to back down.

The October "events"

The stalemate lasted until September 21, when Yeltsin brought things to a head by dissolving Congress with a decree of dubious legality. In response, almost 200 **deputies occupied the White House**, voted to strip Yeltsin of his powers and swore in Rutskoy as president, who promptly authorized the execution of officials guilty of "illegal actions". A motley band of supporters, consisting of pensioners carrying placards denouncing "Yeltsin the Drunk and his Yid Cabinet", Cossacks and neo-Nazis, erected flimsy barricades. The police cordon thrown around the area was so porous that hundreds of firearms were brought into the White House. As the "siege" continued into its second week Rutskoy appealed to the police to switch sides, while the government tried to break parliament's morale by cutting off its electricity, gas and phones, and playing a tape-loop of the song *Happy Nation* day and night. Meanwhile, the Federation Council tried to mediate a solution to the crisis, and appeared likely to blame the imbroglio on Yeltsin rather than parliament.

During the third week parliamentary supporters rallied on Smolenskaya ploshchad and set cars ablaze as the Militia stood by, and on October 3 they broke through the cordon round the White House, seizing trucks and riot shields (see p.180). As they rallied in triumph outside the White House, snipers opened fire from nearby buildings, goading Khasbulatov to call for the storming of the Mayoralty, the Ostankino Television Centre and the Kremlin. The Mayoralty was soon captured, and a convoy of trucks headed for Ostankino. Though the **battle for the TV Centre** (see box, p.283) was televised abroad, Russian viewers simply heard Ostankino warn "We're under attack", and assumed the worst when it went off the air. Actually, Ostankino was held by a unit of commandos which massacred the attackers, but at the time it seemed that Yeltsin had lost control of the TV network and the streets of Moscow.

The ex-Prime Minister Gaidar appealed over local radio for democrats to defend the City Council on Tverskaya ulitsa, which was assumed to be the next target. Hundreds turned up, barricaded Tverskaya with trucks and benches, and spent the night expecting attack. Gun battles flared across the city, as parliamentary supporters attacked the offices of pro-government newspapers. Meanwhile, Yeltsin was in the Defence Ministry, trying to persuade the top brass to obey him and crush the rebellion. They only agreed in the small hours, while the Alpha Force refused until one of their own was shot by a sniper.

The **assault on the White House** began at 7am on October 4. For ten hours tanks shelled the building, watched by crowds of spectators from nearby vantage points, some of whom were killed by stray bullets. Civilians were also slain on the

New Arbat, by snipers whose identity has never been established. By nightfall the White House's occupants had been bundled into prison and the rebellion was over. Isolated shoot-outs continued, however, and a curfew was imposed for a fortnight. With his parliamentary foes behind bars Yeltsin turned on his other opponents: local councils all over Russia were abolished and new elections declared, leaving power concentrated in the hands of local mayors and their bureaucrats. Moscow's Mayor **Yuri Luzhkov** proved as skilful a populist as Yeltsin had been two years earlier, while Yeltsin distanced himself from the party created to represent his government in the forthcoming elections, which bore the presumptuous name of **Russia's Choice** and campaigned as if its triumph were a foregone conclusion.

Zhirinovsky, crime and Chechnya

The result of the December **1993 elections** to the new parliament or Duma was a stunning rebuff for Russia's Choice, which won only 14 percent of the vote, compared to 23 percent for the so-called Liberal Democratic Party of **Vladimir Zhirinovsky**, an ultra-nationalist with a murky past who threatened to bomb Germany and Japan and to dump radioactive waste in the Baltic States. His success owed much to a superbly run TV campaign, whose effects lasted just long enough to get the LDP into parliament, beside the "red-brown" alliance of other ultra-nationalists and Communists.

While Russian liberals and world opinion were aghast, evidence later emerged of systematic voting fraud in Zhirinovsky's favour, which could only have been organized at the highest level. For Yeltsin, the crucial point was that Zhirinovsky supported the new **Constitution**, giving unprecedented powers to the president, and backed Yeltsin's government in the Duma, despite his aggressive rhetoric. Even so, it seemed a humiliating rebuff when the Duma promulgated an amnesty for the participants in the October "events", and the organizers of the 1991 putsch too.

In the wake of the elections, the government backpedalled on further economic reforms and tried to improve its nationalist credentials by taking a sterner stand on the rights of Russians in the ex-republics, or "Near Abroad". Resurgent **nationalism** was evident across the board in foreign policy, from warnings against expanding NATO into Eastern Europe or the Baltics to arguments with Ukraine over Crimea, and increasingly blatant interventions in civil wars in the Caucasus and Central Asia. The Russian Army's new strategic doctrine identified regional wars as the chief threat to national security and defending the old borders of the USSR as a top priority.

At home, cynicism, **crime and corruption** reached new heights in 1994, when car bombs became the favoured means of disposing of business rivals in Moscow, and the finance ministry estimated that $40 billion had been smuggled out of Russia since the fall of Communism. The funeral of the Mafia boss **Otari Kvantrishvili** underscored the extent to which organized crime had meshed with politics and culture, with deputies and pop stars among the mourners. Later that year thousands of Muscovites were ruined by the collapse of the **MMM** investment fund, whose boss then ran for parliament on a pledge to restore their losses, only to scornfully dismiss them once elected. In a further blow to public morale, the murder of a journalist for exposing corruption in the Army was followed early in 1995 by the assassination of the crusading TV presenter **Vladislav Listev**, the director of the national channel ORT, facing a takeover bid by the oligarch Berezovsky.

In December 1994 the Kremlin embarked on a **war in Chechnya** to subdue the breakaway Caucasian republic. The Chechens put up fierce resistance in their capital Grozny, which Defence Minister Grachev had boasted could be taken by a regiment of paratroops in two hours, but in fact only fell after weeks of bombardment, leaving the city in ruins and up to 120,000 dead – including tens of thousands of Russian conscripts. Back home, the debacle was attributed to the so-called "**Party of War**", a shadowy alliance of figures within the military, security and economic ministries, whose geopolitical or personal interests coincided. It was even said that Grachev and other commanders deliberately sacrificed their own troops to write off hundreds of armoured vehicles, in order to cover up the illicit sale of 1600 tanks from the Soviet Army in East Germany.

As the war dragged on throughout 1995, there was a huge protest vote for the Communists in the December parliamentary elections, which boded ill for Yeltsin's chances in the **Presidential election** of June 1996. Fearing the consequences of a victory by the Communist leader **Gennady Zyuganov**, Russia's financiers and journalists gave unstinting support to Yeltsin, with television, in particular, demonizing Zyuganov and denying the Communists any chance to state their case. Yeltsin's campaign was masterminded by Deputy Prime Minister **Anatoly Chubais**, who banked on the anti-Yeltsin vote being split between Zyuganov and the ex-paratroop general **Alexander Lebed** – as indeed happened. Having gained half the vote, Yeltsin co-opted Lebed by offering him the post of security overlord, and subsequently ordered him to end the war in Chechnya. Lebed duly negotiated the withdrawal of Russian forces – leaving the issue of Chechen independence to be resolved at a future date – only to be sacked from the government soon afterwards, having served his purpose.

Despite the war, Russia managed to keep its budget deficit low enough to qualify for a $6.3 billion loan from the International Monetary Fund. Inflation fell as the ruble stabilized, and in Moscow an **economic boom** was led by the new banks and conglomerates such as **Gazprom**, which profited from the huge tax breaks and privatization scams devised by their allies in government.

Yeltsin's second term

With the Communist threat dispelled, the **oligarchs** behind Yeltsin's re-election soon fell out over the remaining spoils. **Vladimir Potanin** acquired thirty percent of the world's nickel reserves for a mere $70 million and a controlling stake in the telecom giant Svyazinvest due to the intervention of Chubais – enraging **Boris Berezovsky**, whose TV station ORT aired a 29-minute diatribe against Potanin during a news show. Along with the banking and media moguls **Vladimir Gusinsky** and **Mikhail Khodorkovsky**, and oil or gas barons such as Roman Abramovich (later famous abroad for buying Chelsea football club), they became synonymous with a series of scandals – including "book advances" to Chubais and his privatization chief Alfred Kokh which were patently bribes. After Chubais had to resign as a sop to public opinion (he became boss of the electricity monopoly), Berezovsky's influence in the Kremlin grew even greater, and he was widely seen as the "kingmaker" of Russian politics.

Meanwhile, St Petersburg's 1996 mayoral election saw Sobchak ousted by his own deputy, following a bitter campaign dominated by allegations of corruption and nepotism. Though it didn't seem important at the time, one of Sobchak's protégés – an ex-KGB officer **Vladimir Putin** – reacted to this by leaving St Petersburg politics to work in the Kremlin, where he would soon become noticed and destined for greater things.

Mayor Luzhkov

Whereas the oligarchs were universally hated, **Mayor Luzhkov** won ninety percent of the vote at the 1996 mayoral elections, reflecting his genuine popularity among Muscovites, who admired his can-do management and staunch defence of local interests. Unlike other cities, Moscow was exempt from rises in housing and heating bills, and retained the Soviet *propiska* system that forbade outsiders to move in without a residency permit – despite this contradicting civil rights enshrined in the new constitution. But as Luzhkov himself said, "It is probably proper to view Moscow as a [separate] state" – and his electorate knew that there were millions who would move to Moscow if it was made easier, since the capital's estimated **population** had already risen by four million people despite a huge drop in the birth rate. Moreover, public services and amenities had visibly improved since their low point in the early 1990s, and the city was rapidly becoming as vibrant as any European capital, with shopping malls and nightclubs vying for big spenders, and confidence in the air. Like autocrats of yore, Luzhkov also gave Moscow some unforgettable **monuments** – the Cathedral of Christ the Saviour, the Resurrection Gate and the Kazan Cathedral, all re-created sixty years after they were destroyed by the Bolsheviks – and mind-bendingly kitsch monuments to Peter the Great and the Great Patriotic War, designed by his favourite artist, Zurab Tsereteli.

Luzhkov's **presidential ambitions** were an open secret. While always careful to assist Yeltsin, he compared Chubais's privatizations to "the way a drunk sells his possessions in the street for nothing", and could rely on favourable media coverage from his long-standing ally Gusinsky. But his strengths were also fatal handicaps, for outside Moscow voters deeply resented the capital where eighty percent of the nation's wealth was concentrated, and his alliance with Gusinsky entailed the enmity of Berezovsky. However, the killer blow was not to fall until after Luzhkov had founded his own party and won pledges of support from regional governors – when a spate of media "exposés" of the Mayor's links to organized crime and the murder of a US businessman undermined his reputation with Muscovites, only months before a new challenger emerged to claim the presidency (see "Yeltsin's endgame", p.436).

The 1998 crash

In the late 1990s prime ministers and cabinets changed with bewildering frequency, as Yeltsin manoeuvred to build or neutralize coalitions in the Duma and its upper house the Federation Council (dominated by regional governors), and find scapegoats for Russia's economic problems. First he encouraged Russia's creditors by appointing the energetic reformer **Boris Nemtsov** to the cabinet – only to sacrifice him a few months later to placate Chernomyrdin and the Duma. By April 1998 Russia's foreign debt stood at $117 billion, workers were owed $9 billion in unpaid wages, and pensioners over $13 billion. With a crisis imminent, Yeltsin stunned the world by dismissing Chernomyrdin's entire cabinet and nominating 35-year-old **Sergei Kirienko** as prime minister. A low-profile technocrat with no power base, his nomination was twice rejected by the Duma, until Yeltsin warned deputies that their Moscow flats and sinecures would be forfeit if they did so a third time.

Unfortunately, Kirienko's rescue plan depended on a "final loan" from the International Monetary Fund, at a time when the collapse of economies across Asia raised fears of a global crash, and pushed down the price of Russia's chief exports, oil and gas. As the IMF loan stalled and hard currency reserves evaporated, the pressure to default or devalue became intolerable, until the Central Bank caved in. In August, the **ruble crashed** and many banks and businesses went into liquidation; the capitalist bubble had burst. Kirienko was promptly sacked and replaced by the veteran diplomat and spymaster **Yevgeny Primakov**, a "safe" candidate accepted across the political spectrum, and also internationally. The US sent 3 million tonnes of emergency food aid to avert the possibility of food riots during the winter.

Yet the crash had some positive results. With imports so costly, shoppers switched back to domestic products, rewarding firms that survived the crisis with a larger share of the market. It also cut a few of the oligarchs down to size – though others seized the chance to snap up rivals' assets or dump all their own liabilities. By the end of the decade, these changes combined with arms sales and the rising price of gas and oil to produce a modest economic revival, which would contribute to the groundswell of support for Russia's next leader.

Yeltsin's endgame

While his government grappled with governing, Yeltsin was preoccupied with ensuring his own future – if not by running for President again in 2000, then by choosing a successor who would safeguard "**the Family**". By now, the term was widely used to describe his inner circle of advisers and relatives, whose backroom deals with Berezovsky were the source of constant speculation in parts of the media they didn't control. With his health so uncertain that even Prime Minister Primakov expressed doubts that Yeltsin could function as President, Yeltsin had no alternative but to find a successor whom he could trust to guarantee the Family's security after they left the Kremlin. There would be no mercy if the Communists won, nor any sympathy from Lebed; Mayor Luzhkov or the recently dismissed Primakov offered little hope either – but any of them could win the next election.

Meanwhile State Prosecutor **Yuri Skuratov** was uncovering the **Mabetex Scandal** which threatened to lay the Family wide open to criminal charges. Skuratov lost his job after state TV broadcast a video of him with two prostitutes (attributed to the KGB's successor, the FSB), but Swiss prosecutors picked up the trail and sought to question a top Kremlin aide, Pavel Borodin, about millions laundered through Kremlin construction deals and Aeroflot ticket sales. Time was running out for the Family.

Yeltsin's chosen successor emerged as suddenly and mysteriously as the apartment-block **bombings** that killed over 300 people in September 1999 – most terrifyingly in Moscow, where 220 died in two massive blasts. Coming only a month after a Chechen warlord seized thousands of hostages in Daghestan, most Russians readily believed that Chechen terrorists were responsible (foreign journalists speculated that the FSB was behind the bombings) and demanded action. The first response was a crackdown on people living in Moscow without a *propiska*, which saw thousands of mostly non-ethnic Russians deported from the city.

Simultaneously, the new acting prime minister, **Vladimir Putin**, made his name by pledging "We will wipe the terrorists out wherever we find them – even on the toilet." Within weeks Russia launched a **second war in Chechnya**, using overwhelming firepower from the start. By December eighty percent of Grozny was in ruins and the plight of its besieged civilians was an international issue, but in Russia the city's fall was hailed as just revenge for the defeat five years earlier. Berezovsky's media went into overdrive, casting Putin as the resolute, honest leader that Russia needed, while tarring Primakov as old and sick and Luzhkov as hand-in-glove with the Mafia. A new party nicknamed "Bear" (real name United Russia) materialized overnight to back Putin's candidacy, and was soon riding high in the polls.

The final masterstroke was **Yeltsin's surprise resignation** during his New Year message to the nation on the last night of the old millennium, when Russians would be more inclined to raise a rueful toast than ponder how power had been so deftly passed to Putin. His first decree as acting president was to grant Yeltsin and his family lifelong immunity from arrest, prosecution or seizure of assets, and confer on Yeltsin the title of "First President" in perpetuity.

President Putin: 2000–2008

Ensconced in the Kremlin as acting president, Putin enjoyed every advantage in the forthcoming election, which most of his opponents tacitly conceded was a foregone conclusion. His **inauguration** on May 5, 2000 was heralded as the first peaceful democratic transfer of power in Russian history, replete with ceremonial trappings harking back to Tsarist times, invented for the occasion. His pledge to restore Russia's greatness was followed by decrees doubling military spending, increasing the powers of the security agencies, and appointing seven "Super Governors" to oversee the regions. Five of these were army or ex-KGB officers, while twenty percent of the new regional governors were from the military or navy. The FSB regained all the powers of the KGB in Soviet times. Putin spoke openly of the need to create "**a strong vertical**" power in Russia – the *vertikal* became as much a mantra of his presidency as "all power to the Soviets" had been in the days of his grandfather (who had been a cook for Lenin and Stalin). Putin's view of Russian history embraced the Soviet, Tsarist and post-Soviet eras as equally worthwhile – symbolized by his decision to restore the Tsarist eagle as the state symbol, and the old Soviet national anthem (with revised words).

For those who feared that totalitarianism was creeping back, an early sign was the **campaign against NTV** and the Media-MOST group, which infuriated the Kremlin by revealing human rights abuses in Chechnya and casualties among Russian troops. Media-MOST's boss, Gusinsky, was arrested and spent several days in Butyrka prison, in what was seen by liberals as a warning to the entire media, but welcomed by most Russians as a blow against the oligarchs. Putin then convened a meeting of the oligarchs that pointedly excluded Gusinsky, Berezovsky and Abramovich, where the invitees reportedly pledged to pay more taxes and quit meddling in state affairs. Gusinsky prudently left Russia, soon to be followed by Berezovsky, who accused Putin of reneging on their deal by authorizing an investigation of the Aeroflot tickets scam. Besides alleging that millions of dollars had been used to finance Putin's election campaign, Berezovsky also implied that he had paid the Chechen warlord to invade Daghestan, to set the stage for a new war in Chechnya and Putin's presidency.

However, Putin's reputation suffered more from a spate of high-profile **disasters** – a bomb in a Moscow subway that killed twelve and injured scores; a fire at the Ostankino TV Tower that blacked out national television for several days; and the loss of 118 men aboard the submarine *Kursk*, a tragedy which cast both navy and Kremlin in the role of villains after they had rejected offers of foreign help at a time when it was still possible to save some survivors.

Nonetheless, his objectives were broadly accepted by the Duma, and foreign heads of state queued up to meet him. On the **foreign agenda** were the prospect of NATO forces on Russia's borders, once Poland and the Baltic States joined the alliance; the status of the Russian enclave of Kaliningrad within the European Union; and whether to ratify the Kyoto Treaty on climate change. On the first issue Putin could only register objections; the others allowed more scope for bargaining, but Russia's prestige had been so dissipated in the Yeltsin years that it no longer commanded respect. If foreign leaders were bothered by Russia's systematic human rights abuses in **Chechnya**, it was barely mentioned in public, while Russian TV viewers had no difficulty in believing that the situation was being "normalized". Putin's claim to be fighting Islamic terrorism became even easier to sell after **September 11**, 2001, when the US needed Russian help to sweep the Taliban from power in Afghanistan. The Northern Alliance was rearmed with Russian munitions and spares; US Special Forces were launched and supplied from an air base in Tajikistan (whose ruler was equally quick in seizing the chance to whitewash his own human rights abuses).

At home, Putin's popularity remained sky-high. Among his claimed achievements was the revival of the **economy**, with growth averaging more than five percent a year and inflation low during his first term. Revamped light industries began catering to a growing middle class no longer ashamed to buy local products and Russian clothes. New sectors like telecoms and advertising began to thrive, while industries that traditionally earned Russia hard currency – such as arms sales – bounced back from their sharp decline in the 1990s.

Yet many economists argue that Putin's successful record was due to the windfall of high world prices for Russia's major natural resources. Today, about a third of Russia's population live below the official **poverty** line ($78 a month, almost half the $150 that independent experts reckon is needed) – and entitlements for vulnerable groups are being cut back. Income inequality is grotesque; the top ten percent have 23 times more than the bottom ten percent (the same ratio in Britain is twelve, in Poland, seven), and a quarter of the nation's **wealth** is owned by a hundred people. Moscow boasts more billionaires than any city in the world (33, two more than in New York); this phenomenal wealth underpins the city's retail economy and property market, which are growing almost exponentially. Yet even Moscow isn't immune to some national trends. Alcoholism, a collapsing health system, unemployment and despair have sent male life expectancy plummeting – the average is now 56 years, less than what it was in the late nineteenth century. Having children is simply too expensive for many Russians; although the government has bought in a programme of incentives, such as doubling family allowance for the first child and a one-off payment of R250,000 for the second child, the weekly state child benefit is still only R125 and it's estimated that for every ten live births, thirteen pregnancies are terminated. Since the Soviet Union's collapse, Russia's **population** has shrunk by 5.3 million to about 142 million – an unprecedented decline for an industrialized nation in peacetime – and is falling at a rate of about a million a year, leading to fears that it could drop to 123 million in a decade.

Terrorism and Chechnya

Putin will also be remembered for his handling of the intractable and interrelated problems of **terrorism** and Chechnya. In October 2002, there was universal shock that dozens of Chechen gunmen and women were able to take more than 800 people hostage at the **Dubrovka Theatre** in southeast Moscow. The storming of the theatre by Special Forces backfired and raised a storm of controversy, when 130 hostages died from the effects of the gas used to subdue the Chechens (see box, p.256). The following year, female **suicide bombers** (dubbed "Black Widows" by the media) killed thirteen people at a suburban rock festival and six passers-by outside the *National Hotel*, followed by a bomb on the metro in February 2004 that left 39 dead and 122 injured.

In late August, two suicide bombers bribed their way past controls at **Domodedovo** airport and downed two passenger jets, killing everyone aboard. A week later, terrorists seized a school in the North Ossetian town of **Beslan**, confining children, parents and teachers in a hall wired with explosives. Hundreds died after an unplanned rescue bid by local militia ignited a firefight and Special Forces moved in to save the fleeing survivors. As after Dubrovka, Putin rejected a parliamentary inquiry and urged strengthening the *vertikal*. However, his demand to make governors state-appointed (rather than elected) officials, and prohibit the media from reporting terrorist situations, was too much for the media and the Duma, and even ex-president Yeltsin warned that Putin risked throwing away the "democratic achievements" of the 1990s.

However, there was widespread approval for the posting of a multi-million dollar bounty on the Chechen militant **Shamil Basayev** (who claimed "credit" for Beslan) and president-in-exile **Aslan Maskhadov** (who deplored the atrocity and denied any involvement) – and for Russia's right to strike pre-emptively at terrorists anywhere in the world. Negotiations with moderate separatists were ruled out, and Putin's "Chechen policy" of using local satraps to do the dirty work of counter-insurgency behind a fig leaf of legitimacy conferred by rigged elections, continues. With ethnic tensions and the influence of Al-Qaida growing in the Caucasus, the prospects for peace in Chechnya remain poor and further terrorist outrages in Russia seem inevitable.

President Medvedev 2008–

Barred by the constitution from a third term as president, Putin put himself forward as prime minister and endorsed **Dmitri Medvedev**, a lawyer and former CEO of Gazprom, as president. Approved by United Russia's majority in the Duma and elected by the Russian people in the March 2008 elections, Medvedev was sworn in as Russia's third president in May 2008, though many believe that little has changed in the power structure at the top. As prime minister, Putin remains very much in control, and laws have been modified so that control of foreign policy, the military and the secret services now rest with the office of the prime minister. In the meantime, inflation has risen dramatically to around fifteen percent and xenophobia is becoming an increasing problem. Despite its huge revenues from oil and gas exports, Russia has invested very little in the infrastructure of the country, and foreign investment is becoming increasingly worried as the government takes over successful companies and forces their competition out of business through Byzantine tax laws. Almost all the **petroleum and gas** in Russia is now controlled by Gazprom and Rosneft, who are in turn controlled by the government, giving it enormous financial clout. It remains to be seen whether Medvedev will break away from his mentor's influence over the next few years, or whether Putin will continue to wield effective control from his office as prime minister.

Books

The number of books available about Russia and the old Soviet Union is vast. We have concentrated on works specifically related to Moscow and on useful general surveys of Russian and Soviet history, politics and the arts. Out-of-print books are designated o/p. Books tagged with the ★ symbol are particularly recommended.

General travel accounts and specific guides

Baedeker's Handbooks (o/p). The 1914 *Baedeker's Handbook to Russia* was a stupendous work that almost bankrupted the company, with dozens of maps and reams of information that were soon rendered irrelevant by the Revolution. A facsimile edition was produced in the 1970s, but nowadays this too is almost as rare as the original, copies of which sell for up to £500 in antiquarian bookshops.

★ **Kathleen Berton** *Moscow: An Architectural History*. Enjoyably erudite study of Moscow's evolution, illuminating scores of buildings and centuries of history, with assured critical appreciations and dozens of photos.

Bruce Chatwin *What Am I Doing Here?* Two accounts of the Moscow art world and a lively essay on Russian Futurism are among the gems in this collection of *pensées* and travel pieces.

★ **Marquis de Custine** *Empire of the Czar*. Classic account of Tsarist Russia by a waspish French diplomat, whose observations on Moscow often ring as true today as when de Custine penned them in the 1830s.

★ **John Freeman & Kathleen Berton** *Moscow Revealed*. Gorgeous photos of Moscow's finest interiors – metro stations, palaces, churches and private homes – in every style from Baroque to Stalin-Gothic. Berton's text provides an essential context and exposes certain aspects of Muscovite life in the early years of perestroika.

Lawrence Kelly (ed.) *Moscow: A Travellers' Companion*. Alternately dull and amusing descriptions of court life, eyewitness accounts of historic events and excerpts from books long out of print, which stop short of the Revolution.

Robert Bruce Lockhart *Memoirs of a British Agent* (o/p). Vivid personal account of Lockhart's efforts to subvert the fledgling Soviet state, which brought him into contact with Trotsky and Dzerzhinsky and resulted in his imprisonment in the Kremlin.

The Armoury: A Guide A profusely illustrated, clearly laid out guide to the treasures of the Kremlin Armoury Museum, which is sold on the premises.

★ **Colin Thubron** *Among the Russians*; *In Siberia*. The first includes a chapter on Moscow, a visit to which formed part of Thubron's angst-ridden journey around the USSR in the early 1980s; the second is as lapidary and even more gloom-inducing, given such locales as Kolyma and Vorkuta, the worst hells of the Gulag.

Tretyakov Gallery Guidebook A well-illustrated room-by-room guide to Moscow's foremost collection of Russian art, from medieval times until the Revolution. A bit large to fit in your pocket, but handy enough to carry round the gallery, where the book is sold in the foyer.

James Young *Moscow Mule*. A mordantly amusing account of Moscow lowlife in 1993, by the author of *Nico: Songs They Never Play on the Radio*.

History, politics and society

John T. Alexander *Catherine the Great: Life and Legend*. Just what the title says, with rather more credence given to some of the wilder stories than Vincent Cronin's book (see below).

Anne Applebaum *Gulag: A History of the Soviet Camps*. This Pulitzer Prize-winning tome emphasizes the human cost and economic futility of the Gulag, drawing on extensive archival material, but its assertion that only fellow travellers on the left had a soft spot for Stalinism is wrong, since *Time* magazine made Stalin its man of the year in 1939 and 1941, and many European conservatives lauded him as a "splendid fellow".

Antony Beevor *Stalingrad* and *The Fall of Berlin 1945*. Military history told from the standpoint of ordinary soldiers on both sides and the civilians caught in the middle. Stalingrad was one of the decisive battles of World War II, its epic scale matched by its ferocity. In 1945, the Red Army took revenge on the German capital, where isolated acts of decency were submerged in an orgy of rapine, licensed by Stalin's order and Soviet propaganda.

Bruce Clark *An Empire's New Clothes*. A provocative assessment of the *realpolitik* behind the dramas of the 1990s, by a former *Times* correspondent. Clark argues that Yeltsin's "democrats" did more to lay the foundations of a resurgent Russian empire than those who accused them of selling out to the West.

Robert Conquest *Stalin: Breaker of Nations; The Great Terror. A Reassessment*. The first is a short, withering biography; the second perhaps the best study of the Terror. In 1990, this was revised on the basis of new evidence suggesting that Conquest's initial tally of the number of victims had been underestimated – he had previously been accused of exaggeration.

Vincent Cronin *Catherine, Empress of all the Russias* (o/p). Salacious rumours are dispelled in this sympathetic biography of the shy German princess who made it big in Russia.

Harold Elletson *The General Against the Kremlin*. An intriguing biography of the maverick soldier-turned-politician Alexander Lebed, which stops short of his career's downward trajectory after 1996 and his death in a helicopter crash in 2002.

Marc Ferro *Nicholas II: The Last of the Tsars*. A concise biography of Russia's doomed monarch, by a French historian who argues that some of the Imperial family escaped execution at Yekaterinburg. Most scholars reckon that the sole survivor was the family spaniel, Joy.

Orlando Figes *A People's Tragedy: The Russian Revolution 1891–1924*. Vivid, detailed, anecdotal, closely argued and sure to infuriate Marxists and monarchists alike, it sees the February and October revolutions and the Civil War as a continuum. A *tour de force*.

Stephen Handleman *Comrade Criminal: The Theft of the Second Russian Revolution*. Fascinating study of how organized crime spread through every level of Russian society and the Communist *apparatchiki* transformed themselves into *bisnesmeni*.

Michel Heller & Aleksandr Nekrich *Utopia in Power*. A trenchant *tour de force* by two émigré historians, covering Soviet history from 1917 until the onset of Gorbachev.

Adam Hochschild *The Unquiet Ghost: Russians Remember Stalin*. A searching enquiry into the nature of guilt and denial, ranging from the penal camps of Kolyma to the archives of the Lubyanka. Hochschild concludes that the road to hell is paved with good intentions, and most people would behave no better had they lived under the Terror themselves.

Andrew Jack *Inside Putin's Russia*. Written by the *Financial Times*' correspondent in Moscow during Putin's first term as president, it epitomizes the consensual view of Russia as a "managed democracy" of authoritarian, oligarchic rule over an impoverished majority, groping towards prosperity, legality and human rights.

John Kampfner *Inside Yeltsin's Russia*. Racy account of Yeltsin's presidency, focusing on political crises, crime and corruption, with vignettes of the highlights and leading characters up to 1994. Best read in conjunction with Clark's book, for a somewhat different view and conclusions.

David King *The Commissar Vanishes*. An intriguing study of the falsification of photographs in Stalin's time, detailing how his victims were erased from history, their final image being a mugshot in the archives of the Lubyanka.

Dominic Lieven *Nicholas II*. Another post-Soviet study of the last Tsar, which draws comparisons between both the monarchies of Russia and other states of that period, and the downfall of the Tsarist and Soviet regimes.

Robert Massie *Peter the Great*; *Nicholas and Alexandra*. Both the boldest and the weakest of the Romanov Tsars are minutely scrutinized in these two heavyweight but extremely readable biographies – the one on Peter is especially good.

Andrew Meier *Black Earth: Russia After the Fall*. Like Jack's book, this focuses on Putin's efforts to restore "vertical power" and Russia's prestige abroad, but also stresses the cultural tradition and the vastness of the country as crucial to an understanding of its politics and economics. Meier used to be *Time* magazine's reporter in Moscow.

John Reed *Ten Days that Shook the World*. The classic eyewitness account of the 1917 Bolshevik seizure of power that vividly captures the mood of the time and the hopes pinned on the Revolution.

David Remnick *Lenin's Tomb*; *Resurrection: The Struggle for a New Russia*. *Lenin's Tomb* remains the most vivid account of the collapse of the Soviet Union, though some of its judgements seem simplistic with hindsight. *Resurrection* is also riveting, but the jury is still out on Remnick's analysis of the Yeltsin era.

Robert Service *History of Modern Russia from Nicholas II to Putin*; *Russia: Experiment with a People*. The first is a magisterial survey of twentieth-century Russian history; the second focuses on the corruption, authoritarianism and missed opportunities of the Yeltsin era. Service is a professor of Russian history at London's School of Slavonic Studies.

Henri Troyat *Alexander of Russia; Ivan the Terrible.* A sympathetic portrayal of the "Tsar Liberator", Alexander II, and a more salacious romp through the misdeeds of Ivan.

Peter Truscott *Putin's Progress.* Whilst adhering to the consensual view of Putin's Russia (see Jack's and Meier's books, opposite), this one contains more biographical detail about Russia's judo-loving president than the others.

John Ure *The Cossacks.* A lively history of the freebooting warriors who rocked the Romanov dynasty but also served as its most faithful instrument of repression, by a former British diplomat who began his career in Russia.

Dmitri Volkogonov *Stalin: Triumph and Tragedy.* Weighty study of the Soviet dictator, drawing on long-withheld archive material, by Russia's foremost military historian.

The arts

Anna Benn & Rosamund Bartlett *Literary Russia: A Guide.* Comprehensive guide to Russian writers and places associated with their lives and works, including such Muscovites as Chekhov, Tolstoy, Pasternak and Bulgakov. Highly recommended.

Ronald Bergan *Eisenstein: A Life in Conflict.* A new biography of the great Soviet director, which argues that he fared better under Stalinism than in Hollywood, despite his admiration for Walt Disney.

Alan Bird *A History of Russian Painting.* A comprehensive survey of Russian painting from medieval times to the Brezhnev era, including numerous black-and-white illustrations and potted biographies.

John E. Bowlt (ed.) *Russian Art of the Avant-Garde.* An illustrated volume of critical essays on this seminal movement, which anticipated many trends in Western art that have occurred since World War II.

Matthew Cullerne Brown *Art Under Stalin; Contemporary Russian Art.* The former is a fascinating study of totalitarian aesthetics, ranging from ballet to sports stadiums and from films to sculpture; the latter covers art in the Brezhnev and Gorbachev eras.

William Craft Brumfield *A History of Russian Architecture.* The most comprehensive study of the subject, ranging from early Novgorod churches to Olympic sports halls, by way of Naryshkin Baroque monasteries and Style Moderne mansions, illustrated by hundreds of photos and line drawings.

Leslie Chamberlain *The Food and Cooking of Russia.* Informative and amusing cook book, full of delicious if somewhat vague recipes.

Camilla Gray *The Russian Experiment in Art 1863–1922.* A concise guide to the multitude of movements that constituted the Russian avant-garde, prior to the imposition of the dead hand of Socialist Realism.

George Heard Hamilton *The Art and Architecture of Russia.* An exhaustive rundown of the major trends in painting, sculpture and architecture, from the Kievan Rus to the turn of this century.

Geir Kjetsaa *Fyodor Dostoyevsky: A Writer's Life*. Readable yet scholarly, this is the best one-volume biography of Russia's most famous writer, by a Finnish academic.

Jay Leyda *Kino* (o/p). A weighty history of Soviet film up until the early 1980s.

Artemy Troitsky *Back in the USSR: The True Story of Rock in Russia* and *Tsusovka: Who's Who in the New Soviet Rock Culture*. Two first-hand accounts of 30 years of rock music in Russia, by the country's leading music journalist and critic, who later edited the Russian edition of *Playboy* magazine and is now a director at state television.

A.N. Wilson *Tolstoy*. Heavyweight but immensely readable biography of the great novelist and appalling family man.

Russian fiction and poetry

Boris Akunin *The Winter Queen*. Wildly popular in Russia at present, Akunin's detective stories set in Pushkin's time are being promoted abroad in translation, but have yet to inspire the same rapture, and are slated at home by some critics as shallow pastiches.

Mikhail Bulgakov *The Master and Margarita; The Heart of the Dog; The White Guard. The Master and Margarita* is a brilliant satire about Satanic deeds in Moscow, entwined with the story of Pontius Pilate. Unpublished in Bulgakov's lifetime, it became *the* cult novel of the Brezhnev era. *The Heart of the Dog* is an earlier, trenchant allegory on the folly of Bolshevism, while *The White Guard* is a sympathetic portrayal of a monarchist family in Kiev during the Civil War. Stalin so enjoyed the play of the last that Bulgakov was spared during the purges.

Fyodor Dostoyevsky *Crime and Punishment; Notes from the Underground; Poor Folk and Other Stories; The Brothers Karamazov; The Gambler; The House of the Dead; The Idiot; The Possessed*. Pessimistic, brooding tales, often semi-autobiographical (particularly *The Gambler* and *The House of the Dead*). Though few of them are set in Moscow, their atmosphere is evocative of life there in the past.

Boris Pasternak *Doctor Zhivago*. A multi-layered story of love and destiny, war and revolution, for which Pasternak was awarded the Nobel Prize for Literature, but forced to decline it. Russians regard him as a poet first and a novelist second. His *dacha* and grave outside Moscow are revered (see p.303).

Victor Pelevin *A Werewolf Problem in Central Russia and Other Stories; Omon Ra; The Blue Lantern: Stories; Buddha's Little Finger; The Life of Insects; The Clay Machine-Gun*. Digital-age fables by the literary voice of Russia's "Generation P", for whom Pepsi, not the Party, set the tone. Essential reading.

Anatoli Rybakov *Children of the Arbat; Fear; Heavy Sand*. Rybakov's prolix trilogy traces the lives of a dozen Muscovites through the era of the show trials, the Great Terror and the war. Its portrait of Stalin is compelling.

Nina Sadur *Witch's Tears and Other Stories*. Strikingly original tales of late Soviet times and afterwards, by one of the best writers in Moscow today. Pain and loss are at the heart of them, whether it's the legacy of Chernobyl, emigration to Israel, or Gagarin's mother, talking to her long-dead son.

Alexander Solzhenitsyn *August 1914* and *Cancer Ward*; *First Circle*; *The Gulag Archipelago*; *One Day in the Life of Ivan Denisovich*. The last two books listed here constitute a stunning indictment of the camps and the purges, for which Russia's most famous modern dissident was exiled abroad in 1974; he returned to live in Russia twenty years later.

Lev Tolstoy *Anna Karenina* and *War and Peace*. The latter is the ultimate epic novel, tracing the fortunes of dozens of characters over decades. Its depiction of the Patriotic War of 1812 cast common folk in a heroic mould, while the main, aristocratic characters are flawed – an idealization of the masses that made *War and Peace* politically acceptable in Soviet times.

Venedikt Yerofeev *Moscow Stations*. An underground classic of the Brezhnev era (known to Russians as *Moskva–Petushki*), its 1995 stage adaptation was a hit in London with Tom Courtenay in the role of Venya, whose alcoholic odyssey from Kursk Station to Petushki has the profundity of *Ulysses* and the tragi-comedy of Gogol.

Yevgeny Yevtushenko *Don't Die Before You're Dead*. Better known as a poet, Yevtushenko's second novel is a melodramatic *roman à clef* of the 1991 putsch, in which Yevtushenko himself makes an appearance, to recite his "very best bad poem" from the balcony of the White House.

Foreign fiction

Alan Brien *Lenin – The Novel* (o/p). Brilliant evocation of Lenin's life and character, in the form of a diary by the man himself, every page of which conveys his steely determination and sly irascibility.

George Feifer *Moscow Farewell*; *The Girl From Petrovka*. Two bittersweet tales of involvement in Moscow lowlife, based on the American author's own experiences as an exchange student. Laced with sex in a very 1970s way.

Robert Littell *Mother Russia*; *The Debriefing*. One is a piquant comedy about a manic black-marketeer who moves into a commune in "the last wooden house in central Moscow" and becomes a pawn of the KGB and CIA; the other a more conventional tale of espionage with an equally odd cast of Muscovite characters. Two early works by America's foremost spy novelist.

Emanuel Litvinov *A Death Out of Season*; *Blood on the Snow*; *The Face of Terror*. A moving epic trilogy that follows a disparate group of revolutionaries from Edwardian Whitechapel to the cellars of the Lubyanka. The second and third volumes are partly set in Moscow.

Stuart M. Kaminsky *A Fine Red Rain*; *A Cold Red Sunrise*; *The Man Who Walked Like A Bear*. Three Soviet police procedurals starring the weightlifting Inspector Rostnkiov. Self-consciously modelled on Ed McBain's *87th Precinct* series, and just as formulaic.

Fridrikh Neznansky & Edward Topol *Red Square*; *Deadly Games*; *The Fair at Sokolniki*. Another trio in the same genre, by two Russian crime writers who missed out on the success now enjoyed in their homeland by Alexandra Marinina and Nikolai Leonov, by emigrating in the Gorbachev years.

Martin Cruz Smith *Gorky Park*; *Polar Star*; *Red Square*. A trio of atmospheric thrillers featuring the maverick homicide detective Arkady Renko. The first was deservedly acclaimed for its evocation of Moscow in the Era of Stagnation; the second finds Renko in exile aboard an Arctic trawler; and the third returns him to Moscow in time for the putsch of 1991.

Boris Starling *Vodka*. Crime, corruption and – of course – vodka turn the head of an American banker stationed in Moscow, who falls in love with the gangster owner of a distillery. Its wealth of secondary detail adds to its appeal.

Jonathan Treitel *The Red Cabbage Café*. Amusing story of an English idealist working on the Moscow metro in the 1920s, which turns darkly surreal and ends with a savage twist. Good holiday reading.

Language

Language

Language

The official language of the Russian Federation is Russian (*russkiy yazik*), a highly complex eastern Slav tongue. Any attempt to speak Russian will be appreciated, though don't be discouraged if people seem not to understand, as most will be unaccustomed to hearing foreigners stumble through their language. English and German are the most common second languages, especially among the younger generation. Bilingual signs and menus are fairly common in the heart of the city, but being able to read the Cyrillic alphabet makes life a lot easier. For a fuller linguistic rundown than the one below, buy the Rough Guide *Russian Phrasebook*, set out dictionary-style for easy access, with English–Russian and Russian–English sections, cultural tips for tricky situations and a menu reader.

The Cyrillic alphabet

The Cyrillic alphabet – derived from a system invented by Saints Cyril and Methodius, the "Apostles of the Slavs" – is an obstacle that's hard to get around, and is worth trying to learn if you're going to be in Russia for more than a few days. Seven of the 33 letters represent approximately the same sound as they do in the Roman alphabet; others are taken from the Greek alphabet, or are unique to the Slavonic languages. It's often possible to decipher the names of streets or metro stations by focusing on the letters you can recognize, but this won't get you far in other situations. Where signs are bilingual, you'll notice variations in **transliterating** Cyrillic into Latin script (for example "Chajkovskogo" or "Chaykovskovo" for Чайковского). In this book, we've used the English System, with a few modifications to help pronunciation. All proper names appear as they are best known, not as they would be transliterated; for example "Tchaikovsky" not "Chaykovskiy".

The box on p.450 gives the Cyrillic characters in upper- and lower-case form, followed simply by the Latin equivalent. In order to pronounce the words properly, you'll need to consult the pronunciation guide below.

Pronunciation

English-speakers often find Russian difficult to pronounce, partly because even letters that appear to have English equivalents are subtly different. On the other hand, Russian spelling is more phonetically consistent than English and the vast majority of words contain no silent letters. The most important factor that determines pronunciation is stress; if you get this wrong, even the simplest Russian words may be misunderstood. Attuning your ear to how stress affects pronunciation is more useful than striving to master Russian grammar (which shares many features with Latin).

Cyrillic characters

Аа	a	Лл	l	Чч	ch
Бб	b	Мм	m	Шш	sh
Вв	v	Нн	n	Щщ	shch
Гг	g*	Оо	o	Ыы	y*
Дд	d	Пп	p	Ээ	e
Ее	e*	Рр	r	Яя	ya
Ёё	e	Сс	s	Ьь	a silent "soft sign" which softens the preceding consonant
Жж	zh	Тт	t		
Зз	z	Уу	u		
Ии	i	Фф	f	Ъъ	a silent "hard sign" which keeps the preceding consonant hard*
Йй	y	Хх	kh		
Кк	k	Цц	ts		

*To aid pronunciation and readability, we have introduced a handful of **exceptions** to the above transliteration guide:

Гг (g) is written as v when pronounced as such, for example Горкого – Gorkovo.

Ее (e) is written as Ye when at the beginning of a word, for example Елагин – Yelagin.

Ыы (y) is written as i, when it appears immediately before q (y), for example Литейный – Liteyniy.

To confuse matters further, **handwritten Cyrillic** is different again from the printed Cyrillic above – although the only place you're likely to encounter it is on menus. The chief differences are:

б which looks similar to a "d"

г which looks similar to a backwards "s"

и which looks like a "u"

т which looks similar to an "m"

Vowels and word stress

Unlike some Slavonic languages, the stress in a word can fall on any syllable and there's no way of knowing simply by looking at it – it's something you just have to learn, as you do in English. If a word has only one syllable, you can't get it wrong; where there are two or more, we've placed accents over the stressed vowel/syllable, though these do not appear in Russian itself. Once you've located the stressed syllable, you should give it more weight than all the others and far more than you would in English.

Whether a **vowel** is stressed or unstressed sometimes affects the way it's pronounced, most notably with the letter "o" (see below).

а – a – like the *a* in father

я – ya – like the *ya* in yarn, but like the *e* in evil when it appears before a stressed syllable

Ээ – e – always a short *e* as in get

е – e – like the *ye* in yes

и – i – like the *e* in evil

й – y – like the *y* in boy

о – o – like the *o* in port when stressed, but like the *a* in plan when unstressed

ё – e – like the *yo* in yonder. Note that in Russia this letter is often printed without the dots

у – u – like the *oo* in moon

ю – yu – like the *u* in universe

ы – y – like the *i* in ill, but with the tongue drawn back

Consonants

In Russian, **consonants** can be either soft or hard and this difference is an important feature of a "good" accent, but if you're simply trying to get by in the language, you needn't worry. The main features of consonants are:

б – b – like the *b* in bad; at the end of a word like the *p* in dip

в – v – like the *v* in van but with the upper teeth behind the top of the lower lip; at the end of a word, and before certain consonants like *f* in leaf

г – g – like the *g* in goat; at the end of a word like the *k* in lark

д – d – like the *d* in dog but with the tongue pressed against the back of the upper teeth; at the end of a word like the *t* in salt

ж – zh – like the s in pleasure; at the end of a word like the *sh* in bush

з – z – like the *z* in zoo; at the end of a word like the s in loose

л – l – like the *l* in milk, but with the tongue kept low and touching the back of the upper teeth

н – n – like the *n* in no but with the tongue pressed against the upper teeth

р – r – trilled as the Scots speak it

с – s – always as in soft, never as in sure

т – t – like the *t* in tent, but with the tongue brought up against the upper teeth

х – kh – like the *ch* in the Scottish loch

ц – ts – like the *ts* in boats

ч – ch – like the *ch* in chicken

ш – sh – like the *sh* in shop

щ – shch – like the *sh-ch* in fresh cheese

There are of course exceptions to the above pronunciation rules, but if you remember even the ones mentioned, you'll be understood.

Words and phrases

Basics

Yes	*da*	да
No	*net*	нет
Please	*pozháluysta*	пожалуйста
Thank you	*spasíbo*	спасибо
Excuse me	*izvinite*	извините
Sorry	*prostíte*	простите
That's OK/it doesn't matter	*nichevó*	ничего
Hello/goodbye (formal)	*zdrávstvuyte/do svidániya*	здравствуйтеюдо свидания
Good day	*dóbriy den*	добрый день
Good morning	*dóbroe útro*	доброе утро
Good evening	*dóbriy vécher*	добрый вечер
Good night	*spokóynoy nochi*	спокойной ночи
See you later (informal)	*poká*	пока
Bon voyage	*schastlívovo putí*	счастливого пути
Bon appetit	*priyátnovo appetíta*	приятного аппетита
How are you?	*kak delá*	как дела
Fine/OK	*khoroshó*	хорошо
Go away!	*ostavte menya!*	оставте меня
Help!	*na pómoshch*	на помощь
Today	*sevódnya*	сегодня
Yesterday	*vcherá*	вчера
Tomorrow	*závtra*	завтра
The day after tomorrow	*poslezávtra*	послезавтра
Now	*seychás*	сейчас
Later	*popózzhe*	попозже
This one	*éta*	это
A little	*nemnógo*	немного
Large/small	*bolshóy/málenkiy*	большойюмаленький

More/less	*yeshché/ménshe*	ещёюменьше
Good/bad	*khoróshiy/plokhóy*	хорошийюплохой
Hot/cold	*goryáchiy/kholódniy*	горячийюхолодный
With/without	*s/bez*	сюбез

Pronouns, names and introductions

Normally, you should use the **polite form** вы (*vy*, "you" plural) in conversation. The informal ты (*ty*, "you" singular) is for children, close friends and relatives (before the Revolution, the ruling classes also used it to serfs, servants and conscripts). Older Russians often introduce themselves and address others using their first name and **patronymic**, eg. Maria Fyodorovna (Maria, daughter of Fyodor) or Anton Ivanovich (Anton, son of Ivan). At some stage they may suggest that you use their first name only, or begin using *ty* to each other. This is usually a good sign, but remember that such informality isn't appreciated at a business meeting (a Russian boss might call his colleagues by their first names, but they would certainly use his patronymic, too).

I	*ya*	я
you (singular)	*ty*	ты
we	*my*	мы
he, she, it	*on, ona, ono*	он она оно
you (plural)	*vy*	вы
they	*oni*	они
What's your name?	*kak vas zovut?*	как вас зовут?
My name is…	*menya zovut…*	меня зовут
Pleased to meet you	*ochen priyatno*	очень приятно

Getting around

Over there	*tam*	там
Round the corner	*za uglóm*	за углом
Left/right	*nalévo/naprávo*	налевоюнаправо
Straight on	*pryámo*	прямо
Where is … ?	*gde*	где
How do I get to the Arbat?	*kak proíti na Arbat*	как пройти на АрбатЮ
Am I going the right way for the Tretyakov?	*ya právilno idú k Tretyakóvke?*	я правилно иду к ТретяковкеЮ
Is it far?	*etó dalekó?*	то далеко?
By bus	*avtóbusom*	автобусом
By train	*póezdom*	поездом
By car	*na mashine*	на ма шине
On foot	*peshkóm*	пешком
By taxi	*na taksi*	на такси
Ticket	*bilét*	билет
Return (ticket)	*tudá i obrátno*	туда и обратно
Train station	*vokzál*	вокзал
Bus station	*avtóbusniy vokzal*	автобусный вокзал
Bus stop	*ostanóvka*	остановка
Is this train going to Vladimir?	*étot póezd idét vo Vladimir?*	тот поезд идёт во Владимир?
Do I have to change?	*núzhno sdélat peresádku?*	нужно сделать перес адку?
Small change (money)	*meloch*	мелочь

Questions and answers

Do you speak English?	*Vy govoríte po-anglíyski?*	вы говорите по-англ ийски?
I don't speak German	*ya ne govoryú po-nemétsky*	я не говорю по-немецки
I don't understand	*ya ne ponimáyu*	я не понимаю
I understand	*ya ponimáyu*	я понимаю
Speak slowly	*govoríte pomédlenee*	говорите помедленее
I don't know	*ya ne znáyu*	я не знаю
How do you say that in Russian?	*kak po-rússki?*	как по-русски?
Could you write it down?	*zapishíte éto pozháluysta?*	запишите это пожалуйста?
What …	*chto*	что
Where	*gde*	где
When	*kogdá*	когда
Why	*pochemú*	почему
Who	*kto*	кто
How much is it?	*skólko stóit*	сколько стоит?
I would like a double room	*ya khochú nómer na dvoíkh*	я хочу номер на двоих
For one night	*tólko sútki*	только сутки
Shower	*dush*	душ
Are these seats free?	*svobódno?*	свободно?
May I … ?	*mózhno?*	можно?
You can't/it is not allowed	*nelzyá*	нельзя
The bill please	*schet pozháluysta*	счёт пожалуйста
Do you have … ?	*u vas yest*	у вас есть?
That's all	*eto vsé*	это всё
Entrance	*vkhod*	вход
Exit	*vZkhod*	выход
Toilet	*stualét*	туалет
Men's	*múzhi*	мужской
Women's	*zhény*	женский
Pull (a door)	*k sebe*	к себе
Push (a door)	*ot sebya*	от себя
Open	*otkrýto*	открыто
Closed (for repairs)	*zakrýto (na remont)*	закрыто на ремонт
Out of order	*ne rabótaet*	не раБотает
No entry	*vkhóda net*	входа нет
Danger zone	*opasnaya zona*	опасная зона
No smoking	*ne kurít*	не курить
Drinking water	*pitеváya vodá*	питьевая вода
Information	*správka*	справка
Ticket office	*kássa*	касса

Days of the week

Monday	*ponedélnik*	понедельник
Tuesday	*vtórnik*	вторник
Wednesday	*sredá*	среда
Thursday	*chetvérg*	четверг
Friday	*pyátnitsa*	пятница
Saturday	*subbóta*	суббота
Sunday	*voskresénе*	воскресенье

Months of the year

January	*yanvár*	январь
February	*fevrál*	февраль
March	*mart*	март
April	*aprél*	апрель
May	*may*	май
June	*iyún*	июнь
July	*iyúl*	июль
August	*ávgust*	август
September	*sentyábr*	сентябрь
October	*oktyábr*	октябрь
November	*noyábr*	ноябрь
December	*dekábr*	декабрь

Numbers

1	*odín*	один
2	*dva*	два
3	*tri*	три
4	*chetýre*	четыре
5	*pyat*	пять
6	*shest*	шесть
7	*sem*	семь
8	*vósem*	восемь
9	*dévyat*	девять
10	*désyat*	десять
11	*odínnadtsat*	одиннадцать
12	*dvenádtsat*	двенадцать
13	*trinádtsat*	тринадцать
14	*chetýrnadtsat*	четырнадцать
15	*pyatnádtsat*	пятнадцать
16	*shestnádtsat*	шестнадцать
17	*semnádtsat*	семнадцать
18	*vosemnádtsat*	восемнадцать
19	*devyatnádtsat*	девятнадцать
20	*dvádtsat*	двадцать
21	*dvádtsat odín*	двадцать один
30	*trídtsat*	тридцать
40	*sórok*	сорок
50	*pyatdesyát*	пятьдесят
60	*shestdesyát*	шестьдесят
70	*sémdesyat*	семьдесят
80	*vósemdesyat*	восемьдесят
90	*devyanósto*	девяносто
100	*sto*	сто
200	*dvésti*	двести
300	*trísta*	триста
400	*chetýresta*	четыреста
500	*pyatsót*	пятьсот
600	*shestsót*	шестьсот
700	*semsót*	семьсот
800	*vosemsót*	восемьсот

900	*devyatsót*	девятьсот
1000	*týsyacha*	тысяча
2000	*dve týsyachi*	две тысячи
3000	*tri týsyachi*	три тысячи
4000	*chetýre týsyachi*	четыре тысячи
5000	*pyat týsyach*	пять тысяч
10,000	*désyat týsyach*	десять тысяч
50,000	*pyatdesyát týsyach*	пятьдесят тысяч

Food and drink terms

Basics

аджика	*adzhíka*	spicy Georgian relish
бутерброд	*buterbrod*	open sandwich
ч%ка	*cháshka*	cup
десерт	*desért*	dessert
фрукты	*frúkty*	fruit
горчица	*gorchítsa*	mustard
хлеб	*khleb*	bread
ложка	*lózhka*	spoon
масло	*máslo*	butter/oil
мёд	*myod*	honey
молоко	*molokó*	milk
мясо	*myáso*	meat
напиток	*napitok*	drinks
нож	*nozh*	knife
обед	*obéd*	main meal/ lunch
овощи	*ovoshchi*	vegetables
пицца	*pizza*	pizza
рис	*ris*	rice
перец	*pérets*	pepper
плов	*plov*	pilau
пирог	*piróg*	pie
рыба	*ryba*	fish
сахар	*sákhar*	sugar
салат	*salat*	salad
сметана	*smetána*	sour cream
соль	*sol*	salt
суп	*soup*	soup
стакан	*stakán*	glass
тарелка	*tarélka*	plate
ужин	*úzhin*	supper
вилка	*vílka*	fork
яйца	*yáytsa*	eggs

яичница	*yaichnitsa*	fried egg
завтрак	*zavtrak*	breakfast
закуски	*zakúski*	appetizers

Appetizers (zakuski) and salads

ассорти мясное	*assortí myasnóe*	assorted meats
ассорти рыбное	*assortí rybnoe*	assorted fish
бастурма	*basturma*	marinated dried meat
блины	*bliny*	pancakes
блинчики	*blinchiki*	bliny rolled around a filling and browned
брынза	*brynza*	salty white cheese
грибы	*griby*	mushrooms
икра баклажанная	*ikrá baklazhánnaya*	aubergine (eggplant) purée
икра красная	*ikrá krásnaya*	red caviar
икра чёрная	*ikrá chornaya*	black caviar
хачапури	*khachapuri*	Georgian nan-style bread, stuffed with cheese
хачапури по-Мингрелский	*khachapuri po-Mingrelskiy*	khachapuri cooked with an egg in the middle
колбаса копчёная	*kolbasá kopchonaya*	smoked sausage
маслины	*maslíny*	olives
морков по-корейский	*morkov po-koreyskiy*	spicy carrot salad
огурцы	*ogurtsy*	gherkins
осетрина с майонезом	*osetrína s mayonézom*	sturgeon mayonnaise
пельмени	*pelmeni*	Siberian ravioli
салат из огурцов	*salat iz ogurtsóv*	cucumber salad
салат из помидоров	*salát iz pomidórov*	tomato salad
сардины с лимоном	*sardíny s limónom*	sardines with lemon
сельдь	*seld*	herring
селёдка под шубы	*selyodka pod shuby*	pickled herring with beetroot, carrot, egg and mayonnaise
шпроты	*shpróty*	sprats (like a herring)
столичный салат	*stolíchniy salát*	meat and vegetable salad
сыр	*syr*	cheese
ветчина	*vetchiná*	ham
винегрет	*vinegrét*	Russian salad
язык с гарниром	*yazyk s garnórom*	tongue with garnish

Soups

борщ	*borsch*	beetroot soup
бульон	*bulón*	consommé
чихиртми	*chikhirtmi*	lemon-flavoured chicken soup
харчо	*kharcho*	spicy beef or lamb soup

хаш	*khásh*	tripe soup, traditionally drunk as a hang-over cure
клёцки	*klyotski*	Belorussian soup with dumplings
лапша	*lapsha*	chicken-noodle soup
окрошка	*okróshka*	cold vegetable soup
постный борщ	*póstny borsch*	borsch without meat
рассольник	*rassólnik*	brine and cucumber soup
щи	*shchi*	cabbage soup
солянка	*solyánka*	spicy, meaty soup flavoured with lemon and olives
уха	*ukhá*	fish soup

Meat dishes

азу из говядины	*azú iz govyádiny*	beef stew
антрекот	*antrekot*	entrecôte steak
баранина	*baránina*	mutton/lamb
бастурма	*basturma*	thinly sliced, marinated, dried meat
бифстроганов	*bifstróganov*	beef stroganoff
биточки	*bitóchki*	meatballs
бифштекс	*bifshtéks*	beef steak
булкоги	*bulkogi*	spicy stir-fried marinated beef
чахохбили	*chakhokhbili*	slow-cooked chicken with herbs and vegetables
казы	*kazy*	pony-meat sausages
хинкали	*khinkali*	dumplings stuffed with lamb, or beef and pork
котлеты по-киевски	*kotléty po-kíevski*	chicken Kiev
кролик	*królik*	rabbit
курица	*kúritsa*	chicken
рагу	*ragú*	stew
сациви	*satsivi*	chicken in walnut sauce, served cold
шашлык	*shashlyk*	kebab
свинина	*svinína*	pork
телятина	*telyátina*	veal
сосиски	*sosíski*	frankfurter sausages
котлета	*kotlet*	fried meatball

Fish

форель	*forel*	trout
карп	*karp*	carp
лещ	*leshch*	bream
лососина	*lososóna*	salmon
осетрина	*osetrina*	sturgeon

щука	*shchúka*	pike
скумбрия	*skúmbriya*	mackerel
треска	*treská*	chub
сёмга	*syomga*	salmon
судак	*sudak*	pike perch

Vegetables and herbs

баклажан	*baklazhán*	aubergine (eggplant)
чеснок	*chisnok*	garlic
гарниры	*garniry*	any vegetable garnish
горох	*gorókh*	peas
грибы	*griby*	mushrooms
грибы с сметаной	*griby s smentanoy*	mushrooms cooked with sour cream
капуста	*kapústa*	cabbage
картофель	*kartófel*	potatoes
кимичи	*kimichi*	spicy, garlicky pickled cabbage
кинза	*kinza*	coriander
лобио	*lóbio*	red or green bean stew
лук	*luk*	onions
мхали	*mkhali*	beetroot or spinach purée with herbs and walnuts
морковь	*morkóv*	carrots
огурцы	*ogurtsy*	cucumbers
петрушка	*petrushka*	parsley
помидор	*pomidór*	tomato
редиска	*redíska*	radishes
салат	*salát*	lettuce
свёкла	*svyokla*	beetroot
толма	*tolma*	tomatoes, aubergines or vine leaves stuffed with meat and rice
укроп	*ukrop*	dill
зелень	*zélen*	fresh herbs

Fruit

абрикосы	*abrikósy*	apricots
апельсины	*apelsíny*	oranges
арбуз	*arbúz*	watermelon
банан	*banan*	banana
чернослив	*chernoslív*	prunes
дыня	*dynya*	melon
финики	*fíniki*	dates
груши	*grushi*	pears
инжир	*inzhír*	figs
лимон	*limón*	lemon
сливы	*slivy*	plums

виноград	*vinográd*	grapes
вишня	*víshnya*	cherries
яблоки	*yábloki*	apples
ягоды	*yágody*	berries

Common terms

фаршированные	*farshiróvannye*	stuffed
фри	*fri*	fried
копчёные	*kopchonye*	smoked
маринованные	*marinóvannye*	pickled or marinated
паровые	*parovye*	steamed
печёные	*pechonye*	baked
отварные	*otvarnye*	boiled
овощной	*ovoshchnoy*	made from vegetables
на вертеле	*na vertele*	grilled on a skewer
с грибами	*s gribami*	with mushrooms
солёные	*solyonye*	salted
со сметаной	*so smetánoy*	with sour cream
тушёные	*tushonye*	stewed
варёные	*varyonye*	boiled
жареные	*zhárenye*	roast/grilled/fried

Drinks

чай	*chay*	tea
кофе	*kófe*	coffee
с сахаром	*s sakharom*	with sugar
без сахар	*bez sákhara*	without sugar
сок	*sok*	fruit juice
кефир	*kefir*	the Russian equivalent of lassi
квас	*kvas*	a drink made from fermented rye
мёд	*myod*	honey mead
сбитен	*sbiten*	a herbal liquor
тархун	*tarkhun*	a tarragon-flavoured drink
пиво	*pívo*	beer
вино	*vinó*	wine
красное	*krásnoe*	red
белое	*béloe*	white
бутылка	*butylka*	bottle
лёд	*lyod*	ice
минеральная вода	*minerálnaya vodá*	mineral water
водка	*vódka*	vodka
вода	*vodá*	water
шампанское	*shampánskoe*	champagne
брют	*bryut*	extra dry
сухое	*sukhoe*	dry

полусухое	*polsukhóe*	medium dry
сладкое	*sládkoe*	sweet
коньяк	*konyák*	cognac
за здоровье	*za zdaróve*	cheers!

A glossary of Russian words and terms

The accents on Russian words below signify which syllable is stressed, but they are not used in the main text of this book.

bánya bathhouse
báshnya tower
bulvár boulevard
dácha country cottage
dom kultúry communal arts and social centre; literally "house of culture"
dvoréts palace
górod town
kassa ticket office
kládbishche cemetery
kommunalka communal flat, where several tenants or families share a bathroom, kitchen and corridor
krépost fortress
kréml citadel that formed the nucleus of most Russian towns, including Moscow – from this foreigners coined the name "Kremlin"
lavra the highest rank of monastery in the Orthodox Church
monastyr monastery or convent; the distinction is made by specifying whether it is a *muzhskiy* (men's) or *zhenskiy* (women's) *monastyr*
móst bridge
múzhik before the Revolution it meant a peasant; nowadays it means masculine or macho
náberezhnaya embankment
óstrov island
ózero lake
pámyatnik monument
pereúlok lane
plóshchad square
prospékt avenue
reká river
restorán restaurant
rússkiy/rússkaya Russian
rýnok market
sad garden/park
shossé highway
sobór cathedral
teátr theatre
tsérkov church
úlitsa street
vokzál train station
výstavka exhibition
zal room or hall
zámok castle

An art and architectural glossary

Art Nouveau French term for the sinuous and stylized form of architecture dating from the turn of the twentieth century to World War I; known as Style Moderne in Russia.

Atlantes Supports in the form of carved male figures, used instead of columns to support an entablature.

Baroque Exuberant architectural style of the seventeenth and early eighteenth centuries, which spread to Russia via Ukraine and Belarus. Characterized by ornate decoration, complex spatial arrangement and grand vistas. See "Moscow" and "Naryshkin" Baroque on p.462.

Caryatids Sculpted female figures used as a column to support an entablature.

Constructivism Soviet version of modernism that pervaded all the arts during the 1920s. In architecture, functionalism and simplicity were the watchwords – though many Constructivist projects were utterly impractical and never got beyond the drawing board.

Deesis row The third tier of an iconostasis (see p.462), whose central icon depicts Christ in Majesty.

Empire Style Richly decorative version of the Neoclassical style, which prevailed in Russia from 1812 to the 1840s. The French and Russian Empire styles both drew inspiration from Imperial Rome.

Entablature The part of a building supported by a colonnade or column.

Faux marbre Any surface painted to resemble marble.

Fresco Mural painting applied to wet plaster, so that the colours bind chemically with it as they dry.

Futurism Avant-garde art movement glorifying machinery, war, speed and the modern world in general.

Grisaille Painting in grey or other coloured monotone used to represent objects in relief.

Icon Religious image, usually painted on wood and framed upon an iconostasis. See p.215 for more about Russian icons.

Iconostasis A screen that separates the sanctuary from the nave in Orthodox churches, typically consisting of tiers of icons in a gilded frame, with up to three doors that open during services. The central one is known as the Royal Door.

Kokóshniki A purely decorative form of gable that evolved from *zakomary* (see p.463). Semicircular or ogee-shaped, they are often massed in a kind of pyramid below the spire or cupola.

Moscow Baroque Distinctly Russian form of Baroque that prevailed from the 1630s to the 1690s. Churches in this style are often wildly colourful and asymmetrical, with a profusion of tent-roofed spires and onion domes, *kokoshniki* and *nalichniki*.

Nalichniki Mouldings framing a window with pilasters, a scrolled or triangular entablature, and a scalloped or fretted ledge. A leitmotif of Moscow Baroque architecture.

Narthex Vestibule(s) preceding the nave of a church, which are strictly categorized as an esonarthex (if inside the main walls) or an exonarthex (if outside) – many Russian churches had both, to retain warmth. Also see "Refectory", below.

Naryshkin Baroque Late style of Moscow Baroque promoted by the Naryshkin family, characterized by monumental red-brick structures decorated with white stone crenellations and *nalichniki*.

Nave The part of a church where the congregation stands (there are no pews in Orthodox churches). Usually preceded by a narthex.

Neoclassical Late eighteenth- and early nineteenth-century style of architecture and design, returning to classical Greek and Roman models as a reaction against Baroque and Rococo excesses.

Neo-Russian (or Pseudo-Russian) Style of architecture and decorative arts that drew inspiration from Russia's medieval and ancient past, its folk arts and myths. This rejection of Western styles was part of a broader Slavophile movement during the late nineteenth century.

Ogee A shape like the cross-section of an onion, widely found in Russian architecture in the form of gables or arches.

Okhlad Chased metal covering for an icon that left uncovered only the figure of the saint (or sometimes just their face and hands). Usually of gold or silver and studded with gems.

Pendant (or Pendule) An elongated boss hanging down from the apex of an arch, often used for decorative effect.

Pilaster A half-column projecting only slightly from the wall; an engaged column stands almost free from the surface.

Podvóre An irregular ensemble of dwellings, stables and outbuildings, enclosing a yard. Medieval Moscow was an agglomeration of thousands of *podvore*, of which only a few – built of stone – have survived.

Portico Covered entrance to a building.

Refectory The narthex of a medieval Russian church was called a Refectory (*Trapeznaya*), as monks and pilgrims were fed there.

Sanctuary (or Naos) The area around the altar, which in Orthodox churches is always screened by an iconostasis.

Stalinist Declamatory style of architecture prevailing from the 1930s to the death of Stalin in 1953, which returned to Neoclassical and Gothic models as a reaction against Constructivism, and reached its "High Stalinist" apogee after World War II. Also dubbed "Stalin-Gothic" or "Soviet Rococo". Moscow's seven Stalin skyscrapers epitomize the genre.

Stucco Plaster used for decorative effects.

Style Moderne Linear, stylized form of architecture and decorative arts, influenced by French Art Nouveau, which took its own direction in Russia, where its greatest exponent was the architect Fyodor Shekhtel.

Tent-roof Form of spire shaped like a wigwam, associated with stone churches in Moscow and wooden ones in northern Russia during the sixteenth and seventeenth centuries. Also added to towers, notably those of the Kremlin. The Russian term is *shatyor* (literally, "tent").

Terem The upper tower-chambers of the houses of the nobility and the merchant class in medieval Moscow, where womenfolk were secluded.

Trompe l'oeil Painting designed to fool the onlooker into believing that it is actually three-dimensional.

Zakomary Rounded gables that outwardly reflect the vaulting of a church's interior, supporting the cupola. Typical of early churches from Yaroslavl, Novgorod and Pskov, which influenced Muscovite church architecture in the twelfth and thirteenth centuries.

Historical terms and acronyms

Apparatchiki A catch-all term to describe the Communist Party bureaucrats of the Soviet era.

Bolshevik Literally "majority"; the name given to the faction that supported Lenin during the internal disputes within the RSDLP during the 1900s and afterwards.

Boyars Medieval Russian nobility, whose feuds and intrigues provoked Ivan the Terrible's wrath and caused the Time of Troubles. To diminish their power Peter the Great instituted a new "service" aristocracy of fourteen ranks, open to anyone who served the state.

Cheka (Extraordinary Commission for Struggle against Counter-Revolution, Speculation and Sabotage) Bolshevik Party secret police 1917–1921.

CIS Commonwealth of Independent States – loose grouping that was formed in December 1991 following the collapse of the USSR. All of the former Soviet republics have since joined, with the exception of the Baltic States.

Civil War 1918–21 Took place between the Bolsheviks and an assortment of opposition forces including Mensheviks, Socialist Revolutionaries, Cossacks, Tsarists and foreign interventionist armies from the West and Japan (collectively known as the Whites).

Decembrists Those who participated in the abortive coup against the accession of Nicholas I in December 1825.

Duma The name given to three parliaments in the reign of Nicholas II, and the lower house of the parliament of the Russian Federation since 1993 (its upper chamber is called the Federation Council).

February Revolution Overthrow of the tsar which took place in February 1917.

Five Year Plan Centralized master plan for every branch of the Soviet economy. The First Five Year Plan was promulgated in 1928.

FSB (Federal Security Service) The name of Russia's secret police since 1994.

Golden Horde (Zolotaya Orda) Powerful Tatar state in southern Russia whose threat preoccupied the tsars until the seventeenth century.

Gósplan Soviet State Planning Agency, responsible for devising and overseeing the Five Year Plan. Its goals were set by the Politburo.

GPU (State Political Directorate) Soviet secret police 1921–23.

Gulag (Chief Administration of Corrective Labour Camps) Official title for Siberian hard labour camps set up under Lenin and Stalin.

Hetman Cossack leader.

Kadet Party (Constitutional Democratic Party) Liberal political party 1905–1917.

KGB (Committee of State Security) Soviet secret police 1954–91.

Kuptsy Wealthy merchant class, often of serf ancestry, which rose to prominence in the late nineteenth century.

Menshevik Literally "minority"; the name given to the faction opposing Lenin during the internal disputes within the RSDLP during the 1900s and afterwards.

Metropolitan Senior cleric, ranking between an archbishop and the patriarch of the Russian Orthodox Church.

MVD (Ministry of Internal Affairs) Soviet secret police 1946–54; now runs the regular police (Militia) and the OMON (see p.53).

Naródnaya Vólya (People's Will) Terrorist group that assassinated Alexander II in 1881.

New Russians Brash nouveaux riches of the Yeltsin era, mocked by countless "New Russian" jokes.

NKVD (People's Commissariat of Internal Affairs) Soviet secret police 1934–46.

October Revolution Bolshevik coup d'état which overthrew the Provisional Government in October 1917.

OGPU (Unified State Political Directorate) Soviet secret police 1923–34.

Okhrána Tsarist secret police.

Old Believers (Staroobryadtsy) Russian Orthodox schismatics (see p.257).

Oligarchs Immensely rich and shady financiers and powerbrokers of the post-Soviet era.

OMON Paramilitary force used for riot control and fighting civil wars within the Russian Federation.

Opríchniki Mounted troops used by Ivan the Terrible to terrorize the population and destroy any real or imaginary threat to his rule.

Patriarch The head of the Russian Orthodox Church.

Petrine Anything dating from the lifetime (1672–1725) or reign (1682–1725) of Peter the Great; Pre-Petrine means before then.

Populist Amorphous political movement of the second half of the nineteenth century that advocated socialism based on the peasant commune.

Purges The name used for the mass arrests of the Stalin era, but also for any systematic removal of unwanted elements from positions of authority.

RSDLP (Russian Social Democratic Labour Party) First Marxist political party in Russia, which split into Bolshevik and Menshevik factions.

SR Socialist Revolutionary.

Streltsy Riotous musketeers who formed Moscow's army in Pre-Petrine times. Many were beheaded on Red Square in 1682.

Time of Troubles (Smutnoe vreme) Anarchic period (1605–12) of civil wars and foreign invasions, following the death of Boris Godunov.

Tsar Emperor. The title was first adopted by Ivan the Terrible.

Tsarevich Crown prince.

Tsarevna Daughter of a tsar and tsaritsa.

Tsaritsa Empress; the foreign misnomer tsarina is better known.

USSR Union of Soviet Socialist Republics. Official name of the Soviet Union from 1923 to 1991.

Whites Generic term for Tsarist or Kadet forces during the Civil War, which the Bolsheviks applied to almost anyone who opposed them.

Small print and Index

A Rough Guide to Rough Guides

Published in 1982, the first Rough Guide – to Greece – was a student scheme that became a publishing phenomenon. Mark Ellingham, a recent graduate in English from Bristol University, had been travelling in Greece the previous summer and couldn't find the right guidebook. With a small group of friends he wrote his own guide, combining a highly contemporary, journalistic style with a thoroughly practical approach to travellers' needs.

The immediate success of the book spawned a series that rapidly covered dozens of destinations. And, in addition to impecunious backpackers, Rough Guides soon acquired a much broader and older readership that relished the guides' wit and inquisitiveness as much as their enthusiastic, critical approach and value-for-money ethos.

These days, Rough Guides include recommendations from shoestring to luxury and cover more than 200 destinations around the globe, including almost every country in the Americas and Europe, more than half of Africa and most of Asia and Australasia. Our ever-growing team of authors and photographers is spread all over the world, particularly in Europe, the USA and Australia.

In the early 1990s, Rough Guides branched out of travel, with the publication of Rough Guides to World Music, Classical Music and the Internet. All three have become benchmark titles in their fields, spearheading the publication of a wide range of books under the Rough Guide name.

Including the travel series, Rough Guides now number more than 350 titles, covering: phrasebooks, waterproof maps, music guides from Opera to Heavy Metal, reference works as diverse as Conspiracy Theories and Shakespeare, and popular culture books from iPods to Poker. Rough Guides also produce a series of more than 120 World Music CDs in partnership with World Music Network.

Visit www.roughguides.com to see our latest publications.

Rough Guide travel images are available for commercial licensing at www.roughguidespictures.com

Rough Guide credits

Text editor: Amanda Tomlin
Layout: Ankur Guha
Cartography: Jasbir Sandhu
Picture editor: Mark Thomas
Production: Rebecca Short
Proofreader: Jan McCann
Cover design: Chloë Roberts
Photographer: Jon Smith
Editorial: **London** Ruth Blackmore, Andy Turner, Keith Drew, Edward Aves, Alice Park, Lucy White, Jo Kirby, James Smart, Natasha Foges, Róisín Cameron, Emma Traynor, James Rice, Emma Gibbs, Kathryn Lane, Christina Valhouli, Monica Woods, Mani Ramaswamy, Alison Roberts, Joe Staines, Peter Buckley, Matthew Milton, Tracy Hopkins, Ruth Tidball; **New York** Andrew Rosenberg, Steven Horak, AnneLise Sorensen, Ella Steim, Anna Owens, Sean Mahoney, Paula Neudorf; **Delhi** Madhavi Singh, Karen D'Souza, Lubna Shaheen
Design & Pictures: **London** Scott Stickland, Dan May, Diana Jarvis, Chloë Roberts, Nicole Newman, Sarah Cummins, Emily Taylor; **Delhi** Umesh Aggarwal, Ajay Verma, Jessica Subramanian, Pradeep Thapliyal, Sachin Tanwar, Anita Singh, Nikhil Agarwal
Production: Vicky Baldwin
Cartography: **London** Maxine Repath, Ed Wright, Katie Lloyd-Jones; **Delhi** Jai Prakash Mishra, Rajesh Chhibber, Ashutosh Bharti, Rajesh Mishra, Animesh Pathak, Karobi Gogoi, Alakananda Bhattacharya, Swati Handoo, Deshpal Dabas
Online: **London** George Atwell, Faye Hellon, Jeanette Angell, Fergus Day, Justine Bright, Clare Bryson, Áine Fearon, Adrian Low, Ezgi Celebi, Amber Bloomfield; **Delhi** Amit Verma, Rahul Kumar, Narender Kumar, Ravi Yadav, Debojit Borah, Rakesh Kumar, Ganesh Sharma, Shisir Basumatari
Marketing & Publicity: **London** Liz Statham, Niki Hanmer, Louise Maher, Jess Carter, Vanessa Godden, Vivienne Watton, Anna Paynton, Rachel Sprackett, Libby Jellie, Holly Dudley; **New York** Geoff Colquitt, Nancy Lambert, Katy Ball; **Delhi** Ragini Govind
Manager India: Punita Singh
Reference Director: Andrew Lockett
Operations Manager: Helen Phillips
PA to Publishing Director: Nicola Henderson
Publishing Director: Martin Dunford
Commercial Manager: Gino Magnotta
Managing Director: John Duhigg

Publishing information

This fifth edition published March 2009 by
Rough Guides Ltd,
80 Strand, London WC2R 0RL
345 Hudson St, 4th Floor,
New York, NY 10014, USA
14 Local Shopping Centre, Panchsheel Park,
New Delhi 110017, India
Distributed by the Penguin Group
Penguin Books Ltd,
80 Strand, London WC2R 0RL
Penguin Group (USA)
375 Hudson Street, NY 10014, USA
Penguin Group (Australia)
250 Camberwell Road, Camberwell,
Victoria 3124, Australia
Penguin Group (Canada)
195 Harry Walker Parkway N, Newmarket, ON,
L3Y 7B3 Canada
Penguin Group (NZ)
67 Apollo Drive, Mairangi Bay, Auckland 1310,
New Zealand

Cover concept by Peter Dyer.
Typeset in Bembo and Helvetica to an original design by Henry Iles.
Printed and bound in China

480pp includes index
A catalogue record for this book is available from the British Library.
ISBN: 978-1-85828-061-5

1 3 5 7 9 8 6 4 2

Help us update

We've gone to a lot of effort to ensure that the fifth edition of **The Rough Guide to Moscow** is accurate and up to date. However, things change – places get "discovered", opening hours are notoriously fickle, restaurants and rooms raise prices or lower standards. If you feel we've got it wrong or left something out, we'd like to know, and if you can remember the address, the price, the hours, the phone number, so much the better.

Please send your comments with the subject line "**Rough Guide Moscow Update**" to ⓔmail@roughguides.com. We'll credit all contributions and send a copy of the next edition (or any other Rough Guide if you prefer) for the very best emails.

Have your questions answered and tell others about your trip at ⓦcommunity.roughguides.com

Acknowledgements

Jonathon Reynolds would like to thank: Diana Safiullina, Nata Safiullina, Inna Verevkina, Kostik Larionov and my wife Lily Yumagulova – without whom much of this research would not have been possible.

Readers' letters

Thanks to all the readers who have taken the time to write in with comments and suggestions (and apologies if we've inadvertently omitted or misspelt anyone's name):

Antony Aston; Gavin Bell; Phil Colley; Christopher Harrison; Elisabeth Major; Fedde Pruiksma; Svetlana Nogai; Leah Sullivan; and Rene van Woerkom.

Photo credits

All photography by Jon Smith © Rough Guides except the following:

Title page
Red Square © PCL/Alamy

Full page
Moscow at night © Gavin Hellier/Getty Images

Introduction
Detail of church painting © Steven Weinberg/Getty Images
Souvenir Stall, Red Square © Naki Kouyioumtzis/Axiom Photo Agency
Police officer and billboards © Simon C Roberts/Axiom Photo Agency
Stained-glass portrait of Lenin © Jim Holmes/Axiom Photo Agency
Space Obelisk © Paul Quayle/Axiom Photo Agency

Things not to miss
02 Gum © Simon C Roberts/Axiom Photo Agency
05 Ballet © Sergio Barrenechea/Corbis
10 A monument to the workers © Paolo Ragazzini/Corbis
12 Red Square © Jochem D Wijnands/Getty Images
13 Clubbing in Moscow © Gueorgui Pinkhassov/Magnum Photos
14 Banya © David Turnley/Corbis
18 Novodevichie Convent © Jon Arnold Images Ltd/Alamy
19 Congregation in Orthodox Church © Dabid Turnley/Corbis

Moscow: the new New York colour section
Model at Moscow Fashion Week © Sergeo Ilnitsky/Corbis
Interior of GUM © Hemis/Axiom Photo Agency
Designer shops © Heather Elton/Axiom Photo Agency
Woman in fur coat © Lawrence Graham/Alamy
Modern apartment buildings © Ivan Vdovin/Corbis

The Moscow metro colour section
Komsomoloskaya metro station © Getty Images
Komsomoloskaya metro station © Martin Thomas Photography/Getty Images

Black and whites
p.250 Kotelnicheskaya apartment building © Iain Masterton/Alamy
p.367 Ballet © John James/Alamy
p.387 VVT's © David Crossland/Alamy
p.396 Hockey © Tatyana Makeyeva © Getty Images

Index

Map entries are in colour.

I INDEX

G

H

I

J

K

INDEX

INDEX

R

S

INDEX

Map symbols

maps are listed in the full index using coloured text

- Chapter boundary
- Provincial boundary
- Road
- Unpaved Road
- Steps
- Path
- River
- Railway
- Wall
- Bridge
- Gorge
- Bus stop
- Metro
- Airport
- Riverboat/Station
- Parking
- Place of Intrest
- Embassy
- Synagogue
- Gardens
- Internet Café
- Tourist Office
- Post Office
- Phone Office
- Gate
- Statue/memorial
- Battlefield
- Church (town maps)
- Building
- Cemetery
- Park/forest
- Beach

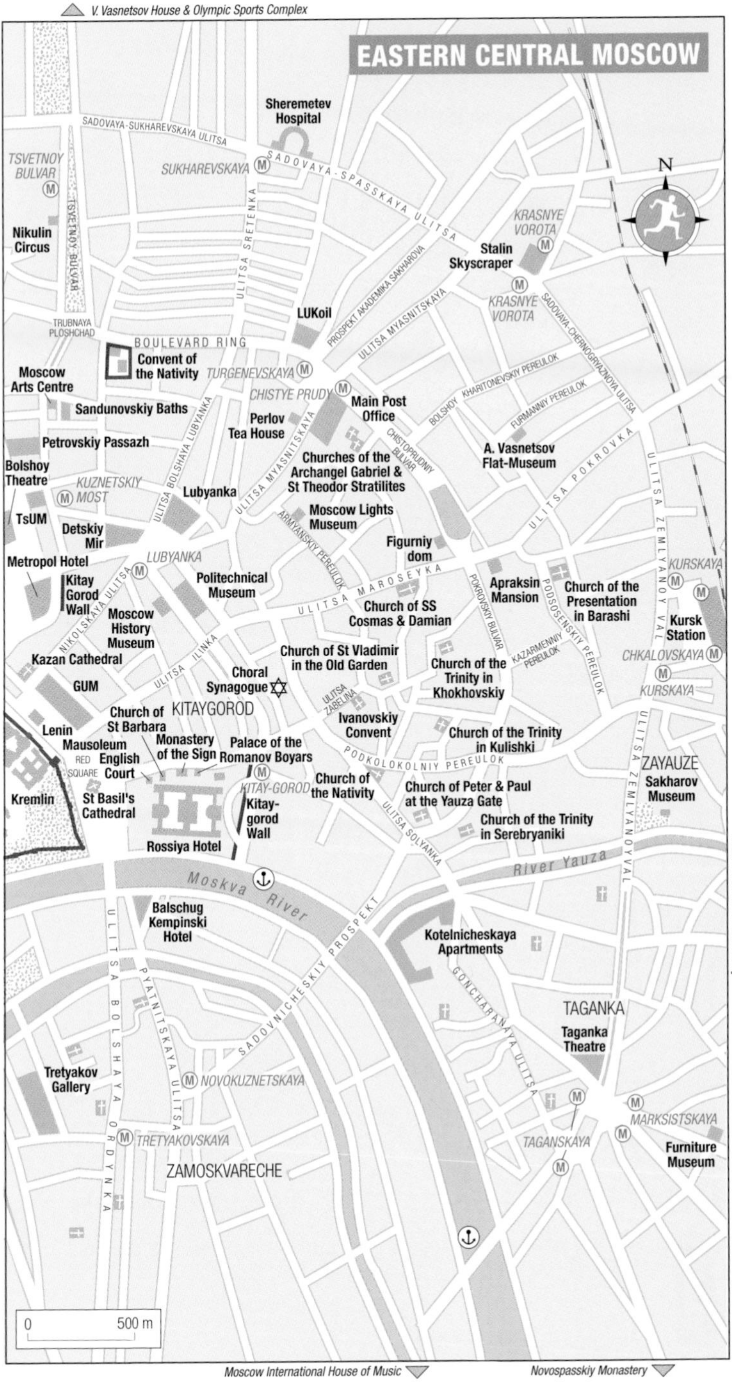

EASTERN CENTRAL MOSCOW

V. Vasnetsov House & Olympic Sports Complex

Sheremetev Hospital
SADOVAYA-SUKHAREVSKAYA ULITSA
SADOVAYA-SPASSKAYA ULITSA
TSVETNOY BULVAR
SUKHAREVSKAYA
TSVETNOY BULVAR
Nikulin Circus
ULITSA SRETENKA
KRASNYE VOROTA
Stalin Skyscraper
PROSPEKT AKADEMIKA SAKHAROVA
ULITSA MYASNITSKAYA
KRASNYE VOROTA
SADOVAYA-CHERNOGRYAZNOVA ULITSA
LUKoil
TRUBNAYA PLOSHCHAD
BOULEVARD RING
Convent of the Nativity
TURGENEVSKAYA
Moscow Arts Centre
CHISTYE PRUDY
Main Post Office
BOLSHOY KHARITONEVSKIY PEREULOK
FURMANNIY PEREULOK
Sandunovskiy Baths
Perlov Tea House
CHISTOPRUDNIY BULVAR
A. Vasnetsov Flat-Museum
Petrovskiy Passazh
ULITSA BOLSHAYA LUBYANKA
Churches of the Archangel Gabriel & St Theodor Stratilites
ULITSA POKROVKA
Bolshoy Theatre
KUZNETSKIY MOST
Lubyanka
ULITSA MYASNITSKAYA
ULITSA ZEMLYANOY VAL
Moscow Lights Museum
TsUM
ARMYANSKIY PEREULOK
Detskiy Mir
Figurniy dom
LUBYANKA
Metropol Hotel
KURSKAYA
Kitay Gorod Wall
Politechnical Museum
ULITSA MAROSEYKA
Apraksin Mansion
Church of the Presentation in Barashi
Moscow History Museum
Church of SS Cosmas & Damian
POKROVSKIY BULVAR
PODSOSENSKIY PEREULOK
Kursk Station
NIKOLSKAYA ULITSA
Kazan Cathedral
ULITSA ILINKA
Church of St Vladimir in the Old Garden
Church of the Trinity in Khokhovskiy
KAZARMENNIY PEREULOK
CHKALOVSKAYA
GUM
Choral Synagogue
KURSKAYA
ULITSA ZABELINA
Church of St Barbara
KITAYGOROD
Ivanovskiy Convent
Lenin Mausoleum
Monastery of the Sign
Palace of the Romanov Boyars
Church of the Trinity in Kulishki
RED SQUARE
English Court
PODKOLOKOLNIY PEREULOK
ZAYAUZE
KITAY-GOROD
Church of the Nativity
Church of Peter & Paul at the Yauza Gate
Sakharov Museum
Kremlin
St Basil's Cathedral
Kitay-gorod Wall
ULITSA SOLYANKA
Church of the Trinity in Serebryaniki
Rossiya Hotel
River Yauza
Moskva River
Andronikov Monastery
Balschug Kempinski Hotel
Kotelnicheskaya Apartments
SADOVNICHESKIY PROSPEKT
GONCHARNAYA ULITSA
ULITSA BOLSHAYA ORDYNKA
PYATNITSKAYA ULITSA
TAGANKA
Taganka Theatre
Tretyakov Gallery
NOVOKUZNETSKAYA
MARKSISTSKAYA
TRETYAKOVSKAYA
TAGANSKAYA
Furniture Museum
ZAMOSKVARECHE
0 500 m

Moscow International House of Music
Novospasskiy Monastery

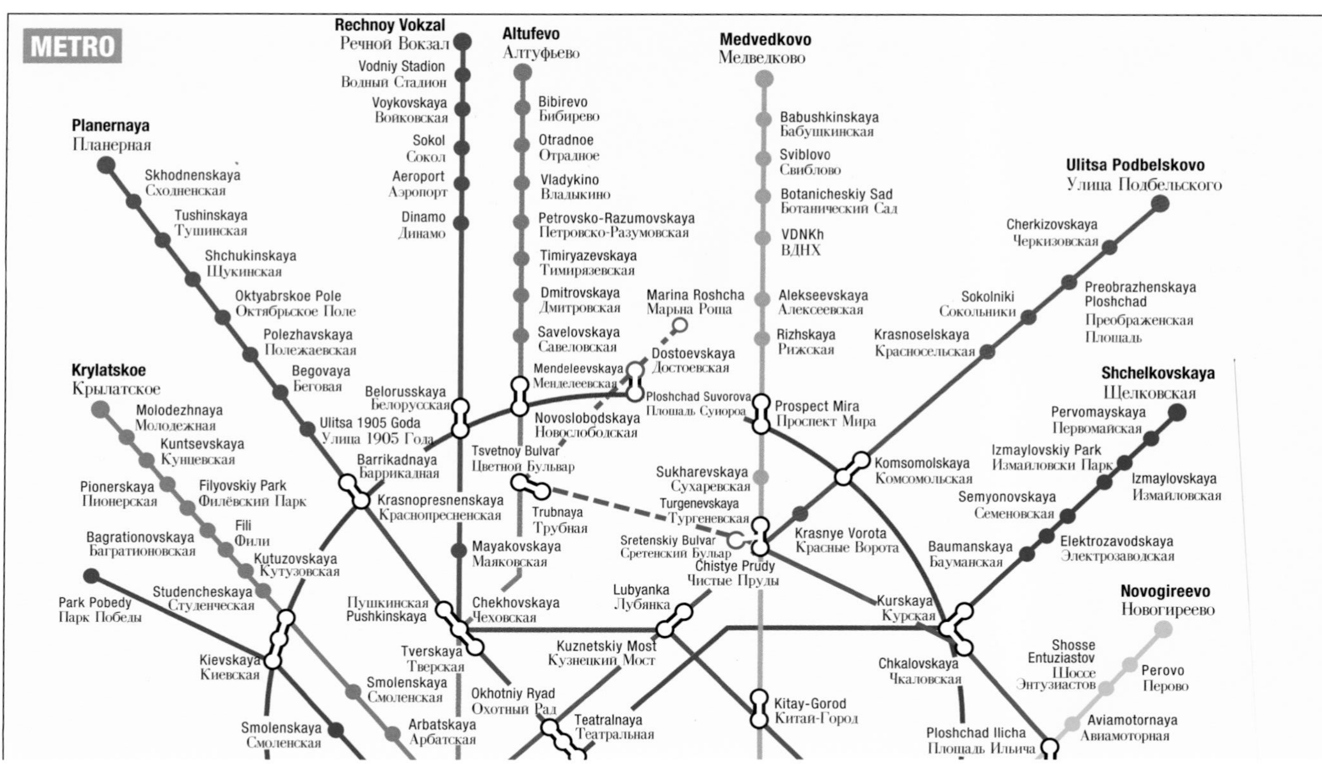
METRO
Rechnoy Vokzal
Речной Вокзал
Vodniy Stadion
Водный Стадион
Voykovskaya
Войковская
Sokol
Сокол
Aeroport
Аэропорт
Dinamo
Динамо
Altufevo
Алтуфьево
Bibirevo
Бибирево
Otradnoe
Отрадное
Vladykino
Владыкино
Petrovsko-Razumovskaya
Петровско-Разумовская
Timiryazevskaya
Тимирязевская
Dmitrovskaya
Дмитровская
Savelovskaya
Савеловская
Medvedkovo
Медведково
Babushkinskaya
Бабушкинская
Sviblovo
Свиблово
Botanicheskiy Sad
Ботанический Сад
VDNKh
ВДНХ
Alekseevskaya
Алексеевская
Rizhskaya
Рижская
Planernaya
Планерная
Skhodnenskaya
Сходненская
Tushinskaya
Тушинская
Shchukinskaya
Щукинская
Oktyabrskoe Pole
Октябрьское Поле
Polezhavskaya
Полежаевская
Begovaya
Беговая
Ulitsa 1905 Goda
Улица 1905 Года
Ulitsa Podbelskovo
Улица Подбельского
Cherkizovskaya
Черкизовская
Preobrazhenskaya Ploshchad
Преображенская Площадь
Sokolniki
Сокольники
Krasnoselskaya
Красносельская
Marina Roshcha
Марьна Роща
Dostoevskaya
Достоевская
Mendeleevskaya
Менделеевская
Ploshchad Suvorova
Плошадь Суюрова
Belorusskaya
Белорусская
Novoslobodskaya
Новослободская
Prospect Mira
Проспект Мира
Krylatskoe
Крылатское
Molodezhnaya
Молодежная
Kuntsevskaya
Кунцевская
Pionerskaya
Пионерская
Filyovskiy Park
Филёвский Парк
Fili
Фили
Bagrationovskaya
Багратионовская
Kutuzovskaya
Кутузовская
Studencheskaya
Студенческая
Park Pobedy
Парк Победы
Kievskaya
Киевская
Smolenskaya
Смоленская
Barrikadnaya
Баррикадная
Krasnopresnenskaya
Краснопресненская
Tsvetnoy Bulvar
Цветной Бульвар
Trubnaya
Трубная
Mayakovskaya
Маяковская
Пушкинская
Pushkinskaya
Chekhovskaya
Чеховская
Tverskaya
Тверская
Smolenskaya
Смоленская
Arbatskaya
Арбатская
Okhotniy Ryad
Охотный Рад
Teatralnaya
Театральная
Kuznetskiy Most
Кузнецкий Мост
Lubyanka
Лубянка
Sukharevskaya
Сухаревская
Turgenevskaya
Тургеневская
Sretenskiy Bulvar
Сретенский Бульвар
Chistye Prudy
Чистые Пруды
Kitay-Gorod
Китай-Город
Komsomolskaya
Комсомольская
Krasnye Vorota
Красные Ворота
Kurskaya
Курская
Chkalovskaya
Чкаловская
Ploshchad Ilicha
Площадь Ильича
Shchelkovskaya
Щелковская
Pervomayskaya
Первомайская
Izmaylovskiy Park
Измайловски Парк
Izmaylovskaya
Измайловская
Semyonovskaya
Семеновская
Elektrozavodskaya
Электрозаводская
Baumanskaya
Бауманская
Novogireevo
Новогиреево
Perovo
Перово
Shosse Entuziastov
Шоссе Энтузиастов
Aviamotornaya
Авиамоторная